ABOUT THE AUTHORS

Nicolás Kanellos has been professor at the University of Houston since 1980. He is founding publisher of the noted Hispanic literary journal *The Americas Review* (formerly *Revista Chicano-Riqueña*) and the nation's oldest and esteemed Hispanic publishing house, Arte Público Press.

Recognized for his scholarly achievements, Dr. Kanellos is the recipient of a 1990 American Book Award, a 1989 award from the Texas Association of Chicanos in Higher Education, the 1988 Hispanic Heritage Award for Literature presented by the White House, as well as various fellowships and other recognitions. His monograph, *A History of Hispanic Theater in the United States: Origins to 1940* (1990), received three book awards, including that of the Southwest Council on Latin American Studies.

Among his other books are the *Biographical Dictionary of Hispanic Literature of the United States* (1989), *Mexican American Theater Legacy and Reality* (1987), and *The Hispanic–American Almanac* (1993), which won an American Library Association Reference and Adult Services Division (RASD) award for outstanding reference source of the year.

Dr. Kanellos is the director of a major national research program, Recovering the Hispanic Literary Heritage of the United States, whose objective is to identify, preserve, study, and make accessible tens of thousands of literary documents of those regions that have become the United States from the colonial period to 1960. In 1994, President Bill Clinton appointed Dr. Kanellos to the National Council for the Humanities.

Cristelia Pérez is the community affairs director for KHOU-TV in Houston. She holds a masters degree in Spanish from the University of Houston and is a frequent collaborator with her husband, Nicolás Kanellos.

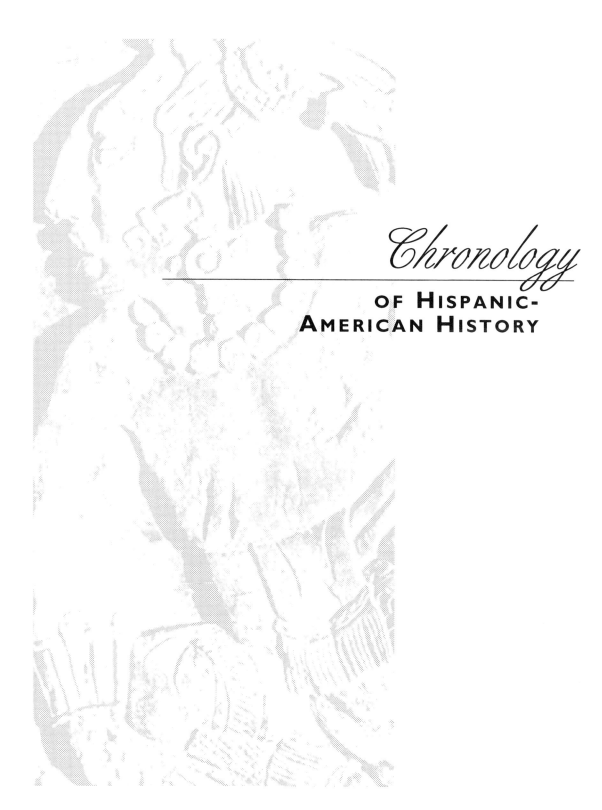

Chronology

OF HISPANIC-
AMERICAN HISTORY

HIGHLIGHTS

The Chronology of Hispanic-American History is a reference source designed for users seeking information on important people, places, and events in the history of Hispanic peoples from pre-Columbian times to the present. Chronologically arranged entries cover numerous topics, including:

- Agriculture
- Anthropology
- Art & Architecture
- Civil Rights & Discrimination
- Economics
- Education
- Film & Theater
- Labor

- Literature
- Media
- Music
- Politics & Law
- Religion
- Science & Medicine
- Sports
- Women's Issues & Feminism

The Chronology of Hispanic-American History provides an abundance of information, and its orderly format makes it easy to use. Special features include:

- Regional histories
- Historical timeline
- Short biographical sketches of prominent Hispanics
- Bibliography
- Excerpts from significant documents
- Glossary
- Category index listing entries by topic
- Subject index listing important names, events, and locations
- Over 145 photos

Chronology

OF HISPANIC-AMERICAN HISTORY

FROM PRE-COLUMBIAN TIMES TO THE PRESENT

NICOLÁS KANELLOS
WITH CRISTELIA PÉREZ

Gale Research Inc.

An International Thomson Publishing Company

I(T)P

Changing the Way the World Learns

NEW YORK • LONDON • BONN • BOSTON • DETROIT • MADRID
MELBOURNE • MEXICO CITY • PARIS • SINGAPORE • TOKYO
TORONTO • WASHINGTON • ALBANY NY • BELMONT CA • CINCINNATI OH

Gale Research Inc. Staff

Rebecca Nelson and Jane Hoehner, *Developmental Editors*; Camille A. Killens, *Associate Developmental Editor*; Lawrence W. Baker, *Managing Editor*

Christine Nasso, *Acquisitions Editor*

Mary Beth Trimper, *Production Director*; Evi Seoud, *Assistant Production Manager*; Mary Kelley, *Production Associate*

Cynthia Baldwin, *Product Design Manager*; Barbara J. Yarrow, *Graphic Services Supervisor*; Pamela A.E. Galbreath, *Cover and Page Designer*

Benita Spight, *Data Entry Services Manager*; Gwendolyn Tucker, *Data Entry Supervisor*; Nancy Sheridan, *Data Entry Associate*

Cover Illustration: Multi-cultural Mural, painted in 1980 by a multi-cultural Artists Collaboration as a gift to New Mexico. Artistic and Project Director: Zara Kriegstein; Co-designers: Zara Kriegstein and Gilberto Guzman; Other Participating Artists: David Bradley, Cassandra Harris, Linda Lomahaftewa, John Sandford, Rosemary Stearus, and Frederico Vigil. The mural as it appears here no longer exists; it is currently being painted over by Gilberto Guzman.

Library of Congress Cataloging-in-Publication Data

Chronology of Hispanic–American history / by Nicolás Kanellos.
p. cm.
Includes bibliographical references and index.
ISBN 0-8103-9200-3
1. Hispanic–Americans—History—Chronology.
2. Latin America—History—Chronology. I. Kanellos, Nicolás.
E184.S75C49 1995
973'.0468—dc20 95-7903
CIP

This book is printed on acid-free paper that meets the minimum requirements of American National Standard for Information Sciences—Permanence Paper for Printed Library Materials, ANSI Z39.48-1984.

ISBN 0-8103-9200-3
Printed in the United States of America by Gale Research Inc.

10 9 8 7 6 5 4 3 2 1

For Emma and José Pérez with love

Para Emma y José Pérez con cariño

TABLE OF CONTENTS

PREFACE xi

REGIONAL HISTORIES xv

HISTORICAL TIMELINE xxxvi

Part 1: THE ENCOUNTER OF PEOPLES (50,000 B.C. TO 1492)

CHAPTER 1 50,000 B.C. TO A.D. 1492 3

Part 2: THE CONQUEST AND COLONIZATION OF THE AMERICAS
(1493 TO 1820)

CHAPTER 2 1493 TO 1599 19

CHAPTER 3 1600 TO 1699 48

CHAPTER 4 1700 TO 1820 53

Part 3: THE BATTLE FOR INDEPENDENCE AND THE EMERGENCE OF
SPANISH AMERICAN REPUBLICS (1821 TO 1898)

CHAPTER 5 1821 TO 1898 77

Part 4: THE STRUGGLE FOR DEMOCRACY AND
CULTURAL IDENTITY (1899 TO 1995)

CHAPTER 6 1899 TO 1949 139

CHAPTER 7 1950 TO 1959 229

CHAPTER 8 1960 TO 1969 242

CHAPTER 9 1970 TO 1979 255

CHAPTER 10 1980 TO 1989 264

CHAPTER 11 1990 TO 1995 276

SIGNIFICANT DOCUMENTS 285

GLOSSARY 363

GENERAL BIBLIOGRAPHY 367

ILLUSTRATIONS CREDITS 371

CATEGORY INDEX 373

SUBJECT INDEX 405

PREFACE

The history of Hispanic culture in the Western Hemisphere is the story of convergence and confluence, processes that were put into motion thousands of years ago when the first Asiatic peoples crossed a land bridge and migrated south to populate the hemisphere to its tip, and processes that were started in Europe when the Iberian Peninsula saw prehistoric man migrating northward from Africa. Over the millennia, the Iberian Peninsula would become a virtual crossroads for the developing cultures of the Mediterranean and northern Africa, as well as for Celtic, Germanic, and other groups migrating westward from northern and eastern Europe. In what came to be known in modern history as the "Americas," the Asiatic peoples over time divided into cultures as diverse in language, custom, and physical appearance as the peoples of Europe and the Iberian Peninsula who confronted each other, violently and culturally, and eventually converged through intermarriage or domination of one group by the other. The inexorable push of migrations westward inevitably brought the Europeans to the Western Hemisphere and into the greatest confrontation of cultures in modern history.

When the Spaniards set foot on the Caribbean islands in 1492, another process was put into motion. Spain and its European neighbors transferred large portions of their populations to the "New World," forcefully transporting as slave labor the peoples of another continent, Africa, to the newly "discovered" lands and subsequently sup-

pressing the native (formerly Asiatic, but now called "Indian") peoples that had developed cultures and civilizations in the Americas.

In Hispanic America, after initial episodes of decimation from European diseases, genocide, and enslavement, the peoples from the three continents—the Americas, Africa, and Europe—interbred and negotiated new racial and cultural identities. In all the Hispanic populations of the Americas, the physiological vestiges of the tricontinental confluence are evident in the diversity that exists in the features of the peoples. What is often not that apparent is the real fusion in the national and regional cultures of Hispanic America. Even in a country thought to be the most racially and culturally European of the Americas—Argentina—the world view, food, music, and folkways nevertheless reveal decidedly Amerindian and African influences. Even in the areas most populated by Amerindians or descendants of Africans, the Spanish language and the Western world view dominate. The cultures of Hispanic America are mestizo and mulatto. The individuals living in those societies are predominantly mestizos and mulattoes regardless of their skin color. Within these general parameters, however, is a diversity of regional histories, cultural admixtures, and substrata that make a Cuban distinguishable from a Chilean, a Mexican from a Puerto Rican. Within the United States, which historically has attempted to superimpose its own official Anglo–European identity on the peoples

An eighteenth-century Spanish painting of the child of a Spaniard and an Indian, illustrating the origin of mestizos. (Courtesy of the Biblioteca Nacional, Madrid.)

of lands it conquered and incorporated into the Union, Hispanic diversity continues both in the Hispanic origin peoples who have always lived in the Southwest, Northeast, and Southeast and in the immigrants who have come here over the last two centuries.

SCOPE OF VOLUME

The Chronology of Hispanic-American History presents a comprehensive listing of historical and cultural events about peoples whose origins or descent is Mexico, Puerto Rico, Cuba, Spain, and the Spanish-speaking countries of Central and South America. We set out to develop the most exhaustive and sensitive chronology about Hispanic issues and events available today. Coverage begins with the pre-Columbian time period of 50,000 to 10,000 B.C. when asian peoples migrated to North and South America and eventually diversified into nations with separate languages and cultures; it ends with the United States' $53-billion loan-guarantee package to Mexico in February 1995. We hope that this volume will contribute to the general understanding of the contributions of the Hispanic peoples in contemporary and historical life.

Within the scope of *The Chronology*, it was our intention to cover many issues and topics that affected and were important to Hispanic Americans, and which influenced Hispanic society. Consequently, *The Chronology* covers historical events in agriculture, anthropology, art & architecture, civil rights and discrimination, economics, education, film and theater, labor, literature, media, music, politics and law, religion, science & medicine, sports, and women's issues and feminism. We have tried not to emphasize one field of events over the other, but rather to provide a short and readily digestible summary of major events in a number of areas that captures the diversity and depth of Hispanic-American historical experiences. The numerous illustrations were designed to complement and augment the chronological entries and should help the reader further understand their significance and meaning.

The book is divided into eleven chronological chapters, all of which include small biographies of key figures. The book is also supplemented with several shorter sections: Regional Histories, which documents the peoples of Mexico and the U.S. Southwest, the Hispanic Caribbean and the Eastern United States, Central America, and South America; a historical timeline; excerpts from or entire important historical legal documents; and a glossary of commonly used terms. A general bibliography provides readers with additional sources on the subject of Hispanics. In addition, a category index lists entries by topic and an extensive general index provides quick access to numerous people, places, and events.

ACKNOWLEDGMENTS

Deepest thanks to Hilda Hinojosa of Arte Público Press and to Christine Nasso, Becky Nelson, Jane Hoehner, and the whole crew at Gale Research Inc.

SUGGESTIONS ARE WELCOME

A work the size of *The Chronology of Hispanic-American History* may contain oversights and errors, and we appreciate any suggestions for correction of factual material or additions that will make future editions more accurate, sympathetic, and useful. Please send comments to:

Editor
The Chronology of Hispanic-American History
Gale Research inc.
835 Penobscot Bldg.
Detroit, MI 48226
Phone: (313) 961-2242
Fax: (313) 961-6741
Toll-free: (800) 347-GALE

Nicolás Kanellos
Cristelia Pérez
April 1995

REGIONAL HISTORIES

MEXICO AND THE UNITED STATES SOUTHWEST

By about A.D. 250, the peoples of the Americas had so well developed their domination of land and animals, and had so developed the organization of their societies—physically, spiritually, and politically—that their civilizations entered into what is known as the Classical Period. Large urban centers with specialized production techniques began trading with other cities. These large cities, especially in Mesoamerica, had ceremonial centers and advanced architecture, art and sciences. In the lake-filled Valley of Mexico, Teotihuacán became the most impressive center with some of the grandest pyramids in the Americas and a population of some 200,000 at its apex. During tenth century A.D., unfortunately, one by one the Classical Period centers began to decline, in the Valley of Mexico and in the tropical lowlands, where the Mayas lived. Newer, warlike tribes appeared, pillaging and sacking the cities. Although these tribes attempted to imitate the older civilizations, they never surpassed them in philosophical or technical achievement. Because of the warlike orientation of the cities, the new era was called the Militaristic Period. This was the state of society when the Spaniards arrived in the fifteenth century.

The Aztecs were the last of a series of Chichimeca tribes migrating into the Valley of Mexico. When they arrived in the thirteenth century, they raided and pillaged and were banished to an island in the center of the great lake in the valley. There, they imitated other great city-states and built their own magnificent city, which surpassed all others in size and beauty; and they began to move against the nations around them. The Aztecs eventually conquered and ruled over a confederacy that stretched from the central valley to both coasts. As a theocracy, political and religious power were centralized in an emperor who was revered as both a god and the head of state. When the Spaniards arrived, Moctezuma II was the most powerful and famous of emperors, enjoying equal status with the sun-god Huitzilopchtli. During 1520 and 1521, Hernán Cortés exploited various Aztec legends and made alliances with nations subjugated by the Aztecs in order to conquer and suppress the most advanced civilization in North America. Cortés had the city of Tenochtitlán razed, and the beginning of Spanish Mexico commenced with the building of a European city on top of the old Aztec capital. The Cathedral of Mexico was erected over and with the very stones of the grand pyramid that had existed in the middle of the Aztec city. The Spaniards then ruled Mexico until 1821, a full three hundred years after the conquest, indelibly stamping their Hispanic mark on Mexican society. Still, much of what is considered Indian remained in many ways, not least of which was the genetic composition of the people. By 1540, liaisons of Spanish men with the subjugated Indian women resulted in numerous

De Yndio y Mestiza

There were racial classifications for the many mixtures of blood that took place with the confluence of people from the Americas, Africa, and Europe. Here an eighteenth-century painting illustrates the making of a "coyote," the child of an Indian and Mestiza. (Courtesy of the Biblioteca Nacional, Madrid.)

offspring who were half-Spanish and half-Indian. They came to be known as *mestizo*; during the next centuries of continuous racial mixing *mestizaje* characterized not only of the biological and genetic makeup of Mexicans but also of their culture as a whole.

Many of the early colonial years were spent in building a society around European models, converting the Indians to Catholicism, and transforming them into economic units that would produce wealth for the mother country. The Indi-

ans were parceled out to religious missions and to conquerors in *encomiendas* (a form of slavery) to clear and work the lands, to acculturate to European ways, to produce the agricultural products needed for domestic consumption, and to mine the gold and silver for export to the Spanish crown. The frontiers of European civilization advanced from the hub of Mexico during the next three centuries as explorers, colonizers, and missionaries struck out northward and southward. From Mexico and the Caribbean, Spanish explorers and conquerors made incursions into many regions of what is today the United States. Using Cuba and Puerto Rico as his base, Juan Ponce de León had landed in Florida as early as 1513, exploring most of the coastal regions and much of the interior. Continuing their maritime adventures, Spanish explorers in the 1520s cruised along the northern shore of the Gulf of Mexico, visiting Alabama, Mississippi, and Texas and sailing up the Atlantic coast to the Carolinas. Between 1539 and 1541, a large group of explorers led by Hernando de Soto journeyed into the interior of North America and through almost all of today's southeastern states and Texas. In 1541, Francisco Vásquez de Coronado set out on an exploratory trek that would take him to present-day Arizona, New Mexico, and Texas in search of the mythical Seven Cities of Cíbola, said to rival Tenochtitlán in wealth and splendor.

During the next two centuries, colonization, and the exploration that it made possible, continued in the interior of today's western United States and all the way up the Pacific coast to Alaska. Colonists and missionaries founded towns and cities, and laid the basis for agricultural and mineral exploitation of areas stretching from what became known as Texas to northern California. They introduced Western-style civilization and its institutions, albeit with a distinctive mestizo imprimatur. In 1776, the Anglo–American colonies of England declared their independence; thirty-four years later, New Spain also declared its independence from Spain. Both countries struggled to invent new forms of government and social organization, and to forge distinctive cultures. Both countries encountered numerous problems in launching their new economies and political structures, but Mexico had the worst of it. Anglo–Americans had a preexisting political structure and economy, which allowed them to make a smoother transition to independent status. The thirteen colonies, moreover, had enjoyed greater freedom than had the Spanish colonies, which were rigidly controlled by the mother country. Spain had imposed a rigid economic and social caste system and had allowed the church inordinate influence over everyday life. In particular, the Spaniards' feudal practice of parceling out im-

mense tracts of lands to the favored, at first explorers and conquerors, and pressing the Indians into peonage on those lands lives on even now throughout Spanish America, in the large private land holdings and in the poverty and disenfranchisement of many Indians and mestizos. The Mexicans thus were not as prepared for the democracy to which they aspired in their constitution of 1824. The result was years of confusion and strife, with one of the first presidents—Agustín de Iturbide—even declaring himself emperor of Mexico.

These unfortunate experiments and false starts kept the economy weak and the nation vulnerable to outside powers. And the area of greatest weakness was the far northern frontier. It was this very area that was to fall into the hands of the expanding, economically dynamic republic that was now known as the United States of America. After the United States had eagerly acquired the Floridas and the Louisiana territory from the French and the Spanish in the opening decades of the nineteenth century, the territories further west, beginning with Texas, beckoned to the growing empire that had even developed a spiritual ideology of expansion and superiority over other peoples and races: Manifest Destiny. Anglo settlers and Mexicans in Texas declared their independence in 1836; Texas was annexed to the United States in 1845 as a slave state. In 1846, the United States provoked a war with Mexico and as a result seized the rest of the northern half of the nascent republic's lands. The Treaty of Guadalupe Hidalgo, signed in 1848, reestablished peace and compensated Mexico with $15 million for almost all of the lands that today form the states of New Mexico, Arizona, and California. The United States rounded out its southwestern border by colluding with the corrupt Mexican president Antonio López de Santa Anna for the sale to the United States of the Mesilla Valley (in what is now New Mexico) in 1853.

What followed in the Southwest during the transition from Spanish/Mexican culture and governance to Anglo–American governance was a decades-long enterprise whereby Mexicans were undone of their lands and their rights, often with the collusion of the authorities. Mexican lands, language, culture, and human and civil rights were all supposedly protected by the terms of the Treaty of Guadalupe Hidalgo. Many of the Mexicans who remained in the U.S. southwestern territories, nevertheless, were denied citizenship, the vote, and appropriate legal recourse for injury. They became the brunt of racial discrimination, even while the very industries, crafts, and arts that they practiced—ranching, mining, and transportation, for example—became the keys to opening and exploitation of the West by the United States.

The thoroughly weakened Mexican republic received other blows from outsiders after losing the great northern expanses of its national territory. The first and most serious came at the hands of Napoleon Bonaparte who, supposedly in retaliation for Mexico's unpaid debts, invaded the country in 1864 and planted a puppet emperor, Maximilian I, in Mexico City. Under the leadership of the first Indian president of the Americas, Benito Juárez, the liberals rallied and were able to drive the French from their soil and found a democratic republic, which unfortunately did not last beyond the death of the great statesman, Juárez.

A heroic *caudillo* (leader of warriors or strongman) who had distinguished himself against the French invaders then took the reins of the government in a fashion that had become familiar throughout Spanish America. He became a dictator. His name was Porfirio Díaz, a mestizo soldier who proceeded to repress the Indian and mestizo elements in the society, to emulate Europe, and to sell out the country's resources to the highest bidders, most notably the United States and Britain. The grand excesses of the landowners, the church, and foreign interests favored by Díaz precipitated a reaction from the landless, the poor, and the intellectuals headed by Francisco Madero, in a wholesale social revolution that broke out in 1910. Díaz was deposed the same year and the revolution proclaimed triumphant, but Madero was soon assassinated and the government was transferred between warring factions as a string of caudillos assumed power and subsequently also were deposed or assassinated.

It was President Plutarco Elías Calles who finally broke the pattern of factionalism and leadership by caudillos that had characterized Mexican politics after the revolution. He brought the postrevolutionary factions together in 1929 in the Partido Nacional Revolucionario (National Revolutionary Party), the forerunner of today's dominant party, the Partido Revolucionario Institucional (Institutional Revolutionary Party) which is widely known as PRI. With the revolutionary family now functioning as the overwhelmingly dominant party in a multiparty system, many of the social and economic changes that were brought about by the Mexican Revolution ushered in an unbroken period of economic and political stability characterized by democracy. Mexico has become one of the most democratic and politically and economically stable countries in the Americas.

In the postrevolutionary society, many of the sectors of the Mexican economy continued to be administered by the government, including the railroads, the oil industry, communications, banking, and others that in the United States have been run by private corporations. But other industries were allowed to grow and prosper as free enterprises. Nevertheless, foreign investors were not allowed to hold more than a 49% interest in Mexican companies. During the 1970s and 1980s, escalating foreign debt and inflation resulted in repeated devaluations of the peso and a considerable lowering of the standard of living. Emigration to the United States, both legal and undocumented, increased to such a degree that it became a social problem in the United States, especially for border states, and a strain on U.S.–Mexico relations. In efforts to control the economy and meet rigorous goals set by the International Monetary Fund, Mexico began to privatize many industries and to remove artificial supports it had lent to various sectors of the economy, most notably agriculture. By the late 1980s, the economy had improved so substantially that Mexico pursued economic integration with its largest trading partner, the United States. In January 1994, the North American Free Trade Agreement (NAFTA) went into effect, eliminating or scaling back trade barriers and in effect creating a free-trade zone for Mexico, the United States, and Canada.

During the twentieth century, Mexican culture in the southwestern United States was profoundly changed by large-scale immigration that escalated during the Mexican Revolution, and has ebbed and flowed up to the present, depending on the need for workers in the United States and the economic conditions in Mexico. The labor needs of the agricultural industry, railway construction firms, and mining during the last decades of the nineteenth century and at the turn of the century made Mexican labor a familiar commodity in the United States. In the 1880s, the Chinese exclusion acts passed by Congress made these industries especially dependent on Mexican labor. When manpower became scarce during World War I, Mexicans were actively recruited from the border by steel mills in the Midwest and as far away as Pennsylvania and by meat packers in Chicago, sugar beet growers in the Northwest, and the automotive industry in Detroit, among many others. The immigrants from the revolution were mostly economic refugees; however, a very large class of wealthy and educated professionals also fled the revolution as political refugees, settling mostly in urban centers with traditionally large Mexican populations, such as El Paso, San Antonio, San Diego, Los Angeles, San Francisco, and Tucson, but also venturing into newer areas such as Chicago, Phoenix, and Houston. These politically active representatives of the Mexican middle and upper classes soon became business and cultural entrepreneurs and fomented an ideology of an internal "colony" of Mexicans on U.S. soil. They set about recreating Mexican culture in the United States to preserve their language, religion, and customs in every way possible so as to be intact when they returned to Mexico after the revolution. But even the common laborer also harbored such sentiments and usually had intentions of returning to the homeland. Of course, many of these immigrants and the families of Mexican Americans that they raised here never returned to Mexico, but they helped to foster a tenacious conservatism in their social and family

patterns that in many ways accounts for the importance of the Spanish language and many Mexican cultural institutions in the Southwest today.

As the Mexican population increased, so did nativist reaction to it, and the long-held, deep-seated prejudices against Mexicans that had facilitated their conversion into an oppressed labor class during the nineteenth century arose again in incidents of discrimination, segregation, police brutality, and abuse in the workplace. Racial persecution increased during the 1921 depression, when many Mexicans suddenly found themselves unemployed and destitute. But when the economy became robust, Mexican labor was once again a sought-after commodity even exempted from the provisions of the 1924 National Origins Quota Act that sought to curtail immigration. Nevertheless, with the onset of the Great Depression, Mexicans became unwanted and subjected to forced as well as voluntary repatriation. Repatriation was massive, especially from cities in the Southwest and the Midwest, with social service agencies, churches, and the police authorities participating in, at times, insensitive splitting up of families and even the deportation of American citizens, the children born in the United States to Mexican immigrants.

For those that remained, Americanization became the overriding goal and, during World War II, Mexican American soldiers strove to prove their allegiance to the United States by becoming proportionately the most decorated of any ethnic or racial group in the country. Having proved their patriotism beyond all expectations, Mexican Americans set about achieving political power, demanding the use of the vote and openly fighting racism and discrimination. They often used their status as veterans of the war as a base for organizing and for claiming their civil rights through such organizations as American Legion posts and the American G.I. Forum, which was founded in 1947. It had been preceded by other alliances in fighting discrimination, such as the Alianza Hispano

Americana, active since the late nineteenth century, and the League of United Latin American Citizens, founded in 1929 and still at the head of the civil rights struggle. With immigration having subsided greatly during the depression and the war, Anglo–American culture wielded great influence, and this generation and its children became the most acculturated in the history of Mexicans in the United States. But programs for visitor workers from Mexico during the 1950s and 1960s, such as the Bracero Program, again opened up the streams of immigration and cultural reinforcement.

Since then, Mexican immigration to the U.S. has continued unabated and, in fact, has provided an avenue for the entrance of Central American political and economic refugees, whose numbers steadily expanded during the civil wars of the 1970s and 1980s in their homelands. Because of the comparatively higher birthrates of Hispanics and the steady and growing flow of immigration from Mexico and Central America during the 1980s, great shifts in economic and political power bases began to take place. By the latter part of the decade, Hispanics ascended to 30, 40, and more than 50 percent of the population in certain regions of the Southwest and promised to constitute a majority in such regions as southern California and Texas by the turn of the century. The 1990s already have seen a southwestern-wide trend of elected representation by Hispanics in municipal and state governments; the growth of Spanish-language communications, most notably represented by three national television networks; and bilingual education in all of the states of the Southwest. But population growth and high immigration figures alone do not explain the progress of Hispanics. Most political and some economic progress has been made because of a century-long history of labor movements, civil rights battles, suits and court decisions, desegregation of public education, the passage of voting rights acts, and the Chicano labor and student movements of the 1960s and 1970s that reformed education to improve its accessibility for Hispanics and made the U.S. workplace more equitable for them.

THE HISPANIC CARIBBEAN AND THE EASTERN UNITED STATES

While it is estimated that some 25 million Indians lived in central Mexico before the conquest, the Indians of the Caribbean lived in far smaller populations, probably numbering no more than one million strong, and did not have as developed a material and urban culture as the Indians of central Mexico. Moreover, the racial and cultural genocide, as well as the decimation through diseases introduced by the Europeans, took a greater toll on the Indians. Despite the total disruption to their lives brought about by the Spanish invasion of the islands of Hispaniola, Cuba, and Puerto Rico, vestiges of the cultural and genetic life of the Arawaks and Caribs are noticeable in the Hispanic Caribbean today. Here and there pockets of people identifying themselves or their ancestors as Taínos (an Arawakan group) still persist. The Taínos lived in a seminomadic society that benefitted from the tropical climate, and from the abundant gathering, hunting, and fishing for food, as well as from farming. Despite their simple means of dressing, feeding, and sheltering themselves, the Taínos had a highly developed social and political system based on fishing and planting and the governance by tribal elders.

Christopher Columbus's first voyages succeeded in encountering the Caribbean Indians and in laying the foundation for colonization and exploitation of the islands and their peoples. The first of the islands to be settled was Hispaniola, then Cuba and Puerto Rico, and the Indians were parceled out with tracts of land to the conquerors and settlers in encomiendas as booty. The Spanish attempted to establish feudal baronies on Hispaniola and the other islands, but failed as the Indians were worked to death in the gold, silver, and copper mines and in farming; the Indians also fell to hitherto unknown diseases, such as the common cold, measles, and smallpox brought by the Spaniards. The Indians eventually were decimated, but not Indian lineage entirely, as many children were born of Spanish and Indian sexual liai-

A drawing of Arawak Indians by Gerolamo Benzoni. (Courtesy of the Library of Congress Prints & Photographs Division.)

sons; thus the mestizo appeared for the first time in the world.

The islands of the Caribbean, especially Hispaniola, became the first seats of European civilization in the New World. On Hispaniola the first churches and schools, even the first university in the hemisphere, were founded. It was from these islands that the rest of Spanish America, including the coast of the Gulf of Mexico, the Floridas, and the Southeast of what became the United States, began to be explored and colonized. It was on these islands that colonial government and its relationship to the church were evolved and then implanted on the mainland. Here, too, many of Spain's attitudes and policies regarding the native peoples of the hemisphere were formulated.

The mining was relatively poor on the islands, and when greater deposits of precious metals were found on the mainland, much of the mining was abandoned and the islands were converted to way stations for the ships transporting riches from the New World to Spain. Because of its fine harbor, Havana became the dominant city in the islands by the mid-sixteenth century. Ships with gold and silver from Mexico and South America were formed into fleets in Havana so that the Spanish navy could protect them from pirates during the journey to Spain.

Following the failure of mining, the island economies were transformed to sustain and benefit from sugar cane. However, the harsh treatment of the Indians, their rapidly falling numbers, and their inexperience with systematic labor rendered them almost useless on the sugar plantations. As a consequence, African slaves were imported to work on the plantations. The population of Africans—and mulattoes, as well—grew steadily throughout the centuries, even to the extent of outnumbering the European population of Cuba. Cuba and Puerto Rico maintained slave economies almost until their separation from Spain at the end of the nineteenth century. In fact, at the height of the sugar boom, some half million slaves were imported to Cuba from 1812 to 1865, in spite of an existing worldwide ban on the slave trade. The importance of the African background in Cuba, Puerto Rico, and the Dominican Republic cannot be minimalized, as the Africans have influenced language, family life, music, art, food, and all aspects of culture and religion.

In 1821, with the euphoria of rebellion sweeping through the Spanish colonies in the Americas, the Dominican Republic proclaimed its independence. The following year it was conquered by Haiti and remained under Haiti's brutally tyrannical rule until 1844, when it successfully liberated itself. After that, the republic felt so defenseless that its leaders sought annexation to the United States and even recolonization by Spain. From 1844 until the turn of the century, just three men dominated politics in the Dominican Republic, establishing the tradition of a long line of dictators. The first two, Pedro Santana and Buenaventura Báez, worked in concert by alternating terms as president of the republic, but by the 1850s they had become enemies. Santana dominated most of the time until his death in 1864, and thereafter Báez until his death in 1882. From 1882 until his assassination in 1899, Ulises Heureaux led a despotic and brutal regime. After his death, so much

chaos reigned in the republic that finally in 1905 the United States acted to forestall European intervention to collect debts. American control gradually increased until 1916, when the United States installed its own military government because of the turmoil that had again overtaken civilian government. During the intervention, which lasted until 1924, the U.S. military government established a national guard as a police force, and modernized the transportation, education, and communications systems. By 1930, a U.S.-backed strongman, Rafael Trujillo, came to power, and put into place one of the longest-lasting dictatorships—he was assassinated in 1961 while still president. While Trujillo developed the government, transportation, and education infrastructure and greatly improved the economy in the Dominican Republic, he ruled with a corrupt regime as a ruthless autocrat. Factionalism again brought the country to violence in the post-Trujillo days, but now the politics of the Dominican Republic became caught up in the cold war tension between rightists and leftists, and President Lyndon Baines Johnson sent in the marines in 1965 to prevent another Cuba from occurring. Eventually, an election was arranged and Joaquín Balaguer was elected with United States backing. He, too, turned out to be a dictator and, at this writing, has been elected to the presidency five times.

Cuba, Puerto Rico, and the Philippines were the only major Spanish colonies that did not gain their independence at the beginning of the nineteenth century. In 1868, a group of Cuban rebels led by a black general, Carlos Manuel de Céspedes, declared independence at Yara and established a provisional government headed by Céspedes in Oriente province. A bloody war, known as the Ten Years' War, ensued during which the Spanish unsuccessfully attempted to evict the rebels from the eastern half of Cuba. The war came to an end when both sides signed the Pact of El Zajón in 1878, which promised home rule and amnesty for the insurgents, as well as freedom for the slaves who had fought on the side of the rebels. Slavery was abolished in 1886, but Spain failed to provide political reform and, thus, the Cuban independence movement gained strength. Throughout the nineteenth century, Cubans had been taking refuge in the United States and attempted either to launch their revolutionary movements from the states or to have the United States annex Cuba to the union as a slave state. In 1869, the United States even tendered an offer of $130 million to purchase Cuba from Spain (in 1848, President James K. Polk had offered $100 million). The sugar economies of both Cuba and Puerto Rico had drawn both Spanish colonies close to the United States because their investors and primary markets were located there. Based on their organizing support and financing in Cuban and Puerto Rican communities in New York, Key West, Tampa, New Orleans, and elsewhere, in 1895 Cuban and Puerto Rican patriots such as José Martí and Ramón Emeterio Betances opened the final battle for independence of Cuba and Puerto Rico. (The Puerto Ricans, who had declared their independence at Lares in 1868, also had met continuous frustration at the hands of the Spaniards.) Finally, in 1897, major concessions were won from Spain, granting both Cuba and Puerto Rico autonomy and home rule. But much of the movement for independence already had been set in motion and involved so much support from the United States that the immediate outcome of the U.S. victory in the Spanish American War of 1898 was that the United States became the new colonial master of both islands.

Cuba was allowed to become independent by 1901, but under the auspices of the Platt Amendment, which was attached to the Cuban constitution, the United States could intervene in Cuba's internal affairs at any time. Puerto Rico, however, did not even have a semblance of independence or the autonomy it had won from Spain; instead it became a full colony of the United States, following classical models of colonialism under an imposed military rule, all authorized by the U.S. Congress under the Foraker Act of 1900. In 1917, the Jones Act extended United States citizenship to all Puerto Ricans, just in time for them to serve in World War I. From then until the creation of commonwealth status in 1953—in

which Puerto Rico became a "free associated state" of the United States and finally was allowed to elect its own governor—the Americanization of the island went ahead full steam. English was mandated as the official language and *the* language of public school education in Puerto Rico for many years (until President Franklin Roosevelt revoked the mandate in 1933)—an imposition that the Puerto Ricans rejected and eventually cast off. But Americanization also meant the building of schools, hospitals, and transportation and communications systems, and the wiping out of previously endemic diseases. Under the Commonwealth of Puerto Rico and Governor Luis Muñoz Marín's Operation Bootstrap, mainland industries were enticed to build factories and subsidiaries in Puerto Rico for substantial tax breaks.

Along with these great improvements came waves of American investors, the transformation of the economy, unemployment and underemployment as the sugar industry was modernized, and increased migration—principally to New York and environs, but then to other U.S. destinations far and wide. In the long run, Puerto Rico's greatest resource was its people; the constant demand for Puerto Rican labor, especially in the service industries, far outstripped the utility of its monocultures: sugar and coffee. After immigration to the U.S. from Europe and Asia was greatly curtailed by two national quota acts in 1921 and 1924, it was far easier to recruit Puerto Rican laborers, who were already citizens. By 1930, there were already 53,000 living in and around New York City. And then, the World War II manpower scarcity triggered one of the most massive migrations in history, most of it effected for the first time by air. Almost two million Puerto Ricans left the island for the mainland. Beginning in the mid-1950s many returned to the island, a movement that balanced out and at times reversed the shift in population. Today, some 2.5 million first- and second-generation Puerto Ricans live on the mainland, with some 3.5 million residing on the island. Puerto Ricans on the mainland are the second largest group of Hispanics in the United States. They traditionally have faced the same types of resistance and prejudice as have Mexicans, except at times more intensely because of the African background of many Puerto Ricans. The Puerto Rican sense of entitlement is greater than that of the other Hispanic groups, because they are citizens and resist being looked upon as immigrants. Nevertheless, to most Americans they are indistinguishable from other Hispanic immigrants and their mixed racial heritage still is anathema to Anglo–Saxon purity. Of the three major Hispanic groups, including Cubans, Puerto Ricans are at the bottom of the scale in educational achievement, employment, earnings, and other such social and economic measures.

With the dislocation and flux of the Puerto Rican population and the island's continued colonial status, even as recognized and declared by the United Nations, the desire for independence among some groups, especially the intellectuals and the labor class on the island, remained alive and fueled a century-long movement to free the island from the United States. The leaders of the independence and socialist movements in Puerto Rico have been at times violently repressed on the island, as in the Ponce Massacre of 1937, and imprisoned on the mainland, as in the case of the great nationalist leader, Pedro Alvizu Campos. The nationalists, however, resorted to terrorist violence to bring attention to their cause: in 1954, a group of nationalists headed by Lolita Lebrón went on a shooting spree in the U.S. House of Representatives, wounding various congressmen, (the island of Puerto Rico is not allowed representation in Congress). Periodically, Puerto Rico undergoes a plebiscite in which the citizens can show their preference for independence, U.S. statehood, or commonwealth status; the latter has remained the majority preference, although the statehood forces are believed to be gaining support.

Cuba, on the other hand, not having to deal with such overt and institutionalized U.S. colonialism, was free to develop its own political and cultural institutions or to follow the models of other Spanish American countries. The model that dominated up until the Revolution of 1959, unfortunately, was that of the caudillo closely allied with and supported by U.S. government and commercial interests. And then, with the socialist revolution instituted, the model of the strongman was resuscitated in the Communist dictatorship of Fidel Castro, the supposedly highly educated and enlightened leader who had ousted the corrupt dictator, Fulgencio Batista. The reaction to the Communist takeover was a massive exodus of the middle and professional classes of Cubans, who were accepted as political refugees in the United States. An immediate pattern of Cuban history was also revived as counterrevolutionaries plotted to launch an invasion of the island from U.S. shores. Such was the Bay of Pigs fiasco in 1961, in which U.S.-trained and -armed Cuban expatriate soldiers attempted to invade the island. They were immediately and mercilessly repressed by Castro's forces. Cuba increasingly became a pawn as well as exploiter of the Cold War, developing long-term ideological, military, and economic relationships with the Soviet Union. The involvement of the Soviet Union in Cuba brought both superpowers to the brink of war when, on October 22, 1962, President John F. Kennedy refused to allow Soviet missiles into Cuba. In exchange for removing the missiles, the Soviets required that the United States not plan or support any further invasions and/or interventions in Cuba's internal affairs. That agreement has stood to this date, albeit with a U.S. embargo of Cuba that is still in effect. With the recent failure of Communist regimes in the Soviet Union and the eastern European countries, Cuba and Castro have suddenly found their chief trading partner and subsidizer, the Soviet Union, no longer to exist and Russia disinterested in using Cuba to further the Cold War. Many Latin American countries are pressuring Cuba and Castro to open the society and reinstate democracy, even as they plead with the United States to end the embargo and resume commercial and diplomatic relations with Cuba. At this writing, many observers around the world predict the imminent end of Castro's dictatorship.

Escapes, defections, and emigration to the United States have continued since the beginning of the Communist regime in Cuba, but in April

1980, a frustrated and embarrassed Castro threw open the doors of Cuba for a brief time and allowed the emigration or escape of another 125,000 people who were literally boatlifted to U.S. shores. This time most of the refugees were from working-class backgrounds, and Castro also availed himself of the opportunity of this exodus from Mariel Harbor—it is consequently known as the Mariel Boatlift—to empty out various jails and mental hospitals. These and the former exiles have settled mainly in Miami, New York, and Union City, New Jersey, but also throughout the nation. In 1994, a growing economic crisis in Cuba led to another widespread exodus by sea, but this time the United States did not openly and unquestioningly accept the escapees as political refugees. The United States' policy changed to one of intercepting the refugee crafts at sea and detaining and processing the refugees back in Guantanamo, Cuba. Today, there are approximately 1.1 million Cubans living in the United States. Like Mexicans and Puerto Ricans, they also make up a racially and socially diverse group of Hispanics whose U.S.-born children are now experiencing stresses and crises of identity similar to those of Puerto Rican and Mexican American youths finding their place within this society.

CENTRAL AMERICA

Guatemala, El Salvador, Honduras, Nicaragua, and Costa Rica emerged from the rule of the captains–general of Guatemala under New Spain when Mexico gained its independence, and then just as quickly separated themselves from Mexico into a Central American confederation, called the United Provinces of Central America, which lasted from 1823 to 1838. While still under Spanish colonial rule, these provinces of New Spain had been mainly a backwater, populated in the majority by Indians, and had lagged economically and culturally behind other centers of Spanish colonial culture. As an independent federation, their new constitution provided for a federal president administering the union from Guatemala and for provisional presidents in each of the five constitu-

ent states. It restricted voting rights in order to maintain land and power in the hands of the propertied and educated class and declared Catholicism to be the only religion of the federation. The constitution also emancipated the slaves. Continuous battles between liberals and conservatives, attacks on the power of the church, and intervention in the neighboring provinces' internal affairs brought the federation to dissolution by 1838, when the Guatemalan Indian leader, Rafael Carrera, occupied Guatemala City with a ragtag army and proclaimed victory for the conservatives and the church. That same year the congress voted that each of the constituent states was free to go its own way and, by 1841, the five countries as we know them today emerged as Central American republics. Since that time, there have been repeated but vain attempts of reintegration. In 1885, one such attempt was conducted by force by Guatemalan dictator J.R. Barrios when he failed to bring the neighboring republics under his autocratic rule. There have also been numerous threats of intervention from outside, one of which was fully realized when the British claimed their colony of British Honduras (today Belize) just after the Central American federation was founded.

The caudillo Rafael Carrera became the first of a long line of dictators over the newly formed republic of Guatemala. An illiterate but nevertheless shrewd military strategist, of Indian heritage, Carrera ruled over Guatemala for twenty-seven years until his death in 1865. During that time he was successful in making the church a supreme power in Guatemala. The Indians regarded Carrera as their messiah, he was decorated by the pope and by López de Santa Anna of Mexico for his conservatism and supported by all of the large landholders, who ridiculed his ignorance behind his back. Although uneducated, Carrera was successful in maintaining peace and security, improving roads, advancing farming, managing the state's finances honestly, and reducing the national debt. But he was a despot and a ruthless persecutor of the opposition. He also continually intervened in El Salvador, Honduras, and Nicaragua to put conservatives in power.

Unfortunately, the pattern of dictatorship set by Carrera was to be followed in Guatemala almost up to the present. Among its many dictators, two merit particular attention: Justo Rufino Barrios and Manuel Estrada Cabrera—the former because in the 1870s he passed debt-peonage statutes and abolished hundreds of Mayan land titles to create a corps of seasonal workers for the coffee plantations. In 1884 alone, more than 100,000 acres of Mayan municipal land became privately owned. Hundreds of thousands of Mayan farmers were displaced and forced to work as pickers and peons. The problem of land dispossession has persisted and is a cause of major unrest in Guatemala and southern Mexico. Barrios's legacy was the creation of a coffee-centered economy that by 1905 controlled 14 percent of the world trade and brought in 85 percent of Guatemala's revenues. Barrios's statutes remained in force until 1934, when dictator Jorge Rufino Ubico replaced them with vagrancy laws that obligated all campesinos who owned less than two hectares to render manual labor for one hundred days per year. Again, this had the effect of producing a cheap or free labor source to harvest coffee and sugar on the big plantations. Estrada Cabrera had one of the longest dictatorships, from 1898 to 1920, and one of the most brutal, characterized by corruption, murder, and keeping the Indians in the rigidly feudal system of peonage.

In 1945, a social revolution finally unseated the traditional dictatorial regimes supported by the military, the creoles, and the landlords in Guatemala. A new leader, Juan José Arévalo, was installed, supported by a small middle class and workers. Arévalo, serving from 1945 to 1950, and Jacobo Arbenz, who followed him from 1950 to 1954, set about democratizing the country, furthering education and limiting foreign interests. A new constitution, based on the Mexican model and authorizing land reform and guaranteeing the rights of labor and free institutions, was adopted in 1945. In 1950, the Communist Party gained influence and began to attack American-owned enterprises, including the United Fruit Company. An agrarian law was passed in July 1952 to recapture, with compensation to the owners, lands withheld from cultivation and to redistribute them to small farmers. The United Fruit Company bore the brunt of expropriation of hundreds of thousands of acres of land. In May 1954, the United States protested the Arbenz government receiving of arms shipments from the Soviet Union. In June, the Arbenz government was ousted through a coup engineered by the U.S. Central Intelligence Agency (CIA). In July, the government was taken over by a military junta headed by General Carlos Castillo Armas, who was later installed as president. Castillo Armas returned most of the expropriated lands to the United Fruit Company and the U.S. handsomely subsidized his government. His despotic and Communist-baiting regime was terminated with his assassination in July, 1957. But the new pattern of U.S. interventionism had been established: dictatorial regimes in Central America—indeed, the Americas—would be supported by the United States in the battle against Communism from within the context of the cold war.

Unlike its neighboring Central American republics, Costa Rica sought to ensure peace at home and abroad. Its constitution of 1848 provided for the abolition of the army and substituted a relatively limited civil guard. Aside from some minor clashes during its history and an interval (1870–82) under the dictatorship of Tomás Guardia, Costa Rica has developed as a peaceful state free of wars, both internal and external. In 1889, Costa Rica was the first republic to conduct elections with complete freedom of speech and press and to conduct an honest vote count. It was the first Central American republic to institute a complete democracy. In fact, Costa Rica's tradition of peace and democracy became essential in bringing a regionally developed peace plan for Central America under the Contadora process in the 1980s and, specifically, the end of the civil war in Nicaragua between the Sandinistas and the Contras.

During the 1870s, the cultivation of bananas as a cash crop was introduced to Costa Rica. The cultivation and export of the "miracle" fruit grew rapidly throughout Central America and by the turn of the century came to be dominated by a giant Boston-based corporation, the United Fruit Company. The importance of the crop was so great that the Central American republics came to be called "Banana Republics." In 1890, Minor Cooper Kieth, an American adventurer and entrepreneur, completed the railroad from the coast to the capital of Costa Rica. After building the railroad, he decided that he needed freight in order to prosper. Thus was born the idea to start up banana plantations and create the cash crop. From Costa Rica, he extended his banana ventures into Guatemala and El Salvador. During the last three decades of the nineteenth century, there were twenty banana companies in Central America; Kieth consolidated them all into the United Fruit Company in 1899. For this and his other business ventures in Central America, he came to be known as "the uncrowned king of Central America."

From its very early days, the republic of Nicaragua had been afflicted with the strife of warring liberals and conservatives. One of its darkest hours came in 1855, when liberals invited an American adventurer, William Walker, to repress the conservatives. Walker proceeded to take over the country and appointed himself president in 1856. He was finally ousted when the Central American republics each sent forces to extract him. He was executed by the British in Honduras in 1857. In 1858, the republic was once again established, this time through the unity of both liberals and conservatives, who instituted a bicameral legislature and an elected presidency of single four-year terms. The conservative Tomás Martínez was elected the first president of the republic, and the conservatives were able to stay in power for thirty-five years.

In 1893, José Santos Zelaya was elected to the presidency of Nicaragua. He subsequently rewrote the constitution to empower himself to be reelected twice. Although he modernized the country—including the army, which became the strongest in Central America—he was a brutish tyrant who fattened himself and his cronies at the public trough and betrayed his country by selling reckless concessions to foreigners. Under Santos Zelaya, Nicaragua became the premier military power in Central America, a power he used to stir up revolutions in the neighboring countries. Pressure from both the United States and the other Central American republics forced him into exile in 1909. José Santos Zelaya's resignation from the presidency represented the first of a series of Nicaraguan governments that the United States would overthrow. The Nicaraguan congress selected one of Zelaya's men, José Madriz, to succeed as president, but he was not acceptable to the United States, which withheld recognition until the rebels overthrew him. Juan Estrada took his place as president, with the United States heavily involved in reconstructing the government. Estrada's successor, Adolfo Díaz, was so weak that in August 1912, he had to request United States military intervention. The marines soon landed on the Pacific coast and, with the exception of an eighteen-month period (August 1925–January 1927), U.S. military rule lasted until January 1933.

The year 1933 marked the beginning of the government by one of Latin America's most successful dictators, Anastasio Somoza, who as head of the U.S. Marine-trained national guard in Nicaragua was the true power behind the newly elected president, Juan B. Sacasa. In 1937, Somoza himself was elected to the presidency and from then until he was struck down by an assassin's bullet in September 1956, he served as supreme despot. Under Somoza, Nicaragua enjoyed unbroken years of economic and political stability and a very close relationship with the United States, its chief partner in trade. In addition to becoming fabulously wealthy at the expense of the nation, Somoza had instituted a dynasty that was represented by his son, Luis, serving as president of the national congress and his other son, Anastasio, Jr., serving as chief of staff of the national guard. When Somoza was assassinated, the congress quickly ratified his son Luis's ascension to the presidency.

From the middle of the nineteenth century, repeated plans were made for digging a transisthmian canal, at first with both United States and British interests and financing, but gradually with the United States assuming sole responsibility. In 1869, President Ulysses S. Grant announced that the United States would build a transisthmian canal in Nicaragua. The intention of the U.S. to build a canal across the Central American isthmus would be expressed often in the years to come. In 1871, President Rutherford B. Hayes repeated the charge. By the end of the century, there was a national clamor in the United States to construct a canal for commercial, military, and nationalistic reasons. Finally, in 1902, the U.S. Congress authorized the pursuit of a canal in Panama.

In 1903, with support from the U.S., Panamanian rebels declared the independence of Panama from Colombia in order to negotiate separately with the United States for the construction of a canal. (The United States had been unsuccessful in attaining beneficial terms from the Colombian government earlier in the year.) Two days after Panama's declaration of independence from Colombia, the United States recognized the new government. The Hay–Bunau–Varilla Treaty for the construction of an isthmian canal was signed by the U.S. and Panama, preventing Panama from pursuing an independent foreign policy and incurring excessive foreign debt and granting the United States rights to construct sanitation facilities in the terminal cities and to intervene in Panama to maintain internal order. In many respects, Panama became a colony from that point on, with the United States dictating over and intervening in the internal affairs of the country continuously, and U.S. administration of the canal accounting for the largest segment of the Panamanian economy. Over the course of the century, the treaty has been renegotiated a number of times, for the most part increasing the payments to Panama. Under President Jimmy Carter, the turnover of the Canal Zone to Panama was negotiated to occur in the year 2000.

As can be seen by the preceding, up until 1933 the United States had treated the Central American and Caribbean republics as virtual colonies. But in that year, President Franklin Delano Roosevelt announced the "Good Neighbor Policy" and noninterventionism in the internal affairs of Latin America countries. Later in the year, at the Inter-American Conference in Montevideo, Uruguay, U.S. representatives repeated the pledge not to intervene. As part of the new policy, the Marines withdrew from Haiti, the Dominican Republic, and Nicaragua; a new canal treaty was signed with Panama; the Platt Amendment with Cuba was revoked; and recognition was extended to Jorge Ubico in Guatemala, Maximiliano Hernández Martínez in El Salvador, Tiburcio Carías in Honduras, Anastasio Somoza in Nicaragua, Rafael Trujillo in the Dominican Republic, and Francois Duvalier in Haiti, all of whom illegally extended their presidential terms. President Roosevelt's policy and even closer, more open relations predominated throughout World War II until the cold war began to rage. Then, United States interventionism resumed on a grand scale to supposedly forward the battle against Communism in the Hemisphere.

During the 1970s and 1980s brutal authoritarian regimes took power in El Salvador and Guatemala. In its anxiety to rid the nations of Communism, the military in those countries arrested, tortured, exiled, and killed thousands of individuals on the slightest suspicion. Political and civil rights were denied. During this period, the rise in politically motivated violence in Central America spurred a massive increase in undocumented immigration to the United States. Because of the U.S. policy of supporting authoritarian regimes in Central America, the Immigration and Naturalization Service (INS) would not recognize as political refugees the people fleeing from El Salvador and Guatemala. In response, a widespread church-based movement arose in the United States to offer them asylum in churches and religious organizations.

With support from the United States, one dictator followed another. In 1967, Anastasio Somoza Debayle became the latest in the succession of Somozas to rule the country. In March 1969, General Omar Torrijos seized the government of Panama from civilian rule and it passed to dictator Manuel Noriega in 1981 upon Torrijos's death in a plane crash. In 1972, dictator Arturo Molina assumed power in El Salvador. However, on October 15, 1979, a military junta ousted President Carlos Humberto Romero in El Salvador, just as El Salvador was on the verge of civil war. The Farabundo Martí National Liberation Front (FMLN), a leftist guerrilla movement, had gained sufficient strength to challenge the power of the infamous "fourteen families" who dominated the nation's economic, political, and social structures. Years of bloodletting ensued, including the Salvadoran military's persecution and killing of nuns and priests, Archbishop Oscar Romero being the most noted victim of assassination. The civil war there and political upheavals and wars in Nicaragua and Guatemala contributed to even larger migrations of refugees to the United States. Salvadorans, in particular, eventually became a substantial immigrant community in the United States.

Under President Jimmy Carter and his attempt to promote human rights around the world, the United States government finally supported the ouster of dictator Somoza from Nicaragua. After great pressure was exerted by the revolutionary Frente Sandinista de Liberación Nacional (FSLN), as well as from the U.S. and neighboring governments, Somoza fled Nicaragua and the Sandinista revolution was triumphant, even garnering support from the United States. But under President Ronald Reagan, and his successor George Bush as well, all of that would change. President Reagan put Latin American affairs within the context of the cold war and the East–West struggle, denying that such long-standing issues as disparity of wealth, deprivation of social mobility, and restriction of political rights were responsible for contemporary protests and violence in Latin America. Instead, he argued that the Soviet Union, through its Cuban proxies, capitalized on these issues to empower local Marxists, who would destroy the economies and offer no hope for political reform. From these Communist outposts, Moscow threatened the United States interests.

Human rights became a policy of the past as military, not economic and social, solutions received first considerations. Within this context, President Reagan was determined to maintain Central America's old order, except in Nicaragua, where he intended to restore it by overthrowing the Sandinista government through funding and supporting the Contras (counterrevolutionaries). To carry out his policy, Honduras became an American military outpost, over $300 million in military aid was turned over to the government in El Salvador for its battle against the FMLN, and the Nicaraguan Contras were supported in a counterrevolution designed to oust the Sandinistas.

The decade of the 1980s marked a turning point in Central American history, however, when regional initiatives were employed to bring about peace. On January 8–9, 1983, four of the neighboring nations of Central America—Mexico, Venezuela, Colombia, and Panama—met on the Panamanian island of Contadora to negotiate for peace in Central America. By July, the Contadora Group issued its first proposals, which included the withdrawal of all foreign military advisors from Central America, the end of aid to irregular forces, and the cessation of military maneuvers in the border regions. From this beginning the Contadora Group went on to recruit other Spanish American states in the process and to develop a consensus in the Americas that the United States should end its militaristic involvement in the area. The process developed over years, continuously hindered by U.S. funding of the Contras, mining of Nicaraguan ports, invasion of Grenada on October 25, 1983, and troop maneuvers in Honduras in 1983. Regardless of these obstacles and others, on September 21, 1984, the Nicaraguan government became the first of the Central American nations to sign the Contadora Group's "Draft Act on Peace and Cooperation." But again, the United States pursued a course of undermining the Contadora process.

On November 25, 1986, news of the Iran–Contra scandal broke in the United States: the U.S. National Security Council had been diverting money from secret arms sales to Iran to clandestine support for the Contras—which had been prohibited by Congress under the 1982 Boland Amendment. U.S. policy towards Nicaragua, which had been judged illegal by the International Court of Justice in The Hague, was exposed as possibly illegal within the United States as well. Despite opposition from President Reagan, the Central American governments ratified their own peace plan, based on one developed by Costa Rican president Oscar Arias Sánchez, on August 7, 1987. The plan called for withdrawal of all foreign military advisors from the area, a complete ceasefire, and the holding of free and pluralist elections in all of the countries in Central America. Implementation of the accords signed by the five republics was to be overseen by the Group of 8 (the Contadora and Lima Groups), the foreign ministers of the Central American countries, and the secretaries general of the United Nations and the Organization of American States. Despite Nicaragua's proceeding to implement the accords and its unilateral declaration of a ceasefire in three of the northern war zones, President Reagan obtained from Congress another $3.2 million for the Contras on September 23, 1987. Later in the year, when he called for more Contra funding, there was a public outcry and defections from his allies in Congress; the administration's policies towards Nicaragua collapsed. Despite continued efforts by the outgoing Reagan administration and the newly elected Bush administration to block the accords, the peace efforts were promoted unilaterally by the Nicaraguan government, which initiated negotiations with the Contras. The efforts were supported regionally and internationally, and eventually resulted in Nicaragua forging a ceasefire treaty with the Contras in 1988 and holding free elections in 1990, with both Sandinistas and Contras as political parties. The elections resulted in the Sandinistas losing the presidency and considerable power, and nonviolently turning the administration over to the moderates headed by newly elected president Violeta Chamorro. For his efforts in forging a regional peace solution in the face of United States opposition, President Oscar Arias Sánchez was

accorded the Nobel Prize. Many of the ideological struggles that had maintained Central America as a war zone during the 1980s ended with the dissolution of the Soviet Union and the Soviet bloc and the collapse of Communism in eastern Europe. Nicaragua ceased to be a target for the U.S. struggle against Communism and, in February 1992, the Farabundo Martí National Liberation Front ended its guerrilla movement by signing a peace treaty with the government of El Salvador. One of the bloodiest civil wars, one that had killed some 75,000 people, had finally come to an end. In exchange for the FMLN laying down its weapons and becoming a legal political party, the government agreed to sweeping changes in the military, including the retirement of more than one hundred officers believed responsible for widespread human rights abuses. During the 1980s, the United States had poured in more than $6 billion in economic and military aid to defeat the FMLN. On May 24, 1994, the FMLN participated in free and democratic elections as a political party in El Salvador. Former human rights ombudsman Armando Calderón Sol, of the ARENA (Nationalist Republican Alliance) party, became president, although the specter of a still very strong military has maintained an uneasy peace in El Salvador to date. United States adventures in Central America were not completely over, however, as the U.S. turned to a growing domestic and international problem: the so-called "war on drugs." In December 1989, President Bush took a definitive and unusual move against a dictator formerly supported by the United States: the U.S. invaded Panama and captured and removed to be tried in the United States President Manuel Noriega, whom it accused of masterminding an international drug trafficking ring and laundering money. The U.S.-backed Guillermo Endara was made provisional president until truly open and democratic elections on May 8, 1994, resulted in a candidate from Noriega's old party, Ernesto Pérez Balladares, winning the presidency.

At the close of the century, Central America seems to have the greatest opportunity in its history for peace and stability, although economic instability remains a fact of life and a threat to long-lasting peace in the volatile region.

SOUTH AMERICA

The conquest of the indigenous populations of South America was effected in much the same way that the Spaniards subdued the native populations of Mexico and Central America. The most infamous of the conquests, of course, was the ruthless and bloody murder of Atahualpa and the destruction of the Inca empire by Francisco Pizarro in 1532. By 1535 the entire Incan empire, which extended into present-day Argentina, Chile, and Colombia, was completed and supplanted by the viceroyalty of Peru. The Indians of Colombia were subdued by Gonzalo Jiménez de Quesada in 1538 and the viceroyalty of New Granada was later founded there. Despite the mineral wealth of Peru, it was Colombia that provided the greatest amount of gold for the Spanish empire. In 1541, Pedro de Valdivia founded Santiago, in Chile, after strenuous resistance from the Araucanian Indians. In 1536, Santa María de Buenos Aires was founded by Pedro de Mendoza; it was recovered by the local Indian nations. When finally reconquered by the Spaniards in 1580, Spanish domination of the New World was complete. Within this very short period of time, what would be the major cultural and civic centers of the continent (with the exception of Rio de Janeiro, which was Portuguese) had been founded and incorporated into the Spanish colonial administration, and the large Indian populations were well on their way to becoming Christians and many of their descendants to being mestizos. By the end of the seventeenth century, Bogotá, Lima, Quito, and Cuzco had become important centers of Spanish culture and even art. One of the earliest universities of the hemisphere was constructed in Lima.

Despite the suppression of the native populations, there were repeated rebellions of the Indians. A major revolt led by Túpac Amaru in 1780 was successful in extending Indian control over all of Bolivia, southern Peru, and parts of Argentina in an effort to reestablish the Inca empire. Although the movement was brutally quashed, sentiments for reestablishing Inca civilization lived on and even furthered the movement for independence from Spain. The large size of the Indian population and the poverty, dispossession of lands, and marginalization it has been subjected to in South America—especially in Peru, Bolivia and Ecuador—have made indigenous issues important themes in politics, government, economics, literature, and art. While the national cultures are infused with indigenous values and customs, and while national identities have relied on the indigenous past, over the last two centuries the same structures of power—the large landholders (mostly of creole background), the church and the caudillos, and dictators they support—have maintained the marginalization of the Indians. But the underlying unrest has reared its head in one political movement after another, such as Raúl Haya de la Torre's Alianza Popular Revolucionaria Americana (APRA), the American Popular Revolutionary Alliance, a widespread movement that became known as Aprism and whose aim was to rescue the Indians from their misery and create a universal system of social security, redistribute the lands, and raise taxes on the mining, oil and agricultural industries. The ultimate goal was the creation of an integrated economy for all of Spanish America, which also would lead to a politically unified Spanish America.

In 1940, after losing in the very destructive Chaco War with Paraguay, another nationalist revolutionary movement, Movimiento Nacionalista Revolucionario (MNR), was founded by Víctor Paz Estenssoro in Bolivia. It became the third most important social and economic reform movement in Latin America, after the Mexican and Cuban revolutions. The MNR was elected into power in Bolivia in 1952 under Estenssoro and, once in government, the party nationalized the mines, redistributed land through an extensive agrarian reform plan, extended civil rights to the Indians, and instituted many other social reforms. In 1953, the Revolutionary Movement Party passed a land decree to redistribute lands equitably, increase productivity and labor, and to integrate

Explorer on a llama, from Ulrich Schmidel, *Vera Historia* . . . , 1559. (Courtesy of the Library of Congress Rare Book and Special Collections Division.)

peasants into the national economy and society. By 1955, most redistribution had been accomplished by the campesinos themselves, who invaded lands and organized peasant syndicates. Half of Bolivia's rural families became land owners, but it took three decades to process certification or entitlement. Much of the reform was disorganized and agricultural production suffered, but the old feudal system was effectively destroyed in Bolivia. The MNR movement was ended in 1964 through a military rebellion.

Today's movements taking up the cause of the Indians and social justice have at times been militant, such as Peru's Sendero Luminoso (Shining Path) Maoist guerrilla movement that have responded to and even arisen from the injustices committed against the original inhabitants of the hemisphere.

The original revolutionary movements on the South American continent were precipitated in 1807, however, when Napoleon Bonaparte invaded Spain and Portugal. Ferdinand VII, the king of Spain, abdicated and Napoleon named his brother Joseph to the throne. The creoles in the Venezuela, New Granada, and River Plate viceroyalties openly denounced the usurpation and refused to recognize Napoleon's representatives. The creoles took the opportunity to begin plotting for the independence of their countries, using their allegiance to the Spanish crown as an excuse for their rejection of the government. The wars of independence broke out, and two liberators with extensive Spanish military experience returned from Europe to free their homelands: the Argentine José de San Martín and the Venezuelan Simón Bolívar.

In 1812, Lieutenant Colonel San Martín returned to Argentina with other patriots to fight for independence. In Mendoza, Argentina, he organized the "Army of the Andes" and in 1813 liberated Argentina. He then crossed the mountain chain and, with the support of Bernardo O'Higgins, liberated Chile in 1817. In 1820, he invaded Peru from the sea and defeated the Spaniards in various battles. San Martín entered Lima victoriously in 1821 and was proclaimed the "Protector" of Peru. In 1822, he met with Simón Bolívar to discuss the future government of the liberated lands in a secret meeting in Guayaquil, Ecuador, and turned his forces over to Bolívar, who finalized the war. San Martín did not want to participate in the nascent discord regarding the future of the liberated colonies, and he retired to live out his days in voluntary exile in France.

Bolívar, a well-educated and well-rounded man who dreamed of a free and confederated Spanish America, returned to Venezuela to lead armies to defeat the royalists in pitched battles. After liberating Venezuela and Colombia, he was named president of Gran Colombia. Bolívar's lieutenant–general, Antonio José de Sucre, defeated the Spanish in Ecuador. Later, Bolívar and Sucre finalized the war in Peru and freed Alto Peru (Bolivia). Bolívar's dream of a United States of South America was frustrated by factionalism and differences in philosophy among the caudillos, who had prevailed in the struggle for indepen-

dence. On his deathbed on December 17, 1830, he is purported to have vented his disappointment at having failed to unite what had become independent republics: "Aquellos que hemos servido a la Revolución hemos arado en el mar." (Those of us who have served the Revolution have plowed in the sea.) Nevertheless, his dream of a United States of South America lives on in among many intellectuals today and among the South American governments that have repeatedly tried to integrate their economies.

Just as in Central America and Mexico, the construction of new governments in the period following independence was characterized by a succession of caudillos seizing power and ruling autocratically. The difficult task for the nineteenth and twentieth centuries was for these republics to achieve democracy and to shed the legacy of feudal organization and power of the church inherited from the Spanish administration of much of the continent. And, when democratic systems were finally achieved in the political realm, achieving control of their economies without domination from external capital was the next challenge. Such was the situation faced by Chile in its brief adoption of socialism in the early 1970s. But by the mid-twentieth century, South America ceased to be a faraway and isolated region of the world, and had come well within the cold war battleground.

Paraguay, the first republic to gain its independence (1813), was also the first to come under a dictatorship. After the Spanish were expelled by a military junta, José Gaspar Rodríguez Francia took over, had himself proclaimed "Perpetual Dictator of the Republic," and immediately closed off the country to outside influence, effectively shutting down the borders for almost fifty years. He was followed by another autocrat, Francisco Solano López, who built up the military and attempted to expand his domain so much that he precipitated the Triple Alliance War (1865–70) with Argentina, Brazil, and Uruguay. Argentina was ruled by such an uneducated and backward, iron-fisted caudillo, Juan Manuel Rosas, during the 1830s that his name has been preserved in some of the most important works of Argentine and Uruguayan literature, especially for his repression of writers.

Of course, one of the most noted dictators of all times was a modern one, Juan Domingo Perón, who rose to prominence during the expansion of fascism in Europe. In 1939, the government sent Colonel Perón to study the German and Italian armies. He not only familiarized himself with fascism, but also became an acquaintance of Benito Mussolini. In fact, Mussolini became Perón's model, even for rhetorical style, and eventually for forming a dictatorship based on one-party politics. Upon his return from Europe, Perón organized the Argentine military lodge, Grupo de Oficiales Unidos (United Officers Group), with seventeen colonels and lieutenant colonels on March 10, 1943; this was the typical Nazi organization that proliferated among the military in Latin America during the war in such countries as Paraguay, Bolivia, Chile, Peru, Ecuador, and Venezuela. On June 4, 1943, the group effected a bloodless coup to remove President Ramón S. Castillo from power. By 1946, Perón had ingratiated himself with the army and the working classes and on February 24, 1946, he was officially elected president of Argentina. Like many dictators, Perón's record was not completely negative. He was successful in expanding the economy and maintaining order and growth. He instituted total economic reorganization of the country via rapid industrialization under his autocratic and at times violent leadership. Perón brought significant progress to the country in the form of benefits for workers, families, and education; under pressure from his wife, Evita, he also brought greater equality to women. It was Perón's economic policy that was chaotic. While he was successful in establishing a national airline, in constructing natural gas pipelines, dams, and hydroelectric plants, and in developing an efficient merchant marine, other programs were disastrous. He nationalized public utilities and public services, including the railroads. He created large bureaucracies to regulate such industries as agriculture, for which he fixed prices and, to cover the country's spiraling debts, he drastically increased the currency in circulation,

thus causing uncontrollable inflation. His policy to transform Argentina's agrarian economy into an industrial one had the effect of accelerating migration from rural areas to the cities and increasing the need to feed and offer welfare to these great urban masses. To remain in power, Perón continuously enabled these masses of workers to shape public policy via public demonstrations and mass movements. On September 16, 1955, Perón himself was deposed by a revolution. He returned from exile eighteen years later, in 1973, and was again elected to the presidency; his third wife, Estela Martínez, was named to the vice presidency. In July 1974, when Perón died, she ascended to the presidency. She, in turn, was deposed in March 1976. But it was his second wife, Eva Duarte (1919–52), fondly called "Evita" by the nation, who gained world fame for the role she played in Perón's government. An ex-actress, she became a fanatically adored public figure whose personal mission was the betterment of the life of the country's workers, whom she called "los descamisados" (the shirtless one) because of their poverty. Through her influence, supposedly, the workers enjoyed a 50 percent wage increase, paid vacations, a shorter work day, and medical and retirement benefits. Thus in the Peróns were summarized all of the excesses, abuses, and benefits of an authoritarian regime.

The penchant for autocratic and militaristic rule was reinforced during the cold war when the United States supported dictators throughout the Southern Hemisphere in its efforts to stem Communism. But American actions towards Latin America have not always been as coldblooded as the above interventions and sponsorship of coups and dictators. President Franklin Delano Roosevelt's Good Neighbor Policy began a more open and egalitarian relationship with Latin America, although it was curtailed with the outbreak of the cold war. But President John F. Kennedy, nevertheless, took the initiative to extend an open hand and support for industrialization and democracy in Latin America. On March 13, 1961, he announced the creation of the Alliance for Progress, an ambitious, $100 billion, ten-year program to bring political reform and social and economic progress to the Southern Hemisphere. As expressed in the Charter of Punta del Este, the alliance called for a 2.5 percent annual economic growth rate, a more equitable distribution of national wealth, trade diversification, emphasis on industrialization, greater agricultural productivity, an end to illiteracy, agrarian reform, increased life expectancy, public housing for the poor, stable price levels, tax reform, and economic development. All of these were to be carried out within the framework of political democracy. The alliance failed to achieve these goals because Latin American elites that controlled the governments resisted social change, tax reform, and democratization, and, in part, because the United States became progressively more involved in Vietnam. By 1971, there were few signs of the improvement of the quality of life for the masses in Latin America, and many of the Latin American governments had come under military control.

During the 1970s and 1980s brutal authoritarian regimes took power in Argentina, Chile, and Peru (in addition to the ones in Brazil and Central America). In its anxiety to rid their nations of Communism, or at least to use that as an excuse, the military arrested, tortured, exiled, and killed thousands of individuals on the slightest suspicion. Political and civil rights were denied. The United States seconded this effort with foreign aid and other backing. The most notable episode in the United States open and covert support and/or intervention was its participation in the overthrow of the democratically elected president of Chile, Salvador Allende.

Allende was the first freely elected Marxist head of state in Latin America. He intended to socialize the economy and began by nationalizing, without compensation, the copper industries—the largest symbol of U.S. presence in the country. He subsequently intervened in other segments of the foreign-dominated economy. In an appeal to labor, Allende froze prices and decreed hefty wage increases. He implemented an agrarian reform program. He also tried to change the national legislature so that it would be more representative of the masses than the elite. Such programs prompted wholesale opposition from the foreign-owned companies, the Chilean landowners, the middle class, and even the workers themselves, who could not keep up with inflationary prices for scarce goods. United States policy towards Chile exacerbated the situation: President Richard M. Nixon severed U.S. trade relations, forbade private bank loans, and prevented loans from the Inter-American Bank and the World Bank. Soon the country was beset by political protest, labor discord, and a general strike that led to a CIA-engineered military coup and the assassination of Allende in September 1973.

The leaders of the military coup took over and ruled the country until 1990 when the junta transferred power to civilians. It was not until 1994 that democratic elections were reinstituted in Chile, with Eduardo Frei winning over the transitional president. This outcome, and the return to democracy in Argentina, Peru, and elsewhere in South America, also were affected by the end of the cold war. At the end of the century, prospects for instituting long-term reforms and maintaining democracy are very high throughout Latin America, but, again, economic stability and relations with the United States are crucial factors in the equation.

Historical Timeline

50,000 B.C.–10,000 B.C. Asian peoples migrate to North America via a land bridge at the Bering Strait.

1500 B.C.–A.D. 1000 Mayan civilization flourishes in the Yucatan Peninsula, Guatemala, and parts of Honduras and El Salvador.

1150 B.C.–A.D. 500 Olmec culture flourishes in Mesoamerica.

1000 B.C. Celts move into the Iberian Peninsula.

500 B.C. The Carthaginians establish themselves on the south coast of Iberia.

200 B.C.–A.D. 1200 The rise of Toltec culture in the Central Valley of Mexico.

200 B.C. The Iberian Peninsula becomes part of the Roman Empire.

A.D. 500 Vandals and Goths invade and conquer the peoples of the Iberian Peninsula.

A.D. 711 The Moors of northern Africa invade and conquer the Visigothic kingdoms of the Iberian Peninsula.

1000 Incan culture emerges in the Cuzco Valley of South America.

1200 The Aztecs arrive at the central plateau of Mexico.

1466 Moctezuma Xocoyotzín, the last Aztec emperor, is born.

1487 The height of Aztec imperial conquests and construction of their great temple-pyramid to the god of war.

1492 Christopher Columbus arrives at an island he calls San Salvador in the Caribbean and encounters Amerindian culture.

1492 Ferdinand of Aragon marries Isabella of Castile and solidifies Spanish dominion over the Iberian Peninsula, with the exception of Portugal. The couple also expel the Moors and the Jews and organize the state religion of Catholicism.

1493 During his second voyage, Columbus reaches the Virgin Islands and Puerto Rico.

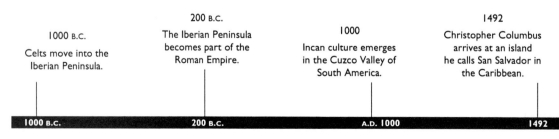

1000 B.C.	200 B.C.	A.D. 1000	1492
Celts move into the Iberian Peninsula.	The Iberian Peninsula becomes part of the Roman Empire.	Incan culture emerges in the Cuzco Valley of South America.	Christopher Columbus arrives at an island he calls San Salvador in the Caribbean.

1493 Pope Alexander VI recognizes the legal claims to land discovered and to be discovered in the Indies by Spain. He authorizes the Catholic monarchs to evangelize the infidels in the New World. He establishes the Line of Demarcation for Spain and Portugal.

1494 During his second voyage, Columbus establishes the first European colony in the New World: Isabella on the island of Hispaniola.

1494 Through the Treaty of Tordesillas, a new Line of Demarcation is established.

1501 Queen Isabella authorizes Nicolás de Ovando to transport slaves from southern Spain to Hispaniola.

1501 Queen Isabella establishes the *encomienda* in the New World.

1503 Construction begins on the first church in the New World: San Nicolás de Bari in the city of Santo Domingo.

1505 The first elementary school is established in the Americas, in Santo Domingo, for children of Spaniards.

1508 The first sugar mill is built in Hispaniola.

1509 Juan Ponce de León explores and settles the island of San Juan Bautista (Puerto Rico) after subduing the native population.

1509 Pope Julius II authorizes the Catholic monarchs to administer the Catholic Church in the Americas.

1510 The official introduction of slavery in the Americas begins when Spain authorizes the importation of 250 slaves to the gold mines in Hispaniola.

1511 After conquering the Indians, Diego Vásquez de Cuéllar begins the settlement of Cuba, founding the cities of Baracoa, Puerto Príncipe, Santiago, and Havana.

1511 The first bishops are installed in Hispaniola and Puerto Rico.

1512 The first cathedral and the first hospital are established in the Americas, in Santo Domingo.

1512 The Laws of Burgos are promulgated to protect the natives.

1513 Antonio de Alaminos explores the Gulf Stream during Juan Ponce de León's expedition of Florida.

1513 Juan Ponce de León explores Florida.

1513 Vasco Núñez de Balboa reaches the Pacific Ocean.

1516 Bartolomé de las Casas is named the official Protector of the Indians.

1516 Juan Díaz de Solís discovers the great River Plate in present-day Argentina and Uruguay.

1517 Francisco Hernández de Córdoba encounters the Yucatan Peninsula and the Mayan Indians.

1519 Alonso Alvarez de Pineda explores the coast of the Gulf of Mexico and claims Texas for Spain.

1501
Queen Isabella establishes
the *encomienda* in the
New World.

1512
The Laws of Burgos are
promulgated to protect
the natives.

1521
The Aztec Empire falls to
the Spaniards.

| 1500 | 1505 | 1515 | 1521 |

1519 Hernán Cortés marches into Tenochtitlán and takes Moctezuma prisoner.

1520 Ferdinand Magellan sets sail on his voyage of circumnavigation.

1521 The Aztec Empire falls to the Spaniards.

1521 In the area called Nicaragua, conquistador Gil González de Avila converts 30,000 Indians to Christianity and sends some 500,000 more as slaves to other parts of New Spain.

1524 Explorer Esteban Gómez sails along the Atlantic coast of North America from Florida to Maine.

1524 King Charles V establishes the Council of the Indies.

1528 Pánfilo de Narváez sails into Tampa Bay and takes possession of the land; later Núñez Cabeza de Vaca becomes shipwrecked and begins nearly ten years of wandering the South and Southwest of the North American continent above the Rio Grande.

1531 Our Lady of Guadalupe miraculously appears to Indian Juan Diego.

1532 Francisco Pizarro invades the Incan Empire, captures and executes Emperor Atahualpa, and conquers the Incas.

1533 The printing press is introduced to the Americas and is brought to Mexico City.

1535 Francisco Pizarro founds the city of Lima as the capital of the conquered lands, which later become the Viceroyalty of Peru.

1536 The city of Santa María de Buenos Aires is founded.

1538 The first university in the Americas is established: St. Thomas Aquinas in the city of Santo Domingo.

1538 Gonzalo Jiménez de Quesada founds the city of Santa Fe de Bogotá.

1539 Hernando de Soto starts to explore the present states of Florida, Mississippi, Tennessee, North Carolina, Arkansas, and Louisiana; he discovers the Mississippi River.

1540 Francisco Vásquez de Coronado begins his expedition in search of Cíbola, or Quivira, the famed cities of gold in the Southwest. He encounters the Grand Canyon, Pike's Peak, and the Rio Grande.

1541 After bloody battles with the Araucan Indians, Pedro de Valdivia founds the city of Santiago in what will become Chile.

1541 Francisco de Orellana discovers the Amazon River in what is now Ecuador.

1542 Juan Rodríguez de Cabrillo discovers the Bay of San Diego in California.

1542 Spain issues its New Laws of the Indies, which officially put an end to the *encomienda*.

1542 Spaniard Bartolomé de las Casas publishes his *Brevísima relación de la destrucción de las Indias* (Brief Account of the Destruction of the Indies).

1544 The Treaty of Crespy is signed by France and Spain.

1550 The *repartimiento*, another form of slavery, is revived to substitute for the outlawed *encomienda*.

1532	1542	1550
Francisco Pizarro invades and conquers the Incan Empire.	Spaniard Bartolomé de las Casas publishes his *Brevísima relación de la destrucción de las Indias* (Brief Account of the Destruction of the Indies).	The *repartimiento*, another form of slavery, is revived to substitute for the outlawed *encomienda*.

1530	1535	1540	1555

1551 Universities are founded in Mexico City and Lima.

1554 Araucan Indian chief Caupolican, allied with Chief Lautaro, offers a series of defeats to the Spaniards, kills Pedro de Valdivia, and on this date defeats the forces of Francisco de Villagrá in Chile.

1560 The Spanish found the first European settlement in what later becomes the continental United States: Santa Elena, in South Carolina.

1562 Bishop Diego de Landa orders the burning of the Mayan codices.

1565 Saint Augustine, Florida, the oldest permanent European settlement on what is now the mainland United States, is founded by Pedro Menéndez de Avilés.

1569 The first part of Spaniard Alonso de Ercilla y Zúñiga's epic poem, *La araucana* (The Araucana), is published.

1580 Spain defeats Portugal and incorporates her and her colonies into the empire.

1580 With the reconquest and settlement of Buenos Aires, the cycle of Spanish conquest is completed in the New World.

1590 Juan de Fuca navigates his ships to the northern coast of present-day Washington State.

1596 The Treaty of the Hague is signed by France, England, and the Netherlands to form an alliance against Spain.

1598 Juan de Oñate begins the colonization of New Mexico.

1600 By 1600, the Spaniards establish the first schools in what will become the continental United States in Florida, New Mexico, and Georgia.

1610 Santa Fe, New Mexico, is founded.

1670 Spain and England sign the Treaty of Madrid.

1680 A Pueblo Indian named Popé leads a rebellion that drives the Spaniards out of northern New Mexico.

1690 San Francisco de los Tejas is founded, the first permanent European settlement in Texas.

1691 Father Eusebio Kino makes his first missionary inroad into Arizona.

1701 The House of Bourbon succeeds the House of Austria to the Spanish throne.

1721 The University of Havana is founded.

1722 The first newspaper appears in the Americas: *La gaceta de México* (The Mexico Gazette).

1722 The first symphony orchestra in the Americas is organized in Caracas, Venezuela.

1760 France cedes to Spain all her claims to lands west of the Mississippi.

1761 The province of Alta California is founded.

1767 King Charles III expels the Jesuits from the Spanish Empire.

1769 The mission at San Diego, California, is established and the colonization of California begins.

1565
Saint Augustine, Florida, the oldest permanent European settlement on what is now the mainland United States, is founded by Pedro Menéndez de Avilés.

1598
Juan de Oñate begins the colonization of New Mexico.

1691
Father Eusebio Kino makes his first missionary inroad into Arizona.

| 1565 | 1600 | 1650 | 1700 |

1773 Spanish expeditions begin to explore the Canadian coast up into Alaska.

1776 San Francisco, California, is founded.

1780 Incan chief Túpac Amaru leads a two-year rebellion against authorities on behalf of the Indians.

1781 Los Angeles, California, is founded.

1783 Academies of fine arts are established in Mexico and Guatemala.

1783 Spain regains Florida.

1793 Spain goes to war with France's Napoleon Bonaparte.

1795 The Pinckney Treaty is signed by Spain and the United States.

1798 The U.S. Congress passes the Naturalization Act.

1800 Spain cedes Louisiana to France through the Treaty of San Ildefonso.

1802 France and England sign the Treaty of Amiens by which Spain cedes Trinidad to England.

1803 The French sell Louisiana to the United States.

1804 President Thomas Jefferson funds the expedition of Lewis and Clark.

1807 Napoleon Bonaparte invades Spain and Portugal. Ferdinand VII abdicates the Spanish throne, and Napoleon names his brother as the successor. Creoles begin plotting the independence of their Spanish American countries.

1810 Under the leadership of Father Miguel de Hidalgo y Costilla, Mexico declares its independence from Spain.

1811 A junta expels the Spanish governor of Venezuela, and Venezuela declares its independence.

1811 Paraguay gains its independence from Spain.

1813 Father José María Morelos y Pavón revives the Mexican independence movement.

1813 José de San Martín and his Army of the Andes liberate Argentina.

1816 José Gaspar y Francia is named Perpetual Dictator of the Republic of Paraguay.

1816 The United Provinces of the River Plate declare their independence.

1817 Bernardo O'Higgins liberates Chile.

1817 The Republic of Gran Colombia is founded.

1817 Spain outlaws the slave trade in all of its provinces to the north of the equator.

1820 Spain outlaws the slave trade in all of its provinces to the south of the equator.

1821 José de San Martín enters Lima in triumph and declares its independence.

1821 Mexico gains its independence.

1821 The United States buys Florida from Spain for $5 million.

1822 Agustín de Iturbide is crowned emperor of Mexico.

1795	1800	1803	1810
The Pinckney Treaty is signed by Spain and the United States.	Spain cedes Louisiana to France through the Treaty of San Ildefonso.	The French sell Louisiana to the United States.	Under the leadership of Father Miguel de Hidalgo y Costilla, Mexico declares its independence from Spain.

| 1750 | 1800 | 1805 | 1810 |

1822 Haiti conquers and absorbs the Dominican Republic shortly after the republic declares its independence from Spain.

1822 Simón Bolívar is ratified as the first president of Gran Colombia.

1823 The Central American Federation is established.

1823 Emperor Iturbide is forced to abdicate the throne of Mexico.

1823 President James Monroe of the United States announces the Monroe Doctrine.

1824 The defeat of the Spanish army at Ayacucho, Peru, signals the end of Spanish rule in Central and South America.

1824 The first conservatory of music in the Americas is founded in Mexico City.

1825 Bolivia gains its independence.

1825 Ferdinand VII returns to the throne of Spain as an absolute monarch.

1826 A Congress of American Republics is held in Panama.

1826 The Spanish surrender their fortress at El Callao, their last stronghold on the continent, effectively ending the wars of independence.

1827 Mexico City's José Joaquín Fernández de Lizardi publishes his powerful novel, *El Periquillo Sarniento.*

1829 Democracy is established in Mexico with the election of its first president, Guadalupe Victoria.

1829 Gran Colombia begins to disintegrate into the countries of Colombia, Ecuador, and Venezuela.

1829 Slavery is abolished by the new republican government in Mexico.

1834 Iron-fisted Miguel Tacón is appointed captain–general of Cuba to quash the independence movement.

1835 The Spanish throne forbids the importation of slaves from Africa to her Caribbean colonies.

1836 Texas declares its independence from Mexico and is victorious over the forces led by General Antonio López de Santa Anna.

1837 The first railroad Spanish America is built in Cuba.

1838–60, Cuba is the world's largest producer of sugar.

1840 The Republic of the Rio Grande is proclaimed.

1844 The regime of dictator Rafael Carrera begins in Guatemala and lasts more than twenty years.

1845 President John Tyler of the United States signs a resolution to annex Texas to the Union.

1846 The Bear Flag Revolt takes place in California.

1846 The United States declares war against Mexico, which brings into the Union territories that form the present states of New Mexico, Colorado, Arizona, and California.

1823
President James Monroe
of the United States
announces the
Monroe Doctrine.

1836
Texas declares its
independence
from Mexico.

1846
The Bear Flag Revolt
takes place in California.

1815   1825   1835   1845

1848 Costa Rica abolishes its army.

1848 President James K. Polk of the United States offers Spain $100 million for Cuba.

1848 The Treaty of Guadalupe Hidalgo is signed by the United States and Mexico, bringing a close to the war.

1849 The Gold Rush lures thousands of Anglos to California.

1850 The Foreign Miners Tax Law is passed in California.

1850 The U.S. Congress passes the Compromise of 1850 to defer the divisiveness of the slavery issue in relation to new states.

1851 The U.S. Congress passes the California Land Act.

1852 President Franklin Pierce of the United States offers Spain $130 million for Cuba.

1853 The United States obtains Mexico's Mesilla Valley through the Gadsden Purchase.

1855 California passes the Anti-Vagrancy Act.

1856 American adventurer William Walker becomes dictator of Nicaragua.

1856 Mexico passes the Lerdo de Tejada Law, forcing the Catholic Church to sell all of its lands and properties not used for religious purposes.

1857 William Walker is driven out of Nicaragua.

1858 Civil war between liberals and conservatives breaks out in Mexico.

1859 President Benito Juárez promulgates the Laws of Reform in Mexico.

1862 The U.S. Congress passes the Homestead Act.

1863 Puerto Rican intellectual Eugenio María de Hostos publishes his attack on Spanish colonialism, *La peregrinación de Bayoán* (The Pilgrimage of Bayoán).

1864 The French intervene in Mexico, with Napoleon III placing the puppet emperor Maximilian on the throne of Mexico.

1865 The Triple Alliance War of Argentina, Brazil, and Uruguay against Paraguay breaks out and lasts until 1870.

1867 After expelling the French, President Juárez marches triumphantly into Mexico City.

1868 Cuban independence from Spain is declared at Yara, thus precipitating the Ten Years' War.

1868 The Fourteenth Amendment to the Constitution of the United States is adopted, declaring all people of Hispanic origin born in the United States to be U.S. citizens.

1868 President Ulysses S. Grant of the United States attempts to annex the Dominican Republic, but the treaty is rejected by the Senate.

1868 Puerto Rican independence is proclaimed at Lares, Puerto Rico, but the insurrection is short-lived.

1871 Esteban Bellán becomes the first Spanish–American to play professional baseball in the United States.

1872 Argentine José Hernández publishes the first part of his epic poem, *Martín Fierro*.

1853	1856	1864
The United States obtains Mexico's Mesilla Valley through the Gadsden Purchase.	American adventurer William Walker becomes dictator of Nicaragua.	The French intervene in Mexico, with Napoleon III placing the puppet emperor Maximilian on the throne of Mexico.

1850	1855	1860	1865

1873 Slavery is finally abolished in Puerto Rico by the Spanish Cortes.

1876 Porfirio Díaz leads a military takeover of the Mexican government and assumes the presidency.

1878 The Cuban professional baseball league is established.

1878 The Pact of El Zajón brings an end to the Ten Years' War in Cuba.

1879 Bolivia and Peru engage in the War of the Pacific with Chile until 1883. As a result, Bolivia becomes landlocked.

1882 Dominican dictator Ulises Heureaux begins his seventeen-year despotic and brutal regime.

1886 The slaves are freed in Cuba.

1889 The first International Congress of the American States is held in Washington, D.C.

1890 The U.S. Congress passes the McKinley Tariff.

1891 José Martí is successful in launching a new independence movement for Cuba.

1894 The Alianza Hispano Americana is founded in Tucson, Arizona.

1898 Autonomy from Spain becomes officially instituted in Cuba and Puerto Rico as does the Law of Universal Suffrage.

1898 The twenty-two-year despotic dictatorship of Manuel Estrada Cabrera begins in Guatemala.

1898 The United States declares war on Spain and, as a result of its victory, obtains dominion over Cuba, Puerto Rico, the Virgin Islands, the Philippines, and Guam through the Treaty of Paris.

1899 The United Fruit Company is formed.

1900 The U.S. Congress passes the Foraker Act, which establishes a civilian government in Puerto Rico under U.S. dominance.

1900 Uruguayan intellectual José Enrique Rodó publishes *Ariel*, contrasting culture in the United States with that of Spanish–American countries.

1901 The Hay–Paunceforte Treaty is signed by the United States and Nicaragua for the building of a transisthmian canal.

1901 Tomás Estrada Palma is elected president of a nominally independent Cuba.

1901 The U.S. Congress passes the Platt Amendment, allowing for U.S. intervention in Cuba.

1902 The U.S. Congress passes the Reclamation Act, dispossessing many Hispanics in the United States of their lands.

1903 Panama rebels against Colombia in order to gain its independence and negotiates separately with the U.S. for the construction of the canal.

1903 The Hay–Bunau–Varilla Treaty is signed by the United States and Panama, allowing for U.S. building of the canal.

1904 President Theodore Roosevelt announces his "Corollary" to the Monroe Doctrine.

1882
Dominican dictator Ulises
Heureaux begins his
seventeen-year despotic
and brutal regime.

1898
Autonomy from Spain
becomes officially
instituted in Cuba and
Puerto Rico as does the
Law of Universal Suffrage.

1870   1880   1890   1900

1905 Upon the assassination of dictator Ulises Heureaux, the U.S. intervenes in the Dominican Republic.

1906 U.S. troops occupy Cuba for three years.

1907 A General Treaty signed by Central American governments, Mexico, and the U.S. calls for nonintervention of Central American governments in each other's affairs and establishes the Central American Court of Justice.

1909 To ward off intervention by the United States, Nicaraguan president José Santos Zelaya resigns. This is the first of a series of Nicaraguan governments that the United States overthrows.

1910 The Mexican Revolution begins.

1911 Emiliano Zapata fights for the Plan of Ayala during the Mexican Revolution.

1911 The regime of Mexican dictator Porfirio Díaz is defeated and the dictator takes flight to Europe after thirty years in power. Francisco Madero is elected to the presidency.

1912 New Mexico achieves statehood.

1912 A period of U.S. military intervention in Nicaragua begins and, with brief interruptions, lasts until 1933.

1913 General Victoriano Huerta, with U.S. backing, has President Madero of Mexico assassinated and seizes the presidency.

1914 Argentina, Chile, Paraguay, Colombia, Venezuela, El Salvador, and Mexico declare neutrality during World War I.

1914 Huerta's army surrenders unconditionally to Carranza's Constitutionalists, who come to power in Mexico.

1914 The Panama Canal goes into operation.

1914 U.S. Marines invade Veracruz, Mexico.

1915 General Francisco "Pancho" Villa is defeated at Celaya.

1915 Mariano Azuela's powerful novel of the Mexican Revolution, *Los de abajo* (The Underdogs), is published.

1916 The United States installs its own military government in the Dominican Republic.

1916 Villa's forces raid the town of Columbus, New Mexico.

1917 The Mexican Revolution is officially over when Venustiano Carranza is elected to the presidency. Under Carranza's leadership, Mexico passes a reform constitution that is the basis for the modern Mexican state.

1917 The U.S. Congress passes the Immigration Act.

1917 The U.S. Congress passes the Jones Act, extending U.S. citizenship to Puerto Ricans.

1918 The U.S. Congress passes the Emergency Tariff Bill, which effectively raises the duty on Cuban sugar by 60 percent.

1919 Adolfo Luque becomes the first Hispanic to play basebell in the World Series.

1919 Zapata is murdered.

1920 Mexican President Venustiano Carranza is assassinated.

1903
The Hay–Bunau–Varilla Treaty is signed by the United States and Panama, allowing for U.S. building of the canal.

1912
A period of U.S. military intervention in Nicaragua begins and, with brief interruptions, lasts until 1933.

1910
The Mexican Revolution begins.

1917
The U.S. Congress passes the Jones Act, extending U.S. citizenship to Puerto Ricans.

| 1900 | 1905 | 1910 | 1915 |

1921 The first of two national origin immigration quota acts is passed by the U.S. Congress.

1921 Mexican muralist David Alfaro Siqueiros publishes his "Manifesto to the Artists in America."

1922 The Partido Nacionalista Puertorriqueño, the nationalist party, is founded in Puerto Rico.

1924 The Alianza Popular Revolucionaria Americana (APRA) is formed by Raúl Haya de la Torre in Peru.

1925 The Border Patrol is created by the U.S. Congress.

1926 In riots in Harlem, Puerto Ricans are attacked by non-Hispanics.

1926 The Mexican government suspends the practice of Catholicism in Mexico. This leads to the Cristero War, which lasts until 1929.

1929 The League of United Latin American Citizens is founded in Texas.

1930 Dictator Rafael L. Trujillo comes to power in the Dominican Republic. He reigns until his assassination in 1961.

1930 *Independent School District (Texas) v. Salvatierra* finds that Mexican Americans have been segregated.

1930 The U.S. Congress passes the Hawley–Smoot Tariff, dealing a serious blow to the Cuban sugar industry.

1931 Between 1931 and 1938, authorities at various levels of government conduct a mass repatriation program of Mexicans from the United States.

1933 The Chaco War breaks out between Bolivia and Paraguay. It lasts until 1938.

1933 Farmworkers begin the El Monte berry strike in Los Angeles County, California.

1933 In a revolt by sergeants in the Cuban army, Fulgencio Batista comes to power and rules through a series of puppets until his election in 1940.

1933 One of Latin America's most infamous dictators, Anastasio Somoza, assumes power in Nicaragua.

1933 President Franklin Delano Roosevelt of the United States announces his "Good Neighbor Policy."

1934 During the presidency of Lázaro Cárdenas, an average of 8.2 million acres per year is redistributed to peasant families in Mexico.

1934 Juan D. Perón founds the Justicialismo (Justicism) movement in Argentina.

1934 President Roosevelt annuls the Platt Amendment.

1934 The Puerto Rican Communist Party is formed.

1935 The first edition of Argentine writer Jorge Luis Borges's *Ficciones* (Fictions) is published.

1936 Argentine statesman and jurist Carlos de Saavedra Lamas wins the Nobel Peace Prize.

1936 The Federation of Agricultural Workers Union of America is established.

1924
The Alianza Popular Revolucionaria Americana (APRA) is formed by Raúl Haya de la Torre in Peru.

1929
The League of United Latin American Citizens is founded in Texas.

1933
President Franklin Delano Roosevelt of the United States announces his "Good Neighbor Policy."

1920   1925   1930   1935

1936 Puerto Rican nationalist Pedro Alvizu Campos is arrested and charged with sedition against the United States.

1936 Sixto Escobar becomes the first Puerto Rican to win a world boxing championship.

1937 Puerto Rican police massacre nationalists during a Palm Sunday demonstration in Ponce, Puerto Rico.

1938 Mexican and Mexican–American pecan shellers strike in San Antonio, Texas.

1938 The Mexican government nationalizes the oil industry.

1938 A national congress of Hispanic peoples is organized in Los Angeles, California.

1940 Fulgencio Batista is elected president of Cuba.

1940 The Movimiento Nacionalista Revolucionario is pioneered by Víctor Paz Estenssoro.

1941 Hispanics in the United States enthusiastically support the involvement of the United States in World War II and become the most decorated ethnic group of soldiers.

1941 President Roosevelt establishes the Office of Inter-American Affairs.

1941 The U.S. Congress passes the Fair Employment Practices Act.

1942 The Mexican Farm Labor Supply Program, or "Bracero Program," is established in the United States. It continues until 1964.

1943 Pedro Alvizu Campos's U.S. citizenship is revoked.

1943 The U.S. Congress passes Public Law 45, which finances and regulates the Bracero Program.

1943 The "Zoot Suit Riots" begin in southern California.

1944 The industrialization program known as "Operation Bootstrap" is initiated in Puerto Rico.

1944 The Partido Independentista Puertorriqueño (Puerto Rican Independence Party) is founded.

1945 Chilean poet Gabriela Mistral becomes Latin America's first Nobel laureate.

1945 Juan José Arévalo is installed as president of Guatemala as the result of a social revolution that ousts the traditional dictatorial regimes.

1945 Mexican American parents in Orange County, California, win a lawsuit (*Méndez et al v. Westminster School District*) alleging segregation of their children.

1945 A popular uprising proclaims Juan Perón as president of Argentina.

1946 The dominant political party in Mexico is rebaptized to its present name: Partido Revolucionario Institucional (Institutional Revolutionary Party).

1947 The American G.I. Forum, a civil rights organization, is established by Mexican–American veterans.

1947 Argentine biologist Bernardo A. Houssay wins the Nobel Prize for physiology and medicine.

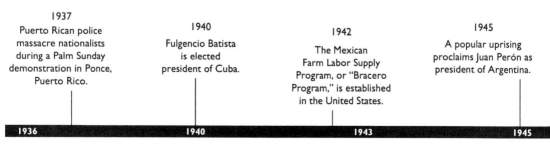

1937
Puerto Rican police massacre nationalists during a Palm Sunday demonstration in Ponce, Puerto Rico.

1940
Fulgencio Batista is elected president of Cuba.

1942
The Mexican Farm Labor Supply Program, or "Bracero Program," is established in the United States.

1945
A popular uprising proclaims Juan Perón as president of Argentina.

1936   1940   1943   1945

1948 Mexican–American tennis player Richard Alonso "Pancho" González becomes singles champion at Forest Hills and plays on the U.S. Davis Cup team.

1949 Luis Muñoz Marín serves as the first Puerto Rican governor elected by the citizens of Puerto Rico.

1950 Puerto Rican nationalists attack President Harry S Truman's residence at Blair House.

1950 The U.S. Congress upgrades Puerto Rico's status from protectorate to commonwealth.

1951 The U.S. Congress passes Public Law 78, which formalizes the Bracero Program as the Migratory Labor Agreement.

1952 The Commonwealth of Puerto Rico is instituted. It continues as the official status of the island to the present time.

1952 Fulgencio Batista comes to power again in Cuba through a coup d'etat.

1952 The Movimiento Nacionalista Revolucionario is elected to power in Bolivia under Víctor Paz Estenssoro.

1952 The U.S. Congress passes the Immigration and Nationality Act.

1953 Puerto Rican René Marqués's play of dislocation and migration, *La carreta* (The Oxcart), makes its debut in New York.

1954 Argentine dictator Perón is overturned by a military and popular democratic movement known as the Liberating Revolution.

1954 The Central Intelligence Agency engineers a coup to oust Jacobo Arbenz from the presidency of Guatemala. He is replaced by military dictator General Carlos Castillo Armas.

1954 General Alfredo Stroessner takes power in Paraguay and becomes the longest-lasting dictator in Latin America.

1954 Puerto Rican nationalists shoot up the U.S. House of Representatives.

1954 Through "Operation Wetback," more than one million Mexicans are deported from the United States.

1954 The United States and Panama sign a new canal zone treaty.

1957 The Civil Rights Act is the first passed by the U.S. Congress since the end of the Civil War.

1958 The Latin American Association for Free Commerce is founded by Argentina, Brazil, Chile, Mexico, Paraguay, Peru, and Uruguay.

1958 Women, for the first time, enjoy full suffrage in elections in Mexico.

1959 Fidel Castro's Cuban Revolution triumphs, sending dictator Fulgencio Batista into exile. In the years that follow, hundreds of thousands of Cubans go into exile in the United States.

1960 Cuba's Fidel Castro establishes diplomatic relations and trade with the Soviet Union. The Cuban government expropriates and nationalizes all property and businesses owned by U.S. citizens and interests.

1960 Mexico establishes a border industrialization program to attract foreign corporations to

1949
Luis Muñoz Marín serves as the first Puerto Rican governor elected by the citizens of Puerto Rico.

1952
The Movimiento Nacionalista Revolucionario is elected to power in Bolivia under Víctor Paz Estenssoro.

1954
The Central Intelligence Agency engineers a coup to oust Jacobo Arbenz from the presidency of Guatemala.

1958
Women, for the first time, enjoy full suffrage in elections in Mexico.

1948   1950   1955   1960

operate assembly plants on its border with the United States.

1961 President John F. Kennedy of the United States announces the creation of the Alliance for Progress.

1961 A U.S.-backed counter-revolutionary invasion at Cuba's Bay of Pigs fails.

1962 Edward R. Roybal is elected to Congress from California's Twenty-fifth District. He subsequently holds his seat in Congress the longest of any Hispanic: more than thirty years.

1962 President John F. Kennedy brings the United States to the brink of nuclear war when he forces the Soviet Union to remove its missiles from Cuba. In return for their removal, he promises the U.S. will not invade or support others' invasions of Cuba.

1963 A popular Mexican–American voter revolt in Crystal City, Texas, leads to the eventual founding (1971) of a Mexican–American political party, the Raza Unida Party.

1963 Reies López Tijerina organizes the Alianza Federal de los Pueblos Libres (Federal Alliance of Free Towns) in New Mexico.

1964 The Organization of American States votes to sever diplomatic and commercial relations with Cuba.

1964 The U.S. Congress passes the Equal Opportunity Act and the Civil Rights Act and creates a host of programs for President Lyndon Baines Johnson's "Great Society" initiative.

1965 César Chávez begins to lead the United Farmworkers through a series of strikes and national boycotts in the creation of a farmworkers' union.

1965 Luis Valdez founds El Teatro Campesino in Delano, California.

1965 President Lyndon Baines Johnson sends the marines to the Dominican Republic to prevent another Cuban-style Communist takeover.

1965 The United States–Mexico border industrialization program is initiated.

1965 The U.S. Congress revises the Immigration and Nationality Act of 1952.

1966 Puerto Rican youths riot in Chicago.

1966 The Texas poll tax is declared unconstitutional.

1967 Guatemalan novelist Miguel Angel Asturias wins the Nobel Prize for literature.

1967 Reies López Tijerina and his followers raid the Tierra Amarilla courthouse in New Mexico.

1967 The U.S. Congress mandates schools to provide programs for children of limited English-speaking ability.

1968 For the first time in history, the Olympic Games take place in Latin America: Mexico City.

1968 General Omar Torrijos overthrows the government in Panama.

1969 An attempt is made to establish a common market by the Andean Group of Bolivia, Colombia, Chile, Ecuador, and Peru.

1962
President John F. Kennedy brings the United States to the brink of nuclear war when he forces the Soviet Union to remove its missiles from Cuba.

1965
César Chávez begins to lead the United Farmworkers through a series of strikes and national boycotts in the creation of a farmworkers' union.

1968
For the first time in history, the Olympic Games take place in Latin America: Mexico City.

| 1962 | 1964 | 1966 | 1968 |

1969 War breaks out between El Salvador and Honduras. It lasts until 1980.

1970 Argentine Luis F. Leloir wins the Nobel Prize for chemistry.

1970 Colombian novelist Gabriel García Márquez publishes *Cien años de soledad* (One Hundred Years of Solitude).

1970 Patrick F. Flores becomes the first Mexican–American to be consecrated as a bishop of the Catholic church.

1970 Salvador Allende becomes the first democratically elected socialist president of Chile.

1971 Chilean poet Pablo Neruda receives the Nobel Prize for literature.

1971 Mexican–American author Tomás Rivera publishes his novel of migrant farm labor *...y no se lo tragó la tierra* (And the Earth Did Not Devour Him).

1971 The Mexican–American political party, Raza Unida Party, is born.

1972 Ramona Acosta Bañuelos becomes the first Hispanic treasurer of the United States.

1973 The Central Intelligence Agency of the United States engineers a coup that results in the assassination of President Allende of Chile and the installation of a military dictatorship.

1974 Puerto Rican jockey Angel Cordero wins the Kentucky Derby.

1974 Puerto Rican Miguel Piñero wins the New York Drama Critics' Circle Award for Best American Play, an Obie, and a Drama Desk Award for *Short Eyes*.

1974 The U.S. Congress passes the Equal Educational Opportunity Act.

1974 The U.S. Supreme Court, in *Lau vs. Nichols*, holds that the San Francisco Unified School District discriminates by not providing programs for limited English-speaking students.

1975 The California Legislature passes the California Labor Relations Act.

1976 Rolando Hinojosa becomes the first U.S. Hispanic to win the international Las Américas Prize for Literature from Cuba.

1977 The Congressional Hispanic Caucus is founded in the United States.

1977 President Jimmy Carter of the United States leads the Congress to approve a new Canal Zone treaty that will turn over the governance of the zone to Panama in the year 2000.

1978 The Sandinista Front for National Liberation begins its revolution to topple the dictatorship of Anastasio Somoza Debayle in Nicaragua.

1978 Thomas Flores becomes the first Hispanic to be named coach of a professional football team in the United States: the Oakland Raiders.

1979 Julián Nava becomes the first Mexican–American to serve as an ambassador to Mexico.

1979 A military junta takes power in El Salvador just as the leftists' guerrilla movement

1971
The Mexican–American political party, Raza Unida Party, is born.

1973
Chilean President Salvador Allende is assassinated.

1977
President Jimmy Carter of the United States leads the Congress to approve a new Canal Zone treaty that will turn over the governance of the zone to Panama in the year 2000.

1970   1972   1974   1976

gains enough power to throw the nation into civil war.

1979 The Sandinista revolution is triumphant in Nicaragua.

1980 The military junta in El Salvador appoints José Napoleón Duarte to the presidency.

1980 Argentine architect and sculptor Adolfo Pérez Esquivel wins the Nobel Peace Prize.

1980 A flotilla of boats assists 125,000 Cubans escaping from the Castro regime through Mariel Harbor.

1980 Ronald Reagan begins his two terms as president of the United States, during which time he considers Latin American affairs solely within the context of the Cold War and the East–West struggle.

1980 The U.S. Congress passes the Refugee Act, redefining the category of "refugee" for immigration purposes.

1982 Argentina attempts to recover its Malvina Islands, held by England since the nineteenth century. This provokes a short war with England, which Argentina loses.

1982 Colombia's Gabriel García Márquez wins the Nobel Prize for literature.

1982 Mexican currency is devalued more than 70 percent.

1982 Mexican diplomat Alfonso García Robles wins the Nobel Peace Prize.

1983 A regional initiative to create peace in Central America, known as the Contadora Process, begins and is eventually successful in

bringing diplomatic solutions to the conflicts in Nicaragua and El Salvador.

1986 Luis Walter Alvarez of the United States wins the Nobel Prize for physics.

1986 News breaks of illegal arrangements by U.S. government officials to surreptitiously fund the Nicaraguan Contras through arms sales to Iran.

1986 The United States creates an alien legalization program through the Immigration Reform and Control Act.

1987 Central American governments ratify the peace plan of the Contadora Process, largely through the initiative of Costa Rican president Oscar Arias Sánchez.

1987 Oscar Arias Sánchez is awarded the Nobel Peace Prize.

1988 President Ronald Reagan appoints Lauro F. Cavazos to the cabinet post of Secretary of Education.

1988 The Sandinistas in Nicaragua forge a peace treaty with the Contras.

1989 The United States invades Panama in its war against the illicit drug trade.

1989 Ileana Ross Lehtinen becomes the first Cuban elected to the U.S. Congress, representing Florida.

1989 Thomas Flores is named president and general manager of the Seattle Seahawks football team, the highest rank ever for an Hispanic in professional sports.

1980
A flotilla of boats assists 125,000 Cubans escaping from the Castro regime through Mariel Harbor.

1983
A regional initiative to create peace in Central America, known as the Contadora Process, begins and is eventually successful in bringing diplomatic solutions to the conflicts

1989
The United States invades Panama in its war against the illicit drug trade.

| 1980 | 1983 | 1986 | 1989 |

1990 Cuban–American novelist Oscar Hijuelos wins a Pulitzer Prize for *The Mambo Kings Play Songs of Love.*

1990 Free elections are held in Nicaragua with both Sandinistas and Contras participating as political parties. The Sandinistas lose power and Violeta Chamorro is elected.

1990 Patricio Aylwin wins a referendum on military rule in Chile and is successful in replacing General Augusto Pinochet as the nation's leader.

1990 The signing of a one-year trade agreement, instead of the usual five, between the Soviet Union and Cuba signals the end of Soviet support of the Cuban economy.

1991 Cuba hosts the XI Pan American Games in Havana.

1991 Guatemalan Indian leader Rigoberta Menchu receives the Nobel Peace Prize.

1991 Mikhail Gorbachev announces the withdrawal of Soviet troops from Cuba.

1991 President George Bush of the United States signs the Cuban Democracy Act, which further bans trade with Cuba.

1992 Mexican poet and essayist Octavio Paz becomes his country's first Nobel laureate in literature.

1993 Chile has peaceful democratic elections for the first time in more than two decades.

1993 Colombia passses the Negritude Law to protect the black population against discrimination.

1993 President Bill Clinton of the United States appoints two Hispanics to his cabinet: former mayors Henry Cisneros and Federico Peña.

1994 El Salvador holds its first free elections in sixty-four years.

1994 Luis Donaldo Colosio, candidate for the Mexican presidency, is assassinated in Tijuana.

1994 Mexico celebrates its first presidential debates in history.

1994 The North American Free Trade Agreement (NAFTA) is instituted to integrate the economies of the U.S., Canada, and Mexico.

1994 The Zapatista National Liberation Army begins a guerrilla war and political movement to improve the plight of dispossessed Indians in Chiapas, Mexico.

1995 The Mexican peso is devalued, losing perhaps one-third of its value against the dollar and causing havoc in the Mexican stock market and among investors abroad. An international loan-guarantee package of $53 billion is made available to Mexico to shore up the peso.

1991
Mikhail Gorbachev
announceÁs the
withdrawal of Soviet
troops from Cuba.

1994
The North American Free
Trade Agreement (NAFTA)
is instituted to integrate the
economies of the U.S.,
Canada, and Mexico

| 1990 | 1992 | 1994 | 1995 |

Part 1

ENCOUNTER OF THE PEOPLES
50,000 B.C. - 1492

Chapter 1

50,000 B.C. TO A.D. 1492

50,000 B.C.–A.D. 1492

50,000–10,000 B.C. Asians Cross Bridge into West. Asian peoples migrate to North and South America via a land bridge at the Bering Strait. The groups bring with them a Neolithic and possibly Paleolithic civilization and, as they descend the length of the hemisphere, they diversify into nations with separate languages and cultures. The indigenous civilizations of the Western Hemisphere rely heavily on agriculture for subsistence and over the centuries develop numerous agricultural products, such as corn, potatoes, and beans that will become the food staples of a great portion of mankind. From 7000 B.C. to 2000 B.C., the indigenous peoples develop an economy based on the cultivation of maize. From 2000 B.C. to 1000 B.C. they establish a village culture. Among their accomplishments over the centuries are architecture, textiles, astronomy, some sciences, the use of precious metals and copper, metallurgy, ceramics, and basketry. But their most important contribution is the discovery and development of corn, without which their advanced civilizations would not have evolved. In addition to serving as the principal staple for many groups, corn thus becomes central to customs, religion, and industry.

1500 B.C.–1000 A.D. Mayan Civilization Flourishes. Mayan civilization prospers in the Yucatan Peninsula, Guatemala, part of Honduras, and El Salvador. The Mayas are superb architects of grand cities carved out of jungles by mathematicians, scientists, and artists. Their calendar, astronomy, mathematics—the Mayas contribute the concept of zero to math and science—and writing are the most advanced in the Americas, beyond even those of European civilization at the time. Making the transition from a nomadic life to a sedentary one in Central America around 2000 B.C. to 1500 B.C., by A.D. 300 they have developed the major characteristics of their civilization, principally in the Petén region of Guatemala. By the year A.D. 900, the Yucatan is the center of Mayan life, and an important cultural exchange with the Toltecs of the central valley of Mexico takes place that brings on a renaissance Mayan–Toltec culture. Of all of the pre-Columbian civilizations of the Americas, the Mayas are the most accomplished in architecture, sculpture, painting, hieroglyphic writing, mathematics, and astronomy. By the fourth or third century B.C. they create the first system of numeration by position that utilizes the concept of zero. Their skill in astronomy is probably more highly developed than that of the Egyptians during the fourth to first centuries, B.C. By the first few centuries after Christ, they are able to predict eclipses and chart the course of Venus; they also develop the concept of the 365-day year. And by the sixth or seventh century, their priests can

A relief produced by Mayan artists in Palenque, Mexico, during the Classical Period. (Courtesy of the Library of Congress Prints & Photographs Division.)

make corrections to the solar year more accurately than was done a thousand years later, in 1582, under the direction of Pope Gregory. In pottery and weaving, the Mayas are behind other civilizations; in government and social organization, the Aztecs exceed them. In the twelfth and fifteenth centuries, Mayan civilization is shaken by internal wars that apparently led to the decline and impotency the Spaniards will encounter in the sixteenth and seventeenth centuries.

1150 B.C.–500 A.D. Olmecs Build Monuments. Olmec culture flourishes in Meso-America, in the area that is currently occupied by the states of Veracruz and Tabasco in Mexico. The Olmecs build stone monuments, including the large stone heads for which their culture is known.

1000 B.C.–1492 A.D. Civilizations Build on Iberian Culture. The Iberian Peninsula, the closest western European crossing point to north Africa, becomes a crossroads for traders and conquerors traveling north and south and westward via the Mediterranean Sea. Numerous peoples and civilizations not only visit the peninsula, leaving their influence on the first Iberians, but also conquer and build their civilizations on the base of Iberian culture. Around 1000 B.C., Celts move into the Iberian Peninsula. In 500 B.C., the Carthaginians establish themselves on the south coast of Iberia. In 200 B.C. the Iberian Peninsula becomes part of the Roman Empire, a culture that contributes the foundation of the Spanish language that in later centuries becomes the language of conquest in the Americas. In A.D. 500 Vandals and Goths invade and conquer the peoples of the Iberian Peninsula, supplanting the Roman Empire. In A.D. 711 the Moors of northern Africa invade and conquer the Visigothic kingdoms of the peninsula and contribute the second largest influence (after the Roman) on what will become Spanish culture: Islam and Arabic culture. The modern nation state of Spain under one king, one religion, and one sword is founded with the final expulsion of the Moors in 1492 and the marriage of King Ferdinand of Aragon and Isabella of Castille, the Catholic monarchs who unite or conquer all of the kingdoms in Iberia, except for Portugal. After seven hundred years of crusades against Islam on their own soil, the Spaniards are ready to spread Christianity to the New World.

200 B.C.–1200 A.D. Toltecs Known for Writing, Architecture. One of the most important indigenous groups is that of the Toltecs, a

Mayan palace at Palenque with observatory. (Courtesy of the Library of Congress Prints & Photographs Division.)

Nahuatl people who are the first to arrive in the central valley of Mexico. While their civilization flourishes, the Toltecs achieve a written culture, in books and scrolls made of paper with an ideographic writing, and construct gigantic monuments and cities decorated with carved and painted stone. They are the architects of the great ceremonial city of Teotihuacán, which is celebrated for its Pyramid of the Sun, Pyramid of the Moon, and Temple of Quetzalcoatl.

1000 A.D.   Incan Empire Flourishes. Incan civi-

lization emerges in the Cuzco Valley of South America, and later expands through conquest to include the modern countries of Peru and Bolivia and parts of Argentina, Chile, and Ecuador. It is the most geographically far-reaching of the ancient American civilizations. The Incas are able to govern this vast expanse, which includes mountains, jungles, and deserts, by creating a sophisticated system of roads, bridges, and communications, even a postal service. Like the Aztecs, Toltecs, and Mayas, the Incas are superb architects, but their civilization is the one most based on order and accounting, with all sectors of life rigorously organized, divided, and subdivided by government functionaries, engineers, and accountants. This organization includes a highly segmented class system, the division of labor and responsibility, and the division of lands and agriculture. Of noteworthy development is medical science; the Incas practice cranial surgery, are able to amputate limbs, and develop drugs and anesthesia. The greatest expansion and flourishing of the Inca Empire begins in 1438 with the ascension to the throne of Pachacuti (1438–93) and ends with the Spanish conquest. Three other emperors rule during this flowering: Túpac Inca (1471–93), Huayna Cápac (1493–1525) and Atahualpa (1500–33). By the time Francisco Pizarro arrives in 1531, the empire reaches to Tucumán in Argentina, to the center of Chile, and to northern Ecuador.

1200 A.D.   Aztec Expansion. The Aztecs, also known as the Mechicas and Tenochas, arrive at the central plateau of Mexico in the thirteenth century and become subjects of the Toltec Empire. By the year 1312, they take possession of an island in the middle of Lake Texcoco. They build pyramids to their gods on this island which they call Tenochtitlán, and develop one of the most grandiose cities in the Americas, the one destined to become Mexico City under the Spaniards. The Aztecs gradually conquer other Amerindian nations in the central valley and as far east and west as both coasts of Mexico and down into Guatemala. The height of their imperial conquests comes in 1487, the same year they consecrate their great temple-pyramid to the god of war, Huitzilopochtli (on the site of today's Cathedral of Mexico in Mexico City), with the sacrifice of twenty thousand prisoners of war. The conquered peoples become part of a confederation ruled by a type of military democracy and is divided into ranks of nobles, priests, soldiers, common folk, and slaves, all headed by a chief of state (the Spaniards erroneously call him an emperor). Aztec

civilization furthers the advances of the Toltecs in art, architecture, literature, education, and, most importantly, military science and social organization. What is most often remembered about the Aztecs is their practice of a highly developed religion based on human sacrifice.

1394   Portuguese Slave Trade. During the reign of Portuguese king Henry the Navigator, the Portuguese trade in African slaves for Europe is centered in the Atlantic islands of the Azores and Madeira. On these islands, the role of the slaves changes from the traditional one of domestic servants to that of workers on sugar plantations and mills. Two centuries later, more or less, when the sugar culture is developed in the Caribbean, expertise in the management of African slaves is readily available for further exploitation.

c. 1451   Christopher Columbus Is Born. Christopher Columbus (1451?–1506) is probably born in this year in Genoa, Italy, into what some scholars say is a family of Jewish merchants. Others claim that he is born into a poor Christian family of weavers. By 1475, he has served as seaman on ships in the Mediterranean. In 1476, while headed for the Atlantic, raiders seize the ship he works on and throw him into the ocean off the coast of Portugal, which thus leads him to Lisbon, the center of navigational activity at that time. From Lisbon, Columbus sails on various expeditions, probably as far north as Iceland. In Lisbon, he gains access to the upper class after marrying a lady of importance; she dies shortly after bearing him a son, Diego. Columbus learns Castilian, the language of the upper-class Portuguese, and most importantly he learns all of the navigational science that the Portuguese have pioneered in their African explorations. It is in Portugal that Columbus's idea to reach Asia by sailing west is born. After seeking the support of various monarchs, Columbus is able to contract with Spain's Catholic monarchs, Isabella and Ferdinand, to search for an ocean route to the Orient in exchange for the hereditary title of admiral, the position of vice-

Columbus bids farewell to the King and Queen of Spain. In *Nova Typis Transacta Navigatio*, 1621. (Courtesy of the Library of Congress Rare Books and Special Collections Division.)

roy and governor of all of the islands and lands that he might discover, and one-tenth of all of the metals and precious stones acquired. Columbus sets out on August 3, 1492, from the Spanish port of Palos de Moguer, and arrives at the island of San Salvador (today's Watling Island or Samana Cay) on October 12, 1492, thus initiating the process of European conquest and colonization of the New World, a process that also begins the blending of races and cultures of the peoples from Europe, Africa, and the Americas. It is estimated that some 35 to 45 million people are living in the Western Hemisphere at that time, a number soon to be greatly diminished by the Spanish conquest and by the infectious diseases that the Spaniards introduce to the New World. Columbus's second voyage, which begins on September 25, 1493, is considered his most important, for it is the first mission in which a colony is established in 1494 at Isabella on the island of Hispaniola. Brought over during this voyage are horses, mules, cows, other livestock and farm animals, sugar cane, seeds, and plants that were introduced to the

Detail of Queen Isabella from a painting by Bartolomé Bermejo. (Courtesy of the National Palace, Madrid.)

one of the most important exploits in history, forming the basis of modern society and culture in the Western Hemisphere. Columbus dies in ignominy, the victim of jealous competitors and politics at court, on May 20, 1506, in the Spanish city of Valladolid. The cathedral of Seville claims to have his bones in a tomb inscribed with "the ingratitude of America."

c. 1460   Ponce de León Is Born. Explorer and political figure Juan Ponce de León is born close to this date in Valladolid, Spain. Some scholars believe him to have come from a distinguished family while others quote Father Bartolomé de las Casas in attributing his origins to a poor family. Las Casas states that Ponce de León came to the Indies as a peon on Christopher Columbus's second voyage in 1493. His name first appears on a document in 1504 as participating in a campaign against the Indian village of Higuey in Hispaniola. For his actions in the campaign, he is promoted to lieutenant and settles in the village of Salvaleón, Hispaniola. In 1509, Ponce de León is engaged in exploration and settlement of the island of San Juan Bautista (Puerto Rico); he then is appointed governor as a reward for his labors. Ponce de León is noted for putting down Indian uprisings in Puerto Rico. He is removed as governor of the island in 1511 and returns to Spain in 1512. In negotiations with the Spanish crown, it is decided that Ponce will lead expeditions to settle Bimini (Florida). He must cover expenses himself, but will receive 10 percent of all royal revenues derived from the exploitation of Bimini. Ponce de León's expedition leaves Spain on March 4, 1513, and arrives at the coast of Florida on April 3. After exploring the coast, he returns to Spain to report to the Council of the Indies and to make new proposals to the crown. He is granted new concessions and appointed captain general of an armada against the Carib Indians. In 1520, Ponce de León sets out on his last journey, to take possession of Florida for the crown. His expedition subsequently is destroyed by the Indians of the peninsula, and he returns to Cuba with an arrow wound that takes his life.

colony for the first time. The voyage also is charged by the Catholic monarchs with Christianizing the natives; thus a Brother Buil and eleven other religious missionaries take part in the enterprise. The record seems to show that Columbus, during these and his two voyages in 1498 and 1502, is convinced that he has found Cathay (China). In all, he discovers and charts for the Spanish crown the islands of Cuba, Hispaniola, Puerto Rico, Jamaica, the Virgin Islands, and others, and the mainland from Venezuela to Honduras. It is without a doubt

Central plaza of the Aztec, c. 1519.

1466 Aztec Emperor Moctezuma Is Born. Moctezuma Xocoyotzín, the last Aztec emperor, is born, the son of Axayácatl. He succeeds his grandfather, Ahuizotl, to the throne and governs over the Aztec federation from 1502 until his death on June 29, 1520. As a celebration of his ascension to the throne, he effects a large military campaign against the Otomí Indians, taking a great deal of booty and some five thousand prisoners, many of whom will be sacrificed to the gods. In 1506, he also conquers the Mixtec Indians. Under his supremely religious rule, the education of the young becomes even more severe than it has been earlier, and he imposes rigorous discipline at court and in other sectors of Aztec life. Because of various religious beliefs and prophecies, he sends emissaries to Hernán Cortés, attempting to persuade him not to venture into the interior of Mexico. Moctezuma finally agrees to receive Cortés at the temple of the goddess Toci, which he does on November 8, 1519. Although Cortés professes friendship, he takes Moctezuma prisoner, which Moctezuma, fearful of Spanish reprisals against his people, keeps secret. Nevertheless, on June 20, there is a popular uprising against the Spaniards. When Cortés returns on May 27, he convinces Moctezuma to present a speech from the roof of his palace in order to calm his people. The exact circumstances of his death are disputed, with versions declaring that he was stabbed by the Spaniards, that he died brokenhearted in his prison cell or that he was wounded by a stone thrown from the crowd during his speech. In any case, the primary cause of Moctezuma's death was the Spanish invasion and takeover, and his problematic leadership and death lead to the defeat of the Aztecs and the end of their civilization.

1470 Díaz de Solís Is Born. Explorer and cartographer Juan Díaz de Solís is born into a prosperous merchant family near Seville, Spain. While growing up, he becomes infected with the desire to travel and, over his family's objections, decides to study cartography. For a while, Díaz de Solís serves the king of Portugal as a cartographer. In 1505, he returns to Spain and, according to some sources, he then leaves on a voyage of exploration that Vicente Yáñez Pinzón carries out along with Christopher Columbus in 1506. It is believed that they sailed to the Greater Antilles, Central America, and northern South America. At a meeting in Burgos,

The myth of the Aztec founding of Tenochtitlán is depicted in this early illustration for a Spanish chronicle. (Courtesy of the Arte Público Press Archives, University of Houston.)

Spain, in 1508, attended by Díaz de Solís, Amerigo Vespucci, Vicente Yáñez Pinzón, and others, it is decided to launch a voyage to find a passage to Asia through the New World continent. That same year, Díaz de Solís participates in a voyage that explores the coasts of Honduras and Mexico, without finding such a passage. When Vespucci dies in 1512, Díaz de Solís is named the head pilot of the Accounting House (Casa de Contratación) in Seville. After Vasco Núñez de Balboa discovers the Pacific Ocean in 1513, Díaz de Solís is again given the mission of finding a passage from the Atlantic Ocean to the Pacific. He leaves Sanlúcar in 1515 at the head of three ships and follows the coast of South America. In February of 1516, he discovers the great Río de la Plata, which he names Mar Dulce (Sweet Sea). He also travels up the Uruguay River and explores inland. In 1516, the Charrua Indians capture him and, it is said, eat him before the eyes of his men on board their ships.

1470 Spanish Missionary Bartolomé de las Casas Is Born. Bartolomé de las Casas, a Dominican missionary famous for his campaigns to protect the Indians, is born into a noble family in Seville, Spain. Las Casas studies humanities, philosophy, and law at the University of Salamanca, where he also becomes acquainted with Thomist doctrine that will inform all of his future written works. After graduating, he departs for the Americas on February 13, 1502, to follow in his father's footsteps as a conquistador, participating in various campaigns against the Indians in Santo Domingo. In 1510, however, Las Casas becomes an ordained Dominican friar; after exercising the faith for a while and being a holder of an encomienda, a form of slavery that is supposed to further the cause of Christianizing the Indians, Las Casas has a spiritual and humane conversion to protecting the same Indians that he had fought and had held in forced service. His first target is the abuses of the conquistadors and colonists against the Indians, and the hated encomienda itself, which he strives to abolish. Las Casas reports inhumane treatment of the Indians, including massacres, rapes, the razing of villages, torture, and dismemberment. After Las Casa pursues his cause at court in Spain, Cardinal Cisneros names him "Protector of the Indians" and he is given a budget to

Bartolomé de las Casas, "Defender of the Indians." (Courtesy of the Library of Congress Prints & Photographs Division.)

carry on his cause. But in the Indies, he meets continuous opposition, including that of the missionary and religious establishment; he thus returns to Spain at various times to pressure for the enactment of laws and their enforcement. After many failures and much frustration in his efforts to enforce the policies that he has worked to create at court, Las Casas returns to Spain definitively in 1523, and becomes a priest and a prolific writer who defends the Indians and seeks to abolish the encomienda. This time, he succeeds in influencing the creation of *Las Leyes de Indias* (The Laws of the Indies). He travels to Santo Domingo, and then to Mexico to personally introduce the laws and to see to their enforcement. In Santo Domingo, he and other friars demonstrate how the Indians could be converted peacefully rather than through conquest. In 1542, in Valladolid, Spain, he was instrumental in writing what becomes the *Nuevas Leyes de las Indias* (The New Laws of the Indies), which officially put an end to the encomienda and enslavement of the Indians. In 1542, Las Casas also finishes writing his famous *Brevísima relación de la destrucción de las Indias* (Brief Account of the Destruction of the Indies), in which he details the history of mistreatment of the Indians. In 1544, Las Casas is named bishop of Chiapas. He dies in Spain in July 1566. In Spanish history Las Casas is seen as one of the initiators of the "Black Legend," a propaganda campaign against the Spanish conquest and colonizing of the Americas, later taken to extreme heights by the English and Dutch in their competition with the Spanish for the new lands. By emphasizing and exaggerating the conquistadors' and colonists' inhuman treatment of the natives, the other colonial powers assumed the moral high ground and justified their designs on Spanish-held territories.

1475   The Culture of Conquest. The reign of the Catholic monarchs begins in Spain and lasts until 1516. The period represents the transition from the Middle Ages to modernity, and is characterized in Spain by the Catholic monarchs unifying the peninsula under one government, one church, and one language. It is also the beginning of the age of exploration and colonization of the Americas by Spain. This transition from a medieval world view to a modern one is particularly evident in the colonization of the Americas. Government and religious forms and institutions relate to a militant church and the creation of Spanish nationalism during the reconquest of the peninsula from the Moslems who are transplanted to the New World just as they are dying out in Spain. The first culture transplanted to the New World by the Spaniards is the culture of conquest, which includes the military and religious apparatus necessary for conquering "heathens" and converting them into Spanish Catholics. One important institution, left over from the Middle Ages, that gains new life and purpose in the Americas is the Spanish Inquisition.

1475   Núñez de Balboa Is Born. Spanish explorer Vasco Núñez de Balboa is born in Jerez de los Caballeros, Spain, into a once noble family now reduced to poverty. For this reason,

at an early age he enters into the service of the lord of Moguer, Pedro Portocarrero, as a page. Attracted by the opportunity for riches and adventure, Núñez de Balboa leaves for the Americas in 1501. In Hispaniola, he establishes a farm worked by Indians, but it is a total failure. In 1510, he stows away on a caravel and escapes penury in Hispaniola. In battles and explorations, Núñez de Balboa rises to distinction and leadership, and eventually is named governor of territories in Central America. On September 25, 1513, an expedition he leads arrives at the shores of the Pacific Ocean (which the Spaniards call the South Sea). He claims for Spain all lands touched by the waters of the South Sea. After a few years of political intrigues, Núñez de Balboa is deposed of his governorship of Darien and reduced to poverty once again. In 1517, he is accused and found guilty of treason, for which he is decapitated in Acla in 1519.

1478   Francisco Pizarro Is Born. Francisco Pizarro is born in Trujillo, Cáceres, Spain, the illegitimate son of a colonel, and is raised in Spain in abject poverty. As a young man, having served in the wars against Italy, he sails for the Caribbean in 1502, where he takes part in various expeditions, including Núñez de Balboa's to the Pacific Ocean. In 1524, he joins the adventurer Diego de Almagro and the rich cleric, Hernando de Luque, in an expedition to conquer the Incas of Peru. They launch two ill-fated expeditions. After their failure, Pizarro prevails upon the Spanish crown, in 1529 to name him governor, captain general, and adelantado, or official explorer and governor, of all the lands that he would conquer. He returns to Panama with his brothers Gonzalo, Hernando, and Juan. In 1531, he leaves with 183 men and 37 horses on three ships sailing southward. He disembarks in San Mateo, founds San Miguel and heads inland, where he is able to take advantage of the civil war raging between the Incas of the emperor Atahualpa and Huácar. Pizarro is able to capture and execute Atahualpa in 1532. He founds the city of Lima, Peru, in

Francisco Pizarro. (Courtesy of the Biblioteca Nacional, Madrid.)

Cortés entering Tenochtitlán. (Courtesy of the Library of Congress Prints & Photographs Division.)

1535 and names it the capital of the conquered lands, which becomes the viceroyalty of Peru in 1544. In June 1541, Pizarro is assassinated by followers of Almagro, who dispute his authority over Cuzco.

1485   Hernán Cortés Is Born. Hernán Cortés, the Spanish conqueror of Mexico, is born a nobleman in Medellin, Spain. After finishing his studies at the University of Salamanca, he leaves for the Indies, where he establishes himself in Hispaniola in 1504. He takes part in the conquest of Cuba under Diego Velásquez de Cuéllar in 1511. On February 10, 1519, Cortés sails for Mexico and, upon his arrival, leads some six hundred men onto the mainland, where he fights Indians in Tabasco and San Juan de Ulloa. He founds the city of Veracruz and separates himself and his men from Velásquez, ordering that his own ships be sunk to prevent the men who did not recognize his authority from returning to Cuba. He works an alliance with various Indian nations and marches his men into the Aztec capital of Tenochtitlán in 1519, where he takes the emperor Moctezuma prisoner after the emperor has received him honorably at his palace. Cortés then travels to

the coast to fight and defeat an expedition sent after him by Velásquez. During this time, the Aztecs revolt and push the Spaniards out of the Tenochtitlán. Cortés reorganizes his forces and, by August 1521, conquers the Aztecs led by Cuauhtémoc, through a siege of the capital that lasts seventy-five days. Cortés later executes Cuauhtémoc. King Charles V rewards Cortés with the titles of governor and captain general of New Spain. He proves to be an able administrator and organizes various expeditions in the directions of Honduras and California. Charles V later names him marquee of the Valley of Oaxaca, but, after years of personal attacks from other colonial officials, Cortés returns to Spain a disillusioned man in 1540. He dies in Castilleja de la Cuesta, near Seville, in 1547. From 1519 to 1526 Cortés writes his own account of the conquest in his *Cartas de relación* (Letters of Account).

c. 1490   Explorer Cabeza de Vaca Is Born. Alvar Núñez Cabeza de Vaca is born in Jerez de la Frontera (some sources say he is born in 1507 in Extremadura), Spain, into a prominent military and political family. His family has enough means to provide a tutor for the children, a fact

Lithograph of Hernán Cortés. (Courtesy of the Library of Congress Prints & Photographs Division.)

that may explain Cabeza de Vaca's ability to write books in a compelling and historic documentary style. After his education, Cabeza de Vaca becomes part of the managerial staff of the duke of Medina–Sidonia in the port of Sanlúcar de Barrameda, a port of departure for voyages to the Americas. Because of this experience, he later secures a position as treasurer for the armada that explores Florida under the leadership of Pánfilo de Narváez, an expedition which sets sail from Sanlúcar in June 1527. After weathering a hurricane, the armada enters Tampa Bay on April 12, 1528. Pánfilo de Narváez takes possession of the land and immediately begins a long and disastrous march inland, plagued by starvation and confrontations with hostile Indians. Lost, and with only two hundred of the six hundred men left, the expedition finally finds the sea and begins to build barges. After more than a month of constructing the vessels while warding off Indian attacks, the men set sail—horse hides have been sewn into sails—and come to the mouth of the Mississippi. Cabeza de Vaca's barge is shipwrecked, and he and his men are taken in by local Indians. By the winter of 1528, there

are only fifteen survivors left. The Indians, who also are ill, force the survivors to become "healers," and Cabeza de Vaca begins his career as a renowned physician among the Indians. During the six years that he remains in this area, he also becomes a merchant, a translator, and what might be considered today an anthropologist or ethnographer, for he records in great detail for the first time many observations about the Indians of the South and Southwest. In 1534, he and four other marooned survivors set out on a march west in search of New Spain. They travel on foot across Texas and into New Mexico, going from one tribe to the next as healers and traders. In 1536, they finally encounter Spaniards in what is today northwestern Mexico. Cabeza de Vaca's ten-year journey from Florida to New Mexico ends when he sets sail from Mexico for Spain in April 1537. The details of the journey and the peoples he encounters are still widely read today in his memoir, *La relación y comentarios* (The Account and Commentary). The memoir may be the first ethnographic study of the Americas, as well as a literary masterpiece, possibly the first book of "American literature" written in a European language. Cabeza de Vaca returns to the Americas in 1540, to become the governor of Río de la Plata, where he meets hostility from the colonists and is accused of abuse of power and arrested. In March 1545, he is allowed to leave for Spain. In Seville, the Council of the Indies condemns him to eight years of banishment from the court. After serving his sentence, Cabeza de Vaca is appointed a judge in Seville. It is in this city that he writes of his experiences in the Americas. He dies in 1557 (other sources give the date of death as 1559 and 1564).

APRIL 17, 1492 Monarchs Meet Columbus's Terms. The contract between the Catholic monarchs and Christopher Columbus to find a route to Cathay and to complete the discovery of the world is signed in Granada. The contract is drafted by the royal secretary, Juan de Colona, the same person who just seventeen days earlier had signed the edict expelling the Jews from

An engraving by Theodore De Bry depicting Columbus meeting the Indians. (Courtesy of the Library of Congress Prints & Photographs Division.)

Spain, and who just 107 days before had conquered the last Moorish stronghold in Spain, Granada. Columbus is represented by Brother Juan Pérez. The terms obtained by Columbus are those that a merchant would request: to be the chief admiral of Spain, the viceroy and governor of newly found lands and the judge over each legal issue brought before him in those lands. Columbus also seeks to retain part of all merchandise found, bought, or traded. All of Columbus's terms are met by his royal patrons, and after his discovery, on May 20, 1493,

the Catholic monarchs even authorize his adding one more lion and one more castle to his coat of arms. (*See also* biography, c. 1451.)

AUGUST 3, 1492 The Santa María, Niña, and Pinta. Columbus sets sail from the Spanish port of Palos de Moguer with three caravels: the admiral's Santa María with 39 men; the Niña commanded by Vicente Yáñez Pinzón with 22 men; and the Pinta, under Martín Alonso Pinzón with 26 men. (*See also* biography, c. 1451.)

Portrait of Christopher Columbus based on a painting by Laurens Lotto dated 1512. (Courtesy of the Library of Congress Prints & Photographs Division.)

OCTOBER 12, 1492 Columbus Lands in Eastern Bahamas. Columbus lands on an island he calls San Salvador—either present-day Watling Island or Samana Cay in the eastern Bahamas. (*See also* biography, c. 1451.)

OCTOBER 27, 1492 Columbus Expects Gold, Finds Poverty. Columbus and his crews land on the northeastern shore of Cuba. Convinced that it is either Cipango or Cathay, Columbus sends representatives to the Great Khan and his gold-domed cities, only to find impoverished Arawak living in *bohíos* (huts). (*See also* biography, c. 1451.)

Part 2

THE CONQUEST
& COLONIZATION OF THE
AMERICAS 1492-1820

Chapter 2

1493–1499

MARCH 15, 1493 Voyagers Return to Spain.
Columbus returns from his first voyage of discovery to his port of departure, Palos de Moguer. (*See also* biography, c. 1451.)

MAY 1493 Pope Divides Lands, Seeks to Expand Church. Spain prevails upon Pope Alexander VI to recognize its legal claims to the lands discovered by Columbus and those that would be found on subsequent voyages. Only the pope has the authority to extend Christianity to other parts of the world. Portugal, which is carrying out similar explorations in Africa and islands in the near Atlantic, also seeks such authorization from the pope. In the papal bull of 1493, Alexander VI draws a Line of Demarcation from north to south, one hundred leagues to the west of the Azores, and declares that all lands to the east will belong to Portugal and all lands to the west will belong to Spain. That line will later be altered. Pope Alexander VI also authorizes the Catholic monarchs to evangelize the infidels in Africa, to subject them to the throne, and to govern them. The pope thus implements the medieval principle that he, as the vicar of Christ, can assign to Christian rulers the territory inhabited by barbarous peoples so that these rulers may extend the church. Similarly, Pope Alexander VI concedes to the Catholic monarchs in May 1493 the right to Christianize the New World. This same royal patronage gives the king and his representatives the right to later construct churches on the ruins of the Pyramid of the Sun in Tenochtitlán.

SEPTEMBER 25, 1493 Columbus' Second Voyage. Christopher Columbus's second voyage is considered his most important, for it is the first mission in which a colony is established at Isabella on the island of Hispaniola. He also discovers the Virgin Islands and Puerto Rico on this voyage. These are the oldest former Spanish possessions that are part of United States patrimony today. Puerto Rico also has the distinction of being the oldest colony in the hemisphere: a colony of Spain from 1493 to 1898, and then of the United States from 1898 to the present. (*See also* biography, c. 1451.)

1494 Line of Demarcation Is Moved. King John II of Portugal pressures Spain to move the Line of Demarcation 370 leagues to the west of the Cape Verde Islands. Both countries sign the Treaty of Tordesillas, agreeing to the new line. In 1500, Portugal discovers Brazil, which is located within that demarcation.

SUMMER 1494 Columbus Sails to Jamaica. After establishing the colony of Isabella on Hispaniola, the first permanent European settlement in the New World, Columbus sets sail and encounters Jamaica. (*See also* biography, c. 1451.)

c. 1496 Prince Cuauhtémoc Is Born. The heroic leader of the Aztec resistance against the Spaniards, Cuauhtémoc, is born around 1496 in Tenochtitlán. His name in Nahuatl signifies descending eagle, or eagle who descends like the sun. Cuauhtémoc receives the privileged education of the royalty and upper classes, learns the traditional discipline, and goes through the rigorous training for future military leaders. By the time of the arrival of Hernán Cortés in Mexico, Cuauhtémoc has already distinguished himself as a military leader and has been named a Supreme Leader. After Cortés leaves the city of Tenochtitlán to head off Pedro de Alvarado's march on the city, Cuauhtémoc leads a fierce attack on the Spaniards left behind, defeats a force of some four hundred, and breaks up Cortés' returning troops. Cortés is successful in getting Moctezuma to try to persuade the Aztecs to lay down their arms of rebellion. Cuauhtémoc is credited by some with challenging Moctezuma and of even hurling the stone from the crowd that kills the bewildered emperor of the Aztecs. Cuauhtémoc is then successful in driving the Spaniards and their Indian allies from the city and inflicting great losses upon them. With Moctezuma dead, and his successor to the empire dead shortly thereafter from smallpox, Cuauhtémoc ascends to the throne and rules until the ultimate defeat of the Aztecs in various battles and a long siege that lasts from May 30 to August 13, 1521. Cuauhtémoc is captured and tortured, but he is not killed by Cortés until February 26, 1525, when the Spanish leader suspects an Indian rebellion.

c. 1497 Pedro de Valdivia Is Born. Pedro de Valdivia, born sometime between 1497 and 1500 in Villanueva de La Serena in Badajoz, Spain, is a nobleman who distinguishes himself in Charles V's wars against Italy. He later joins in expeditions of conquest in Venezuela and Peru under Pizarro. In Peru he becomes a wealthy owner of mines. With two hundred Spaniards and some thousand Indians, Valdivia conquers Chile. After bloody battles to defeat the Araucan Indians, Valdivia founds the city of Santiago on February 12, 1541, and various others, including La Imperial, Valdivia, and Confines. Named governor and captain general of the new province, he also sends expeditions over the Andes into what later becomes Argentina. In the conquest of Chile, Valdivia meets his strongest, most heroic resistance from the Indian chiefs Caupolicán and Lautaro. Valdivia dies in Tucapel, Chile, in January 1554, in battle against the Araucanians led by Lautaro.

1498 Díaz del Castillo, Chronicler of the Conquest of Mexico, Is Born. Bernal Díaz del Castillo, a Spanish soldier who accompanies Hernán Cortés in his conquest of Mexico, is born in Medina del Campo, Spain, into a notable family. As a young man, in 1514 he seeks his fortune in the New World at the side of governor of the mainland, Pedrarias de Avila. Díaz del Castillo soon leaves Pedrarias to enter the service of Cuban governor Diego Velázquez de Cuéllar; from Cuba he participates in the discovery of Yucatan, and in 1518 returns to Cuba with property and station. Almost immediately, he joins Hernán Cortés' expedition to Mexico and participates in the conquest of the Aztecs. As a member of the Spanish army, Díaz de Castillo fights the Aztecs and other nations in 110 battles. For his service against the Aztecs, Cortés rewards Díaz del Castillo with an encomienda in Guatemala. Upon reading inaccurate accounts of the conquest, Castillo feels obligated to set the record straight. He begins to document his experiences and, in so doing, becomes the most famous chronicler of the Americas. Bernal Díaz del Castillo is the author of the historical chronicle and literary masterpiece that details the taking of Mexico: *Verdadera historia de la conquista de la Nueva España* (The True History of the Conquest of New Spain), which he finishes in Guatemala in 1568, the same year as his death. It is first published in Madrid in 1632.

1499   Friar Bernardino de Sahagún Is Born.
Friar Bernardino de Sahagún, a Spanish Franciscan missionary and scholar, is born in Sahagún, León, Spain. He studies at the University of Salamanca, and later teaches in that city. In 1529, he and nineteen other missionaries are sent to Mexico to work among the Indians for the next sixty years. He becomes an expert in Nahuatl, the language of the Aztecs, and in the beliefs and practices of the Aztecs and other Amerindian nations. He is a prolific writer of ethnography, history, and devotional works. His most respected work is *Historia general de las cosas de Nueva España* (General History of the Things of New Spain), which he first writes in Nahuatl and then later translates into Spanish. Unfortunately, it is not published until 1829, some three hundred years after it is written. The book amounts to an encyclopedia of Aztec culture, including their religious beliefs, sciences, and culture. In the volume, Sahagún also transcribes interviews with Aztecs who lived prior to the arrival of Cortés. Sahagún systematically and carefully checks and compares information provided by various sources, attempting to arrive at exact data. He is considered the first "modern anthropologist" of the Americas. He dies in Tlaltelolco, Mexico, on February 5, 1590.

1500–1519

1500   Conquistador de Soto Is Born. Explorer Hernando de Soto is born in Jerez de los Caballeros, Spain, to a Spanish father and a Portuguese mother. At the early age of fourteen, he arrives in the Indies and takes part in the conquest of Nicaragua, after which he serves on the *cabildo,* or city council, of its newly established capital, León. He soon is promoted to captain and also becomes a landowner and businessman. In 1531, de Soto contributes four ships and one hundred men and enlists as a captain in Pizarro's march and assault on Peru. De Soto is documented as having obtained

An illustration of the smallpox epidemic among the Aztecs as a result of contact with the Spaniards, in Sahagún's *Historia general de las cosas de Nueva España.* (Courtesy of the Smithsonian Institution.)

eighty kilos of gold and sixty of silver as booty in the conquest of Peru. During his time in Nicaragua and Peru, de Soto has liaisons with at least two Indian women, with whom he fathers children. He leaves them, although he does include at least his first two children in his will, and returns to Spain alone to enjoy his riches by living in a luxurious fashion. In 1539, de Soto returns to the Americas, this time heading up an expedition to conquer Bimini

(Florida). Prior to his leaving for the Indies, he is named governor of Cuba; when he leaves that island for Bimini, his new Spanish wife remains on the island as governor. From 1539 to 1542, de Soto explores what are now the states of Florida, Alabama, Mississippi, Tennessee, North Carolina, Arkansas, and Louisiana. In May 1541, he arrives at the Mississippi River, the largest river he has ever seen. He names it Río Grande de la Florida (Great River of Florida). During the course of his journeys, de Soto loses one thousand men and he takes ill and also dies at the age of forty-two (1542).

c. 1500   Indian Chief Caupolicán Is Born. Caupolicán, the Indian chief who leads the Araucanians against the Spaniards in Chile, is born sometime around the turn of the sixteenth century. He becomes chief in 1533 and leads his people against the invaders, defeating Spanish forces in the Valley of Tucapel on December 2 and 3 and later executing their leader, Pedro de Valdivia, on December 25. With support from another Indian chief, Lautaro, he is able to defeat the forces of Francisco de Villagrá in April 1554. An Indian traitor later leads García Hurtado de Mendoza in a surprise attack on Caupolicán at Monte Pinto (later named Concepción). Hurtado de Mendoza sentences to death all of the Araucanians that he captures, some six thousand of them. In 1558 Caupolicán suffers a torturous death by impalement.

SEPTEMBER 3, 1501   African Slave Trade Authorized. Queen Isabella authorizes Nicolás de Ovando to transport slaves from southern Spain to Hispaniola. This is the official beginning of the use of African slaves in the New World. The permission is given for the importation of African slaves who belong to Christians and who have been Christianized. It is the Catholic monarchs' duty to keep the New World for Christianity and thus neither Jews nor Moslems, free or enslaved, not even those who have converted to Christianity, are allowed in the Spanish colonies. And it is Spain's role in the New World to bring Christianity to the Indi-

ans. But despite the institution of the encomienda, a form of slavery in which the Indians are to be Christianized and Hispanicized in return for their forced labor, the Indians are neither culturally nor physically accustomed to the hard work imposed by the Spaniards in exploiting mines and running sugar plantations; the Indian populations also are being decimated by diseases imported from Europe. Thus, black slavery becomes a necessity if Spain is to develop the revenues it needs. And many of the first reports assure the crown that the blacks adapt extremely well to the climate and environment as well as to the hard labor in the Indies. There is no accurate way to judge how many slaves are taken from Africa to Spanish America over two centuries; by the time of independence of many of the countries and the abolition of slavery that accompanied independence, it is estimated that some 70,000 slaves are being imported per year. By 1511 the Casa de contratación (Contract House) informs King Ferdinand that one black slave is doing the work of four Indians and that it is necessary to bring more slaves from Guinea. In 1518, a special commission of Jeronymite fathers, sent to Hispaniola for the express purpose of determining the need for African slaves versus the duty to keep the New World for Christians, confirms the need for slaves directly from the west coast of Africa. In that year alone forty new sugar plantations are founded in Hispaniola based on African slave labor. That is the end of bringing in Christianized African slaves and the beginning of more massive importation and exploitation of African slaves. By 1551, King Charles V requires more funds to sustain his wars in Europe and begins selling the licenses for the importation of slaves; that first year alone he sells 123,000 licenses. For the next two centuries, this becomes a lucrative source of revenue for the crown. On June 6, 1556, the crown also begins levying a tariff on the importation of slaves to the New World.

SEPTEMBER 16, 1501   Queen Extends Encomienda to New World. After heavy lobbying by Nicolás de Ovando and other colonists,

An engraving by Theodore De Bry illustrating slaves working in a sugar mill in all of the different processes. In De Bry's *Americae*, 1590. (Courtesy of the Library of Congress Prints & Photograph Division.)

Queen Isabella decides to extend to the New World the system that was being used by Castile to exploit the agricultural lands with conquered Moorish labor: the encomienda, a Christianizing form of slavery. The queen thus dictates on this date and on December 20, 1503, the rules by which Indians would be parceled out (*repartimientos*) to discoverers, conquistadors, and colonists. The encomienda becomes central to colonizing two continents and to the formation of a Catholic, mestizo, Spanish-speaking society there. Ideally, the encomienda is to represent royal patronage over the Indians vested in the *encomendero*, who is supposed to be a benevolent teacher and moral example of faith and citizenship. In actuality, the encomienda creates wealth for the owners and ultimately for the government and crown. Many political and social problems are caused for Spanish colonists by the encomienda, and numerous critics in Spain and in the New World, such as Father Bartolomé de Las Casas, fought for its abolition and for the retreat of the Spaniards from the New World—except for the missionaries, that is.

1503   Church Constructed in Santo Domingo. Spanish American architecture—religious, civil and military—is initiated in the city of Santo Domingo with the construction of the church of San Nicolás de Bari, from 1503 to 1508.

FEBRUARY 14, 1503   Contract House Governs Commerce. Queen Isabella creates the Casa de Contratación (Contract House) in Seville to govern the commerce with Spain's New World colonies. In 1495, the port of Cadiz had been designated as the only port to serve the trade from the Indies, and in 1501 it was declared that anyone who wished to leave for the Indies had to be licensed. The Contract House is to enforce these orders. In 1543, duty is levied on all commerce with the Indies and the Contract House is empowered to collect this duty. In the years that follow, the Contract House becomes the customs office, the court, the post office, the admiralty, the naval school, the center for geographic study, the warehouse, and the market for people and things having to do with Spain's colonies in the Americas. The first head of the Contract House is Amerigo Vespucci.

1505   School Established for Children. The first elementary school is established in the Americas, in Santo Domingo, for the children of the Spaniards. From then on, elementary schools are included in convents, teaching children reading, writing, arithmetic, and religion. Later, the mission system in the Americas functions to instruct the children of Indians and mestizos.

1508   Cuba Circumnavigated. Sebastián de Ocampo circumnavigates Cuba and proves that it is an island, contrary to what Columbus believed.

1508   Ponce de León Governs Puerto Rico. Juan Ponce de León sails in a small caravel for Puerto Rico. He establishes friendly relations with the native chieftain, Agüeybana, who presents him with gold. In 1509 Ponce de León, with soldiers and dogs, subdues the native population of the island and is appointed governor of Puerto Rico. (*See also* biography, c. 1460.)

1508   Sugar Comes to the Americas. The first agricultural product introduced to the Americas by the Spaniards is sugar. Originally from India, the plant is taken to Hispaniola and then to the rest of the Americas for its cultivation. The first sugar mill is built in 1508 or 1509 on Hispaniola, and the first samples of sugar are sent to Spain about 1515. By 1523, there are twenty-four mills operating on the island.

1509   Conqueror of Colombia Is Born. Gonzalo Jiménez de Quesada is born in Córdoba (at the time part of Granada, Spain), a son of the nobility. After studying law in Spain, he becomes a judge in the coastal city of Santa Malta in Colombia in 1535. From there he leads an expedition of eight hundred soldiers by land and river to the interior, looking for El Dorado; takes various Chibcha Indian chiefs as prisoners; subdues the native population; and founds the city of Santa Fe de Bogotá in 1538. The Spanish crown names him governor of all of the lands that he has conquered, an area which in the eighteenth century becomes the viceroyalty of New Granada (1717). He writes an account of the conquest, which he entitles *Relación de la conquista* (The Account of the Conquest). He dies of leprosy in Mariquita, New Granada (present-day Colombia), on February 16, 1579.

1509   First Outpost on Mainland. The Spaniards establish their first outpost on the mainland near present-day Panama. Alonso de Ojeda founds and is declared governor of the eastern part of the Gulf of Darien, which the Spaniards call New Andalusia, and Diego de Nicuesa is given the western part, known as Castilla de Oro (Golden Castle). The Gulf of Darien is to become the center of conquest and colonization for the southern continent.

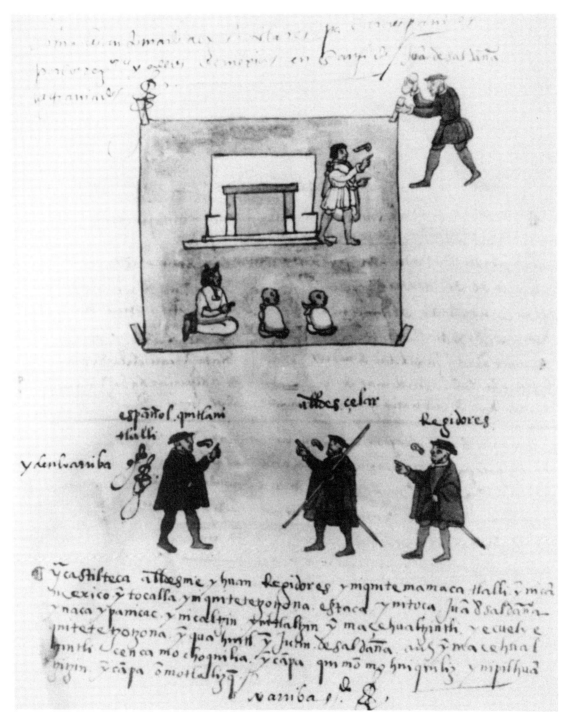

Spanish authorities parceling out land plots to the Indians, according to the *Tudela Codex,* written in Mexico, 1536–66. (Courtesy of the Archivo General de las Indias, Seville.)

1509 Ponce de León Negotiates for Produce. Juan Ponce de León negotiates a treaty with the Carib Indians on St. Croix (then Santa Cruz) for them to supply the Spaniards with agricultural produce. However, his crew's attempt to enslave some of the Carib Indians triggers a war that spreads throughout the Caribbean. By 1600, the Carib Indians have abandoned St. Croix, and also migrated from many of the newly founded Spanish island colonies. (*See also* biography, c. 1460.)

1509 Spaniard Settles Jamaica. Spaniard Juan de Esquivel begins the settlement of Jamaica, near what is today St. Ann's Bay. A small population of Spaniards who ranch cattle is established there, but the area never becomes important to the Spanish crown.

1509 Spanish Kings to Administer Catholic Church in New World. Pope Julius II authorizes the Catholic kings of Spain to administer the Catholic Church in the Americas in exchange for underwriting the costs of evangelization in the New World. In 1511, he issues a bull, the Pontifex Romana, which establishes various dioceses in the New World.

1510 Explorer Francisco Vásquez de Coronado Is Born. Francisco Vásquez de Coronado is born in Santander, Spain. As a youth, he attends the university to study humanities, but soon abandons that career and leaves for the Indies. In 1535, he arrives in Mexico and becomes part of the court of Viceroy Antonio de Mendoza. Politically well-connected through marriage to a noble wife, Coronado eventually becomes the governor of Nueva Galicia. In 1540, he sets out as head of several hundred Spaniards and Indian allies on an expedition financed by his wife to search for Cíbola or Quivira, rumored to be the location of the seven cities of gold. Traveling north into today's Southwest, Coronado conquers various Indian tribes, including Zunis living in what is thought to be the cities of gold. On August 25, 1540, the expedition encounters the Grand Canyon;

they later reach the Rio Grande, which they name Nuestra Señora (Our Lady). Along the way, the Europeans have their first encounters, some peaceful, others violent, with many native groups; included in these are the massacres of the Tiguex and Cicuye Indians. At some points, Indians tell of four, earlier European visitors: Cabeza de Vaca and his companions. Coronado never locates the supposed cities of gold, but travels as far north as today's state of Nebraska. He notifies the king that the lands are poor in metals but rich in livestock and very suitable for farming. In his journey, Coronado covers more territory in a shorter period of time than any other Spanish explorer to date. In so doing, he prepares the way for future settlement of what has become the Southwest of the United States. He returns to Nueva Galicia in 1541. Coronado dies in Mexico City in 1554.

1510 First Slaves Sent to Gold Mines. The beginning of the official, authorized introduction of slavery into the New World occurs when the government of Spain orders its agents at Seville to send 250 slaves to the gold mines in Hispaniola.

1510 Velázquez Leaves to Conquer Cuba. Diego Velázquez de Cuéllar (1465–1524), who has been lieutenant–governor of Hispaniola under Nicolás de Ovando, departs with more than three hundred men to conquer Cuba, and lands at Puerto Escondido. He defeats Arawak chieftain Hatuey's guerrilla raids. In 1511, he founds the cities of Baracoa, Puerto Príncipe, Santiago, Trinidad, and Havana; is named governor; and institutes the encomienda or slavery of the Indians. As a private investment, Velázquez founds these cities as well as some others within the next five years; all of them exist today, albeit with name changes. The first and chief settlement is Santiago in the southeast, because of its proximity to Hispaniola. Later, new trade routes bring Havana to prominence, especially for shipping Cuban gold, tobacco, and sugar. By 1519 Cuba has displaced Hispaniola as the base

Diego Velásquez de Cuéllar. (Courtesy of the Biblioteca Nacional, Madrid.)

for subsequent explorations and conquest of the New World.

1511   Court System Is Established. The Spanish system of justice is instituted in the New World with the establishment of the *audiencia* (tribunal) which, besides serving as a court, also takes on administrative and political functions, basically because the colonies are so far from the central government in Spain. The first audiencia is founded in Santo Domingo in 1511 and the second in New Spain in 1525. During the empire, thirteen audiencias are established.

1511   First Bishop Named. The Diocese of San Juan Bautista (Puerto Rico) is established by Pope Julius II, and the first bishop for Puerto Rico, Alonso Manso, is named. In effect, he becomes the first bishop in the Americas. He says his first mass in Puerto Rico in 1513. Manso also becomes the first inquisitor in the Americas, and functions as such until he is replaced by Rodrigo Bastidas in 1539. Bastidas abolishes the Inquisition, but it is later reinstated under another bishop. This same year, 1511, two bishops also are installed in Hispaniola.

More bishops are named in 1513, to Darien; in 1522 to Mexico; in 1529 to Colombia; and in 1534 to Peru. By the end of the sixteenth century, there are five archbishops and twenty-seven bishops. By the end of the colonial period, there are ten archbishops and thirty-eight bishops.

1511   Taínos Resist. The Taíno Indians in Puerto Rico rebel, but their movement is squashed by the Spaniards at the Battle of Yauco and the Battle of Yagueca. Nevertheless, with the assistance of Carib Indians, the Taínos continue sporadic guerrilla resistance.

1512   First Cathedral Built. The first cathedral, Santo Domingo, and the first hospital, that belonging to the Dominicans and also named Santo Domingo, are built by the Spaniards on the island of Española. The first school also is located here.

1512   Indians and the Laws of Burgos. The Laws of Burgos are promulgated by the Spanish crown in response to the extremely harsh treatment that desperate colonists in the Caribbean are imposing on natives through the deplorable encomienda system. The campaign against abuse and exploitation of the natives had begun in Santo Domingo in 1511 in a sermon preached by Friar Antonio de Montesinos, which Spaniards on the island protested. Montesinos is sent by the Dominicans to plead the cause of the Indians at Court in Spain. As a direct result of his petitions and others, the king's advisors produce the Laws of Burgos, the first European colonial code, which sets down three principles: the Indians are free men, not slaves; they are to be converted to Christianity by peaceful means, not by force; and they are to be made to work. The encomienda and repartimiento are to be continued, but exploitation of the Indians is to be limited. From this point on, enslavement of the Indians is forbidden by law. The greatest defender of the Indians, however, is the Dominican missionary Bartolomé de las Casas, who maintains an

Spaniards beating Indians. Engraving by Theodore De Bry for the German edition of Las Casas' *Breve relación de la destrucción de las Indias.* (Courtesy of the Library of Congress Prints & Photographs Division.)

almost lifelong campaign of sermons, writings, and agitation at all levels of government, including the court, for better laws and enforcement to protect the Indians. His book, *Breve relación de la destrucción de las Indias* (Brief Relation of the Destruction of the Indies), graphically documents atrocities committed against the natives in Hispaniola. In 1516, he is appointed the official Protector of the Indians. Following his appointment, Las Casas conducts years of social experiments to show that the Indians could be taught to be good Chris-tians and engage in civilized life without force or enslavement. (*See also* biography, 1470.) Las Casas's intervention and experiments did bene-fit the Indians of the mainland later, but they come too late to help most of the Indians of the islands, who are decimated. While there is a great cry to protect the Indians, no one speaks up for the Africans. The Indians are subjects of the king of Spain and entitled to protection on legal grounds, but the Africans are the subjects of independent kings who are enslaved as pris-oners of war, as was the custom in most of the

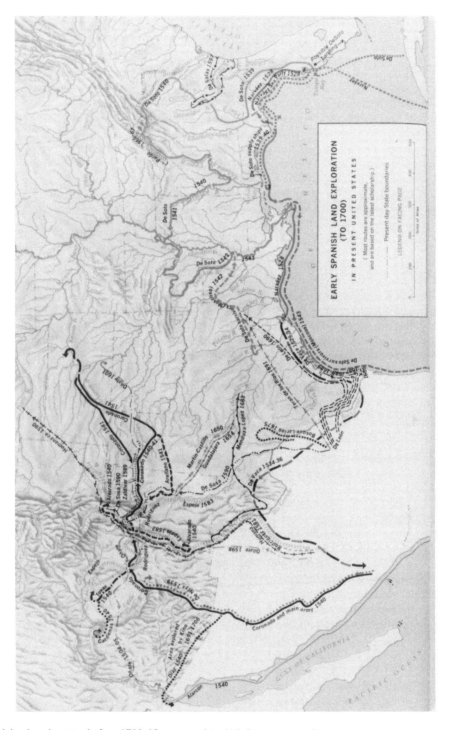

Early Spanish land exploration before 1700. (Courtesy of the U.S. Department of the Interior and National Park Service.)

world, and later precisely for the slave trade, and they have no legal standing in Spain.

1512 Missions Expand. The Jeronymite Fathers in Hispaniola decide to save the decimated Arawak population by gathering them into missions. Soon, missions spread like wildfire throughout the Spanish Empire.

1513 Bishop Establishes Secondary School. The first school, Escuela de Gramática (Grammar School), in Puerto Rico is established at the Cathedral of San Juan by the bishop, Alonso Manso. This secondary school, in which the Latin language and literature, history, science, art, philosophy, and theology are taught, is free to the students. Primary education is soon offered at schools connected to churches. By 1529, the Monastery of Santo Domingo in San Juan has as many as twenty-five students.

1513 Indian Schools Teach Latin. A royal edict is issued ordering the teaching of Latin to select Indians. After that, schools for Indians develop and become important, especially in Mexico and Peru where, besides Latin and religion, painting, sculpture, and other trades are taught.

1513 Indians Defeat Spanish Expeditions. The Indians of Florida attack and destroy nearly every Spanish expedition there from 1513 to 1568. This includes killing eighty men and Juan Ponce de León himself in 1513; 220 men, including the leader of the Lucas Vásquez de Ayllón expedition to the Carolinas in 1526 (the 220 figure also includes men who died of starvation and drowning); the leader and all but five of his men on the Pánfilo de Narváez expedition in 1528; and seven hundred of Hernando de Soto's one thousand men in 1539.

FEBRUARY 4, 1513 Discovery of Gulf Stream Promotes Commerce. The Gulf Stream is discovered by pilot Antonio de Alaminos, during Juan Ponce de León's voyage to Florida. Antonio de Alaminos had served as the pilot on

Columbus's fourth voyage (1502–04). This discovery results in Havana becoming a major port of assembly, and Florida serving as a strategic stopping place for voyages. The current runs from the Florida Strait into the Bahama Channel, past the coast of the Carolinas into the open ocean, where it forks northward to Norway and east to the Azores. Spanish ships thus headed for the Azores, refitted, and returned to Spain.

APRIL 2, 1513 Ponce de León Lands in Florida. Juan Ponce de León, in search of the land of Bimini reported to him by the natives of Puerto Rico, lands on the shores of Florida, exploring most of the coastal regions up to Apalachee Bay and some of the interior. At the time, there are an estimated 100,000 natives living there. Juan Ponce de León records his travels in his diaries, introducing a written language into the area. From this point on, the history of literacy, books, and writing in what is to become the United States is developed by Spanish, mestizo, and mulatto missionaries, soldiers, and settlers. Civil, military, and ecclesiastical records are kept, in what is today the South and Southwest of the United States. This is followed by the importing of books; the penning of original historical and creative writing; later, the use of the printing press; and still later, the publishing of newspapers and other written products. (*See also* biography, 1460.)

SEPTEMBER 25, 1513 Explorer Balboa Reaches Pacific Ocean. Vasco Núñez de Balboa (1475–1517) discovers the Pacific Ocean. (*See also* biography, 1475.)

SEPTEMBER 27, 1514 Colonizing Patent Granted. Ponce de León is granted a patent, empowering him to colonize the island of Bimini and the "island" of Florida. (*See also* biography, c. 1460.)

1515 Velázquez Establishes Cuban Cities. Diego Velázquez de Cuéllar becomes a virtual

Medallion with a likeness of Juan Ponce de León. (Courtesy of the Arte Público Press Archives, University of Houston.)

Vasco Núñez de Balboa. (Courtesy of the Library of Congress Prints & Photographs Division.)

feudal lord of Cuba, and establishes what are to become Cuba's two largest cities, Santiago and Havana. He also directs the explorations of the Mexican Gulf Coast by Francisco Hernández de Córdoba and his nephew, Juan de Grijalva. These expeditions reveal the existence of civilizations in the interior of Mexico.

FEBRUARY 1516 Rio de la Plata Discovered. Juan Díaz de Solís discovers the Río de la Plata in present-day Argentina and Uruguay while he is leading an exploratory voyage in search of a passage to the Pacific Ocean. (*See also* biography, 1470.)

1517 Las Casas Asks for African Slaves. Bartolomé de las Casas petitions the king of Spain to send African slaves to the Indies to substitute for the Indians working in the mines. While Las Casas defends the Indians from the encomienda and abuses, he is not against slavery in and of itself. In this same year, a contract is signed with a foreign company to import slaves to the Indies. (*See also* biography, 1470.)

1517 The Yucatan Peninsula. Francisco

Hernández de Córdoba (1475?–1517) discovers the Yucatan Peninsula.

1518 Cortés Leaves Cuba to Explore Mexico. Hernán Cortés sets out from Cuba to explore the mainland of Mexico in order to confirm reports of the existence of large, native civilizations in the interior. (*See also* biography, 1485.)

1518 Crown Licenses Slave Traders. The Spanish crown begins to grant licenses to private traders to import slaves to the West Indies, this in part to forestall Portuguese smuggling. By the late 1520s, significant problems arise in managing the slave populations: these include a shortage of European supervisors (partly due to the exodus to Mexico), slave mutinies and escapes to hide in the mountains and periodically attacking settlements. Nevertheless, the planters constantly lobby for more slaves; they never have enough. Import is by individual license, and all licensees must buy their slaves from authorized Portuguese dealers. The labor shortage and the difficulty in shipping sugar to distant markets at this point in history limit the development of the sugar industry. Consequently, the African population of the Spanish

Indies never outnumbers the European, as it did later in other areas.

1519   Cortés Documents Conquests. Between 1519 and 1526 Hernán Cortés writes five *Cartas de relación* (Letters of Account) to the king of Spain, documenting his conquests. These documents are considered important for the literature as well as the history of the Americas. (*See also* biography, 1485.)

1519   Cortés Moves into Mexico. Hernán Cortés lands on the coast of Veracruz, Mexico. He makes alliances with local nations subjugated by the Aztecs and moves on Tenochtitlán, the capital of the Aztec confederacy, arriving there on November 8. After various audacious moves, including capturing Moctezuma and then being expelled from the capital, Cortés finally conquers the Aztecs in Tenochtitlán a year later, after a siege of seventy-five days, forcing the retreat of Cuauhtémoc from the city on August 13, 1521. (*See also* biography, 1485.)

1519   Naval Commander Menéndez Is Born. Pedro Menéndez de Avilés, who will become a key figure in the development of Spanish shipping routes in the West Indies, is born in Avilés, Spain, into a distinguished family. At age fourteen, Menéndez de Avilés runs away from home and enlists as a cabin boy on a ship in Santander harbor. Two years later, he returns home and is married off to a ten-year-old bride, but he soon runs off to sea again. During both of his seafaring journeys, he fights against the French. During the 1550s and 1560s, Menéndez de Avilés serves the Spanish crown in high naval commands as a tactician and administrator. Because of his talents, Spain is able to design and implement a system for shipping to and from the West Indies and for protecting its routes from pirates, privateers, and other enemies. Menéndez serves as the commander of the homeward-bound Spanish fleet from 1555 to 1556. In 1561, he is appointed captain general of the Armada de la Carrera de Indias, the largest fleet ever to leave Spain,

Pedro Menéndez de Avilés. (Courtesy of the Library of Congress Prints & Photographs Division.)

with some forty-nine ships. From 1564 to 1566, he advises the Spanish crown on drawing up regulations for the Indies trade. These include trans-Atlantic crossing only by convoy (with a few exceptions), squadrons of well-armed cruisers permanently based to patrol the main routes in the Indies, and fortification of the principal harbors, foremost of which are Santo Domingo, San Juan de Puerto Rico, Havana, and Cartagena. Havana is designated to be the strongest, as the port from which all homeward-bound shipping emanates. In concert with these plans, Menéndez is appointed commander of Florida in 1565 and governor of Cuba in 1567. While planning the creation of an admiralty for the Indies, Menéndez dies in an epidemic in 1574. His labors ensure the protection of the Spanish colonies, the opening up of the mainland to the Spanish crown, and steady, secure communications with Spain during a critical period that lasts some sixty years after his death. He is, nevertheless, greatly disliked by the Cubans and other islanders, because he does not allow them to move to the mainland nor does he build up their societies and institutions. It is his concept to facilitate the exploitation of mainland wealth and to simply develop the Indies as routes of safe passage and support for the fleets traveling from the mainland to the mother country.

1519   Texas Claimed for Spain. Alonso Alvarez de Pineda discovers the coast of the Gulf of Mexico and claims Texas for Spain.

NOVEMBER 8, 1519   Aztec Emperor Meets Spaniard. Moctezuma Xocoyotzín receives Hernán Cortés at the temple of the goddess Toci. Although Cortés professes friendship, he takes Moctezuma prisoner. (*See also* biography, 1466 and biography, 1485.)

1520–1539

1520   Florida Proved to be Part of Continent. Explorer Alonso Alvarez de Pineda settles the question of Florida's geography: he proves it is not an island, but part of a vast continent.

JULY 1, 1520   Aztecs Force Spaniards Out. Under the leadership of Cuitlahuac, Moctezuma's brother, the Aztecs force the Spaniards out of Veracruz, just a year after the Spaniards had come into the city. The Spaniards call this *La Noche Triste* (The Sad Night). Moctezuma killed during this debacle.

AUGUST 10, 1520   Magellan Sails from Spain.

A Portuguese navigator, Ferdinand Magellan (1480?–1521), in the service of the Spanish crown, sets sail from Spain and on November 28 comes to the Pacific Ocean, clearing the passage at Tierra del Fuego between the Atlantic and the Pacific. His mission eventually succeeds in crossing the Pacific to discover and chart the Mariana Islands and, on March 26, 1521, the Philippines, where he dies in a battle with the natives on April 27. His second in command, Juan Sebastián de Elcano, completes the circumnavigation and returns to Spain on December 21, 1521. From that time on, the world is confirmed as round, and humankind has an accurate idea of the physical expanse of this sphere and the effort needed to circumnavigate it.

1521   González de Avila Converts, Enslaves Indians. Of some one million Indians estimated to be in the area called Nicaragua by the natives, Spanish conquistador Gil González de Avila converts some 30,000 to Christianity and sends nearly 500,000 to other parts of New Spain as slaves. Diseases kill many of the original million.

1521   Ponce de León Dies. Juan Ponce de León returns to Florida and explores up to Tampa Bay, where he is mortally wounded by the local Indians. He dies in Cuba. (*See also* biography, 1460.)

AUGUST 13, 1521   Cortés Conquers Aztecs. Hernán Cortés conquers the Aztecs led by Cuauhtémoc through a siege of the capital that lasts seventy-five days. Cortés and his fellow Spaniards level the Aztec empire's city of Tenochtitlán and begin building Mexico City on the same site. (*See also* biography, 1485.)

1522   Slaves Escape in Hispaniola. Black slaves revolt in Hispaniola and escape to the interior, setting up their own communities.

1523   Franciscans Establish Indian School. The Franciscans in Mexico make an effort to broaden the base of education, believing that sound schooling will lift the Indians to an appreciation of Spanish culture. With the support of Viceroy Pedro de Mendoza, the first school for Indians is established at Texcoco in 1523 by Pedro de Gante, a Flemish Franciscan. The school instructs from five hundred to one thousand Indian boys every year in such subjects as Spanish, manual arts, artisanry, and the decoration of churches. Other schools are organized for sons of Indian chieftains, and still others for Indian girls, in preparation for motherhood. In 1547, Viceroy Mendoza founds the school of San Juan de Letrán for unclaimed mestizo children, a school that survives for three centuries. Similar schools also are established in Lima and elsewhere. Many schools are opposed by the *hacendados* landholders and some churchmen, especially the Dominicans, who think the schools will corrupt the Indians. Much of this early experimentation is abandoned by the end of the sixteenth century, and schooling generally becomes limited to the sons of privileged families.

1524 The Council of the Indies. King Charles V establishes the Council of the Indies, designed to oversee the administration of the colonies of the New World. The creation of the council is planned as early as 1511, and takes form by 1524; its functions are further defined in 1571, when King Philip II institutes the Laws of the Indies. Based on the Council of Castile, the Council of the Indies effectively transplants Spanish government and social organization to the Americas. The council is in charge of the courts of justice, government dispositions, authorizing land grants, matters of war and peace, and counseling the king. The government officials who report to the council at first are just the *adelantados,* a type of field marshall, and the governors, but later the empire is divided up among viceroys and captain generals, who rule as representatives of the king. The first two viceroyalties are New Spain (1535) and Peru (1543); two centuries later the viceroyalties of New Granada (1717–21), rein-

stated in 1739) and Río de la Plata (1776) are added.

1524 Spanish Explore the North American Coast. In 1524–25, explorer Esteban Gómez, one of the twenty men who had returned from Magellan's circumnavigation, sails along the coast of North America from Florida to present-day Maine. Gómez goes into Hudson Bay and the Delaware and Connecticut rivers some eighty years before Henry Hudson. His explorations, and those of Giovanni Verrazano for France and John Cabot for England, put Spain and the other two European powers in direct competition for the exploration, charting, and settlement of the regions to the north.

DECEMBER 12, 1531 The Virgin of Guadalupe. According to the Catholic faithful, the Virgin Mary, Our Lady of Guadalupe, a version of the Virgin of Spanish origin, is seen by the Indian Juan Diego on the hill of Tepeyac, just outside Mexico City. She appears to Juan Diego with Indian features on the site of a temple devoted to the Aztec goddess Malintzin, and miraculously causes her image to be emblazoned on his poncho. This image is the one guarded at today's Shrine of the Virgin of Guadalupe, built on the original site, and duplicated in the thousands of churches bearing the Virgin's name, wherever Mexicans live. The Virgin of Guadalupe is named the patron saint of Mexico and the Americas, and has become a symbol of the Catholic Church in Mexico and the Americas, a church for Indians, mestizos, and creoles. The miraculous appearance leads to the rapid and massive conversion of many of the Amerindian peoples in Mexico and the other Indian lands being conquered and incorporated by the Spaniards. By the time of Father Miguel Hidalgo's shout for independence from Spain in 1810, the cult of the Virgin of Guadalupe has become so strong among Indians, mestizos, and creoles that he invokes her name as a rallying cry. From then on she becomes a symbol of Mexican nationalism.

A painting of the Virgin of Guadalupe by Juan de Villegas. (Courtesy of the Arte Público Press Archives, University of Houston.)

Atahualpa. (Courtesy of the Arte Público Press Archives, University of Houston.)

NOVEMBER 16, 1532 Spanish Horsemen Battle Incas. The battle against the Incas is won with the Spanish horsemen slaughtering thousands of Incas and not losing one of their number, and Francisco Pizarro taking Atahualpa prisoner. Pizarro later breaks his promise to free Atahualpa for a ransom of gold and silver, and executes the emperor. The conquest of the Inca Empire is completed by 1535.

1533 Caupolicán Becomes Chief. Caupolicán becomes chief of the Araucanians. (*See also* biography, c. 1500.)

1533 Colombia Produces Gold. Although the gold seized by Cortés and Pizarro from Mexico and Peru is a fabulously wealthy cache, Pedro de Heredia's expedition to Colombia in 1533 yields much more gold. Colombia soon becomes the chief source of gold for the Spanish empire. By the close of the Colonial Period, Colombian mines have produced some thirty million fine troy ounces of gold.

1533 Printers Operate in Mexico City. The printing press is brought to the Americas: to Mexico City. The printer is one Esteban Martín.

By the mid-sixteenth century, seven printers are operating in Mexico City, issuing everything from contracts and religious books to public notices and literary works. Among the first books printed are catechisms, religious books, grammars of the indigenous languages, dictionaries, and some technical and scientific books.

AUGUST 7, 1533 Soldier and Poet Alonso de Ercilla Is Born. Alonso de Ercilla y Zúñiga is a Spanish nobleman born in Madrid. The son of a distinguished judge, he has a privileged education. By age fifteen, he leaves Spain as a soldier and travels in Italy, Germany, and Luxembourg. In 1555, he comes to the New World in search of adventure. In Peru he joins an expedition to pursue the Araucan Indians, which takes him to Chile. Ercilla distinguishes himself in battle, but when not fighting he begins to compose a long, epic poem on the war against the Araucanians. At one point he is to be sentenced for suspected rebellion, but his sentence is commuted and he returns to Spain, where he finishes his poem, *La araucana* (The Araucana). The first part is published in 1569, the second part in 1578. The poem describes the flora and fauna of Chile, the customs of the Araucanians, and their great military leaders, among them the noted Caupolicán and Lautaro. He dies on November 29, 1594, in Madrid. His epic poem remains a classic.

1535 Pizarro Founds City. Francisco Pizarro founds the city of Lima, Peru, and names it the capital of the conquered lands. (*See also* biography, 1478.)

1535 Viceroyalties Are Founded. Spain's first viceroyalty in the New World is founded on the ruins of the Aztec Confederation, and it is meant to be an extension of Spain. It, therefore, is called New Spain, and has Mexico City as its capital. The second viceroyalty to be founded is on the ruins of the Inca Empire: the viceroyalty of Peru in 1542, with Lima as its capital. These two first viceroyalties, the largest administra-

Alonso de Ercilla y Zúñiga, author of *La araucana*. (Courtesy of the Library of Congress Prints & Photographs Division.)

tive divisions of Spain's colonies, are created to cover the expanse of the two great pre-Columbian civilizations, and their administrator is nothing less than the direct representative of the king of Spain. Later, other viceroyalties are created to encompass growing colonies: Nueva Granada in 1717, with Bogotá as its capital, and Río de la Plata in 1776, with Buenos Aires as its capital.

1536 Cabeza de Vaca's Return Starts Ru-

Francisco Pizarro, Diego de Almagro, and Hernando de Luque planning their voyage to conquer to Peru. (Courtesy of the Library of Congress Prints & Photographs Division.)

Medallion with a likeness of Alvar Núñez Cabeza de Vaca.

mors. Alvar Núñez Cabeza de Vaca returns to Mexico, indirectly involving Spain in exploring and colonizing what becomes the American Southwest. In Mexico City there are rumors that Cabeza de Vaca and his companions have discovered cities laden with gold and silver, reviving the legend of the Seven Cities of Cíbola, which dates from the Muslim invasion of the Iberian Peninsula. From 1528 to 1536, Cabeza de Vaca has been shipwrecked, marooned, and living first as a captive and later as a medicine man among natives from present-day Florida to Texas and New Mexico. (*See also* biography, c. 1490.)

1536 Indians Destroy Buenos Aires Fort. The city of Santa María de Buenos Aires is founded on the River Plate by Pedro de Mendoza, accompanied by twelve hundred men. An earlier attempt at establishing a fort, by Sebastián Caboto on the Paraná River, is foiled by the Guaraní Indians, who destroyed it. Again, the Buenos Aires fort is assaulted and destroyed by Indians. Pedro de Mendoza dies at sea on his return to Spain after this defeat.

1537 Asunción Is First Permanent Settlement in La Plata. The Spanish push inland up the River Plate and build a fort called Asunción, which is the first permanent settlement in the La Plata area. Domingo Martínez de Irala is named governor of Asunción.

1538 Dominican College Becomes University. The first university is founded by the Dominicans in the Americas: St. Thomas Aquinas in the city of Santo Domingo. It becomes a university after having functioned as a Dominican college for years. It continues today as the Autonomous University of Santo Domingo.

AUGUST 6, 1538 Jiménez Explores Colombia. The city of Santa Fe de Bogotá is founded by Gonzalo Jiménez de Quesada, who was commissioned to explore and conquer the interior of what was called Cundinamarca, a land thought to be richer than the Inca empire. The region that eventually becomes Colombia is indeed wealthy, and Jiménez de Quesada finds himself battling not only the Indians and the impenetrable forests, but also two other conquistadors racing to claim the same region for themselves. Jiménez de Quesada avoids civil war by putting the decision over the right to conquer the area in the king's hands, and Jiménez prevails. (*See also* biography, 1509.)

1539 Spanish Chronicler Garcilaso de la Vega Is Born. Bernal Garcilaso de la Vega, the son of a conquistador and an Incan princess, becomes a noted chronicler, historian, and man of letters in his native Peru. As a child he learns Spanish and Latin from tutors in his native city of Cuzco; at home he speaks Quechua, the language of the Incas, and hears the stories of his Incan ancestors from parents, relatives, and friends of the family. Upon the death of his father, he travels to Spain but is received coldly by his father's family. He enters the military and participates in some campaigns, after which he retires to a life of study of the humanities and philosophy. His first published work is *La Florida del Inca* (The Incan's Florida), pub-

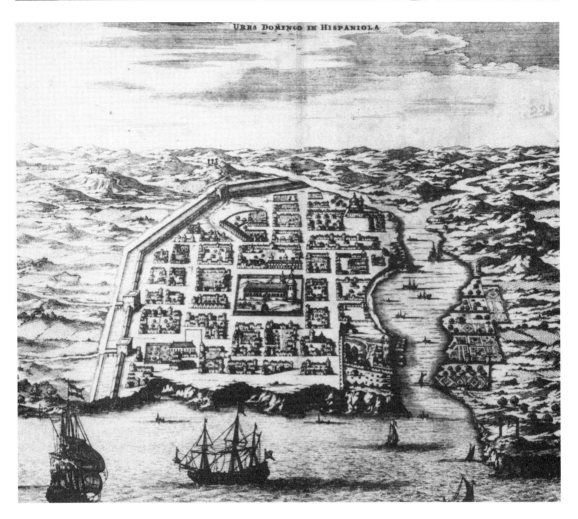

An early map of Santo Domingo. (Courtesy of the Biblioteca Nacional, Madrid.)

lished in 1605. His major work, *Comentarios reales* (Royal Commentaries), is published in two parts in 1609 and 1617, respectively. The commentaries take pride in describing ancient Incan civilization. In fact, the author even takes considerable pride in his mestizo heritage. Although the book contains considerable history, it also is considered a notable work of art and imagination. He dies in 1616.

MAY 18, 1539   De Soto Sails to Florida. From Havana, Cuba, Hernando de Soto (1500?–41) sets sail for Florida; he eventually reaches as far

north as present-day Georgia and South Carolina. His expedition later crosses the Great Smoky Mountains into Tennessee. From the mountains, he heads southwest through what is now Georgia and Alabama. De Soto falls ill and eventually dies on May 21, 1542. He is buried at the mouth of the Mississippi River. (*See also* biography, 1500.)

1540–1599

AUGUST 25, 1540   Coronado's Expedition

Reaches Grand Canyon. The expedition led by explorer Francisco Vásquez de Coronado that set out to reach Quivira—thought to be the legendary Cities of Gold—near present-day Great Bend, Kansas, encounters the Grand Canyon; they later reach the Rio Grande, which they name Nuestra Señora (Our Lady). (*See also* biography, 1510.)

1541 Viceroy Orders Rebuilding of Buenos Aires. Blasco Núñez de Vela, the first viceroy of Peru, dispatches Ortiz de Zárate to rebuild Buenos Aires on the River Plate.

FEBRUARY 12, 1541 City of Santiago Founded. Santiago is founded in Chile by Pedro de Valdivia. In 1539, Francisco Pizarro had commissioned him to conquer Chile. However, on September 11, 1541, Chief Michimalonco, leading the Mapuche Indians, exterminates the Spaniards in Concon and destroys the city of Santiago. Valdivia reconstructs that city and later founds Serena (April 1544), Concepción (1550), Imperial (1551), and Villarrica (1552). In December 1553, he loses his life to the rebel Indian Lautaro, who had served as his stableboy and had learned the tactics of the Spaniards. Leading a rebellion of the Mapuche Indians, Lautaro takes Tucapel, Puren, and Arauco, and defeats Valdivia on the plains of Tucapel. Lautaro also is eventually killed, and is replaced by Caupolicán, who suffers a horrible death by impalement at the hands of the Spanish captain Alonso de Reinoso in vengeance for the assassination of Valdivia. (*See also* biography, c. 1497.)

MAY 8, 1541 De Soto Crosses the Mississippi. Hernando de Soto discovers and crosses the Mississippi River. (*See also* biography, 1500.)

DECEMBER 1541 Expedition Discovers the Amazon River. Francisco de Orellana's expedition discovers the Amazon River in what is now Ecuador. From December to August, the Spaniards travel down the Amazon to its mouth in the Atlantic Ocean. The first written de-scription of the river is produced by a member of the expedition: Friar Gaspar de Carvajal.

1542 Coronado Returns. Francisco Vásquez de Coronado returns to Mexico City with fewer than one hundred of the three hundred Spaniards who are part of his original company. (*See also* biography, 1510.)

1542 King Proclaims New Laws of Indies. The New Laws of the Indies are proclaimed by King Charles V to end the feudal encomienda. The laws prohibit sending the Indians to work in the mines; they also will not be allowed to dive for pearls or to carry them. If the Indians' work is essential, state the laws, then they must be paid for their labor. The law demands that the Indians be treated as free vassals of the crown. By the time the laws are passed, most of the best land is concentrated in the hands of the large plantation (hacienda) holders and the church, and the Indians, except for those in remote villages, have become peons with very few rights as free men.

1542 Spanish Missionary Establishes New Laws. In Valladolid, Spain, Bartolomé de las Casas writes what becomes the *Nuevas Leyes de las Indias* (The New Laws of the Indies), which officially put an end to the encomienda and enslavement of the Indians. He also finishes *Brevísima relación de la destrucción de las Indias* (Brief Account of the Destruction of the Indies), in which he details the history of mistreatment of the Indians. (*See also* biography, 1470.)

SEPTEMBER 28, 1542 Portuguese Sailor Enters California Port. Juan Rodríguez de Cabrillo, a Portuguese sailor commissioned by the viceroy to sail north of Mexico's west coast in search of treasures, enters what he describes as an excellent port—present-day San Diego, California.

1543 Charles V Bans Books. Charles V prohibits the circulation of novels and works of imagination in the Americas so that neither Spaniards nor Indians would read profane works or fictional histories, because such books are thought to be dangerous to spirituality.

1543   Francis Drake Is Born. Sir Francis Drake, the greatest menace to Spanish shipping in the West Indies, is born in England. Drake becomes a pirate and privateer, driving Pedro Menéndez de Avilés to develop defensive plans to protect the shipping routes from the mainland to Spain. Drake sets about preparing a strategy of attack on Spanish shipping much as a businessman would, in the process acquiring great wealth and weakening Spanish maritime dominance. Drake begins his career as a smuggler under Jack Hawkins. In 1570 he transports cargoes of slaves to the Indies and returns with hides and silver. During trips in 1570 and 1571, Drake makes alliances with tribes and groups of runaway slaves along the isthmus. During this time, he also becomes an official English privateer. In 1572, he takes by surprise three mule trains crossing the isthmus, loaded with treasures from Peru. The booty, which makes all of his men extremely wealthy, arrives at Plymouth, England, in 1573. Drake's exploits include a great voyage of circumnavigation from 1577 to 1580. When war between England and Spain breaks out in 1585, Drake once again sails to the Caribbean, this time at the head of a full naval operation of more than twenty ships. He first attacks and captures port towns and cities, including Cartagena, along the mainland, and later captures Havana. Drake hopes to hold both Havana and Cartagena as permanent English military outposts, and thus break up the Spanish supply and trade routes, but he absorbs too many casualties and cannot hold these conquered and sacked cities. He has, nevertheless, inflicted great damage on the Spanish economy and on its reputation for strength in the Caribbean. Drake's strategy and pattern of attack against the Spanish will be duplicated numerous times in the West Indies by the French, Dutch, and English as they attempt to break the Spanish monopoly of trade and territorial power there. This, of course, leads the Spanish to upgrade their fortifications and de-

fenses and, when Drake and Hawkins set out in 1895 for another West Indies campaign, the Spaniards are ready for them. The English are defeated at San Juan de Puerto Rico. Drake dies off the coast of Veragua during this last Indies campaign in 1596.

1543   Painter Bernardo Bitti Is Born. The painter Bernardo Bitti is born in Italy but is considered to have achieved his greatest works of art in the viceroyalty of Peru. In 1568 Bitti becomes a Jesuit brother and in 1573 is sent as a missionary to Peru, where he remains until his death. He travels throughout Peru and Bolivia, decorating churches and missions founded by the Jesuits. Bitti is considered the founder of the Lima and Cuzco schools of mannerist painting. The important Cuzco School follows European canons and is known for a certain naivete in the composition and drawing, the rigidity of lines in the clothing depicted, a great profusion of gold-colored adornments, and the painting of madonnas with indigenous faces. Most of the followers of Bitti who continued the Cuzco School painted anonymously; many of them were Indians. Cuzco becomes the center for an industry of religious painting whose products are distributed throughout New Spain and Spain itself. This period is often referred to as the "Baroque of the Indies." It is not until the eighteenth century that Latin American art begins to separate itself from European models and to develop its own values, including the recognition of indigenous and mestizo traditions. Bitti dies in Peru in 1610.

1544   France and Spain Sign Peace Treaty. The Treaty of Crespy is signed between France and Spain, ending hostilities between the two colonial powers. Prior to this date French-sponsored privateering and piracy was the bane of the Spanish shipping routes on which convoys transported the riches from the New World. In this treaty, Francis I recognizes the Spanish monopoly on Caribbean settlement and trade. Nevertheless, in 1552, a new war once again results in Caribbean raiding. The port of Hava-

The Virgin of Pomata by an anonymous painter of the Cuzco School. (Courtesy of the Secretariat of Culture, La Paz.)

na services the convoys, which originates in the isthmus, on their trans-Atlantic voyages. But Havana (also San Juan, Puerto Rico, and others) is vulnerable to attack by pirates and enemies of the crown. In 1553, François Le Clerc commands a fleet of French warships across the Atlantic and systematically pillages and burns Spanish port towns of the Indies. In 1554, he takes Santiago, Cuba, and the following year Jacques Sores takes Havana. Eventually these threats lead to the creation of a unified com-

mand of the West Indies trade routes, first under Pedro Menéndez de Avilés. Heavy fortifications are constructed around these Spanish ports of the Indies, many of which are still standing, such as the Morros in Havana and San Juan.

1550 Indian Exploitation Continues. With the encomienda outlawed in 1542, another form of slavery, the repartimiento, is revived this year. Indians are seized and forced to work on plantations, in mines, and in the building of churches and roads. Indians are treated cruelly, and their families divided. Again there are outcries to abolish this hated form of exploitation. Even the importation of African slaves, who the Spanish considered to be "natural slaves" and to be innately wicked, did not remove much pressure from the Indians.

1550 Slaves Rebel. African slaves begin to rebel, overthrow their masters, and flee to the backlands in Venezuela.

1551 King Charters Universities. The University of Mexico in Mexico City and the University of San Marcos in Lima, Peru, are founded. The universities are chartered by the king this year, but the University of Mexico does not actually open its doors until 1553 and the University of San Marcos not until 1572. The latter has never had an interruption in its existence and is thus considered the oldest university on the continent. The universities follow the general models of the University of Salamanca and the University of Alcalá de Henares in Spain, offering humanities, theology, law, and medicine. Latin is the official language used in classes at the time, though some universities also teach the indigenous languages for a while. Later, they teach mathematics and physics. The degrees offered are bachelors, masters (or licentiate), and doctorate. The Jesuits are the most important teaching order in the Americas. During the Colonial Period, there were some twenty-six universities, in addition to numerous theological seminaries, founded by

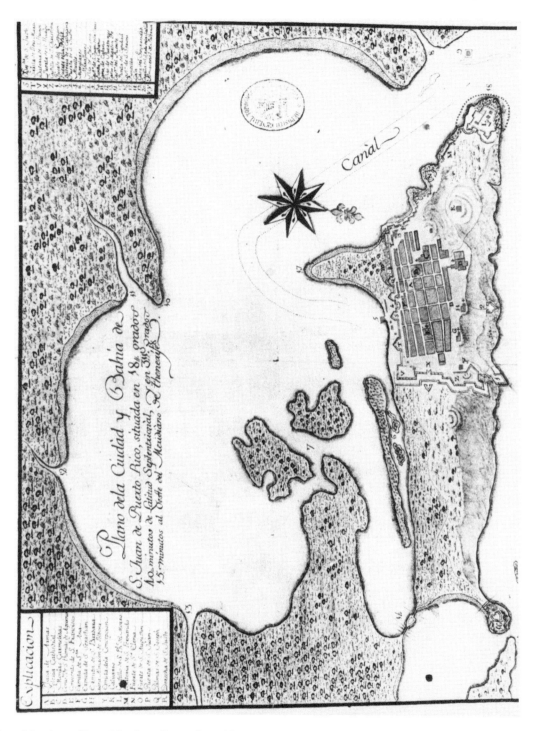

Map of the city and bay of San Juan, Puerto Rico. (Courtesy of the Archivo General de las Indias, Seville.)

Havana in the 16th century. (From *Four Centuries of Spanish Rule in Cuba* by Emilio Canini, 1898.)

the Spaniards in the Americas. During the seventeenth century, the University of Mexico achieves the greatest distinction in the Americas, boasting twenty-three chairs, most in canon law and theology, but others in medicine, surgery, anatomy, astrology, rhetoric, and the Aztec and Otomí languages. In the last quarter of the seventeenth century, the university holds the distinction of being the home for the greatest intellectual of the period: mathematician and historian Carlos de Sigüenza y Góngora.

1553 Argentinean City Founded. The Spanish found Santiago del Estero, the oldest city in Argentina.

1555 Explorer's Document Is Published. Àlvar Núñez Cabeza de Vaca returns to Spain in 1537 and spends some three years writing *La relación y comentarios* (The Account and Commentary), an account of his wanderings in the North American continent. Published in 1555, *La relación y comentarios* is a document of inestimable value because it includes many of the first descriptions of the flora, fauna, and inhabitants in what was to become part of the United States. (*See also* biography, c. 1490.)

1560   Spanish Found Santa Elena. The Spanish found Santa Elena in what is today the state of South Carolina; it is the first European settlement in what will become the continental United States. Both Santa Elena and Saint Augustine predate Jamestown, which is founded in 1607 by the British, and the arrival of the Mayflower in 1620.

1561   Naval Commander Menéndez to Lead Fleet. Pedro Menéndez de Avilés is appointed captain general of the Armada de la Carrera de Indias, the largest fleet ever to leave Spain, with some forty-nine ships. (*See also* biography, 1519.)

1562   Bishop Orders Burning of Mayan Works. Catholic bishop Diego de Landa orders the burning of the Mayan codices that contain the accumulation of the Mayas' knowledge in mathematics, philosophy, astronomy, history, and religion. This act leaves forever unanswered the questions future generations will have about what many scholars believe is the most advanced civilization to have flourished in the Americas.

1562   English Trader Imports Slaves. John Hawkins becomes the first English trader to import slaves into the Indies.

1563   Cathedral of Mexico Is Begun. The largest church built by Spain in the Americas and one of the largest churches in all of Christianity, the Cathedral of Mexico, is begun. Highly influenced by Renaissance architecture, the Mexico City cathedral and others throughout Mexico (Mérida, Guadalajara, Puebla), are also reflective of the cathedrals in Andalusia, southern Spain.

AUGUST 28, 1565   Saint Augustine Is Founded. Saint Augustine, Florida, the oldest permanent European settlement in what is today the mainland United States, is founded by Pedro Menéndez de Avilés. (*See also* biography, 1519.) Menéndez engages in skirmishes with the French and then claims the land for Spain. The Spaniards are welcomed by the Timicua Indians, who give the settlers and soldiers shelter in their huts. The original village of Saint Augustine is moved a year later, 1566, to a more strategic site. Saint Augustine becomes the most successful strategic post for the Spaniards who defend the Florida coast. It is the only one that survived storms, fires, famine, and raids by the French and English. In 1586, the English privateer, Francis Drake, loots and burns Saint Augustine, forcing the villagers to flee to the forest. Once the privateer is gone, they return to rebuild. During the seventeenth century, the city and other areas of Florida receive a considerable amount of migration from Spain and the Spanish Caribbean, and the population grew to 2,000 by the turn of the eighteenth century. The city is afforded more security by the building of the San Marcos Fort, begun in 1672 and finished in 1756. In 1763, the region of the Florida peninsula called "Eastern Florida"—as opposed to "Western Florida," which ranged from the Georgia coast to the Mississippi River—comes under British control as a result of the Treaty of Paris. This includes Saint Augustine. In 1783, under the Treaty of Versailles, Eastern Florida is returned to Spain, whose possession it remains until 1821, when it is surrendered to the United States. Louisiana, which is discovered by the Spanish but settled by the French from Canada, remains a French colony until 1763, when it, too, passes into Spanish hands as a result of the Treaty of Paris. Louisiana is ceded to France in 1801, but is sold to the United States by Napoleon in 1803.

1568   Díaz del Castillo Writes Chronicle. Bernal Díaz del Castillo finishes the historical chronicle and literary masterpiece that details the taking of Mexico: *Verdadera historia de la conquista de la Nueva España* (The True History of the Conquest of New Spain). It is first

A nineteenth-century engraving of a panoramic view of Mexico City, showing the Cathedral of Mexico, begun in 1563, at center. (Courtesy of the Library of Congress Prints & Photographs Division.)

published in Madrid in 1632. (*See also* biography, 1498.)

1569   Alonso de Ercilla Publishes Part I of Poem. Alonso de Ercilla y Zúñiga composes a long, epic poem on the war against the Araucanians called *La araucana* (The Araucana). The first part is published in 1569, the second part in 1578. (*See also* biography, August 7, 1533 and entry, 1578.)

1569   Inquisition Introduced to Americas. The Holy Office of the Inquisition is introduced to the Americas by royal edict. The first inquisitors reach Lima by 1570, and Mexico the following year. The early bishops of the Americas have functioned as deputies of the Holy Office for fifty years, but after 1570 the Inquisition itself claims its important role in colonial life.

1570   Courts Judge Threats to Religious Unity. The Spanish Inquisition is introduced into the New World. Three courts of the faith are established: in Lima (1570), in Mexico City (1591), and in Cartagena, Colombia (1610). The courts judge people accused of blasphemy,

bigamy, heresy, witchcraft, and enchantment and others who are considered a threat to religious unity. Corporal punishment is administered by the civil authorities, not by the Inquisition.

1573   Franciscans Establish Missions. The Franciscan order arrives in Florida to establish missions, which a century later would extend along the east coast of North America, from Saint Augustine, Florida, to North Carolina. The Franciscans also establish a string of missions from Saint Augustine westward to present-day Tallahassee.

1577–89   Sir Francis Drake's Great Voyage. Francis Drake circumnavigates the world. (*See also* biography, 1543.)

1578   Second Part of Epic Poem Published. Alonso de Ercilla y Zúñiga, soldier and poet, publishes the second part of his epic poem, *La araucana* (The Araucana). (*See also* biography, August 7, 1533 and entry, 1569.)

1580   Puerto Rican Indians Fall to Disease. Diseases have all but wiped out the Indians of

Puerto Rico. The flourishing of sugar production would now have to await the importation of large numbers of African slaves.

1580 Spain Defeats Portugal. Spain defeats Portugal and incorporates her and her colonies, including Brazil, into its empire until 1640. Spain's empire now extends to almost every continent, and includes even the Philippines.

1580 Spanish Conquest Is Completed. With the reconquest and permanent settling of Buenos Aires by Juan de Garay, the cycle of Spanish conquest is completed in the New World. This final conquest of the River Plate region and Argentine is preceded by the founding of Tucumán in 1565 and Córdoba in 1573.

1590 Juan de Fuca Sails North. Juan de Fuca navigates his ships to the northern coast of present-day Washington State. Spanish maps from the period show the Strait of Juan de Fuca as a possible Northwest Passage.

1595 King Permits African Slave Trade. Pedro Gómez Reynel obtains permission from the king to import 38,000 slaves from Africa to the Americas.

1596 Treaty of The Hague Is Signed. The Treaty of The Hague is signed by France, England, and the Netherlands to form an alliance against Spain. A combined fleet of English and Dutch ships attacks Cádiz harbor and destroys a Spanish Indies convoy, effectively cutting off communications between Spain and the Indies for almost two years. The alliance breaks up, beginning with the French, who make their peace with Spain through the Treaty of Vervins in 1598. The English also sign a peace treaty, the Treaty of London, in 1604. But the English set forth a principle in this treaty that is uncontested by the Spaniards: England would respect Spanish dominion over all territories effectively occupied by the Spanish, but would not recognize Spanish rights in unoccupied parts of America. This, of course, paves the way for English colonization, as well as Dutch colonization when the Netherlands sign the Truce of Antwerp in 1609 and repeat the same principle.

1598 Soldiers Take Up Pens. Juan de Oñate begins the colonization of New Mexico. Among his men are an amateur playwright, Captain Marcos Farfán de los Godos, who writes a play, which the soldiers perform based on their colonizing adventure. This is the first play in a European language written and performed in what is the present-day United States. The soldiers also have in their repertoire the folk play, often performed on horseback, entitled *Los moros y los cristianos* (The Moors and the Christians), which dramatizes the reconquest of the Spanish peninsula from the Moors during the Crusades. Finally, the poet Gaspar Pérez de Villagrá, also one of Oñate's soldiers, pens a long, epic poem memorializing the expedition, *La conquista de la Nueva Méjico* (The Conquest of New Mexico). It is later published in Spain and, considered an important literary work in the Hispanic world, is still studied today. This is believed to be the first epic or one of the first, written in a European language in the New World.

1600–1649

c. 1600 Painter and Poet Antonio Acero Is Born. The first important artist in the European sense emerges in the viceroyalty of New Granada: Antonio Acero de la Cruz (1600?–67). Born in Bogotá, Acero is a painter, as well as a poet, and is known for his decoration of the tomb of the archbishop of Bogotá in 1633 and for various canvases that hang in churches and in the Colonial Museum of Bogotá.

1600 Spanish Missions Run Schools. By 1600, the Spaniards have established the first schools in what later becomes the United States, at missions in Florida, New Mexico, and Georgia.

1605 Spanish Chronicle Is Published. Bernal Garcilaso de la Vega's first published work is *La Florida del Inca* (The Incan's Florida), describing ancient Incan civilization. (*See also* biography, 1539.)

1610 New Mexican City Founded. Santa Fe, New Mexico, is founded.

1611 Indian Folk Artist Tito Is Born. The Indian painter who is known as the father of folk art in Cuzco, Diego Quispe Tito, is born in Cuzco, viceroyalty of Peru. His paintings are characterized by grand nature scenes. He dies in 1681.

1612 Franciscan Translates Spanish Books into Indian Language. Franciscan missionary by the last name of Pareja is the first to translate books in a European language (Spanish) into an Indian language in what was to become the United States. Pareja translates books into the Timicuan language from about 1612 to 1627 in what is the present state of Georgia.

1626 Quito School Leads Colonial Art. The painting and sculpture executed in Quito, Ecuador, in the mid-seventeenth century is considered the apex of Spanish American colonial art. One of the most outstanding leaders of the Quito School is painter Miguel de Santiago (1626–1706), also known as the "Apeles of America." Both his daughter, Isabel, and his nephew, Nicolás Javier de Goríbar, also contribute significantly to this Baroque artistic movement.

1633 Antonio Acero Decorates Tomb. Antonio Acero de la Cruz completes his decoration of the tomb of the archbishop of Bogotá. (*See also* biography, c. 1600.)

1639 Missions in Paraguay. The Jesuits found missions among the Guaraní Indians in Paraguay, which become virtually independent communities within the Spanish Empire.

1642 First Library Established in Puerto Rico.

The first library in Puerto Rico is established at the Convent of San Francisco.

1645   Sigüenza y Góngora Is Born. The great mathematician, poet, historian, and philosopher, Carlos de Sigüenza y Góngora, is born in Mexico City (or Puebla, according to some sources). At the age of fifteen he joins the Jesuit order and by age seventeen becomes an outstanding scholar of philosophy, history, mathematics, astronomy, and engineering. At the same age, he also composes poetry in Latin describing spring in the torrid zone. But after seven years in the order, Sigüenza y Góngora is expelled from the Jesuits for some unknown reason. Later, he either reenters the order or reestablishes good relations with it. For more than twenty years, Sigüenza y Góngora teaches philosophy and science at the University of Mexico, where he also holds the chair in mathematics. He is appointed Royal Cosmographer by King Charles II. In 1693, the count of Galve invites him on a scientific expedition into what is today the southeastern United States. He publishes his findings in his book, *Descripción de la bahía de Santa María de Galve (antes Pensacola), de la Movila o Mississippi, en la costa septentrional del seno mejicano* (Description of the Bay of Santa María de Galve [previously Pensacola], of Mobile or Mississippi, on the Eastern Coast of the Gulf of Mexico). Sigüenza y Góngora authors numerous books in all the fields of his broad interests and also has the distinction of publishing the first newspaper in Mexico: *El Mercurio Volante* (Winged Mercury). He is one of the first to write in a scholarly manner about territories that would become the United States. In addition to his book about the lands around the northeastern Gulf of Mexico, he also publishes *Historia de la provincia de Tejas* (History of the Province of Texas). Finally, his encyclopedic knowledge and study extends to include what today might be considered anthropology. He researches and writes about the Aztecs and the Chichimecas in his books *Genealogía de los reyes mejicanos* (Geneology of the Mexican Kings) and *Historia del imperio*

de los chichimecas (History of the Chichimeca Empire). Sigüenza y Góngora dies in 1700 in Mexico City. A devastating fire in Mexico City in 1792 consumes many of his manuscripts.

1650–1699

NOVEMBER 12, 1651   Author, Poet Sor Juana Is Born. One of the greatest figures of Spanish American literature, Sor Juana Inés de la Cruz, is born Juan Inés de Asbaje (she changes her name when she becomes a nun in the Carmelite order in 1667) near San Miguel Nepantla, Mexico (then New Spain). At the early age of three, she learns to read and write and, it is also said, she later learned Latin in only twenty lessons. She becomes a serious student of the sciences and, when the viceroy of Mexico hears about her precocity, he incorporates her into his court, where she becomes doted upon and celebrated. She has tremendous difficulty, nonetheless, being admitted to the university, which does not allow women; so she disguises herself as a man. Finally, disenchanted with the court and secular life, she becomes a nun, which probably affords her greater freedom to study and write. However, toward the end of her life she finally gives up her books and scientific experiments to devote herself totally to worship. Sor Juana is the author of religious and secular plays, lyric poetry, and prose works. It is her lyric poetry that results in her inclusion among the great Hispanic poets. But one of her letters of defense of the right of women to study and write leads to her being considered a pioneer of women's rights: her autobiographical *Respuesta a Sor Filotea de la Cruz* (Response to Sister Filotea de la Cruz). She dies during an epidemic, on April 17, 1695.

1665   Bolivian Painter Pérez Is Born. Bolivian painter Melchor Pérez de Holguín, born in Cochabamba, is one of the first great artists in the Americas under Spanish rule. His work, like much of Spanish religious art, is greatly indebted to the Flemish painters of the Ba-

Sor Juana Inés de la Cruz. (Courtesy of the National Museum of History, Mexico City.)

roque Period, as well as to the Spanish painter, Francisco de Zurbarán. Without any signs of the mannerism, or affectation and excessive formalism, Pérez's works are solemn Baroque pieces of the Counter-Reformation. A painter of mystic religiosity, Pérez produces numerous paintings for the Franciscan order. In 1716, Pérez paints a large, three-part scene that is both of historical and artistic importance, in which the panorama of the city of Potosí, popular customs, and dress are depicted: "The Entry of Archbishop Rubio Morello de Aunón

into the City of Potosí." In 1722, he executes a large canvas considered a masterpiece: "The Crucifixion." His last known paintings are of a series of Christ's disciples. He dies in 1724.

1670 Spain and England Sign Treaty of Madrid. Spain and England sign the Treaty of Madrid, in which for the first time Spain formally acknowledges England's presence in the Caribbean and sanctions England's current holdings in the Americas. But trade between the Spanish and British colonies is permitted only with a special license; this restricts commerce severely and leads to the development of smuggling, particularly between New England and the Caribbean. Because of these and other laws and practices, the Spanish and British colonies have little contact with each other.

1678 British Assume Protectorate over Miskito Indians. Without invitation, the British assume a protectorate over the Miskito Indians on the Caribbean coast of Honduras and Nicaragua. After Central America declares independence from Spain and Mexico in 1821, England formally claims British Honduras as a colony of the crown. Over the years, the British attempt to expand their holdings in Central America, but with pressure from the United States and the Central American republics, they concede the Bay Islands to Honduras in 1859 and abandon most of their claims to the Mosquito coast in 1860. The British hold on to British Honduras until September 21, 1981, when it gains its independence. Its name is changed to Belize on June 1, 1973.

AUGUST 9, 1680 Santa Fe Falls. A Pueblo Indian named Popé leads a rebellion that on this date takes Santa Fe, in New Mexico, and forces the Spaniards and Christianized Indians out of northern New Mexico southward toward El Paso; they found Ysleta just north of El Paso. The fall of Santa Fe follows some five years of Indian rebellions. In 1692, Governor Diego de Vargas reconquers northern New

Guardian Angel "Ariel Custos Dei," by an anonymous painter of the Cuzco School. (Courtesy of the Secretariat of Culture, La Paz.)

Mexico for Spain and pacifies it sufficiently for further colonization.

1681   Spain Organizes Laws for Colonies. The *Recopilación de las leyes de las Indias* (Compilation of the Laws of the Indies) is issued by Spain, organizing and reducing to a total of 6,400 the laws applicable to its American colonies. Some 400,000 edicts had been issued by 1635.

1689   First Land Grants. In part due to the need to provide foodstuffs and livestock to the rich mining regions to the south, the first royal *mercedes* (land grants) are granted to Spaniards in the fertile valleys of Monclova, just south of the present U.S.–Mexico border.

MAY 24, 1690   Spanish Settlement in Texas. The first permanent Spanish settlement in Texas, San Francisco de los Tejas, is founded near the Neches River by Father Massanet and Father Fontcubierta.

1691   Governor Named for Texas. Domingo Terán de los Ríos is named governor of the province of Texas. As a response to French explorations and incursions, Spain decides to rapidly settle Texas. Terán de los Ríos is empowered to establish eight missions among the Indian nations in east Texas.

1691   Jesuit Establishes Missions in Arizona. Father Eusebio Kino, an untiring Jesuit missionary, makes the first inroads into Arizona. By 1700, Kino establishes a mission at San Xavier del Bac, near present-day Tucson; he later establishes other missions in Arizona: Nuestra Señora de los Dolores, Santa Gertrudis de Saric, San José de Imuris, Nuestra Señora de los Remedios, and San Cayetano de Tumacácori.

1693   Spanish Abandon Texas. Despite the fact that Texas is made a separate Spanish province with Domingo de Terán de los Ríos as its governor, the Spanish crown orders its abandonment. Fear of Indian uprisings is the reason given by the Spanish authorities.

1700–1749

1700 Operas Continue to Cultivate. By the turn of the century, operas are not only being performed but also composed in Mexico City and Peru.

1701 House of Bourbon Takes Spanish Throne. The House of Bourbon secedes the House of Austria to the Spanish throne and in the years that follow the new kings make substantial changes to the colonial system in the Americas in order to improve the system of government and economic administration. Charles III, the most progressive of the line, introduces many modifications during his reign, 1759–88. The House of Bourbon authorizes the creation of various commercial ports in the New World, creates the new viceroyalties of New Granada and River Plate, concedes patents to various commercial houses for trade with the Americas, reduces taxes, and stimulates the livestock industry and agriculture. However, the most important reforms include enlarging the militia for the defense of the territories, abolishing the encomienda, expelling the Jesuits, and creating a system of economic supervisors responsible for monitoring the exploitation of Indian labor, the payment of taxes, and the general development of the economy. The new Bourbon rulers represent a substantial limit to the power of governors and functionaries, especially in curbing the extensive corruption among officials.

1716 Spaniards Reoccupy Texas. Concerns over possible French encroachment into Texas prompt the Spaniards to reoccupy Texas in 1716 by establishing a series of missions to serve two purposes: convert the natives to Catholicism and ward off the French. Of these missions, San Antonio, founded in 1716 by Alonso de Alarcón, is the most important and most prosperous. During the 1730s and the 1740s, missions spread from east Texas to San Antonio and to La Bahía (Goliad). The east Texas missions are partially abandoned and moved to San Antonio, with San Antonio de Valero, San Juan Capistrano, San Francisco de la Espada, and Purísima Concepción being established along the San Antonio River. The area develops into an important center for trade.

1717 English Company Imports African Slaves in Americas. England's South Sea Company obtains permission to bring 144,000 African slaves into Spanish lands in the Americas at a rate of 4,800 per year for thirty years. France's Company of the Indies also is active at this time.

MAY 1, 1718 Expedition at San Antonio. The Presidio of San Fernando de Béjar and the San Antonio de Béjar and de Valero churches are founded by a colonizing expedition headed by

Unloading slaves in Havana Harbor. (Courtesy of the Library of Congress Prints & Photographs Division.)

Martín de Alarcón, where the city of San Antonio is located today.

1721 Cuban University Established. The University of Havana is founded.

1722 Bolivian Painter Pérez Finishes Masterpiece. Melchor Pérez de Holguín finishes "The Crucifixion," a large canvas considered a masterpiece. (*See also* biography, 1665.)

1722 Newspapers in Americas. The first newspaper appears in the Americas: *La gaceta de*

México (The Mexico Gazette). Shortly thereafter, others appear in Guatemala, Lima, Buenos Aires, and elsewhere.

MARCH 9, 1731 Families Colonize San Antonio. Fifteen families (fifty-six people) of some four hundred authorized families from the Canary Islands arrive to colonize what later becomes the city of San Antonio. This first civil establishment on the banks of the San Antonio River is authorized by a royal decree on February 14, 1729. The settlement, on the banks of the San Antonio River, is named San Fernando de Bexar, a name reflected today in the name of the county where San Antonio is situated: Bexar. Bexar becomes the capital and main nucleus of the Spaniards in Texas.

1750–1759

1750 First Symphony Orchestra. The first symphony orchestra in the Americas is organized in Caracas, Venezuela.

DECEMBER 23, 1751 Colonial Artist Campeche Is Born. One of the greatest colonial artists, José Campeche, is a mulatto born in San Juan, Puerto Rico, the fifth of seven children of María Josefa Jordán Marqués, a Canary Islander, and Tomás de Rivafrecha Campeche, a freed slave who is a painter and musician employed by his local church. As a child, José works in his father's studio, learning both painting and music, while receiving his education at the Dominican convent of St. Thomas Aquinas. In 1772, Campeche begins painting religious figures; his two earliest known paintings are portraits of Brother Sebastián Lorenzo Pizarro and St. Joseph with the Christ Child. In 1776, Campeche becomes an associate of the exiled Spanish painter Luis Paret y Alcázar, recently arrived to Puerto Rico, and receives his influence. Thanks to Paret's influence and instruction, Campeche is transformed from a competent local painter into a colonial master. In the course of his career, Campeche eventually outgrows the rigid academic training of Paret as he develops his own more fluid and humanistic style. In 1785, Campeche paints "La dama a caballo" (The Lady on a Horse), which marks his maturity as a draftsman and colorist. During this period, Campeche becomes one of the leading portrait artists of the nobility and of the government. At the same time, he also develops his career as a musician and teacher of instrumental music at the Cathedral of San Juan. In

San Juan in 1789, he paints portraits of the new king of Spain and the royal family, when Charles IV inherited the throne, and from 1790 on, he becomes the principal portrait artist of the most prominent members of San Juan society. In 1797, Campeche begins to receive commissions from other Spanish colonies. He paints "La Piedad" (Piety) for the Caracas Cathedral in Venezuela, among other works. Campeche receives a number of distinguished commissions to paint religious scenes and portraits of saints; in 1801 he paints "La visión de San Francisco" (St. Frances' Vision) for the Church of St. Frances. On November 7, 1809, José Campeche dies of an infectious disease in the same house where he has lived his entire life. He is buried in the Dominican convent.

MAY 8, 1753 Miguel Hidalgo y Costilla, Mexican Independence Leader, Is Born. Hidalgo, the proclaimer of Mexican independence, is born on this date near Guanajuato, Mexico. Hidalgo is educated in what is today Morelia, Mexico, and is ordained a priest. In 1803 he becomes the parish priest in the small town of Dolores, where he tends to a flock made up mostly of Indians. Hidalgo is a learned man, a liberal who helps his parishioners develop small industries of fabricating silk and winemaking. When Napoleon invades Spain and forces Charles IV to abdicate, Hidalgo joins a group of conspirators for Mexican independence known as the Liberal Club of Querétaro. The club also includes José María Morelos and Agustín de Iturbide. On the morning of September 16, 1810, upon hearing that their conspiracy has been discovered by the authorities, Hidalgo proclaims Mexico's independence from the pulpit of his church, with this famous shout: "Viva Nuestra Señora de Guadalupe i abajo los gachupines" (Long live Our Lady of Guadalupe and death to the Spaniards). That same day, Hidalgo proclaims the abolition of slavery and the end of the Indians' servitude. He is followed by some 60,000 weaponless poor people in a popular uprising. The untrained ragtag army takes over towns and cities that offer little resistance, and finally arrives at the outskirts of Mexico City, where it is wiped out by the viceroy's army. Hidalgo is captured in retreat on his way to the United States to develop support and is executed by a firing squad in Chihuahua on July 31, 1811. Hidalgo is considered the "Father" of his country.

1756   Manuel Tolsá, Sculptor and Architect, Is Born. Until the eighteenth century in Spanish America, most sculpture is of a religious nature and almost always anonymous. In Puebla, Mexico, an important school of sculpture develops, headed by Manuel Tolsá, who is also a noted architect. His most famous piece is the "Caballito," an equestrian sculpture of Charles IV that still stands in Mexico City. Tolsá is credited with introducing neoclassical art into Mexico. He is the architect of the famous Minería Palace in Mexico City.

JUNE 9, 1756   Francisco de Miranda, Activist for Independence, Is Born. An early activist for independence of the Spanish American colonies is the Venezuelan soldier Francisco de Miranda (1756–1816). As a soldier in the Spanish army, he participates in the war of independence of the thirteen British Colonies in North America, and he also takes part in the French Revolution. Inspired by all of those ideas of "liberty, fraternity, equality," Miranda founds the American Lodge, whose members swear their allegiance to democracy and to work for the independence of the Spanish American colonies, in London in 1797. In 1806, Miranda tries to liberate Venezuela by embarking from New York with a group of two hundred soldiers. When they disembark in Coro, Venezuela, they do not find the necessary support and the mission fails. Miranda returns to England, and from there prepares the liberation of his country with Simón Bolívar. When Miranda returns to Venezuela in 1810, he is arrested and sent to Spain, where he dies in jail on July 14, 1816, in Cádiz.

Miguel Hidalgo y Costilla. (Courtesy of the Arte Público Press Archives, University of Houston.)

1760–1769

1760   France Cedes Claims. After the Seven Years' War, which unites France and Spain against Britain, France cedes claims to all lands west of the Mississippi in order to keep them from the victorious British. Overnight, New Spain's territory expands dramatically.

1760   Texas Land Grant. Captain Blas María de la Garza Falcón obtains a grant to 975,000 acres of land in Texas, which he calls Rancho Real de Santa Petronila. In time it would become the largest cattle ranch in the United States: the King Ranch.

1761   Alta California Is Founded. The province of Alta California is founded through the leadership of José de Gálvez who, besides convincing the crown to colonize the area, also outfits two ships, which occupy the port of San Diego in April. After establishing missions and settlements in San Diego, Gaspar de Pórtola and Father Junípero Serra set out for Monterey Bay in July. After discovering San Francisco Bay, Pórtola reaches Monterey Bay in March, 1770.

1762   Cuba and the United States. During the Seven Years' War, the British occupy Havana, Cuba, for ten months. During that time, Cubans come into contact with soldiers and traders from the British North American colonies, and discover the benefits of commercial relations outside of the Spanish empire. This is to have great influence on the future relations of Cuba and the United States, especially as trading partners. During the first half of the nineteenth century, commercial relations expand dramatically, leading as well to the beginnings of Cuban communities in New Orleans, New York, and Philadelphia. Many Cubans come to the United States to pursue higher education. And the United States becomes a refuge for Cuban dissidents, exiles, and revolutionaries plotting the independence of their homeland. These close relations with the United States

José de Gálvez. (Courtesy of the Arte Público Press Archives, University of Houston.)

lead to a strong movement among many Cubans and even U.S. politicians to annex the island to the United States.

SEPTEMBER 17, 1766   Presidio of San Francisco Founded. The presidio of San Francisco is founded. Spain's northernmost frontier outpost is now a reality.

1767   Jesuits Expelled. King Charles III expels the Jesuits from the Spanish Empire. The throne seems to have feared the growing power of the Jesuits. This event opens the door for the Franciscan conquest of California and other lands. In expelling the Jesuits, the king's minister, the count of Aranda, prepares precise, secret orders for the viceroys and governors to follow. Without prior notice, the Jesuits are removed at specific dates and times from their universities, colleges, and convents and are not allowed to take anything with them but a few personal objects. They are shipped en masse to Italy. The expulsion of the popular Jesuits is protested with riots in Mexico, Peru, Chile, and Argentina, uprisings that are quelled by the military. Because of the expulsion, the colonial authorities lose a great deal of respect; the road to independence of Spain's American colonies is now prepared.

1769 San Diego Mission Established. The mission at San Diego, California, is established and the colonization of California begins.

JULY 3, 1769 Father Serra Founds Missions. Father Junípero Serra establishes the first mission of Alta California in what later becomes San Diego. Serra eventually founds ten missions, travels more than ten thousand miles and converts some 6,800 Indians.

1770–1779

1770 Slave Traffic Increases. From 1770 to 1790, there is a striking increase in slave traffic. At least 50,000 Africans arrive in Cuba. At the end of the century, a unique opportunity arises for investors in Cuban sugar production—the collapse of the Haitian sugar industry after rebels ravage that country in the 1790s—leading to an even larger number of slaves on the island.

1773 Alaskan Expeditions. Spanish expeditions begin to explore the Canadian coast up into Alaska over the next few years, making contact with Russians. Their explorations eventually lead to the establishment of a base at Nutka on the coast of Vancouver Island. This is the only European outpost in the expanse from San Francisco to Alaska. In 1789, Spanish soldiers arrest several English sailors at Nutka, which provokes protests and threats from the British government. The Nutka Convention of 1879 results in the Spanish abandoning the base; the convention specifies that all nations will be allowed to engage in trade on the coast of "Columbia," but no nation will be allowed to erect any establishments in the area.

1774 Overland Route to California. Pedro de

Father Junípero Serra. (Courtesy of the Library of Congress Prints & Photographs Division.)

Garcés, a Spanish Franciscan missionary, establishes the first overland route to California.

SEPTEMBER 17, 1776 Moraga Founds San Francisco. José Moraga, a lieutenant in Juan Bautista de Anza's colonizing mission of twenty families (240 people), 700 horses, and 350 cattle to Alta California, founds San Francisco on this date. In 1777, the governor of Alta California, Felipe de Neve, establishes his capital in Monterey and also founds the village of San José with some of the settlers brought by

Moraga. In 1781, de Neve goes south with other settlers and establishes Nuestra Señora la Reina de los Angeles de Portiúncula (Los Angeles).

NOVEMBER 15, 1776 "**The Mexican Think-er**" **Is Born.** José Joaquín Fernández de Lizardi is born in Mexico City. Fernández de Lizardi is considered the first Spanish American novelist. A man of middle-class upbringing and a partial university education, he is known for his liberalism and his promotion in Mexico of ideas from the French Enlightenment. Quite often using the pseudonym of "El Pensador Mexicano" (The Mexican Thinker), he disseminates his reformist ideas through a newspaper that he establishes and edits. Often subjected to censorship, he turns to writing fiction to promote his ideas about the church, education, societal vices, and prejudices under the cover of the dialogues and sermons of his characters. His masterpiece, *El Periquillo Sarniento* (1816), is a picaresque novel in which the main character narrates his autobiography set in the underworld of Mexico City. The work is a wonderful depiction of Mexican society on the eve of independence. He dies of tuberculosis on June 21, 1827.

FEBRUARY 25, 1778   Liberator of Chile and Peru Is Born. José de San Martín, the South American independence leader, is born in Yapeyú, Misiones, in what is today Argentina. He becomes the famous liberator of Chile and Peru. Born in Yapeyú, Argentina, he is raised in Spain, where he is an officer in the Spanish army, and fights against the invading Napoleonic forces in Spain and in Africa. San Martín serves twenty-two years in the Spanish army. In 1812, Lieutenant Colonel San Martín returns to Argentina with other patriots to fight for independence. In Mendoza, Argentina, he organizes the "Army of the Andes" and in 1813 liberates Argentina. He then crosses the mountain chain and, with the support of Bernardo O'Higgins, liberates Chile in 1817. In 1820, he

Portrait of José de San Martín. (Courtesy of the Library of Congress Prints & Photographs Division.)

invades Peru from the sea and defeats the Spaniards in various battles. San Martín enters Lima victoriously in 1821 and is proclaimed the "Protector" of Peru. In 1822, he meets secretly with Simón Bolívar in Guayaquil, Ecuador to discuss the future government of the liberated lands, and turns his forces over to Bolívar, who finalizes the war. San Martín does not want to participate in the nascent discord regarding the future of the liberated colonies, and he retires to live out his days in voluntary exile in Boulogne, France, where he dies on August 17, 1850.

1779   Spain's Role in American Revolution. Spain aligns with France in war on England and thereby gives moral support (but not much military aid) to the North American colonies' revolution.

1780–1789

1780   Incan Chief Battles Authorities. José Gabriel Condorcanqui (1740–81), an Incan chief known as Túpac Amaru and a direct descendant of the Incas, leads a two-year rebellion against the authorities over the Indians. Túpac Amaru has a grand vision of regaining lost Indian lands and of government by the Indians. He puts together a force of some six thousand mostly unarmed Indians, executed in a public plaza (one of the *corregidores*). Within a few months, his forces grow considerably and he controls much of what is now southern Peru, most of Bolivia, and some of Argentina. His army then marches on Cuzco, to ultimate defeat. Túpac Amaru returns with a force of 50,000 Indians, but is quashed mercilessly. He witnesses the execution of his wife and sons, and then is pulled to pieces by the authorities in 1781. The parts of his body are stuck on poles and displayed in villages that supported him, leading more Indians to revolt and to plunder Spaniards wherever they were found. Murder and rapine sweep through the countryside for months thereafter. Despite the bloody end of this rebellion, ideas of reestablishing an Inca monarchy remain alive from 1781 until independence from Spain is declared. In 1805, there is a plan to restore the Inca sociopolitical structure and to crown an Inca. And even after the declaration of independence, at the Congress of Tucumán in Buenos Aires in 1816, the idea of creating a new government based on the Inca empire is proposed. These ideas are often bitterly spurned, and eventually become nostalgic motifs in art and literature rather than sound political programs.

1781   Forerunner of Los Angeles Is Founded. The Pueblo Nuestra Señora de los Angeles de la Portiúncula is founded, later to become the city of Los Angeles.

1781   Spanish Strategy Aids Americans. Brigadier General Bernardo de Gálvez takes Mobile and Pensacola from the English to return these territories to Spanish dominion and to assist George Washington's forces in the War of Independence from England. This strategy forces the British Colonial Army to fight on two fronts. The Spanish also open a route to supply Washington's army with money, food, and weapons. As a result of this support of the Americans, Western Florida comes under the dominion of Spain again through the Treaty of Versailles.

NOVEMBER 29, 1781   Andrés Bello Is Born. Writer, poet, linguist, and political figure Andrés Bello (1781–1865) is born in Caracas, Venezuela. He dedicates himself to the study of the humanities from an early age. In 1810, he goes to live in London, where he works as a teacher, carries out literary studies, and pens some of his early works. From London he also organizes support for the Spanish American independence movements, often in consort with Simón Bolívar. In 1829 he moves to Santiago, Chile, at the invitation of the government. There, he serves as a university professor and one of the founders of the University of Chile (1843); he also is the principal author of the Chilean Civil Code (1855). As a literary figure he is an ardent defender of classicism, but he nevertheless is a fervent Americanist, and even develops a grammar of the Spanish language spoken in the Americas. Most of his poetry is inspired in American themes, as are the legends that he casts in literary form. His literary and intellectual work is encyclopedic in nature, encompassing philology, law, education, literature, history, mathematics, and philosophy. He also translates into Spanish numerous masterpieces from the Latin, Italian, French, and German. His best-known poem is *Silva a la agricultura en la zona tórrida* (Poem Dedicated to the Agriculture in the Torrid Zone), a long poem dedicated to describing the agricultural products of the Americas. He dies in Santiago, Chile, on October 16, 1865.

1783   Fine Arts Schools Established. Academies of Fine Arts are founded in Mexico and Guatemala.

1783   Spain Regains Florida. Through the Peace

Andrés Bello. (Courtesy of the Arte Público Press Archives, University of Houston.)

Treaty of Versailles, England recognizes the independence of the United States and returns Florida to Spain.

JULY 24, 1783 Simón Bolívar, the Liberator, Is Born. Simón Bolívar, the great Liberator, is born in Caracas, Venezuela, into a wealthy family. When Bolívar is three years old, his father dies, and when he is six, his mother dies. At age twenty, Bolívar himself becomes a widower, so he is accustomed to the pain of loss. Bolívar, nevertheless, is left an immense for-

Portrait of Simón Bolívar in Lima, by José Gil de Castro. (Courtesy of the Ministry of Internal Relations, Caracas.)

tune and is able to obtain the best private education money could buy. He receives much of his education in Spain. He reads Locke, Hobbes, Voltaire, Montesquieu, and Rousseau. In Paris he meets the great scientist Alexander von Humbolt, who had just returned from his voyage to the Americas. Humbolt supposedly convinces Bolívar that the Americas are ripe for their independence. Bolívar has become a seasoned officer in the Spanish army. After traveling throughout Europe and the United States, he returns to Venezuela to fight for its independence. He is a well-educated and well-rounded man who dreams of a free and confederated Spanish America. Bolívar leads armies to defeat the royalists in pitched battles, liberating Venezuela and Colombia, after which he is named president of Gran Colombia. Bolívar's lieutenant general, Antonio José de Sucre, defeats the Spanish in Ecuador. Later, Bolívar and Sucre finalize the war in Peru and free Alto Peru (Bolivia). Bolívar's dream of a United States of South America lives on among many intellectuals in the continent today. He dies on December 17, 1830, near the present-day city of Santa Marta, Colombia; his famous last words are reported to have been: "Aquellos que hemos servido a la Revolución hemos arado en el mar" (Those of us who have served the Revolution have plowed in the sea).

1790–1799

1790   Colonial Artist Paints Royalty. José Campeche paints the new royal family of Spain, and becomes the principal portrait artist of the most prominent members of San Juan society. (*See also* biography, December 23, 1751.)

1790   Hispanic Settlements Increase. From the 1790s to the 1820s, the Apache threat subsides because of successful military tactics and negotiations on the part of local leaders, and Hispanic settlements begin to thrive in Pimería Alta (northwestern Mexico and southern Ari-

zona). At one point as many as one thousand Hispanics live in the Santa Cruz Valley.

1790   Northern Exploration. From 1790 to 1792, Spanish ships explore the northern reaches of North America, mapping out portions of Canada and Alaska and starting short-lived settlements, such as those in Valdez and Córdoba.

1792   Mining Schools Established. The Schools of Mining are founded in Mexico City and Guatemala City.

1792   Sigüenza y Góngora's Collection Burns. A devastating fire in Mexico City consumes many of Carlos Sigüenza y Góngora's manuscripts of his scientific expedition of the southeastern United States. (*See also* biography, 1645.)

1793   Father Martínez Is Born. New Mexican priest, politician, and rebel Father José Antonio Martínez is born in Abiquiu into a politically powerful family. Ordained a priest in 1822, Martínez practices his profession in Taos for all but the first four years of his priesthood. In 1833, Martínez founds a school in Taos in which he trains much of the leadership of New Mexico; for the school he acquires what many scholars consider to be the first printing press west of the Mississippi. Under Mexican rule, Martínez serves as a territorial deputy. Prior to the Mexican American War, he is the main adversary to the imminent American civic, cultural, and political takeover. After the war, however, he tries to help his people accommodate as best they can; he becomes a member of the territorial legislature and in the 1848 statehood convention, for which he is elected president. Martínez is also famous for his opposition to new bishop Jean Baptist Lamy, who introduces numbers of French and Spanish priests into New Mexico—priests who were not sympathetic to the religious culture of the Nuevo Mexicanos. Martínez's continued dispute with the bishop leads to his formal excommunication by the bishop in 1857. In response, Martínez founds his own schismatic church and leads a congregation there until his death on July 28, 1867.

1793   Spain and France at War. Spain gets involved in a war with France's Napoleon, which results in the weakening of Spain's Bourbon monarchy, with King Charles IV going into exile. The war lasts until 1795 and is followed by a period where the Spanish Bourbon royalty is in exile and begins to lose some of its New World colonies to France. The first to be lost is Santo Domingo. The greatest loss, however, is that of the Louisiana Territory.

NOVEMBER 3, 1793   Stephen Austin Is Born. Stephen F. Austin, the son of Moses Austin, who was commissioned by Spain to lead settlers into Texas with land grants, is born in Austinville, Virginia. He made his father's vision a reality in firmly establishing the Anglo–American colony in Texas. After establishing the first colony on the Brazos River in 1821, he renegotiates his agreement with the Mexican empire after it achieves independence from Spain. In 1824, he renegotiates once again with the republic of Mexico. By the end of the 1820s, Anglo immigration to Texas has risen to twenty thousand settlers. Mexico grows alarmed and starts to limit this immigration through new laws and the establishment of border presidios and customs houses. Separatist sentiment rises and Austin is arrested and jailed in Mexico in 1833. After his release in September 1834, he is hailed as the only leader who could unite all Texans. After Texas declares its independence from Mexico, Austin is a candidate for the first presidency of the republic of Texas, but is defeated by Sam Houston, the conquering hero at the decisive battle over the Mexicans at San Jacinto. Austin served as Secretary of State, Republic of Texas, until his death on December 27, 1836.

FEBRUARY 21, 1795   Santa Anna Is Born. Antonio López de Santa Anna is born in Jalapa, Veracruz, into a wealthy creole family. At the age of fourteen, he enlists in the royal army of New Spain and fights against Hidalgo and Morelos in their pursuit of Mexican independence. As a youth he idolizes Napoleon Bonaparte, and in his later career has illusions of duplicating some of the emperor's feats. Santa Anna is a mediocre soldier and strategist, and has a flair for the dramatic and the demagogic. He betrays Spain for service with the emperor-to-be Agustín de Iturbide, and later he also betrays Iturbide to forward his own rise to leadership. He betrays the liberals who bring him to power and later betrays the conservatives who use him as a pawn. And later, he betrays Mexico to the United States by selling off a piece of northern Mexico. Santa Anna stole from his country and stole from the church and has gone down in Mexican history as "vende-patrias," vendor of the homeland. In 1832, Santa Anna leads his forces into Mexico City, deposes the president that he had illegally imposed, Anastasio Bustamante, and allows himself to be elected president. He then proceeds to serve as an absentee president, spending much of 1833 and 1834 on his plantation while his vice president, liberal Valentín Gómez Farías, administers the government. In April 1834, Santa Anna ousts Gómez Farías and proceeds to rule as a dictator. Santa Anna's rule is so disorderly and chaotic that the federal system is in grave danger and Zacatecas and Texas both organize revolts. In 1836, with his popularity waning, Santa Anna sets out to prove himself a national hero again by leading troops north to suppress the rebellion in Texas. After defeating forces at the Alamo in San Antonio and ordering the massacre of some three hundred at Goliad City, his forces are defeated and he is captured by Sam Houston's men at the San Jacinto River on April 21. Santa Anna makes treacherous promises to confirm Texan independence. By the time he returns to Mexico in 1836, he has lost face and retires to his hacienda. But his star rises again in 1838 when he ousts the French from Veracruz during the "Pastry War"; he loses a leg in the action. In July 1841, Santa Anna staged a military coup and installs himself as president once again. His rule lasts until 1844, when he is ousted from office. He is driven from Mexico City and then exiled to Havana in 1845. In 1846, Santa Anna again is called to service by the liberals against invading American forces. After winning some battles in the Mexican–American War, Santa Anna returns to power after the war and rules as a despot, deriving all of his power from the army and the church. He drains the national treasury but saves himself by betraying his own nation through the sale of the Mesilla Valley to the United States in 1853 for $10 million. In August 1855, Santa Anna sails to exile in Colombia, after both generals and politicians desert him. He is finally allowed to return to Mexico in 1872, and lives on charity until his death in Mexico City on June 20, 1876.

Antonio López de Santa Anna. (Courtesy of the Library of Congress Prints & Photographs Division.)

OCTOBER 1795 Pinckney's Treaty. Pinckney's Treaty (or Treaty of San Lorenzo) is signed by Spain and the United States, whereby Spain recognizes the 31st parallel as the southern boundary of the United States and grants the United States free navigation of the Mississippi River with the right of deposit at New Orleans.

1796 Colombian Painter Espinosa Is Born. José María Espinosa, the Colombian painter, is born in Bogotá into a leading family. Espinosa studies painting with Pablo Antonio García, but he becomes involved when the war for independence from Spain breaks out in July 1810. Espinosa fights in the revolution until independence is secured in 1819. While held prisoner for a period in San Agustín, he pens caricatures of fellow prisoners and executes several landscapes and battle scenes from memory. He becomes a true painter and chronicler of the war of independence. Even after the war and returning to Bogotá and social prominence, Espinosa continues to depict battle scenes and to paint portraits of the revolutionary heroes, including a famous one of Simón Bolívar. In the history of Latin American art, Espinosa's work represents a transition from colonial art to

that of the period of independence. His style influences many artists who follow, including his own sons. He dies in 1883 in Bogotá.

1796 Spain Allies with France. Spain again allies itself with France against England and loses what comes to be known as British Honduras and the rich island of Trinidad.

1797 American Lodge Founded. Activist Francisco de Miranda founds the American Lodge, whose members swear their allegiance to democracy and to work for the independence of the Spanish American colonies, in London. (*See also* biography, June 9, 1756.)

1798 The Alien Act. The Alien Act of 1798 grants the U.S. president the authority to expel any alien he deems dangerous. Opposed by President Thomas Jefferson, the Alien Act expires under its own terms in 1800, during his presidency.

1798 Naturalization Act. The Naturalization Act of 1798 raises the number of years, from five years to fourteen, an immigrant has to live in the United States to be eligible for citizenship.

1800

1800   Agricultural Products Cross Ocean.
Large, sprawling haciendas with huge herds of
cattle and sheep characterize the economy and
societal life of northeast New Spain. Although
mining is producing a great deal of wealth—
Spain and Portugal are producing ninety percent of the world's precious metals—agricultural products are far more profitable for Spain.
Among the products developed by the Indians
and introduced by the Spaniards to the rest of
the world are corn, varieties of potatoes and
yams, tomatoes, manioc, new species of nuts
and melons, vanilla, cacao (chocolate), quinine,
coca, ipecac, sarsaparilla, and tobacco. Mexico
also introduces the Spaniards to the turkey.
The Spaniards, on the other hand, bring to the
New World numerous crops and livestock,
including sheep, hogs, chickens, goats, and
cattle. Of course, the Spaniards depend on
Indian labor to cultivate and care for these
products. The first and most revolutionary of
the crops is sugar, probably introduced by Columbus in 1493. It becomes the chief export
throughout the Colonial Period. Coffee, a cash
crop that will assume great importance in the
nineteenth and twentieth centuries, is introduced in the eighteenth century. By 1800,
Spanish–American industry is well established,
becoming third in importance after agriculture
and mining. Colonial industry is built on the
craftsmanship of the Indians, who weave cotton and wool and use beautiful and durable
dyes. The wood products, stone work, and
metallurgy of the Indians also are prized. But
the textile industry is by far the most widespread and successful, with cotton and wool
mills multiplying in Mexico and Peru.

1800   Leader of the Californios Is Born. Juan
Bautista Alvarado, a leader of the Californios
(early California residents under the Spanish
and Mexican governments), is born in Monterey.
An educated and literate man, he rises in California politics and economic power and in 1836

leads a revolt against the central government of
Mexico under Antonio López de Santa Anna,
establishing the sovereign state of California
with himself as provisional governor. In 1842,
Alvarado surrenders his authority to a new
Mexican governor, and in 1845 he is elected to
the National Congress in Mexico City. During
the United States invasion of California in
1846, he does not participate in the resistance
against the Americans, but instead withdraws
from public life. He dies in 1882.

1800   Spain Cedes Louisiana. Spain cedes Louisiana to France through the Treaty of San
Ildefonso. This provides Napoleon Bonaparte
with the opportunity to reestablish an empire in
the New World, with an agricultural base in
Louisiana and a naval station on Hispaniola.
But Haiti's independence in 1802 puts an end
to his plans. The French, therefore, sell the
territory to the United States via the Louisiana
Purchase in 1803.

1801

**MARCH 21, 1801   Napoleon and the Treaty
of Luneville.** Charles IV concedes the Louisiana Territory to France's Napoleon. The territory had been ceded to Spain in the previous
century during the Seven Years' War. Through
the Treaty of Luneville, Napoleon promises to
make the territory a dukedom inhabited by
200,000 people. He also pledges not to sell or
turn it over to any other country. But, vying for
dominance in Europe and in need of quick
revenue, Napoleon breaks his promises and
sells the vast territory to the United States in
1803, thus expanding the borders of the infant
nation to connect directly with New Spain.

MAY 5, 1801   Governor Pico Is Born. Pío de
Jesús Pico, the last governor of California under
Mexican rule, is born at San Gabriel Mission
into a family of Californios. As a young man he
becomes successful in business in Los Angeles.
In 1828, he is elected to the territorial legisla-

Hacienda owners and administrator (right). (Courtesy of the Library of Congress Prints & Photographs Division.)

ture and assumes a grand stature as a southern Californio political leader. From January to February, 1832, he serves briefly as governor, but then becomes the civilian administrator of the San Luis Rey Mission. In 1845, he once again becomes governor, this time at the seat in Los Angeles instead of Monterey. He is attacked on various occasions for land grants that he made and his sale of mission lands. When the Americans invade, Pico at first offers some resistance, but soon flees to Baja California. After the signing of the peace treaty, Pico returns to California and assumes the peaceful life of a rancher. He, like many other Californios, loses all of his lands to mortgage companies when he needs funds to defend the titles to the properties against squatters and other usurpers. Under American rule, Pico continues his interest in politics, serving on the Los Angeles City Council and as the Los Angeles County tax assessor. He also owns a large hotel, the Pico House, which still stands in downtown Los Angeles. Pico dies penniless on September 11, 1894.

Pío Pico, the last governor of California under Mexican rule. (Courtesy of the California Historical Society.)

1802

MARCH 27, 1802 The Treaty of Amiens. France and England sign the peace Treaty of Amiens, by which Spain cedes Trinidad to England.

1803

1803 U.S. Buys Louisiana Territory. President Thomas Jefferson convinces a reluctant Congress to purchase the Louisiana Territory from the French for $15 million.

1804

1804 American Expansion Worries Spain. To the consternation of Spain, President Thomas Jefferson funds the historical expedition of Lewis and Clark. Spain worries that the exploration is a prelude to the settlement of the territory by Anglos. In addition, Jefferson leads Congress into passing the Mobile Act, which annexes into the Mississippi Territory all navigable wa-

ters, rivers, creeks, bays, and inlets that are located in the United States and east of the Mississippi River and empty into the Gulf of Mexico.

OCTOBER 21, 1804 The Battle of Trafalgar. In Spain's unholy alliance with Napoleon, the French emperor forces Spain to put its navy under French control in order to destroy the British naval forces. Lord Nelson effects a crushing defeat of the French and Spanish with his twenty-nine ships destroying some thirty-six ships of Marshall Villenueve at Trafalgar on October 21. As a result of this defeat, Spain has no way of protecting itself, much less keeping its New World colonies together.

1805

SEPTEMBER 3, 1805 Poet Echeverría Is Born. Poet Esteban Echeverría is born in Buenos Aires, Argentina. After leaving school in Argentina, Echeverría travels to Paris and on his own studies contemporary philosophers, historians, and writers, as well as Spanish classical writers in order to master his own language. He then returns to Buenos Aires convinced that he can make a contribution to Spanish–American letters and determined to break the cultural link with Spain. He becomes one of the foremost exponents of literary Americanism, rejecting any literary or cultural superiority in Spain. The only legacy that he recognizes from Spain is the language, but he is convinced that Spanish–Americans can improve the Spanish language. In 1832, Echeverría publishes *Elvira o la novia del Plata* (Elvira or The Bride of the River Plate), a poem that is considered to be the first outright romantic work in Spanish–American literature. Echeverría continues publishing poetry and also founds a literary–political society, the Association of May. It is suppressed by dictator Juan Manuel de Rosas, and Echeverría and other associated writers have to take refuge in exile in Uruguay. Echeverría also is credited with having written the first truly Argentine story, *El matadero* (The Slaughterhouse, 1840), an exposé of the atrocities committed by Rosas's followers. The writer who is credited with having introduced Romanticism to Spanish America dies in Montevideo, Uruguay, on January 19, 1851.

1806

1806   Puerto Rican Press Expands. The first newspaper, *La Gaceta de Puerto Rico* (The Puerto Rican Gazette), a government organ, is published in Puerto Rico. The printing press is introduced to Puerto Rico this year and *La Gaceta* became one of the first publications. It lasts until 1898. The development of newspapers and journalism in Puerto Rico is hampered because licenses to publish can be obtained only from the Spanish crown. In 1810, the Spanish *Cortes* (legislative body) creates a Junta Suprema de Censura (Supreme Censorship Commission), which is a further barrier to newspapers. The commission is disbanded in 1814. A second newspaper, *Diario Económico de Puerto Rico* (The Puerto Rican Economic Daily), is established on March 8, 1814, by Alejandro Ramírez, and a third one, *El Cigarrón* (The Cigar), is founded that same year. By 1820, some ten or more printing presses exist in Puerto Rico, and newspapers begin to proliferate. The first real daily newspaper, *Diario Libertad y de Variedades* (The Liberty and Variety Daily), begins publishing on December 6, 1821. But the Cortes once again restricts printing and publishing with its 1820 *Ley de Imprenta* (Law of the Printing Press), and newspapers disappear until 1839. In 1874, General Laureano Sanz becomes governor of the island and enforces a strict and despotic censorship, which actively persecutes publishers and editors, and effectively puts an end to the liberal press.

MARCH 21, 1806   Liberal Leader Benito Juárez Is Born. Benito Juárez (Pablo Juárez García), the first Indian leader of a Spanish–American country, is born into a family of poor Zapotecs

Argentine dictator Juan Manuel de Rosas. (Courtesy of the Columbus Memorial Library.)

in San Pablo Gueletao, Oaxaca, Mexico. Of humble beginnings, Juárez becomes one of the most important figures in Latin America in promoting democracy and liberalism. Orphaned at the age of three, Juárez is raised by an uncle. At the age of twelve, he runs away from home to Oaxaca and finds employment in the home of a Franciscan lay brother, who befriends him, gives him books and introduces him to the world of ideas. By the mid 1820s, Juárez is studying science and law. By 1831, he has become a law clerk, and then later a lawyer defending the property rights of poor Indians. In 1843, he marries Margarita Maza, the daughter of a prominent family. Juárez serves a term in the national congress and then is governor of Oaxaca from 1847 to 1852. In 1853, Santa Anna has Juárez jailed and banished to New Orleans, where other expatriates are planning Santa Anna's overthrow. In 1855, Juárez joins in the march from Acapulco to the capital in Mexico City and helps overthrow the dictatorial government. Juárez subsequently serves in presidential cabinets, as senator, as chief justice of the supreme court and finally as president, elected by a penniless rump congress in Querétaro in 1858. In 1859, Juárez promulgates the Laws of Reform, which call for the immediate confiscation, without compensation, of all church property except the churches themselves; they also call for suppression of the monasteries and for the nationalizing of cemeteries. Marriage becomes a civil contract. These laws are passed as a fiscal measure and as an expedient of a civil war in which the church was financing the conservatives. Juárez and the liberals win the bloody civil war just before the French invade. With the French Intervention in 1861, Juárez suffers imprisonment and exile, and has to establish an itinerant government in Guanajuato, Guadalajara, and other cities. Napoleon III succeeds in placing his puppet, Emperor Maximilian, on the throne of Mexico, only to have him defeated, unseated, and executed by Juárez. In July 1867, Juárez marches at the head of his forces back into Mexico City. He is reelected to the presidency in 1867 and 1871. Among the reforms instituted by Juárez that have lasted are the separation of church and state and the nationalization of church lands. On July 18, 1872, while still in office, Juárez dies of a heart attack in Mexico City.

OCTOBER 27, 1806 Texas Republic Founder Is Born. Politician and one of the founders of the Republic of Texas, Juan N. Seguín is born into a prominent family of French extraction in San Antonio, Texas. At the age of eighteen, he is elected mayor of San Antonio. One of the developers of a nationalist spirit in Texas, Seguín leads Texans in opposition to the centrist government of Antonio López de Santa Anna in the 1830s. In the struggle for independence from Mexico, Seguín serves as a captain in the Texas cavalry, eventually achieving the rank of lieutenant colonel. After the war of independence, Seguín once again serves at the head of San Antonio government, but this time as commander. In 1838, he is elected to the Texas senate, and in 1840 again to the mayoralty of San Antonio. He defends Tejanos against profiteering Anglos who are rushing into the state to make their fortune at all costs.

Unjustly accusing him of favoring invading Mexican forces and betraying the Santa Fe Expedition to foment revolt in New Mexico against Mexico, Anglos force Seguín to resign as mayor in April 1842. Fearing reprisals, he moves with his family across the Río Grande into Mexico. In Mexico, he is jailed and forced to serve in the Mexican army, including in battle against the United States during the Mexican–American War. In 1848, he once again moves to Texas, only to return to live out his days in Nuevo Laredo, Mexico, from 1867 until his death in 1890.

1807

1807 Napoleon Invades; Wars of Independence Begin. Napoleon Bonaparte invades Spain and Portugal. Ferdinand VII, the king of Spain, abdicates and Napoleon names his brother Joseph to the throne. The creoles in the Venezuela, New Granada, and River Plate viceroyalties denounce the usurpation and refuse to recognize Napoleon's governmental representatives. The creoles begin plotting for the independence of their countries, using their allegiance to the Spanish crown as an excuse for their rejection of the government. The wars of independence break out.

1808

JULY 7, 1808 Californio Politician Vallejo Is Born. Mariano G. Vallejo, Californio politician and military leader, is born into an upper-class family in Monterey, the capital of Alta California under Mexican rule. At age fifteen, Vallejo becomes a cadet at the Monterey presidio; at age twenty-one he is already a commander and an elected member of the territorial legislature. In his mid-twenties, Vallejo is appointed military commander of all of northern California and administrator of the San Francisco Solano Mission at the time when missions are being secularized. During his tenure in these positions, Vallejo begins to believe that the American takeover is inevitable and that it would be advantageous for Californios. During the Bear Flag Revolt, Vallejo is jailed for two months but afterwards, under American rule, is named to the legislative council. Later he also serves as the northern Indian agent. In 1849 he is one of only eight Californios elected to the constitutional convention, and is subsequently elected to the state's first senate. Despite his prominence and influence in California politics, Vallejo loses important lands, including the large Soscol land grant, through court action by squatters and speculators. When he dies on January 18, 1890, he owns only 280 acres.

1809

DECEMBER 24, 1809　Kit Carson Is Born. Christopher (Kit) Carson is born in Madison County, Kentucky, and raised on the Missouri frontier. As a teenager he travels west to explore; he becomes a mountain man and learns to trap beaver. In 1826, he becomes a professional trapper and guide in the Rocky Mountains. In 1842, he becomes a guide for John C. Frémont on three expeditions into the west. He becomes involved in the Bear Flag Revolt in California in 1845. After the Mexican–American War, Carson is an Indian agent, a rancher, and a leading citizen in Taos, Mexico. During the Civil War, he is an active commander and is rewarded with the rank of brigadier general. Carson is illiterate almost his whole life, but learns to read in his old age. After the war, he moves to southern Colorado, where he dies on May 23, 1868.

1810

APRIL 19, 1810　French Rule Sparks Wars. The cabildo, the local governmental body, of Caracas deposes the Spanish captain general and replaces him with a junta to rule in the name of the Spanish king, Ferdinand VII, who has been replaced by Napoleon. This is the official start to fourteen years of wars for the independence of Venezuela, Colombia, Peru, and Bolivia. The wealthy creoles use French rule as the spark for their revolution.

SEPTEMBER 16, 1810　Hidalgo Leads Insurrection. Miguel Hidalgo y Costilla (1753–1811), a parish priest in the town of Dolores, Mexico, organizes the grass roots and declares independence from Spain. He leads masses of Indians, mestizos, and creoles in battle with his famous shout *¡Qué viva la Virgen de Guadalupe y qué mueran los gachupines!* (Long live the Virgin of Guadalupe and death to the Spaniards!) In appealing to the Indians he not only invokes their holy patroness, but rallies them about regaining their lands and, presumably, cultural patrimony: "My children, will you be free? Will you make the effort to recover from the hated Spaniards the lands stolen from your forefathers three hundred years ago?" Hidalgo not only goes on to take cities, but also marches on the capital itself, Mexico City, where he finally is defeated by the royalists. While in Guadalajara, Hidalgo organizes a government, abolishes slavery, and begins to redistribute the land to the Indians. In March 1811, he is captured, tried, and convicted by a military court; he also is stripped of his priestly robes. He is executed by a firing squad on July 31. When independence finally does come in 1821, it is not in the form dreamed of by Hidalgo and his followers. In fact, independence brings the "empire" of Agustín de Iturbide, and the land issue is left to be considered again some ninety years later during the Mexican Revolution. With the insurrection of Father Miguel Hidalgo y Costilla, the Spaniards withdraw their troops from the frontier presidios in what will later become the Southwest of the United States. (*See also* biography, May 8, 1753.)

1811

1811 Venezuela Declares Independence. A junta expels the Spanish governor of Venezuela and a national congress is formed in Venezuela, which declares its independence from Spain.

JANUARY 11, 1811 U.S. Seeks to Protect Floridas. The United States Congress meets in a secret session to approve a resolution declaring that the U.S. cannot accept the passing of any part of the Floridas into the hands of a foreign power. It then passes, enabling legislation to authorize the president to negotiate with local authorities an agreement, known as the "no-transfer resolution," to permit the United States to take custody of east Florida should it be threatened by a foreign power. This prepares the way for the annexation of the Floridas by the United States via the Adams–Onís Treaty in 1819.

JANUARY 22, 1811 Mexican War Spreads to Texas. The war for independence of Mexico from Spain spreads to Texas when militia captain Juan Bautista de Casas takes up arms and arrests governor Manuel de Salcedo and the commander of the Spanish auxiliary troops, José Bernardo Gutiérrez de Lara. The insurrection is put down, however, by royalist troops sent from Veracruz and Tampico. By March, Texas again submits to the Spanish throne.

FEBRUARY 14, 1811 Domingo Faustino Sarmiento Is Born. Domingo Faustino Sarmiento, writer, politician, and educator, is born into a poor family in San Juan, Argentina. As a child he is precocious, but he is unable to obtain a university education; he, therefore, instructs himself. As a young man he opposes the regime of dictator Juan Manuel de Rosas and, in 1831, goes into exile in Chile, where he becomes a journalist for *El Mercurio* (The Mercury), a teacher, and the founder of a school, the Escuela Normal de Preceptores, in Santiago. At this point he engages in an historic polemic with Andrés Bello on progressive culture and the

Domingo Faustino Sarmiento. (Courtesy of the Library of Congress Prints & Photographs Division.)

imitation of French models. In 1836, he returns to Buenos Aires, but has to leave again in 1841, when he goes into exile in Europe and the United States. Sarmiento returns to Argentina in 1855 and serves in various political positions, including deputy, senator, and ambassador to the United States. In 1868, he becomes president of the republic. After the war with Paraguay, he is able to establish an observatory in Córdoba, a naval and military academy and various progressive public works. Upon leaving the presidency in 1874, he carries out other political functions and then retires in Asunción, Paraguay, where he dies on September 11, 1888. Sarmiento is the author of some fifty-two works, none of which is solely artistic, for he wrote with pedagogic and polemic intentions. His style is aggressive, devastating, and disorganized, what some have called a "gaucho style." He is considered Argentina's greatest prose writer. His most important work is *Facundo o Civilización y barbarie* (Facundo or Civilization and Barbarie), which originally is published as a newspaper serial. The book is a violent attack on dictator Rosas and his followers, as well as a biting analysis of Argentine society. Sarmiento's ideas were typically liberal; he considered the rough and ready ethos of gaucho life to be an impediment to Argentine progress, and insisted on public education as the means of extracting his country from colonial backwardness. He often took the United States and Europe as models for industrial, scientific, artistic and commercial development.

MAY 14, 1811 Paraguay Leaves Spanish Control. A military junta led by Juan Pedro Caballero executes a successful coup d'etat and wins the independence of Paraguay from Spain. On June 17, a national congress names a five-person junta to govern Paraguay. Paraguay is declared a republic on October 12, 1813.

NOVEMBER 5, 1811 San Salvador Priest Calls for Independence. The first shout for Central American independence is issued by a priest, José Matías Delgado, in San Salvador. It is not until 1821, however, that independence is achieved.

1813

1813 Children of Slaves Become Free. Argentina declares all children born of slaves to be free.

1813 Paraguayan Independence. Under dictator José Gaspar Rodríguez Francia, Paraguay declares its independence of Spain, and of Buenos Aires where a revolutionary junta has included Paraguay in its revolt.

NOVEMBER 1813 Morelos Continues Hidalgo's Fight. Father José María Morelos y Pavón picks up where Hidalgo left off and declares independence from Spain once again at a congress which he organizes in Chilpancingo, Mexico. A constitution is drafted and promulgated in 1814. In 1815, Morelos is defeated and executed by the royalists. He is tried, convicted, stripped of his priestly robes, and executed on December 22, 1815.

1814

1814 Dictatorship Rules Paraguay. Paraguay, the first country in Spanish America to win its independence, becomes a dictatorship when its congress elects José Gaspar y Francia the Supreme Dictator. On June 1, 1816, the congress names Gaspar y Francia "Perpetual Dictator of the Republic." From 1814 to 1840, Paraguay closes its doors to the rest of the world, not permitting foreigners to enter, and becomes extremely isolated. Paraguay seeks to protect itself from the disorder occurring in other countries that are fighting for independence or that are suffering conflict after their wars. No mail is allowed in and the only commerce is with arms salesmen.

MARCH 23, 1814 Writer Gómez de Avellaneda Is Born. One of the most distinguished women writers of the nineteenth century, Gertrudis Gómez de Avellaneda, is born in Puerto Príncipe (name changed later to Camagüey) into a distinguished family. In 1836, her family moves to Spain and she begins her literary career there under the pseudonym of La Peregrina (The Pilgrim). Her first inclination is to be a neoclassical writer, but then she becomes part of the Romanticism sweeping through Europe. She publishes her first book of poems, *Poesías líricas* (Lyric Poems) in 1841, but her greatest contribution is a respectable body of dramas, including *Munio Alfonso* and *El príncipe de Viana* (The Prince of Vina) in 1844 and *Baltasar* (1858). In 1859, Gómez de Avellaneda founds the literary review, *Album Cubano* (Cuban Album) in Cuba. In 1861, she produces her first novel, *El artista banquero* (The Banker Artist). After returning to Spain, Gómez de Avellaneda publishes her complete works, *Obras completas,* from 1869 to 1871. She dies in Madrid on February 1, 1873.

OCTOBER 24, 1814 Rafael Carrera, Dictator of Guatemala, Is Born. Guatemalan dictator Rafael Carrera is born into a poor mestizo-mulatto family in Guatemala City. His father is a mule driver and his mother a servant. When civil war comes in 1826, the unschooled twelve-year-old Carrera enlists in the federal army as a drummer boy. He fights valiantly in various battles and rises to the rank of sergeant. After the war, he becomes a drifter, taking on a number of odd jobs. In 1836, Carrera marries into the family of a wealthy mestizo hacienda owner. Under the tutelage of his father-in-law and his wife, Carrera gains the charisma to organize the peasants of eastern Guatemala against the liberal government in Guatemala City. It is in the rural eastern regions of Guatemala that Carrera eventually emerges as a conservative politician and military leader. He is a leader of the revolution that breaks out in 1937 and is victorious in many battles, eventually overthrowing President Francisco Morazán in 1840. He serves as head of state from 1844 to 1848. Carrera is elected to the presidency in 1851 and, in 1854, names himself president for life. He remains the dictator of Guatemala until his death in 1865.

Guatemalan dictator Rafael Carrera. (Courtesy of the Library of Congress Prints & Photographs Division.)

1816

1816   Lizardi's Masterpiece Published. José Joaquín Fernández de Lizardi publishes *El Periquillo Sarniento,* a picaresque novel set in the underworld of Mexico City. (*See also* biography, November 15, 1776.)

1816   Provinces Proclaim Independence. The United Provinces of the River Plate (Argentina and Uruguay) declare their independence.

1817

1817   Chile Liberated. José de San Martín liberates Chile with the support of Bernardo O'Higgins. (*See also* biography, February 25, 1778.)

1817   Cuban Slave Trade. Spain outlaws the slave trade in all of its colonies to the north of the equator, and signs a treaty with England providing for the suppressing of the slave trade. The first census is taken in Cuba this year and reveals that there are 291,000 whites, 224,000 slaves, and 115,000 free persons of color. Smuggling of slaves, does not abate, and the number of slaves imported continues to rise steadily in the 1820s and 1830s. Another treaty with England signed in 1835 once again emphasizes the will of both nations to end the slave trade. But the trade to Cuba is not effectively suppressed until 1865. Many Cubans are ashamed of slavery and do not support it on humanitarian grounds, but they fear that the sugar industry cannot be maintained without slave labor. Also, the prospect of free slaves and an independent Cuba causes whites to fear living in a black republic. Given that option, they prefer remaining a colony of Spain.

OCTOBER 21, 1817   Antonio Coronel, California Politician, Is Born. Antonio Coronel, educator, politician, and man of letters and theatre, is born in Mexico City. At the age of seventeen he moves with his parents to Los Angeles, Alta California. Under Mexican rule, he serves as a schoolteacher and on various civic commissions and boards. After the Mexican–American War, he continues his public service as an American citizen. During the gold rush, Coronel amasses riches, but returns to Los Angeles when faced with considerable discrimination against Mexicans in the gold fields. He teaches and holds various elected positions in city government, including that of mayor of Los Angeles. He also is a theatrical impresario and owner of the Teatro de la Merced (Merced Theater). In 1867, he is elected state treasurer as a Democrat. He later is elected to the state senate. Coronel dies on April 17, 1894.

DECEMBER 2, 1817 Argentine Writer José Mármol Is Born. Argentine writer José Mármol is born in Buenos Aires. Because of his violent verbal attacks in poetry on dictator Juan Manuel de Rosas, Mármol is forced to spend many years in exile. He is able to write plays and one of the most important romantic novels of Spanish America, *Amalia,* while in exile in Montevideo, Uruguay. The story tells of the amorous and patriotic adventures of an aristocratic widow who falls in love with a young revolutionary. The novel directly attacks dictator Rosas and his police state once again. After the fall of Rosas, Mármol returns to Buenos Aires and is received as a national hero. In 1858, he is named the director of the National Library. He dies on August 9, 1871.

1819

1819 U.S. Buys Florida. The United States purchases Florida from Spain for $5 million under the Adams–Onís Treaty. The treaty establishes the border between the United States' Louisiana territory and Spanish Texas at the Sabine River, and follows a latitude of 42 degrees all the way to the Pacific Ocean. When Mexico gains its independence in 1821, it inherits from Spain an immense territory north of the Rio Grande that has been organized up to

then as the provinces of Texas, New Mexico, and Alta California.

1819 U.S. Takes Over Spanish Sites. Andrew Jackson leads a U.S. military force into the Floridas, capturing two Spanish forts. This results in Spain selling the Florida Territory to the United States for $5 million in 1821. In reality, Spain has suffered an undeclared war by the United States for some thirty years, under the U.S. doctrine of Manifest Destiny, which translated into rights of intervention and annexation, rights to colonize, and to use the soil. During successive interventions and encroachments, Spanish settlements and cities have been occupied or taken over gradually by the United States: Baton Rouge in 1794, Mobile in 1811 and 1814, Amelia Island in 1813 and 1819, Pensacola in 1814 and 1818, and San Marcos de Apalachee in 1818. The South is the first proving ground for this doctrine that justifies to Americans their expansion westward.

JUNE 23, 1819 Spain Seeks to Settle Texas. American Army officer and explorer James Long leads a revolt in Nacogdoches, Texas, ostensibly as part of the independence movement against the Spaniards, but he obviously acts as a filibusterer for his countrymen. Spain finally enters into deliberations with Moses Austin, a Catholic from Missouri, to settle Anglo–Catholic families in Texas, as long as they became nationalized Spaniards. Spain is anxious to settle Texas, even with foreigners, in order to sustain her claim to the territory. The process is still being implemented when Mexico, including Texas, gains its independence in 1821.

1820

1820 Spain Bans Slave Trade. Spain outlaws the slave trade in all of its colonies to the south of the equator.

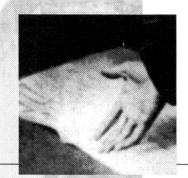

Part 3

THE BATTLE FOR INDEPENDENCE & THE EMERGENCE OF SPANISH AMERICAN REPUBLICS 1821-1898

Chapter 5

1821 TO 1898

1821

1821 Adams–Onís Treaty Approved. The United States Congress finally ratifies the Adams–Onís Treaty.

1821 Santo Domingo Proclaims Independence. Proclaiming its independence as "Spanish Haiti," Santo Domingo sends envoys to Simón Bolívar to request admittance to Gran Colombia. But the president of Haiti, Jean Pierre Boyer, leads his army into Santo Domingo and declares it part of Haiti in 1822. (Haiti had ousted the French in 1803, but the Dominicans remained under the control of Napoleon until 1809, when they were successful in ousting the French. At that point, the Dominicans attempted to establish a free republic but once again fell under the rule of Spain.) Haiti imposes a brutal rule of military, cultural, and racial oppression from 1822 to 1844.

JUNE 1821 Bolívar Leads Gran Colombia. A congress is called to write the Colombian constitution. Simón Bolívar is ratified as president of the new country of Gran Colombia. (*See also* biography, July 24, 1783.)

JULY 28, 1821 Peruvian Independence. José de San Martín declares the independence of Peru. (*See also* biography, February 25, 1778.)

SEPTEMBER 16, 1821 Guatemalan Countries Proclaim Their Independence. The countries declare their independence and, in 1823, later become the United Provinces of Central America. These shortly form the Central American Federation, which because of internal wars lasts only until 1838.

SEPTEMBER 27, 1821 Iturbide Leads Mexico to Independence. Mexico acquires its independence when liberals, Freemasons, and conservative creoles form an alliance in support of the creole Agustín de Iturbide, who in September enters Mexico City triumphant at the head of an army professing three guarantees: union, religion, and independence. Iturbide succeeds in having himself crowned emperor of Mexico in 1822. Iturbide's Plan de Iguala (Iguala Plan) promotes the ideal of equality for all citizens, including Indians and mestizos, but it also is reactionary in supporting the church and praising the culture and achievements of the Spaniards in the Americas, in condemning Hidalgo's insurrection, and in ignoring pre-Colombian indigenous civilizations and the needs of the Indians. Thus, Mexico begins its independence with a newly empowered and optimistic creole and mestizo class living side by side with the traditionally exploited and/or neglected Indians. Both culturally and economically, independence benefits the creoles much and the Indians hardly at all. By the time Mexico acquires its independence from Spain, permanent colonies exist in coastal California, southern Arizona, south Texas, and in most of New Mexico and southern Colorado. The imprint of evolving Mexican culture is stamped on today's Southwest. When Mexico declares the independence of New Spain, it also includes Central America, but the Guatemalan countries quickly declare independence from New Spain/Mexico. Central America remains for a long time a collection of small, fragile political entities, which form a federation in 1823.

1822

1822   Haiti Rules Dominicans. The Dominican Republic falls under Haitian rule. This lasts until 1844, when it successfully liberates itself.

1822   Iturbide Declares Himself Emperor. A former royalist soldier, Agustín de Iturbide, proclaims himself emperor of Mexico, but is forced to abdicate in 1823 by General Antonio López de Santa Anna.

MARCH 8, 1822   U.S. Recognizes Independent Governments. President James Monroe of the United States recommends to Congress the recognition of the Spanish–American governments that have declared their independence from Spain: La Plata (Argentina), Chile, Peru, Republic of Gran Colombia, and Mexico. Monroe states that they are entitled to recognition in order to protect them from European intervention.

JUNE 10, 1822   Mexican Painter Juan Cordero Is Born. Juan Cordero, a distinguished Mexican painter, is born in Teziutlán, Puebla, the son of a Spanish father and a mestiza mother. After studying with Miguel Mata at the San Carlos Academy, he travels to Rome in 1844 to study at the Academy of St. Luke. While there, he is hired as an attaché by the Holy See, which provides him with sufficient funds to continue to study. Most of his paintings of this period deal with religious subjects. His first major

painting is "Columbus before the Catholic Monarchs," which is exhibited at the third San Carlos exposition in 1851. In 1853, Cordero returns to Mexico and to work as a teacher at the San Carlos Academy. He suffers political repercussions because of portraits he paints of dictator Antonio López de Santa Anna. In 1857, he executes his famous murals at the Church of Santa Teresa, and in 1859, those at the Church of San Fernando, which anticipate the techniques used by modern muralists. His last mural is "The Triumph of Science and Work over Ignorance and Sloth" (1874), painted for the National Preparatory School, the institution that would house works by the greatest muralists of the twentieth century. Unfortunately, the mural is destroyed in 1900. During his adult life, Cordero works as a portrait artist all over Mexico, but most notably in the Yucatan. He dies in Popotla, Mexico, on May 28, 1884.

OCTOBER 6, 1822   Manuel Alonso, Puerto Rican Poet and Physician, Is Born. Distinguished Puerto Rican prose writer, poet, doctor, and early nationalist Manuel A. Alonso is born in San Juan. Alonso is educated at home by his mother and obtains his secondary education from the Seminario Conciliar (1836–41). In 1842, he journeys to Barcelona, Spain, to study medicine. In 1848, he receives his medical and surgeon's degree and, in 1849, returns to Puerto Rico to practice his profession in Caguas and surrounding towns. From 1858 to 1862 and from 1866 to 1871, he lives in Spain again, during which time he unites with other Puerto Rican patriots to pressure the throne for reforms of the island governance. Upon his return to Puerto Rico, Alonso is named director of the public hospital, a position that he holds until his death in San Juan on November 4, 1889. As director, Alonso is the first to introduce modern treatment of the mentally ill in Puerto Rico. From his early days as a student in Spain, Alonso writes poetry and he becomes associated with a group of Puerto Ricans who publish an anthology, *Album puertorriqueño*

(1844). The anthology is inspired by Puerto Rican folk customs and song, and is the cultural basis for a proposed Puerto Rican national identity based on grassroots culture. In 1846, Alonso again contributes poetry and prose to an anthology, *El cancionero de Borinqueñ* (The Puerto Rican Song Book), that develops similar folk themes but this time identifies with urban settings. In 1849, Alonso publishes his major work, *El gíbaro* (The Puerto Rican Peasant), which is considered a masterpiece and founding work of Puerto Rican literature. The work, made up of twenty-one local color scenes, describes Puerto Rican customs at mid-century. In 1883, Alonso adds a second volume to *El gíbaro,* in which he includes political criticism.

1823

1823   Argentine Painter Pueyrredón Is Born. Prilidiano P. Pueyrredón, the most important Argentine painter of the nineteenth century, is born in Buenos Aires into an aristocratic family. The son of Juan Martín de Pueyrredón, the director of the United Provinces of Río de la Plata, Martín studies painting in Paris and in Spain. Among his notable works are a portrait of his father, executed in 1848, and one of Manuelita Rosas, finished in 1851, which today is part of the collection of the Museum of Buenos Aires. For the most part, Pueyrredón's works are realist, although some of his landscapes have been considered to exhibit romantic tendencies. Pueyrredón is an academic painter whose work is most distinguished for its use of color and the psychological depth of the portraiture. He dies in 1870.

1823   California Missions. By 1823, the famous mission trail of California includes the following: San Diego de Alcalá (1769), San Carlos de Monterrey (1770), San Antonio de Padua (1771), San Gabriel Arcángel (1771), San Luis Obispo de Tolosa (1772), San Francisco de Asís (1776), San Juan Capistrano (1776), Santa Clara de Asís (1777), San Buenaventura

(1782), Santa Bárbara (1786), La Purísima Concepción (1787), Santa Cruz (1791), San José de Guadalupe (1797), San Juan Bautista (1797), San Miguel Arcángel (1797), San Fernando Rey (1797), San Luis Rey (1798), Santa Inés (1804), San Rafael Arcángel (1817), and San Francisco Solano (1823). Father Junípero Serra dies in 1784 but his death does not stop missionary activity in California. His fellow Franciscans establish another twelve missions.

1823   Guatemalan Territories Join Together. The territories form the United Provinces of Central America, a federation so weak that the president does not even have the power to force compliance with the government's statutes.

1823   John Quincy Adams and Cuba. United States Secretary of State John Quincy Adams informs the Spanish government that the annexation of Cuba would be indispensable to the Union's integrity.

1823–30   Anglos Flock to Texas. Erasmo Seguín, a delegate to the Mexican national congress from Texas, persuades a willing congress to pass a colonization act designed to bring even more Anglo settlers to Texas. Between 1824 and 1830, thousands of Anglo families enter east Texas, acquiring hundreds of thousands of free acres and buying land much cheaper than they could have in the United States. By 1830, Texas has eighteen thousand Anglo inhabitants and their African slaves, who number over two thousand.

FEBRUARY 28, 1823   Puerto Rican Nationalist Román Baldorioty de Castro Is Born. Román Baldorioty de Castro, a distinguished Puerto Rican educator and nationalist, is born in Gauynabo, the son of a poor washerwoman. (He is also thought to have been born sometime in March in Cayey.) After studying at the Seminario Conciliar, he receives a Spanish government subsidy to study in Spain and Europe from 1846 to 1853. In Spain he studies philosophy and physical sciences; later he also is a

San Francisco de la Espada Mission, San Antonio, Texas. Photo by Arthur W. Stewart, 1936. (Courtesy of the Library of Congress Historic American Buildings Survey, Prints & Photographs Division.)

student at the School of Arts and Manufacturing in Paris. In 1853, Baldorioty returns to Puerto Rico to teach. For twenty years he teaches in various towns and cities and is able to found a secondary school in Ponce. In 1869, he is elected to the Spanish Cortes (legislative body), where he works for the abolition of slavery and for the reform of the colonial system. While in dire poverty in 1875, Baldorioty moves to Santo Domingo to earn a living as a teacher; there he establishes the Colegio Antillano, a secondary school for the Caribbean peoples.

The Dominican government also names him director of a nautical academy. In 1878, he returns to Puerto Rico and begins a campaign towards achieving Puerto Rican autonomy from Spain and, in 1887, he is a founder and president of the Autonomist Party of Puerto Rico. On November 8 of that year, he is jailed by the Spanish military for promoting Puerto Rican independence. For the most part, Baldorioty advocates working within the system and pursuing legal means towards autonomy rather than total independence. In fact, he refuses to participate in the Grito de Lares proclamation of independence or in the revolution.

MARCH 19, 1823 Mexican Emperor Steps Down. Agustín de Iturbide, the Emperor of Mexico, abdicates his throne.

JULY 1, 1823 Central Americans Form Federation. The Confederación de Repúblicas Centroamericanas (Central American Federation) is born, and José Manuel Arce of Guatemala is named president. Provincial dissensions and economic and social conflicts lead to the dissolution of the confederation by 1840.

DECEMBER 2, 1823 The Monroe Doctrine. President James Monroe of the United States announces the Monroe Doctrine, guaranteeing the independence of Spanish–American countries from European interference. He states that the Western Hemisphere is off limits to further European expansion and political ideology.

1824

1824 Constitution of the Central American Federation. The Central American Federation drafts one of the most liberal constitutions in all of the Americas. But even before completing the constitution, the government abolishes all titles of distinction, royalty, and nobility and effects numerous anticlerical reforms. Dedicated to "liberty, equality, security and property," the Constitution of 1824 outlaws slavery and guarantees individual liberties, creates a unicameral federal congress to be elected along with an executive branch, and establishes a separate senate and a separately elected supreme court. The constitution also guarantees that Roman Catholicism will be the exclusive religion of state.

1824 First Conservatory Established. The first conservatory of music in the Americas is founded by José Mariano Elízara in Mexico City.

1824 Seguín Becomes Mayor. At the age of eighteen, Juan N. Seguín is elected mayor of San Antonio. (*See also* biography, October 27, 1806.)

1824 Spanish Rule Comes to End. The defeat of the Spanish army at Ayacucho, Peru, for all practical purposes, signals the end of Spanish rule in Central and South America. The wars of independence end in most of Spanish America, with the exception of Cuba and Puerto Rico, which gain their independence from Spain in 1898. As the wars of independence conclude for most of the Spanish–American nations, approximately thirty years of civil wars, revolutions, and the appearance of dictators and even emperors begin.

MAY 16, 1824 Mexican Folk Hero Juan Nepomuceno Cortina Is Born. Juan Nepomuceno Cortina, a rancher, social bandit, and Mexican governor, is born in Camargo on the Mexican side of the Rio Grande. Cortina is raised in a family of Mexican landowners, but after fighting against the United States in the Mexican–American War, he purchases and settles on a ranch near Brownsville, Texas. Recognizing the discrimination that Mexicans face after the war, Cortina strikes out against injustice when he wounds a Texas marshall who is mistreating a Mexican worker. He escapes across the border to avoid arrest and possibly death, whereupon he becomes a folk hero to the oppressed Mexican population in Texas. He soon leads a large force of rebels who cross the border at Matamoros and take over the city of Brownsville, raising the flag of Mexico. As a result of this and other actions, Cortina faces actions by local militia, Texas Rangers, and the U.S. Army. In mid-1860, Cortina is again forced to retreat across the border. In Mexico, he distinguishes himself as an officer in Tamaulipas, fighting against the French intervention. During this time, he becomes acting governor of Tamaulipas for a short term, and is promoted by President Benito Juárez to general. During the American Civil War, he fights on the side of the North. In the

Illustration of the execution of Emperor Agustín de Iturbide by an anonymous artist. (Courtesy of the Library of Congress Prints & Photographs Division.)

mid-1870s he incurs political disfavor in Mexico and is arrested for cattle rustling. After a brief pardon, under General Porfirio Díaz, he returns to the border for a short period, but is again arrested and spends most of his remaining years under local arrest in Mexico City. He dies in 1892.

JULY 19, 1824   Iturbide Killed by Firing Squad. Agustín de Iturbide is executed by a firing squad in Padilla, Tamaulipas, and thus ends Mexico's first European-style empire. Democracy is initiated with the election of Guadalupe Victoria as Mexico's first president, an office he holds until March 21, 1829.

1825

1825   Ferdinand VII Returns. Ferdinand VII of Spain returns to the throne as an absolute monarch after a liberal constitutional government has gained power for a time. He gives unlimited powers to the governors of Cuba and Puerto Rico to repress the independence movements.

1825   Latin–American Congress Fails. Simón Bolívar calls for a congress in Panama to establish a Latin–American League. Only four Latin–American nations send delegates to the congress, which ends in failure. (*See also* biography, July 24, 1783.)

1825   Spain Forces Students Out of U.S. To obtain an education, which Spanish authority does not provide in Puerto Rico, young people begin to travel to Santo Domingo, Cuba, Venezuela, Mexico, and the United States to study medicine, engineering, and other professions. Afraid of American liberalism and democracy, Spanish authorities begin to enforce the Royal Decree of 1799, prohibiting study in the United States. A list of some two hundred Puerto Rican and Cuban students in the United States is developed, and the young people are forced to return home.

AUGUST 6, 1825   Bolivia Becomes Independent. The congress proclaims the independence of the Republic of Bolivara, which later changes its name to Bolivia.

Ferdinand VII, King of Spain, 1814–33. (From Manuel Rivera Cambas's *Los gobernantes de México,* 1873.)

1826

1826　Congress of American Republics. A Congress of American Republics is held in Panama. The United States does not attend, only Gran Colombia, Peru, Mexico, and Central America. Among the topics discussed are developing a common defense force and creating an Assembly of Federated States.

1826　Kit Carson Is Trapper, Guide. Kit Carson becomes a professional trapper and guide in the Rocky Mountains. (*See also* biography, December 24, 1809.)

1826　Spaniards Give Up Fortress. The Spanish surrender their fortress El Callao, Peru, their last stronghold in South America, effectively ending the wars of independence on the continent.

1827

APRIL 8, 1827　Ramón Emeterio Betances, Puerto Rican Patriot, Is Born. Puerto Rican patriot Ramón Emeterio Betances is born in Cabo Rojo. He receives his university education in Paris, graduates as a medical doctor in 1855, and returns to the island to practice his profession. In Puerto Rico, he immediately becomes involved in politics, first in the struggle to abolish slavery and later in the movement for Puerto Rican independence from Spain. He is exiled at various times and suffers numerous death threats. He is credited with being the principal organizer, from his exile in Santo Domingo, of the Grito de Lares proclamation of Puerto Rican independence and the resistance to the Spanish forces that followed. After various failed revolutionary attempts, Betances returns to Paris in 1872 to practice medicine and to continue to plot the independence of Puerto Rico and Cuba. From Paris, he contributes articles to French, Haitian, and Spanish newspapers and magazines in support of independence and liberalism in general. He also publishes many journal articles on medicine and the sciences, and writes literary works in French as well. In his writings and oratory, Betances promotes the idea of an Antillean or Caribbean Federation, because he doubts that Cuba or Puerto Rico can survive alone after independence from Spain. Betances is considered "the Father of His Country." He dies in Paris on September 16, 1898.

1828

1828　Californio Political Leader Elected. Pío de Jesús Pico is elected to the territorial legislature and assumes a grand stature as a southern Californio political leader. (*See also* biography, May 5, 1801).

1828　Uruguay Gains Independence. After a temporary invasion and occupation by Brazil, Uruguay gains its definitive independence.

1829

1829　Friar Bernardino de Sahagún's Work

Ramón Emeterio Betances. (Courtesy of the Institute of Puerto Rican Culture, San Juan.)

Published. A prolific writer of ethnography, history, and devotional works, Sahagún's most respected work is *Historia general de las cosas de Nueva España* (General History of the Things of New Spain), which he first writes in Nahuatl and then later translates into Spanish. It is not published until 1829, some three hundred years after it is written. (*See also* biography, 1499.)

1829 Gran Colombia Splits. From 1829 to 1830, Gran Colombia disintegrates into the modern nation states of Colombia, Ecuador, and Venezuela.

1829 Mexican Government Abolishes Slavery. Slavery in Mexico is abolished by the new republican government of President Vicente Guerrero that emerges after independence.

1830

1830 Uruguayan Painter Juan Manuel Blanes Is Born. Juan Manuel Blanes, the Uruguayan painter, is born in Montevideo to a Spanish father and an Argentine mother. After leaving school at age eleven, Blanes teaches himself to draw. When his parents separate, Blanes moves to Cerrito to work as a typographer for a newspaper, in order to support his mother and sister. From 1844 to 1853, he begins to paint and executes color drawings. In 1855, he moves to Salto, where he teaches painting at the College of Humanities. During this period, he executes military portraits, most notably of General Justo José de Urquiza, and battle scenes. In 1857, he paints "An Episode of Yellow Fever in Buenos Aires," during a trip there. In 1859, Blanes receives a government subsidy to study in Europe. He returns to Montevideo in 1863 and is very productive as a painter of historical and military themes. He goes back to Italy in 1879–80, where he paints "La Paraguaya" (Paraguayan Woman) and "El Ultimo Paraguayo" (The Last Paraguayan), for which he receives a gold medal at an exhibition in Buenos Aires in 1882. Throughout the rest of his career, he continues to paint historical allegories and even creates stamps for the Uruguayan postal service. In 1898, he settles in Pisa, Italy, where he dies two years later of bronchial pneumonia.

SEPTEMBER 1830 Venezuela, Ecuador Leave Gran Colombia. Both Venezuela and Ecuador withdraw from Gran Colombia, effectively putting an end to Simón Bolívar's dream of continental unity. (*See also* biography, July 24, 1783.)

Paraguay: Image of Your Desolate Country, c. 1880, by Juan Manuel Blanes. (Courtesy of the Museo Nacional de Artes Plástucas, Montevideo.)

SEPTEMBER 15, 1830   Mexican Dictator Porfirio Díaz Is Born. Future dictator of Mexico, Porfirio Díaz is born into a poor mestizo family in Oaxaca. He has little schooling and to the end of his life never learns to write proper Spanish. At the age of seventeen, Díaz enters the army. In 1855, he joins the liberal cause and becomes part of the guerrilla force that battles Santa Anna. He fights bravely during the civil war, is elected to congress in 1861, and fight against the French invaders, when he is taken prisoner. He escapes the French and joins Juárez, who appoints him commander in the south, where he becomes a formidable general. Díaz shares in the recapture of Mexico City. After 1867, Díaz becomes resentful of President Juárez, who has cut back the military. He plots and takes part in military revolts against the liberal government. In November 1876, with backing from the church, Díaz leads a military takeover of the capital and assumes the presidency. Díaz rules, with one four-year interregnum, until 1911. During his long dictatorship, Díaz stabilizes Mexico's economy, brings peace and order to political life, and opens the doors to foreign investment and cultural influence. Díaz's regime is successful in great part due to the partnerships that he builds with politicians, the army, the church, foreign capital, and the great landowners. Despite his Indian blood, Díaz is an enemy of indigenism and sets about making Mexico a white man's country by appointing white creoles to high positions, surrounding himself with intellectuals who took leadership from Europe, especially France, and openly courting and welcoming foreign investment. The greatest investment and measure of the growth of the industrial and communications infrastructure under Díaz is the construction of some fifteen thousand miles of railroads by 1910, made possible largely by American, British, and Belgian enterprises. Mining, textiles, petroleum, and other industries grow rapidly with foreign backers. By the time of the revolution, foreign capital controls most of the economic life of the nation. Foreigners also

Porfirio Díaz. (Courtesy of the Library of the Granger Collection.)

grab much of the best land in Mexico. Díaz's partnership with a few thousand land barons, both the domestic owners of haciendas (inheritors of the Spanish encomiendas) and the foreign absentee landlords, is his strength, but it leaves most of the nation's people landless and poor. And, with Díaz's complicity, thousands of mestizo and Indian owners of small farms are dispossessed and their lands taken over by the large haciendas. Díaz is ejected from his eighth office on May 24, 1911, by revolutionaries supporting Francisco Madero for president.

Díaz goes into exile in Europe and dies in Paris on July 2, 1915.

1832

1832   Santa Anna Becomes President. Antonio López de Santa Anna leads his forces into Mexico City, deposes President Anastasio Bustamente, whom he had illegally imposed, and allows himself to be elected president. (*See also* biography, February 21, 1795.)

1832   Spanish Poem Published. Esteban Echeverría publishes *Elvira o la novia del Plata* (Elvira or The Bride of the River Plate), a poem that is considered to be the first outright romantic work in Spanish American literature. (*See also* biography, September 3, 1805.)

APRIL 13, 1832   Writer Juan Montalvo Is Born. Juan Montalvo, known as one of the best prose stylists of the Spanish language, is born in Ambato, Ecuador. Because of the advantageous economic position of his family, he enjoys an international education. He becomes an outspoken enemy of dictators, in particular Gabriel García Moreno (1821–75), and the church, and because of this spends much of his life in exile. He travels and lives in various countries of Europe and the Americas, and is a prolific writer of a vigorous, sonorous, and graphic prose. Although he is religious, he is a committed anticleric and, unlike many of his progressive colleagues, he believes in enlightened despotism or government by the educated minority rather than democracy. In 1866, he founds the newspaper *El Cosmopolita* (The Cosmopolitan). His masterpiece is the *Siete tratados* (Seven Treatises), published in 1882 in Paris; it is made up of a series of essays on such wide-ranging subjects as history, mythology, religion, esthetics, and morality. Such is his control of literary style that he even attempts to continue one of the greatest masterpieces of the Spanish language, *Don Quijote* in his own *Capítulos que se le olvidaron a Cervantes* (Chap-

ters that Cervantes Forgot). He dies in Paris on January 17, 1889.

1833

FEBRUARY 7, 1833   Creator of *Tradición* Literary Genre Ricardo Palma Is Born. Born in Lima, Peru, Ricardo Palma becomes one of the most important figures in the second period of Romanticism in Spanish America. He is a librarian, scholar, and journalist who creates a literary genre called the tradición or "tradition." The tradición is a short story or sketch based on local legends, history, or pre-Columbian myth, written with a sense of nostalgia, humor and, most of all, Americanist pride. Palma publishes ten volumes of *Tradiciones peruanas* (Traditional Peruvians), which are widely circulated as individual narratives as well as in the published volumes. For many years he serves as the director of the National Library of Peru, in Lima. As a scholar, his most important work of philology is represented by two volumes: *Neologismos americanos* (American Neologisms, 1895) and *Papeletas lexicográficas* (Lexicographic Notes, 1903). He dies in Miraflores, Peru, on October 6, 1919.

JULY 17, 1833   Oller, Art Educator and Pioneer of Impressionism, Is Born. Francisco Manuel Oller Cestero, the distinguished painter and pioneer of Impressionism and art education in Puerto Rico, is born in San Juan, the third of four children. Oller is also noted as being one of the first artists to really take his inspiration from the Puerto Rican landscape and the customs of its everyday folk. As a young student in elementary and secondary school, Oller is considered an art prodigy by his teachers. On June 1, 1849, he is hired as an art teacher at the College of St. Thomas, a secondary school; from this date on, Oller accepts commissions from churches to paint religious scenes and portraits of saints. In 1851, he travels to Spain and enrolls at the Academy of San Fernando, where he studies with Federico

Ricardo Palma. (Courtesy of the Arte Público Press Archives, University of Houston.)

Madrazo y Kunts, the director of the Prado Museum. In 1853, Oller returns to Puerto Rico and, in 1854, he receives the silver medal in the first Puerto Rican Exposition Fair. In 1858, Oller moves to Paris, where he studies with Thomas Couture and becomes an official copyist at the Louvre. While living in Paris, Oller takes on a number of jobs, including singing as a baritone with an Italian opera company. In 1859, he becomes a member of the Atelier de Gleyre with Pierre Renoir, Claude Monet, and Alfred Sisley, among others. In the following years, he is associated with many of the pioneers of Impressionism, including Camille Pissarro and Paul Cézanne, with whom he lived for awhile. In 1865, Oller returns to Puerto Rico, but continues to correspond with Cézanne, Pissarro, and other painters in Paris and to send his works there for exhibit and sale. In 1868, Oller exhibits forty-five paintings at the San Juan Fair and is proclaimed the best painter on the island. On September 1 of the same year, Oller opens and directs a free academy of drawing and painting, with an immediate enrollment of two hundred students. On November 10, 1869, Oller is knighted by order of

the king of Spain. On January 22, 1872, he is named painter of the royal court in Spain. From 1873 to 1884, Oller works in Europe. Upon his return to Puerto Rico in 1884, he finds that his school has been shut down. In 1889, he once again establishes a school: the School of Painting and Drawing for Young Ladies. In 1892, Oller finishes his monumental painting, "El Velorio" (The Wake), based on Puerto Rican rural customs. In 1893, he wins the gold medal in the Puerto Rico Exposition for his forty-six works exhibited. In 1895, he settles once again in Paris, where his "El Velorio" also becomes a sensation. In 1896, Oller returns to Puerto Rico with various paintings in the Impressionist "style." In 1901, he opens another academy of drawing in San Juan. In 1902, Oller is named drawing professor in the Normal School that will later become the University of Puerto Rico. Upon being fired from this post in 1904, Oller starts yet another school of art for young ladies. He later works as a teacher in Bayamón and receives a stipend while suffering a long illness that eventually results in his death on May 17, 1917.

1834

1834 **Tacón Governs Cuba.** General Miguel Tacón is appointed captain general of Cuba. Tacón is an extreme conservative who has suffered many defeats in the wars of independence in South America. He is instructed by the government in Madrid to use utmost severity in the governance of Cuba. Spain does not wish to lose its last colonies. Tacón proceeds to concentrate all powers of the colonial administration into his own hands. His governance becomes a period characterized by numerous imprisonments and exiles of dissidents and other Cubans, especially creoles, who are in disfavor. Under Tacón, Cubans lose the right to bear arms, to vote on members of a delegation to send to the Spanish Cortes, and to information about the government. Education suffers as well; many well-trained teachers are not allowed in class-rooms for political reasons. Three-fourths of government revenues are expended on maintaining a built-up military on the island.

NOVEMBER 10, 1834 José Hernández, Defender of Gauchos, Is Born. Writer José Hernández is born in Chacra de Puerredón, Province of Buenos Aires, and is raised among gauchos on the pampas. Hernández does not have a formal education, but is extremely bright and a self-taught intellectual. He is the author of the work known as Argentina's national masterpiece, a long, two-part epic poem about the life of gauchos, *Martín Fierro* (Part I, 1872; Part II, 1879). With the push of modernity and industrialization, both Indians and gauchos fall into disfavor for their refusal to assimilate and for their identification with nature and the wilds; they often are persecuted viciously. *Martín Fierro* is an epic poem that comes to the defense of the gauchos, and somewhat of the Indians. This romanticized version of the gaucho life and ethos catapults the gaucho into a national archetype. Published originally in cheap, popular editions, the book becomes a veritable nineteenth-century bestseller, and it is today a standard text for school children. Hernández dies on October 21, 1886, in Belgrano, near Buenos Aires.

1835

1835 Spain Bans Slave Trade. The Spanish throne forbids the import of slaves from Africa to her Caribbean colonies.

1836

1836 California Established. Juan Bautista Alvarado, leader of the Californios, leads a revolt against the central government of Mexico under Antonio López de Santa Anna, establishing the sovereign state of California with himself as provisional governor. (*See also* biography, 1800.)

1836 Battles Between Texas and Mexico. Mexican troops defeat Texan rebel separatists at the Alamo, February 23–March 6. On April 21, Santa Anna's forces are defeated at the Battle of San Jacinto, leading to Texas's independence from Mexico. The Treaty of Velasco to end hostilities between the new republic and Mexico is signed by Texas president David G. Burnet and Mexican president Antonio López de Santa Anna on May 14, 1836. The 1836 Constitution of the Republic of Texas stipulates that residents in Texas at the time of the rebellion will acquire all the rights of citizens of the new republic, but if they have been disloyal, these rights are forfeited. Numerically superior Anglos, embittered with Mexicans during the rebellion, retaliate by mistreating and forcing Mexicans off their property. Many Mexicans simply cross the border and go to Mexico.

1837

1837 First Spanish–American Railroad. The first railroad in Spanish America is built in Cuba, between Havana and Güines.

APRIL 1, 1837 Colombian Novelist Jorge Isaacs Is Born. Colombian novelist Isaacs is born in Cali, and lives an intense public life as a revolutionary, then later a congressman, a consul, a journalist, and, finally, a failed businessman. Slowly over the years he writes one of the romantic masterpieces of Latin–American literature, *María* (1867). The novel, set in a rural valley in Colombia, deals with an idyllic romance of two star-crossed lovers in the provinces, Efraín and María. The young man is sent by his father to study in Europe and upon his return learns of the death of his beloved. *María* is the most popular novel in Spanish America in the nineteenth and early twentieth centuries, and today is still a favorite of teenagers. Isaacs dies on April 17, 1895, in Ibagué, Colombia.

The Alamo. (Courtesy of the U.S. Department of the Interior and National Parks Service.)

1838

1838   Carrera Rules Guatemala. The caudillo Rafael Carrera becomes the first of a long line of dictators over the newly formed Republic of Guatemala. An illiterate but nevertheless shrewd military strategist, of Indian heritage, Carrera rules over Guatemala for twenty-seven years until his death in 1865. One of his overriding missions during this time is to make of Guatemala the living witness of the glory of the catholic faith. The Indians regard Carrera as their messiah; he is decorated by the pope and by Santa Anna of Mexico for his conservatism and supported by the large landholders, who nevertheless ridiculed his ignorance behind his back. Although uneducated, Carrera is successful in maintaining peace and security, improving roads, advancing farming, managing the state's finances honestly, and reducing the national debt. But he is a despot and a ruthless persecutor of the opposition. He also continually intervenes in El Salvador, Honduras, and

Nicaragua to put conservatives in power. (*See also* biography, October 24, 1814.)

1838   Cuban Sugar Exports. Between 1838 and 1860, Cuba is the world's largest producer of sugar. In 1850, sugar accounts for 83 percent of Cuban exports. By 1860, the island is producing one half million tons per year.

MAY 30, 1838   Federation Authorizes Independence. The congress of the Central American Federation authorizes the individual member countries to develop their own governments. From 1838 to 1841, the federation gradually disintegrates and the independent countries of El Salvador, Nicaragua, Costa Rica, Guatemala, and Honduras are formed.

Eugenio María de Hostos. (Courtesy of Arte Público Press Archives, University of Houston.)

1839

JANUARY 11, 1839   Eugenio María de Hostos Is Born. Eugenio María de Hostos, writer and political figure, is born in Mayagüez, Puerto Rico. Hostos is educated by tutors at home and later attends a Liceum in San Juan, before being sent to Spain for his secondary and university education. He drops out of law school to return to Puerto Rico and become involved in its efforts for independence. While still in Spain, he writes his first book attacking Spain's colonialism in the Americas, *La peregrinación de Bayoán* (Bayoán's Pilgrimage). In 1868, he becomes the editor of a liberal newspaper, *El progreso,* in Barcelona, which is shut down by the authorities. Hostos is deported to France. In 1869, Hostos travels to New York and becomes involved with other distinguished conspirators for the independence of Puerto Rico and Cuba. It is at this stage of his life that he envisions the creation of an Antillean Federation, a government of free, united islands of the Caribbean. From 1870 on, he travels through the countries of Spanish America to raise support for the cause of independence. In Lima, Hostos founds a newspaper, *La patria,* and takes part in the movement to organize labor.

In 1872, he moves to Chile, where he writes many of his most important works on history, art, and politics and a second edition of his *Peregrinación de Bayoán.* He also works as a writer for the newspaper *Ferrocarril* (Railroad) and the magazine *Sud America* (South America), and participates in the struggle for women's rights to education. In 1873, he becomes a university professor of philosophy in Buenos Aires. In 1874, Hostos returns to New York to join the revolutionary movement there but, persecuted by the police, he is forced to move to Venezuela in 1876. From 1878 to 1888, he lives in Santo Domingo, where he dedicates himself to organizing primary and secondary schools and to teaching constitutional law at the university level. In 1889, he is invited to Chile to become the rector of the Miguel Luis Amunátegui Liceum. He remains there until 1898, when he returns to New York to organize the Liga de Patriotas (League of Patriots) to promote independence. Upon the United States invasion of Puerto Rico, he pleads his case for independence to the government in Washington and to his compatriots in Puerto Rico, but his learned arguments and passion fall on deaf ears. He ultimately becomes disillusioned and goes into voluntary exile to Santo Domingo to finish out his life as a teacher. There he dies on August 11, 1903. The twenty volumes of his complete works, which include writings on politics, education, biography, and law, and his own creative writing, are published posthumously in Puerto Rico in 1939. For his internationalist spirit and contribution to education and culture in many countries of Spanish America, Hostos has been called "Citizen of the Americas." His most important literary piece, *La peregrinación de Bayoán* (1863), is a political allegory in the form of a novel, in which his liberal ideas take on flesh and blood. But his best-known work is *Moral social* (Social Morality, 1888), a philosophical treatise in which he illustrates the thesis that individual good and social good are always joined together. Hostos rejects the notion that man's instinctive or animal nature is inherently evil and in need of constant suppression by reason and will; instead, he sees man's reason as inevitably and indissolubly linked to his social and instinctive nature.

1840

1840 Carrera Overthrows Morazán. Rafael Carrera overthrows Guatemalan president Francisco Morazán. (*See also* biography, October 24, 1814.)

1840 Immigrants Aid Cuban Economy. To meet the wage–labor demands, 125,000 Chinese are brought to Cuba between 1840 and 1870 to work as sugar cane cutters, to build railroads in rural areas, and to serve as domestics in the cities. The influx of European immigrants, primarily from Spain, also increases during that period. Newly arrived Spaniards become concentrated in the retail trades and operate small general stores called *bodegas*. In the 1880s, slavery is abolished by Spain in a gradual program that takes eight years. The influx of new people in this period makes Cuba

more heterogeneous, leading to the social diversity that is apparent today.

1840 Landscape Artist Velasco Born in Mexico. The famed Mexican landscape artist José María Velasco is born in Temascalcingo into a bourgeois family. At age nine he moves with his family to Mexico City, where he is educated in Catholic schools until the age of fifteen; he then studies evenings at the San Carlos Academy. He starts full-time instruction there in landscape painting in 1858 under Italian artist Eugenio Landesio. In 1868, Velasco is appointed professor of perspective at the academy. During the 1860s, Velasco executes various large-scale landscapes. In the 1870s he develops an interest in photography, and eventually makes a transition to lithography. In 1875, he is appointed professor of landscape painting at the San Carlos Academy. In 1876, he receives a prize at the Centennial International Exposition in Philadelphia. In 1889, he travels to Europe and exhibits seventy-eight paintings at the Universal Exposition in Paris; he is made a Chevalier de la Légion d'Honneur. In 1890, Velasco receives the highest Austrian award, the Franz Joseph Cross, and in 1893 he is awarded first prize at the Chicago World's Fair. In 1912, Velasco dies in Mexico City.

1840 Puerto Rican Bans Enacted. Because of growing liberalism and the independence movement, foreigners are prohibited from entering Puerto Rico and mustaches and beards are forbidden, since these supposedly are worn by many revolutionaries.

JANUARY 14, 1840 Northern Secessionist Movement Ends. In San Patricio, Texas, General Antonio Canales and a mixed group of Texas-Mexico forces, including Juan N. Seguín, proclaim the independence of the Republic of the Río Grande, to be made up of southern Texas and the Mexican state of Tamaulipas. In the following months, Canales's forces are successful in capturing Laredo, a number of border towns, and Ciudad Victoria, the capital of

Tamaulipas. In his attempts to capture Saltillo, most of Canales's troops go over to the Mexican government side, and the remaining soldiers are forced to withdraw to Texas. Canales finally surrenders to the government in November, and thus ends the northern secessionist effort.

1841

JUNE 1841 The Santa Fe Expedition. Republic of Texas president Mirabeau Buonoparte Lamar sends an armed group of merchants to New Mexico to foment revolt against the Mexican government and union with the Texas Republic. The Santa Fe Expedition is ill-fated. The three hundred Anglo– and Mexican–Texans, led by General Hugh McLeod, encounter hostile Indians and prairie fires and lose their way. Upon reaching New Mexico, they offer no resistance to Governor Manuel Armijo's soldiers, who take them prisoner. Some are executed in Santa Fe and others are marched on foot to prison in Mexico City. Eventually, these *filibusteros,* as they were called in Spanish, are released.

1843

1843 University Founded. Andrés Bello is one of the founders of the University of Chile. (*See also* biography, November 29, 1781.)

SEPTEMBER 14, 1843 Puerto Rican Feminist Lola Rodríguez de Tió Is Born. Puerto Rican patriot and poet Lola Rodríguez de Tió is born in San Germán. She receives an education at religious schools and from private tutors, and begins to write poetry under the influence of poet Ursula Cardona de Quiñones. In 1865, she marries Bonocio Tió, a journalist who shares Rodríguez de Tió's desire for Puerto

Rican independence; they hold literary and political meetings regularly at their home in Mayagüez. In 1868, she writes the nationalist lyrics that will become the Puerto Rican national hymn, "La Borinqueña." In 1877, the government exiles Rodríguez de Tió; she and her family take refuge in Venezuela for three years and then return to Puerto Rico. In 1889, she is exiled again, this time to Cuba, where she continues her revolutionary activities until 1895, when she is exiled yet again. This time she takes up residence in New York and continues to conspire with the leading revolutionaries for Puerto Rican and Cuban independence. In 1899, after the Spanish–American War, she returns to a hero's reception in Cuba. She remains in Cuba and begins to work on fashioning a new society, one in which women would have greater liberty and opportunity. In 1910, she is elected a member of the Cuban Academy of Arts and Letters. Lola Rodríguez de Tió is a romantic poet, as her three books of poems readily attest: *Mis cantares* (My Songs, 1876), *Claros y nieblas* (Clarities and Cloudiness, 1885), and *Mi libro de Cuba* (My Cuban Book, 1893). Rodríguez de Tió is a beloved patriotic and literary figure, as well as an early feminist, in both Puerto Rico and Cuba. She dies on November 10, 1924, in Cuba.

1844

1844 Three Rule Dominican Republic. From 1844, until the turn of the century, just three men dominate politics in the Dominican Republic, establishing the tradition of a long line of dictators. The first two, Pedro Santana and Buenaventura Báez, work in concert by alternating terms as president of the republic, but by the 1850s they have become enemies. Santana dominates most of the time until his death in 1864, and thereafter Báez rules until his death in 1882. Ulises Heureaux reigns in one of the most despotic and brutal regimes, from 1882 until 1899.

1845

MARCH 1, 1845   **Texas Annexed to U.S.** United States President John Tyler signs the resolution to annex Texas to the United States, causing deep anger among Mexicans. Diplomatic relations are ruptured and, later, war breaks out over a skirmish in disputed territory adjacent to the Rio Grande.

1846

1846   **U.S. Invades Mexico.** The United States invades Mexico under the banner of Manifest Destiny, and General Winfield Scott takes Mexico City, which surrenders on September 14, 1847. The United States defeats Mexico in 1848 and forces it to sign the Treaty of Guadalupe Hidalgo. Under the treaty, half the land area of Mexico, including Texas, California, most of Arizona and New Mexico, and parts of Colorado, Utah, and Nevada, is ceded to the United States in exchange for peace and $18 million. The border between the United States and Mexico is set at the Rio Grande and the Gila River. The treaty guarantees former Mexicans their property, civil rights, and freedom of religion. The treaty gives Mexican nationals one year to choose U.S. or Mexican citizenship. Seventy-five thousand Hispanic people choose to remain in the United States and become citizens by conquest.

MAY 13, 1846   **New Mexico Is Attacked.** The United States declares war on Mexico. President James Polk orders General Zachary Taylor to move his force from the Nueces River to the north bank of the Rio Grande. Later, New Mexico is invaded by American Army officer Stephen Kearny.

JUNE 10, 1846   **The Bear Flag Revolt.** Tensions between Mexicans and Anglos run high preceding the Mexican–American War, and

on June 10, Anglo settlers seize a herd of 150 horses being driven south to the Mexican militia. Following this, on June 14, thirty armed Americans, led by William B. Ide and Ezekiel Merritt, take pro-American General Mariano Vallejo a "prisoner of war." At Sonoma, Ide and other Americans declare their independence of Mexico and raise an improvised flag with a grizzly bear and a star. This is called the "Bear Flag Revolt." Following a skirmish on June 24, John C. Frémont merges his troops with the "bear flaggers," declares California to be under martial law and marches to San Francisco, where on July 1 he takes over the presidio, which is in ruins. In the meantime, the United States has declared war on Mexico. By July 11, the United States has raised its flag over California. Thus, the Bear Flag Republic lasts less than a month.

JULY 7, 1846   **California Is Annexed.** Following the conquest of California under commodores John Sloat and Robert Stockton, the United States annexation of California is proclaimed at Monterey.

1848

1848   **Anglos Follow Gold.** The gold rush lures a flood of Anglo settlers to California, which becomes a state in 1850. Settlement in Arizona and New Mexico occurs at a slower pace, and both areas become states in 1912.

1848   **Costa Rica Keeps the Peace.** Unlike its neighboring Central American republics, Costa Rica attempts to ensure peace at home and abroad. Its constitution of 1848 provides for the abolition of the army and substitutes a relatively limited civil guard. Aside from some minor clashes during its history and an interval (1870–82) under the dictatorship of Tomás Guardia, Costa Rica has developed as a peaceful state free of wars, internal and external.

1848   **Invasions of Cuba.** Hoping to ignite a

Battle of Monterrey during the Mexican–American War. (Courtesy of the National Museum of History, Mexico City.)

war of independence in Cuba, Narciso López, a Spanish officer of Venezuelan nationality, organizes three invasions of Cuba from the United States in 1848, 1850, and 1851. López eventually is caught and hanged.

1848   Mexico Offers Aid for Repatriation. Mexico sends commissioners to California, New Mexico, and Texas to assist families who are moving to Mexico as a result of the territories being ceded to the United States under the Treaty of Guadalupe Hidalgo. The commissioners offer land and equipment to those who choose to repatriate; some three thousand accept. In 1855, Mexico once again attempts to repatriate its citizens by offering land in Sonora to Mexicans living in California. Even in the late 1870s there is still some encouragement for repatriation by the Mexican government, but no more than two thousand Mexicans choose to move to Mexico as a result of these efforts.

1848   Presidents Make Offers for Cuba. President James K. Polk of the United States makes an offer to Spain to purchase Cuba for $100 million. Spain responds that the island is not for sale. President Franklin Pierce later increas-es the offer to $130 million, and warns that the United States might move to force Cuban independence from Spain in order to facilitate its annexation to the United States.

JANUARY 6, 1848   Peruvian Poet Manuel González Prada Is Born. Manuel González Prada, poet and polemicist, is born in Lima, Peru. Although raised in an aristocratic family, he repudiates the oligarchy and take up the cause of the Indians, the poor, and the oppressed. He advocates violent revolution in both the political and social realms. His are clear ideas for later indigenist movements and the political and social thought of José Carlos Mariátegui. He is a particularly severe critic of his country's leadership after its defeat in the War of the Pacific, and he has to go into exile. As a poet, González Prada is considered to be original, one of the important precursors of literary modernism. His poetic works show the depth of his knowledge of other languages and cultures. Among his most cited books of poetry are *Minúsculas* (Minute Pieces, 1901), *Libertarias* (Libertarian Pieces, 1938), and *Exóticas* (Exotic Pieces, 1911). He dies on January 22, 1918, in Lima, Peru.

Battle of Churubusco, Mexican–American War. (Courtesy of the National Museum of History, Mexico City.)

FEBRUARY 2, 1848 Mexican–American War Ends. The Treaty of Guadalupe Hidalgo ends the Mexican–American War.

SEPTEMBER 5, 1848 Governor Rejects School for Puerto Rico. Spain never creates a public education system in Puerto Rico. On this date, General Juan Manuel de la Pezuela, the Spanish governor of Puerto Rico, turns down a petition for the establishment of a Colegio Central, a secondary school, stating that "education had lost the Americas [to Spain], and that...it behooves young people to go to Spain to study." When he is informed that the majority of the young people cannot afford to go to Spain, he responds, "...it is enough for the poor to learn reading and writing, Christian doctrine and a trade."

1849

1849 Alonso's Masterpiece Is Published. Manuel Alonso publishes his major work, *El gíbaro*

(The Puerto Rican Peasant), which is considered a masterpiece and founding work of Puerto Rican literature. The work, made up of twenty-one local color scenes, describes Puerto Rican customs at mid-century. (*See also* biography, October 6, 1822.)

APRIL 13, 1849   Cuban Philosopher Varona Is Born. Enrique José Varona y Pera, Cuban philosopher and political figure, is born in Camagüey. Varona becomes a distinguished member of the positivist movement in Latin America. In his thinking, as well, he is characterized as a relativist who has no time for religion or metaphysics. He is an outspoken enemy of political corruption and public vice, including gambling and lying. He is an example of personal morality and ethics and one of the most respected professors at the University of Havana; he is known in Cuba as *the master teacher*. His collected essays and articles, *Desde mi belvedere* (From My Belvedere, 1910), is considered a masterpiece in its genre. In the political realm, Varona is an indefatigable promoter of Cuban independence. In 1895, he writes a manifesto of independence, *Cuna contra España* (Cuba against Spain, 1895). From 1913 to 1917, Varona is able to put some of his thoughts about government into action when he serves as vice president of the Republic of Cuba. He dies in 1933 in Havana.

1850

1850   The Clayton–Bulwar Treaty. The United States and Great Britain sign the Clayton–Bulwar Treaty declaring that any railroad or canal to be built across Central America will be jointly controlled by the two countries; the zone will be neutral and will charge the same toll for both countries. No Central American nation signs the treaty or is even consulted.

1850   Compromise of 1850 Affects Slavery Issue. The so-called Compromise of 1850 refers to a series of laws passed by the U.S. Congress to defer the divisiveness of the slavery issue. After the Mexican–American War, Texas and the other territories of the Southwest pursue admission to the American union as states, but this further complicates the issue of slavery, as debate ensues as to whether they would individually enter as "free" or "slave" states. Also complicating the issue is the fact that New Mexico and southern Texas are populated predominantly by Mexicans. In the compromise, California is admitted as a state and New Mexico as a territory. Texas is given $10,000 to compensate it for land east of the Rio Grande ceded to the New Mexican territory. The New Mexicans are especially disappointed by the denial of statehood.

MAY 20, 1850   The Foreign Miners Tax Law. The Foreign Miners Tax Law, which levies a charge for anyone who is not a U.S. citizen, goes into effect to discourage foreigners from mining in California. This state legislation imposes a tax of $20 per month on all foreign miners. In the preceding year, many Mexicans are expelled from the California gold fields by vigilante groups. And the first California Assembly asks the U.S. Congress to bar all foreigners from the mines. Because it is difficult to collect the tax, as well as to protect those who have paid it, it is largely disregarded. This leads to increased violence against Mexicans by Anglo vigilantes. Many Mexicans are murdered; some are lynched. In 1851, the tax is repealed. But Spanish-speaking people already have been driven from the mines and immigration has declined greatly.

1851

1851   Cordero's Painting on Exhibit. Juan Cordero's first major painting, "Columbus before the Catholic Monarchs," is exhibited at the third San Carlos exposition. (*See also* biography, June 10, 1822.)

FEBRUARY 2, 1851　José Guadalupe Posada, Mexican Illustrator, Is Born. Famous Mexican engraver and illustrator José Guadalupe Posada is born in Aguascalientes into a poor peasant family. Although much of his time as a child is spent working with his father in the fields or with his uncle as a potter, Posada does study under Antonio Varela at a drawing academy for a brief period. During the 1870s, Posada works as an apprentice lithographer in the shop of Trinidad Pedrozo, who also produces the satirical newspaper, *El Jicote,* for which Posada contributes illustrations. After moving to Guanajuato, he teaches lithography at a secondary school in León. In 1888, he opens his first print shop in Mexico City, and prints and illustrates the newspaper, *La Patria Ilustrada* (The Fatherland Illustrated). In 1889, Posada joins the Antonio Vargas Arroyo publishing house as engraver; he works there until his death in 1913. In 1895, Posada introduces the technique of etching on zinc, which he uses in more than twenty thousand engravings. His most famous works are illustrations of *corridos* (ballads) of the Mexican Revolution that are printed on broadsides and sold on the streets by roving singers as a form of news. He also is known for illustrating *calaveras,* folk poems written as epitaphs for living people, often politicians. Posada's most characteristic style for illustrating both the ballads and the calaveras depicts all of the people as skeletons involved in dynamic and sensationalistic motion. Posada also produces hundreds of illustrations for more than fifty newspapers, including the political press, most notably the anti-Porfirio Díaz, *El Hijo de Ahuizotl* (The Son of Ahuizotl). In Posada the Mexican Revolution finds its most graphic and prolific artistic supporter. During his lifetime, Posada is seen as a craftsman. Despite his renown and the wide circulation of his illustrations, he dies a poor man and is buried at the city's expense. He dies on January 20, 1913, in Mexico City.

FEBRUARY 8, 1851　The California Land Act.

Congress passes the California Land Act of 1851 to facilitate legalization of land belonging to Californios prior to the U.S. takeover.

1852

1852　England, France Propose Pact on Cuba. England and France propose that the United States join them in a pact promising never to obtain possession of the island of Cuba, but Washington refuses to tie its hands. The following year, President Franklin Pierce instructs his ministers in Madrid to pursue the purchase of Cuba.

1853

1853　Juárez Jailed. Santa Anna has Benito Juárez jailed and banished to New Orleans, where other expatriates are planning Santa Anna's overthrow. (*See also* biography, March 21, 1806.)

1853　Santa Anna Sells Land to U.S. General Antonio López de Santa Anna returns to power in Mexico and, through the Gadsden Treaty, sells to the United States the region from Yuma along the Gila River to the Mesilla Valley: 44,000 acres in southern Arizona and New Mexico. (*See also* biography, February 21, 1795.)

JANUARY 28, 1853　National Hero Martí Is Born in Cuba. José Martí (José Julián Martí y Pérez), poet, writer, and lawyer, is born in Havana, Cuba. Martí becomes the leading figure in the Cuban revolutionary movement for independence from Spain and he also becomes the most important precursor of the modernist literary movement. In his organizing for the revolution, he serves time in prison in Spain (1871), and suffers long exiles in Mexico (1875), Guatemala (1877), Venezuela (1881), and New

York, which he uses as a base for organizing there and in Philadelphia, Tampa, Key West, and New Orleans. On January 5, 1891, the founding of the Cuban Revolutionary Party is underway in New York. After a military assault from the sea at Dos Playitas, Cuba, he is killed in battle at Boca de Dos Ríos, Cuba, on May 19, 1895. Martí is the Cuban national hero, often called a martyr and apostle of independence. Martí is one of the greatest Spanish–American poets of all time, as well as a distinguished essayist (and orator), journalist, and literary critic. Both his prose and poetry are characterized by clarity and simple elegance. His poetry also is known for its nostalgic and sincere tone. One of his most important books of poetry, *Ismaelillo* (1882), is dedicated to his son and, along with his book of *Versos sencillos* (Simple Verses, 1891), has contributed many verses to the standard elementary education curriculum throughout the Spanish-speaking world. Martí also publishes a magazine for children, *La edad de oro* (The Golden Age, 1889). Finally, Martí is celebrated for his epistolary art, as can be seen in his *Cartas a mi madre* (Letters to My Mother), and as a dramatist and novelist. His plays include *Abdala, Amor con amor se paga* (Love Is Paid with Love), and *Adúltera* (Adulteress). His one known novel is *Amistad funesta* (Unlucky Friendship). Martí's greatest essay, which he also delivers as a speech, "Nuestra América" (Our America), represents his dream, and that of many Spanish–American thinkers and patriots, of a politically united Spanish America, one able to confront the political and cultural threat of the United States (See the Appendix).

José Martí. (Courtesy of Arte Público Press Archives, University of Houston.)

sition Fair for his work. (*See also* biography, July 17, 1833.)

OCTOBER 1854   The Ostend Manifesto and Cuba. President Franklin Pierce of the United States sends three U.S. ministers to meet with representatives from Spain in Aix-la-Chapelle, France, to offer $130 million to purchase Cuba from Spain; they also warn Spain that, if the offer is not accepted, the United States will support Cuba's independence in order to bring about its annexation to the U.S. This declara-

1854

1854   Oller Receives Art Medal. Francisco Manuel Oller Cestero, pioneer of Impressionism and art education in Puerto Rico, receives the silver medal in the first Puerto Rican Expo-

tion, called the Ostend Manifesto, creates a hostile reaction against United States imperialism from the European powers and causes Spain to resist the U.S. initiative even more strenuously. Much of the haggling over Cuba is suspended with the advent of the Civil War. The debate over Cuban annexation is complicated by the slavery issue; Southern congressmen are hoping to add another slave state to the Union.

1855

1855 California Anti-Vagrancy Act. The California Anti-Vagrancy Act of 1855, the so-called "greaser laws" prohibiting bear-baiting, bullfights, and cockfights, is passed, clearly aimed at prohibiting the presence and customs of Californios.

1855 Spanish Newspaper Founded in Los Angeles. *El Clamor Público* (The Public Clamor), Los Angeles's first Spanish-language newspaper, is founded by Francisco P. Ramírez. Throughout its lifespan, the newspaper protests discrimination against Mexicans and Californios and their expulsion from the mines and ranches of Southern California. The newspaper closes shop in 1859.

1855 Supreme Court Rules on Treaty. The Supreme Court rules that the Treaty of Guadalupe Hidalgo does not apply to Texas.

1855 Tennessee Adventurer Heads Nicaragua. Liberals in Nicaragua invite an adventurer from Tennessee, William Walker, and his fifty-seven soldiers of fortune to help them defeat the Conservatives. They defeat the Conservatives and burn down their capital in Granada. Walker allows a Liberal leader to function as president for a time while he keeps control of the army. But in July 1856, he names himself president of Nicaragua, legalizes slavery, and makes English the official language. The United States is not in agreement, will not recognize his government and withdraws its diplomats

William Walker. (Courtesy of the Library of Congress Prints & Photographs Division.)

from Nicaragua. A year later, however, in attempts to gain Southern votes in his reelection bid, President Franklin Pierce exploits feelings about slavery and Manifest Destiny and recognizes Walker's government. After Pierce is not nominated by the Democratic convention, he withdraws recognition. With the support of the British and combined armies of all of the Central American countries, Walker is driven out in 1857. He returns in 1860 and is captured by the British, who execute him in Honduras on September 12.

Street fighting in the Battle of Nicaragua. (Courtesy of the Library of Congress Prints & Photographs Division.)

1856

JUNE 25, 1856 Law Forces Redistribution of Church Lands. The Lerdo de Tejada Law is passed in Mexico, requiring the church to sell all its lands and properties not used for religious purposes. The church is forced to sell its cultivated lands to the sharecroppers and its common lands to the Indians. Secular cemeteries are then founded and fees for weddings and baptisms are set by the state. Although this redistribution of the church assets puts land in the hands of small farmers, the laws soon have the opposite effect of concentrating the majority of the lands into the hands of a very few wealthy ranchers who buy or fraudulently obtain title to the redistributed parcels.

1857

1857 The Cart War. Anglo businessmen attempt to run off Mexican teamsters in south Texas, violating the guarantees offered by the

Treaty of Guadalupe Hidalgo. The "Cart War" eventually results in the death of some seventy-five people.

1857   Father Martínez Is Excommunicated. Father José Antonio Martínez is excommunicated by bishop Jean Baptist Lamy, who is unsympathetic to the religious culture of the Nuevo Mexicanos.) (*See also* biography, 1793.)

1857   Mexico Adopts New Constitution. Mexico adopts a new constitution which will remain in effect until 1917. The constitution represents an important step towards the democratic evolution of the country. It guarantees freedom of speech and freedom of the press and prohibits monopolies and hereditary titles. It establishes a republican form of government and separates Church and State.

MAY 6, 1857   Composer Juan Morel Campos Is Born. One of Puerto Rico's greatest composers, Juan Morel Campos, is born in Ponce. He studies instrumental music with Antonio Egipciano, and, later, harmony and composition with another important Puerto Rican composer, Manuel G. Tavárez. After playing for a time with a battalion band of the Spanish army, Campos founds the Ponce Fire Brigade Band and the Lira Ponceña, a musical society, both in 1877. He also works as an orchestra director, giving concerts in theaters, clubs, and the open air of various cities and towns. At the 1893 commemoration of the discovery of Puerto Rico, Campos receives first prize and diploma of honor for his symphony *Puerto Rico*. Morel directs the *zarzuela* (Spanish operetta) orchestra at the Perla Theater in Ponce for many years; he also tours South America with the zarzuela company. Campos's varied compositions include zarzuelas, some sixty religious works (choral pieces, masses, litanies, etc.), symphonies, overtures, waltzes, and *danzas,* Puerto Rico's salon dance music that often resembles ragtime in its syncopation. Campos's danzas are classics of the genre: *Ten Piedad* (Have Pity), *Influencia del Arte* (Art Influence),

Mis Penas (My Suffering), *Idilio* (Idyll), *No Me Toques* (Don't Touch Me), and many more. Campos is important in the development of a national music for Puerto Rico. He dies of heart disease on May 12, 1896, in Ponce.

JULY 26, 1857   Barbosa, Puerto Rican Doctor and Political Activist, Is Born. Physician and political activist José "Pepito" Celso Barbosa is born in Bayamón into a family of free black artisans. Barbosa's maternal aunt, Lucía, impressed with his intelligence, sees to it that he is enrolled in public elementary school. After he graduates, Lucía sends him to Jesuit Seminary in San Juan over protests from his father that blacks cannot be admitted and the expense is to great. After graduation, Barbosa returns to Bayamón and begins teaching. In 1876, he travels to New York where he learns his fourth language, English (he mastered French, Latin, and Greek at the Seminary). Columbia University rejects Barbosa for admission, and he enters the University of Michigan School of Medicine—the first Puerto Rican to do so. He graduates in 1880, the first in his class of 95 students. Barbosa returns to San Juan, but the local authorities refuse to recognize his degree. The United States Consul intercedes on his behalf and he is certified as a physician in Puerto Rico. Soon after, a smallpox epidemic breaks out and he is able to demonstrate his medical methods. Impressed with his ability, patients flock to him. He becomes involved in politics after receiving encouragement from conservative Spanish government officials. Much to their dismay, he speaks out against the government and joins the Liberal Reform party where he espouses belief in self-government and social justice for Puerto Rico. On March 4, 1897, he cofounds the Partido Autonomista Histórico u Ortodoxo (Historic or Orthodox Autonomist Party) to oppose the Autonomist pact. Barbosa founds and chairs El Ahorro Colectivo, a cooperative society and credit union. In 1898, the Spanish government grants Puerto Rico autonomous regime—the first system of home rule for the island—and Barbosa joins the government as education minister. Less than a year later, Puerto Rico is under the control of the United States and Barbosa works with the colonial government to help draft many of the early social reforms, particularly in health and education. He cofounds the Partido Puertorriqueño Republicano (Puerto Rican Republican Party) to gain statehood for the island. In 1917, he is elected to the newly formed Puerto Rican senate, where he works tirelessly for statehood until his death. Barbosa dies on September 21, 1921, in Santurce, and is buried in the old cemetery in San Juan, Puerto Rico.

1858

1858   Mármol Named Library Director. José Mármol is named the director of the National Library in Buenos Aires. (*See also* biography, December 2, 1817.)

1858   Mexican Civil War. Civil war between liberals and conservatives breaks out in Mexico. Known as the War of Reform or the Three Years War, it lasts until 1860, when the liberals under Benito Juárez prevail.

1858   Parties Unite to Make Nicaragua a Republic. After ridding itself of American interloper William Walker, who has become the dictator of Nicaragua, the Liberals and Conservatives unite to make Nicaragua a republic with a bicameral legislature and an elected president that will serve single four-year terms. The Conservative Tomás Martínez is elected the first president of the republic. The Conservatives are able to stay in power for thirty-five years.

1859

1859   Cortina Leads Rebellion in Texas. During 1859 and 1860, Juan Nepomuceno Cortina leads a guerrilla war on the Anglo-controlled settlements in Texas's Lower Rio Grande Valley. Cortina's rebellion is a response to Anglo abuses against Mexicans. (*See also* biography, May 16, 1824.)

JULY 12, 1859   Reform Laws Enacted in Mexico. In the middle of the civil war in Mexico, the Reform Laws are decreed, nationalizing the holdings of the church, dissolving the monastic orders, making marriage a civil contract, and making state registration of births, deaths and weddings the law. It also decrees freedom of worship and regulates religious festivities.

OCTOBER 17, 1859   New Mexico Governor Otero Is Born. Miguel A. Otero, Jr., governor and businessman, is born in Albuquerque, New Mexico, into the distinguished family of his namesake, an outstanding business and political figure. Educated in St. Louis, Annapolis, and at Notre Dame University, he learns his business acumen in the offices of his father's company, Otero, Sellar & Co., which serves him well when he takes the major role in the firm after his father's death. With significant business interests in mining, ranching, real estate, and banking, Otero enters politics as a republican. During the course of his early career, he holds various elected and appointed positions, and is a candidate for the republican vice presidential nomination in 1894. In 1897, Otero is appointed by President William McKinley to the governorship of the New Mexico Territory. Because he opposes President Theodore Roosevelt's National Forest Project, Otero is not reappointed to a second term as governor. At this point, Otero switches to the Democratic Party. Under President Woodrow Wilson, Otero is appointed United States Marshall of the Panama Canal Zone in 1917. He remains active in politics in the 1920s. He also finds time during his career to write various memoirs of historical value: *My Life on the Frontier, 1864–1882* (1935), *My Life on the Frontier, 1882–1897* (1939), *My Nine Years as Governor of the Territory of New Mexico, 1897–1906* (1940). Four years after the publication of

Miguel A. Otero. (Courtesy of Special Collections, General Library, University of New Mexico.)

his last book, he dies in Albuquerque at the age of eighty-four.

1860

1860 The Cigar Industry. Protectionist tariffs in the United States allow the cigar industry to burgeon. Many working-class Cubans are drawn to Florida, Louisiana, and New York to work in the cigar factories. Very high tariffs on cigars and relatively low ones on the tobacco leaf itself allow the factories to produce a genuine Cuban product within the United States. The McKinley Tariff of 1890, however, is so high that virtually all cigar shipments to the United States are curtailed, and the industry expands rapidly, especially in Tampa, where entire factories have relocated from Cuba.

1860 Colombian Painter Andrés de Santa María Is Born. Colombian painter Andrés de Santa María is born in Bogotá, but at age two moves with his family to London and spends the next thirty-three years of his life in Europe. In the 1880s, de Santa María studies at the Ecole de Beaux Arts in Paris and also at the workshops of Fernando Humberto, Enrique Gervex, and Ignacio Zuloaga in Paris and with Santiago Rusiñol in Spain. The first exhibitions of his paintings are in Paris at the Salon de Artistes Francais and at the Salon des Tuileries. In 1904, he is appointed director of the School of Fine Arts in Bogotá, where he also founds the Professional School of Industrial and Fine Arts. From then until 1910, de Santa María exhibits his Impressionist-inspired works extensively in Colombia. He leaves Colombia in 1911 to settle in Brussels. From then until 1927, his work shows the influence of Van Gogh and is exhibited repeatedly in Brussels, Paris, and Bogotá. In the late 1920s, de Santa María turns towards Expressionism. In 1930, he is named academic correspondent of the Academy of San Fernando in Madrid. He dies in Brussels in 1945. De Santa Maria's work has benefitted from numerous international exhibitions and major retrospectives in Belgium, England, and Colombia.

1861

1861 Avellaneda's First Novel. Gertrudis Gómez de Avellaneda produces her first novel, *El artista banquero* (The Banker Artist). (*See also* biography, March 23, 1814.)

1861 The French Intervention. Benito Juárez

suspends Mexico's foreign debt, which provokes the French Intervention. (*See also* biography, March 21, 1806.)

1861   Spain Reoccupies Dominican Republic. President Pedro Santana of the Dominican Republic and his followers, fearful of Haiti's expansionism, request of Spain the reassumption of its colonial rule. Spain reoccupies the Dominican Republic, but revolts sprout throughout the colony in 1863 and 1864 in reaction to Spain's despotic rule. As soon as the United States emerges from the Civil War, Spain decides to withdraw.

1862

1862   School Mandatory in Puerto Rico. Elementary education is made obligatory in Puerto Rico.

MAY 17, 1862   The Homestead Act. The Homestead Act is passed in Congress, allowing squatters in the West to settle and claim vacant lands, often those owned by Mexicans.

1863

1863   Patriot and Writer Marín Born in Puerto Rico. Francisco "Pachín" González Marín, Puerto Rican patriot and literary figure, is born in Arecibo, where he receives only a rudimentary elementary education. He learns the trade of typesetter, and earns his living as such throughout his life. It is this trade that eventually develops him into an intellectual and man of letters. In 1884, "Pachín" Marín publishes his first book of poems, *Flores nacientes* (Newborn Flowers). While living in Ponce with a journalist uncle during the 1880s, he becomes an advocate of Puerto Rican autonomy from Spain and dedicates his second book of poems, *Mi óbolo* (My Little Bit) to the apostle of autonomy, Román Baldorioty de Castro, in 1887. In 1887 in Arecibo, he founds the newspaper *El*

Postillón (The Postilion), an organ for the anti-Spanish group, La Torre del Viejo. This leads to his exile in Santo Domingo, where he works as a teacher. His ideas lead to his becoming persona non grata; he subsequently moves to Venezuela, and from there he is deported to Martinique. "Pachín" Marín returns to Puerto Rico in 1890 and begins publishing his combative *El Postillón* again, which once more leads to exile, this time to New York in 1891, where he also establishes a print shop and joins the Junta Revolucionaria de Cuba y de Puerto Rico (Revolutionary Junta for Cuba and Puerto Rico). From there, he becomes an important conspirator and fundraiser for the independence movement. In New York, he publishes his book of poems, *Romances* (Ballads) in 1892. In 1896, he joins the revolutionary forces in Cuba and dies in battle at Turiguanó in 1897. While serving in Cuba, he writes his last book of poems, *En la arena* (In the Sand), published posthumously in 1898. Many of Marín's poems and writings in newspapers have not yet been collected and studied. In his literary corpus, there is also a play, *El 27 de febrero* (February 27), which takes the independence of Santo Domingo as a theme. "Pachín" Marín is considered one of Puerto Rico's national heroes.

1864

1864   Juárez Opposes Maximilian. French troops sent by Napoleon III occupy Mexico and impose Archduke Maximilian of Austria as the emperor of Mexico. Benito Juárez establishes a Mexican government in the north of the country and fights back gradually, expelling the French and executing Maximilian in 1867. (*See also* biography, March 21, 1806.)

1865

1865   Public Education in Puerto Rico. Spain finally establishes public education in Puerto Rico, by means of the Decreto Orgánico, the

Emperor Maximilian of Mexico and Archduke of Austria. (Courtesy of the National Museum of History, Mexico City.)

Organic Decree. Under this decree, it becomes the responsibility of each municipality to operate its own schools with public funds. The decree also empowers the government to create a Normal School to prepare teachers, but one is not started until 1890. The appointment of teachers is a responsibility of the governor of the island, but school administration is in the hands of a Junta Superior de Instrucción Pública, a board of public instruction. The system authorized by the Decreto Orgánico breaks down

within a year because of social, economic, and political conditions on the island, and chaos reigns for more than a decade. One governor, Laureano Sanz, interprets education to be solely the learning of allegiance to the Mother Country and hires only teachers imported from Spain. In 1898, the United States government names a commission made up of two Puerto Ricans and two Anglo–Americans to study the condition of public education in Puerto Rico. As a U.S. colony, public education in Puerto Rico progresses rapidly. In 1899, Puerto Rico has 380 public schools for males and 158 for female students. Secondary education is offered at the Provincial Institute, which follows the Spanish system. In 1899, an island-wide board of education is established and in 1900, the Escuela Normal Insular (Island Normal School) is founded in Fajardo. This school moved to Río Piedras in 1903 and becomes the University of Puerto Rico.

1865   The Triple Alliance War. Under dictator Francisco Solano López, Paraguay builds up its military and in 1864 requests permission of Argentina to cross through its northern territory in order to attack Brazil. Argentina denies Paraguay permission and in 1865 the triple alliance of Argentina, Brazil, and Uruguay engages in a bloody war with Paraguay. The Triple Alliance War lasts until 1870, when General Solano López's forces are attacked and he is killed in Cerro Corá, Paraguay. As a result of the war, Paraguay loses part of its national territory.

1866

1866   *El Cosmopolita* Launched. Juan Montalvo founds the newspaper *El Cosmopolita* (The Cosmopolitan). (*See also* biography, April 13, 1832.)

1867

1867   Coronel Becomes Treasurer. Antonio

Coronel is elected state treasurer of California. (*See also* biography, October 21, 1817.)

1867   Isaacs Publishes Spanish American Classic. Colombian novelist Jorge Isaacs publishes his romantic masterpiece, *María. (See also* biography, April 1, 1837.)

JANUARY 18, 1867   Poet Rubén Darío, Promoter of Literary Modernism, Is Born. Rubén Darío, probably Spanish America's greatest modern poet, is born Félix Rubén García into a poor family in rural Metapa, Nicaragua. He chooses the poetic pen name as part of the persona he creates in his self-education, given that as a child he did not have access to schools in the city. As a young man Darío is able to work as a newspaper correspondent in South America and Europe, where he meets many writers and artists. Darío is often credited with single-handedly introducing literary modernism to Spanish America and promoting it in his travels throughout the Americas. Modernism is the first Spanish–American literary movement said to have originated in Spanish America and influenced Spain, quite opposite from the previous cultural imperialism of Spain. Modernism under Darío looks to Europe, and France in particular, for many of its models and sources. Darío and modernism introduce metric innovations and a new approach to the sound and refinement of poetry that have greatly determined the evolution of modern poetry in the Spanish language. Darío's own poetry is known for its technical virtuosity and its originality of themes and images, as well as its innovative sounds and rhythms. His greatest sources are the French symbolist and Parnassian poets, and Greek and Roman archeology and mythology. Despite his great reliance on classical and modern European sources, Darío is an Americanist who, especially in later works, proclaimed the cultures of the Americas and confronted United States imperialism. Almost all of his books of poetry are considered masterpieces: *Azul* (Blue, 1888), *Prosas Profanas* (Profane Prose, 1896), *Cantos de vida y esperanza* (Songs of Life

Rubén Darío. (Courtesy of the Arte Público Press Archives, University of Houston.)

and Hope, 1905), *El canto errante* (The Errant Song, 1907), *Canto a la Argentina* (Song to Argentina, 1910), and *Poema del otoño y otros poemas,* (The Poem of Autumn and Other Poems, 1910). He dies in León, Nicaragua, on February 6, 1916.

APRIL 27, 1867   Troops Executed. Spanish troops stationed on Puerto Rico mutiny and are executed by the colonial governor.

1868

1868   Dominican Annexation Fails. With the complicity of Dominican dictator Buenaventura Báez, President Ulysses S. Grant attempts to annex the Dominican Republic to the United States, but the treaty is rejected by the United States Senate.

1868   National Hymn Lyrics Written. Feminist Lola Rodríguez de Tió writes the nationalist lyrics that will become the Puerto Rican national hymn, "La Borinqueña." (*See also* biography, September 14, 1843.)

1868   Sermiento Becomes President. Domingo Faustino Sermiento becomes president of the republic of Argentina. (*See also* biography, February 14, 1811.)

JULY 28, 1868   The Fourteenth Amendment. The Fourteenth Amendment to the U.S. Constitution is adopted, declaring all people of Hispanic origin born in the United States to be U.S. citizens.

SEPTEMBER 17, 1868   Children of Slaves. A decree in Puerto Rico frees all children born of slaves after September 17.

SEPTEMBER 23, 1868   The Lares Revolt. El Grito de Lares, the shout for Puerto Rican independence, takes place, with its disorganized insurrectionists easily defeated by the Spanish. Largely planned under the leadership of Ramón Emeterio Betances and Segundo Ruiz Belvis from exile in Santo Domingo and New York, the thousand or so insurrectionists who raise the Puerto Rican flag in Lares are not enough to battle the Spanish military. The popular uprising in various towns lacks coordination and is stifled. Betances's ship to transport men and munitions is confiscated at the island of St. Thomas. Many of the rebels are killed and the survivors disperse in the mountains. Hundreds of suspects are jailed by the Spanish military during the weeks that follow, with about eighty of the imprisoned dying during of a yellow fever epidemic in the prison. Although the Lares revolt fails, it is important in calling international attention to the plight of Puerto Rico. It is seen in Puerto Rican history as the first great heroic act for Puerto Rican independence.

OCTOBER 10, 1868   Struggle for Cuban Independence. A lawyer, poet, and follower of the French Enlightenment, Carlos Manuel de Céspedes proclaims Cuba's independence and the equality of all men at Yara, on the eastern

Carlos Manuel de Céspedes. (Courtesy of the Cuban Archives, Florida International University.)

part of the island. He then frees his slaves and leads an uprising of all races and classes against the Spanish. The majority of the insurgent groups recognize Céspedes as the president of the emerging republic. Cities are taken, a constitution written (on April 10, 1869), and delegates and ambassadors named, with Bayamo serving as the capital of the independent republic. The war rages for ten years, with the Cubans burning down the capital rather than turning it over to the Spanish. There are divisions and infighting among the insurgents and their new republic, and Céspedes is deposed on October 27, 1873. The divisiveness continues, however, and causes great damage to the cause of independence. The Spanish prevail in the Ten Years' War and, in 1878, force a peace plan on the Cubans: the Pact of El Zajón. By May 21 a complete ceasefire has been effected. In 1878, many Cubans left for Europe and the United States to once again plot for their independence. One such effort takes shape as early as October 1878, when defeated rebel general Calixto García issues a manifesto in New York inviting all Cubans to unite to fight against Spanish tyranny.

1869

1869   Baldorioty Elected to Legislative Body. Román Baldorioty de Castro is elected to the Spanish Cortes (legislative body), where he works for the abolition of slavery and for the reform of the colonial system. (*See also* biography, February 28, 1823.)

1869   The Panama Canal. United States President Ulysses S. Grant announces that the United States will build a transisthmian canal in Nicaragua. The intention of the U.S. to build a canal across the Central American isthmus will be stated often in the years to come. In 1871, President Rutherford B. Hayes repeats the charge. By the end of the century, there is a clamor in the United States to create a canal for commercial, military, and nationalistic reasons.

NOVEMBER 10, 1869   Oller Knighted. Francisco Manuel Oller Cestero is knighted by order of the king of Spain. (*See also* biography, July 17, 1833.)

1870

1870   Amnesty in Puerto Rico. Amnesty is extended to all those who participated in the Lares rebellion in Puerto Rico.

1870   The Banana Trade. During the 1870s, bananas as a cash crop are introduced to Costa Rica. The cultivation and export of the "miracle" fruit increases rapidly throughout Central America and by the turn of the century is dominated by a giant Boston-based corporation, the United Fruit Company. The importance of the crop is so great that the Central American republics come to be called "Banana Republics."

1870   Guatemala Dispossesses Mayas. During the 1870s under Justo Rufino Barrios, Guatemala passes debt-peonage statutes and abolishes hundreds of Mayan land titles to create a corps of seasonal workers for the coffee plantations. In 1884 alone, more than 100,000 acres of Mayan-owned municipal land becomes privately owned. Hundreds of thousands of Mayan farmers are displaced and forced to work as pickers and peons. Barrios's legacy is the creation of a coffee-centered economy that by 1905 controls 14 percent of the world trade and brings in 85 percent of Guatemala's revenues. Barrios's statutes remain in force until 1934, when dictator Jorge Ubico replaces them with vagrancy laws that obligate all campesinos who own less than two hectares to render manual labor for one hundred days per year. Again, this has the effect of producing a cheap or free labor source for the coffee and sugar harvests on the big plantations. The problem of land dispossession persists to the present and is a cause of major unrest in Guatemala and southern Mexico.

1870   State-Owned Slaves Freed. All slaves who are state property are freed, among various other classes of slaves in Cuba and Puerto Rico.

FEBRUARY 22, 1870   Labor Organizer Pantín Is Born. Santiago Iglesias Pantín, the Puerto Rican labor leader and politician, is born in La Coruña, Spain, where he receives an elementary education and becomes a carpenter. He relocates to Cuba, where he actively organizes labor through the Círculo de Trabajadores de la Habana (Havana Workers' Circle) from 1889 to 1896. In 1899, he moves to Puerto Rico, where he is instrumental in organizing the Partido Obrero Social (Workers' Social Party). In the following years, Iglesias Patín is an organizer for the American Federation of Labor for Puerto Rico and Cuba; in 1917, he establishes the Federación Libre de Trabajadores de Puerto Rico (Free Federation of Puerto Rican Workers) and the Socialist Party. From 1917 to 1933, Iglesias Patín serves as a legislator in the Puerto Rican Senate. From 1925 to 1933, he is secretary of the Federación Panamericana de Trabajo (Panamerican Federation of Labor). In 1932 and 1936, he is elected Resident Commissioner to represent Puerto Rico in Washington, D.C. During his years as a labor organizer, Iglesias Patín also founds and directs three newspapers: *El Porvenir Social* (The Future of Society, 1898), *La Unión Obrera* (Worker Unity, 1903), and *Justicia* (Justice). He dies on December 16, 1939, in Washington, D.C.

AUGUST 27, 1870 Amado Nervo, Mexican Modernist Poet, Is Born. Amado Nervo, one of Mexico's most famous modernist poets, is born in Tepic. Nervo receives religious training as a youth and enters the seminary, but later chooses not to become a priest. The sheer volume of poetry, short stories, and novels by Nervo attests to his lifelong career as a writer. However, he earns his living as a journalist from 1894 on, except when he serves as a diplomat for Mexico in Madrid (1905 to 1918) and Argentina and Uruguay (1919). Nervo's works are imbued with religion, philosophy, and mysticism, but what makes his poetry a favorite of the common man are his sentimental, nostalgic, and romantic pieces in honor of love, motherhood, God, and other popular topics, articulated in highly lyrical and resonant verses. Nervo is highly influenced by the French symbolists, especially in his choice of language and the ineffable and mystic quality emitted from their verse. In his poetry, Nervo is the poet of spirituality in search of truth and the meaning of existence. His neverending spiritual quest takes him eventually to explore the religions of the East, Hinduism and Buddhism, which also influence his later verse. His best-known work, *La amada inmóvil* (The Immobile Beloved One, 1920), is a product of this later period in his life when he is free of his pioneering mission of modernism and the influence of French symbolists and Parnassians. Some of Nervo's best-known works are *Perlas negras* (Black Pearls, 1898), *Poemas* (Poems, 1901) and, of course, his complete works, *Obras completas,* published from 1920 to 1922. His most celebrated novels are *El bachiller* (The College Graduate, 1895) and *Pascual Aguilera* (1896). His most important

nonfiction work is *Juan de Asbaje* (1910). Nervo dies on May 24, 1919, in Montevideo, Uruguay.

1871

1871   Cuban Immigrants Found Institute. The Instituto San Carlos is founded in Key West, Florida, as a mutual aid society for Cuban immigrants, but it quickly develops into the most important exile center for Cubans plotting their independence from Spain.

1871   Hispanics in the Major Leagues. Esteban Bellán becomes the first Spanish–American to play professional baseball in the United States. Bellán is a black Cuban recruited from Fordham College to play for the Troy Haymakers the same year the National Baseball Association is founded. He plays three years in the majors, but by the turn of the century, no blacks are allowed. Until Jackie Robinson breaks the color barrier, Hispanic blacks are regular players in the Negro leagues of the United States. Hispanics who look white, however, are allowed to play throughout professional baseball in the United States. At times, teams go to extremes to prove the racial purity of their Hispanic players, as do the Cincinnati Reds in 1911 in preparing affidavits to prove that their new Cuban players, Armando Marsans and Rafael Almeida, have pure Castillian blood running through their veins.

1872

1872   *Martín Fierro,* Part I, Is Published. Writer José Hernández publishes part I of the work known as Argentina's national masterpiece, *Martín Fierro.* A long, two-part epic poem about the life of gauchos, this romanticized version of the gaucho life and ethos catapults the gaucho into a national archetype. Today it is a standard text for school children. *See also* biography, November 10, 1834 and entry, 1879).

1872   Puerto Rican Civil Rights. Puerto Rican representatives in the Spanish Cortes win equal civil rights for the colony.

JULY 15, 1872   Writer and Humanist José Enrique Rodó Is Born. José Enrique Rodó, the Uruguayan writer, thinker, and humanist, is born in Montevideo. Rodó is a university professor of vast erudition, who is able to develop a life in letters and politics. As a writer, Rodó becomes Spanish America's greatest modernist prose writer, principally in the genre of the essay, where he expresses in figurative, poetic language some of the greatest fears and preoccupations that Spanish–Americans hold about the growth of United States imperialism at the end of the nineteenth century and beginning of the twentieth. These preoccupations are best articulated in his masterpiece *Ariel* (1900) and become the founding basis for a movement called Arielism. *Ariel* takes the form of lectures and dialogue of a university class given by Próspero—of course the characters and title are drawn from Shakespeare's *The Tempest*—who lectures on the nobility of spirit represented by Ariel and the materialism and evil as represented by Caliban. The lower, base materialist values, of course, are assigned to the United States and its tyranny of the masses, with its unrefined and materialist culture. However, Radó does praise the energy and spirit of action and pragmatism, the work ethic of the Anglo–Saxon, and United States culture. Arielism, as proposed by Rodó, consists of a harmonious combination of classical, Christian, Hispanic, and Anglo–Saxon ideals that permits the development of a fully integrated human personality in a representative democracy. Rodó, an unabashed elitist, believes in a democracy directed by an aristocracy of intellectuals and idealists. In the political realm, Rodó and Arielism are the latest manifestation of reaction against United States imperialism and intervention in the internal affairs of Latin America. In the intellectual and cultural realm, later thinkers completely disregard Rodó's paradigm to posit, instead, the identity of the Ameri-

cas as Caliban, the natural man—the Indian, the mestizo, the mulatto—as captured and exploited by European man, Próspero. In the end, it seems that Rodó identifies more with European culture than the mixed and indigenous cultures of the Americas. He dies in Palermo, Italy in May 1917.

1873

JANUARY 1, 1873   Mexican Writer Azuela Is Born. Mariano Azuela, one of Mexico's greatest novelists and chroniclers of the Mexican Revolution, is born in Lagos de Moreno, Jalisco, Mexico. Educated as a physician (University of Guadalajara, M.D., 1898), Azuela develops his career as a writer while continuing to practice medicine. Azuela's early writing in fact, is accomplished while he is participating in the revolution firsthand as a physician in the army of Francisco "Pancho" Villa. Azuela writes more than forty novels, most of them based on Mexico's political life from the point of view of a skeptic and critic bent on reforming social and political life in his native land. In many of his works, he documents the loss or corruption of the ideals that were fought for during the revolution. True to his immediate appreciation of social reality, Azuela's keen ear for dialogue and deft appropriation of characters from social reality contribute a recognition of grassroots Mexican culture that had not really appeared in Mexican letters before, especially within the context of a political analysis through literature. True to a tradition of Hispanic literature in exile, Azuela's greatest and most renowned novel, *Los de abajo* (The Underdogs, 1915), is written while he is a fugitive in El Paso, Texas. In *Los de abajo*, Azuela examines the revolution through the eyes of a common soldier and comes to condemn the uncontrollable whirlwind of violence that the revolution has become. But Azuela's condemnation is a pointed indictment of the forces of corruption and greed in converting the revolution into the murderer of those it is meant to protect and vindicate, such as the rural, grassroots protagonist who is ultimately killed on the very spot where his involvement in the struggle began. Throughout his career Azuela is a productive novelist. His other works include *María Luisa* (1907), *Los fracasados* (The Failures, 1908), *Mala yerba* (1909; translated as *Marcela: A Mexican Love Story* in 1932), *Andrés Pérez* (1911), *Sin amor* (Without Love, 1912), *Los caciques* (1917; translated as *The Bosses* in 1956), *Las moscas* (1918; translated as *The Flies* in 1956), *Las tribulaciones de una familia decente* (1918; translated as *The Trials of a Respectable Family* in 1963), and many others. Azuela dies of a heart attack in Mexico City on March 1, 1952.

MARCH 22, 1873   Puerto Rican Slavery Ends. Slavery is finally abolished in Puerto Rico by the Spanish Cortes. The newly freed slaves, however, are not given political rights—i.e., the vote—until five years later. Freedom is accorded to 29,182 slaves.

1874

1874   Cordero's Last Mural. Juan Cordero's last mural, "The Triumph of Science and Work over Ignorance and Sloth," is painted for the National Preparatory School. Unfortunately, the mural is destroyed in 1900. (*See also* biography, June 10, 1822.)

JANUARY 24, 1874   Historian Schomburg Is Born. Bibliophile, curator, writer, and mason Arturo Alfonso Schomburg is born to Carlos and Maria Schomburg in San Juan, Puerto Rico. He attends public schools in San Juan and graduates from the Instituto de Instrucción and the Instituto de Enseñanza Popular. Schomburg attends St. Thomas College in the Virgin Islands and begins to collect books and photographs about Puerto Ricans of African descent. (The passion for collecting material sprang from an incident in grade school—a teacher

asked him to write an essay on his heritage and he was unable to find any material.) Schomburg expands his collection to include all people of African descent—by 1926 his collection has over 5,000 books, 3,000 manuscripts, 2,000 etchings, and several thousand pamphlets. In April 1891, he comes to New York City and becomes a member of the Puerto Rico Revolutionary Party. Schomburg becomes a mason in 1892. In 1911, he is master of his lodge, El Sol de Cuba No. 38. and becomes grand secretary in 1918 of the Grand Lodge until 1926. Schomburg writes *Racial Integrity: A Plea for the Establishment of a Chair of Negro History in Our Schools, Colleges, etc.*, and magazine articles and brochures on masonry, including some defending Negro masons. In 1927, he receives the William E. Harmon Award for his outstanding work. He serves as curator in 1932 for the Division of Negro Literature, History, and Prints at the New York Public Library. Schomburg dies June 10, 1938.

JULY 28, 1874   Uruguayan Painter Torres-Garcia Is Born. Joaquín Torres-García, painter and world pioneer of abstract and constructivist art, is born in Montevideo to his Caalan merchant father and his Uruguayan mother. In 1891, the family moves to Spain, where he studies painting and drawing at the Academia Baixas. In 1900, he continues his studies at the Escuela Ofical de Bellas Artes in Barcelona, and becomes involved in bohemian art circles. From 1903 to 1907, Torres-Garcia works with architect Antonio Gaudí on stained glass windows for the Church of the Sacred Family in Barcelona and the cathedral in Palma de Mallorca. He also paints frescoes at various churches in Caalonia. From 1910 on, Torres-García travels extensively in Europe. In 1912, he paints a series of murals in Barcelona at the Palace of the Generalitat. During this period, he also begins designing theatrical scenery and creating toys. In 1920, he travels to New York, becomes associated with Gertrude Vanderbilt Whitney, the sculptor and sponsor of artists, and her husband, William Collins Whitney, the financier and politician, and exhibits at the Whitney Studio Club in 1921. He then returns to travels in Europe, has various exhibitions in Paris, and is associated with such avant-garde artists as Theo van Doesburg, Piet Mondrian, and Vantongerloo. With Michel Seuphor, he founds an artists' group and review, *Cercle et Carré*, which promotes the first international exhibition of constructivist and abstract art. In 1932, Torres-Garcia organizes the first Paris exhibition of Latin–American art. In 1934, he returns to Montevideo and, in 1935, founds the Asociación de Arte Constructivo. In 1936, Torres-Garcia begins publishing a review, *Círculo y Cuadrado* (Circle and Square), to disseminate his theories. His autobiography, *Historia de mi vida* (History of My Life), is published in 1939. In 1944, he publishes *Universalismo constructivo* (Constructive Universalism) and establishes his workshop, Taller Torres-García. Torres-García has had retrospectives in many countries and is acknowledged as a major artist of the twentieth century. He dies in Montevideo in 1949.

1875

1875   Court Rules on Immigration. The U.S. Supreme Court in *Henderson v. Mayor of New York* rules that power to regulate immigration is held solely by the federal government.

1875   Pacheco Governs California. Romualdo Pacheco becomes the first and only Hispanic governor of California under United States rule.

1876

MAY 14, 1876   Puerto Rican Poet Torres Is Born. The greatest modernist poet of Puerto Rico, Luis Llorens Torres, is born in Juana Díaz. After receiving his primary and secondary education in Puerto Rico, Llorens Torres studies law in Barcelona, Spain, and later at the University of Granada, where he also receives a doctorate in philosophy and letters. Although Llorens Torres has been writing poetry since the age of twelve, he publishes his first book of poetry in Granada: *Al pie de la Alhambra* (At the Foot of the Alhambra, 1899). Upon returning to Puerto Rico in 1901, he practices law. In 1913, he founded the magazine for literary modernism, *Revista de las Antillas* (Caribbean Review), where he publishes a collection of poems entitled *Visiones de mi musa* (Visions of My Muse). In 1915, with Nemesio R. Canales, he establishes the weekly satirical newspaper, *Juan Bobo*. Although Llorens Torres is a devotee of modernism, with its universalist ideology and cultivation of beautiful sound and structure, much of his work is a celebration of the history, culture, and customs of Puerto Rico, the Caribbean, and Spanish America. The following all attest to this: his famous sonnet "Bolívar," his "Velas épicas" (Epic Sales) inspired by Columbus's discovery, his heroic drama *El Grito de Lares* (The Shout at Lares, 1914), *La canción de las Antillas y otros poemas* (Song of the Indies and Other Poems, 1929), and *Alturas de América* (The Heights of the Americas, 1940). In addition, Llorens Torres also celebrates the regional and folk culture of Puerto Rico, adapting the rural voice and the verse forms of *jíbaro* (mountain folk) ten-line songs. In these and other poems and writings, Llorens Torres is a nationalist and an Americanist. He dies on June 16, 1944, in Santurce, Puerto Rico.

NOVEMBER 1876   Díaz Takes Power in Mexico. General Porfirio Díaz, a hero in the Mexican war against the French, defeats the government forces, takes power, and is recognized by the Mexican Congress as president. Under Díaz's dictatorship, foreign investment in Mexico escalates, railroads are built, and the industries of mining, metallurgy and textiles prosper, as do the oligarchy and corrupt officials and businessmen. The Laws of Reform are forgotten and the privileged classes are protected against the impoverished masses. The excesses of the Díaz regime precipitate the Mexican Revolution of 1910, which leads to the end of the regime in 1911. (*See also* biography, September 15, 1830.)

1877

1877 Composer Juan Morel Campos Founds Society. Campos founds the Ponce Fire Brigade Band and the Lira Ponceña, a musical society. (*See also* biography, May 6, 1857.)

1877 The Salt War. Anglo politicians and profiteers outside El Paso, Texas, attempt to take over communal salt mines, leading to the Mexican and Mexican–American population reacting violently in what becomes known as the "Salt War." There are many deaths and much destruction of property.

1878

1878 Cuba Starts Professional Baseball League. The Liga de Béisbol Profesional Cubana, the Cuban professional baseball league, is founded just seven years after the National Baseball League is established in the United States. Professional baseball in Spanish America is almost as old as it is in the United States.

MAY 21, 1878 Cuba Returns to Colonial Rule. A complete ceasefire brings an end to Cuba's Ten Years' War for independence. The Pact of El Zajón peace plan is forced upon the Cuban independence movement, returning the nascent republic to colonial rule.

JUNE 5, 1878 Bandit and Revolutionary General Villa Is Born. Doroteo Arango, known to history and legend as the colorful bandit and revolutionary general Francisco "Pancho" Villa, is born a peon on the Hacienda de Río Grande, San Juan del Río, close to Durango, Mexico. As a boy laborer on a ranch, Villa

becomes an outstanding horseman. According to legend, Villa flees the ranch after striking back at the owner for some offense; he then becomes a feared bandit leader in the mountains. When the Mexican Revolution breaks out in 1910, Villa joins the forces of Francisco Madero and later Venustiano Carranza's army. After defeating Victoriano Huerta, Villa splits with Carranza and suffers various defeats, most importantly at Celaya in 1915. Villa rises to national fame and legendary status when he escapes and humiliates Colonel John J. Pershing's punitive expedition into Mexico in pursuit of Villa for his attack on Columbus, New Mexico. Villa had attacked the city as a reprimand to President Woodrow Wilson for supporting Carranza against his own leadership. Where Villa has been seen by the folk as an uncontrollable and fierce personification of the chaotic revolution, he immediately becomes a defender of the national honor against the American bully. Many of the ballads of the Mexican Revolution that have world fame, such as "La Cucaracha" (The Cockroach), "La Persecución de Villa" (In Pursuit of Villa), and "Corrido Villista" (Villista Ballad), come from this period when "Pancho" Villa captures the imagination of the Mexican masses. After the revolution, Villa retires to the quiet life of ranching in 1920. On June 20, 1923, he is mysteriously assassinated by gunmen near Hidalgo del Parral, Chihuahua. According to folk legend, the assassination has been commissioned either by higher-ups in the government or by "gringos." Legend further embellishes the Villa story and heightens Mexican nationalism: it is said that the Americans even feared Villa in death, and so they dug up his grave and beheaded his corpse, removing the head to a great distance. In 1976, the government of Mexico transfers his remains to the monument of the revolution in Mexico City.

DECEMBER 31, 1878 Quiroga, Uruguayan Short-Story Writer, Is Born. Horacio Quiroga, one of the greatest Spanish–American short-story writers, is born in Salto, Uruguay. Quiroga spends a great deal of his youth in the jungles of Misiones, Argentina, where he becomes more than familiar with the natural world that often provides settings for his stories. Quiroga makes his debut as a modernist writer, but soon becomes a part of the Americanist movement known as *criollismo* (creolism), devoting his efforts to an understanding of the culture and environment of lower South America, in particular. Frequently compared to Poe and Kipling for his development of a sense of mystery and the ominous presence of death in his stories, Quiroga often examines the battle between nature and man, with nature always prevailing in the end. Quiroga pits his neurotic characters, whether from the city or the backwoods, against the heat, torrential rains, droughts, floods, snakes, and other wild animals of the jungles and deserts in dramatic, often tragic, confrontations. His most renowned book is *Cuentos de amor, de locura y de muerte* (Stories of love, of madness and of death, 1917). Many of his stories are considered by scholars of Spanish–American literature to be masterpieces that have never been surpassed. Quiroga commits suicide in a Buenos Aires charity hospital on February 19, 1937, after being diagnosed with inoperable cancer.

1879

1879 *Martín Fierro,* **Part II, Is Published.** Part II of José Hernández's epic poem is published. *See also* biography, November 10, 1834 and entry, 1872.)

1879 **The War of the Pacific.** Chilean forces invade Bolivian territory, which in the last century reached to the Pacific Ocean, in order to protect its nitrate mining interests in southwest Bolivia after Bolivia has broken its treaty on mining concessions. Bolivia and its ally Peru engage in the War of the Pacific with Chile, which wins in 1883 when its forces take the city of Lima. As a result of the war, Bolivia loses territories that give her an outlet to the sea. Since then, Bolivia has been landlocked.

AUGUST 8, 1879 **Revolutionary General Zapata Is Born in Mexico.** Emiliano Zapata, the southern Mexican poet who rises to revolutionary general and symbol of agrarian revolt is born in the town of Anenecuilco in Morelos into a poor mestizo family. He is about thirty years old when he sets off on the revolutionary trail after rich hacendados (hacienda owners) seize and fence in the village farms that had belonged to the peasants for seven generations. Zapata at the time is the elected president of the council of elders for the village. He goes into the fields with eighty armed men and announces that the land belongs to his village and that the villagers will continue to farm it. Zapata joined the revolution when it broke out in 1910. When Francisco Madero fails to redistribute lands to the peasants, Zapata takes up arms under the Plan of Ayala. By March 1911, Zapata inspires an insurrection in the nearby Villa de Ayala. There, his men disarm the local police and recruit seventy men to his cause. In the following months, thousands of men rise to support the small farmers and the Indians and follow Zapata, whose aim is to return expropriated lands to the peasants. This is the cause that has lived on in history and continues to revive to the present day in Mexico—and always Zapata's memory is revived when the principle reappears. In 1914, Zapata is successful in having the Plan of Ayala incorporated into the revolutionary goals of the Aguascalientes convention. At the peak of his power, Zapata rides into Mexico City and joins forces with the famous general of the north, Francisco Villa, against General Venustiano Carranza. Both Zapata and Villa believe they have been successful and have won the revolution. Instead of grasping power and becoming president, Zapata returns home with his forces. From 1915 until his death, Zapata leads guerrilla forces in the mountains of Morelos. On April 10, 1919, he is ambushed by federal soldiers in a meeting he has arranged with a treacherous cavalry officer,

The meeting of Francisco "Pancho" Villa and Emiliano Zapata in the Presidential Palace, Mexico City, c. 1916. Photo by Agustín Casasola. (Courtesy of the National Museum of History, Mexico City.)

Colonel Jesús Guajardo, some thirty miles from the village of Ayala. Soldiers waiting in ambush fire volleys of bullets killing Zapata before he can even draw his gun. Zapata is still revered throughout Mexico as the purest of the revolutionaries. In folk legendary and song, Zapata is always seen as the defender of the poor and a battler for redistribution of land.

AUGUST 29, 1879 The "Little War" in Cuba. Following organizational efforts led by General Calixto García, who is in exile in New York, the "Guerra Chiquita" (Little War) begins in Cuba. The Spanish response to the rebels is forceful, García is captured eight months after his landing on the shores of Oriente Province, and the rebellion is gradually quelled. By September 1880, defeat of the rebels is complete.

1880

1880   Luisa Capetillo, Advocate for Women's

Mural portrait of Emiliano Zapata (1931) by David Alfaro Siqueiros. (Courtesy of the National Institute for Fine Arts, Mexico City.)

Rights, Is Born. Puerto Rican labor leader and feminist Luisa Capetillo is born in Arecibo in 1880 or 1882. She receives her early education in a private school, where she wins prizes in grammar, history, and geography. Shortly after graduating, she works as a journalist and labor organizer. In 1912, she lives in New York City, and in 1913 she moves to Florida to organize cigar workers. From 1914 to 1915, she lives in Cuba, presumably continuing her organizing among cigar workers. Thereafter, she returns to Puerto Rico and becomes involved in the labor and feminist movements as a socialist. She is particularly outstanding in militating for women's suffrage. She is known as the first woman in Puerto Rico to dress in pants in public, as an exterior sign of her rebellion. She advocates free love, has children out of wedlock, and works for a society without social classes. She is the founder and editor of the magazine *La mujer* (Woman) and authors various books: *Ensayos libertarios* (Libertarian Essays, 1909), *La humanidad en el futuro* (Humanity in the Future, 1910), *Mi opinión sobre las libertades, derechos y deberes e la mujer* (My Opinion on the Liberties, Rights and Duties of Women, 1911), and

Influencia de las ideas modernas (The Influence of Modern Ideas, 1916). She dies of tuberculosis in Río Piedras, Puerto Rico, in 1922.

1882

1882   Blanes Receives Art Medal. Juan Manuel Blanes paints "El Ultimo Paraguayo" (The Last Paraguayan), for which he receives a gold medal at an exhibition in Buenos Aires in 1882. (*See also* biography, 1830.)

1882   Dominican Republic Institutes Reign of Terror. One of the most brutal dictatorships in the history of the Americas is that of the Dominican Republic's Ulises Heureaux, who in 1882 institutes a seventeen-year reign of terror characterized by corruption and murder. After draining the treasury, Heureaux attempts to replenish it by exacting forced loans from leading citizens, printing unsupported paper money, and floating bonds issued in Europe. In 1899, he is assassinated in a coup.

1882   Montalvo Publishes Major Work. Juan Montalvo's masterpiece, the *Siete tratados* (Seven Treatises), is published in Paris. (*See also* biography, April 13, 1832.)

FEBRUARY 28, 1882   Educator Vasconcelos Born in Mexico. One of the greatest Latin-American essayists and outstanding figures in education, José Vasconcelos, is born in Oaxaca, Mexico. An active political figure as well as a beloved teacher, Vasconcelos becomes the minister of education under the revolutionary government, which seeks to democratize and re-form the Mexican educational system. Vasconcelos hires Diego Rivera at his ministry and supports the nascent muralist movement that will revolutionize the world of art. The basic ideas for which he worked throughout his career include the following: eliminating historical prejudices from everyday life in Spanish America, an intimate Christianity, a philosophy based not on logic but on ineffable truths, and the blending of races and cultures in the social sphere for a better evolution of humanity. In the latter, Vasconcelos is really the first theorist to ennoble and empower the mestizo and his culture, which is so essential to understanding life in Latin America. His ideology is aimed at stimulating further blending of all the races, without favoring one over the other. These and other ideas are best developed in his book, *La raza cósmica* (The Cosmic Race, 1925). Vasconcelos also writes an important historical memoir, *Ulises criollo* (Creole Ulysses, 1935), and books on various subjects, such as *La intelectualidad mexicana* (The Mexican Intellectual Establishment, 1916) and *El momento estético* (The Aesthetic Moment, 1918). Vasconcelos's prodigious output also includes books of short stories, such as *La cita* (The Date, 1945), and plays, such as *Prometeo vencedor* (Victorious Prometheus, 1916). Vasconcelos dies in Mexico City on June 30, 1959.

1883

NOVEMBER 23, 1883   Mexican Muralist Orozco Is Born. One of the three greats (with Diego Rivera, b. 1886, and David Alfaro Siqueiros, b. 1896) of Mexican mural painting and modern art, José Clemente Orozco (1883–1949) is born in Ciudad Guzmán, Jalisco. Son of middle-class parents, Orozco moves to Mexico City with his family in 1890, where as a child he frequents the study of José Guadalupe Posada. He attends the School of Agriculture and then the National Preparatory School, intending to become an architect. But while attending the San Carlos Academy, where he studies under Dr. Atl (Gerardo Murillo) from 1902 to 1914, he begins working as a cartoonist for revolutionary newspapers and executing watercolors. Orozco has his first exhibition in Mexico City in 1916 and is given his first mural commission in 1920 at the National Preparatory School. He lives in the United States from 1927 to 1934, where he executes murals at the New School for

Social Research in New York, Claremont College in California, and Dartmouth College in New Hampshire. He returns to Mexico in 1934, and thereafter paints some of his most famous murals in Mexico City and Guadalajara, such as *Catharsis* at the Palace of Fine Arts in Mexico City. During the 1940s, Orozco paints a series of portraits and completes anticlerical and antimilitary paintings as well as murals, such as *Juárez, the Clergy and the Imperialists* at the Chapultepec Castle. Orozco has had major retrospectives and is celebrated internationally as one of the artistic greats of this century. He dies in Mexico City on September 7, 1949.

1884

1884   Francisco "Pachín" González Marín Is Published. Marín, Puerto Rican patriot and literary figure, publishes his first book of poems, *Flores nacientes* (Newborn Flowers). (*See also* biography, 1863.)

1885

1885   Central America Unity Attempt Fails. Guatemalan dictator J.R. Barrios fails in an attempt to unite Central America, this time by force under the rule of an autocrat.

1886

1886   Cuba Liberates Slaves. The slaves are freed in Cuba.

FEBRUARY 13, 1886   Novelist Güiraldes Is Born. Ricardo Güiraldes is born in Buenos Aires into a wealthy ranching family. Güiraldes studies law and architecture, but never practices either. He does become the most famous Argentine novelist of the early twentieth century. He is an assiduous student of European literature, especially French and German volumes, which he reads in the original languages;

he travels at various times to the continent. In fact, in his early twenties, he takes a two-year trip around the world. What Güiraldes does and which highly influences the course of Argentine and Latin–American letters, is to combine his knowledge of European literature with Argentine national history and folklore. His crowning achievement is *Don Segundo Sombra* (1926), a novel that not only becomes a masterpiece of Latin–American literature, but is looked upon as *the* Argentine novel, just as José Hernández's *Martín Fierro* is looked upon as *the* Argentine national epic poem. *Don Segundo Sombra*, winner of the Argentine national prize for literature, is a tale about the dignified life of the Argentine gaucho, a national figure that is passing from the modern scene. Written in the gaucho dialect, the novel follows the adventures of a young apprentice to the master gaucho, Don Segundo Sombra, in a style that is lyrical, but never maudlin, in its nostalgic evocation of life on the pampas. It has been seen as one of the finest examples of how rudimentary material, such as folklore and common dialects, can be transformed into a work of high art. Although Güiraldes dies of Hodgkin's disease at the early age of 41, he is an extremely productive writer. Included among his other works are *El cencerro de cristal* (The Crystal Cowbell, 1915), *Raucho: Momentos de una juventud contemporánea* (Raucho: Moments in the Life of a Contemporary Youth, 1917), *Rosaura* (1922) and various other collections of poetry and narrative. He dies in Paris on October 8, 1927.

OCTOBER 24, 1886 Agustini, Uruguayan Poet, Is Born. Delmira Agustini, a famous Spanish–American poet, is born in Montevideo, Uruguay. She publishes her first book of poems, *El libro blanco* (The White Book, 1907) when she is just twenty-one, which causes a scandal in Uruguayan society because of the book's sensuous nature. However, her next two books not only confirm her poetic talent but also make it evident that her sensuality is spiritual: *Cantos de la mañana* (Morning Songs,

1910) and *Los cálices vacíos* (The Empty Chalices, 1913). But most of her poetry is published posthumously, after her untimely death (she is murdered by her husband on July 6, 1914). Among her most famous works are *Los astros del abismo* (The Stars of the Abysm, 1924), *El rosario de Eros* (Eros' Rosary, 1924), and *Por campos de ensueño* (Through Fields of Dreams, 1927). Since *Obras poéticas* (Poetic Works) was published in 1940, various collections of her complete and selected works have been issued.

DECEMBER 8, 1886 Diego Rivera, Master Painter and Muralist, Is Born. The master painter and muralist, Diego Rivera, is born in Guanajuato, Mexico. Both his parents are teachers. Rivera studies art at the San Carlos Academy from 1896 to 1905 under Félix Parra, José María Velasco, and Santiago Rebull. In 1907, Rivera travels to Europe on a government scholarship. In Spain and France, he studies and works with some of the leading artists of the time. In 1911, he has a successful exhibition in Mexico City that leaves him with enough funds to return to Paris, where he joins Mexican artists Angel Zárraga, Dr. Atl (Gerardo Murillo), Roberto Montenegro, and Adolfo Best-Maugard. Under the influence of Piet Mondrian, Rivera produces some two hundred cubist works from 1913 to 1917. Rivera becomes associated with the Parisian avant-garde that includes Léger, Chagall, Modigliani, Picasso, and others. On his return to Mexico in 1921, José Vasconcelos, minister of education, appoints Rivera to an arts administrative post. From 1922 on, he is a pioneer of mural painting in Mexico, first with "Creation," painted at the National Preparatory School, and then with numerous others. In 1922, Rivera cofounds the Union of Technical Workers, Painters and Sculptors. He becomes a Communist and visits the Soviet Union in 1927 to work with the October Group of artists in Moscow. In 1929, Rivera is appointed director of the San Carlos Academy, but resigns the following year over internal disputes. In 1930, Rivera travels, exhibits, and paints on both coasts of the United States and in Detroit,

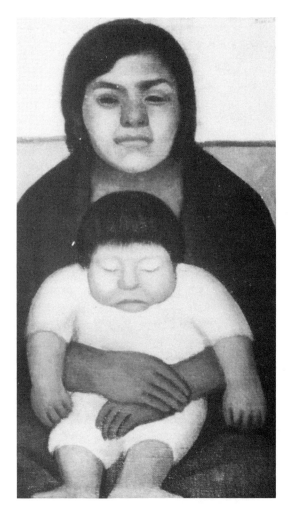

"Mother and Child" (1926) by Diego Rivera. (Courtesy of the National Institute for Fine Arts, Mexico City.)

Michigan. This is the period when he executes murals at Rockefeller Center in New York City, in which he depicted Lenin and the triumph of Communism, which later were destroyed by his embarrassed and incensed patron, John D. Rockefeller. From 1937 to 1942, Rivera receives no public wall commissions in Mexico; in the hiatus, he paints genre scenes. In 1942, he executes a mural at San Francisco City College. In 1953, Rivera is appointed to the Mexican National College to represent the arts and to the faculty of the National School of

Painting and Sculpture in Mexico City. In 1947, with José Clemente Orozco and David Alfaro Siqueiros, he creates a commission on mural painting as a division of the Palace of Fine Arts. In 1949, Rivera has his first major retrospective at the Palace of Fine Arts, and in 1950 he is awarded the National Prize in Art from the government. Before his death of heart failure in Mexico City on November 25, 1957, Rivera travels extensively, including trips to Moscow and East Germany. He is buried in the Rotunda of Illustrious Men in Mexico City. Rivera wills all of his art to the Mexican nation.

DECEMBER 8, 1886 Mexican Composer Ponce Is Born. Mexican composer Manuel M. Ponce is born in Fresnillo. He is raised in Aguascalientes, Mexico, where he begins to take piano lessons and becomes a precocious student. By 1901, when he has already composed numerous pieces for the piano, he starts to study at the Conservatorio Nacional de Música. He is forced to take beginning classes despite his advanced knowledge of music and composition. He leaves the conservatory after a year and returns to Aguascalientes to give private piano lessons. In 1904, he travels to Europe, where he spends two years studying in Bologna, Italy, with Enrico Bossi and Luigi Torchi, and two years in Germany with Martin Krause at the conservatory in Berlin. Upon returning to Mexico in 1909, he is named to the teaching faculty of the same national conservatory that gave him such a hard time as a student. From 1925 to 1933, he once again lives in Europe, this time in Paris. Upon returning to Mexico, he is hired as a professor of folkloric music in the Universidad Nacional Autónoma de México (UNAM), and in 1945 he becomes the director of the music school of the UNAM. He dies in Mexico City on April 4, 1948.

1887

1887 Baldorioty Founds Autonomist Party. Román Baldorioty de Castro is a founder and president of the Autonomist Party of Puerto Rico. (*See also* biography, February 28, 1823.)

SEPTEMBER 26, 1887 Spanish Actor Moreno Is Born. Actor Antonio Moreno is born in Madrid. He plays a dapper "Latin lover" in numerous Hollywood silent films. He begins his career in 1912 under D.W. Griffith and is quite popular during the 1920s, when he plays leads opposite such actresses as Gloria Swanson, Greta Garbo, Pola Negri, and Bebe Daniels. His foreign accent limits his career in talkies, where he is mainly plays character roles. He appears in hundreds of films, including *Voice of the Million* and *The Musketeers of Pig Alley* (1912); *The Song of the Ghetto, The Loan Shark King, In the Latin Quarter,* and *Sunshine and Shadows* (1914); *The Quality of Mercy* and *The Gypsy Trail* (1915); *My American Wife* and *The Spanish Dancer* (1923); *One Year to Live* (1925); *Mare Nostrum* and *The Temptress* (1926); *Venus of Venice* and *The Whip Woman* (1928); *Romance of the Rio Grande* (1929); *One Mad Kiss* (1930); *The Bohemian Girl* and *Rose of the Rio Grande* (1938); *Seven Sinners* (1940); *Notorious* (1946); *Captain from Castille* (1947); *Crisis* and *Dallas* (1950); *Wings of the Hawk* (1953); *Creature From the Black Lagoon* (1954); and *The Searchers* (1956). He dies in 1967.

1888

1888 Cuban Negro League Pitcher Is Born. Cuban José Méndez, an outstanding pitcher and infielder, is born. Because of his African ancestry and dark skin, he is never allowed to play in the majors. Instead, he plays in the Negro National Leagues and in Cuba, and thus many of his statistics are missing. Such witnesses as Hall-of-Famer John Henry Lloyd said that he never saw a pitcher superior to Méndez, and Giants Manager John McGraw said that Méndez would have been worth $50,000 in the majors, an unusually high figure at that time. Méndez travels to the United States in 1908 with the Cuban Stars. In 1909, he has a win-

loss record of 44–2 as a pitcher for the Stars. During the winters he plays in Cuba, where he compiles a record of 62–17 by 1914. From 1912 to 1916, Méndez plays for the All-Nations of Kansas City, a racially mixed barnstorming club. From 1920 to 1926, he serves as a player–manager for the Kansas City Monarchs, leading them to three straight Negro National League pennants from 1923 to 1925. During his long career, he also plays for the Los Angeles White Sox, the Chicago American Giants, and the Detroit Stars.

1888 Posada Starts Print Shop, Newspaper. José Guadalupe Posada, Mexican illustrator, opens his first print shop in Mexico City, and prints and illustrates the newspaper, *La Patria Ilustrada* (The Fatherland Illustrated). (*See also* biography, February 2, 1851.)

1889

1889 American Republics Form Union. In 1888–90, at the initiative of the United States, the First International Conference of the American States is held in Washington, D.C. Various resolutions are passed, including one to create the International Union of American Republics, later named the Panamerican Union, to be headquartered in Washington, D.C. The union is the forerunner of the today's system of international cooperation, the Organization of American States, which includes many agencies, organizations, conferences, and services throughout the hemisphere. The U.S. originally sought the conference in order to promote the establishment of a hemispheric customs union; the United States had an adverse balance of trade of some $100 million due to buying raw materials from Latin–American countries, which then purchased manufactured goods from Europe. The United States hoped to lower trade barriers and attract purchases of manufactured goods at home and to tap further into the Latin–American market. This strategy fails, but it results in the founding of one of the most important hemispheric institutions.

1889   Costa Rica Holds Free, Fair Elections.
Costa Rica holds its first elections under which there is full freedom of speech and of the press, and an honest counting of votes. It becomes the first Central American republic to institute a full democracy. Throughout the twentieth century Costa Rican has one of the most stable and democratic governments in the Americas. There are threats, however, to this political stability, one in the form of a two-year (1917–18) failed dictatorship in the person of Federico A. Tinoco and another in the form of an attempted revolution in 1932.

APRIL 7, 1889   Nobel Winner Mistral Is Born.
Nobel Prize-winning poet Gabriela Mistral is born in Vicuna, Chile. Trained as a teacher, Lucia Godly Alcayaga takes her pen name while still serving as a primary and secondary school teacher. As she becomes well known in the world of letters, she leaves teaching to serve as a consul and later Chile's ambassador to the League of Nations and to the United Nations. As Latin America's first Nobel laureate (1945), she travels extensively throughout the Americas, where she becomes known as a great humanitarian, an active promoter of public education, and an outstanding speaker. She never marries, a fact some attribute to the pain she suffers in her youth when her boyfriend commits suicide. In her poetry, Mistral is a great humanitarian of broad erudition in world literature and the classics. But her overriding theme is always love. Her work also is rooted in a deep religiosity and a concern for the condition and circumstances of women, spanning the gamut of preoccupations from maternity to sterility. Mistral's first book, *Desolación* (Desolation), is published in New York by the Hispanic Institute in 1922. Of her more than twenty books of poetry, *Desolación* and *Tala* (1938) are considered her best works. She dies in Hempstead, New York, on January 10, 1957.

Poet Gabriela Mistral. (Courtesy of the Library of Congress Prints & Photographs Division.)

MAY 10, 1889   Venezuelan Painter Reverón Is Born. Armando Reverón, Venezuelan painter, is born in Caracas and raised by a foster family. He suffers from ill health after contracting typhoid during his childhood. After receiving initial art instruction from his uncle, Ricardo Montilla, Reverón studies at the Academy of Fine Arts in Caracas, graduating in 1911. With a scholarship from Caracas, He travels to Spain to study at the Academy of San Fernando in Madrid, from 1912 to 1913. Back in Caracas in 1915, Reverón joins a group of impressionist painters. From then on, he is an active exhibitor in Venezuela. From 1925 to 1932 almost all of his paintings are near-monochrome white works; a period of paintings in sepia follows this, then a period of studies of nude female figures, and later, the fabrication of lifesize dolls. In the 1940s he returns to painting landscapes, but only in shades of sepia. Before and after his death, Reverón's works are exhibited widely, in Venezuela, France, and the United States. He dies in Caracas on September 1, 1954.

MAY 17, 1889   Mexican Poet and Educator Reyes Is Born. Alfonso Reyes, considered one of Latin America's greatest humanists of the twentieth century, is born in Monterrey, Mexico. In his erudition and his dedication to the humanities and literature, he is the natural successor of Andrés Bello, the great Venezuelan scholar. A student of Ramón Menéndez Pidal, the great Spanish philologist, at the Center for Historical Studies in Madrid, Reyes has his base in the encyclopedic knowledge of the late nineteenth-century positivists. In Mexico, he develops a dual career as a poet and educator, and eventually rises to become the director of Mexico's distinguished graduate school, the Colegio de México. In 1956, Reyes is nominated for the Nobel Prize in Literature. He also serves in various diplomatic positions. His productivity spans various disciplines, including history, criticism, essays, poetry, short stories, and esthetics. Among his most noteworthy books are *Visión de Anáhuac* (A View of Anáhuac, 1917), *Reloj de sol* (Sun Dial, 1956), *Cuestiones gongorinas* (Góngora Issues, 1958), and *La experiencia literaria* (The Literary Experience, 1962). His books of poetry include *Huellas* (Footprints) and *Homero en Cuernavaca* (Homer in Cuernavaca). For many years Reyes edits the journal *Nueva Revista de Filología Española* (New Journal of Spanish Philology). He dies in Mexico City on December 17, 1959.

1890

1890   The United Fruit Company Is Created. Minor Cooper Kieth, an American adventurer and entrepreneur, completes the railroad from the coast to the capital, Limón, of Costa Rica at a cost of about $8 million and some four thousand lives. After building the railroad, he decides he needs freight for the railroad to prosper. Thus is born the idea to start up banana plantations and create a cash crop. From Costa Rica, he extends his banana ventures into Guatemala and El Salvador. During the last three decades there are twenty banana companies in Central America; Kieth consoli-

dates them all into the United Fruit Company in 1899. For this and his other business ventures, he comes to be known as "the uncrowned king of Central America."

1891

1891   Party Organizes for Independence. The Partido Revolucionario Cubano is created to organize the Cuban and Puerto Rican independence movement.

JANUARY 5, 1891   Separatist Clubs Approve Revolutionary Group. Following years of actively organizing Cuban expatriates in the United States, Cuban rebel leader José Martí is successful in winning approval from twenty-seven Cuban separatist clubs for his Partido Revolucionario Cuban (Cuban Revolutionary Party) and thus launches a new independence movement for his island. The party's program is later ratified by other separatist organizations in the South, in New York, and in Philadelphia in late March. In April, the party's program is published in the first issue of its official organ, the newspaper *La Patria* (The Fatherland), which is launched in New York. The official goal of the party is to obtain the complete independence of Cuba and to "promote and aid that of Puerto Rico." It further states that its ultimate goal is the establishment in Cuba of "a new and honestly democratic nation." Only after the party gains broad approval and becomes the recognized leader of the Cuban independence movement does Martí approach the generals who would be essential in implementing the military phase of the revolution: Antonio Maceo, Máximo Gómez, and others. Martí requires them to recognize and accept the authority of the party before becoming involved once again in the movement. They agree and, in August 1892, Máximo Gómez is chosen as the director of all military operations. The Second War of Cuban Independence is

Antonio Maceo. (Courtesy of the Cuban Archives, Florida International University.)

ready to break out. After various false starts, it does so in 1895.

SEPTEMBER 12, 1891   Puerto Rican Activist Campos Is Born. Pedro Alvizu Campos, the greatest activist for Puerto Rican independence from the United States, is born into a mulatto family in Ponce, where he receives his primary and elementary education. In 1912, he goes to Vermont to study engineering, but eventually transfers to Harvard, where he obtains a law degree. During his eight years at Harvard, he is

Pedro Alvizu Campos at a press conference in Puerto Rico, December 16, 1947.

a distinguished student leader, serving as president of various clubs and directing movements for the independence of India and Ireland. He enlists in the U.S. Army when World War I begins. Despite being offered positions as a clerk for the U.S. Supreme Court and as a foreign service officer when he graduates from Harvard, Alvizu Campos decides to return to Puerto Rico in 1921 without graduating, because of racial discrimination that he has encountered at Harvard. He, nevertheless, is sent an exam he must have to graduate; he passes it and obtains his law degree that same year. In Puerto Rico he becomes a member of the Unión de Puerto Rico political party, which is pro-independence. In 1924, Alvizu Campos becomes a member of the Nationalist Party, which is founded in 1922, and shortly thereafter (1924) he is elected its vice president. In 1926, he sells all of the family's belongings and moves his wife and children to his wife's family home in Peru. He leaves on a two-year-long pilgrimage throughout the Americas to raise funds for the Puerto Rican independence movement. Pedro Alvizu Campos is always an eloquent and moving speaker in and out of Puerto

Rico. In Cuba and Santo Domingo, he founds two organizations to work for Puerto Rican independence, and he builds relations with other leaders, such as José Vasconcelos, in many other countries. Alvizu Campos returns with his family to Puerto Rico in 1930, and is elected president of the Nationalist Party. Against his will, the party runs him for senator in 1932, but the result is a humbling loss. During the early 1930s, Alvizu Campos and his party are involved in labor organizing, directing and winning various strikes, such as those against Puerto Rico Railway, Light and Power Company in 1933 and the sugar industry in 1934. During this time, reaction to and persecution of Alvizu Campos and his party intensifies, culminating with a police massacre of supporters in Río Piedras in 1935. In 1936, various leaders are killed and Alvizu Campos is arrested and charged with breaking U.S. sedition laws. He is sentenced to ten years of imprisonment in exile by a jury of ten Anglo–Americans and two Puerto Ricans; he also is disbarred. While Alvizu Campos is in prison, the police carry out another famous massacre on Palm Sunday, 1937, in Ponce. That same year, he is transferred to a federal penitentiary in Atlanta, Georgia; in 1943, in ill health, he is transferred to Columbus Hospital in New York, where he stays for two years. In 1943, his U.S. citizenship is revoked. Upon his release from prison in New York, Alvizu Campos returns to Puerto Rico and to leadership of the independence movement. The nationalists attack Blair House, President Harry S Truman's residence, in 1950, and Alvizu Campos and hundreds of nationalists are immediately arrested. He is tried and sentenced to a long term, but Governor Luis Muñoz Marín suspends his sentence in 1953, due to local and international pressure. In 1954, when the Puerto Rican nationalists shoot up the U.S. House of Representatives to call attention to Puerto Rico's colonial status, Alvizu Campos's sentence is renewed. While still in prison in 1956, he suffers a cerebral stroke, resulting in loss of speech and paralysis of his right side. He is then transferred to Presbyterian Hospital in San Juan; he remains a prisoner there until November 1964, when Muñoz Marín once again suspends his sentence. Alvizu Campos dies in San Juan on April 25, 1965.

DECEMBER 2, 1891   Guatemalan Painter Mérida Is Born. Painter sculptor, printmaker Carlos Mérida, of Mayan Quiché descent, is born in Quezaltenango, Guatemala. At the age of seventeen he meets the artist Carlos Valenti, who takes him to Europe; Mérida stays there until 1914 and becomes involved in the art culture, meeting and working with such notables as Pablo Picasso and others of the Paris School. When he returns to Guatemala, he founds, with sculptor Yela Gunther, an indigenist movement attempting to find an authentic American art. In the late teens and early 1920s, he spends considerable time in Mexico City, working with Diego Rivera, exhibiting at the Palace of Fine Arts (1920), and painting his first mural at the Children's Library, Ministry of Education. In 1926, Mérida has his first New York exhibition and in 1927 he goes back to Europe, where he develops a relationship with Paul Klee and Joan Miró. He exhibits in Paris and returns to Guatemala in 1929, showing the influence of abstraction and surrealism. His interest in theatre and dance led him to found the School of Ballet for the Secretary of Public Education in Mexico City in 1931, and, in fact, Mérida's "Dances," a series of kings and pre-Hispanic figures he painted on parchment during the 1950s, are among his most famous works. Mérida's art is guided by two principles: re-introducing the plane, traditional in the work of creole and mestizo craftsmen of the colonial period, and exploring the connection between art, music, and dance. These principles guided him to learn from Mayan decorative motifs and the rhythms of pre-Colombian dance, and to rediscover the values of pre-Colombian art. In 1940, he exhibits in the International Surrealist show in Mexico City. After 1950, he turns to architectural art, creating relief murals and mosaics. One of his most famous works in the

United States is his mosaic mural *La confluencia de las civilizaciónes en América* (The Confluence of Civilizations in the Americas). Two of his best known mural projects are the exterior decoration of the Benito Juárez multifamily dwellings in Mexico City (1952) and a mural for the Guatemala City Municipal Building (1956). He continues painting and constructing murals until his death in Mexico City in 1984.

1892

MARCH 16, 1892 César Vallejo, Poet and Political Activist, Is Born. César Vallejo, internationally renowned Latin–American poet, is born in Santiago de Chuco, Peru, of mixed European and Peruvian Indian heritage. Though he is a graduate in law from the University of Trujillo in 1915, he works variously in mine offices and as a tutor, teacher, and journalist, rather than a lawyer. From 1920 to 1921, he is imprisoned because of political activity. Vallejo's poetry is deeply humanistic and known for its originality and authenticity. One of the predominant notes is an awareness of the suffering of others, a suffering he shares in prison as an expatriate political activist from 1923 until his death, and as a witness to the holocaust of the Spanish Civil War—he is an ardent anti-Fascist. He also lives a life of poverty and chronic illness. Other themes that dominate are alienation and the senselessness of his own suffering. Initiated as a modernist, which his first book *Los heraldos negros* (The Black Messengers, 1918) fully demonstrates, he later gravitates toward surrealism in *Trilce* (1922), which is printed at the penitentiary in Lima. In *Trilce*, Vallejo uses the metaphor of imprisonment as a constant of the human condition: one is constrained not only by government, society, and culture, but also by the limits of time, space, and the human body. His third book, *Poemas humanos* (Human Poems, 1939), published in Paris posthumously by his widow, is highly influenced by the war in Spain and portrays

great human suffering through a very personal idiom. Other works are published posthumously in the book, *España, apartado de mí este cáliz* (Spain, Take that Chalice Away from Me, 1940), and in his complete works, anthologies of his works, and new editions of his books. Most of Vallejo's worldwide fame comes after his death on April 15, 1938, from tuberculosis or an acute intestinal infection (the cause of his death has not been documented well).

MAY 29, 1892 Poet and Feminist Storni Is Born. One of Latin America's major poets and early feminists, Alfonsina Storni, is born in Sala Capriasca, Switzerland, the daughter of beer manufacturer Alfonso Storni and his wife Paula Martignoni. She emigrates to Argentina in 1896 and becomes a naturalized citizen in 1920. In 1911, Storni begins work as an elementary school teacher in Rosario, Argentina, but soon thereafter moves to Buenos Aires and pursues a series of jobs, including teaching. She is one of the first feminist writers to emerge in Argentina. Her work is characterized for its expression of passionate internal conflicts and desires and for its opposition to the injustices of male-dominated culture. While her early poetry is known for its lyricism and passion, her later works are more abstract and more innovative in form and language, especially in her two highly acclaimed last books: *Mundo de siete pozos* (World of Seven Wells, 1934) and *Mascarilla y trébol* (Mask and Clover, 1938). Her other poetic works include *La inquietud del rosal* (The Disquietude of the Rosebush, 1916), *El dulce daño* (Sweet Damage, 1918), and *Languidez* (Languor, 1920). Storni also writes novels, short fiction, and drama. She commits suicide by drowning in Mar del Plata, Argentina, on October 25, 1938.

OCTOBER 24, 1892 Rafael Hernández, Composer of Popular Music, Is Born. Puerto Rico's greatest composer of popular music, Rafael Hernández, is born in Aguadilla into an Afro–Puerto Rican family. At the age of twelve, he begins to study instrumental music formally with José Rullán Lequerica. He later studies music at a conservatory, but although he writes operas and zarzuelas, it is in the world of popular, commercial music that he becomes known in the Americas. Even from his first hits, Hernández is an intellectual in the popular music scene, composing music to the verse of famous Puerto Rican poets such as José Guatier Benítez, in his "A Mis Amigos" (To My Friends, 1924), and José de Diego, in "Laura Mía" (My Laura, 1924). Many of his songs and lyrics also develop patriotic, even nationalist themes, such as "Pobre Borinquen" (Poor Puerto Rico), "Mi Patria Tiembla" (My Fatherland Shivers), "¡Oh Patria Mía!" (Oh, My Country!), "El Buen Borincano" (The Good Puerto Rican), and "Lamento Borincano" (Puerto Rican Lament). To develop his career as a musician and com- poser, Hernández spends a great deal of time in New York, which by World War II has become the center of the Latin music publishing and recording business. In 1926, Hernández forms a performing group, Trío Borinquen, and later begins publishing his compositions with Peer- Southern Music for recordings mostly on the Columbia label. In 1934, he forms another group, the Cuarteto Victoria, in New York. Compositions that have become classics of Latin music are "El Cumbanchero," "Preciosa" (Pre- cious One, in honor of Puerto Rico), "Capullito de Alelí" (Oleander Bud), and his most famous "Lamento Borincano," which details the pov- erty in Puerto Rico's countryside. His other music includes "Ballet Imaginario" (Imaginary Ballet), "Rapsodia Borincana I y II" (Puerto Rican Rhapsody I and II), "Nueve Danzas Clásicas" (Nine Classical Danzas), "Seis Caprichos Musicales" (Six Musical Caprices), and four operettas. He dies in San Juan on December 11, 1965.

Puerto Rican composer Rafael Hernández. (Courtesy of the Arte Público Press Archives, University of Houston.)

José María Velasco is awarded first prize at the Chicago World's Fair. (*See also* biography, 1840.)

MAY 29, 1893 Nicaragua Elects Zelaya. José Santos Zelaya is elected to the presidency of Nicaragua. He subsequently rewrites the con- stitution to empower him to be reelected twice, thus serving sixteen years. Under his tenure, a railroad connecting the major cities is built, the number of schools is increased, agriculture is diversified, and the army is modernized. But Santos Zelaya is also a brutish tyrant who fattens himself and his cronies at the public trough and betrays his country by selling reck- less concessions to foreigners. Under Santos Zelaya, Nicaragua becomes the premier mili- tary power in Central America, a power he uses to stir up revolutions in the neighboring coun- tries. Pressure from both the United States and the other Central American republics forces Santos Zelaya into exile in 1909.

1893

1893 Artist Wins First Prize. Landscape artist

1894

1894 The Alianza Hispano Americano, Civil Rights Group, Is Founded. The Alianza

Hispano Americana, an early civil rights organization, is founded in Tucson, Arizona, and quickly spreads throughout the Southwest. The Alianza originally is a mutualist society organized along Masonic lines. By 1930, it has spread throughout the Southwest and has grown to more than ten thousand members. In the post-World War II period, the organization becomes very active in protecting the civil rights of Mexican–Americans. Today, it still counts over three hundred chapters in its membership.

1895

1895 Cuban Batter Oms Is Born. Alejandro Oms, considered the best batter in Cuban baseball, is born into a poor family in Santa Clara, Cuba. As a child, he has to work in an iron foundry. He starts playing organized baseball in 1910 as a center fielder. He plays in the Negro league on the Cuban Stars and the New York Cubans from 1921 to 1935, while still managing to put in outstanding seasons during the winter in Cuban professional ball. On the most famous Cuban team of all time, Santa Clara, Oms bats .436 in the 1922–23 season. In Cuba, Oms achieves a lifetime batting average of .352; his average in the U.S. is not known. He is batting champion on the island three times: in 1924–25 with .393; in 1928–29 with .432; and in 1929–30 with .380. In 1928, he establishes a Cuban record for most consecutive games with hits: 30. In his last years, he is penniless and his vision starts to fail; he dies at the age of 51 in 1946.

1895 Posada Creates New Art Technique. José Guadalupe Posada introduces the technique of etching on zinc, which he uses in more than twenty thousand engravings. (*See also* biography, February 2, 1851.)

JANUARY 12, 1895 War of Cuban Independence. United States authorities seize war material and detain ships from embarking from U.S. shores to begin the war of Cuban indepen-

dence. In February, however, the rebels are successful in starting the war.

FEBRUARY 24, 1895 Martí and Weyler Battle. José Martí and his Partido Revolucionario Cubano (Cuban Revolutionary Party) open the final battle for independence. Spain sends Captain General Valeriano Weyler with instructions to put down the insurrection at all costs. Weyler implements a brutal campaign to reconcentrate the peasants into the cities, destroy the agricultural fields, and kill the livestock on the island in order to starve out the rebels. Nevertheless, the support system that the rebels have developed in the communities in New York, Key West, and Tampa allows them to continue the war, and Weyler's inhumanity leads the United States to protest to Spain and prepare for intervention.

MARCH 8, 1895 Poet Juana de América Is Born. Juanita Fernández Morales (who uses her married name, Juana de Ibarbourou, as a writer), is born in Melo, Cerro Largo, Uruguay. She becomes one of the most beloved poets in Spanish America, so much so that she is known affectionately as "Juana de América" (Juana of the Americas), a title consecrated by a law the Uruguayan legislature passes in 1919. Her highly lyrical but simple poems celebrate nature and love. She is a poet within the reach of the common man as well as the academic. Her prodigious output extends to more than thirty collections of verse. But it is her first three books that establish her reputation and remain her best known works: *Las lenguas de diamante* (Tongues of Diamond, 1919), *El cántaro fresco* (The Pitcher of Fresh Water, 1920), and *Raíz salvaje* (Savage Root, 1922). Her complete works are published in Madrid in 1953; the third and last edition of these works appears in Madrid in 1968. Ibarbourou dies in Melo in July, 1979.

JUNE 14, 1895 José Carlos Mariátegui, Peruvian Activist, Is Born. José Carlos Mariátegui, Peruvian essayist, thinker, activist, is born into a poor family in Lima. He works as a

Juana de Ibarbourou. (Courtesy of the Arte Público Press Archives, University of Houston.)

journalist from a very early age, and in 1919 travels to study in Italy on a scholarship. There, he becomes a disciple of the Italian philosopher Antonio Gramsci. Through his writings and organizational efforts, Mariátegui provides one of the most important bases for the indigenist movement in Spanish America. On his return to Peru, Mariátegui joins the Alianza Popular Revolucionaria Americana (APRA). A confirmed Marxist, he attacks Spanish colonialism, the feudalist mentality in the Americas, the large land holdings, and the literary reliance on Europe and Spain. He promotes agrarian reform and political reform, the development of nationalism, and strategies for raising the Indians from poverty and oppression. In 1925, he forms a group called Amauta to promote all of these ideas; the group publishes a magazine by the same title to further disseminate its theories. Mariátegui's most highly regarded work is his *Siete ensayos de interpretación de la realidad peruana* (Seven Interpretive Essays of Peruvian Reality, 1928). Another book, *La escena contemporánea* (The Contemporary Scene, 1925), is a call to Peruvian intellectuals to

become involved in the social issues of their country. He dies in Lima on April 16, 1930.

OCTOBER 8, 1895 Juan Perón, Argentine General and Politician, Is Born. Juan Domingo Perón, the Argentine general and politician, is born in Lobos, near Buenos Aires, and becomes the most prominent figure in Argentine history of the twentieth century. His military training starts at an early age, he authors important books on strategy and military organization, and he becomes a teacher at the national war college (Escuela Superior de Guerra). In 1939, the government sends him to study the German and Italian armies, and he not only becomes familiar with fascism, but also makes the acquaintance of Benito Mussolini—Perón spoke Italian fluently, as do many Argentines. He is, however, repulsed by German Naziism, which he calls racist, and feel more attracted to Italian fascism. In fact, Mussolini becomes his model, even for Perón's rhetorical style and, eventually, for forming a dictatorship based on one-party politics. Upon his return from Europe, Perón organizes the Argentine military lodge, Grupo de Oficiales Unidos (United Officers Group) with seventeen colonels and lieutenant colonels on March 10, 1943; this is the typical Nazi organization that proliferates among the military in Latin America during the war in such countries as Paraguay, Bolivia, Chile, Peru, Ecuador, and Venezuela. On June 4, 1943, the group effects a bloodless coup to remove Argentine president Ramón S. Castillo from power. On July 7, 1944, a second coup results in Colonel Perón becoming vice president of the republic. Perón is a charismatic figure among the oligarchy, the military, and the working classes, which only results in the country's leadership sending him to prison in October 1945. But on October 17, a spontaneous uprising of more than one million workers in the main plaza of Buenos Aires succeeds in obtaining his release. The workers carry him on their shoulders to be installed as president and commander in chief of the armed forces. On February 24, 1946, he is officially elected president of Argentina. Perón institutes total economic reorganization of the country via rapid industrialization under his autocratic and at times violent leadership. Perón also brings significant progress to the country in the form of benefits for workers, families, and education; under pressure from his wife, Evita, he also affords greater equality to women. It is Perón's economic policy that is chaotic. While he is successful in establishing a national airline, in constructing natural gas pipelines, dams, and hydroelectric plants; and in developing an efficient merchant marine, other programs are disastrous. He nationalizes public utilities and public services, including the railroads; he creates large bureaucracies to regulate such industries as agriculture, for which he fixes prices, and to cover the country's spiraling debts he drastically increases the currency in circulation, thus causing uncontrollable inflation. At the beginning of Perón's administration the exchange rate with the United States is four pesos to the dollar; at the end, in 1955, it is thirty to the dollar. His policy to transform Argentina's agrarian economy into an industrial one has the effect of accelerating migration from rural areas to the cities, and increasing the need to feed and offer welfare to these great urban masses. The population of Buenos Aires rises from 4.6 million in 1946 to 6.8 million in 1960 and 8 million in 1970. To remain in power, Perón continuously empowers the workers to shape public policy via public demonstrations and mass movements. On September 16, 1955, Perón himself is deposed by a revolution. He returns from exile eight years later, in 1973, and is again elected to the presidency; his third wife, Estela Martínez, is named to the vice presidency. In July 1974, when Perón dies, she ascends to the presidency. She, in turn, is deposed in March 1976. But it is his second wife, Eva Duarte (1919–52), fondly called "Evita" by the nation, who gains world fame for the role she plays in Perón's government. An ex-actress, she becomes a fanatically adored public figure whose personal mission is the betterment of the life of the country's

workers, whom she calls "los descamisados" (shirtless) because of their poverty. Because of her influence, supposedly, the workers enjoy a 50 percent wage increase, paid vacations, a shorter work day, and medical and retirement benefits. Juan Perón dies in Buenos Aires on July 1, 1974.

1896

1896 New York Puerto Ricans Form Junta. A revolutionary junta is formed in New York to lead the Puerto Rican independence movement.

AUGUST 7, 1896 Cuban Composer Lecuona Is Born. The beloved Cuban composer of popular and semiclassical music, Ernesto Lecuona, is born in Guanabacoa into a family of musical performers. Having been afforded piano lessons from early childhood, Lecuona is composing by the age of eleven and teaching music in the city schools by the age of sixteen. At seventeen, he graduates from the Conservatorio Nacional de Cuba, and later studies with the famous Spanish pianist and musicologist Joaquín Nin. His musical training and virtuosity as a pianist take him to the founding of what becomes a very successful and historically important band, Lecuona's Cuban Boys, which cuts numerous records. Much of the Latin music recording business emanates out of New York during the 1940s, and Lecuona spends considerable time there. Some of his popular compositions are considered standards of Latin music, most noteworthy of which are "Siboney" (the name of a pre-Colombian Indian tribe of Cuba) and "Malagueña" (Girl from Málaga, Spain). These and other songs by Lecuona "cross-over" and become standards of American popular music as well. Lecuona also composes serious pieces, such as his *Rapsodia Negra* (Black Rhapsody) for piano and orchestra, as well as numerous zarzuelas and radio scores. After the triumph of the Cuban Revolution, Lecuona goes into exile in the Santa Cruz de

Tenerife, Canary Islands, where he dies on November 19, 1963.

NOVEMBER 11, 1896 Historian Carlos Castañeda Is Born. Carlos Eduardo Castañeda is born in Ciudad Camargo, Chihuahua, Mexico. He moves with his family to Brownsville, Texas, in 1906, where he receives his early education, graduating as valedictorian from Brownsville High School in 1916. After high school, his scholarship studies at the University of Texas are interrupted by his service in World War I. He receives his B.A. and M.A. from the University of Texas in 1921 and 1923, respectively. In 1923, he is appointed associate professor at the College of William and Mary in Virginia. He returns to the University of Texas in 1927 as a librarian and receives his Ph.D. in history there in 1932. Castañeda is best known for his *Our Catholic Heritage in Texas,* a six-volume history of Texas from 1519 to 1836 and a history of the Catholic Church in Texas from 1836. Castañeda works on the voluminous history from 1936 to 1950. In 1939, he joins the faculty of the history department at the University of Texas and in 1946 he is made full professor. Over the course of his career, he serves at various times as editor of the *Hispanic American Historical Review, The Americas,* and *The Handbook of Latin American Studies.* Over all, Castañeda produces twelve books and more than eighty articles on Mexican and Southwest history. Carlos Castañeda dies in 1958.

DECEMBER 3, 1896 Muralist Xavier Guerrero Is Born in Mexico. Painter Xavier Guerrero is born the son of a house painter in San Pedro de las Colonias, Mexico. Because of his working-class background and his father's union activities, Guerrero develops an ideology of painting as a communal activity. Guerrero also serves as a soldier in the revolution, which contributes to his working-class and nationalist sentiments. In Mexico City from 1921 on, he is involved in mural painting, working with Roberto Montenegro, Diego Rivera, and others on many of their famed mural projects. He becomes a founding member of the Union of Technical Workers, Painters and Sculptors and of various arts. In 1929, he travels to Europe and the Soviet Union, staying abroad for nearly ten years. In 1939 he accompanies David Alfaro Siqueiros on a cultural mission to Chile to paint nearly 400 meters of murals. In 1941, he is awarded a prize for industrial design by the Museum of Modern Art in New York, and in later years he has exhibitions there. Through the 1950s, he continues to paint murals in Mexico, principally in Mexico City, Cuernavaca, and Guadalajara. He dies in Mexico City on August 31, 1974.

DECEMBER 19, 1896 David Siqueiros, Modern Artist and Intellectual, Is Born. Mexican grand master artist, muralist, and controversial intellectual David Alfaro Siqueiros is born in Chihuahua. From 1911 to 1913, Siqueiros studies at the San Carlos Academy in Mexico City and the Open Air Painting School in Santa Anita. He serves with the Constitutionalist forces during the Mexican Revolution. In 1919, he goes to Europe to study on a government grant, during which time he meets Diego Rivera in Paris; both are enthusiastic about French modernist painting. In Barcelona in 1921, Siqueiros publishes his "Manifesto to the Artists in America," in which he explains his ideology about public art and the relationship between art and politics. Back in Mexico in 1922, he begins to execute murals, including those at the National Preparatory School. With Diego Rivera, he founds the Union of Technical Workers, Painters and Sculptors and edits its publication, *El Machete.* He works as a union organizer from 1925 to 1930; in 1930, he is imprisoned for six months in Taxco for his activities but he continues to paint. Siqueiros has his first solo exhibition in 1930 at the Casino Espinel in Mexico City. Also in 1930, he paints murals in Los Angeles, where he becomes interested in using industrial materials in his murals. He is deported from the United States because of his communist activities that same year. During the rest of the 1930s, he travels extensively in Latin America, the United States, and Spain. From 1937 to 1939, Siqueiros serves in the Republican Army in Spain. From 1939 to 1947, he conducts major mural projects in Mexico, Chile, and Cuba. He receives his first retrospective exhibition at the Palace of Fine Arts in Mexico City in 1947. In 1960, he is imprisoned in Mexico for his Communist activities. Upon his release in 1964, Siqueiros begins work on his last grand-scale project, *The March of Humanity,* which is installed at the Siqueiros Cultural Polyforum in Mexico City. In 1966, the same government that had imprisoned him awards him its highest honor, the National Prize for Art. In 1967, he receives the Lenin Peace Prize from the Soviet Union. Upon his death in Cuernavaca on January 6, 1974, his remains are taken to Mexico City and buried at the Rotunda of Illustrious Men. Siqueiros continues to be considered one of the giants of modern art.

1897

1897   Cuban Painter Amelia Peláez Is Born. Painter and ceramist Amelia Peláez is born in Yaguajay, Cuba, one of nine children of a country doctor and his wife. However, she is familiar with the art world, because she is the sister of one of Cuba's most famous poets, Julián del Casal. At the age of fifteen, Peláez begins to study painting with Magadalena Peñarredonda. From 1916 to 1924, she studies at the San Alejandro Academy in Havana, and also with the painter Leopoldo Romañach. She continues her studies in New York at the Art Students' League with George Bridgman, and from 1927 to 1934 she studies in Paris at the Grand Chaumier. She eventually becomes a leader, with René Portocarrero and Wilfredo Lam, of the generation that is to bring Cuban painting into the twentieth century. All three insist on the artist's freedom to reinvent and represent reality. Her solo exhibits include shows in Paris, New York, Havana, and Bogotá. Peláez

wins national awards in Havana and a first prize from the Gulf Caribbean Art Exhibition of the Museum of Fine Arts, Houston, in 1956. Among her most famous paintings is "Hibiscus" (1943), which demonstrates a fusion of native, creole, and imported elements. Peláez also has a distinguished career as a teacher, illustrator for books and magazines, and ceramist. She dies in Havana in 1968.

1897   Otero Appointed Governor. Republican Miguel A. Otero, Jr., is appointed to the governorship of the New Mexico Territory by President William McKinley. (*See also* biography, October 17, 1859.)

FEBRUARY 20, 1897   Telephone Service Begins in Puerto Rico. Sociedad Anónima del Teléfono (Telephone Corporation) begins offering telephone service in San Juan, Puerto Rico.

NOVEMBER 25, 1897   Spain Issues Letter of Autonomy. Spain, upon recognizing the growing interest of the United States in the Caribbean wars of independence, by royal decree issues a letter of autonomy on this date, granting Cuba and Puerto Rico autonomy and home rule. General Weyler is withdrawn from Cuba and his campaign ends.

1898

1898   Cabrera Launches Guatemalan Dictatorship. The despotic, twenty-two-year dictatorship of Manuel Estrada Cabrera begins in Guatemala. His reign is characterized by theft, murder, emptying the treasury, keeping the Indians in peonage, and starving the army. He is overthrown in 1920.

JANUARY 1, 1898   Cuban and Puerto Rican Independence Established. Autonomy in Cuba and Puerto Rico is officially instituted, as is universal suffrage. Cubans and Puerto Ricans are now allowed to legislate their own public affairs through their own bicameral parliaments, and cabinets of secretaries, and other forms of government.

FEBRUARY 15, 1898 U.S. Battleship Destroyed.
The U.S. battleship USS *Maine,* which has been sent to Cuba to protect the lives and property of U.S. citizens, is blown up in the Havana harbor, thus offering the United States a pretext to enter the Cuban war against Spain.

FEBRUARY 18, 1898 Luis Muñoz Marín, Puerto Rican Political Leader, Is Born. Puerto Rican politician and man of letters, Luis Muñoz Marín, is born in San Juan, the son of the patriot of Puerto Rican independence, Luis Muñoz Rivera. Muñoz Marín receives his early education on the island and then attends Georgetown University, where he studies journalism and also earns a degree in law. Besides developing his career as a politician, Muñoz Marín also works as a journalist, serving as publisher of the *Revista de Indians* (Review of the Indies) and editor of various newspapers, including *El Imparcial* (The Impartial), *El Batey* (The Beaten Ground), and *La Democracia* (Democracy). Muñoz Marín also serves as secretary to the resident commissioner for Puerto Rico in Washington, D.C. (1916–18); is a labor organizer; serves in the Secretariat of the Pan American Union; is first elected to the Puerto Rican senate in 1932; and founds the Popular Democratic Party in 1940. In 1941, he is elected president of the senate. He is the first governor of Puerto Rico, from 1949 to 1965, and is one of the principal architects of the Commonwealth of Puerto Rico, a political and governmental organization that establishes Puerto Rico as a "Free Associated State" of the United States—a contradiction in terms that really is a liberal definition of a colony. He is chief architect of "Operation Bootstrap," a program that offers tax incentives for American industries to locate in Puerto Rico and thus contribute to the economic development of the island's population. Muñoz Marín spearheads many reforms and programs that improve the economy, the

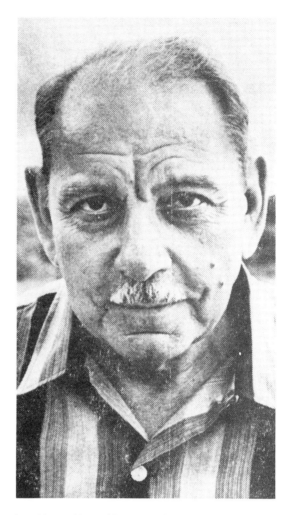

Luis Muñoz Marín. (Courtesy of the Arte Público Press Archives, University of Houston.)

transportation infrastructure, and education and health delivery systems. One constant criticism, however, is that much of the success of his programs and the improvement of the Puerto Rican economy has come at the high cost shifting of its working-class population to the urban centers of the United States, most notably New York City and surrounding areas. Luis Muñoz Marín is a well-read and admired poet and essayist with various books to his credit. In 1982, his autobiography, *Memorias: Autobiografía pública* (Memories: Public Autobiography), is

Luis Muñoz Rivera. (Courtesy of Arte Público Press Archives, University of Houston.)

published posthumously. Muñoz Marín dies of a heart attack on April 30, 1980.

MARCH 20, 1898   Poet Luis Palés Matos Is Born. Puerto Rico's most important poet, Luis Palés Matos, is born in Guayama into a prominent family, and continues in his father Vicente Palés's footsteps as a poet. Palés Matos, although never pursuing a formal education, is a distinguished exponent of modernist poetry in Puerto Rico and goes on to found, with José de Diego, a postmodernist movement called "Diepalismo" (from the combination of their names: "Die" and "Pal"), which advocates the use of onomatopoeia. At the age of seventeen, Palés Matos publishes his first book of poems, *Azaleas*. Despite his leadership in Caribbean letters, only one period of his literary productivity brings him international fame; this comes when he dedicates himself to exploring the exotic sounds and customs of blacks in Puerto Rico, the Caribbean, and Africa as a source of poetic sound and rhythm. In writing his masterpiece, *Tun tun de pasa y grifería* (loosely translated as "Tun Tun of Raisins and Negritude," 1937), Palés Matos demonstrates to Latin America how to exploit onomatopoeia and to

create neologisms based on the native cultures of the Americas. Despite his upper-class origins and the stereotypes that he furthers in this type of poetry, popular bards and the national popular culture, including the educational system, quickly adopt his Afro–Caribbean poems as their own symbols of identity. He is often compared with Cuban mulatto poet, Nicolás Guillén, whose rhythmic verse emerges from the authentic Afro–Caribbean folklore and culture. Palés Matos's collected poems are published as *Poesía, 1915—1956* (1957) and his complete works in two volumes of *Obras (1914—59)* (1984). He dies on February 23, 1959, in Santurce, Puerto Rico. During his lifetime, Palés Matos is celebrated in Puerto Rico; in 1950, he is named poet in residence of the University of Puerto Rico.

APRIL 11, 1898   U.S. Involvement in Cuban Revolution. U.S. president William McKinley refuses to recognize the Cuban revolutionary government, which is making progress against the Spanish military. While on the one hand the McKinley administration is pushing aside the insurgents, on the other hand the U.S. Congress declares war on Spain on April 19, using the pretext of the mysterious explosive destruction of the battleship USS *Maine* in Havana Harbor on February 15. However, via the Teller Amendment, the United States pledges that it has no "intention to exercise sovereignty, jurisdiction, or control over said island except for the pacification thereof, and asserts its determination, when that is accomplished, to leave the government and control of the Island to its people." This pledge is incorporated into the Treaty of Paris in December.

APRIL 19, 1898   U.S. Declares War on Spain. The United States declares war on Spain in support of the Cuban independence movement. The war lasts less than three months, ending on August 12.

MAY 18, 1898   U.S. Army Moves into Puer-

to Rico. U.S. forces invade Puerto Rico during the Spanish–American War. San Juan harbor is bombarded and the American Army occupies the island to welcoming crowds.

AUGUST 12, 1898   Armistice Is Signed. After the United States wins decisive battles, destroying much of the Spanish fleet in Cuba, Puerto Rico, and Spain, the United States sign an armistice in Washington, D.C.

DECEMBER 10, 1898   The Treaty of Paris. Spain signs the Treaty of Paris, freeing Cuba and transferring Puerto Rico and the Philippines to the United States for the sum of $20 million.

Part 4

THE STRUGGLE FOR DEMOCRACY & CULTURAL IDENTITY 1899-1995

1899

1899   Cuban Actor O'Farrill Is Born. Alberto O'Farrill is born in Santa Clara, Cuba. He begins his career as an actor and playwright in Havana in 1921, before emigrating to the United States. In New York O'Farrill is the ubiquitous *negrito* (black face) of *obras bufas cubanas* (Cuban farce) and Cuban zarzuelas who makes a career playing all the major Hispanic stages in New York's stock and itinerant companies. O'Farrill is also an intensely literate man who has been the editor of *Proteo*, a magazine in Havana. In 1927, he is the first editor of New York's *Gráfico* newspaper, which becomes the principal organ for the publication and commentary of literature and theatre. In *Gráfico*, O'Farrill also publishes various stories and essays of his own. Despite his literary interests, as of 1926 none of O'Farrill's dramatic works has been published. He debuts two zarzuelas at the Teatro Esmeralda in Havana in 1921: *Un negro misterioso* (A Mysterious Black Man) and *Las pamplinas de Agapito* (Agapito's Adventures in Pamplona). His other known works all debuted at the Apollo Theater in 1926: one sainete (comedy), *Un doctor accidental* (An Accidental Doctor), and four zarzuelas, *Los misterios de Changó* (The Mysteries of Changó), *Un negro en Adalucía* (A Black Man in Andalusia) *Una viuda como no hay dos* (A Widow like None Other), and *Kid Chocolate*. In most of these, as

in his acting, he seems to have been concerned with Afro–Cuban themes.

1899   Ecuadorean Painter Egas Is Born. The famed Ecuadorean painter Camilo Egas is born in Quito. After secondary school, Egas attends the Academy of Fine Arts in Quito in 1905. Between 1909 and 1909 he receives local recognition by winning awards for his paintings in national competitions. In 1918, he studies at the Academy of Rome on an Ecuadorean government scholarship, and in 1919 he does the same for study at Madrid's San Fernando Academy. In 1922, he studies in Paris, and meets Picasso. In 1924 and 1925, Egas begins showing his works at galleries and exhibitions in Paris, but then returns to Quito in 1926 to teach at the normal school and to serve as art director for the national theater. From that time on, he dedicates his easel to painting indigenist subjects from social and political perspectives. In 1927, he moves to New York, and in 1929 begins teaching art at the New School for Social Research. From 1935 until his death, Egas serves as the director of the art department. During his career, Egas is highly influenced by the Mexican muralists, in particular José Clemente Orozco, and he executes murals as well as easel paintings. Egas exhibits internationally and his works are found in museums around the world. In 1962, he receives an award for artistic merit from the American

Alberto O'Farrill. (Courtesy of Recovering the U.S. Hispanic Literary Heritage Project, University of Houston.)

Academy of Arts and Letters. He dies that same year in New York City.

1899 Pantín Founds Socialist Party. The Partido Obrero Socialista (Socialist Workers Party) is founded in Puerto Rico by Santiago Iglesias Pantín. He introduces the program of the Socialist Party of the United States into the new U.S. colony. After initial disorganization, the party is reestablished in 1915 as part of the Federación de Trabajadores (Workers' Federation). Iglesias Pantín, his union, and its party

promote annexation of Puerto Rico to the United States in order to further their cause of social democracy. The party, nevertheless, never wins an election by itself. Also in 1899, José Celso Barboso founds the Partido Republicano (Republican Party), which presses for Puerto Rico becoming a state of the United States as soon as possible. (*See also* biography, February 22, 1870.)

1899 The United Fruit Company's Influence. The United Fruit Company, headquartered in Boston, Massachusetts, is formed to take over the interests of some twenty companies in Central America. It becomes the largest grower and distributor of fruit in the Americas, inordinately influencing not only the economies but also the politics of the small Central American republics. For the greater part of the twentieth century, Latin–American intellectuals and revolutionaries have pointed to the United Fruit Company as an example of American exploitation of the natural and human resources of Latin America. More recently, the company has emerged as a responsible corporate citizen, paying higher wages and creating educational, social, and living conditions for its workers far superior to those instituted by national companies in Central America. But the extent of penetration and power of the company has been greatly curbed by modern governments in Central America and elsewhere. Its holdings in Cuba have been expropriated by Fidel Castro.

JANUARY 1, 1899 U.S. Institutes Military Rule. The last of the Spanish military forces leaves Cuba and Puerto Rico, and the United States immediately institutes a military government in each island. Independence is not recognized or instituted; the United States explains that a period of political preparation is needed before the islands can govern themselves. In the case of Puerto Rico, to this day it remains a colony of the United States. The wars that the Cubans and Puerto Ricans have fought so long and so valiantly for independence are almost for naught; they are once again colonies of a world power. They were better off with the autonomy they had gained from Spain a year earlier.

FEBRUARY 6, 1899   Ramón Novarro, Silent Film Idol, Is Born. Ramón Novarro, famous silent film actor, is born the son of a dentist in Durango, Mexico. His name by baptism is Ramón Gil Samaniega. In 1913, he moves to Los Angeles, California, with his family as refugees from the Mexican Revolution. The family experiences abject poverty, which leads Novarro to work as a child, including taking small acting and dancing parts on screen and stage. Largely because of his ability as a dancer, he is cast in a leading role in the 1923 film, *Prisoner of Zenda.* Novarro quickly becomes a success as a romantic matinee idol, rivaled only by Rudolph Valentino in sexy Latin and Arab lover roles. Among his notable films are *Ben Hur* (1926); *The Student Prince* (1927); *Son of India* and *Mata Hari* (1932); and *The Cat and the Fiddle* (1934). His last film is *Heller in Pink Tights* (1960). On October 31, 1968, Novarro is found dead at his home after having been beaten by intruders.

JUNE 13, 1899   Carlos Chávez y Ramírez, Composer of Classical Music, Is Born. Mexico's leading composer of classical music, Carlos Chávez y Ramírez, is born in a suburb of Mexico City, one of six children raised by a widowed mother. Chávez's first music lessons comes from his older brother, who is studying piano with the famed composer, Manuel M. Ponce; Carlos later studies with Ponce himself, from 1909 to 1914. For the most part he is a self-taught composer. He begins writing piano pieces and arrangements for popular songs when he is sixteen and completes a symphony by the age of nineteen. In 1921, he begins presenting his own works and wins a government commission for a ballet, *El nuevo fuego* (The New Fire), which is based on an Aztec story. From 1926 to 1928, Chávez lives in New York City, where he composes a great deal of abstract music and works with American composer and exponent

Carlos Chávez. (Courtesy of the National Institute for Fine Arts, Mexico City.)

of experimental music, Edgard Varese. In 1928, he returns to Mexico City to direct the newly founded Orquesta Sinfónica de México and to lead the Conservatorio Nacional de Música. In 1931, he debuts his ballet *H.P.* (Horsepower), which has been written while he is in New York. Over the years he writes significant pieces of chamber and symphonic music. During the 1930s, infused with revolutionary spirit and class consciousness, Chávez offers concerts for workers, producing such works as *Sinfonía India* (Indian Symphony); *Obertura Republicana* (Republican Overture); *Cantos de Méjico* (Mexican Cantos), based on folk songs and instruments; *Llamadas* (Calls), a "proletarian symphony"; and *Xochipilli–Macuilxochitl,* in which he attempts to recreate ancient Aztec music. During the 1940s, his most productive decade as a composer, he writes the ballet *La Hija de Cólquide* (The Daughter of Colchis) for Martha Graham (who produces it as *Dark Meadow*), a great deal of choral music, concertos, and chamber music. From 1947 to 1952, Chávez serves as the director of the Instituto Nacional de Bellas Artes (National Fine Arts Institute). After leaving the institute, he composes five more symphonies and his only opera, *The Visitors,* which premieres at Columbia University in New York in 1957. Chávez is considered to have been the most important unifying force in Mexican serious music.

AUGUST 24, 1899 Writer and Poet Borges Born in Argentina. World-famous short-story writer and poet Jorge Luis Borges is born in Buenos Aires, Argentina, the son of a lawyer and teacher, Jorge Guillermo Borges, and a translator, Leonor Acevedo Suárez. After receiving his early education in Argentina, Borges studies at and graduates from College Calvin in Geneva, Switzerland, in 1918. Although always developing his career as a writer, Borges works as a librarian in Buenos Aires from 1937 to 1946, and as a teacher and lecturer off and on for the rest of his life at institutions of higher learning in the United States and Argentina. Borges is best known for his tightly wrought short stories that deal with metaphysical and philosophical problems. They are at once entertaining and challenging while obviously based on a tremendous amount of erudition. His best-known collection, *Ficciones* (Fictions), published in various editions from 1935 to 1944, has been translated into numerous languages and has been seen as an international literary metaphor, drawing from the literary traditions of people who speak English, French, German, or Spanish. It is commonplace, upon commenting on *Ficciones* and Borge's other works, to compare him with Franz Kafka, James Joyce, and other world masters, but the comment always is added that his style is unique. His style, in fact, gives rise to the term "Borgesian" in literary criticism, applicable works that create magical worlds similar to those that Borges invented in his stories. Borges' seems to be as influential in United States literature as he is in Latin–American literature. Such contemporary greats of U.S. letters as Raymond Carver, Donald Barthelme, John Gardner, and John Barth readily acknowledge Borges's influence. In addition to *Ficciones,* Borges publishes numerous other short story collections, including

Historia universal de la infamia (Universal History of Infamy, 1935), *El jardín de los senderos que se bifurcar* (The Garden with the Paths that Part, 1941), *El Aleph* (The Aleph, 1949), *El informe de Brodie* (Dr. Brodie's Report, 1970), *El congreso* (The Congress of the World, 1971), and *Veinticinco de agosto y otros cuentos de Jorge Luis Borges* (August 25 and Other Stories by Jorge Luis Borges, 1983). Borges is also an important poet in Latin America, one of the leaders of the school of "Ultraísmo" or Ultimatism, very much in the modernist vanguard. At the end of his career, he has some fifteen collections of verse to his credit. Finally, and also as important, is Borges's renown as a productive essayist, whose intelligence ponders the depths of philosophy, literary criticism, and linguistics. He especially turns his attention to evaluating Argentina's literary heritage, with studies on poets José Hernández, Leopoldo Lugones, gaucho literature, and other relevant topics. During his career, Borges is honored with the highest awards for literature offered by Argentina, the United States, European countries, and Latin–American countries. Although his name is repeatedly considered for the Nobel Prize, he is never accorded that honor. Borges dies of liver cancer in Geneva, Switzerland, on June 14, 1986.

AUGUST 26, 1899 Rufino Tamayo, Mexican Painter, Is Born. Mexican painter Rufino Tamayo is born in Oaxaca into a Zapotec Indian family. Upon being orphaned in 1911, Tamayo moves to Mexico City, where he works for an aunt selling produce at the La Merced market. He studies part-time at the San Carlos Academy and becomes associated with Roberto Montenegro and his belief in cultural nationalism. In 1921, Tamayo is appointed head of the Department of Ethnographic Drawing at the National Archeological Museum. From 1928 to 1930, he teaches at the National School of Fine Arts and at the San Carlos Academy. From 1930 to 1949, Tamayo lives in New York City and exhibits at galleries there; he also works for a time for the WPA. During the

1930s and 1940s he enjoys various one-man exhibitions in Mexico, and has his first retrospective at the Palace of Fine Arts in 1948. In 1957, Tamayo moves to Paris, but he remained active internationally as a muralist. Tamayo's paintings have been exhibited all over the world in museums and major biannual shows. His honors include the Grand Prize for Painting of the Sao Paulo Biennial (1953), Chevalier de la Légion d'Honneur (1956), Guggenheim International Award (1960), American Academy of Arts and Letters (1961), and others. Tamayo returns to Mexico in 1964, where he receives the National Prize for Fine Arts that same year. The Rufino Tamayo Museum of Contemporary Art is inaugurated in 1974 in Mexico City to house his collection of contemporary European and American art; Tamayo bequeaths his collection of pre-Columbian art to the people of Oaxaca for their Museum of Pre-Hispanic Art in 1981. Tamayo dies on June 24, 1991, in Mexico City.

OCTOBER 19, 1899 Guatemalan Novelist Asturias Is Born. Nobel Prize-winning novelist Miguel Angel Asturias is born in Guatemala City, Guatemala. The son of a Supreme Court magistrate, Asturias is raised in a political household and, as a student and writer, he becomes directly involved in politics, but it is the politics of opposition, most notably to the dictatorship of Manuel Estrada Cabrera. He receives a law degree from the University of San Carlos in Guatemala in 1923, and later studies anthropology at the Sorbonne (1923–28) during a forced exile from Guatemala, when he is actually stripped of Guatemalan citizenship because of his political activity against the dictatorship. Abroad, and later back in Guatemala, he works as a journalist; he is later elected to political office in Guatemala and still later appointed a diplomat abroad. Although he is the author of at least eight books of poems and various anthropological studies of the Central American Indians, their religion, and their legends, Asturias is best known for his novels. The most celebrated of his novels are *El señor Presidente* (Mr.

Novelist Miguel Angel Asturias. (Courtesy of Arte Público Press Archives, University of Houston.)

President, 1946) and *Hombres de Maíz* (Men of Corn, 1949). The former is a scathing but poetic indictment of Latin–American dictators, while the latter penetrates the mind and culture of Guatemalan Indians as their world view and survival is threatened by the interests of farmers and others who exploit the land. In these and his other novels and poetry, Asturias often blends the mythology and folklore of the Indians with surrealism and social critique. Asturias's other novels are a trilogy made up of works on the theme of "banana republics"— *Viento fuerte* (String Wind, 1950), *El papá verde* (The Green Father, 1954), and *Los ojos de los enterrados* (The Eyes of the Buried, 1960)— and *Mulata de tal* (Mulata, 1963). Asturias receives the Nobel Prize in 1967. He dies in 1974, leaving behind a large legacy of creative writing, ethnographic studies, and even children's stories. He dies in Madrid on June 9, 1974.

DECEMBER 31, 1899 Composer Silvestre Revueltas Is Born. The famed Mexican composer of serious music, Silvestre Revueltas, is born in Santiago, Papasquiaro, Durango. At the age of eight he begins studying the violin; in 1911, he studies at Durango's Instituto Juárez and later in Mexico City with José Rocambruna and with Rafael J. Tello. From 1918 to 1920, he studies at St. Edwards College, in Austin, Texas, and also spends a period of time in Chicago under Félix Browski at the Chicago Musical College. Beginning in 1920, he performs violin recitals, and participates in musical programs directed by Carlos Chávez y Ramírez, the greatest Mexican composer of his time. He also directs theater orchestras in the southern and southwestern United States. In 1928, he is named assistant director of the Orquesta Sinfónica de México by Carlos Chávez. In 1937, Revueltas tours Spain and Europe, directing his own symphonic works and concertos. Upon returning to Mexico, he concentrates on composing rather than teaching and directing. During the remainder of his career, he also writes numerous film scores. He dies in 1940.

1900

1900 Civilians Govern Puerto Rico. The Foraker Act establishes a civilian government in Puerto Rico under U.S. dominance. The law allows for islanders to elect their own House of Representatives, but not to have a vote in Washington. The newly founded (1899) Partido Republicano (Republican Party) wins the elections in 1900 and 1902 under the banner of annexation, pushing for rapid admission to United States statehood. A Puerto Rican Socialist Party also is founded.

1900 Mexicans Hired by Railroads. At the turn of the century, American railway companies begin recruiting Mexican workers at El Paso for six-month contracts to construct lines in the north. The most active companies hiring Mexican labor are the Southern Pacific Railroad and the Atchison, Topeka and Santa Fe, which heavily recruit workers to lay track in California. It is estimated that some sixteen thousand Mexicans are working on the railroad in the Southwest and West by 1908. The importation of Mexican labor by the railroads

Silvestre Revueltas. (Courtesy of the National Institute for Fine Arts, Mexico City.)

reaches its peak between 1910 and 1912. During World War I, thousands of Mexican workers are brought to the Midwest to build railways there. During World War II, the Bracero Program authorizes further recruitment of Mexican workers for the railroads; during the war 80,273 Mexican nationals are employed on some thirty-two American railroads. More than half of these work on the Southern Pacific and Santa Fe. By April 1946, all of the Bracero Program workers are repatriated.

1900 Writer José Enrique Rodó Publishes Masterpiece. Rodó's masterpiece, *Ariel,* is published, and becomes the founding basis for a movement called Arielism. (*See also* biography, July 15, 1872.)

MAY 20, 1900 Writer Lydia Cabrera Born in Cuba. Short-story writer and folklorist Lydia Cabrera is born and educated in Havana, Cuba. She emigrates to the United States in 1960 after the Cuban Revolution. Throughout her career both in Cuba and in Miami, where she has resided since 1960, Cabrera collects, studies, and publishes Afro–Cuban legends and tales. She also studies and documents Nañigo secret societies and other manifestations of African religious and Catholic syncretism. Most of Cabrera's fiction is based on Afro–Cuban folklore that surrounds her as she grows up. In addition, her narrative style is direct and owes much to the modes of oral performance and delivery of Afro–Cuban folklore. In both Cuba and the United States, Cabrera's work enriches literature by introducing the themes and culture of a previously ignored and misunderstood base of Cuban and Caribbean literature and culture. Her first, most groundbreaking collection, *Cuentos negros de Cuba* (Black Tales from Cuba) is published in Havana in 1940, although it was written and already circulating as early as 1936. Among her important fiction works are: *Ayapá: Cuentos de Jicotea* (Ayapá: Stories from Jicotea) in 1971, *Francisco y Francisca: Chascarrillos de negros viejos* (Francisco and Francisca: Spicy Tales of Old Black Men) in 1976, and *Cuentos para adultos, niños y retrasados mentales* (Stories for Grown-Ups, Children and the Mentally Retarded) in 1983.

SUMMER 1900 Cuban Fencer Wins Medal. Cuba's Ramón Fonst takes a gold medal in fencing at the Olympic Games in Paris, France.

1901

1901 Puerto Rican Journalist and Activist Jesús

Colón Is Born. Jesús Colón, noted Puerto Rican journalist and political activist, is born into a working-class, Afro–Puerto Rican family in Cayey, Puerto Rico. Jesús Colón's writings are considered to be landmarks in the development of Puerto Rican literature in the continental United States; he is one of the first writers to become well known through his use of English, his identification with the working class, and his ideas on race. These three factors in the essays that he writes in the 1940s and 1950s make him a clear forerunner of the Nuyorican writers who appear two decades later. At the age of sixteen, Colón stows away on a ship that lands at Brooklyn. In New York, he works in a series of jobs that expose him to the exploitation and abuse of lower-class and unskilled workers. He becomes involved in literary and journalistic endeavors while working as a laborer, trying to establish a newspaper, and writing translations of English-language poetry. As he strives to develop his literary and journalistic career, he encounters racial prejudice, mainly because of his dark skin color. Despite discrimination, he is active in white and black community and political activities. Colón becomes a columnist for the *Daily Worker,* the publication of the national office of the Communist Party, as an outgrowth of these activities and his literary interests. He also founds and operates a publishing house, Hispanic Publishers (Editorial Hispánica), which offers history and literary books, as well as political information, in Spanish. In 1952 and 1969, Colón runs for public office on the Communist Party ticket, but is unsuccessful. A selection of Jesús Colón's newspaper columns and essays is collected and published in 1961 in book form under the title of *A Puerto Rican in New York and Other Sketches.* In 1993, another collection is published under the title of *The Way It Was and Other Sketches.* In these essays, or sketches, as Colón preferred to call them, his major themes are the creation and development of a political consciousness, his own literary development and worth, advocacy for the work-

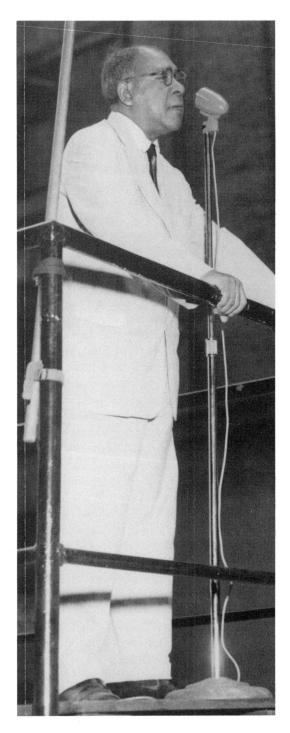

Jesús Colón, c. 1960. (Courtesy of the Center for Puerto Rican Studies Library, Hunter College, CUNY.)

ing-class poor, and the injustices of capitalist society in which racial and class discrimination are all-too-frequent and individual worth seems not to exist. The collections are richly expressive of a socially conscious and humanistic point of view. Colón dies in 1974.

1901   Treaty Permits U.S. to Build Canal. The Hay–Paunceforte Treaty is signed, permitting the United States to build and fortify a transisthmian canal. The Walker Commission recommends that the United States pursue the Nicaraguan route at an estimated cost of $189 million, as opposed to the $149 million that the Panama route would cost. The latter figure does not include the $109 million that the New Panama Canal Company will want for its rights and property. With later negotiations and jockeying for position by all interested parties, including the governments of Colombia, Nicaragua, and Costa Rica, the New Panama Canal Company drops its price to $40 million, causing the Walker Commission to change its recommendation to the Panama route. In June 1902, the Spooner amendment to the Hepburn bill authorizes the president to pursue the Panama route first; if this proves unsuccessful, the president would be permitted to turn to Nicaragua. Under Theodore Roosevelt, the 1903 Hay–Herrán Treaty grants the United States the right to build a canal in a six-mile-wide zone across Panama in return for a $10 million cash payment and an annual subsidy of $250,000.

1901   Workers Group Joins AFL. The Federación Libre de los Trabajadores (Workers Labor Federation) affiliates with the American Federation of Labor; the AFL has thus broken from its usual policy of exclusion toward nonwhites.

MARCH 1, 1901   Cuba and the Platt Amendment. The Platt Amendment is passed by The United States Congress. Drafted by and named

Senator Orville Platt. (Courtesy of the Library of Congress Prints & Photographs Division.)

Tomás Estrada Palma, 1902. (Courtesy of the Library of Congress Prints & Photographs Division.)

for Republican Senator from Connecticut, Orville Platt, the measure, an amendment to the Army Appropriation Act of 1901, comes as a total surprise to Cubans who, still under U.S. military occupation, believe they have negotiated their complete independence from Spain and the United States as a result of the Spanish–American War. The Platt Amendment proscribes U.S.–Cuba relations by pledging the republic to a low public debt; preventing it from signing any treaty that impairs U.S. interests; granting the United States intervention rights to protect life, liberty, and property; and granting the U.S. the right to construct naval facilities. Before withdrawing from Cuba, U.S. authorities ensure that the Platt Amendment is annexed to the 1901 Cuban constitution and formalized by treaty two years later. The principles of the Platt Amendment are duplicated in the Hay–Bunau–Varilla Treaty with Panama in 1903.

DECEMBER 28, 1901   Cuba Elects Palma. Tomás Estrada Palma is elected president of a nominally independent Cuba under a constitutional election, but also under the shadow of the Platt Amendment.

1902

1902   Alvarez Bravo, Mexican Photographer, Is Born. Famed Mexican photographer Manuel Alvarez Bravo is born in Mexico City into a family of painters and photographers. From 1915 to 1918 he studies accounting and works for the Mexican Treasury, but gives that up to study art at the San Carlos Academy. He begins his career in photography in 1923 after meeting the German photographer Hugo Brehme. Alvarez Bravo associates with the great Mexican muralists Diego Rivera and Pablo O'Higgins, and, under Rivera's direction, he photographs works of the great muralists for Frances Toor's historically important book *A Treasury of Mexican Folkways,* 1947. His first one-person exhibition takes place in 1932 at the Galería Posada in Mexico City. In 1935, he exhibits at the Palace of Fine Arts in Mexico City. After meeting French poet André Breton, one of the founders of surrealism, Alvarez Bravo participates in surrealist exhibitions in Mexico City and Paris in 1938. From the 1930s through the 1950s he works as a cameraman in Mexican films with such greats as directors Sergei

Eisenstein, Luis Buñuel, and John Ford. In 1959, he cofounds a fund for the publication of Mexican art. In 1980, he organizes and serves as director of the Museum of Mexican Photography.

1902 Argentine Painter Forner Is Born. Painter Raquel Forner is born in Buenos Aires, Argentina. After studying at the Academia Nacional de Bellas Artes in Buenos Aires in 1922, Forner begins extensive travels through Europe, North America, Latin America, and Africa. She studies at the Othon Friesz Art School in Paris from 1929 to 1930. Forner comes to the forefront in Argentina in the 1930s with a series of scenes from the Spanish Civil War. Although painted in a highly personal surrealist style, her apocalyptic visions of the war are very dramatic. Her more recent work has turned to a science fiction interpretation of the cosmos, as exemplified by her "Astroseres Negros" (Black Astrobeings, 1961). Most of Forner's solo exhibitions have taken place in Argentina, with a few exceptions; the Organization of American States dedicates a solo show to her in 1957. Her awards include national prizes in Argentina, a Gold Medal from the International Exhibition in Paris in 1937, and the Press Prize for the Mexico City Biennial in 1958.

1902 Cuban Independence. Cuba declares its independence from the United States.

1902 The Reclamation Act. The Reclamation Act is passed in the United States, dispossessing many Hispanic–Americans of their land.

1902 Wilfredo Lam, Modern Artist, Born in Cuba. Cuban painter Wilfredo Lam, one of the world's masters of modern art, is born in Sagua La Grande, Cuba, into a family of mixed Chinese, African, and European heritage. He attends the Academy of San Alejandro in Havana from 1918 to 1920, and from 1920 to 1923 begins exhibiting in the Salon of the Association of Painters and Sculptors in Hava-

na. From 1923 to 1930 he studies with the curator of the Prado Museum, Fernández Alvarez de Sotomayor, and at the Free Academy of the Alhambra in Granada, Spain. In Paris in the late '30s and early '40s, Lam associates with Pablo Picasso, André Breton, and Benjamin Péret, and also becomes connected with the surrealists. During the years of World War II, he travels throughout the Caribbean and is greatly influenced by Afro–Caribbean folk arts and religion. His famous *The Jungle* (1943), in fact, is inspired by the black culture and native flora in Cuba. With various stints in New York, he finally settles in Paris in 1952. By the 1960s, his international reputation is well established and he receives major awards, including the Guggenheim International Award in 1964–65. His work is in major museum collections throughout the world and has been the subject of prestigious retrospectives in Amsterdam, Paris, Havana, and Brussels, among other cities. He dies in 1982.

MAY 1902 Cuba Breaks with United States. Cuba declares its independence from the United States. Military Governor Leonard Wood turns over the government to President Tomás Estrada Palma and returns to the United States. During his four-year term, Estrada Palma signs a reciprocal trade agreement with the United States, in 1903, under which Cuban sugar is given a 20 percent reduction in tariffs—an arrangement that lasts up until the Castro era. He also persuades Washington to give up its claims on numerous coaling and naval bases, with the exception of Guantanamo Bay and a smaller site, which is relinquished in 1912. The United States holds steadfastly to the Guantanamo Naval Base to this day.

JULY 10, 1902 Cuban Poet Nicolás Guillén Is Born. Cuba's greatest poet of the twentieth century, Nicolás Guillén, is born in Camagüey. The son of middle-class mulattoes, Nicolás, a silversmith and newspaper editor, and Argelia, Guillén is educated in the provinces. He attends the University of Havana from 1920 to 1921, where he has intended to study law. Instead, economic hardship forces him to abandon his studies and work as a journalist. This also is the period when he begins to publish his poetry. Journalism took him to Spain during the civil war to serve as a correspondent and to various countries of Europe and Latin America. An early socialist, Guillén becomes for all practical purposes, the poet laureate of Communist Cuba. Under Communism, he serves as the editor in chief of *La gactea de Cuba* (The Cuban Gazette), the official magazine of the Cuban National Union of Writers and Artists. In 1953, Guillén is accorded the Stalin Prize and, in 1964, the Lenin Peace Prize, both from the Soviet Union. During the last twenty years of his life, he receives the highest awards from Cuba, Haiti, and Bulgaria. Guillén's long trajectory as a poet takes him from modernism to an Afro–Cuban and mulatto style, to a pan-Caribbean and pan-Latin American style as his appreciation and hopes extend progressively to the uniting of all working-class and postcolonial peoples and an exploration of their art and culture. Guillén is best known for his poems that build upon the music and folklore of Afro–Caribbean peoples, capturing their sounds, dialects, and spirituality. His two principal influences when he is defining his poetic voice and breaking the barriers of conventional language and structure are the Spanish poet Federico García Lorca and the American poet Langston Hughes, both of whom he knew before they died. Of Guillén's forty-some books and collections of poetry, his best known and most highly regarded are the following: *Motivos del son* (Motifs of Sound, 1930), *Sóngoro cosongo* (no translation, 1931), *West Indies Ltd.: Poemas* (1934), and *El gran zoo* (The Great Zoo, 1967). In 1974, two large volumes of his complete poetry are published under the title, *Obra poética, 1920–1972* (Poetic Works, 1920–1972). Throughout his career, various collections of selected poems are published. He dies on July 16, 1989, in Havana.

1903

MARCH 12, 1903   University of Puerto Rico.
The University of Puerto Rico is founded by expanding the Normal School in Río Piedras. Over the years, it offered more and more degrees in varying disciplines and extends to campuses in various parts of the island. It starts its College of Liberal Arts in 1910, Agricultural and Mechanical College in Mayagüez in 1911, Law School and School of Pharmacy in 1913, School of Education in 1925, Business Administration School in 1926, and School of Social Work in 1934.

JUNE 1903   Arizona Copper Miners Strike.
One of the earliest and most important copper mine strikes in the Southwest occurs the first two weeks in June in Arizona, when Mexican and Mexican–American workers walk out. The Clifton–Morenci Strike fails because Anglo workers do not join the Mexicans in the walkout and because a major flood created havoc in Clifton on June 9.

AUGUST 20, 1903   La Chata Noloesca, Stage Personality, Is Born. Beatriz Escalona, known by her stage name of La Chata Noloesca (a rearranged spelling of Escalona), is the greatest stage personality to come out of U.S. Hispanic communities. Born on this date in San Antonio, Texas, Escalona is discovered while working as an usherette and box office cashier at the Teatro Nacional. She becomes associated with the Spanish–Cuban troupe of Hermanos Areu—she marries José Areu—and plays everything from melodrama to vaudeville with them, beginning in 1920, when she makes her stage debut in El Paso. Over the course of the 1920s, Escalona develops and perfects her comic persona of the streetwise maid, a *peladita*, or underdog character, that maintains a spicy and satirical banter. By 1930, La Chata Noloesca has split from the Areus and formed her own company, Atracciones Noloesca; she continues to tour the Southwest and northern Mexico. In

Vaudeville actress Beatriz "La Chata Noloesca" Escalona and Pedro "Ramirín" González. (Courtesy of the Arte Público Press Archives, University of Houston.)

1936 she reforms her company in her native San Antonio and sets out to weather the Depression by performing in Tampa, Chicago, and New York—as well as in Puerto Rico and Cuba—as the Compañía Mexicana. La Chata's novel idea is to bring to the Cubans, Puerto Ricans, and others Mexican vaudeville, music, folklore, and her own brand of humor. In 1941, the company puts down roots in New York for a stretch of nine years, during which time it is a mainstay on the Hispanic vaudeville circuit comprising the Teatro Hispano, the Teatro Puerto Rico, the Teatro Triboro, and the 53rd Street Theater. Back in San Antonio, she periodically performs for special community events until her death in 1980.

NOVEMBER 1, 1903 The Hay–Bunau–Varilla Convention. The Hay–Bunau–Varilla Convention between the United States and Panama is signed. It prevents Panama from pursuing an independent foreign policy and incurring excessive foreign debt and grants the United States rights to construct sanitation facilities in the terminal cities and to intervene in Panama to maintain internal order.

NOVEMBER 2, 1903 Panama, U.S. Negotiate on Canal. Panama rebels against Colombia in order to gain its independence and negotiate separately with the United States for the construction of a canal. Signed earlier in the year, the Hay–Herrán Treaty granted the United States the right to build a canal in a six-mile-wide zone in Panama in exchange for a payment of $10 million and an annual subsidy of $250,000. The Colombian senate, however, rejects the treaty and calls for new negotiations in order to obtain greater financial considerations from the United States. Two days after Panama's declaration of independence from Colombia, the United States recognizes the new government.

1904

1904 Painter Andrés de Santa María Becomes Director. De Santa María is appointed director of the School of Fine Arts in Bogotá, where he also founds the Professional School of Industrial and Fine Arts. (*See also* biography, 1860.)

1904 Roosevelt's Corollary to Monroe Doctrine. President Theodore Roosevelt enunciates his famous "Corollary" to the Monroe Doctrine to discourage interventions in the Americas by foreign powers. It also implies the

Political cartoon satirizing the United States' Theodore Roosevelt fomenting Panamanian independence and pushing Colombia out of the way of canal negotiations. (Courtesy of the Library of Congress Prints & Photographs Division.)

intention of the United States to exercise a supervisory role over the internal affairs of the countries of the Americas, thus underpinning its continuous interventionist policies.

1904 Union Party Takes Power in Puerto Rico. Under the leadership of the patriot of independence, Luis Muñoz Rivera, the Partido Unión (Union Party) is founded in Puerto Rico. The party postulates three options—1) United States statehood, 2) autonomy, or 3) a dependent republic—as a final solution for Puerto Rico. In the meantime, a maximum of self-government is sought. The party stays in power from 1904 to 1924. One of its major successes is the passage of the Jones Act by the United States Congress in 1917, extending U.S. citizenship to Puerto Ricans.

MARCH 26, 1904 Actor and Director "El Indio" Fernández Is Born. Emilio "El Indio" Fernández, famous director and actor, is born in El Seco, Coahuila, Mexico. One of the most important figures of Mexican cinema, he is born to a Spanish Mexican father and Indian mother (hence the nickname, "El Indio"). At nineteen he takes part in the Mexican Revolution; in 1923 he is sentenced to twenty years of imprisonment, but escapes to California. There he plays bit parts and supporting roles until returning to Mexico first as an actor, debuting in the role of an Indian in *Janitizio* (1934), and then as Mexico's most prominent director. His film *María Candelaria* wins Grand Prize at Cannes and *La Perla/The Pearl* wins the International Prize at San Sebastián. As a Hollywood actor he has a few notable parts in Sam Peckinpah films. Among the films he directs are *Soy puro mexicano* (I am Full-blooded Mexican, 1942); *Flor silvestre* (Wildflower) and *María Candelaria* (1943); *Bugambilla* (Bougainvillea, 1944); *La perla/The Pearl* (Mexico and U.S., 1946); *El gesticulador* (The Gesticulator, 1957); and *A Loyal Soldier of Pancho Villa* (U.S., 1966). He is an actor in *The Reward* (1965); *The Appaloosa* and *Return of the Seven* (1966); *A Covenant with Death* and *The War*

Wagon (1967); *The Wild Bunch* (1969); *Pat Garrett and Billy the Kid* (1973); *Bring Me the Head of Alfredo García* (1974); *Lucky Lady* (1975); *Under the Volcano* (1984); and *Pirates* (1986). Fernández dies in 1986.

SUMMER 1904 Olympic Gold Medalists. Cuban teammates Ramón Fonst, Manuel Díaz, Carlos Tatham, and Albertson Van Zo Post take gold medals in individual and team fencing at the Olympic Games in St. Louis, Missouri.

JULY 12, 1904 Chilean Pablo Neruda, Poet and Nobel Laureate, Is Born. One of the greatest poets of the twentieth century, Pablo Neruda is born in the backwoods town of Parral, Chile, where he attends local schools under his given name, Ricardo Eliezer Neftalí Reyes y Basoalto (he changes his name legally to the pseudonym in 1946). Although his father, a railroad worker, and his mother do not encourage his interest in poetry, Neruda's talent as a boy is discovered by the Nobel laureate Gabriela Mistral and is encouraged by her. In the 1920s, Neruda attends the Instituto Tecnológico and, in 1926, the University of Chile. The next year, he serves as Chilean consul in Rangoon, Burma, and continues in the foreign service until 1944, serving in Java, Siam, and Cambodia, as well as in Madrid, Mexico City, and Buenos Aires. In 1945, Neruda begins serving in the Chilean senate as a Communist, and he agitates against the president of Chile until, in 1948, he has to flee to Mexico to avoid arrest. From 1945 to 1953, he lives in Mexico and also travels extensively in Europe and Red China. He returns to Chile in 1953. In 1970, he is nominated for the presidency of the Chilean Communist Party. Under Salvador Allende, Neruda serves as ambassador to France (1971–72). He dies on September 23, 1973, of heart failure following an operation for prostate cancer. Neruda's career as a writer spans many decades and includes a evolution from modernism to surrealism to the personal minimalist style of his last decades. This evolution also mirrors his political trajectory from the general idealism of youth to an leader in the Chilean Communist Party, and the fulfillment of his dreams when Salvador Allende is elected. Neruda's early book, *Veinte poemas de amor y una canción desesperada* (Twenty Love Poems and a Song of Despair, 1924) is an unabashed success in the world of Hispanic literature, and one of the most reprinted, recited, and best loved collections of poetry in Spanish to this date. This modernist work revolutionizes the writing of love poetry in the Spanish language, not only does he compare woman's body with nature, he elevates it to a universal force. But it is Neruda's work in *Residencia en la tierra* (Residence on Earth, Vol I: 1925–1931; Vol. II: 1931–1935) that brings him recognition as a leading poet of Spanish America and Spain. In these largely surrealistic poems, Neruda portrays a world that is falling apart, riddled by chaos and incomprehensible. Some critics see these poems as foreshadows of World War II and existentialism. It is said that Communism rescues Neruda from the despair that he feels in *Residencia en la tierra* and opens up new paths for his poetry. He comes to believe that the work of art, when rooted in human need, is inseparable from the historic and political context and process. From this point on, Neruda's poetry, and his prose as well, promote social change. Neruda explains his poetic and political ideology in his poetry book, *Canto general* (General Canto, 1950), an epic poem about the struggle for justice in the New World. The poem has the resonance and epic formula that make it a public poem appropriate for performance before masses of people; it is a type of poetry mural, similar to or perhaps greater in scope than the works of Rivera, Siqueiros, and Orozco. After 1953, when Neruda is again in Chile, he produces a variety of poetic genres: love poetry, as in *Cien sonetos de amor* (One Hundred Love Sonnets, 1959); nature poetry, as in *Las piedras de Chile* (The Stones of Chile, 1961); public and epic poetry, as in *Incitación al Nixonicidio y alabanza de la Revolución Chilena* (Inciting Nixonocide and Praise of the Chilean

Revolution, 1974); and numerous minimalist odes in very clear, direct language. Neruda writes more than fifty books of poetry, some of which have been compiled in various collections; as yet, no one has collected all of Neruda's works between two covers. Included among his numerous prizes are the Chilean National Prize (1945), the Lenin and Stalin Peace Prize (1953), and the Nobel Prize (1971).

DECEMBER 26, 1904   Novelist Carpentier Born in Cuba. Alejo Carpentier, one of Latin America's most outstanding novelists, is born in Havana, Cuba. Trained and experienced as an journalist, an ethnomusicologist, and a professor, Carpentier develops his career as a writer of fiction along with his other pursuits while in Cuba and during his exile from 1943 to 1959. He returns to Cuba for the triumph of the revolution. Throughout his prose fiction, Carpentier examines native culture in the Caribbean with particular attention to Afro–Cuban history, literature, and music. Ever enchanted with the qualities of Latin–American fauna and flora and the cultures that have evolved there, Carpentier is a magic realist who looks for the marvelous and fantastic behind everyday reality. Through his fiction, he is able to study the great social movements of Latin America as embodied by individuals who are swept up in these movements. Among his most noteworthy novels are *El siglo de las luces* (1962), published in translation as *Explosion in a Cathedral*; *Los pasos perdidos* (1953), published in English as *The Lost Steps*; and *El recurso del método* (1974), published in English translation as *Reasons of State*. In *El siglo de las luces,* Carpentier revisits the Haitian revolution and examines Afro–Caribbean culture and history as a uniting force for the whole region. In *El recurso el método*, he turns his attention to a fictional South American dictatorship and its relationship to European and US imperialism. *Los pasos pedidos,* considered his masterpiece, while set in the present, is a search for origins: the origin of music and the origin of civilization. Carpentier dies in Havana on April 24, 1980, after a long illness.

He leaves behind more than two-score books and numerous international prizes.

1905

1905 Antonio Berni, Argentine Painter and Muralist, Is Born. Painter and muralist Antonio Berni is born in Rosario, Argentina, the son of a poor Italian tailor. He studies drawing and painting as a youth in Rosario and, in 1925, wins a scholarship to study abroad, whereupon he travels widely in Europe. He studies at the school of André Lhote and at the Grand Chaumier in Paris. In 1929, he meets French writer Louis Aragon, one of the founders of surrealism, and affiliates with the surrealist movement. Upon his return to Argentina in 1930, he becomes a Communist and begins to develop social realist art. In 1932, he founds the New Realism movement in Argentina. In 1933, he works with the great Mexican muralist, David Alfaro Siqueiros. From 1936 to 1946, Berni teaches at the National School of Fine Arts in Buenos Aires. During the 1930s and 1940s his international reputation grows. From this period he travels up and down the Pacific coast of the Americas, painting scenes of Indian life. During the 1960s, Berni experiments and develops a distinct style in creating collage constructions. One of his most famous is the collage series on the life of *Juanito Laguna,* for which he wins the Grand Award for Etching at the Venice Biennale in 1962. His work is featured in major retrospectives from the 1960s to the 1980s, including such cities as Santiago, Rio de Janeiro, Caracas, and Paris.

1905 O'Gorman, Mexican Muralist, Is Born. Juan O'Gorman, one of the great Mexican muralists and architects, is born in Coyoacán. O'Gorman receives his early education in Guanajuato. He later attends the National Preparatory School in Mexico City and meets Diego Rivera, who is painting his mural *Creación* (Creation) there. O'Gorman graduates as an architect from the National University of Mexico

in 1927. Over his career, O'Gorman evolves from the functionalist architectural ideas of Le Corbusier to the organic architecture of Frank Lloyd Wright. In 1932, O'Gorman becomes a professor at the Polytechnic Institute and, in that function, is responsible for building 28 new public schools. In 1935, he leaves his position to dedicate himself to painting. He starts painting extensively, receiving commissions for murals, such as those at the Mexico City airport, and portraits. In 1950, he is given a solo exhibition at the Palace of Fine Arts, the same year that he designs the famed library of the National University and covers it with a mosaic mural. Another of his famous murals is the *Retablo de la Independencia* (The Altarpiece of Independence) at the Chapultepec Castle, 1960–61. In 1982, he commits suicide.

1905 Palma Resigns. Cuban president Tomás Estrada Palma is greeted with an armed revolt after his reelection to the presidency. After failed negotiations and arbitration, Estrada Palma and his vice president resign, leaving the government without a head. Various Cuban parties encourage the United States to intervene under the provisions of the Platt Amendment. The occupation lasts from 1906 to just after the supervised elections of 1909.

1905 U.S. Moves in Dominican Republic. The assassination of dictator Ulises Heureaux of the Dominican Republic in 1899 leaves the government in chaos and burdened with public debt. Various European governments escalate their means to extract payment on behalf of creditors in their countries. In 1905, to forestall intervention from Europe, the United States forces the Dominicans to accept collection of customs by American officers. To do this, the United States relies on what has come to be called the "Roosevelt Corollary" to the Monroe Doctrine, named for President Theodore Roosevelt upon his invoking the earlier doctrine as justification for intervening in the Dominican Republic to stave off European intervention. American fiscal and political control gradually increases and culminates with the installation of an American military government in 1916. The United States steps in when, in 1916, President Juan Isidro Jiménez resigns and leaves the country without a government.

FEBRUARY 20, 1905 Folklorist and Scholar Campa Is Born. Mexican–American folklorist Arthur León Campa is born in Guaymas, Sonora, Mexico, of American parents. (His father was a Methodist missionary killed by Francisco Villa during the revolution.) Campa is raised in El Paso, Texas. He receives his B.A. and M.A. degrees from the University of New Mexico in 1928 and 1930, respectively, and his Ph.D. in Spanish from Columbia University in 1940. From 1933 to 1942 Campa rises from instructor to full professor at the University of New Mexico. From 1942 to 1945, he serves in World War II as a combat intelligence officer, suffering a back injury and winning a Bronze Star. After the war, he returns to the University of New Mexico. During the postwar years, he serves as a Department of State lecturer in Spain (1953) and as a cultural affairs officer at the U.S. Embassy in Lima, Peru. During the 1960s, he is a language training coordinator for the Peace Corps and directs Peace Corps training projects in Peru, Ecuador, and Venezuela. Among his many fellowships are the Guggenheim and the Rockefeller. He is named to the national academies of scholars in Argentina, Brazil, Chile, Mexico, Peru, and Spain. Campa also served as the regional editor for *Western Folklore* and on various other editorial boards. Campa has won many awards for his numerous books, most of which are pioneering collections and analyses of Hispanic folklore of the Southwest. His last, all-embracing vision is represented by his book, *Hispanic Culture in the Southwest.*

AUGUST 3, 1905 Actress Dolores del Río Is Born. Dolores del Río (Lolita Dolores Martínez Asunsolo López Negrete) is born in Durango, Mexico, and educated in a convent. By age sixteen she is married to writer Jaime del Río. Director Edwin Carewe is struck by her beauty

Arthur León Campa. (Courtesy of the Arte Público Press Archives, University of Houston.)

and invites her to Hollywood where she appears in *Joanna* in 1925. She becomes a star in many silent films but her career suffers from frequent typecasting in ethnic and exotic roles, particularly after the advent of sound. Dissatisfied with Hollywood, she returns to Mexico in 1943 to do many important films of the 1940s, including *María Candelaria* (1943) and John Ford's *The Fugitive* (1947), filmed on location in Mexico. She finally returns to Hollywood in character parts in the 1960s. Her films include *Resurrection* and *The Loves of Carmen* (1927); *Ramona* and *Revenge* (1928); *Evangeline* (1929); *The Bad One* (1930); *The Girl of the Río* (1932); *Flying Down to Río* (1933); *Madame Du Barry* (1934); *In Caliente* (1935); *Devil's Playground* (1937); *Doña Perfecta* (Mexico, 1950); *La cucaracha* (The Cockroach, Mexico, 1958); *Flaming Star* (1960); *Cheyenne Autumn* (1964); and *The Children of Sánchez* (1978). Del Río dies in 1983.

NOVEMBER 17, 1905 Playwright and Diplomat Usigli Born in Mexico. Rodolfo Usigli, considered one of Mexico's greatest playwrights, is born in Mexico City. He begins his artistic education in 1923 at the Escuela Popular

Nocturna de Música y Declamación in Mexico City and from 1935 to 1936 studies at Yale University with a fellowship from the Rockefeller Foundation. He develops a career as a professor of theatre at the National University of Mexico in Mexico City and as a playwright, one of the first to create a dramatic literature based on Mexican national themes. From 1942 to 1972, he serves as a diplomat representing Mexico in France, Lebanon, and Norway. Late in his career, in 1972, he receives Mexico's National Prize for Literature. Rodolfo Usigli is considered one of the modern masters of Mexican theatre, who was able to create a social interaction on stage that realistically addressed the great national questions. One of those grand questions dealt with the problems of creating a modern society in the wake of the Mexican Revolution, a question considered in his highly acclaimed *El gesticulador* (The Gesticulator, 1938), and the trilogy of "crowns": written from the 1940s to the 1960s *Corona de Sombra* (Crown of Shade), *Corona de luz* (Crown of Light) and *Corona de fuego* (Crown of Fire). As a playwright, theorist, and teacher, Rodolfo Usigli is the most important figure in Mexican theatre of the twentieth century.

DECEMBER 11, 1905   Gilbert Roland, the Cisco Kid, Is Born. Famed movie star Gilbert Roland is born in Juárez, Mexico, as Luis Antonio Dámaso de Alonso. He follows his father's footsteps into the bullfighting ring, but turns to acting when the family moves to California. In films from the 1920s through the 1980s, Roland plays Mexican/Hispanic lovers, ranchers, and bandits in both comedic and dramatic films. His most famous role is as Armand in the 1927 hit *Camille*. His most historic role, however, is that of the Cisco Kid in eleven B-pictures, starting in the 1940s. Roland plays the bandit with dignity, showing that he was educated and intelligent: "My Cisco Kid might have been a bandit, but he fought for the poor and was a civilized man in the true sense of the word." The Cisco Kid, a character created by writer O. Henry in his *The Caballero's Way*, is

one of the few positive depictions of Hispanics in early film. During World War II, Roland serves as an air force intelligence officer. He dies on May 15, 1994.

1906

MARCH 3, 1906   Enrique Laguerre, Puerto Rican Writer and Teacher, Is Born. Puerto Rican novelist Enrique Laguerre is born in Moca into a rural farming family. He receives his early education in his small town and later in Aguadilla, where he becomes a "rural teacher." He becomes a licensed teacher in 1927; he receives his bachelor's and master's degrees in Spanish–American literature from the University of Puerto Rico in 1936 and 1941, respectively. Throughout his career, Laguerre teaches, first in rural areas and then as a professor at the University of Puerto Rico and the Catholic University of Ponce. In his novels, Laguerre is an avid and incisive observer of Puerto Rico, bringing to life social, political, and economic themes in the everyday people that populate his novelistic world. Laguerre states that he believes it is the duty of all novelists to contribute to an understanding of the world in which they live, through the creation of characters who profess a social ideology; but this must be presented in a poetic ambiance and with high craftsmanship. Laguerre is known for elaborating the creole, regional themes of rural Puerto Rican life, of which he has firsthand experience. Laguerre's works include *La llamarada* (The Flames, 1935), *Solar Montoya* (Montoya's Plot of Land, 1941), *El 30 de febrero* (February 30, 1943), *Los dedos de la mano* (The Fingers on a Hand, 1951), *La ceiba en el tiesto* (The Ceiba Tree in the Clay Pot, 1956), *El laberinto* (The Labyrinth, 1959), *El fuego y su aire* (Fire and Its Air, 1971), *La resaca* (The Whirlpool, 1971), *Los amos benévolos* (Benevolent Bosses, 1976), and *Infiernos privados* (Private Hells, 1986). It is Laguerre's first novel, *La llamarada* that catches the attention of literary critics; it is now considered a modern classic of Puerto Rican literature. The book deals with conflicts between the sugar cane workers and the landowners. It is followed by *Solar Montoya*, which is about Puerto Rico's other monoculture: coffee. Laguerre is also a prolific short-story writer, an essayist, and a literary critic with various published volumes of these genres to his credit. In 1962, Laguerre publishes his autobiographical essay, *Cauce sin río: Diario de mi generación* (Riverbed without a River: A Diary of My Generation), in which he considers the conflict between contemporary social life and Puerto Rican tradition.

OCTOBER 4, 1906 Educator and Civil Rights Advocate George Sánchez Is Born. George Sánchez is born in Albuquerque, New Mexico, to parents with long histories in the territory. Sánchez becomes a teacher while he is still a student at the University of New Mexico, which he attends only during the summer months. He graduates from the University of New Mexico in 1930 with a B.A. degree in Spanish. He later receives a master's degree in educational psychology at the University of Texas and an Ed.D. in educational administration from the University of California, Berkeley, in 1934. During the next thirty-five years, Sánchez becomes the foremost expert on the education of Hispanic children and a tireless and effective civil rights leader on their behalf. He is also an expert on Latin–American education and a pioneer in bilingual, bicultural education. Among his many writings are *Mexico: A Revolution by Education* (1936) and *Forgotten People* (1940), the latter a work that documents the educational neglect of Mexican–American children in New Mexico. Sánchez joins the faculty of the University of Texas in 1940, and in 1941, becomes president of the League of United Latin American Citizens (LULAC). From then on, he uses LULAC as a forum to struggle against practices that inhibit the civil and educational rights of Hispanics. In 1951 he founds a national organization to bring together all of the civil rights-oriented Hispanic organiza-

tions and to focus their efforts: the American Council of Spanish-Speaking People. It is this council that experiences early civil rights legal victories and prepares the way for many of the gains made during the 1960s and for the later emergence of the Mexican American Legal Defense and Education Fund. Because of his many pioneering studies, articles, and books, as well as his role in preparing the ground for the Hispanic civil rights and education movements, George I. Sánchez has been the subject of numerous books, articles, and homages. Many schools in the Southwest are named in his honor.

1907

1907 Mexican Workers Repatriated. A recession in the United States leads to the repatriation of thousands of Mexican workers who have been fired from factories and mines across the border.

1907 Nicaragua Invades Honduras. After building up Nicaragua's army, President José Santos Zelaya invades Honduras, replaces its president and prepares to invade El Salvador. Instability in the region is seen by the United States as endangering its plans for the Panama Canal.

1907 Poet Agustini Is Published. Uruguayan poet Delmira Agustini publishes her first book of poems, *El libro blanco* (The White Book) when she is just twenty-one years old. (*See also* biography, October 24, 1886.)

FEBRUARY 15, 1907 Movie Star César Romero Is Born. Cuban–American movie star César Romero is born in New York City, the son of a machinery exporter, César Julio Romero, and singer María Mantilla, supposedly the daughter of poet and patriot José Martí. Romero begins his artistic career as a nightclub dancer. Romero makes his stage debut as a dancer in the New York show *Lady Do* in 1927. His first

Broadway performance is as the character Ricci in *Dinner at Eight* in 1932. After dancing and acting in numerous Broadway shows, he begins work in Hollywood films in 1934 with *The Thin Man*. He is best known for the string of musical comedy films that he made with the 20th Century Fox Studio from the 1930s to the 1950s and his role as the Cisco Kid in a series of films. Throughout much of his career he is cast as the suave "Latin lover" and the mysterious foreigner. Among his films in the 1930s and '40s are the following: *British Agent* (1934); *Show Them No Mercy* (1935); *Love before Breakfast* (1936); *Wee Willie Winkle* (1937); *Happy Landing* and *My Lucky Star* (1938); *The Return of the Cisco Kid* (1939); *The Gay Caballero* (1940); *Weekend in Havana* (1941); *Orchestra Wives* (1942); *Coney Island* and *Wintertime* (1943); and *Carnival in Costa Rica* and *Captain from Castile* (1947). His later films include *Love that Brute* (1950); *Happy Go Lovely* and *Lost Continent* (1951); *Prisoners of the Casbah* (1953); *Vera Cruz* (1954); *The Americano* (1955); *The Castilian* (1963); *Sergeant Deadhead* (1964); *Marriage on the Rocks* (1965); and *A Talent for Loving* (1969). While his film career continues into the 1960s, he also frequently appears on television, most memorably as The Joker in the *Batman* series. Romero dies in 1994.

APRIL 24, 1907   Noted Cinema Photographer Figueroa Born in Mexico. The famed director of cinematic photography, Gabriel Figueroa, is born in Mexico City. An orphan, he is forced to seek work as a boy, yet still pursues painting and photography on his own. In 1935, he goes to Hollywood to study motion picture photography. He returns to Mexico the following year, when he began a prolific career as the cameraman of more than a hundred films. He works for Luis Buñuel, John Ford, and Emilio Fernández and ranks among the leading directors of photography in world cinema. His films include (primarily Mexican): *Allá en el rancho grande* (Out on the Big Ranch, 1936), *Flor silvestre* (Wildflower), *María Candelaria* (1943), *Bugambilla* (Bougainvillea, 1944), *La perla/The*

Pearl (Mexico and U.S., 1946), *The Fugitive* (1947), *Los olvidados* (The Forgotten, 1952), *La cucaracha* (The Cockroach, 1958), *Nazarín* (1959), *Macario* (1960), *Animas Trujano* (1961), *El angel exterminador* (The Exterminating Angel, 1962), *The Night of the Iguana* (U.S., 1964), *Simón del desierto* (Simon in the Desert, 1965), *Two Mules for Sister Sara* (U.S.,1970), *The Children of Sánchez* (U.S., 1978), and *Under the Volcano* (U.S., 1984).

JULY 6, 1907   Modern Artist Frida Kahlo Born in Mexico. Frida Kahlo, one of the most celebrated figures in modern art, is born in Coyoacán, Mexico, to a German–Jewish father and a Mexican mestiza mother who is a devout Catholic. As a youth, Kahlo is an active anarchist. In 1916, she contracts polio, a disease which affects her greatly and, in 1925, she is involved in a traffic accident that leaves her a semi-invalid for the rest of her life. These two afflictions, plus her stormy but undying relationship with painter Diego Rivera, convert her life into an agony that is graphically depicted on her canvases. Because of her passionate pursuit of art and her suffering at the hands of Rivera, who in life cast a shadow that often obscured her greatness as a painter, Kahlo is a heroine for modern feminists throughout the world. Although she studies painting for a time with printmaker Fernando Fernández, Kahlo is a truly original painter in style and content, so original, in fact, that she is most assuredly self-taught and with very few models. Almost all of her work is highly autobiographical, depicting scenes of intense sorrow and anguish over her physical disabilities and her tempestuous relationship with Diego Rivera. Her style reveals a personal adaptation of both expressionism and naive art. After marrying Diego Rivera in 1929, Kahlo accompanies him to his commissions in the United States in 1930 to 1934, this despite her open membership in the Communist Party. Back in Mexico City in 1936, she meets and befriended Leon Trosky, who is assassinated while living in Kahlo's house in 1940. Through the efforts of André Breton and Marcel Duchamp,

"The Two Fridas" (1939) by Frida Kahlo. (Courtesy of the National Institute for Fine Arts, Mexico City.)

Kahlo's works are exhibited in 1938 at the Julian Levy Gallery in New York, and in 1939 and 1940, at Pierre Colle Gallery in Paris. During and after World War II, Kahlo remains active in politics as an anti-fascist and anti-imperialist. She has a leg amputated in 1953 and dies the following year on July 13.

JULY 18, 1907 Lupe Vélez, Screen Actress, Is Born. Lupe Vélez (María Guadalupe Vélez de Villalobos) is born in San Luis Potosí, Mexico, and becomes one of the most famous Hispanic screen actresses of all time. Originally a dancer, she debuts in film in 1926 under Hal Roach's direction. The next year she stars as the leading lady in *The Gaucho* opposite Douglas Fairbanks. Known as a fiery leading lady, both in silent and sound films, she later makes positive use of her Spanish-accented English to reposition herself as a comedienne in the "Mexican Spitfire" series. Her volatile personal life, including a romance with Gary Cooper and marriage to Johnny Weismuller, ends in suicide in 1944. Her films include *The Gaucho*

(1927); *Stand and Deliver* (1928); *Lady of the Pavements* (1929); *The Squaw Man* and *The Cuban Love Song* (1931); *Hot Pepper* (1933); *The Girl from Mexico* (1939); *Mexican Spitfire* (1940); and *Redhead from Manhattan* (1943).

SEPTEMBER 17, 1907   Luis Leal, Scholar and Teacher, Is Born. Luis Leal is born in Linares, Mexico. He receives his B.A. degree from Northwestern University in 1940 and his M.A. and Ph.D. degrees from the University of Chicago in 1941 and 1951, respectively. Leal is one of the most productive, respected, and honored scholars of Latin–American and Chicano literature, a true pioneer in both disciplines. In his long career, he teaches at the University of Chicago, the University of Mississippi, Emory University, and the University of Illinois (professor emeritus since 1976), and the University of California, Santa Barbara, (visiting professor and acting director of Chicano studies since 1980). He is the author of sixteen books, including his important *El cuento hispanoamericano* (The Spanish American Short Story, 1967) and *Breve historia de la literatura hispanoamericana* (Brief History of Spanish American Literature, 1971). He is the editor of twenty-one anthologies and other books, besides publishing scores of articles. In 1978, a conference is held and a book published in his praise: *Homenaje a Luis Leal* (Homage to Luis Leal), edited by Donald W. Bleznick and Juan O. Valencia. Today, Luis Leal is an Emeritus Professor of the University of Illinois and an Adjunct Professor of the University of California–Santa Barbara.

NOVEMBER 14, 1907   United States, Mexico Hold Peace Conference. To protect the Canal Zone and ward off aggression from Nicaragua towards Panama, United States president Theodore Roosevelt, along with Mexican president Porfirio Díaz is determined to establish constitutional governments in Central America. To that end, both leaders call for a general peace conference in Washington, D.C. The conference develops the General Treaty, calling for

Luis Leal. (Courtesy of the Arte Público Press Archives, University of Houston.)

nonrecognition of governments that come to power through coup d'etat and banning the Central American governments from interfering in each other's internal affairs. It also establishes the Central American Court of Justice.

NOVEMBER 26, 1907   Lefty Gómez, Record-Holding Baseball Pitcher, Is Born. One of baseball's greatest pitchers, Vernon Louis "Lefty" Gómez, is born in Rodeo, California. He ranks third in regular season wins, with 189 for the New York Yankees. He also holds the record for World Series wins without a loss (6–0) and three wins against one loss in All-Star play. Gómez is active from 1930 to 1943, pitching 2,503 innings and winning 189 games to 102 losses, with an ERA of 3.34. He scores twenty wins or more in 1931, 1932, 1934, and 1937. Gómez is number thirteen on the all-time winning percentage list. He makes the All-Star teams every year from 1933 to 1939, and he is a member of the Baseball Hall of Fame. During winter seasons, he plays in Cuba, where he also serves as manager of the Cienfuegos team. At one time, he teaches a class on pitching at the University of Havana. Gómez dies on February 2, 1989, in San Rafael, California.

1908

MARCH 3, 1908 Corretjer, Poet and Activist, Born in Puerto Rico. Puerto Rican poet and political activist Juan Antonio Corretjer is born in Ciales, where he also attends elementary and secondary school. He receives no further formal education; however, he becomes a writer while he is still a child. As early as 1923, he is active politically, founding a pro-independence group named after the romantic poet, Sociedad José Gautier Benítez. Throughout his subsequent verse and his life's work, themes of the pursuit of nationhood and independence dominate. In 1927, Corretjer starts to work as a journalist for *La Democracia,* a profession which he pursues in Puerto Rico, Cuba, and the United States. In 1928, he becomes associated with the Puerto Rican literary movement entitled Atalayismo (literally Guardianism, but in reality an invented term). By 1930, he is a leader of the Partido Nacionalist Puertorriqueño, the nationalist party, and he becomes involved in various organizing activities, including the 1932 assault on the island's capitol building. He continues his party activities in the Dominican Republic, Haiti, and Cuba, where he lands in jail in 1935. On his return to Puerto Rico in 1936, he is again jailed—a year in Puerto Rico for his political activities and ten years in Atlanta, Georgia, on federal charges. Upon being paroled from prison in 1947, he settles in New York, where he edits the newspaper *Pueblos Hispanos* (Hispanic Peoples). In 1950, Corretjer again is arrested, this time for inciting a riot. In his later years, he declares himself a Communist. Corretjer's poetry is deeply rooted in Puerto Rican tradition, folklore, the indigenous past, and his people's ever-present desire for independence. His approximately twenty books of poetry make him one of the most productive and widely read poets in Puerto Rican history. Among his highly regarded titles are *Agüeybana* [Name of Taíno Indian Chief] (1932), *Ulisas* (Ulysses 1933), *Amor de Puerto Rico* (Love of Puerto Rico, 1937), *Alabanza en la torre de Ciales* (Uplifting Praise at the Tower of Ciales, 1953), *Yerba bruja* (Witch's Weed, 1957), and *Pausa para el amor* (Pause for Love, 1967). His historical and political writings are represented by numerous books, including *La revolución de Lares* (The Lares Revolution, 1947), *La lucha por la independencia de Puerto Rico* (The Struggle for Puerto Rican Independence, 1949), *Hostos y Alvizu Campos* [named after the Puerto Rican patriots] (1965), *Alvizu Campos, hombre histórico* (Alvizu Campos, Historical Man, 1966), and *Semblanza polémica de Pedro Alvizu Campos* (A Polemical Portrait of Pedro Alvizu Campos, 1973).

1909

NOVEMBER 4, 1909 Ciro Alegría, Peruvian Novelist, Is Born. Peruvian novelist Ciro Alegría is born in Trujillo, the son of Spanish Irish parents. Alegría grows up among the Indians of the Marañón River, and the Indians and their plight in Peru became the predominant theme in his writings. After attending the University of Trujillo, Alegría writes for *El Norte* (The North) newspaper. During the 1930s he is active in the founding of the Aprista party, which advocates social and economic reforms; his activities eventually lead to his imprisonment (1931–33) and exile in Chile (1934). His career as a novelist actually begins in Chile, when he starts his first novel, *La serpiente de oro* (The Golden Serpent, 1935) as a recollection of growing up along the Marañón and observing the plight of the Indians. He continues to develop his career as a writer of fiction while in the United States from 1941 to 1948 and in Puerto Rico during the 1950s, where he also teaches at the University of Puerto Rico. His most renowned work, considered a classic in the genre of indigenist literature, is *El mundo es ancho y ajeno* (Broad and Alien Is the World, 1941); it documents the destruction of the way of life of northern Peruvian Indians by landowners who exploit the land and Indian labor.

This novel, which wins the first Latin American Novel Contest of the Pan American Union, has often been compared to John Steinbeck's *Grapes of Wrath*. Among Alegría's other novels are *Los perros hambrientos* (The Hungry Dogs, 1939), *Lázaro* (Lazarus, 1973), and *El dilema de Krause: Penitenciaría e Lima* (Krause's Dilemma: The Lima Penitentiary, 1979). Alegría is also a prolific short-story writer and children's author. Alegría dies of a heart attack on February 17, 1967 in Lima.

DECEMBER 16, 1909   United States Intervenes in Nicaragua. To ward off intervention by the United States, which has already unofficially backed a small, unsuccessful revolution in Nicaragua, President José Santos Zelaya tenders his resignation. This represents the first of a series of Nicaraguan governments that the United States will overthrow. The Nicaraguan Congress selects one of Zelaya's men, José Madriz, to succeed as president. He is not acceptable to the United States, however, which withholds recognition until the rebels overthrow him. Juan Estrada takes his place as president, with the United States heavily involved in reconstructing the government. Estrada's successor, Adolfo Díaz, is so weak that in August 1912, he has to request United States military intervention. The marines soon land on the Pacific coast and, with the exception of an eighteen-month period (August 1925–January 1927), the intervention lasts until January 1933.

Brother Angélico Chávez. (Courtesy of Special Collections, General Library, University of New Mexico.)

1910

1910   Philosopher Varona Publishes Collected Works. Enrique José Varona y Pera, Cuban philosopher and political figure, publishes his collected essays and articles, *Desde mi belvedere* (From My Belvedere). It is considered a masterpiece in its genre. (*See also* biography, April 13, 1849.)

APRIL 10, 1910   Franciscan Angélico Chávez, Religious Poet, Is Born. Brother Angélico

Chávez, one of the most renowned religious poets in the United States, is born in Wagonmound, New Mexico. Named Manuel Chávez by his parents, he is raised in Mora and attends St. Francis Seminary in Cincinnati, Ohio, and colleges in the Midwest. In 1917, he is the first native New Mexican to become a Franciscan friar. From the time of his ordination at age 27 until age 62, he serves as pastor in several towns and Indian pueblos in New Mexico. Chávez is the author of nineteen books and a historian of his order and of the Catholic

Church in New Mexico. What unifies Chávez's large output as a poet and historian is his interest in New Mexico's past, and his own Catholicism. Beginning as a religious poet, he later takes an interest in historical fiction and, finally, in the history of the region itself, as in his most famous historical essay, *My Penitent Land: Reflections on Spanish New Mexico* (1947). Chávez's reputation as a creative writer rests upon an important body of poetic works that include *Clothed with the Sun* (1939), *Eleven Lady Lyrics and Other Poems* (1945), *The Single Rose; The Rose Unica and Commentary of fray Manuel de Santa Clara* (1948), and *The Virgin of Port Lligat* (1959). Although Chávez's poetry and all of his works are grounded in New Mexico Catholicism, his poems are not local color pieces celebrating New Mexico's picturesque landscape; instead they depict Chávez's inner life.

JUNE 8, 1910   Novelist María Bombal Is Born. Chilean novelist and filmwriter María Luisa Bombal is born in Viña del Mar, Chile. After receiving much of her education in France and graduating from the Sorbonne in Paris, Bombal works as a screenwriter for Sonofilm in Argentina from 1937 to 1940. With the publication of her first novella, *La última niebla* (The Final Mist) in 1935, Bombal becomes one of Latin America's most beloved writers of the twentieth century. Considered an early feminist and among the avant-garde writers, she departs from the masculine, regionalistic, and realistic trends that dominate Latin–American fiction. Bombal's writings focus on women protagonists who escape their lonely and unfulfilled lives through fantasy. Bombal's 1938 novella, *La amortajada* (The Shrouded Woman), one of her most famous, is narrated from the perspective of a dead woman reflecting on her life. Because of the fantasy world that she develops, Bombal is considered a forerunner of the Latin–American style of magic realism, so well developed in younger generations of writers that include Gabriel García Márquez, Ernesto Sábato, and her compatriot Isabel Allende.

María Luisa Bombal also writes numerous stories that are published both separately and in collections. Her later works include *La historia de María Griselda* (The History of María Griselda) in 1962 and an English translation of some of her stories, *New Islands, and Other Stories,* in 1982. She dies on May 6, 1980, in Chile.

OCTOBER 28, 1910   Cuban Boxer Eligio Sardiñas Is Born. Cuba's "Kid Chocolate" is the first Hispanic boxer to win a world title in the junior lightweight class. Born in Havana, Sardiñas' career becomes an example of the fate of boxers who battle their way out of poverty into fame and fortune. After winning eighty-six amateur fights and twenty-one professional fights in Cuba, he makes his New York debut in 1928 and fights over one hundred bouts in the United States in the next ten years. He becomes a true champion, supports his community, and is memorialized on stage and screen. However, he is seriously exploited by his managers and owners and ultimately is done in by poverty and alcoholism.

NOVEMBER 20, 1910   The Mexican Revolution. On this date, at 6:00 P.M., the Plan de San Luis calls for the Mexican Revolution to begin. Under the leadership of Francisco I. Madero, elections are declared null, and the reelected regime illegitimate. Madero is named president of the United Mexican States. (The revolution does not erupt suddenly, the call for revolution finally takes effect by May of 1911.) The Mexican Revolution starts as a national socialist effort to overthrow Dictator Porfirio Díaz and institute social justice. As it gains steam as a full-fledged social upheaval, strong issues come to the fore: agrarian reform, wresting power from the church, nationalism, democracy. Two ideologues of the revolution, Ricardo and Enrique Flores Magón, attack the Díaz regime from their exile in the United States. Their anarchist movement to organize workers on both sides of the border coincides with Madero's liberal democratic movement. By May

Ricardo and Enrique Flores Magón in Leavenworth Federal Penitentiary in 1922. (Courtesy of the *Los Angeles Times*.)

Mexican state. Not only does the revolution cause societal upheaval in Mexico, it also creates great disorder and social transformation in the United States border states, which not only experience raids and streams of refugees on United States soil, but also become the home for hundreds of thousands of people fleeing north from Mexico. Hispanic culture in the United States, in particular, is greatly transformed, as political refugees of the elite class settle in major cities and take up leadership in Mexican and Hispanic communities. The great numbers of economic refugees transform the racial and ideological composition of the working classes in many industries in the United States. In fact, the large-scale immigration of Mexicans into the United States continues into the present, although at a significantly reduced rate.

1911, the Díaz regime has been defeated and the dictator flees to Europe after having been in power for thirty-four years. Madero is elected to the presidency of a newly democratic Mexican Republic while the revolution is still in force. Liberals and conservative and agrarian reformers form various armed factions and, in February 1913, General Victoriano Huerta betrays Madero, who is then assassinated. The counterrevolution, now led by Huerta, is opposed by Venustiano Carranza, Francisco Villa, and Emiliano Zapata. After Huerta and his followers are driven across the border into the United States, Villa and Zapata unite against Carranza to dispute the type of reforms that either side would bring to Mexico. Carranza's forces finally win and his government is quickly recognized by the United States, which leads to Villa's historic raid on Columbus, New Mexico. President Woodrow Wilson sends General John J. Pershing into Mexico in pursuit of "Pancho" Villa, who succeeds in evading and humiliating Pershing and gains immortality as a hero of Mexican nationalism. President Carranza accepts the reform Constitution of 1917, which becomes the basis for the modern

1911

1911 Roberto Matta, Surrealist Painter, Born in Chile. Chilean painter and printmaker Roberto Matta is born in Santiago. He is to become his country's and one of Latin America's leading surrealists. Matta moves to Paris in 1934, where he works as an assistant to the architect Le Corbusier. He is part of the surrealist group in Paris in 1937, recognizes its cosmic character, and attempts in the rest of his art to give structure to the surrealist experience. From 1938 to 1948, Matta lives in New York City, where he influences the upcoming generation of American abstract expressionists. One of his most influential paintings of this period is "The Vertigo of Eros" (1944), which now belongs to the Museum of Modern Art in New York. From 1949 to 1954, Matta lives in Rome and travels extensively throughout Europe, but especially Paris. His solo exhibitions include venues throughout Europe, the United States, and Latin America, from Paris to London, New York to Minneapolis, Caracas to Buenos Aires. In 1974, the Museum of Modern Art in Mexico City mounts "Matta: Homage to Jorge Zalamea," which travels to Bogotá and Caracas. In 1968, an exhibition at the Museum of Modern Art in Paris honors Latin–American masters Matta, Wilfredo Lam, and Rodrigo Peñalba.

JANUARY 18, 1911   Peruvian Novelist Arguedas Is Born. José María Arguedas, one of Peru's greatest novelists, is born in Andahuaylas, Peru, the son of a traveling judge. Arguedas receives a doctorate from the University of San Marcos in Lima and goes on to teach Spanish and later to direct national programs in folklore and popular culture at museums, the Ministry of Public Education, and the University of San Marcos. In addition to his expertise in literature and folklore, in his later years he becomes a professor of the Quechua language at the Universidad Nacional Agraria, from 1963 until 1969, when he commits suicide. During his life, Arguedas champions the cause of the Quechua Indians, the descendants of the Incas. He is responsible for creating a space for Quechua language, culture, and realistic depiction of Indians in Peruvian literature. In his novels and short stories, Arguedas develops a style that intertwines Spanish and Quechua and creates a bridge between the cultures. Among his major novels are *Yawar fiesta* (Blood Feast, 1941), in which he shows the incivility of nonindigenous society toward the Indians, and *Todas las sangres* (All of the Races, 1964), a story of epic proportions that deals with the rivalry of two brothers and the unrest in all stratas of Peruvian society. On November 28, 1969, he shoots himself in an empty classroom of the University of Lima.

MAY 21, 1911   Peace Treaty Signed in Mexico. In Mexico, a peace treaty is signed between the revolutionary forces of Francisco I. Madero and those of dictator Porfirio Díaz, which appears to be a sign of early success and an end to the revolution. Under the terms of the treaty, Díaz is to renounce his presidency by the end of the month.

MAY 24, 1911   Díaz Is Ousted. Porfirio Díaz is ejected from his eighth office by revolutionaries supporting Francisco Madero for president. (*See also* biography, September 15, 1830.)

JUNE 7, 1911   Madero, Supporters Enter Mexico City. Francisco Madero enters Mexico City, the military phase of his revolution triumphant. He is accompanied by more than 100,000 supporters.

JUNE 13, 1911   Physicist Alvarez, Nobel Prize Winner, Is Born. Luis Walter Alvarez, Nobel Prize-winning physicist, is born in San Francisco, California. He is one of the United States' most distinguished and respected physicists. With a B.S. (1932) and a Ph.D. (1936) from the University of Chicago, Alvarez also holds honorary degrees from universities in the United States and abroad. He develops most of his work at the University of California–Berkeley from 1936 to the present, where he is Emeritus Professor. From 1954 to 1959 and from 1976 to 1978, Alvarez serves as associate director of the prestigious Lawrence Berkeley Lab. In 1986, he is awarded the Nobel Prize in physics; earlier, he receives the Collier Trophy (1946), the Scott Medal (1953), the Einstein Medal (1961), the National Medal of Science (1964), and many other awards. Alvarez is a pioneer in particle physics, astrophysics, ophthalmic and television optics, geophysics, and air navigation.

JUNE 24, 1911   Argentine Racing Driver Fangio Is Born. Argentine racing car driver Juan Manuel Fangio is born in Balcarce. He becomes the most successful race car driver of all time. He wins the world championship five times—1951, 1954, 1955, 1956, and 1957—and some twenty-four important racing prizes. Fangio becomes the oldest racer in the world to win international titles when he wins the World Race Car Championship in 1957 at the age of forty-six.

OCTOBER 1, 1911   Mexico Elects Madero President in Landslide Francisco Madero is elected president of a constitutionally democratic Mexico, receiving 98 percent of the vote.

NOVEMBER 6, 1911　Madero Takes Office. Francisco I. Madero assumes the presidency of the Republic of Mexico after being constitutionally elected. He does so under unique circumstances, given the previous dictatorial administration: freedom of the press, a political environment for bringing about social justice, and two enemy armies at his command (the revolutionary forces and an unreformed federal army). The Maderist revolution has triumphed politically, but now his supporters await the implementation of a socioeconomic revolution. Conservatives and the federal army must be dealt with, as well as numerous revolutionary uprisings around the country that either do not recognize Madero's government or are pressing for economic and social reform.

1912

1912　Ambassador Protests Mistreatment of Mexicans. Brutality against Mexican–Americans in the Southwest territories is commonplace as it has been since the turn of the century. Lynchings and murders of Mexican–Americans become so frequent in California and Texas that, in 1912, the Mexican ambassador formally protests the mistreatment of Mexicans and cites several brutal incidents that have recently taken place.

1912　Film Career Begins for Spanish Actor. Antonio Moreno begins his career in 1912 under D.W. Griffith. He is quite popular during the 1920s, when he plays leads opposite such actresses as Gloria Swanson, Greta Garbo, Pola Negri, and Bebe Daniels. (*See also* biography, September 26, 1887.)

1912　Marines Are Sent to Cuba. The violent Colored Independents' revolt in Cuba prompts Washington to send the U.S. Marines, despite Cuban president Máximo Gómez's protests.

The intervention is authorized under the principles of the Platt Amendment.

1912　Medical Institute Founded. The world-famous Institute for Tropical Medicine is established in Puerto Rico. In 1926, the institute becomes the School for Tropical Medicine of the University of Puerto Rico, affiliated with Columbia University School of Medicine. In 1949, the School of Medicine of the University of Puerto Rico is established, again in association with Columbia University. In 1966, the school became the Campus for Medical Sciences of the University of Puerto Rico, bringing together under one roof the schools of medicine, dentistry, and health sciences.

1912　New Party Established in Puerto Rico. The first pro-independence party, Partido de la Independencia, is founded in Puerto Rico under United States rule. Among the notable founders of the party are writers Manuel Zeno Gandía, José de Diego, and Luis Llorens Torres.

1912　René Portocarrero, Cuban Painter, Is Born. Cuban painter René Portocarrero is born in Cerro, Cuba. As a child, he attends classes at the Academia de Villate y San Alejandro in Havana. By 1938, he is teaching at the Eduardo Abela art school and at the Havana prison. His works show the influence of the Spanish baroque (*Interiors* 1943) and the Afro–Cuban popular tradition, as in *Small Devil* (1962). Most of Portocarrero's exuberant work is related to Cuba, especially Havana. He explores his fantasy cityscapes in his post-Impressionist "Imaginary Cities" and Cuban folk culture in his carnival pictures, which date from the 1970s. In 1963, he is awarded the International Prize at the Sao Paulo Bienal. Solo exhibitions of his work are held internationally, most notably at the Julian Levy Gallery in New York in 1945, the Organization of American States Museum in Washington, D.C., in 1956, the Museum of Modern Art in Mexico City in 1965, and the National Museum in Havana in 1967. Portocarrero is one of the most noted and respected contemporary Cuban painters. He dies in 1986.

JANUARY 6, 1912 New Mexico Becomes a State. New Mexico achieves statehood. Repeated attempts have failed since it became a territory of the United States in 1850. Many historians and political scientists agree that the reason for denial of statehood for so long is that the majority of the residents are Mexican–American, and they hold considerable political and economic power. California, on the other hand, was admitted to statehood in 1850 without having to pass through the territorial stage. By 1912, the economic and political power of Mexican–Americans in New Mexico is waning, but their numbers remain the largest percent of a state population until the 1930s.

JANUARY 8, 1912 Actor, Director, and Producer José Ferrer Is Born. José Ferrer is one of the most distinguished actors of Hispanic background to have made a career in the mainstream films and on stage in the United States. The star of numerous Hollywood films and of many stage productions, he is born in Santurce, Puerto Rico. Raised and educated in Puerto Rico, he graduates from Princeton University in 1933. As an actor and/or director, his stage credits include *Let's Face It* (1942), *Strange Fruit* (1945), *Design for Living* (1947), *Twentieth Century* (1950), *Stalag 17* (1951), *Man of La Mancha (1966),* and *Cyrano de Bergerac* (1975), among many others. As an actor, director, or producer, he is associated with some of the most famous Hollywood films, including *Joan of Arc* (1947), *Moulin Rouge* (1952), *Caine Mutiny* (1953), *Return to Peyton Place* (1962), *Lawrence of Arabia* (1963), *Ship of Fools* (1966), and others. His awards include the Gold Medal from the American Academy of Arts and Sciences (1949), the Academy Award for Best Actor in *Cyrano de Bergerac* (1950), and induction into the Theater Hall of Fame (1981). Ferrer dies in 1992.

MAY 9, 1912 Mexican Film Star Pedro

José Ferrer. (Courtesy of the Arte Público Press Archives, University of Houston.)

Armendáriz, Sr., Is Born. Pedro Armendáriz, one of Mexico's most successful film stars, is born in Mexico City. During his career, he appears in more than forty films, many directed by Emilio "El Indio" Fernández. He is internationally recognized for *María Candelaria* (1943) and his work with major directors, including Luis Buñuel and John Ford. His son, Pedro Armendáriz, Jr., also is an actor. Among Pedro Sr.'s films are (primarily U.S.) *María Candelaria* (Mexico, 1943); *La Perla/The Pearl* (U.S. and Mexico, 1945); *Fort Apache* (1948); *Three Godfathers, We Were Strangers,* and *Tulsa* (1949); *Border River* (1954); *The Littlest Outlaw* (U.S. and Mexico, 1955); *The Wonderful Country* (1959); *Francis of Assisi* (1961); and *Captain Sinbad* (1963). Armendáriz dies in 1963.

JUNE 1912 United States Takes Control in Nicaragua. United States Marines are sent to Nicaragua to supervise the presidential elections. They are sent again for the same reason in 1916 and 1920. Except for an eighteen-month period (August 1925–January 1927), the United States military intervention in Nicaragua lasts until 1933. By 1912, Nicaragua has become virtually a ward of New York banks, which act informally for the American government; the considerable commercial interests of the United States are protected throughout this period by the United States military on the soil of a foreign, sovereign nation. The policy has been called by Latin–American scholars and critics "dollar imperialism." During this period, the United States organizes Nicaragua's national finances, supervises budget expenditures, collects customs revenues, manages the national bank and the railroad, and supervises elections. By 1925, the New York bankers recover the funds they risked in Nicaragua, and the United States decides that it is safe to withdraw the marines. But they return in 1927 when the president, Adolfo Díaz, is on the verge of losing power. After the United States restores order and supervises elections in 1928, only one revolutionary force escapes repression by the marines and continues its guerrilla attacks: the force headed by César Augusto Sandino, regarded today as Nicaragua's greatest hero. In 1934, after Sandino officially lays down his arms, he is assassinated by military officers.

1913

1913   Poet Establishes Magazine. Luis Llorens Torres founds the magazine for literary modernism, *Revista de las Antillas* (Caribbean Review), where he publishes a collection of poems entitled *Visiones de mi musa* (Visions of My Muse). (*See also* biography, May 14, 1876.)

FEBRUARY 10, 1913   United States Backs Huerta. United States ambassador Henry Lane Wilson promises Mexican General Victoriano Huerta that the United States will recognize "any government capable of establishing peace and order in place of the government of Señor Madero." After consulting with the representatives of Spain, Germany, and England about possible cooperation in a political intervention, Ambassador Wilson visits Madero on February 11 to threaten intervention. On February 14 and 15, Wilson requests Madero's resignation

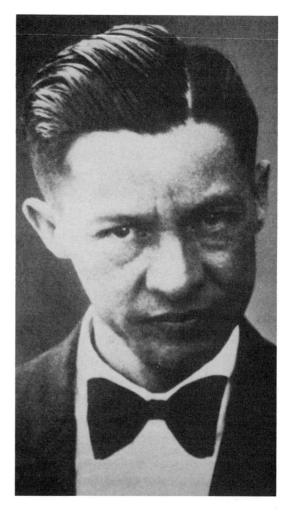

César Augusto Sandino, 1928. (Courtesy of the Library of Congress Prints & Photographs Division)

or else the United States will send in four thousand soldiers to Mexico to establish order. On February 17, Wilson works out negotiations with the coup forces inside the American embassy itself: he will support the new government and not intervene. On February 18, at 1:30 P.M., Huerta's troops detain Madero. Within two hours, Wilson brings together the diplomatic corps to issue a vote of confidence for Huerta and his army. And, shortly thereafter, Wilson receives Huerta and his coconspirators at the embassy to plan for the transition of power; Wilson proposes that Huerta be named the interim president.

FEBRUARY 19, 1913   General Forces Out Officials. General Victoriano Huerta seizes the presidency of Mexico, forcing President Francisco I. Madero and Vice President Pino Suárez to resign. On February 22, both deposed officials are executed against a penitentiary wall. By the end of the year, Huerta has dissolved congress, imprisoned several legislators, assassinated opponents, and assumed extraordinary powers in war, finance, and government. He also puts off indefinitely the October elections for president and vice president. Dictator Huerta's seizure of the presidency precipitates the bloodiest phase of the Mexican Revolution.

MARCH 4, 1913   Wilson Backs New Policy toward Mexico. Newly elected President Woodrow Wilson orders a new U.S. policy toward Mexico; he hopes to encourage free enterprise and a parliamentary democracy. Thus, Wilson immediately falls into conflict with Dictator Victoriano Huerta, who has seized power with United States support. Wilson involves himself in the internal affairs of Mexico, gradually increasing pressure on Huerta to resign.

1914

1914   Countries Side with Allies in War. During World War I, all of the Spanish–American countries join the Allies, except for those that declare neutrality: Argentina, Chile, Paraguay, Colombia, Venezuela, El Salvador, and Mexico. Puerto Rican soldiers fight for the first time under the United States flag.

1914   Disputes Arise between U.S. and Panama. Within the opening of the Panama Canal, the largest segment of the population of the Republic of Panama begins to owe their incomes directly or indirectly to the canal and the business it generates. Despite the profitability of the canal for Panamanians, over the years

there are numerous disputes. One of the earliest is the United States breaking its promise to withdraw the Jamaicans and West Indians it has imported to construct the canal. There also is great resistance to Panama being considered a "protectorate" of the United States. Another dispute concerns the segregation and discrimination imposed by the Canal Zone. All employees of the Canal Zone are divided into "gold" and "silver" categories: gold for U.S. citizens and silver for all others. Those on the gold list are paid twice as much money for the same amount of work. Gold employees also are segregated from silver ones in myriad daily ways, including separate postal windows. And, of course, Panamanian politics are characterized by American interventionism.

1914   President Wilson Sends Troops. President Woodrow Wilson orders the invasion of Veracruz in an effort to depose Victoriano Huerta.

JANUARY 17, 1914   Héctor García Pérez, Civil Rights Leader and Government Official, Is Born. García Pérez, the Mexican–American civil rights leader, is born in Llera, Tamaulipas, Mexico. Educated in the United States after his parents emigrate to Texas, he receives his B.A. in 1936 and his M.D. in 1940, both from the University of Texas. During World War II, he serves with distinction in the Army Medical Corps, earning the Bronze Star and six Battle Stars. At the end of the war, he opens a medical practice in Corpus Christi and, outraged at the refusal of local authorities to bury a Mexican–American veteran in the city cemetery, he organizes the American G.I. Forum, which is still one of the largest and most influential Hispanic civil rights organizations. Besides participating in a wide variety of civil rights organizations, García Pérez also becomes active in the Democratic Party and is appointed to the Democratic National Committee in 1954. In the 1960 presidential campaign, García Pérez is the national coordinator of the Viva Kennedy Clubs, and he is later appointed to various national positions by presidents Kennedy and Johnson. In 1967, President Johnson names García Pérez alternate delegate to the United Nations with the rank of ambassador, and he also appoints him the first Mexican–American member of the United States Commission on Civil Rights. In 1965, the president of Panama awards García Pérez the Order of Vasco Núñez de Balboa, in recognition of his services to humanity. In 1984, he is awarded the United States of America Medal of Freedom.

MARCH 31, 1914 Octavio Paz, Nobel Laureate, Is Born. Mexico's first Nobel laureate for literature, Octavio Paz, is born in Mexico City, the son of a lawyer and a housewife. He receives all of his formal education in Mexico City, where he also attends the National Autonomous University from 1932 to 1937. While developing his career as a poet and essayist, Paz holds several positions in Mexico's foreign service from 1945 to 1968, including ambassador to India from 1962 to 1968. At various times he is a visiting professor at the University of Texas, University of Pittsburgh, Harvard University, and Cambridge University. He is also the founder and publisher of Spanish America's most distinguished magazine of literature and commentary, *Vuelta* (Return), which he establishes in 1976. He founds and is the editor (1943–46) of *El Hijo Pródigo* (The Prodigal Child) and from 1971 to 1975 he is the editor of Mexico's important magazine of news and commentary, *Plural* (Plural). In both his poetry and his essays, Paz makes his mark as a deep thinker of universal breadth, pondering themes important to both world culture and Mexican civilization. He is a voluminous reader and student of world history, art, and culture, and allows such diverse influences as Eastern religions and music, as well as Freudian psychology, into his work. A distinct characteristic of his work is the tendency to blend genres: Paz writes poetic prose and allows prose to enter into his poetry. This can be most readily observed, for instance, in *El mono gramático* (The Monkey Grammarian, 1974), which is both an essay and a poem that

explores the nature and dimensions of language. Another tendency in Paz is the fusion of opposites, which may be influenced by the Eastern concepts of yin and yang. Paz also at times uses from two to four languages in the same poem, as a symbol of his attempts to create community or communion, which he finds lacking in contemporary society. Through his juxtaposition of contrary thoughts and dualities, Paz's attempts to create a more harmonious world. He is also a student of the indigenous past of Aztec poetry and thought from which he captures dualities, as in his book titled after the Mexican coin with the Aztec sun on one side and the Mexican eagle on the other: *¿Águila o Sol?* (Eagle or Sun [as in flipping a coin], 1973). In this book, he explores the Aztec concept of burnt water, which is a duality unto itself; for Paz there are no barriers between fire and water, men and women, life and death—all of these opposites merge and are resolved. Paz's meditation on Mexican culture and its development, *El laberinto de la soledad* (The Labyrinth of Solitude, 1950) is perhaps one of the two most influential books in contemporary Mexico, the other being José Vasconcelos's *La raza cósmica*. Although Paz's book is a deep and detailed examination of Mexican existential values, many critics and thinkers around the world see it as universal and highly influential in its method of examining the self within a contemporary culture. Paz's works include forty books of poetry. Various editions of selected and collected poems appear in Spanish and English translation, one of the latest being the bilingual edition of *Collected Poems, 1957–1987* in 1987. Paz also writes some thirty books of essay, art and literary criticism, and commentary on history and politics. He is a copious anthologizer and editor, as well as translator. He wins the highest prizes awarded by various nations, including Belgium, France, Israel, Mexico, and Spain. In 1990, he receives the Nobel Prize for literature.

APRIL 21, 1914 Wilson Orders Marines to Veracruz. Following the February occupation of the port of Veracruz by United States forces, President Woodrow Wilson orders the invasion of Veracruz by U.S. Marines in an effort to depose Victoriano Huerta.

AUGUST 14, 1914 Huerta's Army Surrenders. Huerta's federal army surrenders unconditionally to Venustiano Carranza's Constitutionalists.

AUGUST 14, 1914 Panama Canal Opens. The first ship clears the newly constructed Panama Canal. Notwithstanding this historic commercial and strategic success, the United States moves to establish claim on a future canal route by Lake Nicaragua and the San Juan River. The Bryan–Chamorro Treaty, finally ratified by the United States Senate in 1916, concedes rights to the route to the United States for $3 million. Costa Rica protests because it also shares the boundary of the San Juan River, and El Salvador protests the provision calling for United States naval bases in the Bay of Fonseca, which threaten her territory. Costa Rica and El Salvador win their suit against the United States and Nicaragua in the Central American Court. The United States refuses to honor the decision and, in 1918, helps to destroy the court which it had participated in establishing. The treaty also angers Nicaraguans when the United States decides to pay amounts of the $3 million to Nicaragua's creditors instead of directly to Nicaragua.

AUGUST 26, 1914 Argentine Novelist Cortázar Is Born. Julio Cortázar (Julio Denís), internationally famous Argentine novelist, is born in Brussels, Belgium. He holds dual citizenship throughout his life. After receiving degrees in education and translation, Cortázar becomes a high school, and later a university, teacher. One of the leading novelists of the Latin–American "Boom," Cortázar is considered an experimenter in novelistic form as well as one who explores the meaning of life through interpretation of novelistic form. He rebels against false realism in form and in thought; he suspects other

General Venustiano Carranza during the Revolution. (Courtesy of Recovering the U.S. Hispanic Literary Heritage Project, University of Houston.)

nonsystematic, more mysterious orders in life that are not so simplistically real and or empirical. He encourages the reader to engage in arranging and rearranging the parts of the narrative, thus participating in the creation of the novel. His most noted novel, *Hopscotch*, exemplifies all of these tendencies. It is considered the first Latin–American novel to deal with the writing of itself. Cortázar's other experimental works include *62: Modelo para armar* (62: A Model Kit, 1959); *Libro de Manuel* (A

Manual for Manuel, 1973); *Ultimo round* (Last Round, 1969); and *Fantomas contra los vampiros internacionales* (Fantomas Takes on the Multinational Vampires, 1975). Cortázar confronts readers with humor, surprise, fantasy, and unexpected forms; he challenges his reader to be as creative and intuitive as the novelist and to take a similar approach to life. In his later years, Cortázar lives in exile in Paris, where he dies of a heart attack on February 12, 1984.

NOVEMBER 13, 1914 Constitutionalists Come to Power. The Constitutionalists, headed by First Chief Venustiano Carranza, come to power with United States support. The Constitutionalist government issues a demand for the unconditional withdrawal of the United States forces from the port of Veracruz, and thereafter remains wary against U.S. interventionism.

1915

1915 Mariano Azuela Writes. True to a tradition of Hispanic literature in exile, Azuela's greatest and most renowned novel, *Los de abajo* (The Underdogs), is written while he is a fugitive in El Paso, Texas. (*See also* biography, January 1, 1873.)

JANUARY 6, 1915 Agrarian Reform in Mexico. The Venustiano Carranza administration in Mexico passes an agrarian reform law, which mandates the return of lands to communities and proclaims the right of all peasants to own a plot of land. This is the first of many agrarian reform laws to come under Carranza. But, during the next five years, only 427,000 acres are parceled out to some 44,000 peasants. On the other hand, Carranza also arranges to return to their owners numerous haciendas that have been confiscated during the revolution.

FEBRUARY 20, 1915 Plan de San Diego. On this date the Supreme Revolutionary Congress

of San Diego intends a general uprising among Mexican–Americans in the area of San Diego, Texas, in order to create a separate republic, with possible future union to Mexico. A written Plan de San Diego is found in the possession of a Mexican–American arrested in January. It calls for the killing of all Anglo-Americans over the age of sixteen, except for the elderly. The plan is discovered at the height of the Mexican Revolution and leads to increased military presence, border patrols and vigilantism against Mexicans and Mexican–Americans.

APRIL 21, 1915 Anthony Quinn, Academy Award-Winning Actor, Is Born. Anthony Quinn, born in Chihuahua, Mexico, of Irish-Mexican parentage, lives in the United States from childhood. He begins his career as a film actor in 1936. The following year marries Cecil B. de Mille's adopted daughter, Katherine (they later divorce), but his father-in-law does nothing to advance Quinn's career. Quinn does not attain star status until 1952 when he wins the Academy Award for his role as Zapata's brother in *Viva Zapata!* Quinn goes on to win a second Academy Award for *Lust for Life* (1956) and he begins playing leads that emphasize his earthy and exotic qualities. He appears in over one hundred films and writes his autobiography, *The Original Sin* (1972). Among his many films are *Parole!* (1936); *The Buccaneer* and *King of Alcatraz* (1938); *Texas Rangers Ride Again* (1940); *Blood and Sand* (1941); *The Ox-Bow Incident* and *Guadalcanal Diary* (1943); *Back to Bataan* (1945); *California, Sinbad the Sailor,* and *Black Gold* (1947); *The Brave Bulls* (1951); *Viva Zapata!* and *Against All Flags* (1952); *Ride Vaquero* (1953); *Lust for Life* and *Man From Del Rio* (1956); *The Black Orchid* (1958); *The Guns of Navarone* and *Barabbas* (1961); *Requiem for a Heavyweight* and *Lawrence of Arabia* (1962); *Zorba the Greek* (1964); *A High Wind in Jamaica* (1965); *The Shoes of the Fisherman* and *The Magus* (1968); *The Secret of Santa Vittoria* (1969); *The Greek Tycoon* and *The Children of Sánchez*

(1978); *The Salamander* (1981); and *Ghosts Can't Do It* and *Revenge* (1990).

JULY 15, 1915   Dictator Huerta Steps Down. Pressed by Venustiano Carranza's constitutionalist army and by the United States, dictator Victoriano Huerta renounces the presidency of Mexico and goes into exile.

SEPTEMBER 3, 1915   Américo Paredes, Folklorist and Teacher, Is Born. Américo Paredes is born in Brownsville, Texas. A famed folklorist, writer, and teacher, Paredes receives his B.A., M.A., and Ph.D. degrees from the University of Texas in 1951, 1953, and 1956, respectively. After working at a variety of jobs, including journalist, and serving in the armed forces, Paredes receives an advanced education later in life and becomes one of the most distinguished Hispanic scholars in U.S. history. He teaches at the University of Texas from 1951 on and is currently professor emeritus of English and anthropology there. He is instrumental in the development of the field of folklore in academia as well as in the field of Mexican–American studies. He has served as president of the American Folklore Society and been recognized for his leadership internationally. In the United States, he is awarded one of the nation's highest awards for a humanist, the Charles Frankel Prize given by the National Endowment for the Arts (1989), and in Mexico, the highest award given a foreigner by the Mexican government, the Águila Azteca (the Aztec Eagle) medal (1991). Besides publishing numerous research articles, he is the author of *With a Pistol in His Hand: A Border Ballad and Its Hero* (1958), *Folktales of Mexico* (1970), *A Texas Mexican Cancionero* (1976), and *Uncle Remus con chile* (Uncle Remus with Chile, 1992). He is also the author of a novel, *George Washington Gomez* (1990), a book of poems, *Between Two Worlds* (1991), and a collection of short stories, *The Hammon and the Beans* (1994).

OCTOBER 17, 1915   U.S. Recognizes Carranza Government. The United States recognizes the Carranza regime as the government of Mexico.

NOVEMBER 15, 1915   Physicist and Teacher Alberto Baez Is Born. Alberto Vinicio Baez, noted physicist, is born in Puebla, Mexico. Baez receives his B.S. from Drew University in 1933, his M.A. from Syracuse University in 1935, and his Ph.D. from Stanford University in 1950. Over his long career he teaches and conducts research at various universities, including Cornell, Drew, Stanford, Wagner, Redlands, and Harvey Mudd. Between 1961 and 1974, he works in science education for UNESCO in New York and Paris. He also holds various international board and committee positions and, from 1974 to 1978, serves as chairman of the Committee on Teaching Sciences of the International Council of Science Unions. Since 1984, he has been the chairman emeritus of community education, International Union for the Conservation of Nature and Natural Resources, Glantz, Switzerland. In 1991, Baez and his co-researcher, Paul Kirkpatrick win the Dennis Gabor Award for their important role in the development of X-ray imaging optics. Their early discoveries show that grazing incidence optical systems could be used to focus X-rays. Their pioneering contributions to this field include the Kirkpatrick–Baez X-ray double reflecting imaging system and the Kirkpatrick–Baez Lamar X-ray telescope, which has been approved for flight on the Freedom Space Station. In his research, Baez specializes in X-ray radiation, optics, and microscopy, as well as science and environmental education.

1916

1916   Debut Art Exhibition. José Clemente Orozco has his first exhibition in Mexico City. (*See also* biography, November 23, 1883.)

1916   Mexican–American Governs New Mexi-

Alberto Vinicio Baez. (Courtesy of the Arte Público Press Archives, University of Houston.)

co. Ezequiel Cabeza de Vaca is the first Mexican–American elected to the governorship of the state of New Mexico.

1916 U.S. Installs Military Government in Dominican Republic. The United States intervenes in the Dominican Republic and installs its own military government as a response to the chaos reigning in the Dominican government. As early as 1905, Theodore Roosevelt established a customs receivership in the Dominican Republic, and financial and political conditions improved steadily in the country until 1911, when President Ramón Cáceres was assassinated. From then until 1916, various political rivals serve in the presidency, loot the treasury, and are deposed. Thus, President Woodrow Wilson sends in the marines and insists on new financial and military reforms and supervision of the next presidential election. General Harry Knapp reorganizes the government to carry out the reforms, creates a U.S.-style court system, and establishes a national guard to act as a police force. Over time, transportation, communications, and educational systems also are modernized. The intervention, nevertheless, is opposed by numerous

armed revolts and finally ends in 1924, with the election of Horacio Vásquez to the presidency. But the collection of customs on the island remains under American control.

FEBRUARY 10, 1916 Edward Roybal, U.S. Congressman, Is Born. Edward R. Roybal, the U.S. congressman to hold his seat in Congress the longest of any Hispanic, is born into a middle-class Mexican–American family in Albuquerque, New Mexico. When he is four, his family moves to Boyle Heights, Los Angeles, where he begins his education in the public schools. Roybal graduates high school in 1934 and works for the Civilian Conservation Corps. Later, he continues his education at the University of California and Southwestern University. He serves in World War II, and after the war accepts a position as director of health education for the Los Angeles County Tuberculosis and Health Association. In 1949, Roybal is elected to the Los Angeles City Council as a representative of East Los Angeles, as a result of a drive by returning war veterans to get representation. He thus becomes the first Mexican–American to serve on the board since 1881. Roybal is first elected to Congress in 1962 as a Democrat from the Twenty-fifth District. During his three decades in Congress, Roybal works for social and economic reforms. In 1967, he introduces legislation that becomes the first bilingual education act. In 1982, as chairman of the Congressional Hispanic Caucus, he leads the opposition to employer sanctions for hiring the undocumented, which ultimately is enacted as the Reform and Control Act of 1986. Throughout his tenure, congressman Roybal consistently advocates greater citizenship participation in party politics and in the federal and local government.

MARCH 9, 1916 Villa's Troops Attack. General Francisco "Pancho" Villa's troops sack the town of Columbus, New Mexico, killing seventeen American citizens. (*See also* biography, June 5, 1878.)

APRIL 1, 1916   Composer Ginastera Born in Buenos Aires. The famed Argentine composer, Alberto Ginastera, is born in Buenos Aires. He becomes a student at the Conservatorio Nacional de Música at an early age and graduates in 1938. A year earlier, in 1937, he debuts his suite *Panambí* at the Colón Theater in Buenos Aires; from that time on his name becomes known throughout the music world as one of Latin America's greatest composers. In 1941, he writes the music for "Estancia" (Sojourn) for New York's Caravan Ballet. He travels to New York with a Guggenheim Fellowship in 1946, and sees his *Panambí* performed by the NBC Symphonic Orchestra. In the following years, many institutions in the United States commission Ginastera compositions, including the Pittsburgh Festival, the Louisville Symphony Orchestra, the Coolidge Foundation, the New York Philharmonic for the inauguration of Lincoln Center, and others. During the 1950s Ginastera's works are featured at numerous international festivals, including those in Washington, D.C., Stockholm, Rome, and Frankfurt. In 1954, Igor Markevitch chooses his "Variaciones Concertantes" (Concert Variations) as a required work in his course on conducting in Salzburg. The "Variaciones" also wins the Cinzano Prize in 1957 and is later adopted by the City Center Ballet of New York as a ballet titled "Tender Night." Ginastera has won numerous national and international awards and participates on various international music councils. Ginastera is a founder of the School of Music of the Catholic University of Argentina.

MAY 3, 1916   Mexican–American Politician González Is Born. Henry Barbosa González, one of six children, is born in San Antonio, Texas, to Mexican political refugees Leónides and Genevieve González. He attends San Antonio public schools, San Antonio Junior College, the University of Texas at Austin, and, in 1943, graduates from St. Mary's University School of Law in San Antonio. He serves as the chief probation officer for Bexar county from 1946–51. In 1950, González runs for his first elected office, the San Antonio city council, but loses in a narrow race. In 1953, he tries again and is elected. While on the city council he works for passage of an ordinance ending segregation practices in city facilities. In 1953, he is the first Mexican–American elected to the Texas senate in 110 years. In November 1961, González wins a special election to fill a Texas seat in the United States House of Representatives. In Congress, González introduces and pushes bills to protect the civil rights of minorities and improve their economic and educational opportunities, including bills for better housing, farm worker benefits, minimum wage, a youth conservation corps, adult basic education, and terminating the Mexican bracero program. González serves as cochairman of both the Viva Kennedy organization during the 1960 presidential election and the Viva Johnson 1964 election campaign. He is critical of Chicano activists in the 1960s and 1970s, accusing the activists of advocating reverse racism. This results in many Mexican–Americans accusing González of being a conservative. In 1965, his alma mater bestows on him an honorary doctor of laws (LL.D) degree. He writes a weekly column for the San Antonio *Express News.* González becomes chairman of the Housing Subcommittee on Banking in 1981. During the Whitewater scandal that surrounds the Clinton presidency, González works to thwart the Republican's investigations.

SEPTEMBER 16, 1916   Carranza Calls for Constitutional Congress. Venustiano Carranza calls for a Constitutional Congress in the wake of winning the revolution in Mexico. On October 22, elections are held to name the delegates to the congress.

1917

1917   Acosta García Wins in Costa Rica. Federico Tinoco seizes the presidency of Costa Rica. Despite requests from United States business interests, including the United Fruit Company and the Canal Zone, for President Woodrow Wilson to recognize Tinoco's government, Wilson refuses; instead, without authorization, U.S. Naval Commander L.B. Porterfield takes his ship to the port of Limón on the Costa Rican coast and threatens to land the marines. Tinoco resigns. Julio Acosta García wins the elections that follow the resignation, and he is recognized immediately by the United States.

1917   Brother Chávez Becomes Friar. Brother Angélico Chávez, one of the most renowned religious poets in the United States, is the first native New Mexican to become a Franciscan friar. (*See also* biography, April 10, 1910.)

1917   Horacio Quiroga Publishes Most Renowned Book. Uruguayan writer Horacio Quiroga publishes *Cuentos de amor, de locura y de muerte* (Stories of Love, of Madness and of Death). (*See also* biography, December 31, 1878.)

1917   The Jones Act. The Jones Act is passed, extending U.S. citizenship to all Puerto Ricans and creating two Puerto Rican houses of legislature whose representatives are elected by the people. English is decreed the official language of Puerto Rico. This new citizenship allows the United States to enlist Puerto Ricans as soldiers to serve during World War I.

1917   The Mexican Constitution. Right in the middle of the Mexican Revolution, the Mexican government approves a new constitution containing important reforms. All land and the water running through it belong to the state, it is declared, and the state has the exclusive right to transfer them to individuals as private property. All mines and mineral and gas deposits belong exclusively to the state. The constitution recognizes workers' rights, their right to form unions and participate in profits from their work. It establishes an elaborate system of public education and limited property rights for the public good. The constitution also empowers the government to begin the redistribution

of lands and the development of small properties and farms. This first agrarian reform turns over parcels, called *ejidos*, to small farmers in rural communities, but they cannot be sold or mortgaged by the individual holders. To this date, about half of Mexico's rural land is still parceled out in this fashion. Many economists today believe that this is not efficient use of the land and that it both historically and currently retards Mexico's economic development. This 1917 constitution survives in great part today; it is democratic, but also contains some socialistic reforms.

1917   Navy, Marines Go to Cuba. Armed revolts and political unrest in Cuba lead the United States to invoke the Platt Amendment and send the navy and marines to Cuba, where U.S. forces eventually occupy a large portion of the island. While World War I rages, the United States wants to protect sugar mills, mines, and railroads. But the occupation goes far beyond what is authorized by the Platt Amendment. Some 2,600 marines are stationed in Oriente and Camagüey until 1922.

1917   Otero Becomes U.S. Marshall. Miguel A. Otero, Jr., having switched to the Democratic Party, is appointed United States Marshall of the Panama Canal Zone under President Woodrow Wilson. (*See also* biography, October 17, 1859.)

1917   U.S. Restricts Immigration. During World War I, "temporary" Mexican farmworkers, railroad laborers and miners are permitted to enter the United States to work. But throughout 1917, the United States begins to limit immigration by passing restrictive laws. Immigrants are now required to pay a head tax and demonstrate their ability to read. For those workers contracted by employers, their stay in the United States is not to exceed six months.

JANUARY 16, 1917   The Zimmerman Telegram. A telegram, known as the "Zimmerman Telegram," from the German government to

President Venustiano Carranza of Mexico is intercepted and revealed to the United States government. The German government offers to return the southwestern part of the United States to Mexico in return for Mexico's alliance with Germany. The prospect of a German–Mexican alliance leads to further mistrust of Mexicans and Mexican–Americans.

FEBRUARY 1917 U.S. Immigration Act. The United States Congress enacts the Immigration Act, imposing a literacy requirement on all individual immigrants, aimed at curbing the influx of immigrants from southern and eastern Europe but ultimately inhibiting immigration from Mexico.

FEBRUARY 17, 1917 Julia de Burgos, Puerto Rican Poet, Is Born. Julia de Burgos, one of Puerto Rico's greatest poets, is born in Carolina, where she receives her elementary education. In 1933, she receives her teaching certificate from the University of Puerto Rico and pursues teaching off and on during the rest of her life. From 1935 to 1937, Julia de Burgos writes political poetry, including her famous "Domingo de Ramos" (Palm Sunday). In 1940 she leaves Puerto Rico, never to return, when she goes to study at the University of Havana. In 1942 she moves to New York City. Her published books of poetry include *Poemas exactos a mí misma* (Exact Poems to Myself, 1938), *Poemas en veinte surcos* (Poems in Twenty Furrows, 1938), *Canción de la verdad sencilla* (Song of Simple Truth, 1939) and *El mar y tú* (The Sea and You, 1954). Borgo's poetry is inspired in the Puerto Rican landscape and the need for a national identity and freedom, as in her famous "Rio Grande de Loíza" (Big River of Loíza), but they are also intimate songs of love, death, and passion. Burgos dies an alcoholic in abject poverty in New York City on July 6, 1953.

MARCH 2, 1917 Desi Arnaz, Cuban Bandleader and Actor, Is Born. Actor, musician, and producer Desidero Alberto Arnaz y de Acha III is born in Santiago, Cuba, to Desidero

Julia de Burgos. (Courtesy of the Center for Puerto Rican Studies Library, Hunter College, CUNY.)

Alberto II, senator and mayor of Santiago, Cuba, and his wife, Lolita. After the Cuban Revolution in 1933, his family emigrates to Miami, Florida. Arnaz has a career as a drummer, guitarist, and singer from 1934 until 1939. He performs on Broadway as a Cuban football star in the musical *Too Many Girls* and reprises his role for the RKO film version in 1940. During the filming he meets Lucille Ball and they marry later that year. He serves as musical director for Bob Hope's radio show (1946–47) and tours with his band throughout the 1940s.

In 1950, he cofounds Desilu Productions with Lucille Ball and they tour as a husband and wife comedy act. Arnaz and Ball approach television networks with the idea of a husband–wife situation comedy to star Arnaz and Ball as Ricky and Lucy Ricardo, a Cuban bandleader and his wacky, high-spirited wife. Producers argue that audiences won't accept Ball's marriage to a Cuban. To prove them wrong, the couple makes the pilot of *I Love Lucy* with $5,000 of their own money. CBS Television agrees to air the show, but insists that it be filmed live. To accomplish this, the show pioneers the "three camera technique," a filming technique using three different angles, allowing for close-ups and long shots. *I Love Lucy* is an immediate success and runs until 1959. Desilu Productions purchases RKO Studios and begins producing other shows, including *The Untouchables* and *Our Miss Brooks*. In 1960, Arnaz and Ball divorce, and he goes on to create and produce other television pilots. Arnaz dies December 2, 1986, in Del Mar, California, of lung cancer at the age of 69.

MAY 1917 The Selective Service Act. The Selective Service Act becomes law in the United States, obligating noncitizen Mexicans in the United States to register with their local draft boards, even though they are not eligible for the draft.

MAY 1, 1917 Revolution Ends. The Mexican Revolution is officially over when General Venustiano Carranza is elected to the presidency of Mexico under the constitution, the product of a constitutional convention of six sessions in 1916 and 1917. That constitution is still in force today.

AUGUST 15, 1917 Archbishop, Human Rights Advocate Romero is Born. Oscar Arnulfo Romero y Galdamez is born to a railway employee, Santos, and his wife, Guadalupe de Jesús Galdamez, in Ciudad Barrios, El Salvador. Romero is apprenticed to a carpenter before attending secondary school in San Miguel.

He spends two years at the minor seminary of the Claretians before continuing his theological studies in Rome. In 1942, he receives his ordination. Romero is named assistant bishop of San Salvador in 1971, and four years later becomes the titular bishop of the dioceses of San Miguel. In 1977, the Vatican appoints Monsignor Romero to the Archbishopric of San Salvador. Outraged by the murder of a Jesuit friend, Archbishop Romero begins to denounce political violence and calls for social changes, including redistribution of wealth, land reform, and justice and equality for the poor. He is nominated for the Nobel Peace Prize by 18 British Members of Parliament and 23 U.S. congressmen in 1979. In the chapel of the Hospital of Divine Providence, an institution he founded for terminally ill cancer patients, while celebrating mass in memory of a well-known opposition journalist, Romero is assassinated. His funeral mass is held in the Metropolitan Cathedral in San Salvador with more than 30,000 mourners in attendance.

1918

1918 The Rise and Fall of Sugar. The United States Sugar Equalization Board contracts to buy all of the Cuban sugar crop for 1918–19, what amounts to four million tons or 25 percent of the entire world supply. (In 1898, Cuba produces only some 1.5 million tons. In 1909, sugar accounted for just 54 percent of Cuban exports.) This elevates sugar to account for 89 percent of Cuba's exports. Cuba–United States relations always are conditioned by the sugar industry, and Cuba readily accepts United States price fixing in order to trade for the goods and services that the U.S. could readily supply. After the war ends in 1918, the price of sugar continues to rise, with the Sugar Equalization Board reaping windfalls of profit, to the protest of Cuban producers and numerous investigations by the government authorities for fraud and corruption. The 1919–20 crop is not turned over to the board and instead is put on the world open market. A boom ensues in Cuba as the price of sugar quadruples. But since the 1918 sugar sabotage is largely the figment of speculators' imagination, the boom turns to bust almost immediately, with the price per pound returning to almost the same level it was at war's end. Numerous sugar producers, mills, transport companies, and others that had borrowed heavily to expand business find themselves in difficulty. The final blow is the U.S. Congress's passage, in February 1921, of the Emergency Tariff Bill, which raises the duty on Cuban sugar by 60 percent. Many sugar mills and plantations fall into the hands of United States entrepreneurs through forced sale or foreclosure. Eventually, the banks that have underwritten the expansion of the industry also close their doors and most of them fail. The government, too, finds its revenues depleted and must rely on foreign assistance to save the republic from bankruptcy. As a result, the island economy becomes increasingly controlled by a relatively small group of New York financiers. By the time of the 1926–27 sugar crop, 62 percent of the sugar is produced by American-owned mills, 8 percent by jointly owned Cuban and American interests, and 4 percent by Canadian-owned mills.

1918 Vallejo Has First Book Published. César Vallejo, poet and political activist, has his first book, *Los heraldos negros* (The Black Messengers), published. The book fully demonstrates his modernist views. (*See also* biography, March 16, 1892.)

MAY 29, 1918 Bert Corona, Founder of Labor Groups, Is Born. Union organizer and political activist Bert Corona is born in El Paso, Texas. He is educated in El Paso public schools and attends the University of Southern California and the University of California, Los Angeles, where he studies commercial law. Between 1936 and 1942, Corona is involved in labor activities in the Southwest, especially organizing cannery and warehouse workers. His later

activities are directed more toward political action and, in 1959, he is instrumental in founding the Mexican American Political Association. Among the many other organizations that he helped to found are the Hermanded General de Trabajadores, the National Congress of Spanish-speaking People, and the Mexican American Youth Conference.

SEPTEMBER 12, 1918 Writer Arreola Born in Mexico. Juan José Arreola, one of Latin America's outstanding writers of short narratives, is born in Ciudad Guzmán, Jalisco, Mexico. A professional actor and man of letters, Arreola is best known for a plethora of brief, often surrealistic narratives, some of which can be considered short stories. Arreola's unique works often defy tradition because of their lack of such conventions as plot and characterization. His best-known collection *Confabulario* (Confabulations, 1952) is full of whimsy, innovative structure, satire, and allegories to the human condition. Arreola's novel, *La feria* (The Fair, 1963), continues this fragmented view of reality and break with conventions, tying together unrelated scenes, partial conversations, and portions of letters and diaries that require the reader to piece together the narrative. Among Arreola's many collections of narratives are *Varia invención* (Various Inventions, 1946), *Bestiario* (Bestiaries, 1958), *Punta de Plata* (Silver Point, 1958), *Cuentos* (Stories, 1969), *Palindroma* (Palindrome, 1971), and *Zoo en cuarta dimensión* (Zoo in Fourth Dimension, 1973). Arreola is also an actor and a playwright who in 1954 wins first prize in the National Institute for Fine Arts Drama Festival for his play *La hora de todos* (Everyone's Hour).

SEPTEMBER 26, 1918 Alegría, Chilean Scholar and Novelist, Is Born. Chilean literary critic, professor, and novelist Fernando Alegría is born in Santiago, Chile. Alegría receives his early education in Chile, his M.A. from Bowling Green State University in 1941, and his Ph.D. in Spanish from the University of California–Berkeley in 1947. After receiving his

Fernando Alegría. (Courtesy of the Arte Público Press Archives, University of Houston.)

Ph.D., he makes his entire career at Stanford University, where he ascends the ranks to full professor with a Chair, and finally professor emeritus, which is his current status. Alegría is a pioneer in the study of Latin–American narrative literature. He is a distinguished novelist, essayist, and poet, recognized in both the Spanish- and English-speaking worlds. His book, *Historia de la novela hispanoamericana* (History of the Spanish American Novel, 1965), goes through various editions and serves as a standard text of Latin–American literature. He has been a Guggenheim Fellow and has won numerous other awards and distinctions. Alegría also is one of the first and most influential scholars to acknowledge and promote Hispanic literature of the United States in academia.

OCTOBER 17, 1918   Rita Hayworth, Dancer and Actress, Is Born. Rita Hayworth (Margarita Carmen Cansino) is born in Brooklyn N.Y., the daughter of Spanish-born dancer Eduardo Cansino and his *Ziegfeld Follies* partner Volga Hayworth. Hayworth dances professionally by the age of thirteen at Mexican night spots in Tijuana and Agua Caliente, where she eventually is noticed by Hollywood. She makes her screen debut in 1935, playing bit parts under her real name. In 1937, she marries Edward Judson, under whose guidance she changes her name and is transformed into an auburn-haired sophisticate. For the remainder of the 1930s Hayworth is confined to leads in B pictures, but through much of the 1940s she is the undisputed sex goddess of Hollywood films and the hottest star at Columbia Studios. Her tempestuous personal life includes marriages to Orson Welles, Prince Aly Khan, and singer Dick Haymes. As Rita Cansino her films include *Under the Pampas Moon, Charlie Chan in Egypt,* and *Dante's Inferno* (1935); *Meet Nero Wolfe* (1936); and *Trouble in Texas, Old Louisiana,* and *Hit the Saddle* (1937). As Rita Hayworth she acts in *The Shadow* (1937); *Angels Over Broadway* (1940); *The Strawberry Blonde* and *Blood and Sand* (1941); *Cover Girl* (1944); *Gilda* (1946); *The Lady from Shanghai* and *The Loves of Carmen* (1948); *Salome* and *Miss Sadie Thompson* (1953); *Pal Joey* (1957); *Separate Tables* (1958); *They Came to Cordura* (1959); *The Happy Thieves* (1962); *The Money Trap* (1966); *The Wrath of God* (1972); and *Circle* (1976). Hayworth, a sufferer of Alzheimer's Disease, dies in 1987.

1919

1919   Cuban Pitches in Two World Series. Adolfo Luque becomes the first Hispanic–American to play in the World Series of baseball, as a member of the Cincinnati Reds. Luque, a dark-skinned Cuban, breaks into the majors in 1924 with the Boston Braves, where he is incessantly jeered and subjected to racial epithets. Despite his emotionally rocky career, because of the racism he faces, he has one of the longest careers of any Hispanic baseball player, serving until 1935 for the Boston, Cincinnati, Brooklyn, and New York teams. Luque pitches in two World Series, and is credited with the decisive win in one of them. See Fall 1923.

1919   Guayasamín, Prize-Winning Painter

and Muralist, Is Born. Painter Oswaldo Guayasamín is born the eldest of ten children in an Indian–mestizo family in Quito, Ecuador. From 1933 to 1940, Guayasamín studies painting under Pedro León Donoso at the National School of Fine Arts in Quito and has his first solo exhibition in 1940. Through the influence of Nelson Rockefeller, who collect his works, Guayasamín is able to travel extensively in the United States and exhibit widely there. He also travels and exhibits in Latin America. In 1943, he studies fresco painting with José Clemente Orozco in Mexico. Highly influenced by pre-Columbian art, Guayasamín also becomes a muralist and fresco painter. In 1948 he completes his famous fresco, *El incario y la Conquista* (The Incan and the Conquest). In 1952, he has more than one hundred works exhibited under the title of *Huacayñan* at the Museum of Fine Arts in Caracas. A notable series is his 250 paintings of *La edad de la ira* (The Age of Anger) on the theme of political prisoners. Guayasamín wins numerous international prizes, including the Grand Prize for Painting at the Spanish Bienal and the Sao Paolo Bienal.

OCTOBER 4, 1919 René Marqués, Puerto Rican Playwright and Author, Is Born. René Marqués, considered Puerto Rico's foremost playwright and writer of short fiction, is born in Arecibo, Puerto Rico, into a family of agrarian background. Marqués studies agronomy at the College of Agriculture in Mayagüez and actually works for two years for the Department of Agriculture. But his interest in literature takes him to Spain in 1946 to study the classics. Upon his return, Marqués founds a small theatre group dedicated to producing and furthering the creation of Puerto Rican theatre. In 1948 he receives a Rockefeller Foundation fellowship to study playwriting in the United States, which allows him to study at Columbia University and at the Piscator Dramatic Workshop in New York City. After his return to San Juan, he establishes the Teatro Experimental del Ateneo (the Atheneum Society Experimental Theater). From that time on, Marqués

Poster for the production of René Márques's famous play *La Carreta* (The Oxcart). (Courtesy of the Arte Público Press Archives, University of Houston.)

maintains a heavy involvement not only in playwriting, but also in development of Puerto Rican theatre. He produces a continuous flow of short stories, novels, essays, and anthologies. Marqués's best-known work is still the all-important play *La Carreta* (debuted in 1953, published in Spanish in 1961, and in English *The Oxcart*, in 1969). He starts writing in 1944, when he publishes his first collection of poems, *Peregrinación* (Pilgrimage). Of his many published works his plays include *El hombre y sus sueños* (Man and His Dreams, 1948), *Palm Sunday* (1949), *Otro día nuestro* (Another of Our Days, 1955), *Juan Bobo y la Dama de Occidente* (Juan Bobo and the Western Lady, 1956), *El sol y los MacDonald* (The Sun and the MacDonalds, 1957), and a collection, *Teatro* (1959), which includes three of his most important plays: *Los soles truncos* (The Fan Lights), *Un niño azul para esa sombra* (A Blue Child for that Shadow), and *La muerte no entrará en palacio* (Death Will Not Enter the Palace). Marqués is one of the few Puerto Rican writers who have had international audiences and impact; he is truly one of the greats of all Latin–American dramatists. The style, philosophy, and craft of his works, as produced in New York, have had long-lasting influence on the development of Hispanic theatre in the United States. René Marqués dies in 1979.

1920

1920 Amado Nervo Publishes Poetry. Mexican poet Nervo publishes his best-known work, *La amada inmóvil* (The Immobile Beloved One). (*See also* biography, August 27, 1870.)

MARCH 1, 1920 Julián Samora, Hispanic Sociologist, Is Born. Julián Samora is born in Pagosa Springs, Colorado. Samora receives his B.A. degree from Adams State College in 1942, his M.S. degree from Colorado State University in 1974, and his Ph.D. degree from Washington University in 1953. From 1955 to 1957, he is an assistant professor at the University of Colorado Medical School, associate professor at Michigan State University from 1957 to 1959, and a full professor at the University of Notre Dame from 1959 to 1985, when he becomes professor emeritus. One of the pioneer Hispanic sociologists, Samora trains a generation of important sociologists whose ranks include the noted Mexican sociologist, Jorge Bustamante. Among his many honors are the White House Hispanic Heritage Award (1985),

the Mexican government's highest award given to a foreigner, and the Águila Azteca (Aztec Eagle) medal (1991). His books include *A History of the Mexican American People* (1977) and *Gunpowder Justice: A Reassessment of the Texas Rangers* (1979). In 1991, a research center at Michigan State University is named in his honor.

MAY 21, 1920 Carranza Is Killed. Mexican President Venustiano Carranza is assassinated in Taxcalantongo, in the mountains of Mexico.

SUMMER 1920 Olympic Medal Winners. Brazil's Afranio Da Costa takes the Silver Medal in the free pistol competition at the Olympic Games in Antwerp, Belgium. Teammate Guilherme Paraense wins the gold in the rapid-fire competition.

NOVEMBER 25, 1920 Actor Ricardo Montalbán Is Born in Mexico. Actor Ricardo Montalbán is born in Mexico City. He plays bit roles in several Broadway productions before debuting on the screen in Mexico in the early 1940s and subsequently being recruited as a "Latin lover" type by Metro-Goldwyn-Mayer (MGM) in 1947. He serves as a strong force in Hollywood for the establishment of better opportunities for Hispanics. His films include *Fiesta* (1947); *The Kissing Bandit* (1948); *Neptune's Daughter* and *Border Incident* (1949); *Right Cross* and *Two Weeks with Love* (1950); *Across the Wide Missouri* and *Mark of the Renegade* (1951); *Sombrero* and *Latin Lovers* (1953); *The Saracen Blade* (1954); *A Life in the Balance* (1955); *Sayonara* (1957); *Let No Man Write My Epitaph* (1960); *Cheyenne Autumn* (1964); *The Money Trap* and *The Singing Nun* (1966); *Sweet Charity* (1969); *Escape from the Planet of the Apes* (1971); *Conquest of the Planet of the Apes* (1972); *The Train Robbers* (1973); *Joe Panther* (1976); and *Star Trek II: The Wrath of Khan* (1982). He eventually is given an opportunity to demonstrate a wider acting range on television, including segments of *The Loretta Young Show* and his most well-known role as Mr.

Roarke in the dramatic series *Fantasy Island*, which ran from 1978 to 1984.

1921

1921   Composer Chávez Wins Commission. Carlos Chávez y Ramírez begins presenting his own works and wins a government commission for a ballet, *El nuevo fuego* (The New Fire), which is based on an Aztec story. (*See also* biography, June 13, 1899.)

1921   Immigration Restrictions. Limits on the number of immigrants allowed to enter the United States during a single year are imposed for the first time in the country's history. As the first of two national origin quota acts designed to curtail immigration from eastern and southern Europe and Asia is passed, Mexico and Puerto Rico become major sources of workers.

1922

1922   Artists' Union Founded. Diego Rivera cofounds the Union of Technical Workers, Painters and Sculptors. (*See also* biography, December 8, 1886.)

1922   Nationalist Party Founded in Puerto Rico. The Partido Nacionalista Puertorriqueño, the nationalist party, is founded in Puerto Rico, with José Coll y Cuchí as president. The party struggles for Puerto Rican independence even to the present. Under the leadership of Pedro Alvizu Campos, the party becomes increasingly militant and even violent, and sees many of its members persecuted and imprisoned. One of the tragic reprisals against the nationalists is the 1937 Ponce Massacre, where the police kill twenty-two young people, mostly students, and wound some two hundred others. It is the Partido Nacionalista Puertorriqueño that plans and executes revolutionary uprisings on the island and the attacks on the United States

House of Representatives and President Truman's residence at Blair House in 1954.

DECEMBER 1922   Central American Conference Adopts Accords. Concerned that political unrest in Central America will spill over into Panama, the United States government calls for a Central American conference in Washington, D.C. The conference ends in 1923 with a series of accords that rigidly define revolutionary government not worthy of recognition, establish a new Central American Court, and force arms limitations. Despite these accords, the United States soon finds reason to intervene in the internal affairs of Honduras, Nicaragua, El Salvador, and Guatemala.

1923

1923   Jesús Rafael Soto, Venezuelan Painter, Is Born. Venezuelan painter Jesús Rafael Soto is born in Ciudad Bolívar, the eldest of five peasant children later abandoned by their father. In his youth, he is highly influenced by the natural surroundings and Indian life and culture in rural Venezuela. He begins his life as an artist at age fifteen, painting signs for the local movie house. By age nineteen he has won a scholarship to the Cristóbal Rojas School of Fine and Applied Arts in Caracas. In 1947, he is named the director of the School of Fine Arts in Maracaibo. After his first solo exhibition in 1949 at the Taller Libre de Arte (Free Art Workshop), the next year he travels to Paris on a grant and exhibits there through 1955. While in Paris, he becomes interested in kinetic art and experiments with integrating movement into painting. He later experiments with hanging elements in front of geometric structures and kinetic murals. Soto's international reputation grows and he wins numerous awards, including prizes at the Sao Paolo Bienel, the Venice Biennale, and the American Bienal at Córdoba, Argentina. Among his numerous architectural works are the *Volume Suspendu* for the Montreal World's Fair in 1967 and wall sculptures for the UNESCO Building in Paris (1970). He has had various retrospectives, including one at the Museo de Bellas Arts in Caracas (1971) and one at the Solomon R. Guggenheim Museum in New York (1974).

1923   Mexican Film Idol Sees Success in Movie Role. Ramón Novarro, is cast in a leading role in the 1923 film, *Prisoner of Zenda*, largely because of his ability as a dancer. He quickly becomes a success as a romantic matinee idol. (*See also* biography, February 6, 1899.)

FALL 1923   Luque Wins Pitching Championship. Adolfo Luque becomes the first Hispanic American ballplayer to win the pitching championship in professional baseball in the United States. His earned run average for Cleveland that year is 1.93, with 27 wins and 8 losses (including 6 shutouts).

1924

1924   The Aprism Movement. In Peru, the Alianza Popular Revolucionaria Americana (APRA)—the American Popular Revolutionary Alliance—is formed by Raúl Haya de la Torre. The alliance spearheads a widespread movement that becomes known as Aprism to rescue the Indians from their misery and create a universal system of social security, redistribute the lands, and raise taxes on the mining, oil, and agricultural industries. The ultimate goal is to create an integrated economy for all of Spanish America, which would also lead to a politically unified Spanish America.

1924   Border Patrol Established. The United States Border Patrol is created this year to supervise and control migration, especially from Mexico.

SUMMER 1924   Olympic Medal Winners. Argentina's Luis Angel Bruneto wins the triple jump competition at the Olympics in Paris,

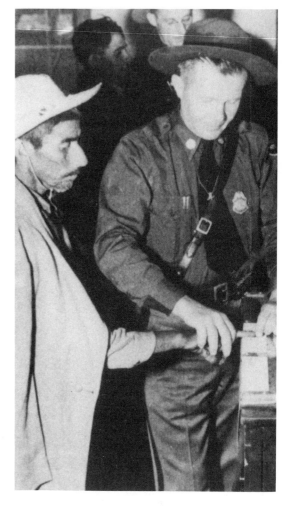

Border patrol agent fingerprinting an undocumented worker before deporting him. (Courtesy of the Library of Congress Prints & Photographs Division.)

France, with 15 meters 42.5 centimeters. Uruguay wins the gold medal in soccer.

1925

1925   Activist Forms Political Group. Peruvian activist Juan Carlos Mariátegu forms a group called Amauta to promote agrarian and political reform, the development of nationalism, and strategies for raising Indians from poverty and oppression. (*See also* biography, June 14, 1895.)

1925   Mexican Educator Vasconcelos Publishes Book. Vasconceles's ideology of the blending of all races is published in his book, *La raza cósmica* (The Cosmic Race). (*See also* biography, February 28, 1882.)

1925   New Church Leader Disavows Rome. As a result of anticlerical actions taken by the Mexican government, a schismatic Mexican Catholic Church is established, under the leadership of patriarch José Joaquín Pérez. He disavows Rome and considers celibacy immoral. Numerous attacks on the Catholic church follow, including a decree by the legislature of the state of Tabasco making it illegal for any unmarried priest to serve Mass.

JANUARY 20, 1925   Author and Priest Cardenal Born in Nicaragua. Nicaragua's poet–priest–revolutionary, Ernesto Cardenal, is born in Granada, Nicaragua. Cardenal attends the National Autonomous University of Mexico from 1944 to 1948 and Columbia University from 1948 to 1949. In 1965, he is ordained as a Roman Catholic priest. From 1948 to the present he has published copious volumes of poetry, and today he is considered a major Latin–American poet. Cardenal uses his poetry in the struggle to overthrow Nicaraguan dictator Anastasio Somoza in 1979 and to further literacy and educate the young in postrevolutionary society when he becomes Minister of Culture for the Sandinista regime. Although a "Christian Marxist" with a firm belief in the relationship of art and politics, Cardenal attacks socialist realism and creates nonrhetorical, nonstrident verse. His work is highly lyrical and technically innovative, but harkens back to classical Roman poets, such as Catullus and Martial, both of whose works Cardenal has translated. Among the themes that Cardenal explores in his poems are the following: materialistic values corrupting human values in modern society, the importance of truthfulness and precision in lan-

guage, and a quest in past history for models applicable to today's society. And Cardenal consistently revisits Nicaragua's and Latin America's history, as can readily be seen in his collections of selected works: *Antología de Ernesto Cardenal* (Ernesto Cardenal Anthology, 1967) and *With Walker in Nicaragua and Other Early Poems, 1949–1954*. Two other volumes have brought together selected later poems: *Antología: Ernesto Cardenal* (Anthology: Ernesto Cardenal, 1983) and *From Nicaragua with Love: Poems, 1979–1986* (1986). In much of Cardenal's production the uniting of Marxism and Catholicism and the support of the Marxist revolution, particularly in Nicaragua, is evident. But much of his work, too, is deeply religious and even mystical in the grand tradition of ascetic and mystic writers; he produces numerous psalms and prayers and meditations. Pope John Paul II has reprimanded Cardenal on more than one occasion for promoting liberation theology, which the pope finds divergent from Catholic teachings. With more than thirty books and numerous translations to other languages, Cardenal is one of the most accessible and highly regarded poets in Latin America.

MAY 25, 1925   Castellanos, Mexican Poet, Novelist, and Feminist, Is Born. Mexican poet and novelist Rosario Castellanos is born in Mexico City. She is considered to have been a leading feminist and an advocate for Mexico's Indians. Raised in Comitán, Chiapas, she encounters the plight of the Maya Indians there and in her later life she devotes much of her writing to them. Among her other works of poetry are *De la vigilia estéril* (From the Sterile Vigil, 1950), *Poemas, 1935–1955* (Poems, 1957), *Al pie de la letra* (Literally Speaking, 1959), and *Lívida luz* (Livid Light, 1960). Her selected poems are published in 1972 in *Poesía no eres tú: obra poética, 1948–1971* (You Are Poetry: The Poetic Works, 1948–1971). Her novels include *Balún–Canán* (published in 1957, translated as *The Nine Guardians* in 1960) and *Oficio de tinieblas* (Shadow Trade, 1962). Castellanos is also a prolific short-story writer and essayist.

Her writings on feminist topics include *Sobre cultura femenina* (On Women's Culture, 1950), *Mujer que sabe latín* (Woman Who Knows Latin, 1973) and *El uso de la palabra* (The Use of the Word, 1975). Castellanos dies in Tel-Aviv, Israel, on August 7, 1974, where she was serving as the Mexican ambassador.

1926

1926   Güiraldes' Prize-Winning Novel Published. Novelist Ricardo Güiraldes' crowning achievement is *Don Segundo Sombra,* a masterpiece of Latin American literature and winner of the Argentine national prize for literature, is published. (*See also* biography, February 13, 1886.)

1926   Pentecostal Minister López Tijerina Is Born. Reies López Tijerina, a Pentecostal minister who founds and leads a major movement to regain for families their ancestral Spanish and Mexican land grants in New Mexico, is born into a poor sharecropper family near San Antonio, Texas. Because his family joins the migrant farm labor stream, he receives little formal education. After graduating from a Texas Bible school in 1940, López Tijerina conducts evangelistic work along the border as a traveling preacher. During independent study and research in the 1950s, López Tijerina becomes convinced that many of the Mexican–Americans' social and political problems are traceable to the loss of their ancestral lands, given to them in Spanish and Mexican grants or mercedes. In 1963, in Albuquerque, López Tijerina and his five brothers found the Alianza Federal de Mercedes (Federal Alliance of Grants)—later changed to Alianza Federal de Pubelos Libres (Federal Alliance of Free Towns)—to work toward returning the lands to their heirs. By 1966, the movement claims twenty thousand followers. In October of that year, López Tijerina leads a group in a takeover of part of the Kit Carson National Forest, which they declare to be the Republic of Río Chama.

Because of this clash with authorities and others, including a raid on the Tierra Amarilla courthouse on June 5, 1967, where various members of the movement have been jailed, López Tijerina is arrested, tried and sentenced in both state and federal proceedings to two one-to-five and two two-to-ten-year prison terms, to run concurrently. During his repeated clashes with authorities, his trial, and the beginning of his sentences, López Tijerina becomes a national hero to liberals and for the Chicano civil rights movement. On July 27, 1971, López Tijerina is paroled from prison; he subsequently is a moderating influence on the Chicano Movement and dedicates himself to preaching brotherhood, although he remains dedicated to the land-grant issue.

1926   Puerto Ricans Attacked in New York City. In rioting in Harlem, Puerto Ricans are attacked by non-Hispanics as their numbers become larger in Manhattan neighborhoods (by 1930 they will reach 53,000).

MARCH 8, 1926   José González, Novelist and Short-Story Writer, Is Born. José Luis González, Puerto Rico's leading novelist and short story writer, is born in Santo Domingo, the Dominican Republic, but moves to Puerto Rico at the age of eight. He receives his primary education in Guaynabo and his secondary education in Santurce, and receives his bachelor's degree in social sciences from the University of Puerto Rico in 1946. He later obtains a master's degree in literature from the National Autonomous University of Mexico. During the late '40s and early '50s, González lives and travels in the United States, Europe, and Mexico. In 1953, he is back in Puerto Rico writing scripts for radio crime programs. Since 1953, he has lived in Mexico, where he has taught for many years at the National Autonomous University; he has given up U.S. citizenship to become a Mexican citizen. González is a Communist and a lifelong supporter of independence for Puerto Rico. His literary reputation is gained in Mexico and most important narratives are written

José Luis González. (Courtesy of the Arte Público Press Archives, University of Houston.)

there, although they almost always deal with Puerto Rico and its culture. Most of his stories detail the life of the common man of Puerto Rico, whether in an urban or rural setting. Of all of the Puerto Rican prose writers, it is González who has most participated in the boom of Latin–American writing and has garnered an international following. His collections of stories include *En la sombra* (In the Shade, 1953), *Cinco cuentos de sangre* (Five Stories of Blood, 1945), *El hombre en la calle* (Man in the Street, 1948), *En este lado* (On this Side, 1954), *Mambrú se fue a la guerra* (Mambrú Went Off to War, 1973), *En Nueva York y otras desgracias* (In New York and Other Misfortunes, 1973), and *Cuento de cuentos y once más* (The Story of Stories and Eleven More, 1973). Among his novels are *Balada de otro tiempo* (Ballad from Another Time, 1978) and *La llegada* (The Arrival, 1980). In 1978, González is awarded Mexico's most prestigious literary award, the Xavier Villaurrutia Prize for Fiction for his *Balada de otro tiempo*.

JULY 31, 1926 Mexican Government Ends Catholic Practices. The Mexican government suspends the practice of Catholicism in Mexi-

co. Following disputes between the government and the high leadership of the Church because of the anticlerical tenets of the 1917 constitution, the government enacts laws prohibiting the celebration of Mass and the administering of the holy sacraments, including weddings and baptisms. Earlier in the year, the Plutarch Elías Calles regime ordered the closing of several convents and churches, and expelled two hundred foreign priests from the country. The number of priests allowed in certain states was limited and the bishop of Huejutla was arrested. Calles also introduced a new penal code that instituted penalties of one to five years imprisonment for priests and clerics who criticized the laws or conducted religious acts outside of church, including the wearing of religious clothes in public. On July 25, the Catholic bishops in Mexico announced in a pastoral letter their suspension of Catholicism in Mexico. Calles's ratification of the bishops' decision is supported on August 1 by a rally of 40,000 workers in front of the National Palace. When the bishops are unsuccessful in September at getting the Mexican Congress to rescind the laws, dozens of radical priests and their followers are ready for war. The Cristero War (1926–29) is an uprising of more than 50,000, mainly in the states of Colima, Durango, Guerrero, Jalisco, Michoacán, Nayarit, and Zacatecas. Some 90,000 lives are lost, and another wave of refugees enters the United States. Neither side is strong enough to prevail in the bloody war, and it is finally negotiated to an end by the religious hierarchy and the government of Emilio Portes Gil. An agreement is signed on June 21, 1929, in which the government and the Church agree to restrict themselves to their respective realms.

1927

MAY 3, 1927 César Chávez, Advocate for Farmworkers, Is Born. César Chávez, the famed Mexican–American labor organizer and

César Chávez exhorting people to start a new grape boycott. (Courtesy of the Arte Público Press Archives, University of Houston.)

leader, is born near Yuma, Arizona, to a family of migrant farmworkers. Chávez attends nearly thirty schools, eventually achieving a seventh-grade education. During World War II he serves in the navy, after which he returns to migrant farm labor. He eventually settles down in 1948 in the barrio of Sal Si Puedes (Get Out If You Can) in San Jose, California. It is in San Jose that he begins working for the Community Service Organization as a community organizer. By 1958, he has become general director of the CSO in California and Arizona. In 1962,

wishing to organize farmworkers, he resigns the CSO directorship and moves to Delano, California, where he becomes head of the United Farm Workers Organizing Committee, which is today the United Farm Workers, AFL-CIO. From 1965 on, Chávez and his fledgling union embark on a number of history making strikes and national boycotts of agricultural products that became the most successful in the history of farm labor in the United States. Due principally to Chávez and his organization's efforts, the California legislature passes the

California Labor Relations Act in 1975, which provides secret ballot union elections for farmworkers. Due to his efforts, as well, many other improvements are made in wage, health, and housing conditions for farmworkers in California and Arizona. Chávez is known as a selfless and spiritual leader of farmworkers everywhere, bringing to national attention their plight through media appearances and interviews, hunger strikes, and well-organized boycotts. He dies in 1993 of a heart attack near the place of his birth. On August 8, 1994, President Bill Clinton posthumously bestows on Chávez the Medal of Freedom—the nation's highest honor for civilians.

JUNE 19, 1927 Julián Nava, Educator and Ambassador, Is Born. Julián Nava, the Mexican-American educator and ambassador, is born in Los Angeles, California, to a family that fled Mexico during the Revolution. Nava grows up in East Los Angeles, where he begins his higher education, at East Los Angeles Junior College. He serves in the Navy Air Corps during World War II and, upon return, obtains an education through the G.I. Bill. Nava graduates from Pomona College with an A.B. in 1951 and from Harvard University with an A.M. degree in 1952 and a Ph.D. in 1955. After graduation he serves as a lecturer and professor at various universities in Colombia, Venezuela, Puerto Rico, Spain, and California; he is currently a tenured professor of history at California State University at Northridge. In 1967, Nava is elected to the Los Angeles school board and later serves as president of the board. Nava serves as ambassador to Mexico from 1979 to 1981; he is the first Mexican-American to ever hold that post. Nava is a productive researcher and writer on Mexican-American history and education. Among his books are a high school textbook *Mexican Americans: Past, Present and Future* (1969), *Mexican Americans: A Brief Look at Their History* (a college textbook co-authored with Robert Barger, 1970), *A General History of California* (1976), and *Cali-*

fornia: Five Centuries of Cultural Contrasts, (also with Barger).

1928

1928 Composer Becomes Musical Director. Composer Silvestre Revueltas is named assistant director of the Orquesta Sinfónica de México by Carlos Chávez. (*See also* biography, December 31, 1899.)

1928 Oms Sets Baseball Record. Batter Alejandro Oms establishes a Cuban record for most consecutive games with hits: 30. (*See also* biography, 1895.)

MARCH 6, 1928 Novelist and Nobel Laureate Gabriel García Márquez Is Born. Gabriel García Márquez, distinguished Colombian novelist and Nobel laureate in 1982, is born. He graduates in journalism from the National University of Colombia and later obtains a degree in law. For many years, he develops his career as a journalist for *El Heraldo* (The Herald) in Barranquilla, as well as in Cartagena and Bogotá. He also works as a correspondent in Rome, Barcelona, and Mexico City. García Márquez begins his literary career by writing short stories for the newspapers at which he worked. Many of these early works are published in 1955 in the collection entitled *La Hojarasca* (The Leafstorm). One of his early novels, *Cien años de soledad* (One Hundred Years of Solitude, 1970), is his best known and is considered a masterpiece of Latin-American and world literature. In this generational novel set in Macondo, a mythical small town in a South American jungle, he becomes the primary exponent of the style which has characterized and made famous Latin-American literature of the twentieth century: magic realism. Among his many other famous works are *El coronel no tiene quien le escriba* (Nobody Writes the Colonel, 1961), *Los funerales de la Mamá Grande* (The Funeral of Mamá Grande, 1962), *El otoño del patriarca* (The Autumn of the Patriarch, 1978),

Gabriel García Márquez. (Courtesy of the Arte Público Press Archives, University of Houston.)

La increíble y triste historia de la cándida Eréndira y de su abuela desalmada (The Incredible and Sad Story of Candid Eréndira and Her Soulless Grandmother, 1978), *Crónica de una muerte anunciada* (Chronicle of a Death Foretold, 1981), *El amor en los tiempos del cólera* (Love in the Time of Cholera, 1985), and *El general en su laberinto* (The General in His Labyrinth, 1989). García Márquez's journalistic writings are collected and published as *Crónicas y reportajes* (Chronicles and News Articles, 1976). He is also a productive and acclaimed writer for the

screen. In all, he is the giant figure of Latin-American literature in this century. García Márquez wins the Nobel Prize for Literature in 1982.

MAY 9, 1928   Tennis Champion Pancho González Is Born. One of the greatest tennis professionals ever, Richard "Pancho" González is born in Los Angeles, California, to Mexican immigrant parents. His father, Manuel, fits furniture and paints movie sets, and his mother, Carmen, is an occasional seamstress. González is a self-taught tennis player, having started at age 12 on the public courts of Los Angeles. He wins his first tournament as an Edison Junior High School student, but because of excessive absenteeism, he is not allowed to compete in high school. González serves in the U.S. Navy and competes in the U.S. singles championship upon his return in 1947. In 1948, at age twenty, González, ranked seventeenth nationally and seeded eighth becomes the U.S. singles champion at Forest Hills and plays on the U.S. Davis Cup Team. He wins Forest Hills again in 1949. After winning the U.S. grass, clay, and indoor championships, González turns pro. From 1954 to 1962, he is world professional singles champion. In 1968, he coaches the U.S. Davis Cup team, and is named to the International Tennis Hall of Fame.

SUMMER 1928   Hispanics Win Olympic Medals. Chile's Miguel I. Plaza wins the silver in the marathon at the Olympic Games in Amsterdam, Holland. Argentina wins the bronze medal in the team foil fencing competition and Argentina's Alberto Zorilla wins the gold medal in the 400 free style swimming. Argentina's Victorio Angel Avendaño wins the gold medal in light heavyweight boxing and Arturo Rodriguez Jurado the gold in heavyweight; Victor Peralta wins the silver in featherweight boxing and Raul Landini the silver in welterweight. Argentina also takes the silver medal in soccer, while Uruguay wins the gold—its second straight Olympic soccer championship.

Richard Alonso "Pancho" González. (Courtesy of the National Archives.)

Ché Guevara.

JUNE 14, 1928 Ernesto "Ché" Guevara, Castro Aide and Revolutionary, Is Born. The Marxist revolutionary and intellectual Ernesto "Ché" Guevara is born in Rosario, Argentina, the son of an architect. Guevara has a comfortable upbringing in Argentina and graduates as a medical doctor and surgeon from the University of Buenos Aires Medical School in 1953. In 1954, Guevara is hired as an inspector for the Guatemalan government agrarian reform agency and by 1956 emerges in Cuba as a commander of the July 26th Guerrilla Movement to depose dictator Fulgencio Batista. After the triumph of the revolution, Guevara serves in various posts in the Castro government, including as president of the national bank (1959–61). One of his major successes is the working out of a trade agreement with the Soviet Union whereby Cuban sugar is traded for capital goods and, thus, the United States-imposed boycott and blockade of Cuba is circumvented. Guevara is believed to be one of the principal supporters who leads Fidel Castro to nationalize Cuban industries. Guevara seeks to industrialize the island rapidly in order to break Cuba's historic dependence on sugar. He discusses many of the

reasons behind his economic and social architecture in numerous articles, as well as in his speeches. In his writings, Guevara also presents his concept of the socialist "new man" and other social and political issues: Third World foreign debt, the terms of trade between socialist and market economies, and economic development in Latin America. Many of the articles are translated and published in *Ché Guevara Speaks: Selected Speeches and Writing* (1967) and *¡Venceremos! The Speeches and Writings of Ernesto Ché Guevara* (1968). Various other compilations of his short and book-length essays are published in Spanish; in 1968, his last diary is published as *El diario de Ché en Bolivia* (The Diary of Ché Guevara in Bolivia). From 1966 until his execution in 1967 by the Bolivian army, Guevara serves as the commander in chief of the National Liberation Army guerrilla organization in Bolivia. Guevara has believed that the rest of Latin America is ripe for revolution, but he is unsuccessful in recruiting Castro for continental insurgency; he, therefore, sets out on his own to foment and organize rebellion in the region that seems most ready. Guevara was to the generation of the 1960s in Latin America and the United States the quintessence of the selfless and idealistic guerrilla fighter and Marxist intellectual. He is still a hero to leftists throughout the world.

JULY 17, 1928 Mexican President Assassinated. Mexican President Alvaro Obregón is assassinated as president re-elect, about to begin his second term. Under Plutarch Elías Calles, who succeeds to the presidency, and the presidents who follow him until 1934, Mexico finally achieves peaceful institutionalization of the reforms brought about by the revolution and also effects the peaceful transfer of power from one election to the next. The period of government by revolutionary commanders (*caudillos*) is over at last and modern Mexico is born.

NOVEMBER 11, 1928 Carlos Fuentes, Novelist, Essayist, and Teacher, Is Born. The internationally famous Mexican novelist and essayist, Carlos Fuentes, is born in Panama City, Panama, the son of a career diplomat. Fuentes graduates as a lawyer from the National Autonomous University of Mexico in 1948 and pursues graduate study at the Institute es Haute Etudes in Geneva, Switzerland. Besides beginning his career as a writer during the 1950s, he works in Mexico's foreign service. From 1975 to 1977, he serves as the Mexican ambassador to France. During the 1970s he is a visiting professor at universities in the United States, France, and Chile, and he holds a chair at Princeton University. As a novelist, Fuentes has won all of Mexico's major awards, as well as major awards in Spain, Nicaragua, and Venezuela. All of Fuentes's novels, and most of his other writings, explore the history and culture of Mexico, from the indigenous past to the revolution and contemporary modernization. No other novelist has pondered with such depth what it is to be a Mexican; his queries extend to consideration of Mexico's bittersweet relations with the United States throughout history. Fuentes himself has said that, "In a sense my novels are one book with many chapters: *Where the Air Is Clean* is a biography of Mexico City;

The Death of Artemio Cruz deals with an individual in that city; *A Change of Skin* is that city, that society, facing the world, coming to grips with the fact that it is part of civilization and that there is a world outside that intrudes into Mexico." Fuentes's output is prodigious, with more than a dozen novels, seven collections of short stories, and more than a dozen nonfiction works varying from literary criticism to essays on human rights. Fuentes's acknowledged masterpieces are *La región más transparente* (Where the Air Is Clear, 1958), *La muerte de Artemio Cruz* (The Death of Artemio Cruz, 1964), *Cambio de piel* (Change of Skin, 1967), and *Terra Nostra* (Our Land, 1975).

DECEMBER 2, 1928 Mari Bras, Activist for Puerto Rican Independence, Is Born. Political activist in the pro-independence for Puerto Rico movement Juan Mari Bras is born in Mayagüez. His first notable leadership role is in student strikes at the University of Puerto Rico in 1948, for which he is expelled. He finishes his undergraduate education at the University of Florida and later obtains a law degree from Georgetown University in 1954. In 1959, he is one of the founders of the Movimiento Pro Independencia (Pro Independence Movement) and serves as its secretary general. He participates in various political actions, including the movement against taking a popular vote on Puerto Rico's political status in 1967, the campaign against the military draft in Puerto Rico and the movement against mining in Puerto Rico. In 1971, the Movimiento Pro Independencia becomes the Partido Socialista Puertorriqueño (Puerto Rican Socialist Party), with Mari Bras as its secretary general. One of his main programs to lobby the United Nations to declare Puerto Rico a colony of the United States and is to move that institution to press the United States to allow for Puerto Rican independence. Mari Bras is also the editor of the party's organ, *Claridad* (Clarity).

DECEMBER 11, 1928 Director/Screenwriter Gutiérrez Alea Born in Cuba. Cuba's outstanding film director and screenwriter, Tomás Gutiérrez Alea, is born in Havana. He studies law at the University of Havana and then film at the Centro Sperimentale di Cinematografia in Rome, where he is influenced by Italian neorealism. Upon his return to Havana in 1953, he joins the radical culture society, Nuestro Tiempo (Our Time), and begins his career working on films. In 1955, he codirects a 16-mm documentary that is seized by dictator Fulgencio Batista's police because of its political content. After the success of the Cuban Revolution in 1959, Gutiérrez Alea cofounds the national revolutionary film institute, Instituto del Arte e Industria Cinematográfica (Cinematographic Art and Industry Institute—ICAIC), in which he continues to function as one of the leaders. Over his career, Gutiérrez Alea experiments with a broad range of styles and themes, running the gamut from his neo-realistic first feature film, *Stories of the Revolution* (1960) to magic realism as in his best-known film *The Last Supper* (1976), which deals with the eighteenth-century slave revolts. In three satires, Gutiérrez Alea attacks the legacy of bourgeois society in postrevolutionary Cuba: *The Twelve Chairs* (1962), *Death of a Bureaucrat* (1966), and *The Survivors* (1979). Gutiérrez Alea's masterpiece is *Memories of Underdevelopment* (1968), in which he blends documentary and drama to portray a politically uncommitted intellectual in the early days of the Cuban Revolution. Gutiérrez Alea has coscripted all of his films in accordance with the ICAIC's collective approach to filmmaking, in which he works with many of Cuba's young filmmakers. His 1994 film, *Strawberry and Chocolate*, is nominated for an Academy Award in the category of best foreign language film—the first Cuban film ever nominated for an Oscar.

1929

1929 Artist Gironella Born in Mexico City.

Alberto Gironella, a distinguished artist, is born in Mexico City to a Catalan father and a mother from the Yucatan. After studying literature at the National Autonomous University, Gironella first becomes known as a poet. In 1952, he begins to make his mark as a painter with an exhibition in the Galería Prisse in Mexico City, in which he develops a personal style that does not follow the political art of the Mexican School. In 1959, he travels to New York and creates a series of paintings and constructions based on the Diego Velásquez's portrait of Queen Mariana that is hanging in the Metropolitan Museum of Art; these are exhibited in Mexico City in 1963. That same year he travels to Madrid and Paris, and becomes associated with the group Phases, with which he exhibits at the University of Paris. Back in Mexico, Gironella attempts to encourage other artists to revive surrealism. Since the 1960s, Gironella has exhibited widely throughout Mexico and the United States, and has participated in numerous international group exhibitions, including the Sao Paulo Bienal in 1961 and the Salon de Mai in Paris in 1964 and 1966. In 1975 Gironella illustrates novelist Carlos Fuentes's *Terra Nostra*.

1929 Depression Alters Migration. With the onset of the Great Depression, Mexican immigration to the United States virtually ceases and return migration increases sharply.

1929 The League of United Latin American Citizens. The League of United Latin American Citizens is founded in Texas by frustrated Mexican–Americans who find avenues for opportunity in the United States blocked.

JANUARY 21, 1929 Rolando Hinojosa, Hispanic Writer, Is Born. Rolando Hinojosa is the most prolific and bilingual of the Hispanic novelists of the United States. Not only does he create memorable Mexican–American and Anglo characters, but he completely populates a fictional county in the Lower Rio Grande Valley of Texas through his continuing generational

Rolando Hinojosa. (Courtesy of the Arte Público Press Archives, University of Houston.)

narrative that he calls the "Klail City Death Trip Series." Hinojosa is born in Mercedes, Texas, to a Mexican–American father and a bilingual Anglo–American mother; his paternal ancestors arrive in the Lower Rio Grande Valley in 1749 as part of the José Escandón expedition. Hinojosa is educated at first in Mexican schools in Mercedes and later in the segregated public schools of the area where all of his classmates are Mexican–Americans. He begins integrated classes in junior high. It is in high school that Hinojosa begins to write, with his first pieces in English published in an annual literary magazine, *Creative Bits.* Hinojosa leaves the valley in 1946 when he graduates from college, but the language, culture, and history of the area form the substance of all of Hinojosa's novels. The ensuing years see a stretch in the army, studies at the University of Texas, reactivation into the army to fight in the Korean War (an experience which informs his poetic narrative *Korean Love Songs*), graduation from the University of Texas in 1954 with a degree in Spanish, and back to Brownsville as a teacher, among a variety of other jobs, and finally on to graduate school. In 1969 he ob-

tains his Ph.D. in Spanish from the University of Illinois, returning to Texas to teach at colleges. Hinojosa remains in academia in a variety of positions and universities; today he serves as Ellen Clayton Garwood Professor of English and Creative Writing at the University of Texas. Although he continues writing throughout his life, Rolando Hinojosa does not publish a book until 1973, his *Estampas del Valle y otras obras* (which he recreates in English and publishes as *The Valley* in 1983), winner of the national award for Chicano literature, Premio Quinto Sol. From that time on he has become the most prolific Chicano novelist, publishing one novel after another in his generational narrative that centers around the lives of two of his alter-egos, Rafa Buenrostro and Jehú Malacara, in individual installments that vary in form from poetry and dialogue to the picaresque novel and the detective novel. His titles in English alone include *Korean Love Songs* (1980), *Rites and Witnesses* (1982), *Dear Rafe* (1985), *Partners in Crime: A Rafe Buenrostro Mystery* (1985), *Claros varones de Belken/Fair Gentlemen of Belken County* (1986, bilingual edition), *Klail City* (1987), *Becky and Her Friends* (1989), and *The Useless Servants*. His original Spanish version of *Klail City,* entitled *Klail City y sus alrededores* (1976), wins the international award for fiction, Premio Casa de las Américas, from Cuba in 1976; it is issued there under this title and a year later a version is published in the United States under the title of *Generaciónes y semblanzas* (Generations and Likenesses). The book is also published in German two years later. Hinojosa publishes many short stories and essays, as well as installments of a satirical running commentary on life and current events in the United States, known as "The Mexican American Devil's Dictionary," supposedly created by another of his alter-egos, who is also one of the narrators of the "Klail City Death Trip Series": P. Galindo (meaning "right on target," in Spanish). Hinojosa is hailed as a master satirist, an acute observer of the human comedy, a Chicano William Faulkner for his creation of the history and people of Belken County, a faithful recorder of the customs and dialects in Spanish and English of both Anglos and Mexicans in the Lower Rio Grande Valley. He is one of the best loved and most highly regarded Hispanic writers; he is totally committed to the novelistic world that he has created and that has helped readers to understand Mexican–American life so well.

MARCH 1929 Revolutionary Party Formed. The Partido Nacional Revolucionario (National Revolutionary Party), the forerunner of today's Partido Revolucionario Institucional (Institutional Revolutionary Party) is founded in Mexico. Over time the party puts an end to the proliferation of parties that characterized electoral politics after the revolution, and it comes to dominate popular elections. President Plutarch Elías Calles paves the way for this party to unite the revolutionary family and put an end to factionalism and the power of the revolutionary caudillos to change government through individual, at times violent, action.

APRIL 22, 1929 Cabrera Infante, Cuban Novelist and Critic, Is Born. The internationally famous novelist Guillermo Cabrera Infante is born in Gibara, Cuba. The son of a journalist, Cabrera Infante follows in his father's footsteps and graduates in journalism in 1956 from the University of Havana. He teaches in the school of journalism there from 1960 to 1961. From 1962 to 1965, Cabrera Infante works in Cuba's foreign service. In 1966, he emigrates to London and becomes a naturalized British citizen. Thereafter, he pursues his career as a fiction writer, a screenwriter, and a film critic. His award-winning first novel, *Tres tristres tigres* (published in 1967, translated as *Three Trapped Tigers* in 1971), is considered a masterpiece of contemporary Latin–American fiction for its innovative use of language, its linguistic experimentation, and its narrative perspectivism— the story is told from various points of view. The emphasis on spoken language, puns, double entendres, and Havana street dialects all

make for a linguistic roller coaster that the author calls "a joke lasting five hundred pages." He also states that the book is an antidote to the seriousness of so much Latin–American fiction. Besides copious film criticism and nonfiction, Cabrera Infante writes other novels: *Así en la paz como en la guerra* (In Peace as in War, 1960), *Vista del amanecer en el trópico* (View of Dawn in the Tropics, 1978), and *La Habana para un infante difunto* (published in 1979, translated as *Infante's Inferno* in 1984).

JUNE 21, 1929 Government and Church Sign Peace Agreement. The Mexican government and the Catholic Church sign a peace agreement, putting an end to the bloody Cristero War that broke out in 1926 as a result of anticlerical laws and practices of the government.

JULY 26, 1929 Flores, First Hispanic Bishop, Is Born. Patrick F. Flores is the first Mexican–American to be named a bishop of the Catholic Church. Born Patricio Fernández Flores in Ganado, Texas, the seventh of nine children, Flores receives his early education in Ganado and Pearland, and he graduates from Kirwin High School in Galveston. He then attends St. Mary's Seminary in La Porte, Texas, and St. Mary's Seminary in Houston. He is ordained a Catholic priest on May 26, 1956, and serves in a variety of functions in the Diocese of Galveston–Houston, including becoming the director of the Bishop's Committee for the Spanish-Speaking, until March 18, 1970, when Pope Paul VI appoints him to serve as auxiliary to the archbishop of San Antonio. On May 5, 1970, he is consecrated a bishop. Bishop Flores is the first Mexican–American elevated to the hierarchy of the Catholic Church in the United States. On May 29, 1978, he is installed as the bishop of the Diocese of El Paso, where he serves until he is installed as the archbishop of San Antonio on October 13, 1979. Bishop Flores receives many honors and pioneers programs in the church and in government on behalf of the civil rights of Hispanics and immigrants. In 1983 he is one of four

Bishop Patrick Flores. (Courtesy of the Arte Público Press Archives, University of Houston.)

bishops elected to represent the hierarchy of the United States at the Synod of Bishops in Rome. In 1986, he is awarded the Medal of Freedom (Ellis Island Medal of Honor) in honor of the Statue of Liberty's 100th birthday.

1930

1930   Coffee Crash Precipitates Revolution. The price of coffee crashes on the world market, causing much social unrest and precipitating a revolution in El Salvador that brings to power dictator Maximiliano Hernández Martínez for fourteen years. He is unseated by a military coup in 1944.

1930   The Hawley–Smoot Tariff Affects Sugar Industry. The United States Congress passes the Hawley–Smoot Tariff, thus dealing a serious blow to the Cuban sugar industry, which was itself perennially dependent on the American economy, as was the economy of the whole of Cuba. By 1934, however, the negotiations bring the tariff down from 2.5 cents per pound of sugar to .9 cent per pound, and fix a quota for imported Cuban sugar.

1930   Juan Antonio Corretjer Heads Party. Puerto Rican poet and political activist Juan Antonio Corretjer becomes a leader of the Partido Nacionalist Puertorriqueño, the nationalist party, where he becomes involved in various organizing activities, including the 1932 assault on the island's capitol building. (*See also* biography, March 3, 1908.)

1930   Mexican–Americans Use Courts to Fight Segregation. Segregation characterizes education for Mexican–Americans for all the years since the Mexican–American War. At first, Mexican–American communities establish their own schools in response. But during the 1930s, these communities begin to use the courts to attack segregation. In the 1930 case of *Independent School District (Texas) v. Salvatierra*, the courts find that Mexican–Americans have indeed been segregated, without regard for individual ability. The only legitimate use of segregation should be for special education. Many other court victories follow.

1930   Puerto Ricans Go Back to Island. Within the next four years, approximately 20 percent of the Puerto Ricans living in the United States will return to the island.

1930   Southern Migrants Displace Mexicans. With the onset of the Great Depression, many Mexican workers are displaced by the dominant southern whites and blacks of the migrant agricultural labor force.

1930   Spanish Cinematographer Almendros Is Born. Academy award-winning cinematographer and director, Nestor Almendros, is born in Barcelona, Spain, on October 30, 1930. At the age of fourteen, he emigrates with his family to Cuba, where he graduates from the University of Havana in philosophy and literature. Almendros begins his career in film with an amateur 8-mm film with the great Cuban director, Tomás Gutiérrez Alea, in 1950. He later studies film with Hans Richter at the City University of New York, and also studies

Worker on relief line during the Depression. (Courtesy of the Library of Congress Prints & Photographs Division.)

cinematography at the Centro Sperimentale di Cinematografia in Rome. Almendros works as a cameraman and/or director on several documentaries of the early Castro era for the Cuban film institute, Instituto del Arte e Industria Cinematográfica (Cinematographic Art and Industry Institute), then moves to France where he works for television and on film shorts. In the mid-1960s he collaborates regularly with director Erich Rohmer and later with director Francois Truffaut. He wins the Academy Award for cinematography for the 1978 film, *Days of*

Heaven. Included among his many outstanding films are *The Wild Racers* and *Gun Runner* (U.S., 1968); *Ma nuit chez Maud/My Night at Maud's* (France 1969); *L'enfant sauvage/The Wild Child* (France 1970); *Le genou de Claire/Claire's Knee* (France 1971); *L'amour l'après-midi/Chloe in the Afternoon* (France 1972); *Chinatown* (1974); *L'histoire d'Adele/The Story of Adele H.* (France 1975); *Days of Heaven* (U.S., 1978); *Kramer vs. Kramer* (1979); *The Blue Lagoon* and *The Last Metro* (France) (1980); *Sophie's Choice* (1982); *Improper Conduct* (1983); *Places in the Heart* (1984); *Heartburn* (1986); and *New York Stories* (1989). Almendros also directed some very noteworthy documentaries, including *Improper Conduct* and the anti-Castro *Nobody Listened* (1988). Almendros also writes an important autobiographical book on cinematography, published first in French in 1980, and then in English translation in 1984: *Un Homme a la caméra A Man with a Camera.* Almendros dies in 1993.

1930 Trujillo, Dictator of Dominican Republic, Comes to Power. General Rafael L. Trujillo, head of the national police force, comes to power in the Dominican Republic and puts in place one of the longest lasting dictatorships (until his assassination in 1961). First, Trujillo rebuilds the capital, Santo Domingo, which had been destroyed by a hurricane and, in 1936, names the city after himself (Ciudad Trujillo). In 1930, Trujillo takes over a nation that is in chaos, bankrupt and poverty stricken, with a foreign debt of $20 million. By 1957, he liquidates both the foreign and domestic debts and the national income has been multiplied some forty times. By 1957, the national budget reaches a high point of $131 million, and the yearly budget has been balanced already for some twenty years. Trujillo administers many programs that improved the lot of citizens and the economy, including land colonization, communications, industrialization, transportation, hydroelectric power, agricultural programs, and social legislation. But a lion's share of the

Nestor Almendros. (Courtesy of the Arte Público Press Archives, University of Houston.)

relative economic prosperity that ensues goes into the private coffers of the Trujillo family. And Trujillo himself rules as a ruthless autocrat assisted by a brutal secret police force.

1930   Uruguayan Soccer Champions. Thirteen teams gather in Montevideo, Uruguay to play the first World Cup. The home-team emerges as the champion.

1930   U.S. Controls Much of Puerto Rico. By 1930, the United States controls 44 percent of the cultivated land in Puerto Rico; U.S. capital-

ists control 60 percent of the banks and public services, and all of the maritime lines.

1931

1931   Mexican–Americans Deported. As the Depression intensifies, authorities in the United States become increasingly hostile towards Mexican immigrants. The federal authorities, including the secretary of labor, begin to express the opinion that removing Mexicans from the United States will help bring an end to the Depression by taking them off of the welfare rolls and by opening up jobs for American citizens. The federal government conducts anti-alien drives across the country, especially in southern California, where by 1932 some 75,000 Mexicans are forced to leave. Between 1931 and 1934, local police, sheriffs' offices, and welfare authorities join forces with the federal authorities in repatriating trainloads of Mexicans. In these deportation drives, thousands of American citizens—many of them Mexican–American children—are driven from the country. This type of wholesale, indiscriminate repatriation of Mexicans spreads from the Southwest to the Midwest during the early years of the Depression. In some Midwestern cities, such as Gary, East Chicago, and Detroit, many families are forcefully deported. By 1938, most of the repatriation drives end, and by World War II, Mexican immigration is once again welcome and encouraged in the United States.

JULY 15, 1931   Cuban Wins World Boxing Title. Cuba's Eligio "Kid Chocolate" Sardiñas is the first Hispanic boxer to win a world title in the junior lightweight class. (*See also* biography, October 28, 1910.)

DECEMBER 11, 1931   Actress Rita Moreno Is Born. Rita Moreno (Rosita Dolores Alverio), Academy Award-winning actress, dancer, and singer, is born in Humacao, Puerto Rico. A dancer from childhood, she reaches Broadway at age thirteen and Hollywood at fourteen. She wins an Academy Award in 1961 as best supporting actress for *West Side Story* and is in several films important for understanding the Hollywood depiction of Hispanics, including *The Ring* (1952), *A Medal for Benny* (1954), and *Popi* (1969). Her other films include: *Pagan Love Song* (1950); *Singin' in the Rain* (1952); *Latin Lovers* and *Fort Vengeance* (1953); *Jivaro* and *Garden of Evil* (1954); *The King and I* and *The Vagabond King* (1956); *The Deerslayer* (1957); *West Side Story* and *Summer and Smoke*

Eligio "Kid Chocolate" Sardiñas. (Courtesy of the Arte Público Press Archives, University of Houston.)

(1961); *Marlowe* (1969); *Carnal Knowledge* (1971); *The Ritz* (1976); *The Boss' Son* (1978); *Happy Birthday* and *Gemini* (1980); *The Four Seasons* (1981); and *Life in the Food Chain* (1991).

1932

1932   Painter Fernando Botero Born in Cuba. Painter Fernando Botero is born in Medellín, Colombia. Botero works his way into a career in fine art as an illustrator for a Sunday newspaper supplement. After graduating from the Liceo de Antioquia in 1950, Botero moves to Bogotá, and in 1951 has his first solo gallery exhibition, and another in 1952. In 1952, Botero studies at the San Fernando Academy in Madrid, Spain; in 1953, he studies fresco painting at the San Marco Academy in Florence, Italy. In the following years, he returns to Colombia and also moves to Mexico City and New York. He participates in exhibitions in the United States. From 1958 to 1960 he serves as a professor of art at the National University in Bogotá, but in 1960 establishes himself definitively in New York. From that time on, Botero has enjoyed one of the most prestigious reputations in modern art in the world. Botero has developed a highly personal and characteristic style that has been imitated often; it includes chubby figures which harken back to the opulence of colonial times. And, in much of his work, there is evident a sense of humor and anticlericalism. His paintings are part of the permanent collections of the most important museums in Latin America, the United States, and Europe, where he often has had solo exhibitions and retrospectives. When he is given a major retrospective at the Museo de Arte contemporáneo in Caracas, he is awarded the Venezuelan order of Andrés Bello.

1932   Painter Organizes Exhibition. Joaquín Torres-García organizes the first Paris exhibi-

"Rubén's Wife" (1963), by Fernando Botero. (Courtesy of the National Institute for Fine Arts, Mexico City.)

tion of Latin American art. (*See also* biography, July 28, 1874.)

JANUARY 20, 1932   Poet Heberto Padilla Is Born. Cuban poet Heberto Padilla is born in Puerta de Golpe, Pinar del Río, Cuba, the son of a lawyer and a housewife. After attending the University of Havana, Padilla works as a journalist in Miami, New York, London, and Moscow from 1957 to 1963. After the fall of Batista, Padilla returns enthusiastically to take part in the making of a new society in Cuba, but he becomes greatly disillusioned over the next decade. From 1959 to 1963, he is also a contributing editor to *Lunes de Revolución* (Monday of Revolution), a literary supplement to the newspaper *Revolución*. From 1963 to 1970, Padilla works in a variety of positions, including lecturer at the University of Havana. In 1968 his *Fuera del juego* (Out of the Game) is awarded the Julián del Casal prize, a Cuban-sponsored literary award given by the Cuban Union of Writers and Artists. However, following the publication of this book and with readings from his *Provocaciones* (Provocations) text in preparation, he falls out of favor with the government. He is imprisoned in 1971, tortured, and later "rehabilitated." Padilla's imprisonment and mistreatment by the authorities and writers in Cuba becomes a celebrated cause to writers throughout Latin America, who also become progressively disillusioned with the Castro regime. From 1971 to 1980, he works in obscurity as a translator in Cumanayagua. He is not allowed to leave Cuba or to publish new writings. In 1980, Castro allows many dissidents to leave Cuba; after pleadings from novelist Bernard Malamud and U.S. Senator Edward Kennedy, Padilla is permitted to leave. He and his wife, novelist Belkis Cuza Malé, move to New York and then to Princeton, where they have edited the literary journal *Linden Lane* since 1982. Much of Padilla's poetry since moving to the United States is concerned with the revolution and with political oppression in Cuba. The critics almost unanimously prefer Padilla's earlier poetic works, such as those in *El hombre junto al mar* (The Man by the Sea, 1981), to the political works he writes after he emigrates. Padilla has two collections of poetry in English translation: *Sent Off the Field: A Selection from the Poetry of Heberto Padilla* (1971) and *Legacies: Selected Poems* (1982). In addition, he is the author of a novel about the revolution, *En mi jardín pastan héroes* (published in 1981; translated as *Heroes Are Grazing in My Garden* in 1984) and a memoir, *Autorretrato del otro: La mala memoria* (published in 1988; translated as *Self-Portrait of the Other* in 1990).

SUMMER 1932 Olympic Medal Winners. Argentine athletes take gold medals at the Olympic Games in Los Angeles, California: Juan Zabala is the athlete to run away with marathon gold with a time of 2:31:36.0. Mexico's Gustavo Huet wins the silver in the men's smallbore free rifle competition, scoring 294 points. Teammate Francisco Cabañás win a silver medal in flyweight boxing. Carmelo Ambrosio Robledo wins the gold in featherweight boxing and Santiago Lovell in heavyweight boxing. Two Hispanics from the United States are part of the US Olympic team:

triple jumper Roland Lee Romero and Fencer Miguel de Capriles.

1933

1933 Bolivia and Paraguay Fight Chaco War. The Chaco War breaks out between Bolivia and Paraguay. The bloody struggle, which starts over disagreements on the border line running through the inhospitable Chaco jungle (an area rich in oil deposits), lasts until 1938. The prolonged struggle is not only a bloodletting but also a waste of human and financial resources, driving both countries toward bankruptcy. In 1935, after Paraguay succeeds in occupying most of the land that it wants, friendly countries intervene to call a halt to the war. The peace treaty is finally signed in Buenos Aires in 1938.

1933 Confederation Advocates for California Workers. In May, farmworkers establish the El Monte Berry Strike in Los Angeles County. In June, members of the Mexican Farm Labor Union, an affiliate of the Confederation of Mexican Farm Workers Unions (founded in 1927 by the Los Angeles Federation of Mexican Societies, based on the model of unions in Mexico), officially sanction the strike and call for a 25-cent per hour minimum wage. The strike spreads from Los Angeles County to Orange County and the union grows rapidly. In June, the strike ends with the concession of a small increase in wages and recognition of the confederation. That same year, the confederation becomes the largest and most active agricultural union in California. In 1935, the confederation is responsible for six of the eighteen strikes in California agriculture and also is effective in winning negotiations without striking. In 1936, it is a leader in establishing the Federation of Agricultural Workers Union of America. By the end of the 1930s, however, the confederation's power wanes in the face of increased resistance from the growers and leg-

A farmworker during the Depression. Photo by Dorothea Lange. (Courtesy of the Library of Congress Prints & Photographs Division.)

islators, jurisdictional disputes between the AFL and the CIO, and a surplus of workers.

1933   Language Policy Changed. The Roosevelt Administration reverses the policy, established by the Jones Act in 1917, of English as the official language in Puerto Rico.

1933   Somoza Wins Power in Nicaragua. The year 1933 marks the beginning of the government by one of Latin America's most successful

dictators, Anastasio Somoza, who as head of the U.S. Marine-trained national guard in Nicaragua is the true power behind the newly elected president, Juan B. Sacasa. In 1937, Somoza is elected himself to the presidency and from then until he is struck down by an assassin's bullet in September 1956, he serves as supreme despot. Under Somoza, Nicaragua enjoys unbroken years of economic and political stability and a very close relationship with the United States, its chief partner in trade. In addition to becoming fabulously wealthy at the cost of the nation, Somoza institutes a dynasty that is represented in his son Luis serving as president of the national congress, and his other son, Anastasio, Jr., serving as chief of staff of the national guard. When Somoza is assassinated, the congress quickly ratifies his son Luis's ascension to the presidency.

JANUARY 1933   The "Good Neighbor" Policy. President Franklin D. Roosevelt announces during his inaugural address the "Good Neighbor Policy" and noninterventionism in the internal affairs of Latin America countries. Later in the year, at the Inter-American Conference in Montevideo, Uruguay, the United States representatives repeat the pledge not to intervene. As part of the new policy, the marines withdraw from Haiti, the Dominican Republic, and Nicaragua; a new canal treaty is signed with Panama; the Platt amendment with Cuba is revoked; and recognition is extended to Jorge Ubico in Guatemala, Maximiliano Hernández Martínez in El Salvador, Tiburcio Carías in Honduras, Anastasio Somoza in Nicaragua, Rafael Trujillo in the Dominican Republic, and Francois Duvalier in Haiti, all of whom illegally extend their presidential terms.

SEPTEMBER 4, 1933   Batista Comes to Power in Cuba. A revolt led by sergeants in the Cuban army, including Fulgencio Batista, eventually results in the downfall of dictator Gerardo Machado. The revolt marks a turning point in the modern development of Cuba: the army is converted into a political party that now dis-

Political cartoon satirizing the "Good Neighbor Policy." (Courtesy of the Library of Congress Prints & Photographs Division.)

Fulgencio Batista as president of Cuba, 1956. (Courtesy of the Library of Congress Prints & Photographs Division.)

putes power with another rebelling group, the Auténtico (Authentic) party, centered among faculty and students at the University of Havana. But Batista and the army essentially run Cuba until losing power to Fidel Castro's revolutionaries in 1959. Until his "election" to the presidency in 1940, Batista rules essentially through puppets: Carlos Mendieta, Miguel Mariano Gómez, and Federico Laredo Brú. During the 1930s, the United States no longer intervenes and instead acquiesces to military

rule in Cuba in the name of stability and favorable treatment for U.S. government and business. Batista becomes a symbol of order and stability to the United States. Despite Batista not being the head of state, the United States recognizes the new puppet government replacing Machado, and treats Batista as if he were the head of state long before his election in 1940 to the presidency. The United States adds to Batista's prestige by finally revoking the hated Platt amendment. When Batista stages a coup in 1952, the United States moves to recognize Batista just three months later.

OCTOBER 1933 The San Joaquín Cotton Strike. Mexican farmworkers strike the cotton industry in the counties of the Central Valley, California. The San Joaquín Cotton Strike is the largest and best organized of labor actions initiated by the radical Cannery and Agricultural Workers Industrial Union in the 1930s. Some 12,000 to 18,000 pickers walk out, demanding a raise from 60 cents to one dollar a pound for picked cotton. Growers and vigilante groups attempt to repress the strike violently and, in fact, kill two strikers and wound others. California governor James Rolf calls in the

National Guard and establishes a fact-finding board, that eventually creates the basis for a compromise: 75 cents per pound and a condemnation of the growers for violation of the strikers' civil rights.

1934

1934 Cárdenas Redistributes Land. During the Lázaro Cárdenas presidency in Mexico, running from 1934 to 1940, an average of 8.2 million acres per year is distributed to some 771,640 peasant families grouped on 11,347 acres. By the time he leaves office, more than half of all Mexicans belonged to ejido communities with lands of their own. Almost half of all of the crop land is owned and worked in this manner. Cárdenas is the president who redistributes the most land. Yet, more than 200 million acres remain in private hands, much of it as individual haciendas, and approximately 35 percent of all Mexicans still work for meager wages on the land of others.

1934 Communists Organize. The Puerto Rican Communist Party is formed.

1934 Mexican Painter Cuevas Is Born. Famed Mexican painter José Luis Cuevas is born in Mexico City. Although he takes classes at the Escuela Nacional de Pintura y Escultura in Mexico City, he claims to be self taught. Cuevas breaks away from the overriding influence of the masters of the Mexican School by cultivating a highly personal and psychological art whose aim it is to convey the solitude of contemporary man and his inability to communicate. His figurative work is often distorted as in hallucinations. Technically, all of Cuevas's work relies heavily on drawing and draftsmanship, and thus departs from the freer interpretations of his contemporary artists, mostly expressionists. Cuevas benefits from solo exhibitions at the major museums in Europe, North America, and South America. Among his many awards are first prizes from biennials and international

shows in Sao Paulo (1959); Lugano, Switzerland (1962); Santiago, Chile (1964); New Delhi, India (1968); San Juan, Puerto Rico (1977); Stuttgart, Germany (1978), and Mexico City (1981).

1934 Movie Star César Romero Goes to Hollywood. After dancing and acting in numerous Broadway shows, Romero begins work in Hollywood films with *The Thin Man.* (*See also* biography, February 15, 1907.)

1934 Perón Starts Political Movement in Argentina. In Argentina, Juan D. Perón founds a movement called *justicialismo* (Justicism), which later is called "Peronism," advocating the free determination of countries, humanitarian capitalism, humanistic and Christian education, social equality, and, above all, protection of the workers and unions, who are Perón's primary supporters. Known as the *descamisados* ("shirtless" have-nots), they prevail in electing Perón to the presidency from 1946 to 1952, and he effects great social and economic reforms, including industrialization and nationalizing the economy. After his legal presidency, Perón leads a dictatorial regime riddled with corruption and persecution of intellectuals, as well as of the church. He is finally overthrown in 1955 by the military and a popular democratic movement, known as the Revolución Libertadora (Liberating Revolution). In the 1970s, there is a resurgence of Peronism in Argentina. (*See also* biography, October 8, 1895.)

MAY 29, 1934 Platt Amendment Annulled. President Franklin Delano Roosevelt annuls the Platt Amendment, which was so hated by the Cubans.

AUGUST 11, 1934 Educator and Author Carmelo Mesa-Lago Is Born. Born in Havana, Cuba, Carmelo Mesa-Lago receives his LL.M. degree in civil law from the University of Havana in 1965, his LL.D. degree from the University of Madrid in 1958, his M.A. degree in economics from the University of Miami in

1965, and his Ph.D. degree in labor economics from Cornell University in 1968. From 1967 on, Mesa-Lago develops his career at the University of Pittsburgh, beginning as an assistant professor in economics and rising to the rank of full professor in 1980. During his tenure there, he also serves as the director of the Center for Latin American Studies (1974–86). He lectures and teaches in Europe and Latin America as well and holds prestigious fellowships, including the Ford, Rockefeller, and Tinker. Mesa-Lago also serves as the president of the Latin American Studies Association (1980) and as regional advisor for the United Nations on Social Security and Development (1983–84). Among his many honors are the Hoover Institution Prize for Best Article on Latin America (1986), the Bicentennial Medallion of the University of Pittsburgh (1987), and the Alexander von Humbolt Senior Research Award on Social Security (1990–92). His recent books include *The Economy of Socialist Cuba* (1981), *Portfolio Performance of Selected Social Security Institutes in Latin America* (1991), *Social Security and Prospects for Equity in Latin America,* (1991), and *Health Care for the Poor in Latin America and the Caribbean: Problems, Cases and Solutions* (1992).

AUGUST 18, 1934 Star Outfielder Roberto Clemente Born in Puerto Rico. One of the greatest baseball players of all time, Roberto Clemente, is born in Carolina, Puerto Rico. He rises from an impoverished background to be a star outfielder for the Pittsburgh Pirates from 1955 to 1972. He assists the Pirates in winning two World Series in 1960 and 1971. Clemente is four times the National League batting champion—1961, 1964, 1965, and 1967—and he is voted the league's most valuable player in 1966. He is awarded twelve Golden Gloves and sets a major league record by leading the National League in assists five times. He serves on fourteen All-Star teams, and is one of only sixteen players to have three thousand or more hits. In his career, Clemente accumulates 240 home runs and a lifetime batting average of .317.

Clemente dies in 1972 in a plane crash while bringing relief to victims of an earthquake in Nicaragua. Upon his death, the Baseball Hall of Fame waives its five-year waiting period after a player's retirement and immediately elects him to membership. For his generosity, leadership, outstanding athletic achievements, and heroism, Roberto Clemente is considered by Puerto Ricans to be a national hero to this day.

DECEMBER 4, 1934 Guerrilla Guzmán Is Born. Abimael Guzmán Reynoso, the founder and leader of Peru's fiercest guerrilla movement, is born in Arequipa, Peru. Although he is an only child born out of wedlock to a woman of very modest means, he is able to attend the prestigious La Salle Catholic school. His mother dies when he is twelve years old and he then lives with his father and continues his education. In secondary school and college he becomes obsessed by political philosophy and becomes a Marxist activist. During the 1950s, Guzmán is particularly affected by the brutal dictatorship of General Manuel Odría and is convinced that peaceful means to socialism are impossible. By 1962, he is teaching at the University of San Cristóbal of Huamanga in Ayacucho, where he becomes increasingly involved with the Indians and outraged at the state of feudalism in which they live. He studies Mao's teachings and travels to China in 1965 and 1967 to learn firsthand what it is like to live in a communist state. In China and later in Albania, Guzmán makes high-level communist contacts and allegiances. By 1975, he is the leader of a pro-Maoist splinter group of the Peruvian communist party; the group, El Sendero Luminoso, or Shining Path, promotes change through violence. In 1976, Guzmán resigns his academic post and disappears from the public eye; and here begins his life in legend, his life almost as an omnipresent shadow on Peruvian politics. His first terrorist attack is launched in 1980, when his group sets fire to ballot boxes in a remote Andean village. From here, his path of violence broadens and intensifies in a quest to establish a

People's Republic of Peru fashioned on Mao's China. His terrorist activities include killing and torturing children and adults, and setting fire to entire villages. Many of the attacks are against peasants who refuse to join the Shining Path. The army employs equally brutal methods to battle the Shining Path, and the two sides create a death toll of some 27,000 lives since 1980. When Alberto Fujimoro takes office as president in 1990, the Shining Path steps up its attacks in the provinces and in Lima. On September 12, 1992, the national antiterrorism squad captures Guzmán, and he remains imprisoned to this day. However, Shining Path bombings and assassinations continue.

Lionel G. García. (Courtesy of the Arte Público Press Archives, University of Houston.)

1935

1935 Novelist Bombal Publishes First Novel. With the publication of her first novella, *La última niebla* (The Final Mist), María Bombal becomes one of Latin America's most beloved writers of the twentieth century. (*See also* biography, June 8, 1910.)

AUGUST 20, 1935 Lionel García, Author and Veterinarian, Is Born. Lionel G. García, a novelist who creates some of the most memorable characters in Chicano literature in a style steeped in the traditions of Texas tall-tales and Mexican–American folk narratives, is born in San Diego, Texas. García grows up in an environment in which Mexican–Americans are the majority in his small town and on the ranches where he works and plays. His father, a paint-and-body man, and his mother a teacher, García lives inn a middle-class background and does so well in school that he is one of the very few Mexican–Americans admitted to Texas A & M University. He majors in biology but also is encouraged by one of his English professors to write. After graduating he attempts to become a fulltime writer but is unsuccessful in getting his works published. He serves in the army and, after being discharged honorably, he returns to Texas A & M and graduates from the

institution in 1969 as a Doctor of Veterinary Science. He then develops a successful career as a veterinarian. Throughout this time he continues to write. In the early 1980s he once again attempts to publish, and finds many more opportunities. In 1983 he wins the PEN Southwest Discovery Award for his novel in progress, *Leaving Home,* which is published in 1985. This and his second novel, *A Shroud in the Family* (1987), draw heavily on his family experiences and small-town background. In part, *A Shroud in the Family* also demythologizes the "great" Texas heroes, such as Sam Houston and Jim Bowie who have become symbols of Anglo–Texans' defeat of and superiority over Mexicans; this is García's contribution to the Texas Sesquicentennial celebrations. His novel, *Hardscrub* (1989), is a departure from his former works; it is a realistically drawn chronicle of the life of an Anglo child in an abusive family relationship. *Hardscrub* is awarded the two most prestigious prizes for fiction in the Southwest: the Texas Institute of Letters Award for the Best Novel and the Southwest Booksellers Association Prize for Fiction. Lionel García's latest novel, *To a Widow with Children*

(1994), is a warm-hearted tale, set in rural south Texas, about a humorous love triangle that becomes the talk of the town. García also publishes short stories in magazines, newspapers, and anthologies.

SEPTEMBER 4, 1935 Batista Tries to Overthrow Cuban President. Fulgencio Batista leads a barracks revolt to overthrow President Gerardo Machado of Cuba. Eventually Batista becomes a dictator himself.

OCTOBER 23, 1935 Golfer Chi Chi Rodríguez Born in Puerto Rico. One of golf's all-time greats, Juan "Chi Chi" Rodríguez, is born in Río Piedras, Puerto Rico. Rodríguez comes from an extremely impoverished family and finds his way into golf as a caddy on the links that serve Puerto Rico's booming tourism. His is one of the most famous Hispanic "rags to riches through sports" tales, his career earnings having now passed the $3 million mark. He contributes financially to numerous charities and to the Chi Chi Rodríguez Youth Foundation in Clearwater, Florida. He wins a number of important tournaments, including the Denver Open (1963), the Lucky Strike International Open (1964), the Western Open (1964), the Dorado Pro-Am (1965), the Texas Open (1967), and the Tallahassee Open (1979). He later wins tournaments as a member on the Senior PGA Tour, including the Silver Pages Classic (1987), the GTE Northwest Classic (1987), and the Sunwest Senior Classic (1990).

NOVEMBER 1, 1935 Author Nicholasa Mohr Is Born. To date, Nicholasa Mohr is the only U.S. Hispanic woman to have developed a long career as a creative writer for the major publishing houses. Since 1973 her books for such publishers as Dell/Dial, Harper & Row, and Bantam, in both the adult and children's literature categories, have won numerous awards and outstanding reviews. Part and parcel of her work is the experience of growing up female, Hispanic, and a minority in New York City. Born in New York City, Nicholasa Mohr is

Nicholasa Mohr. Photo by Cindy Grossman. (Courtesy of the Arte Público Press Archives, University of Houston.)

raised in Spanish Harlem. Educated in New York City schools, she finally escapes poverty after graduating from the Pratt Center for Contemporary Printmaking in 1969. From that date until the publication of her first book, *Nilda* (1973), Mohr develops a successful career as a graphic artist. *Nilda,* a novel that traces the life of a young Puerto Rican girl confronting prejudice and coming of age during World War II, wins the Jane Addams Children's Book Award and is selected by *School Library Journal* as a Best Book of the Year. After *Nilda*'s success, Mohr produces numerous stories, scripts, and the following titles: *El Bronx Remembered* (1975), *In Nueva York* (1977), *Felita* (1979), *Rituals of Survival: A Woman's Portfolio* (1985), and *Going Home* (1986). Mohr's works are praised for depicting the life of Puerto Ricans in New York with empathy, realism, and humor. In her stories for children, Mohr handles the most serious and tragic of subjects, from incest to the death of a loved one, in a sensitive and humane way. Mohr contributes to the world of commercial publishing some of the most honest and memorable depictions of Puerto Ricans in the United States. In this and in her crusade to open the doors of publishing and the literary world to Hispanics, Nicholasa Mohr is a true pioneer.

DECEMBER 22, 1935 Tomás Rivera, Leader in Chicano Literature, Is Born. Mexican–American novelist Tomás Rivera is one of the principal founders of Chicano literature as a concept and the author of the universally acknowledged classic of that literature, *...y no se lo tragó la tierra* (And the Earth Did Not Devour Him, 1971). Born into a family of migrant workers in Crystal City, Texas, Rivera has to fit his early schooling as well as his college education in between the seasons of field work. He, nevertheless, achieves an outstanding educational career, earning the following degrees: B.A. and M.Ed. from Southwest Texas State College in 1958 and 1964, respectively; an M.A. in French literature and a Ph.D. in Spanish from the University of Oklahoma, both in 1969. In addition, Rivera pursues a career as a college professor and an administrator. He becomes chancellor of the University of California–Riverside in 1978, the position he holds when he dies of heart disease on May 16, 1984, in Fontana, California. Rivera's outwardly simple, but inwardly complex novel, *...y no se lo tragó la tierra,* is much in the line of experimental Latin–American fiction, demanding that readers take part in unraveling the story and in coming to their own conclusions about the identity and relationships of the characters, as well as the meaning. Drawing upon his own life as a migrant worker from Texas, Rivera constructs the novel in the straightforward, but poetic, language of migrant workers; a nameless central character attempts to find himself by reconstructing overheard conversations and stories, as well as events that take place during a metaphorical year, which really represents his whole life. In many ways, *...y no se lo tragó la tierra* has come to be the most influential book in the Chicano's search for identity. Rivera also writes and publishes other stories, essays, and poems. Through his essays, such as "Chicano Literature: Fiesta of the Living" (1979) and

"Into the Labyrinth: The Chicano in Literature" (1971), and his personal and scholarly activities, he is one of the prime movers in the promotion of Chicano authors, in the creation of the concept of Chicano literature, and in the development of Chicano literature and culture as legitimate academic areas in the college curriculum. In 1989 his stories are collected and published under the title of *The Harvest,* also the title of one of his stories, and in 1990 his poems are collected and published under the title of *The Searchers. Tomás Rivera: The Complete Works* is published in 1990. Tomás Rivera remains an outstanding and influential figure in the literature of Mexican peoples in the United States, and is fast achieving a place in the canon of Spanish-language literature in the world.

1936

1936 Argentine Wins Peace Prize. Argentine statesman and international jurist Carlos de Saavdera Lamas (1878–1959) wins the Nobel Peace Prize.

1936 La Chata Noloesca's Compañía Mexicana. Stage personality La Chata Noloesca reforms her theatre company in her native San Antonio as the Compañía Mexicana. (*See also* biography, August 20, 1903 and entry, 1941.)

1936 Olympians Win Medals. At the Summer Games in Berlin, Jeanette Campbell of Argentina wins the silver medal in the women's 100 meters freestyle in swimming and Mexico wins the bronze medal in basketball. Argentina's Oscar Casanovas wins the gold in featherweight boxing.

1936 Panama and U.S. Agree on Canal Zone Treaty. Panama and the United States work out a new Canal Zone treaty, which cancels Panama's "protectorate" status and guarantees Panama's independence. The United States also foreswears intervention in Panamanian affairs. The treaty is not ratified by the U.S.

Senate until 1939, after assurances that the United States would be free to shoot first and consult later in case of a threat to the canal.

AUGUST 31, 1936 Puerto Rican Boxer Is Champion. Sixto Escobar becomes the first Puerto Rican boxer to win a world championship when he knocks out Tony Marino. Fighting as a bantamweight boxer, Escobar is one of only a very few boxers to have regained his crown: twice.

1937

1937 Composer Ginastera Debuts. While still a student at the Conservatorio Nacional de Música, Alberto Ginastera debuts his suite, *Panambí,* at the Colón Theater in Buenos Aires. From that time on his name becomes known throughout the music world as one of Latin America's greatest composers. (*See also* biography, April 1, 1916.)

1937 Juan Marichal, Dominican Baseball Pitcher, Is Born. Juan Marichal starts with the San Francisco Giants in 1962, and from 1962 to 1971 he averages twenty wins per year. He leads the National League in wins in 1963 with a record of 25–8 and in 1968 with 26–9, in shutouts in 1965 with ten, and in 1969 with an ERA of 2.10. He pitches in eight All-Star games with a record of 2–0 and a 0.50 ERA for eighteen innings. Marichal's innings pitched total 3,509, for a record of 243–142 and an ERA of 2.89. He is an All-Star from 1962 to 1969 and again in 1972, and is inducted into the Hall of Fame in 1983.

1937 Palés Matos Publishes Masterpiece. Luis Palés Matos publishes his masterpiece, *Tun tun de pasa y grifería* (loosely translated as "Tun Tun of raisins and negritude"), demonstrating to Latin America how to exploit onomatopoeia and create neologisms based on the native cultures of the Americas. (*See also* biography, March 20, 1898.)

1937 The Ponce Massacre. Police attack and break up a pro-independence demonstration on the anniversary of the abolition of slavery, attended by some two thousand people, in Ponce, Puerto Rico. Known as the Ponce Massacre, the police kill twenty-two demonstrators and wound two hundred others.

MARCH 21, 1937 Football Coach Thomas Flores Is Born. Flores, born in Fresno, California, into a family of Mexican–American farmworkers, becomes one of the most successful coaches in the history of the National Football League. In 1978, Flores becomes the first Hispanic–American to be named a coach of a professional football team in the United States. He succeeds John Madden to the post for the Oakland Raiders in 1978 and is officially named in 1979. He leads the Raiders to two Super Bowl championships. In 1989, Flores is named president and general manager of the Seattle Seahawks, the highest rank ever attained by an Hispanic in professional sports in the United States.

OCTOBER 30, 1937 Rudolfo Anaya, Novelist and Teacher, Is Born. Novelist Rudolfo A. Anaya is born in the village of Pastura, New Mexico, in surroundings similar to those celebrated in his famous novel about growing up in the rural culture of New Mexico: *Bless Me, Ultima.* He attends public schools in Santa Rosa and Albuquerque and earns both his B.A. (1963) and his M.A. (1968) in English from the University of New Mexico. In 1972 he also earns an M.A. in guidance counseling from the same university. From 1963 to 1970 he teaches in the public schools, but in 1974 he becomes a member of the English Department of the University of New Mexico. With the success of his writing career, Anaya rises to head the creative writing program at the university. Among his many awards are the following: an honorary doctorate from the University of Albuquerque, the New Mexico Governor's Award for Excellence, the Premio Quinto Sol in 1972 for *Bless Me, Ultima,* and the President's National Salute to American Poets and Writers in 1980. Anaya is also a fellow of the National Endowment for the Arts and the Kellogg Foundations, through whose auspices he travels to China and other countries for study. Anaya is very much a believer in and promoter of a return to pre-Columbian literature and thought through the reflowering of Aztec civilization in Aztlán, the mythic homeland of the Aztecs (corresponding to the five states of today's Southwest). He sees his role in literature as that of the shaman; his task as a storyteller is to heal and reestablish balance and harmony. These ideas are present throughout his works, but are most successfully represented in his prize-winning novel, *Bless Me, Ultima* (1972), in which the folk healer Ultima works to reestablish harmony and social order in the life of the Mares family and to bring psychological well-being to Antonio, the protagonist who is struggling to understand the roles of Good and Evil in life. Anaya's other books are: *Heart of Aztlán* (1976), *Tortuga* (1979), *The Silence of the Llano* (1982), *The Legend of La Llorona* (1984), *The Adventures of Juan Chicaspatas* (1985), *A Chicano in China* (1986), *The Farolitas of Christmas* (1987), *Lord of the Dawn: The Legend of Quetzalcoatl* (1987), and *Albuquerque* (1992). In 1994, Warner Books announced its intentions of reissuing all of Anaya's works, including *Bless Me, Ultima* in a new hardback edition.

1938

1938 Hispanic Civil Rights Congress Founded. A national congress of Spanish-speaking people, the Congreso de Pueblos de Habla Hispana, is founded in Los Angeles by Bert Corona, Luisa Moreno, and others to protect the civil rights of Hispanics in the United States. After years of investigation by the FBI, which considers the congress subversive, and the advent of World War II, the organization declines in the mid-1940s.

JANUARY 1938 Pecan Shellers on Strike. Young

Mexican and Mexican–American pecan shellers strike in San Antonio, Texas. Since the late nineteenth century, the Texas pecan industry has been centered in San Antonio and has traditionally used predominantly Mexican-American labor. Paying only two or three cents a pound for shelling pecans, the industry rejects the National Recovery Administration's higher wage code. By 1937, various unions make incursions into the pecan industry and, in January 1938, announcement of a 15 percent wage cut leads to spontaneous strikes throughout the industry. A Mexican–American pecan sheller, Emma Tenayuca, emerges as a leader. She joins the Communist Party, because she believes that it is the only entity willing to help the shellers. The strike and management reaction to it becomes increasingly strife-ridden: more than 1,000 out of 6,000 strikers are arrested, and a great deal of violence is employed against the strikers. In March the strike is settled through arbitration: the union is recognized but a 7.5 percent decrease in wages is enforced. This decision is rendered moot in October when the Fair Labor Standards Act enforces a twenty-five cents per hour minimum wage. This is stimulus for the industry to mechanize and eventually reduce its labor force drastically.

MARCH 8, 1938 Mexican Oil Industry Nationalized. The Mexican government nationalizes the oil industry.

1939

1939 Collected Works of Hostos Published. The twenty volumes of Eugenio María de Hostos' complete works, which include writings on politics, education, biography, law, and his own creative writing, are published posthumously in Puerto Rico. (*See also* biography, January 11, 1839.)

1939 Painter Publishes Autobiography. Joaquín Torres-García publishes his autobiography,

Pecan shellers in San Antonio during the 1930s. (Courtesy of the Library of Congress Prints & Photographs Division.)

Historia de mi vida (History of My Life). (*See also* biography, July 28, 1874.)

1939 Spanish–American Nations Align with Allies. During World War II, all of the Spanish–American countries eventually declare war against the Axis (Germany, Italy, Japan) and join the Allies.

MARCH 23, 1939 George Castro, Chemist and IBM Lab Leader, Is Born. Mexican–American Chemist George Castro is born in Los Angeles, California. Castro receives his B.S. in chemistry from the University of California–Los Angeles in 1960 and his Ph.D. in physical chemistry from the University of California–Riverside in 1965. At various times, he is a post doctoral fellow at the University of Pennsylvania, Cal Tech, and Dartmouth, but works as a researcher for IBM after 1968. Castro assumes the leadership of the physical sciences at the IBM San Jose Research Lab in 1975, three years after its formation, and builds the organization into one that is world famous for its scientific discoveries. These include the discovery of the first superconducting polymer, novel organic metals and superconductors, high resolution laser techniques, and new methods

of investigating magnetic materials. In 1978, he receives the Outstanding Innovation Award from IBM. Since 1986, he has been the manager of synchrotron studies for IBM at the Almaden Research Center. In 1990, he is elected a fellow of the American Physical Society. Castro is the discoverer of the mechanism of the intrinsic charge carrier of organic photoconductors. Years later, such materials in the form of organic polymeric films become the basis for flexible photoconductors that are used in photocopying machines and high-speed printers.

DECEMBER 1, 1939 Lee Treviño, Champion Golfer, Is Born. The famous Mexican–American golfer, Lee Buck Treviño, is born in Dallas, Texas, to a cleaning lady. Treviño is raised by his mother and her father, a gravedigger, in a four-room farmhouse located at the back of the Glen Lakes Country Club fairways. As a boy, Treviño studies the form of golfers on the course from his own back yard. He drops out of school in the seventh grade and makes his way into what was then an exclusively Anglo rich man's sport by working as a caddy and greenskeeper. In 1966, Treviño becomes a professional golfer and achieves his first major victory in 1968 at the U.S. Open, where he is the first player in history to shoot under par in all four rounds of the event. In 1970, he is the leading money winner on the Professional Golf Association tour. In 1971, Treviño captures the U.S. Open for a second time and wins five tournaments between April and July, as well as the British Open in that year and again in 1972. In 1971, Treviño is named PGA Player of the Year, Associated Press Athlete of the Year, and *Sports Illustrated* Sportsman of the Year. In 1974, he wins the PGA again, among many other tournaments. In 1975, Treviño and two other golfers are struck by lightning on a course near Chicago. To this day, he suffers from back problems due to the accident; it seriously affects his game, and he is winless in 1976 and 1978. In 1980, he makes a comeback by winning the Texas Open and the Memphis Classic, and earning $385,814 for the year. He also is awarded the Vardon Trophy for the fewest strokes per round (69.73 for 82 rounds), the lowest since Sam Snead in 1958. Treviño retires from the PGA tour in 1985, with his thirty victories and total career earnings of over $3 million (third highest). Treviño is a member of the Texas Sports, American Golf, and World Golf halls of fame.

1940

1940s   Actor Gilbert Roland Portrays the Cisco Kid. Starting in the 1940s, Roland plays his most historic role, that of the Cisco Kid, in eleven B-pictures. (*See also* biography, December 11, 1905.)

1940   Bolivian Revolutionary Movement. After losing the Chaco War, in Bolivia a nationalist revolutionary movement, Movimiento Nacionalista Revolucionario (MNR), is led by Víctor Paz Estenssoro. The movement is the third most important social and economic reform movement in Latin America, after the Mexican and Cuban revolutions.

1940   Cubans Elect Batista. Fulgencio Batista is elected president of Cuba.

1940   Independent Labor Union Formed. The independent union, Confederación de Trabajadores Generales, is formed and soon becomes the major labor organization in Puerto Rico.

1940   Industrialization and Urbanization in Mexico. With the phase of socialist reform in Mexico now in the past, the administration of President Manuel Avila Camacho sets in motion a policy that is followed to the present: industrialization. The focus now shifts to the urban centers, as the urban working class, the bourgeoisie, and the middle class grow, and once again foreign investment and technology become a significant part of the economy. The result is a "mixed" economy in which the government invests one-third and the private sector two-thirds. Between 1940 and 1960, production more than triples and between 1960 and 1978, it increases 2.7 times. Average annual growth is 6 percent. In 1940, agriculture is 10 percent of the economy; in 1977, only 5 percent. Manufacturing increases from less than 19 percent to 23 percent. In 1940, only 20 percent of the population lives in urban centers; in 1977, more than 50 percent. The population increases from 19.6 million in 1940 to 67 million in 1977.

1940   Muñoz Marín Heads New Party in Puerto Rico. The Partido Popular Democrático is formed with future governor Luis Muñoz Marín at its head. It is the ruling party from 1940 to 1964. After 1972 it alternates power with the Partido Republicano (Republican Party). The Partido Popular Democrático begins as a pro-independence party, but under Muñoz Marín's leadership converts to pro-autonomy, equivalent to the present commonwealth status. It is this party that is successful in having the United States Congress authorize the creation of the Commonwealth of Puerto Rico. (*See also* biography, February 18, 1898.)

MARCH 9, 1940   Raúl Julia, Puerto Rican Star of Stage and Screen, Is Born. International stage and screen actor Raúl Rafael Carlos Julia y Arcelay, the oldest of four children, is born to Raúl, a restaurateur and his wife, Olga, in San Juan, Puerto Rico. He graduates from the University of Puerto Rico. While still a student at the university, comedian Orson Bean sees Julia in a local stage revue and recommends him to the American Place Theater in New York. In 1964, he moves to New York and lands a few stage roles, including a Spanish-language production of *Life Is a Dream*. Julia begins working for the New York Shakespeare Festival in 1967. He receives Tony Award nominations for his stage performances in *Two Gentlemen of Verona* (1971), *Where's Charley* (1974), *The Threepenny Opera* (1976), and *Nine* (1982). Julia begins to appear on television in such roles as Raphaél on *Sesame Street* and Aristotle Onassis in the television mini-series *Onassis: The Richest Man in the World* (1988). In the 1990s, Julia stars in a revival on Broadway of *Man of Lá Mancha*. He is also one of the few stage actors to make a successful transition to film. His movies include *Panic in Needle Park* (1971); *The Eyes of Laura Mars* (1978); *Kiss of the Spider Woman* and *Compromising Positions* (1985); *The Moon Over Parador* and *Tequila Sunrise* (1988); *Mack the Knife* (1989); *Frankenstein Unbound, Havana,* and *A Life of Sin* (1990); and *The Plague* (1993). He is described as a performer with a social conscience and a flair for comedy. Julia demonstrates his political and social conscience in films such as *Romero,* which is based on the life of Archbishop of El Salvador Oscar Arnulfo Romero, and *The Burning Season,* an HBO movie about Chico Mendes, the Brazilian labor-unionist assassinated in 1988. Julia receives critical acclaim for his supporting role as attorney Sandy Stern in *Presumed Innocent* (1990). In 1991, he takes the lead role as Gómez, the Latin-lover husband in the macabre comedy *The Addams Family,* and again in its 1993 sequel, *Addams Family Values*. Julia dies October 24, 1994, from complications of a stroke in Manhasset, Long Island. He receives a state funeral in San Juan, Puerto Rico.

MAY 11, 1940   Novelist Victor Villaseñor Is Born. Victor Villaseñor, novelist and screenwriter, is born in Carlsbad, California, the son of Mexican immigrants. Villaseñor brings Chicano literature to the widest of audiences through his novel of immigration, *Macho!* issued in 1973 by the world's largest paperback publisher, Bantam; through the epic saga of his own family in *Rain of Gold* (1991); and through the television screenplay of "The Ballad of Gregorio Cortéz." Villaseñor is raised on a ranch in Oceanside and experiences great difficulty with the educational system, because he is both a Spanish-speaker and dyslexic. He drops out of high school and works on the ranch and in the fields and as a construction worker. After attempting college at the University of San Diego for a brief period, he again drops out and goes to live in Mexico, where he discovers the world of books and learns to take pride in his identity and cultural heritage. From then on he reads extensively and teaches himself the art of writing fiction. During years of work in California as a construction worker, he completes nine novels and sixty-five short stories, all of which are rejected for publication, except for *Macho!* which launches his professional writing career. His second publishing venture is the nonfiction narrative of the life and trial of a serial killer, *Jury: The People versus Juan Corona* (1977). Negative experiences with stereotyping and discrimination toward Hispanics in commercial publishing lead Villaseñor to publish his most important literary effort with a small, not-for-profit Hispanic press, Arté Publico Press of Houston. The popularity of his bestselling family autobiography, *Rain of Gold,* brings to millions of Americans the family stories of the social, economic, and political struggles that result in Mexican immigration to the United States, where new stories of racism, discrimination, and the triumph over some of these barriers continue to develop in the epic of Mexican-American life. In 1994, Villaseñor publishes a

Victor Villaseñor. (Courtesy of the Arte Público Press Archives, University of Houston.)

Luis Valdez. (Courtesy of the Arte Público Press Archives, University of Houston.)

collection of stories, *Walking Stars,* which continue the *Rain of Gold* saga.

JUNE 26, 1940 Luis Valdez, the Father of Chicano Theatre, Is Born. Luis Valdez is born in Delano, California. He distinguishes himself as an actor, director, playwright, and filmmaker; however, it is in his role as the founding director of El Teatro Campesino, a theater of farmworkers in California, that his efforts inspire young Chicano activists across the country to use theatre as a means of organizing students, communities, and labor unions. Luis Valdez is born into a family of migrant farm workers in Delano, California. The second of ten children, he begins to work the fields at age six and to follow the crops. Valdez's education is constantly interrupted; he, nevertheless, finishes high school and goes on to San Jose State College, where he majors in English and pursues his interest in theatre. While there he wins a playwriting contest with his one-act, *The Theft* (1961), and in 1963 the drama department produces his play, *The Shrunken Head of Pancho Villa.* After graduating from college in 1964, Valdez joins the San Francisco Mime Troupe and learns the techniques of agit–prop

(agitation and propaganda) theatre and of the Italian *commedia dell'arte* (comedy of art), both of which influence Valdez's development of the basic format of Chicano theatre: the one-act presentational *acto* or "act." In 1965 Valdez enlists in César Chávez's mission to organize farmworkers in Delano into a union. It is there that Valdez brings together farmworkers and students into El Teatro Campesino to dramatize the plight of the farmworkers. The publicity and success gained by the troupe lead to the spontaneous appearance of a national Chicano theatre movement. In 1967 Valdez and El Teatro Campesino leave the unionizing effort to expand their theater beyond agit–prop and farmworker concerns. From then on Valdez and the theater explore most of the theatrical genres that are important to Mexicans in the United States, including religious pageants, vaudeville with the down-and-out *pelado* or underdog figure, and dramas corridos, or ballads. During the late 1960s and the 1970s El Teatro Campesino produces many of Valdez's plays, including *Los vendidos* (The Sell-Outs, 1967), *The Shrunken Head of Pancho Villa* (1968), *Bernabé* (1970), *Dark Root of a Scream* (1971),

La Carpa de los Rascuachis (1974), and *El Fin del Mundo* (1976). In 1978, Valdez breaks into mainstream theatre in Los Angeles, with the Mark Taper Forum's production of his *Zoot Suit* and the 1979 Broadway production of the same play. In 1986 he has a successful run of his play *I Don't Have to Show You No Stinking Badges* at the Los Angeles Theater Center. Valdez's screenwriting career begins with early film and television versions of Corky González's poem, "I Am Joaquín" (1969) and *Los Vendidos,* and later with a film version of *Zoot Suit* (1982). But his real incursion into major Hollywood productions and success comes with his writing and directing of *La Bamba* (the name of a dance from Veracruz), the screen biography of Chicano rock and roll star, Ritchie Valens. Valdez's plays, essays, and poems are widely anthologized. He publishes two collections of plays: *Luis Valdez—The Early Works* (1990) and *Zoot Suit and Other Plays* (1992). Valdez's awards include an Obie (1968), Los Angeles Drama Critics Awards (1969, 1972, and 1978), a special Emmy Award (1973) for Best Musical from the San Francisco Bay Critics Circle (1983), and honorary doctorates from San Jose Sate University, Columbia College, and the California Institute of the Arts.

JULY 19, 1940 Singer Vikki Carr Is Born. Vikki Carr, internationally famous singer of popular music, is born in El Paso, Texas, and baptized Florencia Bisenta de Casillas Martínez Cardona. Under her stage name of Vikki Carr, she becomes one of the most successful Hispanic recording artists and international performers of popular music in history. She begins her singing career while still in high school in the Los Angeles area. After touring with a band for a while, she signs her first recording contract with Liberty Records in 1961. Her first recording successes, however, are in Australia and England. By 1967 Carr's international popularity is so great that she is invited to perform for Queen Elizabeth II in London. The following year, she sets a precedent for sold-out concerts in Germany, Spain, France,

England, Australia, Japan, and Holland. In the United States, she becomes a favorite of the White House, performing repeatedly for Presidents Carter, Reagan, and Bush. To date, Carr has recorded forty-nine best-selling records, including fifteen gold albums. In 1985, she wins a Grammy for her Spanish-language album, "Simplemente Mujer" (Simply Woman). Her Spanish-language records have gone gold, platinum, and diamond. Her 1989 album, "Esos Hombres" (Those Men) wins gold records in Mexico, Chile, Puerto Rico, and the United States. Among her other awards are the *Los Angeles Times* 1970 "Woman of the Year," the American Guild of Variety Artists' 1972 "Entertainer of the Year," the 1984 "Hispanic Woman of the Year," and the 1991 Girl Scouts of America Award. In 1971, Carr founds the Vikki Carr Scholarship Foundation to provide higher education scholarships to Mexican-American youths. She is active in a number of other charities, as well.

SEPTEMBER 5, 1940 Raquel Welch, International Film Star, Is Born. International film star and sex-symbol Raquel Tejada is born to Armand Tejada, a Bolivian immigrant, and Josephine Hall, in Chicago, Illinois. She marries her high school sweetheart, James Welch, on May 8, 1959. After divorcing in 1964, Welch and her two children move to southern California where she gets small roles in films such as *A House Is Not a Home* and *Roustabout* (1964) with Elvis Presley. She goes on to star in *Fantastic Voyage* (1966); *The Queens: The Oldest Profession* (1967); *Bandolero!* (1968); *100 Rifles* (1969); *The Fuzz Bluebeard* and *Kansas City Bomber* (1972); *The Last of Sheila* (1973); *Mother, Jugs, and Speed* (1976); *Right to Die* (1987); and *Scandal in a Small Town* (1988). She produces and stars in the home exercise videos *Raquel: Lose 10 Lbs in 3 weeks, Body and Mind, Total Relaxation and Stress Relief Program,* and *A Week with Raquel.* She wins a Golden Globe in 1974 for her performance in *The Three Musketeers* and in 1990 is named Woman of the Year by The Los Angeles Hispanic Women's

Council. She currently produces films through the Raquel Welch Productions company.

OCTOBER 7, 1940 Agronomist Pedro Sánchez Is Born. Pedro Antonio Sánchez is born in Havana, Cuba. Sánchez receives his B.S., M.S., and Ph.D. in soil science from Cornell University in 1962, 1964, and 1968, respectively. After 1968, to the present, he is associated with North Carolina State University. In 1979 he becomes a professor of soil science and leader of the Tropical Soils Program. His research and consultancies take him abroad, most frequently to Latin America. For his outstanding service, the government of Peru awards him the Orden de Mérito Agrícola Medal. Currently, Sánchez is professor emeritus at North Carolina State University and director of the International Centre for Research in Agroforestry (ICRAF), Nairobi, Kenya. The ICRAF is devoted to alleviating poverty, tropical deforestation, and land degradation through improved agroforestry systems. He also serves as chairman of the board of the worldwide Tropical Soil Biology and Fertility Program and chairman of the National Academy of Sciences' panel on Sustainable Agriculture and the Environment in the Humid Tropics. Sánchez's research concerns the fertility and management of tropical soils, especially rice soils and tropical pastures.

1941

1941 Ciro Alegría Publishes Famous Work. Peruvian novelist Alegría publishes *El mundo es ancho y ajeno* (Broad and Alien Is the World), his most renowned work, and considered a classic in the genre of indigenist literature. It wins the first Latin American Novel Contest of the Pan American Union. (*See also* biography, November 4, 1909.)

1941 Compañía Mexicana Moves to New York. La Chata Noloesca's theatre company, the Compañía Mexicana puts down roots in New York for a stretch of nine years, during which time it is a mainstay on the Hispanic vaudeville circuit comprising the Teatro Hispano, the Teatro Puerto Rico, the Teatro Triboro, and the 53rd Street Theater. (*See also* biography, August 20, 1903 and entry, 1936.)

1941 Congress Outlaws Discrimination in Employment. The Fair Employment Practices Act is passed in the United States, eliminating discrimination in employment.

1941 George Sánchez Is President of LULAC. Educator and civil rights activist Sánchez becomes president of the League of United Latin American Citizens (LULAC). From then on, he uses LULAC as a forum to struggle against practices that inhibit the civil and educational rights of Hispanics. (*See also* biography, October 4, 1906.)

1941 Hispanics Support War Effort. With the U.S. declaration of war in 1941, Hispanics throughout the country enthusiastically respond to the war effort.

MARCH 29, 1941 Ricardo Sánchez, Autobiographical Chicano Poet, Is Born. Ricardo Sánchez, one of the most prolific Chicano poets, one of the first creators of a bilingual literary style, and one of the first to be identified with the Chicano Movement, is born the youngest of thirteen children in the notorious Barrio del Diablo (Devil's Neighborhood) in El Paso, Texas. He receives his early education there and becomes a high school dropout, an army enlistee, and later a repeat offender sentenced to prison terms in Soledad Prison in California and Ramsey Prison Farm Number One in Texas. At these prisons he begins his literary career before his last parole in 1969. Much of his early life experiences of oppressive poverty and overwhelming racism, as well as his suffering in prisons and his self-education and rise to a level of political and social consciousness, are chronicled in his poetry, which, although very lyrical, is also the most autobiographic of all the

Hispanic poets. Once his writing career is established and Sánchez begins to publish his works with both mainstream and alternative literary presses, he assumes various visiting appointments as a professor or writer in residence at several universities. He is a founder of the short-lived Mictla Publications in El Paso; he edits special issues of literary magazines, such as *De Colores* (Of Colors) and *Wood/Ibis*; he is a columnist for the *San Antonio Express*, a bookseller, a migrant worker counselor, and to this date he is still an active performer of his poetry on tours in the United States and abroad. Since 1991, Sánchez has been teaching Chicano studies at Washington State University in Bellingham. Sánchez's poetry is characterized by an unbridled linguistic inventiveness that not only calls upon both English and Spanish lexicon, but also is a source of neologisms and surprising combinations of the sounds and symbols of both languages in single works. His work can be virile and violent at one moment and delicate and sentimental at the next, as he follows the formulas and dictates of a poetry written for oral performance. His is often the exaggerated gesture and emotion of the *declamador*, or poetic orator, whose works are performed to inspire a protest rally, inaugurate a mural, celebrate a patriotic holiday, or eulogize the dead. Most of all, Sánchez is the autobiographical poet who casts himself as a Chicano Everyman participating in the epic history of his people through his poetry. His bilingual facility and immense vocabulary and inventiveness are legendary in Chicano literature. Besides publishing hundreds of poems in magazines and anthologies, Sánchez authors the following collections: *Canto y grito mi liberación (y lloro mis desmadrazgos)* (I Sing and Shout for My Liberation [and Cry for My Insults], 1971), republished in expanded form in 1973; *Hechizospells: Poetry/Stories/Vignettes/Articles/Notes on the Human Condition of Chicanos & Pícaros, Words & Hopes within Soul & Mind* (1976); *Milhuas Blues and Gritos Norteños* (Milwaukee Blues and Northern Shouts, 1980); *Amsterdam cantos y poemas pistos* (Amsterdam Cantos and Drunken Poems, 1983); and *Selected Poems* (1985).

JULY 30, 1941   The Office of Inter-American Affairs Is Established. President Franklin Delano Roosevelt institutes the Office of Inter-American Affairs to improve relations with Latin America, now that there is a perceived threat of Axis influence there. In April 1942, author–journalist Carey McWilliams heads up a Spanish-Speaking Division of the office to reduce discrimination against Mexican–Americans and help to integrate them into American society. In April 1946, President Harry S Truman terminates the Office of Inter-American Affairs.

1942

JULY 1942   The Bracero Program. Not long after the entry of the United States into World War II, the governments of the United States and Mexico enter into a bilateral agreement entitled the Mexican Farm Labor Supply Program. Informally known as the Bracero Program (from the Spanish word *brazo*, referring to workers using the strength of their arms), the program permits Mexicans to enter farm labor in the Southwest while U.S. manpower is drained for the war effort and for heavier industry. The program continues, however, after the war, and expands to the fields in the Midwest. The program is the subject of considerable controversy over the years, with various interest groups, such as farmers and organized labor, arguing for or against it. Congress extends the program in 1947 and again in 1951. During the Great Society program of President Lyndon B. Johnson, the program is unilaterally terminated by the United States in December 1964. During the twenty-two years of its existence, some 4.8 million Mexican workers come to the United States.

AUGUST 2, 1942   Isabel Allende, Chilean Novelist, Is Born. Chilean novelist Isabel

Migrant farm workers under the Bracero Program. (Courtesy of the Library of Congress Prints & Photographs Division.)

Allende is born in Lima, Peru, the daughter of Chilean diplomat Tomás Allende and Francisca Llona Barros. Isabel Allende is the niece of slain Chilean president, Salvador Allende. After 1975 she lives outside of Chile, first because of possible persecution from the same military dictatorship that killed her uncle, and later because of her marriage (in 1988) to American lawyer William Gordon. She and her husband now reside in northern California. Isabel Allende is one of Latin America's leading novelists and a primary exponent of magic realism. What Allende brings to contemporary Latin–American literature is a woman's perspective in understanding the history and politics of the region. Her original female characters, their particular upbringing and involvement in society, especially their political and economic participation, and their ability to spin their own tales and weave them into the social reality, has led to greater international understanding and appreciation of Latin America. To date her most important novel is *La casa de los espíritus,* (The House of the Spirits, 1982), which is a grand, sweeping, poetic recreation of her family and her country during this century. Her magic realist depiction of three generations of the

fictitious Trueba family is reminiscent of Gabriel García Márquez's Buendía family in *Cien años de soledad* (One Hundred Years of Solitude); and for this she is criticized by some. But her true originality and artistry is borne out in the rest of her narrative production: *De amor de sombra* (Of Love and Shadows, 1984), *Eva Luna* (1987), *Los cuentos de Eva Luna* (The Tales of Eva Luna, 1992), and *El plan infinito* (The Infinite Plan, 1992). Allende is also the author of plays, short stories, and children's stories.

SEPTEMBER 5, 1942 Symphony Conductor Eduardo Mata Born in Mexico City. Eduardo Mata, the renowned Mexican conductor, is born in Mexico City. Mata dedicates his life to music and becomes one of Mexico's most outstanding symphonic directors. Educated at the National Conservatory of Music from 1954 to 1963, and through private instruction, he begins his conducting career in 1964 with the Guadalajara Symphony Orchestra. From 1966 to 1975, he is music director and conductor of the Orquesta Filarmónica of the National University in Mexico City. In 1975 he becomes the director of the National Symphony in Mexico

Isabel Allende. (Courtesy of the Arte Público Press Archives, University of Houston.)

City and also directs a number of international music festivals, including the 1976 Casals Festival in Mexico. Mata has been a guest conductor around the world and throughout the United States. Starting in 1977, Mata leads the Dallas Symphony as music director, while also touring extensively and even continuing to serve as the principal conductor and musical advisor of the Phoenix Symphony (1974 to 1978), and the principal guest conductor of the Pittsburgh Symphony (since 1989). Mata is named conductor emeritus of the Dallas Symphony beginning with the 1994 season. Mata also maintains a busy schedule recording albums of his conducting some of the world's leading orchestras. In Mexico, his honors include the Golden Lyre Award (1974), the Elías Sourasky Prize in the Arts (1975), and the Mozart Medal conferred by the president of Mexico (1991). In the United States, he is a recipient of the White House Hispanic Heritage Award (1991).

1943

1943   Film Star Dolores del Rio Returns to Mexico. Actress Dolores del Río, dissatisfied

with Hollywood, returns to Mexico to do many important films of the 1940s, including *María Candelaria* (1943) and John Ford's *The Fugitive* (1947), filmed on location in Mexico. (*See also* biography, August 3, 1905.)

JANUARY 13, 1943   The "Sleepy Lagoon" Murder Case. In the famous "Sleepy Lagoon" murder case, a jury finds three Mexican–American youths guilty of first-degree murder, nine guilty of second-degree murder, five guilty of assault, and five others not guilty. The controversial case is infamous for the anti-Mexican bias introduced into the proceedings as well as for the "yellow journalism" of the press that covered the trial and inflamed public opinion against Mexicans in general and Pachucos in particular. On August 2, 1942, a Mexican–American youth, José Díaz, is found dead as the result of a fight among gangs near a popular swimming hole, which the press dubbed "Sleepy Lagoon." Twenty-two members of the 38th Street gang are tried en masse on sixty charges. A Sleepy Lagoon Defense Committee, headed up by Carey McWilliams, is successful in appealing the case, and on October 4, 1944, the District Court of Appeals reverses the decision for lack of evidence. During and after the case, the Los Angeles Police Department and the press emphasize Mexican–American crime, an important factor in precipitating the "Zoot Suit Riots" in June.

APRIL 29, 1943   Congress Passes Act to Regulate Bracero Program. Prompted by the labor shortage of World War II, the U.S. Congress passes Public Law 45 which ratifies a July 1942 agreement with the Mexican government to supply temporary workers, known as "braceros," for American agricultural work. The law finances and regulates the Bracero Program, which is later extended and amended on various occasions.

MAY 14, 1943   Cuban Singer Tania León Is Born. Tania León, Cuban singer of classical music, is born in Havana. She receives degrees

Defendants in the Sleepy Lagoon Court Case, 1944. (Courtesy of the *Los Angeles Times.*)

from the National Conservatory of Music in Havana, a B.S. in music education from New York University in 1973, and an M.A. in music composition from New York University in 1975. One year after arriving in the United States in 1968, Tania León becomes became the first music director of the Dance Theater of Harlem, and she continues to be an important composer for the Dance Theater. From then on, León studies conducting under such teachers and coaches as Laszlo Halasz, Leonard Bernstein, and Seiji Ozawa. She maintains a busy schedule

as a composer and recording artist, and as a guest conductor at most of the important symphonies throughout the United States and Puerto Rico, as well as in Paris, London, Spoleto, Berlin, and Munich. From 1977 to 1988, she directs the family concert series for the Brooklyn Philharmonic Community. In 1985, León joins the faculty of Brooklyn College as an associate professor, teaching both composition and conducting. She also serves as music director for Broadway musicals, such as "The Wiz." León is one of just a handful of women who

Tania León. (Courtesy of the Arte Público Press Archives, University of Houston.)

have had a successful career as a conductor. Her honors include the Dean Dixon Achievement Award in 1985, the ASCAP Composer's Award from 1987 to 1989, the National Council of Women Achievement Award in 1980, and the 1991 Academy-Institute Award in Music of the American Academy and Institute of Arts and Letters.

JUNE 3, 1943   The "Zoot Suit" Riots. The so-called "Zoot Suit Riots" begin in southern California. What they are, in fact, is a campaign spearheaded by the press to perceive Mexicans as foreigners and to persecute them as scapegoats. Bands of hundreds of sailors, marines, and soldiers in southern California move through barrio streets looking for Mexican youths wearing zoot suits so they can beat them and tear their clothes from their bodies. In response, the authorities often arrest the victims of these assaults. The press and the soldiers are far from reality in their perception and persecution of Mexicans youths. Though it is not publicized at the time, Mexicans are proportionately overrepresented in the armed services and later they are awarded proportionately more medals

of honor and decorations than any other ethnic group in the United States.

JUNE 4, 1943   Perón Begins to Take Over. The Argentine military lodge, Grupo de Oficiales Unidos (United Officers Group), effects a bloodless coup to remove Argentine president Ramón S. Castillo from power. A second coup (on July 7, 1944) results in Colonel Juan Perón becoming vice president of the republic. (*See also* biography, October 8, 1895 and entry, February 24, 1946.)

JULY 4, 1943   Reporter, TV Personality Geraldo Rivera Is Born. Geraldo Miguel Rivera, journalist and television personality, is born in New York City. Rivera studies at the University of Arizona and Brooklyn Law School, and receives a law degree from the University of Pennsylvania and a degree in journalism from Columbia University. Rivera is one of the nation's best-known investigative television journalists, writing and producing various award-winning documentaries. He has won a Peabody Award and ten Emmies for distinguished broadcast journalism. After beginning his career as a reporter for WABC-TV in New York in 1970, he becomes a reporter, producer, and host for television news and entertainment shows. Starting in 1987, he hosts and produces his own *Geraldo* talk show, which is nationally syndicated. Rivera is also the author of books including *Puerto Rico, Island of Contrast* (1973), *Miguel Robles: So Far* (1973), *A Special Kind of Coverage* (1976), and his very controversial autobiography, *Geraldo* (1993), which was published in 1991.

JULY 16, 1943   Reinaldo Arenas, Cuban Novelist, Is Born. Cuban exile novelist Reinaldo Arenas is born in Holguín, Oriente, Cuba. Educated at the University of Havana and Columbia University, Arenas launches his career as a writer in Communist Cuba, while he works as a researcher and journalist. Arenas is politically active in the overthrow of dictator Fulgencio Batista. From 1968 to 1974, he serves as the editor of *La gaceta de Cuba* (The Cuban Gazette), a literary magazine. He is imprisoned and "rehabilitated" by the government from 1974 to 1976 for his dissidence. He emigrates to the United States in 1980 through the Mariel Boatlift, and much of his life as a writer and speaker is dedicated to revealing political and homophobic repression and atrocities that occur in Castro's Cuba. As a gay intellectual, Arenas is doubly persecuted in the Communist country. Before Arenas leaves Cuba, his manuscripts are confiscated by the government, and he arrives in the United States penniless and without the product of his years of writing. In the United States, Arenas is a prolific writer and sees some of his earlier works translated to English and published. While some critics are taken aback by the political content and anti-Communist passion of the works, they agree on the power and beauty of Arenas's style and his placement in the mainstream of Latin–American magic realism. Arenas's novels include *Celestino antes del alba* (published in 1967, translated in 1987 as *Singing from the Well*), *El mundo alucinante* (published in 1967, translated in 1971 as *Being an Account of the Life and Adventures of Friar Servando Teresa de Mier*), *La vieja Rosa* (published in 1980, translated as *Old Rose: A Novel in Two Stories* in 1989), *Otra vez el mar* (published in 1982, translated as *Farewell to the Sea* in 1986), *La loma del ángel* (published in 1987 and translated as *Graveyard of the Angels*), *El portero* (The Gatekeeper, 1988), and *Palacio de las blanquísimas mofetas* (Palace of the White Skunks, 1990). In addition, Arenas has written short stories, essays, and plays. Reinaldo Arenas commits suicide in 1990.

1944

1944 Batista Retires from Politics. Dictator Fulgencio Batista retires from Cuban politics in favor of his successor, Ramón Grau San Martín, and leaves to live in Florida on the millions of dollars that he accrues during his rule. In 1952, he will return and install himself as president once again.

1944 Operation Bootstrap in Puerto Rico. Operation Bootstrap, a program initiated by the Puerto Rican government to meet U.S. labor demands of World War II and encourage industrialization on the island, stimulates a major wave of migration of workers to the United States. Under the program, U.S. factories that relocate to Puerto Rico receive a ten-year tax exemption. In addition to industrializing the island, the program also results in stimulating migration to urban centers from the countryside and emigration to the continental United States; agriculture suffers greatly. The program lasts until 1960.

1945

1945 Miriam Colón, Hispanic Theatre Leader, Is Born. Miriam Colón, the first lady of Hispanic theatre in New York, is born in Ponce, Puerto Rico. She is the founder and artistic director of the Puerto Rican Traveling Theater and a genuine pioneer in bringing Hispanic theatre to broad audiences. Raised in Ponce and in New York, Colón attends the University of Puerto Rico and the Erwin Piscator Dramatic Workshop and Technical Institute, as well as the famed Actors Studio, both in New York. Colón develops a long and distinguished career on New York stages and in Hollywood films and television series. Among her stage credits are *The Innkeepers* (1956); *Me* and *Cándido* (1965); *The Oxcart* (1966); *Winterset* (1968); *The Passion of Antígona Pérez* (1972); *Julius Caesar* (1979); and *Orinoco* and *Simpson Street* (1985). In 1989, she is made an honorary doctor of letters by Montclair State College; she also receives the White House Hispanic Heritage Award in 1990.

1945 Mistral Awarded Nobel Prize. Chilean poet Gabriela Mistral wins the Nobel Prize for

Literature, becoming Latin America's first Nobel Laureate. (*See also* biography, April 7, 1889.)

1945   Ponce Becomes Musical Director. Composer Manuel M. Ponce becomes the director of the music school of the Universidad Nacional Autónoma de México (UNAM). (*See also* biography, December 8, 1886.)

1945   Revolution in Guatemala. A social revolution unseats the traditional dictatorial regimes supported by the military, the creoles and the landlords in Guatemala. A new leader, Juan José Arévalo, is installed, supported instead by a small middle class and workers. Arévalo, serving from 1945 to 1950, and Jacobo Arbenz, who follows him from 1950 to 1954, set about democratizing the country, furthering education, and limiting foreign interests. A new constitution, based on the Mexican model and authorizing land reform and guaranteeing the rights of labor and free institutions, is adopted in 1945. In 1950, the Communist party gains influence and begins to attack American-owned enterprises, including the United Fruit Company. In July 1952, an agrarian law is passed to recapture, with compensation to the owners, lands withheld from cultivation and to redistribute them to small farmers. The United Fruit Company bears the brunt of expropriation of hundreds of thousands of acres of land. In May 1954, Washington protests the Arbenz government receiving arms shipments from the Soviet Union. In June, the Arbenz government is ousted through a CIA-engineered coup. In July, the government is taken over by a military junta headed by General Carlos Castillo Armas, who later is installed as president. Castillo Armas returns most of the expropriated lands to the United Fruit Company, and Washington handsomely subsidizes his government. His despotic and Communist-baiting regime is terminated with his assassination in July 1957.

1945   The United Nations. All of the Spanish–American countries join the United Nations.

Jacobo Arbenz. (Courtesy of the National Archives).

MARCH 21, 1945   Parents Win Rights Case in California. Mexican–American parents win a suit alleging segregation in four Orange County elementary school districts (*Méndez et al v. Westminster School District et al*) in California. They argue that segregation deprive more than five thousand Mexican–American students of the constitutional guarantees of due process and equal protection under the law. Despite the school districts' appeal to the Ninth Circuit Court in 1947, the lower court ruling is upheld.

Vice President Richard M. Nixon receiving General Carlos Castillo Armas in Washington, D.C., with an honor guard. (Courtesy of the National Archives.)

1946

1946   Mexican Political Party Takes New Name. The dominant political party in Mexico is rebaptized and takes on the name that it still bears today: Partido Revolucionario Institucional (Institutional Revolutionary Party). Until 1938, it had been the Partido Nacional Revolucionario (National Revolutionary Party), but the name is changed in that year to the Partido de la Revolución Mexicana (Party of the Mexican Revolution).

1946   Puerto Rican Independence Party Created. The Partido Independentista Puertorriqueño (Puerto Rican Independence Party) is created under the leadership of Gilberto Concepción de Gracia. Unlike the nationalist party, it proposes to move towards independence through peaceful means, including participating in the electoral process. The party, promotes a socialist ideology.

1946   Truman Appoints Puerto Rican Governor. The first Puerto Rican governor, Jesús T. Piñero, is appointed by President Harry S Truman.

FEBRUARY 24, 1946   Perón Elected President. Juan Perón is officially elected president of Argentina. (*See also* biography, October 8, 1895 and entry, June 4, 1943.)

DECEMBER 19, 1946   Miguel Piñero, Dramatist of Nuyorican School, Is Born. Miguel Piñero, the most famous dramatist to come out of the Nuyorican school, is born in Gurabo, Puerto Rico. He was raised on the Lower East Side of New York, the site of many of his plays and poems. Shortly after moving to New York, his father abandons the family, and they have to live on the streets until his mother can find a source of income. Piñero is a gang leader and involved in petty crime and drugs while an adolescent; he is a junior high dropout and by the time he is twenty-four he has been sent to Sing Sing Prison for armed robbery. While at Sing Sing, he begins writing and acting in a theatre workshop there. By the time of his release, his most famous play, *Short Eyes* (1975) has been prepared in draft form. The play is produced and soon moves to Broadway after getting favorable reviews. During the successful run of his play and afterwards, Piñero becomes involved with a group of Nuyorican writers in the Lower East Side and becomes one of the principal spokespersons and models for the new school of Nuyorican literature, which is furthered by the publication of *Nuyorican Poets: An Anthology of Puerto Rican Words and Feelings,* compiled and edited by him and Miguel Algarín in 1975. During this time, as well, Piñero begins his career as a scriptwriter for such television dramatic series as *Barreta, Kojak,* and *Miami Vice.* In all, Piñero writes some eleven plays that are produced, most of which are included in his two collections, *The Sun Always Shines for the Cool, A Midnight Moon at the Greasy Spoon, Eulogy for a Small-Time Thief* (1983) and *Outrageous One-Act Plays* (1986). Piñero is also author of a book of poems, *La Bodega Sold Dreams* (1986). Among his awards are a Guggenheim Fellowship (1982) and the New York Drama Critics Circle Award for Best American Play, an Obie, and the Drama Desk Award, all in 1974, for *Short Eyes.* Piñero dies of sclerosis of the liver in 1988, after many years of hard living and recurrent illnesses resulting from drug addiction.

1947

1947   Actor Ricardo Montalbán Goes to Hollywood. Montalbán is recruited as a "Latin lover" type by Metro-Goldwyn-Mayer (MGM). (*See also* biography, November 25, 1920.)

1947   The American G.I. Forum Movement. The American G.I. Forum is organized by Mexican–American veterans after a funeral home in Three Rivers, Texas, refuses to bury a Mexican–American serviceman killed in the Pacific. The G.I. Forum movement subsequently spreads throughout the Southwest and even to Puerto Ricans in the Northeast in one of the largest organized efforts by Hispanics to protect their civil rights.

1947   Argentinean Wins Nobel Prize. Argentine doctor and biologist Bernardo A. Houssay (1887–1947) wins the Nobel Prize for physiology and medicine for his studies of glandular secretion.

1947   Painter Jesús Rafael Soto Becomes Art Director. Soto is named director of the School of Fine Arts in Maracaibo. (*See also* biography, 1923.)

1947   Puerto Ricans Fly Away. More than twenty airlines provide service between San Juan and Miami and San Juan and New York, facilitating the first large migration by air in history.

FEBRUARY 24, 1947   Mexican–American Actor Olmos Is Born. Edward James Olmos, the second of three children born to Pedro Olmos, a Mexican immigrant, and the former Eleanor Huizar, is born in Los Angeles, California. In elementary school Olmos wins the Golden State batting championship. At the age of 15, his interest in baseball is replaced with an interest in music, and he teaches himself to play the piano. Shortly thereafter he forms a band called Pacific Ocean. He earns his associate's degree in sociology from East Los Angeles City College. Olmos takes acting lessons to help with his singing career, and finds he prefers acting. In the 1970s and 1980s, he has small parts in several television police series, including *Kojak, Hawaii Five-O,* and *Hill Street Blues.* Olmos lands a major part in *Zoot Suit,* a musical drama about a group of Mexican–Americans being sentenced on bogus murder charges in 1942 in Los Angeles. The play moves from the Mark Tapper Forum in Los Angeles to Broadway in March of 1979. For his 1978 performance in *Zoot Suit,* Olmos wins the Los Angeles Drama Critics Circle Award. In 1979, he receives the Theater World Award for Most Outstanding New Performer and is nominated for a Tony Award for Best Actor in a Featured Role in a Play. Olmos collaborates with director Robert Young in filming and promoting *The Ballad of Gregorio Cortéz,* the true story of a Mexican cowhand who was the victim of ethnic prejudice in Texas in 1901. After the movie is shown on television, Olmos negotiates for corporate sponsors to distribute copies of the film to libraries, schools, and youth clubs. In 1984, Olmos takes the role of Lieutenant Martin Castillo in the blockbuster police series *Miami Vice*. He wins an Emmy for Best Supporting Actor in a Dramatic Series in 1985 and the Golden Globe Award in 1986 for that role. His next project is playing the barrio math teacher, Jaime Escalante in *Stand and Deliver*, for which he receives an Academy Award nomination for Best Actor. In 1992, Olmos coproduces *American Me*, a motion picture about crime and violence in America. Olmos' other films include *Wolfen* (1981), *Triumph of the Spirit* (1989), and *Talent for the Game* (1991). Eastman Kodak awards him the Eastman Second Century Award for his encouragement of young filmmakers. After the 1993 riots in Los Angeles following the acquittal of the police in the Rodney King trial, Olmos becomes a member of the Rebuild LA Committee to restore destroyed inner-city neighborhoods.

MARCH 15, 1947   Federico Peña, Secretary of Transportation, Is Born. Federico Peña, presidential cabinet member and former mayor of Denver, Colorado, is born in Laredo, Texas. Peña is raised in Brownsville and receives his early education there. He later attends the University of Texas at Austin, where he receives both an undergraduate degree and a law degree. Federico Peña follows in a tradition of public service in his family. One of his great-grandfathers served as mayor of Laredo during the Civil War and another was a member of that city's first school board. Peña's grandfather held the office of alderman in Laredo for almost a quarter of a century. At age thirty-six Federico Peña is elected Denver, Colorado's 37th mayor in 1983 and is reelected to a second term in 1987. Mayor Peña's efforts to strengthen Denver's economy place the city in the

national spotlight. During his tenure, the U.S. Conference of Mayors selects Denver over one hundred other cities as the winner of its prestigious "City Liveability Award." Mayor Peña did not seek a third term. In 1993, he was named by President Bill Clinton to the position of Secretary of Transportation; he is the first Hispanic to hold that post.

JUNE 11, 1947   Henry Cisneros, HUD Secretary, Is Born. Henry G. Cisneros, Secretary of Housing and Urban Development (HUD) and former mayor of San Antonio, Texas, is born in a west-side Mexican barrio of San Antonio, the son of a civil servant. He is educated in the city's parochial schools and attends Texas Agricultural and Mechanical University, where he receives a B.A. and a master's degree in urban planning in 1970. In 1971, Cisneros moves to Washington, D.C., where he works for the National League of Cities and begins fulltime graduate studies in public administration at George Washington University. In 1971, at age twenty-two, Cisneros becomes the youngest White House Fellow in U.S. history. When his fellowship ends, he earns a second master's degree, in public administration, at Harvard University. He then completes his work at George Washington University and received a Ph.D in public administration. He returns to San Antonio to teach government at the University of Texas. In 1975, Cisneros runs for the city council on the Good Government League ticket and wins. He gains a reputation as a bright young politician, and in 1977 he is reelected in a landslide. In 1981, Cisneros run for mayor of San Antonio, the ninth largest city in the U.S., and wins 62 percent of the vote. In 1983, he is reelected with 94 percent of the vote, reelected in 1985 with 72 percent, and reelected in 1987 with twice as many votes as his closest opponent. In 1993, he is named by President Bill Clinton to the cabinet position of Secretary of Housing and Urban Development, the first Hispanic to hold that post.

AUGUST 8, 1947   Alurista, Poet and Pioneer in Chicano Literature, Is Born. Alurista (Alberto Baltazar Urista), pioneer of Chicano literature, is born in Mexico City. He spends his early years in the states of Morelos and Guerrero. At age thirteen he emigrates to the United States with his family, which settles in San Diego, California. He begins writing poetry at an early age, and is a restless and widely read student. He enters Chapman College in 1965 and transfers to and graduates from San Diego State University in 1970 with a B.A. in psychology. He later obtains an M.A. from that institution and a Ph.D. in literature from the University of California–San Diego in 1983. Around 1966 he writes poetry seriously for publication and assumes the pen name of Alurista, which is virtually the only name he uses to this date. He is one of the first poets to support the Chicano Movement through his poetry. He writes and signs important manifestos of the movement, and is a founder of the Movimiento Estudiantil de Aztlán (MECHA, Chicano Student Movement of Aztlán) in 1967. Alurista is one of the first to establish the concept of Aztlán in literature, which forecasts a return to the glories of Aztec civilization by the Chicanos in the mythic homeland of the Aztecs, what is today roughly the five southwestern states of the Southwest. He is a prolific and talented poet, a pioneer of bilingualism in Chicano poetry. Throughout his career his study of the Nahuatl and Mayan languages and mythology enrich his poetic works and inspire his promotion of the ideology of Aztlán. But it is Alurista's bilingualism that opens new frontiers in poetry, with his free experimentation in combining the sounds, meanings, and graphic representations of Spanish and English in the same poem, quite often achieving surprising and beautiful effects. Alurista's published poetry includes these books: *Floricanto en Aztlán* (1971), *Nationchild Plumaroja, 1967–1972* (1972), *Timespace Huracán: Poems, 1972–1975* (1976), *A'nque* (1979), *Spik in Glyph?* (1981), and *Return: Poems Collected and New* (1982).

1948

1948   Oswaldo Guayasamín Completes Fresco, Wins Fellowship. Guayasamín completes his famous fresco, *El incario y la Conquista* (The Incan and the Conquest), and he receives a Rockefeller Foundation fellowship to study playwriting in the United States, which allows him to study at Columbia University and at the Piscator Dramatic Workshop in New York City. (*See also* biography, 1919.)

1948   Pancho González Is Tennis Champion. Richard "Pancho" González wins the U.S. men's singles tennis championships at Forest Hills (New York). He repeats the feat in 1949, and also wins the men's doubles championships at Wimbledon, England. González, native of Los Angeles, is a top-ranked professional player from 1954 to 1961. (*See also* biography, May 9, 1928 and entry, 1968.)

JANUARY 29, 1948   TV and Radio Talk Show Host Cristina Saralegui Is Born. Cristina Saralegui, journalist and television personality, is born in Havana, Cuba, into a distinguished family of journalists. Her grandfather, Francisco Saralegui, known throughout Latin America as the "paper czar," initiates his granddaughter into the world of publishing as an editor at such popular magazines as *Bohemia*, *Carteles*, and *Vanidades*. In 1960 she emigrates to Miami's Cuban exile community, but continues in the family profession by majoring in mass communications and creative writing at the University of Miami. In her last year at the university, she works for *Vanidades*, the leading ladies' service magazine in Latin America. By 1979, she is named editor in chief of the internationally distributed *Cosmopolitan-en-Español*. In 1989, she resigns that position to become the host of *The Cristina Show*, which is now the top-rated daytime talk show on Spanish-language television in the United States. Saralegui also hosts (since 1991) a daily nationally syndicated radio show, *Cristina Opina* (Cristina's Opinions) and

Cristina Saralegui on her internationally televised talk show. (Courtesy of the Arte Público Press Archives, University of Houston.)

is the editor in chief of a new monthly magazine *Cristina—La Revista* (Cristina—The Magazine), published by Editorial América in Miami. Through radio and television, Cristina reaches 6.5 million Hispanics daily throughout the United States and in twelve Latin–American countries.

SUMMER 1948   Hispanic Olympic Medalists. Panama's Lloyd La Beach wins the bronze in both the 100 meters with a time of 10.4 and the 200 meters in 21.2 in the Olympic Games in London, England. Argentine athletes Noemí Simonetto de Portela wins a silver medal in the women's long jump with a jump of 5 meters 60 centimeters, Delfo Cabrera wins the marathon with a time of 2:34:51.6, and Carlos Enrique Díaz Saenz Valiente wins the rapid-fire pistol competition with 571 points. Mexico's Humberto Mariles Cortes, Rubén Uriza, and Alberto Valdes Lacarra take the gold medal in the team equestrian competition (Nations Grand Prize), and Cortes takes the gold in the individual equestrian. Mexico's Joaquín Capilla Pérez takes the bronze in platform diving, with 113.52 points. Peru's Edwin Vásquez Cam wins the

Olympic free pistol competition with 545 points. Uruguay's Eduardo Risso is awarded the silver medal in sculling (7:38.2). Team Brazil wins the bronze in basketball.

JULY 4, 1948   Puerto Rican Politics. The pro-statehood Republican Party is founded in Puerto Rico. Also, a newly formed independence party, the Partido Independentista, participates for the first time in the Puerto Rican elections.

1949

1949–65   Muñoz Marín Is Governor. Politician Luis Muñoz Marín serves as the first governor of Puerto Rico. (*See also* biography, February 18, 1898.)

FEBRUARY 6, 1949   Nuyorican Poet Victor Hernández Cruz Is Born. Victor Hernández Cruz, the Nuyorican poet most recognized and acclaimed by the mainstream, is born in Aguas Buenas, Puerto Rico; he moves with his family to New York's Spanish Harlem at the age of five. Cruz attends Benjamin Franklin High School, where he begins writing poetry. In the years following graduation, his poetry appears in *Evergreen Review, New York Review of Books, Ramparts, Down Here,* and in small magazines. In 1973 Cruz leaves New York and takes up residence in San Francisco, where he works for the U.S. Postal Service. In 1989 he moves back to Puerto Rico, where he currently resides. Victor Hernández Cruz's poetry books include *Papo Got His Gun* (1966), *Snaps* (1969), *Mainland* (1973), *Tropicalization* (1976), *By Lingual Wholes* (1982), and *Rhythm, Content and Flavor* (1989). Classifying his poetry as Afro–Latin, Cruz is a consummate bilingual poet and experimenter who consistently explores the relationship of music to poetry in a multiracial, multicultural context. Cruz is often considered a jazz poet, and an African–American poet. The April 1981 issue of *Life* magazine, includes Cruz among a handful of outstanding American poets.

Chapter 7

1950 TO 1959

1950

1950s   Mexican Immigration Increases. During the 1950s, immigration from Mexico doubles from 5.9 percent to 11.9 percent of the total number of immigrants to the United States.

1950   Arnaz Starts Production Company. Desi Arnaz and his wife, actress Lucille Ball, cofound Desilu Productions. (*See also* biography, March 2, 1917.)

1950   Juan O'Gorman Has Exhibition, Designs Library. Juan O'Gorman, one of the great Mexican muralists and architects, is given a solo exhibition at the Palace of Fine Arts, the same year that he designs the famed library of the National University and covers it with a mosaic mural. (*See also* biography, 1905.)

1950   Migrant Workers. During the 1950s and 1960s in the United States, black workers continue as the most numerous migrant workers in the eastern seaboard states, while Mexican and Mexican–American workers soon dominate the migrant labor paths between Texas and the Great Lakes, the Rocky Mountain region, and the area from California to the Pacific Northwest.

1950   Puerto Rican Actor Ferrer Wins an Oscar. José Ferrer wins the Academy Award for Best Actor in *Cyrano de Bergerac.* (*See also* biography, January 8, 1912.)

1950   Segregation Banned in Southwest. From the 1950s through the early 1960s, segregation is abolished in Texas, Arizona, and many other communities, largely through the efforts of the League of United Latin American Citizens (LULAC) and the Alianza Hispano Americana.

1950   World Cup Winners. Uruguay wins its second World Cup in soccer. Uruguay and Argentina are the only two countries in the world to win the international soccer championship twice.

JULY 3, 1950   Puerto Rico Becomes Commonwealth. The U.S. Congress upgrades Puerto Rico's political status from protectorate to commonwealth. Puerto Rico also is authorized to write its own constitution, which is accepted by the Puerto Ricans in a popular vote on March 3, 1952. This constitution gives rise to the commonwealth status of Puerto Rico that is still in effect today. Many of the rights, privileges, and guarantees of the constitution are similar to those in the U.S. Constitution and the Bill of Rights, and the government structure that it calls for, including the bicameral legislature, is modeled upon the government structure of the United States. Because of the commonwealth status, nationalist groups demonstrate and attack authorities all over the island during this year. Blanca Canales Torresola and her followers declare the independent Republic of Jayuya, a small mountain town; she is arrested and eventually spends more than ten years in prison. Other nationalist groups attack the fortifications at San Juan and other targets in Arecibo and Mayagüez. Pedro Alvizu Campos is arrested again. The activities culminate with a nationalist attack on Blair House, in Washington, D.C., where President Harry S Truman resides while the White House is renovated. In all, there are more than two thousand arrests of nationalists on the island in 1950.

SEPTEMBER 5, 1950 Tato Laviera, Popular Hispanic Poet, Is Born. Jesús Abraham "Tato" Laviera is the best-selling Hispanic poet of the United States, and he has the distinction of still having all of his books in print. Born in Santurce, Puerto Rico, he migrates to New York at the age of ten with his family, which settles in a poor area of the Lower East Side. After finding himself in an alien society and with virtually no English language skills, Laviera is able to adjust and eventually graduates from high school as an honor student. Despite having no other degrees, his intelligence, aggressiveness, and thorough knowledge of his community lead to a career in the administration of social service agencies. After the publication of his first book, *La Carreta Made a U-Turn* (1979), Laviera gives up administrative work to dedicate his time to writing. After 1980 Laviera's career includes not only writing but touring nationally as a performer of his poetry, directing plays, and producing cultural events. On January 3, 1980, he is received by President Jimmy Carter at the White House gathering of American poets. In 1981 his second book, *Enclave,* is the recipient of the American Book Award of the Before Columbus Foundation. All of Tato Laviera's books are well received by critics, most of whom place him within the context of Afro–Caribbean poetry and U.S. Hispanic bilingualism. *La Carreta Made a U-Turn* is bilingual, jazz- or *salsa*-poetry that presents the reader with a slice of life drawn from the

Tato Laviera. (Courtesy of the Arte Público Press Archives, University of Houston.)

Puerto Rican community of the Lower East Side. As such, it examines both oppression of the migrant community and its alienation through such popular culture forms as soap operas; it examines crime and drug addiction while affirming the spiritual and social values of the community, and the place of art, poetry, and music in what many may consider to be the unlikeliest of social environments. Laviera, here as in the rest of his books, acknowledges and supports the existence of a true Puerto Rican and Latino culture within the heart of the metropolis and the United States. He further affirms that there is no need to return to a homeland on an island or south of the border, for Latinos have made their home here and are transforming mainstream culture not only in the United States, but also throughout the hemisphere. In *Enclave,* Laviera celebrates such cultural heroes, both real and imagined, as Alicia Alonso, Suni Paz, John Lennon, and Miriam Makeba, and the fictitious Afro–Puerto Rican Tito Madera Smith, the barrio gossip Juana Bochisme, and the neighborhood tough Esquina Dude. As in *La Carreta Made a U-Turn,* Laviera acknowledges his debt to Afro–Caribbean music and poetry in his eulogies of salsa composer Rafael Cortijo, of the famed poetry recitator Juan Boria, and of master poets Luis Palés Matos and Nicolás Guillén. *American* (1986), published on the occasion of the centennial celebration of the Statue of Liberty, is a poetic reconsideration of immigrant life in New York City and the United States. *Mainstream Ethics* (1988) proposes transforming the United States from a Eurocentric culture to one that is ethnically and racially pluralistic in its official identity.

1951

1951   Cuban Player Has Most Stolen Bases. Cuban Orestes (Minnie) Miñoso becomes the first Hispanic–American ballplayer to win the championship in stolen bases (31) in professional baseball in the United States. Miñoso makes his debut with the New York Cubans of the Negro Leagues in 1948, but goes to the Cleveland Indians in 1949 when the color line is broken. Miñoso has a long career playing for various teams, and in 1976, when he serves as a designated hitter for the Chicago White Sox, he becomes one of only six players to be active over four decades.

1951   Painter Botero Has Exhibition. Fernando Botero has his first solo gallery exhibition in Bogotá, Colombia. (*See also* biography, 1932.)

JULY 10, 1951   Carrasquel Is First Hispanic in All-Star Game. After participating in professional baseball since its beginning in the United States, a Hispanic–American ballplayer is finally selected for the All-Star game: Venezuelan shortstop Alfonso (Chico) Carrasquel. Carrasquel serves as the opening player in that position on this date.

JULY 12, 1951   The Migratory Labor Agreement. Under Public Law 78 passed by Congress on this date, the Bracero Program is formalized as the Migratory Labor Agreement, and will bring an annual average of 350,000 Mexican workers to the United States until its end more than a decade later. The law is passed because of the alleged need for manpower during the Korean War and the needs of the Southwestern agribusiness. P.L. 78 empowers the Secretary of Labor to recruit, transport, process, negotiate contracts for, and regulate the use of Mexican laborers. It also authorizes contracting undocumented workers who have resided in the United States for five years or more. Employers are supposed to reimburse the government for transportation and agree to minimum wage and working conditions. After years of complaints against the program and abuses by agribusiness, the program is allowed to lapse without renewal in 1964.

AUGUST 24, 1951   Pulitzer Prize-Winning Writer Oscar Hijuelos Is Born. Oscar Hijuelos is the first Hispanic writer to win the Pulitzer Prize for fiction (1990). Born to Cuban–American working-class parents in New York City, Hijuelos is educated in public schools and obtains a B.A. in 1975 and an M.A. in 1976, both in English, from City College of the City University of New York. While at City College he studies creative writing with and is guided by the noted novelist Donald Barthelme. Hijuelos is one of the few Hispanic writers to formally study creative writing and then to break into Anglo-dominated creative writing circles, participating in prestigious workshops, such as the Breadloaf Writers Conference, and benefitting from highly competitive fellowships, such as the Fellowship from the American Academy in Rome and the Institute for Arts and Letters (1985), the National Endowment for the Arts Fellowship (1985), and the Guggenheim Fellowship (1990). Hijuelos is the author of various short stories and three novels, *Our House in the Last World* (1983), *The Mambo Kings Play Songs of Love* (1989), and *The Fourteen Sisters of Emilio Montez O'Brien* (1993). His first novel follows in the tradition of ethnic autobiography and the novel of immigration, as it chronicles the life and maladjustment of a Cuban immigrant family in the United States during the 1940s. *The Mambo Kings Play Songs of Love,* the winner of the Pulitzer Prize, is more than just a story of immigration as it examines a period in time when Hispanic culture is highly visible in the United States and influences American popular culture: the 1950s during the height of the mambo craze and the overwhelming success of Desi Arnaz's television show, *I Love Lucy.* Written in a poetic but almost documentary style, the novel follows two brothers who are musicians trying to ride the crest of the Latin music wave. While providing a picture of one segment of American life never before seen in English-language fiction, the novel also indicts, as does *Our House in the Last World,* womanizing and alcoholism as particularly Cuban flaws.

SEPTEMBER 24, 1951 Novelist Roberto Fernández Born in Cuba. Cuban–American novelist Roberto Fernández is born in Sagua la Grande, Cuba, just eight years before the Cuban Revolution. He goes into exile with his family at the age of eleven. His family settles in southern Florida, not in the Cuban community of Miami but in areas where Anglo–American culture is dominant. This leads to periods of adjustment to what seemed like a hostile environment to the young boy, an impression that accounts for some of the culture conflict that is narrated in his writings. The Fernández family nevertheless maintains close ties with the Miami community, and this too becomes subject

matter for the writer. As an adolescent, Fernández is interested in writing, and this interest takes him to college and graduate school. In 1978 he completes a Ph.D. in linguistics at Florida State University; by that time he has already published two collections of stories: *Cuentos sin rumbo,* (Directionless Tales, 1975) and *El jardín de la luna* (The Garden of the Moon, 1976). At this point he also starts his career as an academic, teaching linguistics and Hispanic literature at Florida State University in Tallahassee. Roberto Fernández is in the vanguard of Cuban–American literature, having made the transition from the literature of exile to a literature very much of the culture and social conditions of Cubans in the United States, and having made the transition from producing works in Spanish to writing in English. Roberto Fernández is the author of three open-formed novels that have gained him the reputation of being a satirist and humorist of the Miami Cuban community. In all three, he is also a master at capturing the nuances of Cuban dialect in Spanish and English. *La vida es un special* (Life Is on Special, 1982), *La montaña rusa* (The Roller Coaster, 1985), and *Raining Backwards* (1988) are all mosaics made up of monologues, dialogues, letters, phone conversations, speeches, and other types of oral performance that, in the composite, make up a continuing tale of the development of the exile community and its younger generations of increasingly acculturated Cuban–Americans. Through the pages of these books the author charts the goings-on at social clubs, coming-out parties, counterrevolutionary guerrilla movements in the Florida swamps, the emergence of a Cuban pope, a mystery novel, a poetry and art contest, and many other episodic bits and pieces that create a broad and epic spectrum of a dynamic community caught between two cultures, two sets of values, two languages, and two political systems. *Raining Backwards,* Fernández's first book to be published in English, becomes somewhat of a small press hit, receiving outstanding reviews from coast to coast in major newspapers and magazines; it is optioned to become a feature film. In 1994, he publishes a sequel to *Raining Backwards* called *Holy Radishes!*

1952

1952　Agrarian Reform in Bolivia. Before the 1952 revolution, more than 92 percent of all farmland in Bolivia is held in units of 1,000 hectares or more, but 82 percent of all owners only controlled 1 percent of the land. After the revolution, agrarian reform begins, and in 1953, the Revolutionary Movement Party passes a land decree to redistribute lands equitably, in order to increase productivity and labor and to integrate peasants into the national economy and society. By 1955, most redistribution has been accomplished by the campesinos themselves who invade lands and organize peasant syndicates. Half of Bolivia's rural families become land owners, but it takes three decades to process certification or entitlement.

1952　Agrarian Reform in Guatemala. The government of Jacobo Arbenz in Guatemala passes a decree expropriating abandoned and uncultivated lands, and those owned in absentia, and redistributing them. This agrarian reform proceeds rapidly and even includes the expropriation of some 420,000 acres from the powerful United Fruit Company. The effort halts in 1954, when Arbenz is deposed. The program is then substituted with a one to open up undeveloped lands for cultivation.

1952　Anthony Quinn Wins the Oscar. Quinn wins the Academy Award for his role as Zapata's brother in *Viva Zapata!* (*See also* biography, April 21, 1915 and entry, 1956.)

1952　McCarran–Walter Act Regulates Immigration. The United States Congress passes the Immigration and Nationality Act of 1952, also known as the McCarran–Walter Act. The act reaffirms the basic features of the 1924 quota law by maintaining a restrictive limit on immigration from particular countries. Immigration from the Western Hemisphere remains exempt, except that applicants must clear a long list of barriers devised to exclude homosexuals, Communists, and others.

1952　Revolutionary Movement Wins in Bolivia. The nationalist revolutionary movement, Movimiento Nacionalista Revolucionario, is elected into power in Bolivia under Víctor Paz Estenssoro. Once in government, the party nationalizes the mines, redistributes land through an extensive agrarian reform plan, extends civil rights to the Indians, and institutes many other social reforms. The movement is ended in 1964 through a military rebellion.

1952　Writer Juan José Arreola Publishes Collection. One of Latin America's outstanding writers of short narratives, Arreola publishes his best-known collection *Confabulario* (Confabulations). (*See also* biography, September 12, 1918.)

FEBRUARY 24, 1952　Judith Ortiz Cofer, Poet, Novelist, and Teacher, Is Born. Poet and novelist Judith Ortiz Cofer is born in Puerto Rico into a family that moves back and forth between Puerto Rico and Paterson, New Jersey. Her father, Jesús Ortiz Lugo, is a navy man, first assigned to the Brooklyn Navy Yard and then other points around the world. In Puerto Rico, the young Judith attends San José Catholic School in San Germán and in Paterson she goes to public schools at first, and then to Saint Joseph's Catholic School in Paterson, as well. In 1968, after her father retires from the navy with a nervous breakdown, the family moves to Augusta, Georgia, where she attends high school and Augusta College. She meets John Cofer at the college and they marry. After graduation and the birth of her daughter, they move to West Palm Beach, Florida, and she earns an M.A. degree at Florida Atlantic University. She also is awarded a scholarship by the English-Speaking Union of America to do graduate work at Oxford University. Among many other awards are fellowships from the Florida Arts Council (1980), the Bread Loaf Writers Conference (1981), and the National Endowment for the Arts (1989). While teaching English in south Florida area colleges, Ortiz Cofer begins writing poetry, and her works are soon appearing in such magazines as the *New Mexico Humanities Review, Kansas Quarterly, Prairie Schooner, Revista Chicano-Riqueña, Southern Humanities Review, Southern Poetry Review,* and elsewhere. Her collections of poetry include four chapbooks—*Latin Women Pray* (1980), *Among the Ancestors* (1981), *The Native Dancer* (1981), *Peregrina* (1986)—and two books: *Reaching for the Mainland* (1987) and *Terms of Survival* (1987). Her well-crafted poetry reflects her struggle as a writer to create a history for herself out of the cultural ambiguity of a childhood spent traveling between the United States and Puerto Rico. Through her poetry she also explores from a feminist perspective her relationship with her father, mother, and grandmother, while also considering the different expectations for the males and females in Anglo–American and Hispanic cultures. Her book of autobiographical essays, in particular, follows this question: *Silent Dancing: A Remembrance of a Puerto Rican Childhood* (1990). *Silent Dancing* is awarded a commendation from PEN and chosen as an outstanding book for the teenage years by the New York Public Library in 1991. Her novel, *The Line of the Sun* (1990), is based on her family's gradual immigration to the United States, and chronicles the years from the Depression to the 1960s. Currently, Ortiz Cofer teaches creative writing at the University of Georgia.

MARCH 10, 1952   Batista Seizes Power Again; Castro Opposes. Fulgencio Batista, foreseeing his loss in the constitutional elections to be held on June 1, seizes power again in Cuba, this time as an arrogant dictator. Batista then takes Cuba

Judith Ortiz Cofer. (Courtesy of the Arte Público Press Archives, University of Houston.)

to new extremes of repression and corruption. A twenty-six-year old lawyer, Fidel Castro, pursues court action against Batista for violating six articles of the constitution, and demands action from the judges or their resignations. Unsuccessful in court, Castro founds a small newspaper, *El Acusador* to continue the attack on Batista, and finally he takes up arms against the dictator.

JULY 25, 1952   Puerto Rican Commonwealth Takes Effect. The Commonwealth of Puerto Rico, in Spanish called the Estado Libre Asociado (Free Associated State), goes into effect on this date and continues as the political and governmental status of Puerto Rico to this date. Under this form of colonial government, Puerto Ricans remain U.S. citizens with all the rights appertaining to them, except to elect representatives and senators to the U.S. Congress. Under this arrangement, Puerto Rico may not conduct a foreign policy, engage in foreign commerce or act in many other ways as an independent nation, but its citizens are subject to federal taxation, serving in the military, and fulfilling other duties of citizens in the states. After taking up residence in any of the states, Puerto Ricans are entitled to full rights of citizenship, including the vote in all federal elections.

1953

1953   Agrarian Reform in Bolivia. The Bolivian government under the leadership of President Victor Paz Estenssoro begins expropriating the large, dormant ranches (latifundios) and breaking them up to be parceled out to the Indians of the Andean central plateau and valleys. Much of this agrarian reform took years to effect, and much of it was disorganized and without sufficient planning. Agricultural production suffered, but the old feudal system was effectively destroyed in Bolivia.

1953   Cuban Poet Wins Soviet Award. Cuba's greatest poet of the twentieth century, Nicolás Guillén, is accorded the Stalin Prize. (*See also* biography, July 10, 1902.)

FEBRUARY 15, 1953   Biodiversity and Conservation Biologist Gómez-Dallmeier Is Born. Francisco Gómez-Dallmeier, wildlife biologist, is born in Caracas, Venezuela. He receives his Licentiate in Biology from the Central University of Venezuela in 1979 and his M.S. and Ph.D. in wildlife biology from the University of Colorado in 1984 and 1986, respectively. From 1973 to 1977, he is the director of the La Salle Museum of Natural History and a member of the ecology team of the Institute of Tropical Zoology of the Central University of Venezuela. From 1977 to 1986, he works as a biologist and researcher in various positions in Venezuela and the United States. After 1986, he works for the Smithsonian Institution in Washington, D.C., for which he serves as the director of the Man and the Biosphere Biological Diversity Program from 1989 to the present. In that capacity, he coordinates field biodiversity research and training in

Francisco Gómez-Dallmeier. (Courtesy of the Arte Público Press Archives, University of Houston.)

Bolivia, Brazil, Peru, Ecuador, Guatemala, Panama, Puerto Rico, the Virgin Islands, Tennessee, and Washington, D.C. His major research focuses on the integration of biological diversity and natural resources conservation and management programs. He latest studies concern neotropical waterfowl and wetlands ecology and management.

JULY 26, 1953   Cuban Guerillas Take Up Arms. Fidel Castro and his young revolutionaries begin their armed struggle against dictator Fulgencio Batista with an assault on the Monada military post. The inexperienced and outnumbered (15 to 1) guerrillas suffer significant casualties and take refuge in the mountains. Castro is later captured and sentenced to fifteen years in prison.

1954

1954   Avila Wins Batting Championship. Mexican second baseman Roberto (Beto) Avila becomes the first Hispanic–American to win the batting championship in professional baseball in the United States. That year for Cleveland, he bats .341, drives in 67 runs, and scores 112, with 15 home runs.

1954   General Rules Paraguay. General Alfreo Stroessner takes power in Paraguay and eventually becomes the longest-lasting dictator in Latin America.

1954   Juan José Arreola Wins Prize for Play. Arreola wins first prize in the National Institute for Fine Arts Drama Festival for his play, *La hora de todos* (Everyone's Hour). (*See also* biography, September 12, 1918.)

1954   Supreme Court Rules on Hispanic Discrimination. In the landmark case of *Hernández v. Texas,* the Supreme Court of the United States recognizes Hispanics as a separate class of people suffering profound discrimination. Previously, Hispanics were officially recognized as "white" and, therefore, not a separate, minority class. This is the first Mexican–American discrimination case to reach the Supreme Court. The court rules that Pete Hernández, who has been convicted of murder, is denied equal protection under the law because the jury selection process excludes Mexican–Americans. (In Jackson County, Texas, where the suit originates, no Mexican–Americans are selected for jury duty in the previous twenty-five years, despite the county's 14 percent Mexican–American population.) The 1954 decision paves the way for Hispanic–Americans to use legal means to attack all types of discrimination throughout the United States. It is also the first U.S. Supreme Court case to be argued and briefed by Mexican–American attorneys.

1954   U.S. Deports Mexicans. Through "Operation Wetback," more than one million persons of Mexican descent are deported from the United States between 1954 and 1958. Only a small fraction of that amount are allowed hearings prior to being deported. Thousands more

Lorna Dee Cervantes. Photo by Georgia McInnis. (Courtesy of the Arte Público Press Archives, University of Houston.)

legitimate U.S. citizens of Mexican descent are also arrested and detained. Attorney General Herbert Boswell, Jr., creates a special mobile force to effect a dragnet to deport and otherwise encourage undocumented workers to return to Mexico.

MARCH 1, 1954   Puerto Rican Nationalists Attack Congress. A group of nationalists headed by Lolita Lebrón attacks the U.S. House of Representatives firing 20–25 random pistol

A rally in support of Puerto Rican independence in Manhattan. (Courtesy of the Jesús Colón Papers, Center for Puerto Rican Studies Library, Hunter College, CUNY.)

shots and wounding five representatives, in order to bring national attention to the colonial status of Puerto Rico. She and her followers, including Ramón Cancel Miranda, Irving Flores, and Oscar Collazo, are arrested. Lebrón spends twenty-five years in federal prison without recanting and becomes a heroine and martyr of the independence movement to the present.

AUGUST 6, 1954 Poet and Teacher Lorna Dee Cervantes Is Born. Of Mexican and Amerindian ancestry, poet Lorna Dee Cervantes

is born into a very poor family in the Mission District of San Francisco, California. Cervantes's parents separate and, at the age of five she moves to San Jose with her mother and brother to live with her grandmother. She discovers the world of books at a very early age, and begins writing poetry when she is six years old; poems written when she is fourteen are eventually published in a magazine after Cervantes establishes her career as a writer. In 1990, she obtains a Ph.D. from the University of California, Santa Cruz, where she studies philosophy and aesthetics. She then teaches creative writing at the University of Colorado in Denver. *Emplumada* (Plumed, 1981), Cervantes's first collection of poems, is made up of works published in literary magazines throughout the Southwest. The book's popularity makes it the best-selling title in the University of Pittsburgh's prestigious poetry series. *Emplumada* as a whole presents a young woman coming of age, discovering the gap that exists in life between one's hopes and desires and what life eventually offers in reality. The predominant themes include culture conflict, oppression of women and minorities, and alienation from one's roots. Cervantes's poetry is very well crafted and has the distinction of using highly lyrical language while at the same time being direct and powerful. The same can be said of her second book, *From the Cables of Genocide,* which is the work of a mature poet dealing with the great themes of life, death, social conflict, and poverty. In 1992 *From the Cables of Genocide* is awarded the Paterson Poetry Prize and the Latin American Writers Institute Award. Cervantes is also the founding editor of a literary magazine, *Mango,* which published for about three years in the early 1970s. Currently, she teaches creative writing at the University of Houston.

1955

1955 Spanish-Language Television Begins. The first Spanish-language television station in the United States, KCOR-TV, begins broadcasting in San Antonio, Texas.

JULY 9, 1955 Jimmy Smits, Puerto Rican Actor, Is Born. Jimmy Smits is born in Brooklyn, New York, to a merchant seaman of Dutch and South American Indian descent, and a Puerto Rican-born mother. Smits receives a bachelor of arts from Brooklyn College in 1974 and a master of fine arts degree from Cornell University in 1978. He works as a community organizer before beginning his stage career with

small parts in public theater. Smits' career in television begins with appearances in soap operas, including *All My Children, Another World, The Guiding Light,* and *One Life to Live.* Smits' film appearances include *Running Scared* (1986); *The Believers* (1987); *Glitz* (1988); *Old Gringo* (1989); *The Fires Within* and *Switch* (1991); Stephen King's *The Tommyknockers* (1993); and *The Cisco Kid* (1994). He has a guest appearance on the prime time television police series *Miami Vice* before landing starring roles in the television dramas *LA Law,* and, in 1994, *NYPD Blue.* Smits receives the Hispanic Media Image Task Force Imagen Award in 1987.

1956

1956 Actor Anthony Quinn Takes Second Oscar. Quinn wins a second Academy Award for his role in *Lust for Life.* (*See also* biography, April 21, 1915 and entry, 1952.)

1956 Luis Aparicio Is Baseball's Outstanding Rookie. Venezuelan shortstop Luis Aparicio becomes the first Hispanic–American in professional baseball in the United States to be named "Rookie of the Year." During this season for Baltimore, Aparicio drives in 56 runs, scores 69 runs, and leads the leagues in stolen bases.

1956 Mexican Poet Nominated. Alfonso Reyes is nominated for the Nobel Prize in Literature. (*See also* biography, May 17, 1889.)

FALL 1956 Hispanics Take Medals in Summer Olympics. In Melbourne, Australia, at the first Olympics to be held in the Southern Hemisphere—where seasons are reversed—Chile's Marlene Ahrens wins a silver medal in the women's javelin throw with a distance of 50 meters 38 centimeters. Humberto Selvetti wins the bronze medal in the 110 kg weightlifting category. Mexico's Joaquín Capilla Pérez wins a gold medal in platform diving. Uruguay wins the bronze medal in basketball for the second straight Olympiad. The United States Olympic team includes a record eleven U.S. Hispanics, including José Torres, later to become a world professional boxing champion, who wins a silver medal in the middleweight division. Included in the American Winter Olympic team is the U.S. Senior Women's Figure Skating champion, Catherine Machado, the first Hispanic ever to compete on the U.S. winter Olympic team.

DECEMBER 2, 1956 Castro and His Men Land in Cuba. Fidel Castro lands in Cuba with a force of eighty-two men that he trains in Veracruz, Mexico, after he is released from prison on a general amnesty. He raises funds for this endeavor from supporters in Miami, Tampa, and New York. Having been discovered from the air by a military plane, on December 5 all but twelve of Castro's men are killed in an ambush by the army. Once again Castro and the survivors take refuge in the mountains. From there, he builds up his forces, conducts a propaganda campaign against Batista and the government, and eventually succeeds in winning the revolution.

1957

1957 The Civil Rights Commission. The 1957 Civil Rights Act is the first passed by Congress since the end of the Civil War. The act creates the Civil Rights Commission to investigate and report on the denial of voting rights for reasons of color, race, creed, or national origin. It also is commissioned to advise Congress in creating civil rights policy and laws.

1957 Land Redistribution Starts in Venezuela. A well organized program to redistribute lands is put into effect by the government of Rómulo Betancourt in Venezuela. First, the government buys the lands for prices that go up to $30,000 dollars, paid part in cash and part in bonds. And then the land is redistributed by a commission made up of representatives of all

Nancy López. (Courtesy of the Arte Público Press Archives, University of Houston.)

the interested parties. The government also provides agricultural technical assistance to all those receiving land. Not only does the government distribute large quantities of land; it also raises its agricultural productivity.

JANUARY 6, 1957 Nancy López, Golf Champion, Is Born. One of the greatest women's golf champions of all time, Nancy López, is born to Mexican–American parents in Torrance, California. She is raised in Roswell, New Mexico, and becomes one of the youngest women golfers to experience professional success. She learns golf from her father and, by age eleven is already beating him. López wins the New Mexico Women's Open when she is only twelve. In high school, she is the only female member of the golf team, and as an eighteen-year-old senior, she places second in the U.S. Women's Open. In 1978, during López's first full season as a pro, she wins nine tournaments, including the Ladies Professional Golf Association. She is named "Rookie of the Year," "Player of the Year," and "Female Athlete of the Year"; she also wins the Vare Trophy. Also in 1978, she sets a new record for earnings by a rookie: $189,813. In 1983, she has a break from her career when she gives birth to Ashley Marie, the product of her marriage to baseball star Ray Knight. Two months after having Ashley, López begins touring again, and by 1987, she has won thirty-five tournaments and qualifies to become the eleventh member of the Ladies Professional Golf Association Hall of Fame. López's most outstanding year is 1985, when she wins five tournaments and finishes in the top ten at twenty-five others; that year she also wins the LPGA again. Through 1987, she earns over $2 million.

AUGUST 18, 1957 Fangio Wins World Race Car Championship. Argentine racing car driver Juan Manuel Fangio becomes the oldest racer in the world to win international titles when he wins the World Race Car Championship at the age of forty-six. (*See also* biography, June 24, 1911.)

1959

1959 Activist Mari Bras Founds Movement. Bras is one of the founders of the Movimiento Pro Independencia (Pro Independence Movement) and serves as its secretary general. (*See also* biography, December 2, 1928.)

1959 Countries Seek Free Trade Zone. The Latin American Association for Free Com-

merce (ALALC) is founded by Argentina, Brazil, Chile, Paraguay, Peru, and Uruguay with the objective of establishing a free trade zone among the partners that eventually will evolve into a common market. Ecuador, Colombia, Mexico, and Venezuela join later. Due to continued protectionism of the industries in various countries, however, the agreements and the removal of trade barriers are slow in coming; also, the internal political unrest in various member countries does not make for stability of the organization. Then, too, the industrial and agricultural production of many of the trade partners are too similar to constitute a basis for real trade.

1959 Cuban Immigration. Large-scale Cuban immigration to the United States occurs much more quickly than that from either Puerto Rico or Mexico. In fact, over one million Cubans enter the country after the Cuban Revolution of 1959. On the other hand, most of the two million Puerto Ricans who trek to the U.S. mainland in this century are World War II or postwar-era entries. Unlike the immigrant experience of Mexicans, or Cubans before 1959, the vast majority of Puerto Ricans enter with little or no red tape.

1959 Director and Screenwriter Gutiérrez Alea Founds Institute. After the success of the Cuban Revolution in 1959, Gutiérrez Alea cofounds the national revolutionary film institute, Instituto del Arte e Industria Cinematográfica (Cinematographic Art and Industry Institute—ICAIC), in which he continues to function as one of the leaders. (*See also* biography, December 11, 1928.)

1959 Union Organizer Corona Founds Political Association. Political activist Bert Corona is instrumental in founding the Mexican American Political Association. (*See also* biography, May 29, 1918.)

JANUARY 1, 1959 The Cuban Revolution. In late December 1958, Dictator Fulgencio Batista

Fidel Castro.

abandons Cuba and goes into exile in the Dominican Republic. The Cuban Revolution officially triumphs on New Years Day after five years and five months of struggle; in the process, Fidel Castro spends two years in jail, a year and a half in exile, and twenty-five months in battle. On January 8, Castro marches into Havana at the head of his revolutionary army. At the national capital, he announced the dissolution of Batista's government, the army, the political parties, and the congress, and many of the members of these entities go into immediate exile. During the course of the year, Castro sets up a revolutionary government and sets about introducing numerous reforms, nationalizing industries, redistributing lands, and constructing schools and hospitals. Most of the reforms and new laws are dictated in an autocratic manner and are based upon and forwarded the ideology of class struggle, which frightens the landed and propertied classes of Cuba. The vast majority of Cuban–Americans presently residing in the United States emigrate here after 1959. Between 1959 and 1962, twenty-five thousand Cubans are "paroled" to the United States using a special immigration rule.

MAY 17, 1959   Cuba's Agrarian Reform Law. Among the many changes and reforms put in place by Fidel Castro's revolutionary government in Cuba, on this date the Agrarian Reform Law is announced, empowering the peasants to take over the lands on which they work or have sharecropped, limiting each family to approximately one thousand acres.

Chapter 8
1960 TO 1969

1960

1960   The Chicano Movement. During the decade of the 1960s and into the early 1970s, intellectual foment and rebellion reign in the United States. Caught up in the mood, young Mexican–Americans throughout the country seek a new identity while struggling for the same civil rights objectives of previous generations. This struggle becomes known as the Chicano Movement. The word "Chicano" is elevated from its pejorative usage in the 1920s— to denote lower-class Mexican immigrants— and from its slang usage of the 1940s and 1950s as a substitute for Mexicano.

1960   Employers Recruit Foreign Workers. During the 1960s and 1970s, the migrant agricultural work force is changing rapidly. With the rise of the black power and Chicano movements, the appearance of modest protective legislation, and the increasingly successful unionization efforts of farm workers, employers increasingly seek to recruit and hire foreign workers to replace the citizens.

1960   Labor Migration Patterns Change. During the 1960s a third phase of labor migration to the United States begins when the established patterns of movement from Mexico and Puerto Rico to the United States are modified, and migration from other countries increases. The Bracero Program ends in 1964, and, after a brief decline in immigration, workers from Mexico increasingly arrive to work under the auspices of the H-2 Program of the Immigration and Nationality Act of 1952, as well as for family unification purposes or as undocumented workers. During the 1960s, immigration from Mexico rises to 13.3 percent of the total number of immigrants to the United States.

1960   Miñoso Leads Leagues in Hits. Cuban Orestes (Minnie) Miñoso becomes the first Hispanic–American ballplayer in professional baseball in the United States to lead both leagues in hits, with 184 for the Chicago White Sox.

1960   The Rise of the Maquiladoras. Mexico establishes the Programa Nacional Fronterizo (National Border Program), which five years later leads to the Border Industrialization Program, whereby foreign corporations are permitted to operate assembly plants on the border. These plants, known as *maquiladoras*, multiply rapidly and transform the border region in Mexico and the United States. The lower wages in Mexico attract corporations from the United States and multinational companies who wish to cut labor costs for assembly work. Other incentives include weak unions, weak environmental regulations, and cooperative Mexican officials, and the proximity to

U.S. markets. Besides employing hundreds of thousands of Mexicans, mostly women, in assembly work, the maquiladoras become by the late 1980s the second most important generator of foreign exchange, thus allowing Mexico to cope with its foreign debt problem. In the border towns and cities in Mexico, the growth of maquiladoras has not been supported by sufficient growth in sanitation and social services, schools, and hospitals for the burgeoning populations drawn to work there. Increased population and overpopulation have led to many health risks and disease. In the United States, the growth of the maquiladoras has meant the loss of jobs, which have been exported, and the concomitant weakening of labor unions.

JANUARY 1960 Eisenhower Moves against Cuba. President Dwight D. Eisenhower, beginning to apply pressure to Cuba's increasingly radical government, requests of the U.S. Congress authorization to reduce sugar imports from Cuba. Eisenhower continues to escalate pressure throughout the spring and in May suspends all technical assistance to Cuba.

MAY 8, 1960 Cuba Turns to Soviets for Help. Cuba reacts to pressure against Fidel Castro's government from the United States by establishing diplomatic relations with the Soviet Union, and begins to export sugar to the Communist country and to import oil from there.

SUMMER 1960 Olympic Athletes Win Bronze Medals. Mexico's Juan Botella wins a bronze medal in diving at the Olympic Games in Rome, Italy. Venezuela's Enrique Forcella Pelliccioni wins bronze in the smallbore free rifle competition and team Brazil takes the bronze in basketball.

JULY 6, 1960 Cuba Nationalizes U.S. Owned Property. Cuba passes Law 851, expropriating and nationalizing all property and businesses owned by U.S. citizens and interests. From this point on, the United States considers the Cuban government to be an openly Communist

dictatorship. On May 1, 1961, two weeks after the Bay of Pigs fiasco, Castro finally announces that he is a Marxist–Leninist and will remain so until his death.

1961

1961 Aspira Promotes Education. Aspira (Aspire) of America is founded in the United States to promote the education of youth by raising public and private sector funds. Aspira acquires a national following, serving Puerto Ricans in locales where they live in large numbers. It sponsors a variety of in-school and out-of-school programs in tutoring, counseling, assistance in filling out applications for higher education, and also runs alternative schools and programs for dropouts.

1961 Cepeda Hits Most Home Runs. Puerto Rican Orlando Cepeda becomes the first Hispanic–American home run champ in professional baseball in the United States, with 46 home runs hit for the San Francisco Giants. He also bats .311, with 182 hits and 105 runs scored. This year, he also became the first Hispanic–American to be the champion of runs driven in: 142.

1961 Colón's Essays Published. A selection of Jesús Colón's newspaper columns and essays is collected and published in book form under the title of *A Puerto Rican in New York and Other Sketches. (See also* biography, 1901.)

1961 Land Reform in Colombia. The Colombian government passes Law 135, which provides for agrarian reform. In the first phase of the reform program, the Instituto Colombiano de la Reforma Agraria grants land titles to small farmers on public lands. But from 1968 to 1972, some 200,000 hectares of land are expropriated and formed into collective farms. But, overall, the program remains marginal, and the policy of land redistribution is abandoned during the 1970s.

1961   Puerto Rican Actress Moreno Wins Oscar. Rita Moreno wins an Academy Award in 1961 as best supporting actress for *West Side Story.* (*See also* biography, December 11, 1931.)

1961   Trujillo Assassinated. President Rafael Trujillo, the iron-fisted dictator of the Dominican Republic is assassinated, and thirty years of dictatorship come to an end, at least for the time being. Juan Bosch administers the country in the interim, but he is seen by the military and by Washington as leaning to the left, and is therefore ousted in 1963. The generals install a triumvirate headed by Donald Reid Cabral, but this leads to demonstrations and political unrest. Cabral is ousted in 1965 by a group of younger officers who look to Bosch as their leader. Old-line officers fear that Bosch will bring in the communists, and gunfire is exchanged between the two factions. President Lyndon B. Johnson sends in the marines to prevent another Cuba, stating that communists already have infiltrated the revolution. His exaggeration is met with derision from the Latin-American countries. Eventually an election is arranged and Joaquín Balaguer is chosen to guide the U.S.-controlled democratic experiment.

MARCH 13, 1961   The Alliance for Progress. President John F. Kennedy announces the Alliance for Progress, an ambitious, $100 billion, ten-year program to bring political reform and social and economic progress to the Southern Hemisphere. As expressed in the Charter of Punta del Este, the alliance calls for a 2.5 percent annual economic growth rate, a more equitable distribution of national wealth, trade diversification, emphasis on industrialization, greater agricultural productivity, an end to illiteracy, agrarian reform, increased life expectancy, public housing for the poor, stable price levels, tax reform, and economic development. All of these are to be carried out within the framework of political democracy. The alliance fails to achieve these goals because Latin-American elites that control the governments resist social change, tax reform, and democratization,

and, in part, because the United States becomes progressively more involved in Vietnam. By 1971, there are few signs that the quality of life has improved for the masses in Latin America, and many of the Latin-American governments have come under military control.

APRIL 1961   The Bay of Pigs Invasion. Cuban exiles who are trained and armed by the United States attempt to oust Castro and Communism, but do not receive direct military support in their invasion. They attempt a foray into Cuba that is doomed from the beginning, especially since they expect a spontaneous uprising in their homeland to support their invasion. None occurred. The failure of the infamous Bay of Pigs invasion embitters the thousands of Cubans who are in exile, but Castro's position at home is strengthened. To many observers throughout the world, especially in the Third World, the United States is clearly taking the side of the usurpers, who attempt to overthrow a legitimately based government. In 1961, the United States officially breaks off diplomatic relations with Cuba.

AUGUST 27, 1961   Bowling Champion Monacelli Is Born. Amleto Andrés Monacelli, a champion bowler, is born in Barquisimeto, Venezuela. Monacelli is a college graduate who joins the Professional Bowling Association tour in 1982. By 1991, he is winning $81,000 in prizes annually, and in 1989 achieves a record $213,815. The list of tournaments he wins includes the Japan Cup (1987), the Showboat Invitational (1988), the Miller Challenge (1989), the Wichita Open (1989 and 1990), the Budweiser Touring Players Championship (1989), the Cambridge Mixed Doubles (1989 and 1990), the Columbus Professional Bowling Classic (1990), the Quaker State Open (1991), and the True Value Open (1991). Among his many awards are the Professional Bowlers Association Player of the Year (1989 and 1990) and the Harry Smith Point Leader Award in 1989. In 1990, he wins the Budweiser Kingpin Competition for the highest average of the year. And in

1990, the sportswriters name him Bowler of the Year; this is the first time that a foreigner achieves that distinction in the United States. In his professional career, Monacelli rolls sixteen perfect games, seven of them during the 1989 season, establishing a new record for perfect games in a year. Three of these are accomplished during one week, thus tying the record.

1962

1962   Chile Establishes Agencies for Land Reform. The Alessandri administration in Chile passes a law establishing two new agencies to carry out land reform: the Corporación de Reforma Agraria (Agrarian Reform Corporation) and the Instituto de Desarrollo Agropecuario (Institute for Agricultural and Fishing Industry Development), which is to provide credit and other services to families receiving land.

1962   Dictator Heads El Salvador. Dictator Colonel Julio Adalberto Rivera is elected president of El Salvador. He is the first in a string of military dictators, all colonels and generals, to rule El Salvador in the following years.

1962   Edward R. Roybal Becomes Congressman. Roybal is first elected to Congress in 1962 as a Democrat from the Twenty-fifth District. He will hold the longest seat in Congress of any Hispanic. (*See also* biography, February 10, 1916 and entry, 1982.)

1962   Enrique Laguerre Publishes Essay. Laguerre publishes his autobiographical essay, *Cauce sin río: Diario de mi generación* (Riverbed without a River: A Diary of My Generation), in which he considers the conflict between contemporary social life and Puerto Rican tradition. (*See also* biography, March 3, 1906.)

1962   Painter Antonio Berni Wins Award. Argentine painter wins the Grand Award for Etching at the Venice Biennale for his most

Amleto Andrés Monacelli. (Courtesy of the Arte Público Press Archives, University of Houston.)

famous work, the collage series on the life of *Juanito Laguna*. (*See also* biography, 1905.)

1962   Painter Egas Accepts Merit Award. Camilo Egas receives an award for artistic merit from the American Academy of Arts and Letters. (*See also* biography, 1899.)

1962   United Farm Workers Organizing Committee. The United Farm Workers Organizing Committee in California, begun as an independent organization, is led by César Chávez. In

1965 it organizes its successful Delano grape strike and first national boycott. It becomes part of the AFL–CIO in 1966. Today it is known as the United Farm Workers of America.

APRIL 21, 1962   Carlos Ortiz Becomes Boxing Champion. Puerto Rico's Carlos Ortiz wins the lightweight boxing championship from Joe Brown. He successfully defends his crown various times until April 10, 1965, when he loses to Panama's Ismael Laguna. But he recovers the title on November 13 of the same year in San Juan, Puerto Rico. Again, he successfully defends his crown until losing it on June 29, 1968, to Dominican Carlos "Teo" Cruz. Ortiz is the second Puerto Rican boxer to win a world championship.

OCTOBER 22, 1962   The Cuban Missile Crisis. United States President John F. Kennedy redeems himself from the Bay of Pigs defeat by backing down the Soviet Union on a Russian plan to establish missile bases in Cuba. Because of a small island in the Caribbean, two world leaders, Kennedy and Nikita Khrushchev, bring the world to the brink of nuclear war, for such is the threat issued by Kennedy. Following what becomes known as the Cuban Missile crisis, Fidel Castro complains to Kennedy that Cuba's self-determination and sovereignty has been violated by the United States, and he states before the United Nations that Cuba has a right to arm itself. On October 28, Kennedy promises Khrushchev, in return, that the United States will not invade Cuba and will not cooperate with any other nation in an invasion there. From then on, the only viable policy alternative for the United States is to expand the Cuban refugee program. There will be no recurrence of a "Bay of Pigs"; this is the standoff: no missiles for no invasion.

1963

1963   Ecuador Passes Land Reform Act. Ec-
uador embarks on a program to begin to change centuries-old land and labor relations by passing the Reform Law of 1964, which institutes agrarian reform in its highlands. Peasants, many of whom are working under debt peonage, are given a plot of their own land to work. About 17,000 plots were parceled out.

1963   La Raza Unida. In Crystal City, Texas, where Mexican–Americans make up 85 percent of the population, the community ousts five Anglo city council members and elects five Mexican–Americans. This is the first time that Hispanic political action has such a success in the United States. With the assistance of the Teamsters Union at the local Del Monte cannery and the Political Association of Spanish-speaking Organizations, the new city government undertakes important positive reforms, but Anglo resistance and factionalism make the job difficult. A second revolt takes place in 1969 and leads to greater, more successful reforms. As a result of this revolt and a protest against discrimination in the Crystal City schools in 1971, a political party is formed, La Raza Unida, which expands rapidly throughout Texas under the leadership of José Angel Gutiérrez. By 1972, the Raza Unida Party has chapters in seventeen states and the District of Columbia. Crystal City becomes the first city in the United States to have a Chicano third party controlling the local government. Later on, La Raza Unida gains control of the government of Zavala County and makes inroads into other areas. By 1981, however, the party is in decline, especially as the Democratic party starts to make reforms and become more inclusive of Mexican–Americans and their issues. La Raza Unida and Crystal City are important historically for bringing about political change and forcing the two-party system in the United States to take Hispanics into account.

1963   Painter René Portocarrero Wins Prize. Cuban Painter Portocarrero is awarded the International Prize at the Sao Paulo Bienal. (*See also* biography, 1912.)

JULY 1963   OAS Votes to Sever Relations with Cuba. The Organization of American States, meeting in Washington, D.C., votes to sever diplomatic and commercial relations with Cuba, except in food and medical supplies, and to impose restrictions on travel to Cuba. The Latin–Americans go along with U.S. policy because many of them fear a similar revolution themselves.

JULY 15, 1963   Marichal Throws No-Hitter. Dominican pitcher Juan Marichal becomes the first Hispanic–American to throw a no-hitter in professional baseball in the United States. Pitching for the San Francisco Giants, he beats Houston 1–0 on this date. (*See also* biography, 1937.)

SEPTEMBER 1963   López Tijerina Founds Alianza. In Albuquerque, New Mexico, Reies López Tijerina founds the Alianza Federal de Pueblos Libres (Federal Alliance of Free Towns), an organization of people descended from original Spanish and Mexican land-grant holders, to work through the courts to gain back the lands that had been lost or stolen from their ancestors. By 1965, the Alianza claims a membership of twenty thousand (the press claims the membership is three thousand), largely small farmers and ranchers who are losing the right to graze their stock on federal land. The organization increases its militancy and public acts and suffers repression from the authorities for acts of vandalism and arson; it is disbanded early in 1967. The organization is reestablished in June 1967, and, following a meeting broken up by the district attorney, the group raids the Tierra Amarilla courthouse on June 5, 1967, an act that becomes celebrated by Chicano militants throughout the Southwest. For his militant activities as leader of the Alianza, López Tijerina is sentenced to two concurrent terms in prison of one to five years and two to seven years, beginning in 1970. He is released in 1971, and finishes his five-year term of probation in 1976, whereupon he returns to the

presidency of the Alianza. (*See also* biography, 1926.)

1964

1964   Congress Passes Historic Acts to Expand Opportunities. The United States Congress and the president of the United States enact historic "Great Society" programs to end decades of discrimination and to extend social, economic, and educational opportunity to all segments of the society. The Economic Opportunity Act (EOA) of 1964 is the centerpiece of President Lyndon B. Johnson's War on Poverty. The EOA also creates the Office of Economic Opportunity (OEO) to administer a number of programs on behalf of the nation's poor. These include the Job Corps, the Community Action Program (CAP), and the Volunteers in Service to America (VISTA). But of more far-reaching consequence, Congress enacts the first comprehensive civil rights law since the Reconstruction period when it passes the Civil Rights Act of 1964. One result of the act is the establishment of affirmative action programs. Title VII of the Civil Rights Act of 1964 comprises the most important statute of the War on Poverty addressing employment discrimination. It prohibits discrimination on the basis of gender, creed, race, or ethnic background, "to achieve equality of employment opportunities and remove barriers that have operated in the past." Discrimination is prohibited in advertising, recruitment, hiring, job classification, promotion, discharge, wages and salaries, and other terms and conditions of employment. Title VII also establishes the Equal Employment Opportunity Commission (EEOC) as a monitoring device to prevent job discrimination.

1964   Cuban Poet Accorded Award. Poet Nicolás Guillén is awarded the Lenin Peace Prize. (*See also* biography, July 10, 1902.)

1964   Revolutionary Movement Ousted in Bo-

livia. The Movimiento Nacionalista Revolucionario in Bolivia is ousted from power by a military revolt that brings René Barrientos into the presidency, and later General Ovando Gandia and other dictators.

1964 Tony Oliva Leads in Baseball Categories. Cuban ballplayer Tony Oliva becomes the first Hispanic–American in professional baseball in the United States to win the scoring title, with 109 runs. He also is the leader in hits (217), doubles (43), and batting average (.323). Playing for the Minnesota Twins, Oliva is the only player to win batting championships during his first two major league seasons: 1964 and 1965. He wins it again in 1971. In 1964, he is named "Rookie of the Year."

SUMMER 1964 Cuban, Argentine Win Silver Medals. Cuban runner Enrique Figuerola wins the silver in the 100 meters with a time of 10.2 at the Olympic Games in Tokyo, Japan. Argentina's Carlos Moratorio wins the silver in the individual three-day equestrian event. Mexico's Juan Fabila Mendoza and Uruguay's Washington Rodriguez tie for the bronze in bantamweight boxing.

1964–65 Cuban Painter Wins Award. Cuban painter Wilfredo Lam wins the Guggenheim International Award. (*See also* biography, 1902.)

1965

1965 Cubans Transport Relatives to Miami. Fidel Castro himself announces as early as 1965 that Cubans can leave Cuba if they have relatives in the United States. Castro stipulates, however, that Cubans already in Florida must come and get them at Camarioca Bay. Nautical crafts of all types systematically leave Miami to Camarioca, returning laden with anxious Cubans eager to rejoin their families on the mainland.

1965 El Teatro Campesino, Labor-Related Theatre Movement. The most important and long-standing Hispanic theater, El Teatro Campesino, is founded as a labor theater in the agricultural fields, under the directorship of Luis Valdez. Valdez, a beginning playwright who has graduated from San Jose State University and spent some time learning agit–prop theatre with the San Francisco Mime Troupe, takes his skills and places them at the service of the United Farm Workers Organization in creating a union for agricultural workers. The new type of socially engaged theatre that El Teatro Campesino pioneers leads to the creation of a full-blown theatrical movement in fields and barrios across the country. For nearly three decades, El Teatro Campesino and Luis Valdez dramatize the political and cultural concerns of Hispanics, initially among workers and their supporters, but later among students in universities and to the general public through the legitimate stage, television, and film. In establishing the canon of what *teatro chicano* should be, Valdez and El Teatro Campesino publish their actos (short one-act agit–prop pieces) with a preface that outlines their theatrical principles: (1) Chicanos must be seen as a nation with geographic, religious, cultural, and racial roots in the Southwest; the teatros must further the idea of nationalism and create a national theater based on identification with the Amerindian past; (2) the organizational support of the national theater must be from within and totally independent; (3) "Teatros must never get away from La Raza.... If the Raza will not come to the theater, then the theater must go to the Raza. This, in the long run, will determine the shape, style, content, spirit and form of *el teatro chicano*." (*See also* biography, June 26, 1940.)

1965 Héctor García Pérez Awarded Panamanian Prize. The president of Panama awards García Pérez the Order of Vasco Núñez de Balboa in recognition of his services to humanity. (*See also* biography, January 17, 1914.)

A scene from *Zoot Suit,* by Luis Valdez and El Teatro Campesino Productions. (Courtesy of the Arte Público Press Archives, University of Houston.)

1965   Novelist Fernando Alegría Publishes Book. Chilean novelist Fernando Alegría publishes *Historia de la novela hispanoamericana* (History of the Spanish American Novel), which goes through various editions and serves as a standard text of Latin American literature. (*See also* biography, September 26, 1918.)

1965   U.S. Military Intervenes in Dominican Republic. The United States intervenes militarily in the Dominican Republic. Within the context of the Cold War and in order to prevent another Cuba, President Lyndon B. Johnson dispatchs the marines to the Dominican Republic when dictator Donald Reid Cabral is ousted by a military coup in favor of former dictator Juan Bosch.

1965   U.S. Revises Immigration Law. The United States revises the Immigration and Nationality Act of 1952, abolishes the quota system and places a cap on immigration from the Western Hemisphere for the first time, a cap that becomes effective in 1968.

1965　The Voting Rights Act. In the United States, the Voting Rights Act of 1965 is passed by Congress. Although the single aim of the Voting Rights Act is African–American enfranchisement in the South, obstacles to registration and voting are faced by all minorities. The act's potential as a tool for Hispanic–Americans, however, is not fully realized for nearly a decade.

APRIL 1965　The Maquiladora Program. A United States–Mexico border industrialization program, the maquiladora (assembly plant) program, is initiated. Mexico hopes to raise the standard of living in the northern border region, while both the U.S. and Mexican governments are concerned about the possible negative political and economic consequences of leaving hundreds of thousands of Mexican workers stranded on the border without employment when the Bracero Program ends. Industrialists are eager to reap the benefits offered by tax and tariff breaks and by the availability of unemployed and underemployed workers in Mexico. Those Mexican workers who had experience in the Bracero Program encourage many others to emigrate to the United States in search of work. When the program is over, many former braceros stay in the United States or return after being delivered to Mexico.

SEPTEMBER 16, 1965　César Chávez and the Delano Grape Strike. César Chávez, head of the National Farm Organizing Committee, leads his organization into a strike started by Filipino grape pickers in Delano, California. Chávez and his organization successfully convert the strike into one of the most significant movements for social justice for farm workers, especially the Mexican/Mexican–American farm workers who form the majority of pickers. From this humble beginning, the National Farmworkers Association (NFWA) develops into the largest union of agricultural workers through more than a decade of struggles, national boycotts, court cases, and legislative action in California. From table grapes, the labor

actions spread to lettuce and other crops, and eventually win concessions and contracts on wages, working conditions, safe use of pesticides, and the right to unionize and strike. In his pacifist tactics, hunger strikes, and crusades, César Chávez enlists and receives the support of national politicians, such as Robert F. Kennedy, as well as the Catholic Conference of Bishops and eventually organized labor. When Chávez dies in 1993, he is mourned in the United States as a national hero. (*See also* biography, May 3, 1927.)

1966

1966　The Crusade for Justice and the Spiritual Plan of Aztlán. One of the most successful Mexican–American civil rights organizations, the Crusade for Justice, is founded in Denver, Colorado, by Rodolfo "Corky" Gonzales, a former boxer. The organization militates for better housing and educational opportunity, as well as jobs. The crusade also buys a building and converts it into a multipurpose center for the community, including classrooms, a gym, a nursery, and a library. During the late 1960s, the crusade leads protest marches and walkouts against the Denver public schools that at times erupt in violence. From March 27 to 31, 1969, the crusade sponsors the first national Chicano Youth Liberation Conference. The conference addresses political, economic, and educational concerns of Chicanos and drafts a document which lives on as an historical expression of the nationalistic sentiments of Chicanos: El Plan Espiritual de Aztlán (The Spiritual Plan of Aztlán). The plan calls for economic, political, social, and educational independence for Chicanos in their homeland: Aztlán, the southwestern states (formerly the cradle of Aztec civilization). During the late '60s and early '70s, the crusade articulates many of the demands, philosophy, and policies essential for the Chicano Movement. The crusade's director, "Corky" Gonzales, is the author of a widely distributed

A "maquiladora" plant at the Texas-Juárez border. (Courtesy of the *Texas Catholic Herald*.)

epic poem, *Yo soy Joaquín* (I Am Joaquín), which eloquently expresses the history and aspirations of Chicanos.

1966 The Cuban Airlift. A program is initiated to airlift Cubans to the United States, but it is halted by Castro in 1973. Over 250,000 Cubans are airlifted to the United States during that period. About 10 percent of the island's population emigrates to the United States between 1966 and 1973.

1966 Ernesto "Ché" Guevara Is Commander in Chief. Castro aide and revolutionary Guevara serves as the commander in chief of the National Liberation Army guerrilla organization in Bolivia from 1966 until his execution in 1967 by the Bolivian army. (*See also* biography, June 14, 1928.)

1966 Outfielder Clemente Named MVP. Star outfielder for the Pittsburgh Pirates Roberto Clemente is voted the National League's most valuable player. (*See also* biography, August 18, 1934.)

1966 Puerto Rican Youths Riot in Chicago. Hundreds of Chicago Puerto Rican youths go on a rampage, breaking windows and burning down many of the businesses in their neighborhoods. Ostensibly, the riots are in response to an incident of police brutality, but the underlying causes are broader, linked to the urban blight that characterizes their life in Chicago.

1966 Siqueiros Receives Art Award. The same government that had imprisoned him for his pro-union activism awards David Siqueiros its highest honor, the National Prize for Art. (*See also* biography, December 19, 1896.)

1966 Texas Tax on Voting. The Texas poll tax, which prevents many minorities from voting, is declared unconstitutional.

OCTOBER 1966 Reies López Tijerina Reclaims Forest. López Tijerina leads a group in a takeover of part of the Kit Carson National Forest, which they declare to be the Republic of Río Chama. (*See also* biography, 1926.)

1967

1967 Colonel Sánchez Elected in El Salva-

dor. Dictator Colonel Fidel Sánchez is elected president of El Salvador.

1967   Guatemalan Wins Nobel Prize. Guatemalan novelist Miguel Angel Asturias wins the Nobel Prize for literature. (*See also* biography, October 19, 1899.)

1967   Guillermo Cabrera Infante Publishes Award-Winning Novel. Cabrera's first novel, *Tres tristres tigres* (translated as *Three Trapped Tigers* in 1971), is published. It is considered a masterpiece of contemporary Latin American fiction for its innovative use of language, its linguistic experimentation, and its narrative perspectivism. (*See also* biography, April 22, 1929.)

1967   Héctor García Pérez Appointed by President Johnson. Civil rights leader García Pérez is named alternate delegate to the United Nations with the rank of ambassador, and is appointed the first Mexican American member of the United States Commission on Civil Rights, by U.S. President Lyndon Johnson. (*See also* biography, January 17, 1914.)

1967   New Dictator Heads Nicaragua. General Anastasio Somoza Debayle, scion of the oligarchy and latest in a line of dictators, is elected to the presidency of Nicaragua. A long, protracted war will eventually topple him from leadership and take Nicaragua to its present democracy.

1967   Reform Leads to Assassination. The Frei administration in Chile passes an agrarian reform law that provides for quick-taking procedures. This represents a base that the succeeding president, Salvador Allende, will use to accelerate agrarian reform. Of course, this is one of the policies that leads to his overthrow and assassination. The military dictatorship that replaces Allende returns many of the reform lands to their previous owners.

1967   Rosemary Casals Becomes Tennis Champion. The daughter of Salvadoran immigrants

to the United States, Rosemary Casals joins with Billie Jean King to win the doubles tennis championship at Wimbledon. They go on to win it again another four times. They also win the U.S. Lawn Tennis doubles championship twice at Forest Hills.

1967   School Programs Aid Bilingual Children. The United States Congress enacts legislation mandating schools to provide programs for children of limited English-speaking ability. By 1971 in New York City alone there are some 450 full- or part-time teachers of bilingual education and/or English as a Second Language, reaching some 122,000 children of Hispanic background.

1967   Siqueiros Awarded Soviet Prize. David Siqueiros receives the Lenin Peace Prize from the Soviet Union. (*See also* biography, December 19, 1896.)

1967   Writer Alurista Founds Chicano Movement. Alurista (Alberto Baltazar Urista) is a founder of the Movimiento Estudiantil de Aztlán (MECHA, Chicano Student Movement of Aztlán). (*See also* biography, August 8, 1947.)

1968

1968   Civil Rights Act of 1968. The Civil Rights Act of 1968 prohibits discrimination in housing. It also makes federal offenses of various acts that promote riots.

1968   Cuban Singer Named Music Director. Tania León becomes the first music director of the Dance Theater of Harlem. (*See also* biography, May 14, 1943.)

1968   González Coaches, Becomes Hall-of-Famer. Pancho Gonzáles coaches the U.S. Davis Cup team and is named to the International Tennis Hall of Fame. (*See also* biography, May 9, 1928 and entry, 1948.)

Chicano protest march for fair housing in El Paso, 1968. (Courtesy of the *Texas Catholic Herald*.)

1968 Mexican American Legal Defense and Education Fund. The Ford Foundation establishes the Mexican American Legal Defense and Education Fund to inform Mexican–Americans about their civil rights and to protect their legal rights by preparing civil rights cases.

1968 Torrijos Overthrows Civil Government in Panama. General Omar Torrijos overthrows the civil government in Panama and imposes his dictatorship, which will be passed on to

General Manuel Noriega in 1981, when Torrijos dies in a plane crash. Panama will not have free elections until May 1994.

SUMMER 1968 Olympic Medals Won by Hispanics. For the first time in history the Olympic games are held in Latin America. Practically every country in Latin America sends a team to Mexico City, Mexico, and the Latin–American athletes perform superbly. The Cuban teams win the silver in both the men's and women's 4 x 100 meters track relays with respective times of 38.3 and 43.3. Mexico's José Pedraza won the silver in the twenty kilometers with a time of 1:34:00. Mexico's María Teresa Ramírez takes the bronze in the 800 meters freestyle swimming, and Felipe Muñoz wins the gold in the 200-meter breast stroke. Mexico's Alvaro Gaxiola wins the spring platform diving competition with a score of 154.49. Argentina's Alberto Demiddi wins the kayak competition in 7:57.19.

1969

1969 Border War Affects Common Market. After the establishment of the Central American Common Market in the 1960s results in economic growth in the region, the border war between Honduras and El Salvador leads to the collapse of the common market and the rapid decline of economic conditions in Central America.

1969 El Salvador, Honduras Go to War. Salvadorans living in Honduras are forced to relinquish their lands. A war that breaks out between El Salvador and Honduras will not be resolved until 1980.

1969 Peru Begins Agrarian Reform. Peru institutes a far-reaching agrarian reform program whereby farms over a certain size—the designated size varied by region—are, without exception, subject to expropriation. Most of the expropriated lands are assigned to cooperatives. By 1979, some 38.3 percent of the agricultural land has been redistributed to about 21 percent of all agricultural families (more than 31 percent of families in need of land). The reasons for the vast program are the following: to promote social justice, enlarge the country's internal market, and contribute to capital formation needed for industrialization.

FEBRUARY 18, 1969 Ramos Outboxes Cruz. Mexican–American boxer Armando Ramos wins the world lightweight boxing championship from Carlos Cruz in Los Angeles.

MAY 1969 The Andean Group. An attempt to integrate the markets of the Andean coun-

tries is signed by Bolivia, Colombia, Chile, Ecuador, and Peru. The signatories to this beginning of a common market calls itself the Andean Group. In 1973, Venezuela also joins the group.

OCTOBER 2, 1969 Demonstrators Massacred in Mexico City. The Mexican army and the police massacre demonstrators at the Plaza of the Three Cultures in Tlaltelolco, Mexico City, just before the Olympic Games are to be held in the city. The demonstrators, made up largely of students, are protesting the lack of democracy in Mexico, especially in the workings of the dominating Partido Revolucionario Institucional (Institutional Revolutionary Party).

1970

1970 Affirmative Action vs. Reverse Discrimination. The struggle over affirmative action in the United States continues into the 1970s, when opponents coin the term "reverse discrimination," by which they suggest that white males are victims of discrimination as a result of affirmative action on behalf of women, blacks, Hispanics, and other underrepresented groups.

1970 Allende Elected to Govern Chile. Salvador Allende is elected to the presidency in Chile, becoming the first freely elected Marxist head of state in Latin America. Allende intends to socialize the economy. He begins by nationalizing, without compensation, the copper industries, the largest symbol of United States presence in the country. He subsequently intervenes in other segments of the foreign-dominated economy. In an appeal to labor, Allende freezes prices and decrees hefty wage increases. He implements an agrarian reform program. He also tries to change the national legislature so that it will be more representative of the masses rather than the elite. Such programs prompt wholesale opposition from the foreign-owned companies, the Chilean landowners, the middle class and even the workers themselves, who cannot keep up with inflationary prices for scarce goods. United States policy to Chile exacerbates the situation: President Richard

M. Nixon severs U.S. trade relations, forbids private bank loans, and prevents loans from the Inter-American and World Banks. Soon the country is beset by political protest, labor discord, and a general strike that leads to a CIA-engineered military coup and the assassination of Allende in September 1973.

1970 Argentine Chemist Wins Nobel Prize. Argentine citizen Luis F. Leloir, born in Paris, wins the Nobel Prize for chemistry for his discovery of the nucleotides for sugar and their role in the biosynthesis of carbohydrates.

1970 Authoritarian Regimes Rule Six Countries. During the 1970s and 1980s brutal authoritarian regimes take power in Argentina, Brazil, Chile, Peru, El Salvador, and Guatemala. In its anxiety to rid the nations of Communism, the military arrest, torture, exile, and kill thousands of individuals on the slightest suspicion. Political and civil rights are denied.

1970 Congress Amends Voting Rights Act. In the United States Congress, an amendment to the landmark Voting Rights Act of 1970 adds a provision designed to guard against inventive new barriers to political participation. It requires federal approval of all changes in voting procedures in certain jurisdictions, primarily southern states. This act prevents minority votes from being diluted in gerrymandered districts or through at-large elections.

1970   Ecuador Expropriates Land. To further its agrarian reform program, Ecuador expropriates by decree large tracts of land in its lowlands to create rice cooperatives.

1970   Most Hispanics in U.S. Live in Nine States. The census shows that 82 percent of the Hispanic population of the nation lives in nine states, with the proportion rising to 86 percent in 1990. The major recipients of Hispanic immigration are California, Texas, and New York, and to a lesser degree Florida, Illinois, and New Jersey.

1970   Novelist Gabriel García Márquez Publishes Novel. García Márquez' early novel, *Cien años de soledad* (One Hundred Years of Solitude), is published. It is his best known work, and is considered a masterpiece of Latin American and world literature. (*See also* biography, March 6, 1928.)

1970   Undocumented Immigration Rises. During the 1970s and early 1980s, the rise in politically motivated violence in Central America spurs a massive increase in undocumented immigration to the United States. During the 1970s, Immigration and Naturalization Service (INS) Commissioner Leonard Chapman seeks to increase funding and expand the power of his organization, claiming that there are as many as 12 million undocumented workers in the country. Other observers place the number in the range of 3.5 million to 5 million people. Given the U.S. policy of support to authoritarian regimes in Central America, the INS refuses to recognize the Salvadoran and Guatemalan immigrants as political refugees. A church-based movement to smuggle, support, and offer church asylum to the refugees develops in the United States as a response to this policy.

MAY 5, 1970   First Mexican–American Bishop. Patrick F. Flores is the first Mexican–American to be named a bishop of the Catholic Church. (*See also* biography, July 26, 1929.)

JULY 29, 1970   The Lettuce Boycott Leads to New Labor Law. After prolonged strikes and national boycotts, United Farmworkers Organizing Committee (UFWOC), under the leadership of César Chávez, signs contracts with most of the Central Valley table grape growers of California and immediately chooses the Salinas Valley lettuce growers for the organization's next labor action. In response, some seventy growers sign "sweetheart" contracts with the International Brotherhood of Teamsters. Despite the Teamster contracts, some seven thousand farm workers strike in August. In September, UFWOC launches a national boycott of lettuce. Strikes and lettuce and grape boycotts continue, as does the jurisdictional battle with the Teamsters, on through 1974, when newly elected governor Jerry Brown, Jr., pioneers passage of the California Agriculture Labor Relations Act. Under this legislation, union elections may be held by workers; the result is that the UFWOC, now the United Farm Workers (UFW), wins 65 percent of the elections and regains many lost contracts. In 1977, the UFW–Teamsters dispute is resolved, but the lettuce boycott does not end until February 1978. Definitive victory at unionizing the lettuce fields comes in September 1979, when the UFW successfully signs contracts with major lettuce farmers in the state.

AUGUST 20, 1970   Police Disrupt Chicanos' Vietnam War Protest. In Los Angeles, more than twenty thousand Chicanos and supporters participate in a Chicano Moratorium to the Vietnam War to protest the disproportionately high number of Chicano casualties in that war. On the route from Belvedere to Laguna Park, police begin to break up the march, supposedly in response to rock and bottle throwing. At Laguna Park, where speeches are being heard, the authorities stop the proceedings with tear gas. Two hours of struggle between police and demonstrators ensue. Rubén Salazar, a journalist not involved in the struggle, is accidentally killed by police. Salazar's death becomes a symbol of police brutality and suppression of Hispanic civil rights to this day.

1971

1971–72 Pablo Neruda Is Chilean Ambassador. Poet Pablo Neruda serves as ambassador to France under Salvador Allende. (*See also* biography, July 12, 1904.)

1971 Argentine Composer Wins Pulitzer Prize. Argentine composer Mario Davidovsky wins the Pulitzer Prize for his "Sincronism No. 6." Born in Buenos Aires in 1934, Davidovsky is teaching at Princeton University at the time.

1971 Big Year for Mexican–American Golfer. Lee Treviño is named PGA Player of the Year, Associated Press Athlete of the Year, and *Sports Illustrated* Sportsman of the Year. (*See also* biography, December 1, 1939.)

1971 Chilean Poet Awarded Nobel Prize. Chilean poet Pablo Neruda wins the Nobel Prize for literature. (*See also* biography, July 12, 1904.)

1971 Cuban Poet Imprisoned. Cuban poet Heberto Padilla is imprisoned for falling out of favor with the government due to his political writings. (*See also* biography, January 20, 1932.)

1971 Singer Carr Founds Scholarship Foundation. The Vikki Carr Scholarship Foundation is created by the singer to provide higher education scholarships to Mexican–American youths. (*See also* biography, July 19, 1940.)

AUGUST 1971 California Court Rules on School Financing. In *Serrano v. Priest*, a suit brought by John Serrano against the California state treasurer, alleging that his son was receiving an inferior education in East Los Angeles because schools are financed by local property taxes, the California courts finds in August— and in April 1974 and December 1977 (California Supreme Court)—that financing schools

through local property taxes does not provide equal protection of the law and, therefore, the financing system must be changed. After that, the state legislature mandates that income taxes be used for financing education.

1972

1972 Clemente Recognized by Hall of Fame. The Baseball Hall of Fame waives its five-year waiting period and inducts Pittsburgh Pirates star Roberto Clemente after his untimely, heroic death while bringing aid to Nicaraguan earthquake victims. (*See also* biography, August 18, 1934.)

1972 Dictator Molina Elected in El Salvador. Colonel Arturo Armando Molina, another military dictator, is elected president of El Salvador. There is growing opposition to the military dictatorships and demands from the poor for land and jobs.

1972 Hispanic Woman Named U.S. Treasurer. Ramona Acosta Bañuelos becomes the first Hispanic treasurer of the United States.

1972 Land Reform in the Dominican Republic. The Dominican Republic institutes a long overdue agrarian reform program. In 1960, there are some 450,000 farmers in the Dominican Republic, but only 1 percent of them own over 50 percent of the land. In 1962, land reform laws are passed and the Instituto Agrario Dominicano (Dominican Agrarian Institute) is founded to carry out reform, but throughout the 1960s land concentration remains high. By 1972, political pressure from peasant groups becomes intense, the country needs increased agricultural output, and the Catholic Church through liberation theology supports liberalization. A reform law is passed, which brings about the expropriation of private lands, mostly those dedicated to growing rice. Two-thirds of the expropriation and redistribution project is carried out in the following ten years, with more than 32,000 individuals receiving an average of 5.3 hectares of farm lands, and nearly 16,000 more benefiting through some 118 collectives, with an average of 4 hectares per individual. Today, about one-third of the Dominican Republic's rice is produced by the land reform sector.

1972 Mexican Rosario Castellanos Publishes Poems. Castellanos' selected poems are published in *Poesía no eres tú: obra poética, 1948–1971* (You Are Poetry: The Poetic Works, 1948–1971). (*See also* biography, May 25, 1925.)

1972 Playwright Usigli Awarded National Prize. Rodolfo Usigli, considered one of Mexico's greatest playwrights, receives Mexico's National Prize for Literature. (*See also* biography, November 17, 1905.)

FEBRUARY 19, 1972 Ramos Defeats Carrasco for Boxing Title. Mexican–American boxer Armando Ramos wins the World Boxing Congress lightweight championship over Pedro Carrasco.

MAY 3, 1972 Farah Workers Strike in Texas. Workers strike the Farah Manufacturing Company in El Paso, Texas, and initiate a national boycott. The strikers are represented by the Amalgamated Clothing Workers of America, but the union is not recognized by the owner, William Farah. After various unfair labor practices and antiboycott suits, the strike ends in February 1974, when a vote indicates that two-thirds of the workers want the union to represent them.

SUMMER 1972 Athletes Win Olympic Medals. In Munich, West Germany, Cuba's Silvia Chibas wins an Olympic bronze medal in the women's 100-meter run with a time of 11.24, and Cuban teams win the bronze in the women's 4 x 100 relay with a time of 43.36 and the

bronze in men's basketball competition. Colombia's Helmut Bellingrodt wins the silver in running game target competition.

1973

1973 Author Mohr Publishes Award-Winning Book. Nicholosa Mohr's novel, *Nilda,* wins the Jane Addams Children's Book Award and is selected by *School Library Journal* as a Best Book of the Year. (*See also* biography, November 1, 1935.)

1973 Court Decides Texas School Financing Issue. A suit brought on behalf of poor school children, *San Antonio Independent School District v. Rodríguez,* challenges the Texas system of financing its school system based on local property taxation. The Supreme Court of the United States holds that the system does not violate the constitutional right of the children to equal protection under the Fourteenth Amendment. By a 5–4 majority, the court rules that education is not a fundamental right and poverty is not a reason to hold otherwise.

1973 Hispanics Form Labor Group. The Labor Council of Latin American Advancement (LCLAA) forms to promote the interests of Hispanics within organized labor.

1973 Supreme Court Acts on Farah Case. In the United States, an employment discrimination case, *Espinoza v. Farah Manufacturing Company* is brought against Farah for discrimination toward an employee, Espinoza, on the basis of his citizenship status under the Civil Rights Act. However, the Supreme Court holds that there is nothing in Title VII, the equal employment opportunities provisions of the Civil Rights Act of 1964, that makes it illegal to discriminate on the basis of citizenship or alienage.

1973 UN Action Supports Independence

A bilingual classroom in Crystal City, Texas, 1979. (Courtesy of the *Texas Catholic Herald.*)

Movement. The right of the Puerto Rican people to decide their own future as a nation is approved by the United Nations. In this year, the United Nations officially recognizes Puerto Rico as a colony of the United States. This finding by the United Nations is of great support to the independence movement on the island and in the United States because the U.S. government always refuses to acknowledge it possesses colonies.

1973   Writer Hinojosa Publishes First Book.
Hispanic writer Rolando Hinojosa publishes *Estampas del Valle y otras obras* (which he recreates in English and publishes as *The Valley* in 1983), winner of the national award for Chicano literature, Premio Quinto Sol. (*See also* biography, January 21, 1929.)

1973   Writing Career Launched for Villaseñor.
The professional writing career of Victor Villaseñor is launched with the publication of *Macho!* (*See also* biography, May 11, 1940.)

SEPTEMBER 11, 1973   Chile's Allende Killed in Military Coup. The constitutionally elected Socialist president of Chile, Salvador Allende, is killed in a bloody coup d'etat led by the

military (army, navy, air force, and national police) with support from the Central Intelligence Agency of the United States. A military iron-fisted dictatorship, led by General Augusto Pinochet, is immediately instituted and begins exiling, imprisoning, and executing anyone identified as opposing its regime; many of these are students. Allende had furthered the expropriation of lands initiated by his Christian Democratic predecessor, Eduardo Frei (1964–70), and completed the nationalizing of the copper, steel, sodium nitrate, and coal industries, in some cases without restitution to the owners. Allende saw his government as being in the vanguard of Socialism in the world in reorganizing an industrial society for the benefit of the majority. But he had moved too fast and had misinterpreted the will of many powerful sectors of Chilean society. Allende's government faced continuing waves of strikes, revolutionary movements, domestic and foreign political pressures, and polarization of various right-wing and left-wing groups in the society, all of which led to mounting social disorder and a short supply of basic foods and commodities. As a result, the Christian Democratic party withdrew from the coalition that brought

Allende into office, and the stage was set for one of the most powerful and decisive coups in Latin–American history.

1974

1974–76 Cuban Novelist Imprisoned. Novelist Reinaldo Arenas is imprisoned and "rehabilitated" by the government for his literary dissidence. (*See also* biography, July 16, 1943.)

1974–86 Carmelo Mesa-Lago Serves as Director. During his tenure at the University of Pittsburgh, educator and author Carmelo Mesa-Lago serves as the director of the Center for Latin American Studies. (*See also* biography, August 11, 1934.)

1974 Congressional Act Supports Bilingual Education. The United States Congress passes the Equal Educational Opportunity Act of 1974 to create equality in public schools by making bilingual education available to Hispanic youth. According to the framers of the act, equal education means more than equal facilities and equal access to teachers. Students who have trouble with the English language must be given programs to help them overcome their difficulties with English.

1974 Jockey Runs for the Roses. Puerto Rican jockey Angel Cordero wins the Kentucky Derby. Cordero wins the Derby again in 1976 and 1985. He also wins the Preakness Stakes in 1980 and 1985, and the Belmont Stakes in 1976. In 1982, he is named "Jockey of the Year."

1974 Museum Established for Mexican Painter. The Rufino Tamayo Museum of Contemporary Art is inaugurated in 1974 in Mexico City to house Rufino Tamayo's collection of contemporary European and American art. (*See also* biography, August 26, 1899.)

1974 Nuyorican Poet Has Award-Winning Year. Miguel Piñero, the most famous dramatist to come out of the Nuyorican school, is awarded the New York Drama Critics Circle Award for Best American Play, an Obie, and the Drama Desk Award, all in for *Short Eyes*. (*See also* biography, December 19, 1946.)

JANUARY 1974 Court Decision Backs Bilingual Programs. In *Lau v. Nichols,* the United States Supreme Court holds that the San Francisco Unified School District discriminated against a non-English-speaking student, Kinney Lau, by not providing a program to deal with his language problem and thereby depriving him of meaningful participation in school. This decision serves as a cornerstone for the creation and maintenance of bilingual education programs across the country.

1975

1975–77 Novelist Carlos Fuentes Is Ambassador. Fuentes serves as the Mexican ambassador to France. (*See also* biography, November 11, 1928.)

1975 Abimael Guzmán Reynoso Heads Guerrilla Movement. Guzmán is the leader of a pro-Maoist splinter group of the Peruvian communist party known as El Sendero Luminoso, or Shining Path. The group promotes change through violence. (*See also* biography, December 4, 1934 and entry, September 12, 1992.)

1975 Alberto Gironella Illustrates Fuentes's Book. Distinguished artist Gironella illustrates novelist Carlos Fuentes's *Terra Nostra.* (*See also* biography, 1929.)

1975 Ban on Literacy Tests for Voting Becomes Permanent. The Voting Rights Act Amendments of 1975 extend the provisions of the original Voting Rights Act and make permanent the national ban on literacy tests. Critical for Hispanic–Americans, the amendments make bilingual ballots a requirement in certain locations.

MAY 1975 California Labor Relations Act. Upon his inauguration to office, Governor Jerry Brown, Jr., proposes legislation to protect both farm labor and the growers. In May 1975, the California Labor Relations Act is passed, giving agricultural workers the same benefits that the National Labor Relations Act (1935) guarantees all industrial workers. The law authorizes secret elections among the workers, and thus prepares the way for unions to be voted in.

1976

1976 Octavio Paz Founds Magazine. Mexico's Octavio Paz is founder and publisher of Spanish America's most distinguished magazine of literature and commentary, *Vuelta* (Return). (*See also* biography, March 31, 1914.)

1976 Peso Devaluated. Mexico's peso is devaluated for the first time in twenty-five years. The process is repeated in the following years as Mexico's economic situation worsens, especially after the oil market falls apart.

SUMMER 1976 Hispanics Are Olympic Medalists. In Montreal, Quebec (Canada), Cuba's Alberto Juantorena wins Olympic gold medals in both the 400 and 800 meters with times of 44.26 and 1:43.5, and Alejandro Casanas wins the silver in the 110-meter hurdles. Mexico's Daniel Bautista wins the 20 km with a time of 1:24:40.6.

1977

1977 The Antonio Maceo Brigade. A group of young Cuban exiles called the Antonio Maceo Brigade travels to Cuba from the United States to participate in service work and to achieve a degree of rapprochement with the Cuban government.

1977 Canal Will Go to Panama in 2000. President Jimmy Carter succeeds in leading Congress to sign a new Panama Canal treaty, which provides for the turnover of the canal to Panama in the year 2000.

1977 Ecuador Encourages Colonization of Amazon Region. As part of its agrarian reform program, the Ecuadorean government passes special legislation to encourage colonization of the Amazon region. By 1985, the reform sector of agriculture accounts for some 30 percent of the total national farmland. But more than three-fourths of this is made up of colonization lands. While many peasants do benefit by receiving land, it nevertheless is the medium and larger producers who seem to have benefit the most from Ecuador's agrarian reform program. Faced with the threat of state intervention, many large farmers sell lands and invest in the urban–industrial sector of the economy, while others modernize their farming operations to eliminate their dependence on peons.

1977 Hispanics Form Congressional Caucus. The Congressional Hispanic Caucus is founded. The privately funded caucus brings attention to all governmental issues of concern to Hispanics.

1977 INS Seizes Undocumented Workers. The Immigration and Naturalization Service (INS) is apprehending more than one million undocumented workers each year.

1977 Romero Elected in El Salvador. General Carlos Humberto Romero becomes the latest military dictator to be elected to the presidency of El Salvador.

1978

1978 Big Year for Mexican–American Golfer. Nancy López is named "Rookie of the Year," "Player of the Year," and "Female Athlete of the Year"; she wins the Vare Trophy;

and she sets a new record for earnings by a rookie. (*See also* biography, January 6, 1957.)

1978 Book on Luis Leal Published. A conference is held and a book published in Luis Leal's praise: *Homenaje a Luis Leal* (Homage to Luis Leal), edited by Donald W. Bleznick and Juan O. Valencia. (*See also* biography, September 17, 1907.)

1978 Cinematographer Wins Oscar. Nestor Almendros wins the Academy Award for cinematography for the film *Days of Heaven*. (*See also* biography, 1930.)

1978 Civil War Erupts in Nicaragua. A violent civil war breaks out in Nicaragua when the Sandinista Front for National Liberation (FSNL or Sandinistas) attempts to topple dictator Anastasio Somoza Debayle from power.

1978 Flores Coaches Oakland Raiders. Thomas Flores becomes the first Hispanic–American to be named a coach of a professional football team in the United States. He succeeds John Madden to the post for the Oakland Raiders in 1978 and is officially named in 1979. (*See also* biography, March 21, 1937.)

1978 Hispanic Income Data. The median income of Hispanic families below the poverty level in the United States falls from $7,238 in 1978 to $6,557 in 1978, controlling for inflation. From 1978 to 1988, the proportion of Hispanic children living in poverty rises more than 45 percent, and by 1989, 38 percent of Hispanic children are living in poverty.

1978 Hispanic Women in U.S. Work Force. From 1978 to 1988, Hispanic female participation in the work force in the United States more than doubles, from 1.7 million to 3.6 million. In 1988, 56.6 percent of Hispanic women are in the work force, compared with 66.2 percent of white females and 63.8 percent of black women.

1978 José Luis González Wins Award. González is awarded Mexico's most prestigious literary award, the Xavier Villaurrutia Prize for Fiction, for his *Balada de otro tiempo* (Ballad from Another Time). (*See also* biography, March 8, 1926.)

1978 Writer Tomás Rivera Heads University. Rivera, a leader in Chicano literature, becomes chancellor of the University of California–Riverside. (*See also* biography, December 22, 1935.)

JUNE 11, 1978 González Sets World Record in Walk. Mexico's Raúl González sets a new world record of 3 hours 41 minutes and 19.2 seconds in the 50,000-meter walk in Pobedrady, Czechoslovakia.

1979

1979 Galavisión, Spanish-Language Television, Begins. Galavisión, a subsidiary of Mexico's Televisa, begins as a cable service. It expands to offer over-the-air programming and currently is affiliated with 228 cable systems across the U.S., including stations in Bakersfield, Los Angeles, Palm Springs, San Jose, and Santa Barbara, California; Corpus Cristi, Houston, and San Antonio, Texas; and Phoenix and Tucson, Arizona.

1979 Nationalists Leave Prison. The Puerto Rican nationalists who shot up the House of Representatives in 1954 are released from prison: Lolita Lebrón, Ramón Cancel Miranda, Irving Flores, and Oscar Collazo.

1979 Poet Laviera Publishes Book. Hispanic poet Tato Laviera becomes popular after the publication of his first book, *La Carreta Made a U-Turn*. (*See also* biography, September 5, 1950.)

JULY 17–19, 1979 Sandinistas Come to Power. Dictator Anastasio Somoza abandons Nicaragua after great pressure not only from the Sandinista Front for National Liberation (FSNL) but also from the United States and Mexico and from Central American governments. On

July 20, the Junta of the Government of National Reconstruction is sworn into office. On September 24, President Jimmy Carter meets with the junta in the White House; the United States has not only supported Somoza's ouster but has funneled considerable aid to Nicaragua under Carter—that would change under the presidency of Ronald Reagan. As soon as the Sandinistas comes to power in Nicaragua, they take over the land holdings of former dictator Anastasio Somoza and his close associates, which accounts for about one-fifth of Nicaragua's arable land. The confiscated lands are then set up as state farms under the administration of the Nicaraguan Agrarian Reform Institute established in July. To continue land reform, the Agrarian Reform Act of 1981 is passed, which empowers the government to expropriate lands over 350 hectares in the Pacific region and over 700 hectares in the central region. The most favored reorganization of expropriated lands in Nicaragua is production cooperatives. In 1984, the government begins to grant property titles to squatters, with some 30,000 families receiving titles within two years. After 1984, much of the policy and implementation is decentralized and regionalized. This results, for example, in the Atlantic coast region placing a high priority on titling lands to indigenous communities. To date, some 55 percent of the rural poor have received land under these reforms, representing one of the most far-reaching land reform programs in Latin America.

Chapter 10
1980 TO 1989

1980   Cubans in U.S. Elected to Office. All throughout the 1960s, the majority of Cubans in the United States maintain their Cuban citizenship, hoping to return to a free Cuba someday. In the 1970s, however, their rate of naturalization becomes the highest of any ethnic group, and subsequently leads to their ascendance to political power. After progressively electing Cubans to city councils throughout Dade County, Cubans are able to elect one of their own for the first time to the mayoralty of Miami. In 1982, they elect three Cubans to the state legislature, and the number has grown in the years that have followed. And, finally, in 1989, a Cuban is elected for the first time to the United States Congress: Ileana Ross Lehtinen, representing Florida's 18th Congressional District. Similar trends emerge in Union City and West New York, both Cuban population centers in New Jersey.

1980   Duarte Appointed President of El Salvador. The military junta ruling El Salvador appoints José Napoleón Duarte to the presidency. Duarte initiates reform programs that include redistribution of lands, but nevertheless continues to face protests and widespread discontent. Civil war between government forces and the leftist Farabundo Martí National Liberation Front (FMLN) breaks out and continues during the 1980s.

1980   El Salvador, Honduras End Dispute. El Salvador and Honduras sign a peace treaty, ending their decade-old dispute.

1980   Former Nicaraguan Dictator Assassinated. Recently deposed Nicaraguan dictator Anastasio Somoza Debayle is assassinated in Paraguay.

1980   Hispanic Novelist Wins Award. Rudolfo Anaya, novelist and teacher, is awarded the President's National Salute to American Poets and Writers. (*See also* biography, October 30, 1937.)

1980   Hispanics Are 40 Percent of Immigrants. During the 1980s, the rates of immigration approach the levels of the early 1900s: legal immigration during the first decade of the century reached 8.8 million, while during the 1980s 6.3 million immigrants are granted permanent residence. The immigrants are overwhelmingly young and in search of employment, and Hispanic immigrants continue to account for more than 40 percent of the total. From 1980 to 1988, the number of Hispanics in the work force increases by 48 percent, representing 20 percent of U.S. employment growth.

Guerrillas of the Frente Farabundo Martí in El Salvador. (Courtesy of the Arte Público Press Archives, University of Houston.)

1980   Land Reform in El Salvador. Agrarian reform begins in El Salvador, first with estates larger than 500 hectares being expropriated, then later with sharecroppers empowered to claim for their own up to 7 hectares of land that they work. Most of the expropriated lands are organized in cooperatives. Approximately 22 percent of the rural poor benefit from land redistribution in El Salvador.

1980   The Mexican Economy. Mexico's oil pro-

duction rises to 2.3 million barrels per day, making it the fifth largest producer in the world. Unfortunately, in 1981 oil prices fall by two-thirds, which increases Mexico's foreign debt to unmanageable levels. In 1982, Mexico announces postponement on payments to $80 billion in foreign debt, and the peso falls from 26.50 to the dollar to 150 to the dollar. In 1983, the International Monetary fund provides Mexico with an emergency loan of $4 billion, but only on the conditions that public spending and imports be drastically curbed and taxes raised.

1980   Meza Takes Over Bolivia in Military Coup. Luis García Meza leads a military coup and takes over the government of Bolivia, installing himself as dictator. His efforts are backed by cocaine traffickers and the military government of Argentina. Before his government is ousted in 1981, Meza recruits neo-Nazi paramilitary soldiers from France, Germany, Argentina, and Bolivia to terrorize labor leaders, journalists, and students. Gestapo Chief Klaus Barbie serves as a close advisor to Meza. After García Meza's ouster, Barbie is expelled from Bolivia in 1983 and imprisoned in France for crimes committed during World War II. On March 11, 1994, Meza is arrested in Brazil as a fugitive from Bolivia, where he had been sentenced to thirty years in prison for treason, armed insurrection, genocide, human rights violations, theft, and embezzlement. García Meza has been associated with drug trafficking in Bolivia, Chile, and Brazil.

1980   Nava Named Ambassador to Mexico. Julián Nava becomes the first Mexican–American to be named ambassador to Mexico. (*See also* biography, June 19, 1927.)

1980   Nobel Peace Prize Awarded to Argentine. Argentine architect and sculptor Adolfo Pérez Esquivel wins the Nobel Peace Prize for his efforts on behalf of human rights.

1980   Photographer Bravo Establishes Museum. Manuel Alvarez Bravo organizes and serves as director of the Museum of Mexican Photography. (*See also* biography, 1902.)

1980   Reagan and Affirmative Action. From 1980 to 1988, the Reagan administration maintains that affirmative action programs entail quotas, constituting a form of reverse discrimination.

1980   Reagan Supports Old Order, Except in Nicaragua. Newly elected U.S. president Ronald Reagan puts Latin–American affairs within the context of the Cold War and the East–West struggle, denying that such longstanding issues as the disparity of wealth, deprivation of social mobility, and restriction of political rights are responsible for contemporary protests and violence in Latin America. Instead, Reagan argues that the Soviet Union, through its Cuban proxies, capitalizes on these issues to push local Marxists into power, and that they will destroy the economies and offer no hope for political reform. From these communist outposts, Moscow threatens the United States interests. Human rights becomes a policy of the past as military, not economic and social, solutions receive first consideration. Within this context, Reagan is determined to maintain Central America's old order, except in Nicaragua, where he intends to restore it by overthrowing the Sandinista government through funding and supporting the Contra counterrevolution. To carry out his policy, Honduras is turned into an American military outpost, over $300 million in military aid is given to the government in El Salvador for its battle against the Farabundo Martí National Liberation Front (FMLN), and the Nicaraguan Contras are supported in a counterrevolution designed to oust the Sandinistas from power.

1980   The Refugee Act of 1980. The Refugee Act of 1980 removes the ideological definition of refugee as one who flees from a Communist regime, thus allowing thousands to enter the United States as refugees. While more "refugees" are being admitted, the Immigration and Naturalization Service is implementing numerous programs to apprehend undocumented immigrants; thousands of violations of their civil rights are reported.

JANUARY 3, 1980   Poet Laviera at the White House. Hispanic poet Tato Laviera is received by President Jimmy Carter at the White House gathering of American poets. (*See also* biography, September 5, 1950.)

APRIL 1980   The Mariel Boatlift. A bus carrying a load of discontented Cubans crashes through the gates of the Peruvian embassy in Havana and the passengers receive political asylum from Peru. Fidel Castro begins to revise his policy of gradually allowing Cubans to leave. A flotilla soon converges at Cuba's Mariel Harbor to pick up refugees. By year end, more than 125,000 "Marielitos" migrate to the United States. Castro charges that the Cuban exiles he has allowed to return on visits have contaminated many with the glitter of consumerism.

SUMMER 1980   Cuban Athletes Win Medals. During the U.S.-boycotted Olympics in Moscow, Russia, Daniel Núñez wins a gold medal in 56 kg. weightlifting while Hipolito Ramos (light flyweight silver), Juan Hernández (bantamweight gold), Adolfo Horta (featherweight silver), Angel Herrera (lightweight gold), Jose Aguilar (light welterweight silver), Andres Aldama (welterweight gold), Armando Martinez (light middleweight gold), Jose Gómez (middleweight gold), and Teafilo Sterenson (heavyweight gold) show Cuba's strength in boxing. María Colón becomes the first Latin–American woman to win a gold medal in the javelin.

1981

1981   Ferrer Becomes Hall-of-Famer. Puerto Rican actor José Ferrer is inducted into the

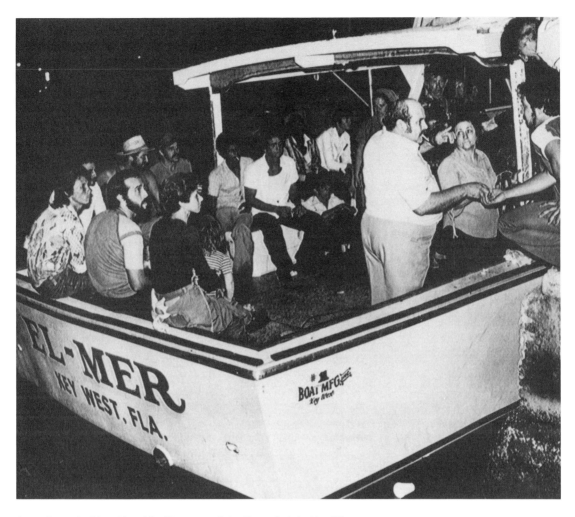

Scene from the Mariel boatlift. (Courtesy of the *Texas Catholic Herald*.)

Theater Hall of Fame. (*See also* biography, January 8, 1912.)

1981   Nuyorican Poet Hernández Cruz in *Life*.
The April 1981 issue of *Life* magazine includes Cruz among a handful of outstanding American poets. (*See also* biography, February 6, 1949.)

JANUARY 1981   U.S. Seeks Ouster of Sandinistas in Nicaragua. When President Ronald Reagan takes office, he begins an all-out military, economic, diplomatic, and ideological cam-

paign to oust the revolutionary government in Nicaragua.

NOVEMBER 17, 1981   Reagan Supports Contras. President Ronald Reagan decides to support the Contras attempts to overthrow the Sandinistas in Nicaragua.

1982

1982   Cordero Named Top U.S. Jockey. Puer-

A protest march against President Reagan's policies towards Nicaragua. (Courtesy of CISPES.)

to Rican jockey Angel Cordero is named United States horse racing's "Jockey of the Year."

1982   García Márquez Wins Nobel Prize. Colombian novelist Gabriel García Márquez wins the Nobel Prize for literature. (*See also* biography, March 6, 1928.)

1982   Hispanic Congressman Roybal Chairs Committee. Edward R. Roybal becomes chairman of the Congressional Hispanic Caucus, where he leads the opposition to employer sanctions for hiring the undocumented, which

ultimately is enacted as the Reform and Control Act of 1986. (*See also* biography, February 10, 1916 and entry, 1962.)

1982   Novelist Allende Publishes Poetic Work. Isabel Allende publishes her most important novel, *La casa de los espíritus* (The House of the Spirits), a sweeping recreation of her family and her country during this century. (*See also* biography, August 2, 1942.)

1982   Robles Co-Winner of Peace Prize. Mexican diplomat Alfonso García Robles wins the

Nobel Peace Prize jointly with Alva Myrdal for developing and promoting the Treaty of Tlaltelolco which declares Latin America to be a nuclear-free zone.

FEBRUARY 1982 Mexico Devalues Its Currency. Mexico devalues its currency more than 70 percent. The country is faced with exorbitant foreign debt and is not even able to service its loans, is running a deficit in its balance of payments, and is experiencing oil prices that are continuously depressed.

APRIL 14, 1982 Argentina Invades Malvinas. The military dictatorship in Argentina, faced with mounting domestic crises, decides to attempt to regain control of the Malvina Islands, whose return to Argentina from British control has been repeatedly requested since 1833. For the English, these "Falkland Islands" are one of the few vestiges left of its once grand colonial empire. After an Argentine invasion, the British fleet succeeds in taking back the islands on June 14. One immediate outcome of the Malvinas fiasco is General Leopoldo Galtieri's resignation as head of Argentina; he is immediately succeeded by another member of the autocratic military junta, Major General Reynaldo Bignone. After peace is reestablished from this undeclared war, the Malvinas resume life much as before.

AUGUST 1982 Mexico Cannot Pay Foreign Debt on Time. Mexico announces that it will not be able to pay its foreign debt on time. The Federal Reserve, the United States Treasury, and eleven large international banks have loaned Mexico almost $2 billion. A large portion of the loan had to be paid back with oil sold at a low price to the U.S. Strategic Oil Reserve. Mexico's economic independence once again is crumbling.

1983

1983 Contras Invade Northeastern Nicara-

gua. Several thousand Nicaraguan counter-revolutionaries (Contras) invade northeastern Nicaragua in efforts to topple the leftist Sandinista regime. The Contras are supported militarily by the United States government.

1983 Dominican Pitcher Is Hall-of-Famer. Pitcher Juan Marichal is inducted into the Baseball Hall of Fame. (*See also* biography, 1937.)

1983 Lionel García Wins Literary Award. Author and veterinarian García wins the PEN Southwest Discovery Award for his novel in progress, *Leaving Home*, which is published in 1985. (*See also* biography, August 20, 1935.)

JANUARY 8–9, 1983 Nations Pursue Peace in Central America. In order to pursue peace in the region, four of the neighboring nations of Central America—Mexico, Venezuela, Colombia, and Panama—meet on the Panamanian island of Contadora. Their goal is a mutually agreed and negotiated peace treaty. In July, the Contadora Group issues its first proposals, which include the withdrawal of all foreign military advisors from Central America, the end of all aid to irregular forces, and the cessation of military maneuvers in the border regions. In September, the group produces a draft 21-point peace treaty. The peace proposals are accompanied by intense diplomatic activity. The Contadora Group meets eleven times in 1983, with the Central American ministers participating on six of those times. In January 1984, the Contadora Group and the Central American nations attempt to strengthen the process by creating three joint committees to cover security, political, and social and economic issues. But all during this time of peacemaking, the United States is preparing for war in the region, with President Reagan issuing bellicose speeches, the United States invading Grenada on October 25, 1983, with U.S. troop maneuvers in Honduras in 1983, funding the Contras, and mining the Nicaraguan ports. Finally, with United States presidential elections approaching, the Contadora Group is successful in urging the United States administration to hold bilateral conversations with the Nicaraguan government. The talks at Manzanillo start in June 1984 and end in January 1985, when the United States unilaterally abandons the bilateral negotiations. On September 21, the Nicaraguan government becomes the first of the Central American nations to sign the Contadora Group's "Draft Act on Peace and Cooperation." But again, the United States pursues a course of undermining the Contadora process, and the pursuit of peace is extended into 1985 and the process enlarged to include Argentina, Brazil, Peru, and Uruguay ("The Lima Group"). The most important next step is the Caraballeda Declaration in January 1986, whereby the Contadora and Lima Groups call on the United States to resume talks with Nicaragua, to suspend aid to the Contras, and to withdraw its troops from the region. The declaration is supported by the Central American presidents and representatives from all the major political parties in Western Europe. The United States refuses, stating that the Nicaraguan government has to negotiate with the Contras. On June 27, 1986, the International Court of Justice in the Hague states that the United States is in breach of international law by intervening economically and politically in Nicaragua, and in November 1986, the secretaries general of the United Nations and the Organization of American States launch a joint initiative to further peace in Central America. Both of these events strengthen the Contadora process. On November 25, 1986, news of the Iran–Contra scandal breaks in the United States: the National Security Council has been diverting money from secret arms sales to Iran to clandestine support for the Contras—which was prohibited by Congress under the 1982 Boland Amendment. U.S. policy towards Nicaragua, which has been judged illegal by the International Court is exposed as possibly illegal with-

in the United States as well. Despite opposition from President Reagan, the Central American governments ratify their own peace plan, based on one developed by Costa Rican president Oscar Arias Sánchez on August 7, 1987. The plan, "Procedure for the Establishment of a Strong and Lasting Peace in Central America," calls for withdrawal of all foreign military advisors from the area, a complete ceasefire, and the holding of free and pluralist elections in all of the countries in Central America. Implementation of the accords signed by the five republics is to be overseen by the Group of 8 (the Contadora and Lima Groups), the foreign ministers of the Central American countries, and the secretaries general of the United Nations and the Organization of American States. Despite Nicaragua's proceeding to implement the accords and its unilateral declaration of a ceasefire in three of the northern war zones, President Reagan obtains from Congress another $3.2 million for the Contras on September 23, 1987. Later in the year, when Reagan calls for more Contra funding, there is a public outcry and defections from his allies in Congress; the administration's policies towards Nicaragua collapse. Despite continued efforts by the outgoing Reagan administration and the newly elected Bush administration to block the accords, the peace efforts are promoted unilaterally by the Nicaraguan government, which initiates negotiations with the Contras. The efforts are supported regionally and internationally, and eventually result in Nicaragua forging a ceasefire treaty with the Contras in 1988 and holding free elections in 1990, with both Sandinistas and Contras as political parties. The elections result in the Sandinistas losing the presidency and considerable power and nonviolently turning the administration over to the moderates headed by newly elected president Violeta Chamorro. For his efforts in forging a regional peace solution in the face of United States opposition, President Oscar Arias Sánchez is accorded the Nobel Prize.

1984

1984   Argentinean Is Co-Winner of Nobel Prize. Doctor César Milstein wins the Nobel Prize for medicine jointly with Georges J.F. Kohler for their experiments on cancer cells.

1984   Baseball Hall of Fame Inducts Aparicio. Venezuelan Luis Aparicio is inducted into the baseball Hall of Fame as one of the greatest shortstops of all time in U.S. professional baseball. He still holds the records for games played, assists, and double plays, and the American League record for putouts. His 506 stolen bases rank among the highest. Playing most of his career for the Chicago White Sox, Aparicio begins his career in 1956 as Rookie of the Year and continues to play inspired baseball until his retirement in 1973. Aparicio plays on All-Star teams from 1958 to 1964 and again from 1970 to 1972. He wins the Golden Glove eleven times.

1984   Duarte Elected in El Salvador. After having been appointed to the presidency by a military junta in 1980, José Napoleón Duarte is elected to the presidency of El Salvador.

1984   Héctor García Pérez Recognized by U.S. García Pérez is awarded the United States of America Medal of Freedom. (*See also* biography, January 17, 1914.)

1984   Ortega Heads Nicaragua. Daniel Ortega, head of the Sandinista revolutionary government, is elected president of Nicaragua.

FEBRUARY 29, 1984   New World Walking Record. Mexico's Raúl González sets another new world record of 3 hours 41 minutes and 38 seconds in the 50 kilometer walk, in Fana, Norway.

MAY 10, 1984   World Court Tells U.S. to Stop Mining Ports. The World Court at the Hague unanimously orders the United States to stop mining Nicaraguan ports. The United

José Napoleón Duarte. (Courtesy of the Library of Congress Prints & Photographs Division.)

States government has been continuously provoking the revolutionary government in Nicaragua, including having the Central Intelligence Agency mine the country's ports.

SUMMER 1984   Cuba Boycotts Olympics. Latin America's greatest sports power, Cuba, boycotts the Olympiad in Los Angeles, California. With the largest Hispanic representation ever on the United States team, a U.S. Hispanic wins a gold medal: Paul Gonzales in light flyweight boxing, while Venezuelan Jose

Daniel Ortega. (Courtesy of the *Texas Catholic Herald*.)

Marcelilno Bolivar ties with a Zambian for the bronze.

OCTOBER 1, 1984   The Iran–Contra Affair. The United States Congress votes to halt aid to the Nicaraguan Contras. The National Security Council under Ronald Reagan nevertheless launches a covert scheme to launder money, pay a ransom to Iran for hostages, and indirectly supply the Contras with military aid. The illegal scheme headed by Oliver North eventually is uncovered and comes to be known as the

"Iran–Contra Affair," tainting the careers of various politicians and military leaders in the United States and even casting suspicions on President Reagan and his vice president, George Bush.

1985

1985   Cuba Reacts to Radio Martí. The Cuban government suspends its immigration agreement with the United States in response to the creation of Radio Martí, a twenty-four hour news/propaganda service created in the United States specifically to broadcast to Cuba.

1985   Hispanic Singer Vikki Carr Wins Grammy. Vikki Carr wins a Grammy for her Spanish-language album, "Simplemente Mujer" (Simply Woman). (*See also* biography, July 19, 1940.)

1986

1986   Argentina Repeats World Cup Win. Argentina wins its second World Cup in soccer. Argentina and Uruguay are the only countries to have won the international soccer championship twice.

1986   Physicist Alvarez Wins Nobel Prize. Physicist Luis Walter Alvarez is awarded the Nobel Prize in physics. (*See also* biography, June 13, 1911.)

1986   Undocumented Hispanics Achieve Legal Status. After more than a decade of debate, Congress enacts the Immigration Reform and Control Act (IRCA), creating an alien legalization program: legal status is given to applicants who held illegal status in the United States before January 1, 1982, until the time of application. The program brings legal status to a large number of undocumented Hispanics and curtailed many abuses of employers who took advantage of them and relieved their flight

Mass citizenship swearing in ceremonies in Houston, 1987. (Courtesy of the *Texas Catholic Herald*.)

from authorities. The bill also called for sanctions against employers of undocumented aliens.

JUNE 27, 1986   International Court Finds U.S. Breaches Law. The International Court of Justice finds the United States in breach of international law for supporting the Contras and for intervening militarily and economically in Nicaragua.

NOVEMBER 25, 1986   The Iran–Contra Affair. News of the Iran–Contra scandal breaks nationally: members of the U.S. National Security Council have engineered an illegal process to divert proceeds from secret arms sales to Iran to clandestine funding of the Nicaraguan Contras despite the U.S. Congress having created a law (the Boland Amendment) that forbids such funding. Shortly thereafter, Colonel Oliver North and Admiral John Poindexter resign from the National Security Council as a result of the congressional investigation into the diversion of funds to the Contras. During 1987, joint hearings on the Iran–Contra Affair are held by the Senate and the House of Representatives, detailing the elaborate private operation run by North.

1987

1987 Costa Rica's President Awarded Peace Prize. Costa Rican president Oscar Arias wins the Nobel Prize for peace in recognition of his efforts to bring about an end to the civil war in Nicaragua based on a Central American peace plan. Arias and representatives from Colombia, Mexico, Panama, and Venezuela create a plan for peace based on regional concerns and solutions; this is known as the "Contadora" process.

1987 Journalist Rivera Launches Talk Show. After beginning his career as a reporter, Geraldo Rivera hosts and produces his own *Geraldo* talk show, which is nationally syndicated. (*See also* biography, July 4, 1943.)

1987 Luis Valdez Writes Hollywood Screenplay. Valdez, the father of Chicano theatre, writes and directs *La Bamba* (the name of a dance from Veracruz), the screen biography of Chicano rock and roll star, Ritchie Valens. (*See also* biography, June 26, 1940.)

JANUARY 1, 1987 Univisión Television Begins. The Former Spanish International Communications Corporation and Spanish International Network are renamed Univisión on this date. In 1992, the station is affiliated with 566 cable operators in the United States and owns and operates over-the-air stations in Albuquerque, New Mexico; Austin, Dallas/Fort Worth, and San Antonio, Texas; Bakersfield, Fresno, Los Angeles, and San Francisco, California; Hartford, Connecticut; Miami, Florida; New York, New York; Philadelphia, Pennsylvania; and Phoenix and Tucson, Arizona.

APRIL 10, 1987 Telemundo Group Begins Broadcasting. Telemundo Group begins broadcasting with stations in Miami, Florida, and San Juan, Puerto Rico. The network currently owns and operates stations in Houston, Odessa, and San Antonio, Texas; Los Angeles, Modesto, Salinas, San Jose, and Stockton, California; Miami, Florida; New York, New York; and San Juan, Puerto Rico. Telemundo is also currently affiliated with stations in 22 other cities.

1988

1988 Cavazos Named Secretary of Education. President Ronald Reagan appoints the first Hispanic Secretary of Education: Dr. Lauro F. Cavazos, the former president of Texas Tech University.

1988 Ceasefire Negotiated in Nicaragua. The Sandinistas and the Contras negotiate a ceasefire in Nicaragua and plan for free and open elections.

1988 Novelist Fernández Publishes Hit Book. *Raining Backwards*, Roberto Fernández's first book to be published in English, becomes somewhat of a small press hit, receiving outstanding reviews from coast to coast in major newspapers and magazines; it is optioned to become a feature film. (*See also* biography, September 24, 1951.)

1989

1989 Américo Paredes Wins Award. In the United States, folklorist and teacher Paredes is awarded one of the nation's highest awards for a humanist, the Charles Frankel Prize, given by the National Endowment for the Arts. (*See also* biography, September 3, 1915.)

1989 Biologist Gómez-Dallmeier Becomes Director at Smithsonian. Francisco Gómez-Dallmeier serves as the director of the Man and the Biosphere Biological Diversity Program at the Smithsonian Institution in Washington, D.C. (*See also* biography, February 15, 1953.)

1989   Christiani Leads El Salvador. Alfredo Christiani is elected to the presidency of El Salvador while the civil war escalates.

1989   First Cuban Member of Congress. Ileana Ross Lehtinen is elected to the United States Congress, representing Florida's 18th Congressional District.

1989   Hispanic Family Income Data. Median family income in the United States for white families is $35,210; for blacks, $20,210; and for Hispanics, $23,450. Per capita income is $14,060 for whites, $8,750 for blacks, and $8,390 for Hispanics. Seventy percent of Hispanic female-headed households live below the poverty level.

1989   Immigration Increases. Immigration from the Americas rises from 44.3 percent of the U.S. total in 1964 to 61.4 percent in 1989. Of the major countries, Mexico accounts for 37.1 percent of total documented immigration to the United States, the next highest number of immigrants being from El Salvador, 5.3 percent.

1989   Journalist Cristina Saralegui Launches Talk Show. Saralegui resigns her position as editor in chief of the internationally distributed *Cosmopolitan-en-Español* to become the host of *The Cristina Show*, which is now the top-rated daytime talk show on Spanish-language television in the United States. (*See also* biography, January 29, 1948.)

1989   Novelist Ortiz Cofer Wins Arts Fellowship. Novelista and poet Judith Ortiz Cofer is awarded a fellowship by the National Endowment for the Arts. (*See also* biography, February 24, 1952.)

1989   Novello Named Surgeon General. U.S. president George W. Bush names Antonia Novello Surgeon General of the United States. Novello is the first Hispanic and the first woman to be named to this post.

JANUARY 20, 1989   Puerto Rican Statehood. President George Bush announces in his State of the Union address his support for Puerto Rican statehood. Later in the year, the U.S. Senate Energy and Resources Committee prepares three bills making arrangements for a plebiscite on status in Puerto Rico. A final bill is killed later that year. Another is killed in 1991, with the conclusion being that the United States is not ready to grant statehood to Puerto Rico.

DECEMBER 1989   Noriega Captured as U.S. Invades Panama. The United States invades Panama in its war against the drug trade, which is using Panama as a communications and banking post, with complicity and support from the Panamanian president, General Manuel Noriega, who is captured and taken to the United States for trial and imprisonment.

DECEMBER 28, 1989   An Open Letter to Fidel Castro. Some four hundred public figures, intellectuals, and artists from Europe and Latin America publish an open letter to Fidel Castro requesting that he hold a referendum on whether he should remain in power.

Chapter 11
1990 TO 1995

1990

1990 Civilian Leads Chile. Civilian Patricio Aylwin forges a center-left coalition in Chile to win in a referendum on military rule and replace dictator Augusto Pinochet as the nation's leader. Power is transferred to him peacefully and the way is paved for peaceful, democratic elections in December 1993.

1990 Hispanic Theatre Leader Wins Award. Miriam Colón receives the White House Hispanic Heritage Award. (*See also* biography, 1945.)

1990 IBM Chemist and Lab Leader Castro Named Fellow. George Castro is elected a fellow of the American Physical Society. (*See also* biography, March 23, 1939.)

1990 Nobel Prize Awarded to Octavio Paz. Mexican poet and essayist Octavio Paz receives the Nobel Prize for literature. (*See also* biography, March 31, 1914.)

1990 Venezuelan Bowler Monacelli Is Bowler of the Year. Amleto Andrés Monacelli is named Bowler of the Year; this is the first time that a foreigner achieves that distinction in the United States. (*See also* biography, August 27, 1961.)

1990 Writer Hijuelos Wins Pulitzer Prize.

Oscar Hijuelos is the first Hispanic writer to win the Pulitzer Prize for fiction for *The Mambo Kings Play Songs of Love*. (*See also* biography, August 24, 1951.)

FEBRUARY 1990 Chamorro Succeeds Ortega in Nicaragua. The revolutionary Sandinista government in Nicaragua is removed from power peacefully when President Daniel Ortega loses the national elections to Violeta Chamorro.

MARCH 20–23, 1990 Cubans Respond to Newspaper Survey. The Mexican newspaper *El Norte* publishes the results of a survey taken of four hundred randomly selected people in Havana. The respondents state that the greatest achievement of the government is a guaranteed education (60%) and free medical care (30%). The greatest problems are: the regime becoming a dictatorship (66%) and that there is no freedom of the press (87%). Many of the respondents (63%) say they are unhappy in Cuba, do not like their jobs (74%) and have relatives abroad (83%).

DECEMBER 1990 Russia and Cuba Sign Treaty. A one-year treaty, instead of the customary five-year treaties, is signed between Russia and Cuba. The beginning of the end of the Cuba–Soviet Union commercial and political relationship is in sight. In the early 1990s, with the Cold War over and the Soviet Union and Eastern Europe undergoing massive transformations, Cuba's position as Moscow's most important Third World client ends. Russia—the Soviet Union has dissolved into independent republics—no longer has the means or the desire to continue to pump massive aid and political support into Cuba. During the 1970s and early 1980s, Cuba receives an estimated 4 to 6 billion dollars worth of economic aid annually from the Soviet Union. It also receives approximately 1.5 billion dollars worth of military equipment between 1960 and 1970, and twice that amount from 1970 to 1975, from the eastern superpower. In addition, throughout the 1970s, approximately 70 percent of Cuba's trade is with the Soviet Union; the entire supply of oil to Cuba and all of its development loans also originate in the Soviet Union. By the late 1980s, trade with the Soviet Union has risen to 85 percent.

1991

1991   Américo Paredes Wins Mexican Award. Paredes wins the Águila Azteca (the Aztec Eagle) medal in Mexico, the highest award given a foreigner by the Mexican government. (*See also* biography, September 3, 1915.)

1991   Conductor Mata Receives Award. Eduardo Mata is a recipient of the White House Hispanic Heritage Award. (*See also* biography, September 5, 1942.)

1991   Hispanic Sociologist Julián Samora Wins Award. Samora receives the Águila Azteca (Aztec Eagle) medal, and a research center at Michigan State University is named in his honor. (*See also* biography, March 1, 1920.)

1991   NAFTA Proposal Expands Maquiladora Concept. The proposed North American Free Trade Agreement (NAFTA) between Mexico, the United States and Canada expands even further the maquiladora concept (in which Mexican factories perform cheap labor on products or semi-finished products that are shipped

back to the United States), offering potentially greater tax abatements for U.S. businesses.

1991   Physicist Alberto Baez Is Co-Winner of Award. Baez and his co-researcher, Paul Kirkpatrick, win the Dennis Gabor Award for their important role in the development of X-ray imaging optics. (*See also* biography, November 15, 1915.)

1991   New Civil Rights Action Sought. The erosion of past civil rights legislation by the Supreme Court during the Reagan and Bush administrations results in efforts by representatives of civil rights, black, and Hispanic organizations to initiate a push for a new Civil Rights Act in 1990 to return to previous standards. A series of compromises produces a watered-down Civil Rights Act in 1991.

1991   Puerto Ricans Favor Statehood. Despite the U.S. Congress's refusal to consider the statehood of Puerto Rico, a referendum is held on the island, clearly showing that the population is in favor of statehood.

MARCH 1991   Hispanic Unemployment High. Unemployment among Hispanics in the U.S. reaches 10.3 percent, roughly double the rate for whites.

MARCH 1991   Minorities Riot. A jury exonerates Los Angeles police of the brutal beating of African–American Rodney King, which was captured on videotape. African–Americans in central Los Angeles are joined by many Latinos in protesting the verdict by rioting for a number of days. The volatile reaction of the minority community leads the country to reassess social and economic policy, as well as police training as it affects minorities.

JULY 17–22, 1991   Spain, Mexico Urge Castro to Democraticize Cuba. At the Guadalajara Summit of Ibero–American presidents, presidents Felipe González of Spain and Carlos Salinas de Gortari of Mexico urge Fidel Castro to democratize Cuba. Castro has faced similar pressures to democratize from other Latin-American heads of state in the past.

AUGUST 5, 1991 Cuba Wins Gold at Pan Am Games. Cuba hosts the XI Pan American Games in Havana; its teams win 140 gold medals.

SEPTEMBER 11, 1991 Soviet Troops to Withdraw from Cuba. Mikhail Gorbachev announces the withdrawal of Soviet troops from Cuba. The withdrawal is to be completed by July 1993.

1992

1992 Guatemalan Woman Wins Peace Prize. Guatemalan Indian leader Rigoberta Menchu receives the Nobel Peace Prize. Her activities in speaking out and writing about the oppressive labor practices and military oppression against the Guatemalan Indians led to her arrest in 1988. In her memoir, *I, Rigoberta Menchu* (1985), she documents the brutal killings of four members of her family by the military.

1992 Poet Cervantes Wins Awards. Poet Lorna Dee Cervantes is awarded the Paterson Poetry Prize and the Latin American Writers Institute Award for *From the Cables of Genocide*. (*See also* biography, August 6, 1954.)

FEBRUARY 1992 FMLN, El Salvador Sign Peace Treaty. The Farabundo Martí National Liberation Front ends its guerrilla movement by signing a peace treaty with the government of El Salvador. One of the bloodiest civil wars, one that had killed some 75,000 people, finally comes to an end. In exchange for the FMLN laying down its weapons and becoming a legal political party, the government agrees to sweeping changes in the military, including the retirement of more than a hundred officers believed responsible for widespread human rights abuses. El Salvador was a key battleground for the Cold War during the 1980s, with the

United States pouring in more than $6 billion in economic and military aid to defeat the FMLN. With the fall of the Communist states in Europe, the end of the Cold War brings considerable peace benefits to Central America.

MARCH 31, 1992 Russia Withdraws Economic Support for Cuba. The dissolution of the Soviet Union under Mikhail Gorbachev, along with subsequent economic problems leads Russia to withdraw economic support from Cuba. Cuba is left foundering with a faltering economy, still suffering severely from an economic blockade enforced by the United States.

SEPTEMBER 12, 1992 Shining Path Leader Jailed. Abimael Guzmán Reynoso, the leader of the fiercest communist guerrilla movement in the Americas, the Sendero Luminoso (Shining Path), is captured in Peru by an antiterrorism squad. He remains in prison to this day. (*See also* biography, December 4, 1934 and entry, 1975.)

OCTOBER 23, 1992 The Cuban Democracy Act. President George Bush signs the Cuban Democracy Act, also known as the Torricelli Bill, which bans trade with Cuba by United States subsidiary companies in third countries and prohibits ships docking in U.S. ports if they have visited Cuba. The Torricelli Bill is heavily backed by Cuban–Americans, and Bush makes a point of signing it in Miami. The passage and signing of the bill illustrate the power of U.S. ethnic groups in creating legislation and affecting foreign policy. Upon passage of the Cuban Democracy Act, the United States is condemned by the United Nations General Assembly for maintaining its 30-year embargo of Cuba; the vote is 59 to 3, with 71 countries abstaining. Even most of the United States' allies either vote to end the embargo or they abstain.

1993

1993 Colombia Passes Anti-Discrimination

Law. After political protests and guerrilla action, the Colombian government passes the Negritude Law, which acknowledges and protects from discrimination Colombia's black population of some 5 million. The law calls for extending land titles to traditional black communities, for promoting black education, and for punishing racial discrimination. In addition, two seats in the Colombian legislature are reserved for black candidates. In 1991, Colombian Indians simultaneously win political power and two seats in the legislature. The Indians are thought to number about 500,000.

1993   Colón's Essays Published. A second collection of Jesús Colón's columns and essays (a first was published in 1961) is published under the title of *The Way It Was and Other Sketches*. (*See also* biography, 1901.)

1993   Federico Peña Named Secretary of Transportation. Peña is named to the position of Secretary of Transportation by President Bill Clinton; he is the first Hispanic to hold that post. (*See also* biography, March 15, 1947.)

1993   Henry Cisneros Named HUD Secretary. Cisneros is named to the cabinet position of Secretary of Housing and Urban Development (HUD) by President Bill Clinton; he is the first Hispanic to hold that post. (*See also* biography, June 11, 1947.)

1993   U.S. President Appoints Hispanics. President Clinton appoints Norma Contú, the former director of the Mexican American Legal Defense and Education Fund, to the position of Assistant Secretary for Civil Rights, Department of Education. The president also appoints twenty-five Hispanics to positions that need confirmation by the Senate, including Nicolás Kanellos to the National Council for the Humanities.

MAY 25, 1993   Carpio Governs Guatemala. Guatemalan president Jorge Serrano, after seizing near-dictatorial powers to silence his critics' charges of corruption and human rights abuses, is toppled from power in a coup. On June 5, the Guatemalan Congress picks Ramiro de León Carpio, a former human rights ombudsman, from a slate of three candidates to fill Serrano's term through 1995. But forced to allegiance with the military and to work with a corrupt congress, human rights abuses actually escalate under de León. According to the Catholic Church's rights office, January 1994 is the bloodiest month in three years, with 46 slayings and executions.

DECEMBER 1993   Frei Wins Free Elections in Chile. Eduardo Frei wins in free and open elections in Chile, defeating a transitional president, Patricio Aylwin, who was appointed by the military junta when it transferred power to civilian rule in 1990. The military was still under control of the right-wing former autocrats.

1994

1994   Mata Named Conductor Emeritus. Eduardo Mata is named conductor emeritus of the Dallas Symphony beginning with the 1994 season. (*See also* biography, September 5, 1942.)

JANUARY 1, 1994   NAFTA Takes Effect. The North American Free Trade Agreement (NAFTA) takes effect to eliminate all tariffs between trading partners Canada, Mexico, and the United States within fifteen years from this date. The measure is a first step towards integrating the economies of the three countries and possibly towards the creation in the future of an American common market that will include the whole hemisphere. Regarding Mexico and the United States, on this date 53.8 percent of U.S. imports from Mexico became duty free, while 31 percent of imports from the U.S., excluding those imported by maquiladoras, became duty free. The most immediately affected industries are energy, automobiles, textiles, agriculture, electricity, banks and insurance, bus and trucking services, ports, railroads, and telecommunications. NAFTA passage is opposed in the United States by labor unions, which fear the continuing loss of jobs to Mexico, and domestic industries artificially protected by tariffs, such as textiles. In Mexico, revolutionary outbreaks by Mayan peasant farmers in Chiapas are timed to coincide with the beginning of NAFTA, and, in fact, they start shortly after 12 A.M. New Year's Day. As many as one thousand Mayan guerrillas, baptizing themselves the Zapatista National Liberation Army (in honor of the revolutionary general Emiliano Zapata), with some of them uniformed and well armed, take over the important southern city of San Cristobal de las Casas, as well as the towns of Ocosingo, Las Margaritas, and others. This leads to bloody confrontations with and repression by the Mexican Army until a ceasefire is accepted by both sides on January 12, with an agreement to dialogue on the problems of the Mayas in Chiapas. The Mayas of southern Mexico, who have suffered poverty and dispossession of their communal lands for years, are now faced with the prospect of imported corn displacing their main farm product and dietary staple. All of this crystallizes in an environment of increasing indigenous overpopulation, poverty, and exploitation as Mexico bows to the demands of foreign debtors, the constraints of the International Monetary Fund to control inflation, and recent devaluations of the peso. With the economic policy of President Carlos Salinas de Gortari straining to bring Mexico into the "first world," the gap between the select few who are rich, and getting richer under new economic programs, and the poor in Mexico is accentuated. After a ceasefire is established, the government and Mayan rebels sign a tentative 32-point accord on March 2, calling for a new local government designed to serve Indian communities and a redrawn Chiapas state legislature to increase Indian representation; it also calls for the government to build roads, improve schools, upgrade health services, and extend electricity and water to remote areas in Chiapas, the poorest state in the Mexican republic. The government

agrees to grant rebels amnesty, to outlaw discrimination against Indians, and to enact laws that would allow officials to confiscate large landholdings in Chiapas and divide them among the peasants. The government also promises to help retrain farmers harmed by NAFTA. In the months following the ceasefire, Mayan farmers proceed to seize some 75,000 acres of ranch lands, claiming that the lands had been stolen from them as far back as 1819. An agrarian court in 1989 had ruled in favor of the Mayas, but the government has done nothing to enforce the ruling. President Carlos Salinas de Gortari announces, however, that redistribution of farmland is no longer an option in Mexico. Thus, the issue of land remains on the table in the continuing negotiations with the Mayas.

FEBRUARY 24–25, 1994 Mexican Farmers Protest Agricultural Crisis, Blame NAFTA. Farmers protest in marches and sit-ins in banks in Chihuahua, Guadalajara, and other northern cities because of their inability to pay off loans. Their impending foreclosures and bankruptcies, they claim, result from a change in government farm policy called for by the North American Free Trade Agreement, abolishing guaranteed prices for agricultural products and allowing increased imports. The changes leave many farmers unable to repay millions owed to private and government banks. Many of the farmers threaten a Chiapas-style armed revolt. As a result of the protests, leaders of various banks promise that no more properties will be seized, but it is uncertain how long that policy will stand. El Barzón, a national independent organization representing farmers in seventeen of Mexico's 32 states, threatens to blockade Mexico's seaports on the Gulf and Pacific coasts if the agricultural crisis, stemming from NAFTA, is not resolved soon by the government.

MARCH 11, 1994 Frei Sworn In as Chilean President. Eduardo Frei, the son of a former Chilean president, is sworn in as the first democratically elected president since the military coup ousts and assassinates Salvador Allende.

The peaceful inauguration to a democracy is facilitated by the absence of Cold War tensions. The way is prepared for the elections when power is peacefully transferred by dictator General Augusto Pinochet to civilian rule in the hands of Patricio Aylwin in 1990. The seventy-eight-year-old Pinochet remains the commander in chief of the army.

MARCH 23, 1994   Mexican Presidential Candidate Assassinated. Luis Donaldo Colosio, presidential candidate for Mexico's Institutional Revolutionary Party (PRI), is assassinated in Tijuana, Mexico, while campaigning. The conspiracy to assassinate the candidate handpicked by President Carlos Salinas de Gortari is assumed to be political in nature and provokes insecurity in Mexico's trading partners through the North American Free Trade Agreement. On March 24, acting unilaterally, the United States extends a $6 billion line of credit to Mexico. This is followed later by both NAFTA partners, the United States and Canada, moving rapidly to create a multibillion-dollar fund to stabilize Mexico's currency and protect it created by onslaughts from global speculation. The centerpiece of the fund is a $6.7 billion line of credit for the Central Bank of Mexico. All three parties to the treaty see their economies as interdependent. Critics charge that the United States has repeatedly shored up and supported the PRI with loans and lines of credit during elections and political transitions to ensure stability. Had it not been for the loans in 1988, they charge, the Party of the Democratic Revolution candidate, Cuauhtémoc Cárdenas, would have defeated Carlos Salinas de Gortari in what was a close election.

APRIL 24, 1994   El Salvador Holds Free Elections. El Salvador holds its first free elections in sixty-four years, with the right-wing Republican National Alliance (ARENA) candidate Armando Calderón Sol winning 70% of the vote. Calderón and ARENA have been associated with dictator Roberto d'Aubuisson, death squads, and the murder of Archbishop

Archbishop Oscar Romero. (Courtesy of the Arte Público Press Archives, University of Houston.)

Oscar Romero. The opposition left-wing alliance of three parties includes the Farabundo Martí National Liberation Front (FMLN), which had waged a guerrilla war for years. The left-wing alliance wins 21 out of 84 legislative seats. Calderón takes office peacefully on June 1.

MAY 8, 1994   Balladares Elected President of Panama. Ernesto Pérez Balladares, of deposed dictator Manuel Noriega's Democratic Revolutionary Party wins the Panamanian elections for president. He succeeds despite the party's record of corruption and a strong challenge from international recording and film star, Rubén Blades, who founds an independent party to break the cycle of dictatorial regimes and corruption. This is the first time in twenty-six years that the country does not vote under the shadow of a military dictatorship.

MAY 12, 1994 Mexico Holds First Presidential Debates. Mexico celebrates its first presidential debates in history in response to great pressure to open up the multiparty system, reduce election fraud, and break the monopoly of the Institutional Revolutionary Party (PRI). The three-way, internationally televised debate comes as the most direct fallout of the assassination of PRI's candidate Luis Donaldo Colosio and its quick drafting of a replacement candidate, Ernesto Zedillo. Added pressure for opening up the political process also comes from Mexico's trading partners in the North American Free Trade Agreement, who are wary of the evident political unrest that resulted not only in the assassination but also in the Indian revolts in Chiapas earlier in the year. General consensus is that Diego Fernández de Cevallos, the conservative National Action Party candidate, has won the day over Zedillo and the longstanding star of the opposition, center-left Party of the Democratic Revolution: Cuauhtémoc Cárdenas. In the 1987 elections, Cárdenas leads a dissident faction of the PRI and runs against Carlos Salinas de Gortari, the winner and current president. All PRI candidates for the presidency of Mexico have traditionally been chosen by "el dedazo," appointment by the incumbent presidency. The PRI has never gone through a primary process similar to the ones used by parties in the United States.

MAY 16, 1994 Dominican Republic Holds Election. Reluctant to give up power after holding his office for twenty of the previous twenty-eight years, eighty-seven-year-old Joaquín Balaguer, president of the Dominican Republic, sponsors long, drawn out elections that take more than a week of vote counting.

According to international observers, the elections were riddled with fraud and effectively disenfranchised thousands of supporters of his opponent, José Francisco Peña Gómez. If Peña Gómez had been elected in this hotly contested race, he would have been the Dominican Republic's first black in a nation that is 87 percent African ancestry. Balaguer is first elected president in 1966, after serving for years as a diplomat and close advisor to the Dominican dictator Rafael Trujillo. In 1990, Balaguer defeats Juan Bosch for the presidency by only 24,000 votes, in an election also characterized by fraud.

AUGUST 8, 1994 César Chávez Wins Medal of Freedom. President Bill Clinton posthumously bestows on Chávez the Medal of Freedom, the nation's highest honor for civilians. (*See also* biography, May 3, 1927.)

AUGUST 14, 1994 Free Elections in Guatemala. The historic free elections in Guatemala result in the conservative party of the former Guatemalan dictator Efraín Ríos Montt winning by a large margin with a campaign that promises to stamp out crime and corruption. Less than one-quarter of the populace vote in the elections, which are considered to be ushering in a new era in Guatemalan politics. The low voter turnout reflects Guatemalan's deep-seated dissatisfaction with Guatemala's traditional parties. The victory for the conservatives in Guatemala is foreshadowed by similar election results in El Salvador, where Armando Calderón Sol wins the presidency in June. Calderón Sol has been associated with dictator Roberto D'Aubuisson and the death squads during the civil war in El Salvador. This is El Salvador's first peacetime transfer of power between civilians in more than six decades.

NOVEMBER 8, 1994 Save Our State Initiative Passes. Californians pass Proposition 187 with 59 percent of the vote. The initiative bans undocumented immigrants from receiving public education and public benefits such as welfare and subsidized health care, except in emergency circumstances; makes it a felony to manufacture, distribute, sell, or use false citizenship or residence documents; and requires teachers, doctors, and other city, county, and state officials to report suspected and apparent illegal aliens to the California attorney general and the Immigration and Naturalization Service (INS). Governor Pete Wilson issues an executive order for state officials to begin following the initiative by cutting off government services to undocumented pregnant women and nursing home patients. On November 9, 1994, eight lawsuits are filed in state and federal courts protesting the measure. On November 16, 1994, Judge William Matthew Byrne, Jr., of the Federal Court in Los Angeles, temporarily blocks California state officials from enforcing the proposition. Mark Slavkin, president of the Los Angeles Unified School District Board, and other officials are threatened with recall efforts for opposing Proposition 187. Similar proposals are being considered on the federal level to severely limit or ban undocumented immigrants from receiving public benefits and attending public schools. Hispanics and other minorities perceive the initiative as an anti-immigrant sentiment stemming from a weak economy.

NOVEMBER 16, 1994 Courts Block Implementation of Proposition 187. In Los Angeles, California, Federal District Court Judge William Matthew Byrne, Jr., temporarily blocks the enforcement of Proposition 187, stating that it raises serious constitutional questions. Judge Byrne exempts the provisions that increase penalties for manufacturing or using false immigration documents.

1995

JANUARY 1995 Efforts to Curb Affirmative Action Laws Begin. Signatures are collected to put an initiative on the 1996 ballot that states "Neither the State of California nor any of its

political subdivision or agents shall use race, sex, color, ethnicity or national origin as a criterion for either discriminating against or granting preferential treatment to any individual or group in the operation of the State's system of public employment, public education or public contracting." The initiative is labeled Son of 187—a reference to Proposition 187, the immigration-control measure passed by Californians on November 8, 1994.

FEBRUARY 14, 1995 Cuban Film Receives Oscar Nomination. Tomás Gutiérrez Alea's 1994 film, *Strawberry and Chocolate,* is nominated for an Academy Award in the category of best foreign language film. This is the first Cuban film ever nominated for an Oscar. (*See also* biography, December 11, 1928.)

FEBRUARY 21, 1995 Mexico Receives International Loan Package. President Bill Clinton of the United States is successful in arranging for an international loan-guarantee package of $53 billion, with $20 million from the United States, to prop up the devalued peso and restore confidence in the Mexican economy. On December 20, 1994, after the PRI ruling party's victory at the polls, outgoing President Carlos Salinas de Gortari allows the peso to float against the dollar, thus revealing the extent of weakness in the economy that has been covered up during the negotiations and implementation of the North American Free Trade Agreement (NAFTA). With additional stress to the economy and international investor confidence in Mexico brought on by the assassination of a presidential candidate during the elections and the armed insurrection by Maya Indians in Chiapas, the peso plunges, losing one-third of its value. During January and February, a monetary and investment crisis takes hold of the economy, and the Mexican stock market, *Bolsa,* loses forty percent of its value. After Clinton is unsuccessful in moving Congress to help abate Mexico's monetary crisis, which also affects the U.S. economy, Clinton taps sources not needing congressional approval to put together the $20 billion package. Clinton goes on to appeal to the International Monetary Fund, Canada, and various European and South American countries to come to the aid of Mexico. As soon as the loan package is announced, both the peso and Mexican stocks stabilize, and the Mexican nation prepares for some of the strictest austerity policies in its history, including placing oil revenues as collateral for the U.S. loans. In the wake of much higher prices for even the most basic of staples, and rising unemployment in Mexico, the United States is bracing for another large wave of immigrant Mexican labor.

SIGNIFICANT DOCUMENTS

THE LAWS OF BURGOS (1512)

Doña Juana, by the Grace of God Queen of Castile, León, Granada, Toledo, Galicia, Sevilla, Córdoba, Murcia, Jaén, the Algarbes, Algeciras, Gibraltar, the Canary Islands, and the Indies, Islands, and Mainland of the Ocean Sea; Princess of Aragón, the Two Sicilies, and Jerusalem; Archduchess of Austria; Duchess of Austria, Burgundy, and Brabant; Countess of Flanders and Tyrol; Lady of Biscay, Molina, etc.

To you, the Alcalde Mayor and constables of the Island of San Juan, which is in the Indies of the Ocean Sea, and to our officers of the said Island, and to all other justices and officers of it whatsoever, present and future, and to the town councils, justices, regidores, knights, squires, officers, and citizens of the said Island, its towns and villages, and to any other persons whatsoever to whom what is contained in this my letter may apply in any way, and to each and every one of you:

Whereas, the King, my Lord and Father, and the Queen, my Mistress and Mother (may she rest in glory!), always desired that the chief and Indians of the Island of Española be brought to a knowledge of our Holy Catholic Faith, and,

Whereas, they commanded that certain ordinances be drawn up, which were indeed drawn up, by their Highnesses, as well as, at their command, by the Comendador Bobadilla and the Comendador Mayor de Alcántara, former governors of the said Island, and afterward by Don Diego Columbus,

our Admiral, Viceroy, and Governor of it, and by our officers who reside there, and,

Whereas, it has become evident through long experience that nothing has sufficed to bring the said chiefs and Indians to a knowledge of our Faith (necessary for their salvation), since by nature they are inclined to idleness and vice, and have no manner of virtue or doctrine (by which Our Lord is disserved), and that the principal obstacle in the way of correcting their vices and having them profit by and impressing them with the doctrine is that their dwellings are remote from the settlements of the Spaniards who go hence to reside in the said Island, because, although at the time the Indians go to serve them they are indoctrinated in and taught the things of our Faith, after serving they return to their dwellings where, because of the distance and their own evil inclinations, they immediately forget what they have been taught and go back to their customary idleness and vice, and when they come to serve again they are as new in the doctrine as they were at the beginning, because, although the Spaniard who accompanies them to their village, as is there ordered, reminds them of it and reprehends them, they having no fear of him, do not profit by it and tell him to leave them in idleness, since that is their reason for returning to their said village, and that their only purpose and desire is to do with themselves what they will, without regard for any virtue, and,

Whereas, this is contrary to our Faith, and,

Whereas, it is our duty to seek a remedy for it in every way possible, it was considered by the King, my Lord and Father, and by several members of my council and by persons of good life, letters, and conscience, and they having informed themselves from others who had much knowledge and experience of the affairs of the said Island, and of the life and customs of the said Indians, gave it as their opinion that the most beneficial thing that could be done at present would be to remove the said chiefs and Indians to the vicinity of the villages and communities of the Spaniards—this for many considerations—thus, by continual association with them, as well as by attendance at church on feast days to hear Mass and the divine offices, and by observing the conduct of the Spaniards, as well as the preparation and care that the Spaniards will display in demonstrating and teaching them, while they are together, the things of our Holy Catholic Faith, it is clear that they will the sooner learn them and, having learned them, will not forget them as they do now. And if some Indian should fall sick he will be quickly succored and treated, and thus the lives of many, with the help of Our Lord, will be saved who now die because no one knows they are sick; and all will be spared the hardship of coming and going, which will be a great relief to them, because their dwellings are now so remote from the Spanish communities, so that those who now die from sickness and hunger on the journey, and who do not receive the sacraments which as Christians they are obligated to receive, will not die [unshriven], because they will be given the sacraments in the said communities as soon as they fall sick; and infants will be baptized at birth; and all will serve with less hardship to themselves and with greater profit to the Spaniards, because they will be with them more continually; and the visitors who have them in charge will visit them better and more frequently and will have them provided with everything they need, and will not permit their wives and daughters to be taken from them, as now happens while they live at a distance; and many other evils and hardships will cease which the Indians now suffer because they are so remote, and which are not described

here because they are notorious; and many other advantages will accrue to them for the salvation of their souls, as well as for the profit and utility of their persons and the conservation of their lives; and so,

Therefore, for these reasons and for many others that could be adduced, it was agreed that the improvement and remedy of all the aforesaid, the said chiefs and Indians should forthwith be brought to dwell near the villages and communities of the Spaniards who inhabit that Island, so that they may be treated and taught and looked after as is right and as we have always desired; and so I command that henceforth that which is contained below be obeyed and observed, as follows;

I

First, since it is our determination to remove the said Indians and have them dwell near the Spaniards, we order and command that the persons to whom the said Indians are given, or shall be given, in encomienda, shall at once and forthwith build, for every fifty Indians, four lodges [*bohíos*] of thirty by fifteen feet, and have the Indians plant 5,000 hillocks (3,000 in cassava and 2,000 in yams), 250 pepper plants, and 50 cotton plants, and so on in like manner, increasing or decreasing the amount according to the number of Indians they have in encomienda, and these shall be settled next the estates of the Spaniards who have them in encomienda, well situated and housed, and under the eyes of you, our said Admiral and judges and officers, and of our visitor who will be in charge of it, or of the person whom you, our said Admiral and judges and officers, shall send for the aforesaid purpose, and he, I charge and command you, shall be such as will be competent in this matter; and the persons who have the said Indians in their charge [in encomienda] shall have them sow, in season, half a *fanega* of maize, and shall also give them a dozen hens and a cock to raise and enjoy the fruit thereof, the chickens as well as the eggs, and as soon as the Indians are brought to the estates they shall be given all the aforesaid as their own property; and the person whom you send for this purpose shall tell them it is for their own use and that it is given them in exchange for what they are leaving behind, to enjoy as their own property. And we command that the persons to whom they are given in encomienda shall keep it for them so that they may enjoy it as their own; and we command that this property shall not be sold or taken from them by any person to whom they may be given in encomienda, or by anyone else, but that it shall belong to the said Indians to whom it is assigned and to their descendants, even though this said person sell the estate in which they are, or the said Indians be removed from him; and we declare and command that the person to whom the said Indians are given in encomienda may utilize the goods that the said Indians abandon when they are brought to the estates of the Spaniards, each according to the number of Indians he has, in order to maintain them with such goods; and after the said persons have removed the said goods I command you, our said Admiral and judges and officers, to have the lodges of the said villages burned, since the Indians will have no further use from them: this so that they will have no reason to return whence they have been brought.

II

After the aforesaid has been done, we order and command that all the chiefs and Indians dwelling on the Island of Española, now or in the future, shall be brought from their present dwelling places to the villages and communities of the Spaniards who reside, now or in the future, on the said Island; and in order that they be brought of their own volition and suffer no harm from the removal, we hereby command Don Diego Columbus, our Admiral, Viceroy, and Governor of the said Island, and our appellate judges and officers of it, to have them brought in the manner that seems best, with the least possible harm to the said chiefs and Indians, to this end encouraging them and urging them with praise; and we charge and command them most earnestly to do this with much care, fidelity, and diligence, with greater regard for the good treatment and conservation of the said Indians than for any other respect, desire, or interest, particular or general.

III

Also, we order and command that the citizen to whom the said Indians are given in encomienda shall, upon the land that is assigned to him, be obliged to erect a structure to be used for a church, on a site selected by you, the said Admiral, judges, and officers, or by the visitor appointed by you; and in the said church he shall place an image of Our Lady and a bell with which to call the Indians to prayer; and the person who has them in encomienda shall be obliged to have them called by the bell at nightfall and go with them to the said church, and have them cross themselves and bless themselves, and together recite the *Ave Maria* the *Pater Noster,* the *Credo,* and the *Salve Regina,* in such wise that all of them shall hear the said person, and the said person hear them, so that he may know who is performing well and who ill, and correct the one who is wrong; and since the period we command to be allowed them for rest before nightfall is principally for the purpose of having them rested at the hour of evening prayer, in case any Indian should fail to come to the said church at the said time, we command that on the day following he shall not be allowed to rest during the said period; but he shall still be urged to go to prayers the next night; and we also command that each morning, before they go to work, they shall be obliged to go to the said church and pray as they do in the evening; but they shall not be obliged on the account to rise earlier than is customary, that is, at full daylight.

IV

Also, in order to discover how each one is progressing in things of the Faith, we command that every two weeks the said person who has them in charge shall examine them to see what each one knows particularly and to teach them what they do not know; and he shall also teach them the Ten Commandments and the Seven Deadly Sins and the Articles of the Faith, that is, to those he thinks has the capacity and ability to learn them; but all this shall be done with great love and gentleness; and the person who fails to obey this shall incur a penalty of six gold pesos, two of which shall be for our treasury, two for his accuser, and two for the judge who sentences him and executes the sentence; and I command that the penalty shall be executed at once upon the persons of those who incur it.

V

Also, because I have been informed that the Spaniards and Indians who live on the estates go for a long time without hearing Mass, and since it is right that they should hear it, at least on feast days and Sundays, and since it is impossible for each estate to maintain a priest to say Mass, we order and command that where four or five estates, more or less, are within the distance of a league, on that estate which is nearest the others a church shall be built, and in this church an image of Our Lady and a bell shall be placed, so that every Sunday and obligatory feast day they may come there to pray and hear Mass, and also to hear the good advice that the priests who say Mass shall give them; and the priests who say Mass shall teach them the Commandments and the Articles of the Faith, and the other things of the Christian doctrine. Therefore, in order that they be instructed in the things of the Faith and become accustomed to pray and hear Mass, we command that the Spaniards who are on the estates with the said Indians and have charge of them shall be obliged to bring them all together to the said church in the morning and remain with them until after Mass is said; and after Mass they shall bring them back to the estates and give them their pots of cooked meat, in such wise that they eat on that day better than on any other day of the week, and, although the priest who says Mass will sometimes be absent, nevertheless they shall bring them even so to the church to pray and receive good advice. If, however, the other estates are in places where the Indians can easily come to hear Mass, the said citizen shall be obliged to bring them thither, on pain that any person who has charge of the said Indians and fails to bring them [to Mass] shall incur a penalty of ten gold pesos: six pesos as prescribed in the preceding article, and of the four remaining, two shall be for the erection of the said church and two for the priest who teaches the Indians.

VI

Also, since it is our will that the best means be sought to persuade the Indians to accept the things of our Holy Catholic Faith, and since if they should have to travel more than a league to hear Mass on Sundays and feast days it would be a grave hardship for them, we order and command that, if beyond the aforesaid league where we command the said church to be built there should be other estates, even though they should be in the same district, a church shall be erected there in the aforesaid manner.

VII

Also we order and command the prelates and priests who, now and in the future, collect the tithes from the estates where the said Indians are, to maintain priests continually in the said churches of the said estates, to say masses on Sundays and obligatory feasts days; and [we order and command] also that the said priests shall have charge of confessing those who know how to confess, and of teaching those who do not. Thus Our Lord will be served, and, if the contrary is done, He has been and will be disserved.

VIII

Also, we order and command that at the mines where there are a sufficient number of Indians churches shall be built, in convenient places approved by you, our said Admiral, judges, and officers, or by the person selected by you, so that all the Indians who are at the mines may hear Mass on the said feast days; and we command the settlers and Spaniards who bring the said Indians to extract gold, to observe with them the same procedure that is followed on the estates, as prescribed above, under the same penalties applied in the same manner.

IX

Also we order and command that whoever has fifty Indians or more in encomienda shall be obliged to have a boy (the one he considers most able) taught to read and write, and the things of our Faith, so that he may later teach the said

Indians, because the Indians will more readily accept what he says than what the Spaniards and settlers tell them; and if the said person has a hundred Indians or more he shall have two boys taught as prescribed; and if the person who has Indians does not have them taught as ordered, we command that the visitor who in our name has charge shall have them taught at the cost of such person. And because the King, my Lord and Father, and I have been informed that several persons are employing Indian boys as pages, we order and command that the person who does so shall be obliged to teach them to read and write, and all the other things that have been prescribed above; and if he fails to do so the boys shall be taken from him and given to another, because the principal aim and desire of the King, my Lord and Father, and mine, is that in the said parts and in each one of them our Holy Catholic Faith shall be planted and deeply rooted, so that the souls of the said Indians may be saved.

X

Also, we order and command that each and every time an Indian falls sick in a place where there is a priest, the priest shall be obliged to go to him and recite the *Credo* and other profitable things of our Holy Catholic Faith, and, if the Indian should know how to confess, he shall confess him, without charging him any fee for it; and, because there are some Indians who already understand the things of our Holy Faith, we command that the said priests shall be obliged to have them confess once a year, and also that they shall go with a Cross to the Indians who die and shall bury them, without charging any fee for it or for the confession; and if the said Indians die on the estates we command that the Christian settlers there shall bury them in the churches of the said estates; and if they die in other places where there are no churches they shall be buried where it seems best, on pain that he who has Indians in his charge and fails to bury them or have them buried, shall pay four gold pesos, which shall be applied and distributed in the following manner: one for our treasury, one for his accuser, one for the judge who sentences him, and

one for the priest at the estate or village where the said Indians are buried.

XI

Also, we order and command that no person having Indians in encomienda, or any other person, shall use Indians as carriers for transporting supplies to Indians at the mines, but that when the latter are removed from one place to another they shall carry their own effects and provisions, because we have been informed that there are no beasts of burden there; and the aforesaid is to be observed and obeyed, on pain that the person who employs the said Indians as carriers against the tenor and form of this article shall pay, for each offense, two gold pesos, which shall be for the hospital of the village where the said settler lives; and if the burden which he thus puts on the Indians is of foodstuffs, he shall lose it also and it shall go to the said hospital.

XII

Also, we order and command that all the Spanish inhabitants and settlers who have Indians in encomienda shall be obliged to have all infants baptized within a week of their birth, or before, if it is necessary; and if there is no priest to do so, the person who has charge of the said estate shall be obliged to baptize them, according to the custom in such emergencies, on pain that he who fails to obey this article shall incur, for each offense, the penalty of three gold pesos, which we command shall be for the church where the said infants are baptized.

XIII

Also, we order and command that, after the Indians have been brought to the estates, all the founding [of gold] that henceforth is done on the said Island shall be done in the manner prescribed below: that is, the said persons who have Indians in encomienda shall extract gold with them for five months in the year and, at the end of these five months, the said Indians shall rest forty days, and the day they cease their labor of extracting gold shall be noted on a certificate, which shall be given to the miners who go to the mines; and upon the day thus designated all the Indians shall be released in the district where the founding is to be done, so that all the Indians of each district shall go to their houses on the same day to rest during the said forty days; and in all the said forty days no one shall employ any Indians in extracting gold, unless it is a slave, on pain that for every Indian that any person brings to the mines in the said period of forty days shall pay half a gold peso, applied in the aforesaid manner; and we command that in the said forty days you, the said officers, shall be obliged to finish the founding. And we command that the Indians who thus leave the mines shall not, during the said forty days, be ordered to do anything whatever, save to plant the hillocks necessary for their subsistence that season; and the persons who have the said Indians in encomienda shall be obliged, during these forty days of rest, to indoctrinate them in the things of our Faith more than on other days, because they will have the opportunity and means to do so.

XIV

Also, since we have been informed that if the Indians are not allowed to perform their customary dances [areytos] they will receive great harm, we order and command that they shall not be prevented from performing their dances on Sundays and feast days, and also, on work days, if they do not on that account neglect their usual work stint.

XV

Also, since the most important consideration for the good treatment and increase of the Indians is their subsistence, we order and command that all persons who have Indians shall be obliged to maintain those who are on their estates and there to keep continually a sufficiency of bread and yams and peppers, and, at least on Sundays and feast days, to give them dishes of cooked meat, as is prescribed in the article that says that on feast days when they go to Mass they shall be given better pots of meat than on other days; and on the days when meat is to be given to the Indians of the said estates it shall be given them in the same manner as is prescribed for the Indians at the mines; that is,

they shall be given bread and peppers and a pound of meat a day, and on feast days fish or sardines or other things for their subsistence; and those who are on the estates shall be allowed to go to their lodges to eat, on pain that the person who has the said Indians and does not fulfill all the aforesaid contained in this article shall incur for each offense the penalty of two gold pesos, which shall be distributed as prescribed above; and if he should be fined three times and still fail to correct himself, at the fourth conviction the Indians he has in encomienda shall be taken from him and given to another.

XVI

Also, we order and command that, among the other things of our Faith that shall be taught to the Indians, they shall be made to understand that they may not have more than one wife at a time, nor may they abandon her; and if the persons who have them in encomienda see that they have sufficient discretion and knowledge to undertake matrimony and govern their households, they shall procure their lawful marriage, as our Holy Mother Church commands, with the wife of their choice; and we especially command that the chiefs be made to understand that they may not take wives related to them, and we command that the visitors shall be responsible for their understanding this, repeating it to them very frequently and telling them, or having them told, all the reasons for their so doing, and how by this action they will save their souls.

XVII

Also, we order and command that now and in the future all the sons of chiefs of the said Island, of the age of thirteen or under, shall be given to the friars of the Order of St. Francis who may reside on the said Island, as the King my Lord has commanded in one of his decrees, so that the said friars may teach them to read and write, and all the other things of our Holy Catholic Faith; and they shall keep them for four years and then return them to the persons who have them in encomienda, so that these sons of chiefs may teach the said Indians, for the Indians will accept it more readily from them;

and if the said chiefs should have two sons they shall give one to the said friars, and the other we command shall be the one who is taught by the person who has him in encomienda.

XVIII

Also, we order and command that no pregnant woman, after the fourth month, shall be sent to the mines, or made to plant hillocks, but shall be kept on the estates and utilized in household tasks, such as making bread, cooking, and weeding; and after she bears her child she shall nurse it until it is three years old, and in all this time she shall not be sent to the mines, or made to plant hillocks, or used in anything else that will harm the infant, on pain that the person who has Indians in encomienda and fails to obey this shall, for the first offense, incur the penalty of six gold pesos, distributed as prescribed above, and for the second offense the woman and her infant shall be taken from him, and for the third, the woman and her husband and six other Indians.

XIX

Also, we order and command that all those on the said Island who have Indians in encomienda, now or in the future, shall be obliged to give to each of them a hammock in which to sleep continually; and they shall not allow them to sleep on the ground, as hitherto they have been doing; and they shall give them this hammock within the twelve months immediately following their receiving the said Indians in encomienda. And we command our visitors carefully to observe whether each Indian has the said hammock, and to urge the said persons who have them in encomienda, if they have not already supplied hammocks, to do so within the said following twelve months, [on pain that the person who fails to obey the aforesaid shall incur the penalty of . . . pesos], and this penalty we command you, our said Admiral and judges, to execute on the person who incurs it. And since it is said that when anything is given to an Indian he immediately wishes to exchange it for something else, we command that the said Indians be admonished by the visitors that they are not to exchange the said hammocks for other things, and if they

exchange them, we command the said visitors to punish the Indians who do so and to void the exchanges they have made.

XX

Also, we order and command that, in order that henceforth the Indians may have wherewith the better to clothe and adorn themselves, the person who has them in encomienda shall give to each of them a gold peso every year, which he shall be obliged to give them in wearing apparel, in the sight of with the consent of our visitor, and this gold peso shall be understood to be in addition to the said hammock that we commanded above to be given to each of them. And since it is just that the said chiefs and their wives should be better dressed and better treated than the other Indians, we command that one *real* be deducted from the gold peso to be paid to the latter, and that with this said *real* the said visitor shall have clothing purchased for the said chiefs and their wives; and we command you, our said Admiral, judges, and officers, to have special care to see that this article is observed, obeyed, and fulfilled.

XXI

Also, in order that each one may employ only the Indians he has in encomienda, and that no one may employ those belonging to another, we order and command that no person or persons shall employ an Indian belonging to another, or receive him in his house or estate or mine, or anywhere; but if an Indian should be traveling from one place to another, we permit him to be detained for one night on an estate, provided that immediately on the following morning he is sent forth to go and serve his master; and we command that the person who fails to obey this, and detains an Indian not given to him in encomienda, shall incur the penalty of the loss of one Indian of his own for every Indian of another he thus detains; and the said Indian shall be given to the accuser and the other returned to his master; and if the said person has no Indians he shall suffer the penalty, for the first offense, of six gold *castellanos;* for the second, twelve; and for the third penalty shall be doubled again and distributed in the prescribed manner;

and if he has no Indians or money the penalty shall be commuted to one hundred lashes.

XXII

Also, we order and command that, in order that the chiefs may the more easily have people to serve them in their personal needs (provided that the Indians of the said chiefs are distributed among more than one person), if a chief has forty subjects two of them shall be given to him for his service; if he has seventy he shall be given three; if a hundred, four; from a hundred to a hundred and fifty, six; and from that point onward, even though he should have more subjects, he shall not be given more; and these said Indians who are to serve him shall be chosen by the said chief, provided they are man and wife and child; and we command that the said Indians shall be chosen from among those belonging to the person who has the largest share of the subjects of the said chief in encomienda. And we command that they [the said chiefs] shall be well treated and not forced to work save at light tasks, so that they may be occupied and not idle, thus avoiding the difficulties that might arise from idleness. And we command our visitors to look carefully after the said chiefs and Indians, and to feed them well and teach them the thing of our Holy Faith better than they teach the others, because [the said chiefs] will be able to indoctrinate the other Indians, who will accept it more readily from them.

XXIII

Also, we order and command that all persons who have in encomienda Indians of the said Island of Española, as well as those brought from other island, shall be obliged to give an accounting to the visitors, within ten days, of those who die and those who are born; and we command that the said visitors shall be obliged to keep a book in which to enter every person who has Indians in encomienda, and the Indians that each one has, with their names, so that those who are born may be entered, and those who die removed, and the visitor have continually a complete record of the increase or decrease of the said Indians, on pain of two pesos gold for each offense, levied against each of the said settlers who fails to do so; and this penalty shall be divided among the treasury and the accuser and the judge who sentences him; and the visitors shall be obliged to bring to each founding an account of all the aforesaid and give it to our officers there, so that they may know how much the Indians have increased or decreased between one founding and the next, and they shall so inform us when they remit us the gold that falls to our share in the said founding.

XXIV

Also, we order and command that no person or persons shall dare to beat any Indian with sticks, or whip him, or call him dog, or address him by any name other than his proper name alone; and if an Indian should deserve to be punished for something he has done, the said person having him in charge shall bring him to the visitor for punishment, on pain that the person who violates this article shall pay, for every time he beats or whips an Indian or Indians, five pesos gold; and if he should call an Indian dog, or address him by any name other than his own, he shall pay one gold peso, to be distributed in the manner stated.

XXV

Also, since we have been informed that many persons having Indians in encomienda employ them in commerce or trade, thereby disserving us, we order and command that each person having Indians in encomienda shall be obliged to bring the third part of them to the mines to extract gold, or more than the third part if he so desires, on pain that if he fails to observe this he shall incur a penalty of three gold pesos for each Indian lacking in the said third part to be sent to the mines; but we permit the residents of La Sabana and Villanueva de Yaquimo to be excused from bringing Indians to the mines, because of their remoteness; but we command them to employ the said Indians in the manufacture of hammocks and cotton shirts, in raising pigs, and in other activities profitable to the community. And whereas I have learned that when the Indians are removed to the estates of the settlers it is necessary to employ some of them at once in the erection of lodges, and in other tasks that the settlers will indicate to them as required for their estates, and because of which they will not immediately be able to send the third part to the mines, I command you, the said Admiral, judges, and officers, forthwith to fix for all this the period you think should be allowed, making it as brief as possible.

XXVI

Also, we order and command that those who have Indians [in encomienda], but whose estates are so remote from the mines that they cannot supply provisions for the said Indians [being sent thither], shall combine their Indians with those of others who have estates in the vicinity, in order to supply provisions for the said Indians, one person supplying the provisions and the other the Indians, provided that the master of the Indians [being sent to the mines] sends along with them a miner who will see to it that they do not lack necessities; and the aforesaid shall not be done through a third party, or in any way other than that prescribed, under the penalty stated above.

XXVII

Also, since many Indians have been brought, and are daily being brought, from the neighboring islands, we order and command that these said Indians be indoctrinated in and taught the things of the Faith, in the form and manner that we have commanded to be observed with the other Indians of the said Island; also, that they shall be inspected by the said visitors, unless they are slaves, for these may be treated by their owner as he pleases; but we command that they shall not be treated with that rigor and harshness with which other slaves are customarily treated, but rather with much love and gentleness, in order the better to incline them to the things of our Faith.

XXVIII

Also, we order and command that each and every time any person vacates the Indians he has in encomienda, either by death or for some other reason for which he may deserve to lose them, the person to whom we grant the said estate in encomienda shall be obliged to purchase it from the one who has vacated the said Indians, or from

his heirs, and it shall be appraised under oath by two persons who are acquainted with it, to be named by you, the said Admiral, judges, and officers; and the said owner shall be obliged to sell it at their appraisal, so that the said Indians do not have to change their residence, because the persons to whom they are given [in encomienda] must be residents of the community to which the said Indians were allotted.

XXIX

Also, we order and command that in each community of the said Island there shall be two visitors in charge of inspecting the whole community, together with its mines and estates, its shepherds and swineherds, and they shall ascertain how the Indians are being taught in the things of our Faith, and how their persons are being treated, and how they are being maintained, and how they or the persons who have them in charge are obeying and fulfilling these our ordinances, and all the other things that each of them is obliged to do; and we command them to have particular care in all this, and we charge their consciences with it.

XXX

Also, we order and command that the said visitors shall be selected and named by you, the said Admiral, judges, and officers, in the form and manner you think best, provided they are selected from among the oldest inhabitants of the communities in which they are to serve; and we command that they shall be given and assigned some Indians in encomienda, in addition to those given them for their responsibility and work in the use and exercise of the said office; and these Indians shall be chosen by you, the said Admiral, judges, and officers; and it is our will that if the said visitors should become negligent in enforcing the said ordinances, or if any of them fail to carry out the aforesaid, especially in the matter of subsistence and hammocks, their own Indians that they have in encomienda shall on that account be removed from them.

XXXI

Also, we order and command that the said visitors shall be obliged twice a year to inspect all the places where there are Indians of their charge, once at the beginning of the year, and again at the middle; and we command that one of them alone shall not make the inspection both times, but each one once, so that each may know what the other is doing and so that everything may be done with the necessary care and diligence.

XXXII

Also, we order and command that no visitor shall bring to his house or estate any lost or runaway Indians he finds in the estates or elsewhere, but that immediately upon finding them he shall deposit them with a person of good conscience whom he shall select; but first he shall endeavor to discover who their master is, and when he has done so he shall deliver the Indians to him at once; otherwise, they shall be deposited as prescribed until the said master is found, on pain that the visitor who is discovered with an Indian in his possession or in his house shall lose an Indian of his own, to be given to his accuser, and the said runaway Indian taken by the visitor shall be restored to his master.

XXXIII

Also, we order and command that the said visitors shall be obliged to have and keep in their possession a copy of these ordinances, signed by the said Admiral, judges, and officers, together with the instructions that we command you, the said Admiral, judges, and officers, to give them, by which they may the better know what they must do, observe, and obey; and upon the visitor who fails to obey, the aforesaid penalties shall be executed.

XXXIV

Also, we order and command that you, the said Admiral, judges, and officers, shall inquire once every two years into the way in which the said visitors are fulfilling their duties, and you shall have their *residencias* taken, in which it shall be ascertained how they have enforced these ordinances, each according to his obligation. And we command that the said visitors shall be obliged, at the time of their residencias, to give you, the said Admiral, judges, and officers, a very complete accounting of all the Indians and their number,

each reporting for the place in his charge, and how many have been born and how many have died in those two years, so that the Admiral, judges, and officers may send us an accounting of it all, which shall be signed by you and the visitors, to the end that I may be well informed of everything.

XXXV

Also, we order and command that no inhabitant or resident of the said communities of the said Island of Española, or of any other island, shall have in encomienda, by grant or otherwise, more than a hundred and fifty Indians, or fewer than forty.

Therefore, I command you, our said Admiral, judges, and officers, and each and every one of you, present and future, and all other persons whatsoever to whom the contents of these ordinances may apply, to consider the ordinances incorporated above and those others mentioned, and to observe and obey them, and to have them observed and obeyed and executed completely, each according to its contents; and you shall execute and cause to be executed the penalties upon such as incur them; and also, you shall observe and obey the said ordinances yourselves, according to the manner and form prescribed therein, under the penalties stated. Moreover, in case of disobedience, you shall incur the loss of the Indians you have in encomienda, and they shall be considered vacated, so that we may assign them to whomsoever we please; and you shall not act counter to their tenor and form, nor shall you permit them to be violated at any time or in any way. And if, in order to fulfill and execute the aforesaid, you should have need of favor and aid, I hereby command all town councils, justices, regidores, knights, squires, officers, and citizens of the said Island of Española to render you such favor and aid as you shall demand of them, under whatever penalties that you in our name shall impose which by these presents I impose and consider imposed; and I hereby give you authority to execute them upon all those who fail to obey you.

Also, so that this my letter may be brought to the attention of all, and that none may plead ignorance of it, I command that it be read in the squares and markets and other customary places of the said Island of Española by the public crier, in the presence of a notary and witnesses, none of whom shall disobey it in any way, on pain of my displeasure and 50,000 *maravedís* for my treasury, to be levied against each offender. Moreover, I command him who shows them this my letter to cite them to appear before my at my court, wherever I may be, within one hundred days of the time they are cited, under the said penalty; and, also, under the same penalty, I command any notary who should be called upon to do so, to give testimony thereof signed with his rubric, so that I may know how my command is being observed.

Done in this City of Burgos, December 27, 1512.

I, the King.

I, Lope Conchillos, Secretary to the Queen our Mistress

The Bishop of Palencia—Count [of Pernia].

AMENDMENTS TO THE LAWS OF BURGOS (1513)

Doña Juana, etc. . .

Know, that the King, my Lord and Father, and I, seeing how necessary it was for the service of God Our Lord, and ours, and for the salvation of souls and the increase and good treatment of the Indians of the said Island, as well as for its citizens, consulted prelates and religious and certain members of our Council, which we convened for the purpose, after which we commanded that certain ordinances be drawn up by which the said Indians were to be indoctrinated and taught and brought to a knowledge of our Holy Catholic Faith, and by which the said Indians were to be well treated and reduced to settlements, as is explained at greater length in the said ordinances. Thereupon the King, my Lord and Father, and I were informed that, although the said ordinances were very useful, profitable, and necessary, as well as fitting, it was said that some of them had need of further elucidation and modification. Therefore, since it has always been our intent, desire, and will, to have

greater regard for the salvation of souls and the indoctrination and good treatment of the said Indians than for any other consideration, we commanded several prelates and religious of the Order of St. Dominic, and several members of our Council, and preachers and learned men of good life and conscience, very prudent and zealous in the service of Our Lord, to consider the said ordinances and amend them, add to them or reduce them, and modify them as might be necessary. Therefore, having considered the said ordinances and listened to the religious who have knowledge of the affairs of the said Island and the conditions and habits of the said Indians, they, together with other prelates and members of our Council, amended and modified the said ordinances as follows:

I

First, we order and command that Indian women married to Indian men who have been given in encomienda shall not be forced to go and come and serve with their husbands, at the mines or elsewhere, unless it is by their own free will, or unless their husbands wish to take them; but the said wives shall be obliged to work on their own land or on that of their husbands, or on the lands of the Spaniards, who shall pay them the wages agreed upon with them or with their husbands; but if the said wives should become pregnant we command that the ordinances we issued covering this situation be observed, on pain that he who does the contrary shall, besides suffering the penalty prescribed in the said ordinance, lose the Indian woman whom he thus forces to work, as well as her husband and children, who shall be given in encomienda to others.

II

Also, we order and command that Indian children under fourteen years of age shall not be compelled to work at tasks [of adults] until they have attained the said age or more; but they shall be compelled to work at, and serve in, tasks proper to children, such as weeding the fields and the like, on their parents' estates (if they have parents); and those above the age of fourteen shall be under the authority of their parents until they are of age and married. Those who have neither father nor mother, we command shall be given in encomienda by the person who has our authority to do so, and he shall give them in charge to persons of good conscience who shall see that they are taught and indoctrinated in the things of our Holy Faith, and employ them on their estates in tasks set by our appellate judges, in which they can work without endangering their health, provided that they [the encomenderos] feed them and pay them their proper wages at the rate fixed by our said judges, and provided that they [the encomenderos] do not prevent their attendance at Christian doctrine at the appointed time. And if any of the said boys should wish to learn a trade they may freely do so, and they may not be compelled to serve in, or work at, anything else while they are learning the said trade.

III

Also, we order and command that unmarried Indian women who are under the authority of their parents, mothers or fathers, shall work with them on their lands, or on the lands of others by agreement with their parents; and those not under authority of their fathers and mothers shall, to prevent their becoming vagabonds and bad women, and to keep them from vice and teach them the doctrine, be constrained to be with the other women and work on their estates, if they have such; otherwise, they shall work on the estates of the Indians and others, who shall pay them their wages at the rate they pay the others who work for them.

IV

Also, we order and command that within two years [of the publication of this ordinance] the men and women shall go about clad. And whereas it may so happen that in the course of time, what with their indoctrination and association with Christians, the Indians will become so apt and ready to become Christians, and so civilized and educated, that they will be capable of governing themselves and leading the kind of life that the said Christians lead there, we declare and command and say that it is our will that those Indians who thus become competent to live by themselves

and govern themselves, under the direction and control of our said judges of the said Island, present or future, shall be allowed to live by themselves and shall be obliged to serve [only] in those things which our vassals in Spain are accustomed to serve, so that they may serve and pay the tribute which they [our vassals] are accustomed to pay to their princes.

Therefore, I order and command that each and every one of you, the said Admiral, governor, judges, and officers, present or future, and any other persons whatsoever to whom the said ordinances apply or shall apply, to consider the first ordinances mentioned [i.e., those of 1512], together with the amendments and modifications here incorporated, to observe, obey, and execute them, in every way and by every means, as is prescribed in the said amendments and modifications; and while observing and obeying them yourselves, you shall execute and cause to be executed the penalties upon those who incur them; and you yourselves shall also obey them in the form and manner prescribed in the said ordinances. Moreover, [in case of disobedience] you shall incur the penalty of the loss of the said property and be forbidden to hold the Indians allotted to you in encomienda, as persons who have failed to indoctrinate or teach them or treat them with the charity with which they should be treated, and as it is our will that they be treated. Also, we avow that those of you who exceed what is here ordered shall be held accountable to God, and that this shall be a charge on your consciences. We say further that we do not give you faculty [to act otherwise], and that [in case of disobedience] you shall lose the Indians you have in encomienda and they shall be declared vacated, so that we may assign them to whomsoever we please; and you shall not act against the tenor and form of these ordinances, nor shall you consent to it at any time or in any way. And if [in order to execute them] you should have need of favor and aid, by this my letter I order all town councils, justices, regidores, alcaldes, and constables [of that Island] and of its towns and villages, and all our officers residing there, to render you such favor and aid as you may require in order to execute everything that is contained in this my letter and in each and every part of it.

And so that this my letter may come to the knowledge of all, I order that it and the ordinances contained therein be proclaimed by the public crier, in the squares, markets, and other customary places of the said Island, in the presence of a notary public and witnesses; and no one shall proceed against it in any way, on pain of my displeasure and a fine of 10,000 *maravedís*, to be paid into my treasury. Further, I order that those who disobey it shall be cited by him who shows them this my letter, to appear before me at my court, wherever I may be, within six months of the day when they are thus cited, under the same penalty. And under the same penalty I command any notary public whatsoever who is called upon for this purpose, to give him who shows him this my letter a certificate to that effect signed with his rubric, so that I may know how this my command is being observed.

Given in the City of Vallodolid, July 28, 1513.

I, the King.

I, Lope Conchillos, Secretary to our Mistress the Queen, caused this to be inscribed, by order of the King her Father.

Registered: Licenciatus Ximénez.

The Bishop of Palencia—Count [of Pernia].

Castañeda, Chancellor.

TREATY OF FRIENDSHIP, LIMITS AND NAVIGATION (THE PINCKNEY TREATY)

Between the United States of America, and the King of Spain

October 27, 1795

His Catholic Majesty and the United States of America, desiring to consolidate, on a permanent basis, the friendship and good correspondence, which happily prevails between the two parties, have determined to establish, by a convention, several points, the settlement whereof will be productive of general advantage and reciprocal utility to both nations.

With this intention, his Catholic Majesty has appointed the most excellent Lord, don Manuel de Godoy, and Alvarez de Faria, Rios, Sanchez, Zarzosa, Prince de la Paz, duke de la Alcudia, lord of the Soto de Roma, and the state of Albalá, Grandee of Spain of the first class, perpetual regidor of the city of Santiago, knight of the illustrious order of the Golden Fleece, and Great Cross of the Royal and distinguished Spanish order of Charles the III, commander of Valencia, del Ventoso, Rivera, and Acenchal in that of Santiago; Knight and Great Cross of the religious order of St. John; Counsellor of state; first Secretary of state and despacho; Secretary to the Queen; Superintendent General of the posts and highways; Protector of the royal Academy of the noble arts, and of the royal societies of natural history, botany, chemistry, and astronomy; Gentleman of the King's chamber in employment; Captain General of his armies; Inspector and Major of the royal corps of body guards &c. &c. &c. and the President of the United States, with the advice and consent of their Senate, has appointed Thomas Pinckney, a citizen of the United States, and their Envoy Extraordinary to his Catholic Majesty. And the said Plenipotentiaries have agreed upon and concluded the following articles:

Article I

There shall be a firm and inviolable peace and sincere friendship between his Catholic Majesty, his successors and subjects, and the United States, and their citizens, without exception of persons or places.

Article II

To prevent all disputes on the subject of the boundaries which separate the territories of the two high contracting parties, it is hereby declared and agreed as follows, to wit. The southern boundary of the United States, which divides their territory from the Spanish colonies of East and West Florida, shall be designated by a line beginning on the river Mississippi, at the northernmost part of the thirty-first degree of latitude north of the equator, which from thence shall be drawn due east to the middle of the river Apalachicola, or

Catahouche, thence along the middle thereof to its junction with the Flint: thence straight to the head of St. Mary's river, and thence down to the middle thereof to the Atlantic ocean. And it is agreed, that if there should be any troops, garrisons, settlements of either party, in the territory of the other, according to the above-mentioned boundaries, they shall be withdrawn from the said territory within the term of six months after the ratification of this treaty, or sooner if it be possible; and that they shall be permitted to take with them all the goods and effects which they possess.

Article III

In order to carry the preceding article into effect, one commissioner and one surveyor shall be appointed by each of the contracting parties, who shall meet at the Natchez, on the left side of the river Mississippi, before the expiration of six months from the ratification of this convention, and they shall proceed to run and mark this boundary according to the stipulations of the said article. They shall make plats and keep journals of their proceedings, which shall be considered as part of this convention, and shall have the same force as if they were inserted therein. And if on any account it should be accompanied by guards, they shall be furnished in equal proportions by the commanding officer of his Majesty's troops in the two Floridas, and the commanding officer of the troops of the United States in their southwestern territory, who shall act by common consent, and amicably, as well with respect to this point as to the furnishing of provisions and instruments, and making every other arrangement which may be necessary of useful for the execution of this article.

Article IV

It is likewise agreed that the Western boundary of the United States which separates them from the Spanish Colony of Louisiana, is in the middle of the channel or bed of the river Mississippi from the northern boundary of the said states to the completion of the thirty-first degree of latitude north of the equator; and his Catholic Majesty has likewise agreed that the navigation of the said River in its whole breadth from its source to the

Ocean shall be free only to his Subjects, and the Citizens of the United States, unless he should extend this privilege to the Subjects of other Powers by special convention.

Article V

The two High contracting Parties shall by all the means in their power maintain peace and harmony among the several Indian Nations who inhabit the country adjacent to the lines and Rivers which by the preceding Articles form the boundaries of the two Floridas; and the better to obtain this effect both Parties oblige themselves expressly to restrain by force all hostilities on the part of the Indian Nations living within their boundaries: so that Spain will not suffer her Indians to attack the Citizens of the United States, nor the Indians inhabiting their territory; nor will the United States permit these last mentioned Indians to commence hostilities against the Subjects of his Catholic Majesty, or his Indians in any manner whatever.

And whereas several treaties of Friendship exist between the two contracting Parties and the said Nations of Indians, it is hereby agreed that in future no treaty of alliance or other whatever (except treaties of Peace) shall be made by either Party with the Indians living within the boundary of the other; but both Parties will endeavour to make the advantages of the Indian trade common and mutually beneficial to their respective Subjects and Citizens observing in all things the most complete reciprocity: so that both Parties may obtain the advantages arising from a good understanding with the said Nations, without being subject to the expence which they have hitherto occasioned.

Article VI

Each Party shall endeavour by all means in their power to protect and defend all Vessels and other effects belonging to the Citizens or Subjects of the other, which shall be within the extent of their jurisdiction by sea or by land, and shall use all their efforts to recover and cause to be restored to the right owners their Vessels and effects which may have been taken from them within the extent of their said jurisdiction whether they are at war or not with the Power whose Subjects have taken possession of the said effects.

Article VII

And it is agreed that the Subjects or Citizens of each of the contracting Parties, their Vessels, or effects shall not be liable to any embargo or detention on the part of the other for any military expedition or other public or private purpose whatever; and in the cases of seizure, detention, or arrest for debts contracted or offences committed by any Citizen or Subject of the one Party within the jurisdiction of the other, the same shall be made and prosecuted by order and authority of law only, and according to the regular course of proceedings usual in such cases. The Citizens and Subjects of both Parties shall be allowed to employ such Advocates, Solicitors, Notaries, Agents, and Factors, as they may judge proper in all their affairs and in all their trials at law in which they may be concerned before the tribunals of the other Party, and such Agents shall have free access to be present at the proceedings in such causes, and at the taking of all examinations and evidence which may be exhibited in the said trials.

Article VIII

In case the Subjects and inhabitants of either Party with their shipping whether public and of war or private and of merchants be forced through stress of weather, pursuits of Pirates, or Enemies, or any other urgent necessity for seeking of shelter and harbor to retreat and enter into any of the Rivers, Bays, Roads, or Ports belonging to the other Party, they shall be received and treated with all humanity, and enjoy all favor, protection and help, and they shall be permitted to refresh and provide themselves at reasonable rates with victuals and all things needful for the sustenance of their persons or reparation of their Ships, and prosecution of their voyage; and they shall no ways be hindered from returning out of the said Ports, or Roads, but may remove and depart when and whither they please without any let or hindrance.

Article IX

All Ships and merchandize of what nature soever which shall be rescued out of the hands of any Pirates or Robbers on the high seas shall be brought into some Port of either State and shall be delivered to the custody of the Officers of that Port in order to be taken care of and restored entire to the true proprietor as soon as due and sufficient proof shall be made concerning the property there of.

Article X

When any Vessel of either Party shall be wrecked, foundered, or otherwise damaged on the coasts or within the dominion of the other, their respective Subjects or Citizens shall receive as well for themselves as for their Vessels and effects the same assistance which would be due to the inhabitants of the Country where the damage happens, and shall pay the same charges and dues only as the said inhabitants would be subject to pay in a like case; and if the operations of repair should require that the whole or any part of the cargo be unladen they shall pay no duties, charges, or fees on the part which they shall relate and carry away.

Article XI

The Citizens and Subjects of each Party shall have power to dispose of their personal goods within the jurisdiction of the other by testament, donation, or otherwise; and their representatives being Subjects or Citizens of the other Party shall succeed to their said personal goods, whether by testament or ab intestato and they may take possession thereof either by themselves or other acting for them, and dispose of the same at their will paying such dues only as the inhabitants of the Country wherein the said goods are shall be subject to pay in like cases, and in case of the absence of the representatives, such care shall be taken of the said goods as would be taken of the goods of a native in like case, until the lawful owner may take measures for receiving them. And if question shall arise among several claimants to which of them the said goods belong the same shall be decided finally by the laws and Judges of the Land wherein the said goods are. And where on the death of any person holding real estate within the territories of the one Party, such real estate would by the laws of the Land descend on a Citizen or Subject of the other were he not disqualified by being an alien, such subject shall be allowed a reasonable time to sell the same and to withdraw the proceeds without molestation, and exempt from all rights of detraction on the part of the Government of the respective states.

Article XII

The merchant Ships of either of the Parties which shall be making into a Port belonging to the enemy of the other Party and concerning whose voyage and the species of goods on board her there shall be just grounds of suspicion shall be obliged to exhibit as well upon the high seas as in the Ports and havens not only her passports but likewise certificates expressly showing that her goods are not of the number of those which have been prohibited as contraband.

Article XIII

For the better promoting of commerce on both sides, it is agreed that if a war shall break out between the said two Nations one year after the proclamation of war shall be allowed to the merchants in the Cities and Towns where they shall live for collecting and transporting their goods and merchandizes, and if any thing be taken from them, or any injury be done them within that term by either Party, or the People or Subjects of either, full satisfaction shall be made for the same by the Government.

Article XIV

No subject of his Catholic Majesty shall apply for or take any commission or letters of marque for arming any Ship or Ships to act as Privateers against the said United States or against the Citizens, People, or inhabitants of the said United States, or against the property of any of the inhabitants of any of them, from any Prince or State with which the said United States shall be at war.

Nor shall any Citizen, Subject, or Inhabitant of the said United States apply for or take any com-

mission of letters of marque for arming any Ship or Ships to act as Privateers against the subjects of his Catholic Majesty or the property of any of them from any Prince or State with which the said King shall be at war. And if any person of either Nation shall take such commissions or letters of marque he shall be punished as a Pirate.

Article XV

It shall be lawful for all and singular the Subjects of his Catholic Majesty, and the Citizens People, and inhabitants of the said United States to sail with their Ships with all manner of liberty and security, no distinction being made who are the proprietors of the merchandizes laden thereon from any Port to the Places of those who now are or hereafter shall be at enmity with his Catholic Majesty or the United States. It shall be likewise lawful for the Subjects and inhabitants aforesaid to sail with the Ships and merchandizes aforementioned, and to trade with the same liberty and security from the Places, Ports, and Havens of those who are Enemies of both or either Party without any opposition or disturbance whatsoever, not only directly from the Places of the Enemy aforementioned to neutral Places but also from one Place belonging to an Enemy to another Place belonging to an Enemy, whether they be under the jurisdiction of the same Prince or under several, and it is hereby stipulated that Free Ships shall also give freedom to goods, and that every thing shall be deemed free and exempt which shall be found on board the Ships belonging to the Subjects of either of the contracting Parties although the whole lading or any part thereof should appertain to the Enemies of either; contraband goods being always excepted. It is also agreed that the same liberty be extended to persons who are on board a free Ship, so that, although they be Enemies to either Party they shall not be made Prisoners or taken out of that free Ship unless they are Soldiers and in actual service of the Enemies.

Article XVI

This liberty of navigation and commerce shall extend to all kinds of merchandizes excepting those only which are distinguished by the name of contraband; and under this name of contraband or prohibited goods shall be comprehended arms, great guns, bombs, with the fusees, and other things belonging to them, cannon ball, gun powder, match, pikes, swords, lances, spears, halberds, mortars, petards, grenades, saltpetre, muskets, musket ball, bucklers, helmets, breast plates, coats of mail, and the like of arms proper for arming soldiers, musket rests, belts, horses with their furniture and all other warlike instruments whatever. These merchandizes which follow shall not be reckoned among contraband or prohibited goods; that is to say, all sorts of cloths and all other manufactures woven of any wool, flax, silk, cotton, or any other materials whatever, all kinds of wearing apparel together with all species whereof they are used to be made, gold and silver as well coined as uncoined, tin, iron, latton, copper, brass, coals, as also wheat, barley, oats, and any other kind of corn and pulse: tobacco and likewise all manner of spices, salted and smoked flesh, salted fish, cheese and butter, beer, oils, wines, sugars, and all sorts of salts, in general all provisions which serve for the sustenance of life. Furthermore all kinds of cotton, hemp, flax, tar, pitch, ropes, cables, sail cloths, anchors, and any parts of anchors, also ships masts, planks, wood of all kind, and all other things proper either for building or repairing ships, and all other goods whatever which have not been worked into the form of any instrument prepared for war by land or be sea, shall not be reputed contraband, much less such as have been already wrought and made up for any other use: all which shall be wholly reckoned among free goods as likewise all other merchandizes and things which are not comprehended and particularly mentioned in the foregoing enumeration of contraband goods: so that they may be transported and carried in the freest manner by the subjects of both parties, even to Places belonging to an Enemy, such towns or Places being only excepted as are at the time besieged, blocked up, or invested. And except the cases in which any Ship of war of Squadron shall in consequence of storms or other accidents at sea be under the necessity or taking the cargo of any trading Vessel or Vessels, in which case they may stop the said Vessel or Vessels and furnish themselves with necessaries, giving a receipt in order that the Power to whom the said ship of war belongs may pay for the articles so taken according to the price thereof at the Port to which they may appear to have been destined by the Ship's papers: and the two contracting Parties engage that the Vessels shall not be detained longer than may be absolutely necessary for their said Ships to supply themselves with necessaries: that they will immediately pay the value of the receipts: and indemnify the proprietor for all losses which he may have sustained in consequence of such transaction.

Article XVII

To the end that all manner of dissentions and quarrels may be avoided and prevented on one side and the other, it is agreed that in case either of the Parties hereto should be engaged in a war, the ships and Vessels belonging to the Subjects or People of the other Party must be furnished with sea letters or passports expressing the name, property, and bulk of the Ship, as also the name and place of habitation of the master or commander of the said Ship, that it may appear thereby that the Ship really and truly belongs to the Subjects of one of the Parties; which passport shall be made out and granted according to the form annexed to this Treaty. They shall likewise be recalled every year, that is, if the ship happens to return home within the space of a year. It is likewise agreed that such ships being laden, are to be provided not only with passports as above mentioned but also with certificates containing the several particulars of the cargo, the place whence the ship sailed, that so it may be known whether any forbidden or contraband goods be on board the same; which certificates shall be made out by the Officers of the place whence the ship sailed, that so it may be known whether any forbidden or contraband goods be on board the same; which certificates shall be made out by the Officers of the place whence the ship sailed in the accustomed form; and if any one shall think it fit or advisable to express in the said certificates the person to whom the goods on board belong he may freely do so: without which requisites they may be sent to one of the Ports of the other contracting Party and adjudged by the competent tribunal according to what is above set forth, that all the circumstances of this omission having been well examined, they shall be adjudged to be legal prizes, unless they shall give legal satisfaction of their property by testimony entirely equivalent.

Article XVIII

If the Ships of the said subjects, People or inhabitants of either of the Parties shall be met with either sailing along the Coasts on the high Seas by any Ship of war of the other or by any Privateer, the said Ship of war or Privateer for the avoiding of any disorder shall remain out of cannon shot, and may send their boats aboard the merchant Ship which they shall so meet with, and may enter her to number of two or three men only to whom the master or commander of such ship or vessel shall exhibit his passports concerning the property of the ship made out according to the form inserted in this present Treaty: and the ship when she shall have shewed such passports shall be free and at liberty to pursue her voyage, so as it shall not be lawful to molest or give her chase in any manner or force her to quit her intended course.

Article XIX

Consuls shall be reciprocally established with the privileges and powers which those of the most favoured Nations enjoy in the Ports where their consuls reside, or are permitted to be.

Article XX

It is also agreed that the inhabitants of the territories of each Party shall respectively have free access to the Courts of Justice of the other, and they shall be permitted to prosecute suits for the recovery of their properties, the payment of their debts and for obtaining satisfaction for the damages which they may have sustained, whether the persons whom they may sue be subjects or Citizens of the Country in which they may be found, or any other persons whatsoever may have taken refuge therein; and the proceedings and sentences of the Court shall be the same as if the contending parties had been subjects or Citizens of the said Country.

Article XXI

In order to terminate all differences on account of the losses sustained by the Citizens of the United States in consequence of their vessels and the cargoes having been taken by the Subjects of his Catholic Majesty during the late war between Spain and France, it is agreed that all such cases shall be referred to the final decision of Commissioners to be appointed in the following manner. His Catholic Majesty shall name one Commissioner, and the President of the United States by and with the advice and consent of their Senate shall appoint another, and the said two Commissioners shall agree on the Choice of a third, or if they cannot agree so they shall each propose one person, and of the two names so proposed one shall be drawn by lot in the presence of the two original Commissioners, and the person whose name shall be so drawn shall be the third Commissioner, and the three Commissioners so appointed shall be sworn impartially to examine and decide the claims in question according to the merits of the several cases, and to justice, equity, and the laws of Nations. The said Commissioners shall meet and sit at Philadelphia and in the case of the death, sickness, or necessary absence of any such commissioner his place shall be supplied in the same manner as he was first appointed, and the new Commissioner shall take the same oaths, and do the same duties. They shall receive all complaints and applications, authorized by this article during eighteen months from the day on which they shall assemble. They shall have power to examine all such persons as come before them on oath or affirmation touching the complaints in question, and also to receive in evidence all written testimony authenticated in such manner as they shall think proper to require or admit. The award of the said Commissioners or any two of them shall be final and conclusive both as to the justice of the claim and the amount of the sum to be paid to the claimants; and his Catholic Majesty undertakes to cause the same to be paid in specie without deduction, at such times and Places and under such conditions as shall be awarded by the said Commissioners.

Article XXII

The two high contracting Parties hoping that the good correspondence and friendship which happily reigns between them will be further increased by this Treaty, and that it will contribute to augment their prosperity and opulence, will in future give to their mutual commerce all the extension and favor which the advantage of both Countries may require; and in consequence of the stipulations contained in the IV. article his Catholic Majesty will permit the Citizens of the United States for the space of three years from this time to deposit their merchandize and effects in the Port of New Orleans, and to export them from thence without paying any other duty than a fair price for the hire of the stores, and his Majesty promises either to continue this permission if he finds during that time that it is not prejudicial to the interests of Spain, or if he should not agree to continue it there, he will assign to them on another part of the banks of the Mississippi an equivalent establishment.

Article XXIII

The present Treaty shall not be in force until ratified by the Contracting Parties, and the ratification shall be exchanged in six months from this time, or sooner if possible.

In Witness whereof We the underwritten Plenipotentiaries of His Catholic Majesty and of the United States of America have signed this present Treaty of Friendship, Limits and Navigation and have thereunto affixed our seals respectively.

Done at San Lorenzo el Real this seven and twenty day of October one thousand seven hundred and ninety five.

THOMAS PINCKNEY

EL PRINCIPE DE LA PAZ

CESSION OF LOUISIANA
Treaty Between the United States of America and the French Republic

The President of the United States of America and the First Consul of the French Republic in the name of the French People desiring to remove all Source of misunderstanding relative to objects of discussion mentioned in the Second and fifth articles of the Convention of the 8th Vendemiaire and 9/30 September 1800 relative to the rights claimed by the United States in virtue of the Treaty concluded at Madrid the 27 of October 1795, between His Catholic Majesty, & the Said United States, & willing to Strengthen the union and friendship which at the time of the Said Convention was happily reestablished between the two nations have respectively named their Plenipotentiaries to wit The President of the United States, by and with the advice and consent of the Senate of Said States; Robert P. Livingston Minister Plenipotentiary of the United States and James Monroe Minister Plenipotentiary and Envoy extraordinary of the Said States near the Government of the French Republic; And the First Consul in the name of the French people, Citizen Francis Barbe Marbois Minister of the public treasury who after having respectively exchanged their full powers have agreed to the following Articles.

Article I

Whereas by the Article the third of the Treaty concluded at St. Idelfonso the 9th Vendemiaire an 9/1 October 1800 between the First Consul of the French Republic and his Catholic Majesty it was agreed as follows.

"His Catholic Majesty promises and engages on his part to cede to the French Republic six months after the full and entire execution of the conditions and Stipulations herein relative to his Royal Highness the Duke of Parma, the Colony or Province of Louisiana with the Same extent that it now has in the hands of Spain, & that it had when France possessed it; and Such as it Should be after the Treaties subsequently entered into between Spain and other States."

And whereas in pursuance of the Treaty and particularly of the third article the French Republic has an incontestible title to the domain and to the possession of the said Territory—The First Consul of the French Republic desiring to give to the United States a strong proof of his friendship doth hereby cede to the said United States in the name of the French Republic for ever and in full Sovereignty the said territory with all its rights and appurtenances as fully and in the Same manner as they have been acquired by the French Republic in virtue of the above mentioned Treaty concluded with his Catholic Majesty.

Article II

In the cession made by the preceding article are included the adjacent Islands belonging to Louisiana, all public lots and Squares, vacant lands and all public buildings, fortifications, barracks and other edifices which are not private property. The Archives, papers & documents relative to the domain and Sovereignty of Louisiana and it dependencies will be left in the possession of the Commissaries of the United States, and copies will be afterwards given in due form to the Magistrates and Municipal officers of Such of the said papers and documents as may be necessary to them.

Article III

The inhabitants of the ceded territory shall be incorporated in the Union of the United States and admitted as soon as possible according to the principles of the federal Constitution to the enjoyment of all the rights, advantages and immunities of citizens of the United States, and in the mean time they shall be maintained and protected in the free enjoyment of their liberty, property and the Religion which they profess.

Article IV

There Shall be Sent by the Government of France a Commissary to Louisiana to the end that he do every act necessary as well to receive from the Officers of his Catholic Majesty the Said country and its dependencies in the name of the French Republic if it has not been already done as to transmit it in the name of the French Republic to the Commissary or agent of the United States.

Article V

Immediately after the ratification of the present Treaty by the President of the United States and in case that of the first Consul's shall have been previously obtained, the Commissary of the French Republic shall remit all military posts of New Orleans and other parts of the ceded territory to the Commissary or Commissaries named by the President to take possession—the troops whether of France or Spain who may be there shall cease to occupy any military post from the time of taking possession and shall be embarked as soon as possible in the course of three months after the ratification of this treaty.

Article VI

The United States promise to execute Such treaties and articles as may have been agreed between Spain and the tribes and nations of Indians until by mutual consent of the United States and the said tribes or nations other Suitable articles Shall have been agreed upon.

Article VII

As it is reciprocally advantageous to the commerce of France and the United States to encourage the communication of both nations for a limited time in the country ceded by the present treaty until general arrangements relative to the commerce of both nations may be agreed on, it has been agreed between the contracting parties that the French Ships coming directly from France or any of her colonies loaded only with the produce and manufactures of France or her Said Colonies; and the Ships of Spain coming directly from Spain or any of her colonies loaded only with the produce or manufactures of Spain or her Colonies Shall be admitted during the Space of twelve years in the Port of New Orleans and in all other legal ports-of-entry within the ceded territory in the Same manner as the Ships of the United States coming directly from France or Spain or any of their Colonies without being Subject to any other or greater duty on merchandise or other or greater tonnage than that paid by the citizens of the United States. During the Space of time above mentioned no other nation Shall have a right to the Same privileges in the Ports of the ceded territory—the twelve years Shall commence three months after the exchange of ratifications if it Shall take place in France or three months after it Shall have been notified at Paris to the French Government if it Shall take place in the United

States; It is however well understood that the object of the above article is to favour the manufactures, Commerce, freight and navigation of France and of Spain So far as relates to the importations that the French and Spanish Shall make into the Said Ports of the United States without in any Sort affecting the regulations that the United States may make concerning the exportation of produce and merchandize of the United States, or any right they may have to make Such regulations.

Article VIII

In future and for ever after the expiration of the twelve years, the Ships of France shall be treated upon the footing of the most favoured nations in the ports above mentioned.

Article IX

The particular Convention Signed this day by the respective Ministers having for its object to provide for the payment of debts due to the Citizens of the United States by the French Republic prior to the 30th Sept 1800 (8 Vendemiaire an 9) is approved and to have its execution in the Same manner as if it had been inserted in this present treaty and it Shall be ratified in the Same form and in the Same time So that the one Shall not be ratified distinct from the other.

Another particular Convention Signed at the Same date as the present treaty relative to a definitive rule between the contracting parties is in the like manner approved and will be ratified in the Same form, and in the Same time and jointly.

Article X

The present treaty Shall be ratified in good and due form and the ratifications Shall be exchanged in the Space of Six months after the date of the Signature by the Ministers Plenipotentiary or Sooner if possible.

In faith whereof the respective Plenipotentiaries have Signed these articles in the French and English languages; declaring nevertheless that the present Treaty was originally agreed to in the French language; and have thereunto affixed their Seals. Done at Paris the tenth day of Floreal in the eleventh year of the French Republic; and the 30th of April 1803.

ROB. R. LIVINGSTON

J.A. MONROE

BARBE MARBOIS

CESSION OF LOUISIANA: FINANCIAL ARRANGEMENT

A Convention Between the United States of America and French Republic

The President of the United States of America and the First Consul of the French Republic in the name of the French people, in consequence the treaty of cession of Louisiana which has been Signed this day; wishing to regulate definitively every thing which has relation to the Said cession have authorized to this effect the Plenipotentiaries that is to say: the President of the United States has, by and with the advice and consent of the Senate of the Said States nominated for their Plenipotentiaries, Robert R. Livingston Minister Plenipotentiary of the United States and James Monroe Minister Plenipotentiary and Envoy-Extraordinary of the Said United States near the Government of the French Republic; and the First Consul of the French Republic in the name of the French People has named as Plenipotentiary the Said Republic the citizen Francis Barb-Marbois: who in virtue of their full powers, which have been exchanged this day have agreed to the following articles:

Article: 1

The Government of the United States engages to pay to the French Government in the manner Specified in the following article the Sum of Sixty millions of francs independent of the Sum which Shall be fixed by another Convention for the payment of the debts due by France to citizens of the United States.

Article: 2

For the payment of the Sum of Sixty millions of francs mentioned in the preceding article the United

States Shall create a Stock of eleven millions, two hundred and fifty thousand Dollars bearing an interest of Six per cent: per annum payable half yearly in London, Amsterdam or Paris amounting by the half year to three hundred and thirty Seven thousand five hundred Dollars according to the proportions which Shall be determined by the French Government to be paid at either place: The principal of the Said Stock to be reimbursed at the treasury of the United States in annual payments of not less than three millions of Dollars each; of which the first payment Shall commence fifteen years after the date of the exchange of ratifications—this Stock Shall be transferred to the Government of France or to Such person or persons as Shall be authorized to receive it in three months at most after the exchange of the ratifications of this treaty and after Louisiana Shall be taken possession of in the name of the Government of the United States.

It is further agreed that if the French Government Should be desirous of disposing of the Said Stock to receive the capital in Europe at Shorter terms that its measures for that purpose Shall be taken So as to favour in the greatest degree possible the credit of the United States and to raise to the highest price the Said Stock.

Article: 3

It is agreed that the Dollar of the United States Specified in the present Convention Shall be fixed at five francs 3333/10000 or five livres eight Sous tournois.

The present Convention Shall be ratified in good and due form, and the ratifications Shall be exchanged in the Space of Six months to date from this day or Sooner if possible.

In faith of which the respective Plenipotentiaries have Signed the above articles both in the French and English languages, declaring nevertheless that the present treaty has been originally agreed on and written in the French language; to which they have hereunto affixed their Seals.

Done at Paris the tenth of Floreal eleventh year of the French Republic (30th April 1803).

ROB. R. LIVINGSTON

J.A. MONROE

BARBE MARBOIS

THE MONROE DOCTRINE

ANNUAL MESSAGE from President James Monroe to the United States Congress, Containing the "Monroe Doctrine," December 2, 1823 (extract)

John Bassett Moore, *A Digest of International Law, VI,* 401

AT THE PROPOSAL of the Russian Imperial Government, made through the minister of the Emperor residing here, a full power and instructions have been transmitted to the minister of the United States at St. Petersburg, to arrange, by amicable negotiation, the respective rights and interests of the two nations on the northwest coast of this continent. A similar proposal has been made by his Imperial Majesty to the Government of Great Britain, which has likewise been acceded to. The Government of the United States has been desirous, by the friendly proceeding, of manifesting the great value which they have invariably attached to the friendship of the Emperor, and their solicitude to cultivate the best understanding with his Government. In the discussions to which this interest has given rise, and in the arrangements by which they may terminate, the occasion has been judged proper for asserting as a principle in which the rights and interests of the United States are involved, that the American continents, by the free and independent condition which they have assumed and maintain, are henceforth not to be considered as subjects for future colonization by any European powers.

It was stated at the commencement of the last session that a great effort was then making in Spain and Portugal to improve the condition of the people of those countries, and that it appeared to be conducted with extraordinary moderation. It need scarcely be remarked that the result has been, so far, very different from what was then anticipated. Of events in that quarter of the globe with which we have so much intercourse, and from which we derive our origin, we have always been anxious and interested spectators. The citizens of the United States cherish sentiments the most friendly in favor of the liberty and happiness of their fellow-men on that side of the Atlantic. In the wars of the European powers in matters relating to themselves we have never taken any part, nor does it comport with our policy so to do. It is only when our rights are invaded or seriously menaced that we resent injuries or make preparation for our defense. With the movements in this hemisphere we are, of necessity, more immediately connected, and by causes which must be obvious to all enlightened and impartial observers. The political system of the allied powers is essentially different in this respect from that of America. This difference proceeds from that which exists in their respective Governments. And to the defense of our own, which has been achieved by the loss of so much blood and treasure, and matured by the wisdom of their most enlightened citizens, and under which we have enjoyed unexampled felicity, this whole nation is devoted. We owe it, therefore, to candor, and to the amicable relations existing between the United States and those powers, to declare that we should consider any attempt on their part to extend their system to any portion of this hemisphere as dangerous to our peace and safety. With the existing colonies or dependencies of any European power we have not interfered and shall not interfere. But with the governments who have declared their independence and maintained it, and whose independence we have, on great consideration and on just principles, acknowledged, we could not view any interposition for the purpose of oppressing them, or controlling in any other manner their destiny, by any European power, in any other light than as the manifestation of an unfriendly disposition toward the United States. In the war between these new governments and Spain we declared our neutrality at the time of their recognition, and to this we have adhered and shall continue to adhere, provided no change shall occur which, in the judgment of the competent authorities of this Government, shall make a cor-

responding change on the part of the United States indispensable to their security.

The late events in Spain and Portugal show that Europe is still unsettled. Of this important fact no stronger proof can be adduced than that the allied powers should have thought it proper, on any principle satisfactory to themselves, to have interposed by force, in the internal concerns of Spain. To what extent such interposition may be carried, on the same principle, is a question in which all independent powers whose governments differ from theirs are interested, even those most remote, and surely none more so than the United States. Our policy in regard to Europe, which was adopted at an early stage of the wars which have so long agitated that quarter of the globe, nevertheless remains the same, which is, not to interfere in the internal concerns of government for us; to cultivate friendly relations with it, and to any of its powers; to consider the government de facto as the legitimate preserve those relations by a frank, firm, and manly policy, meeting, in all instances, the just claims of every power, submitting to injuries from none. But in regard to these continents, circumstances are eminently and conspicuously different. It is impossible that the allied powers should extend their political system to any portion of either continent without endangering our peace and happiness; nor can anyone believe that our southern brethren, if left to themselves, would adopt it of their own accord. It is equally impossible, therefore, that we should behold such interposition, in any form, with indifference. If we look to the comparative strength and resources of Spain and those new governments, and their distance from each other, it must be obvious that she can never subdue them. It is still the true policy of the United States to leave the parties to themselves, in the hope that other powers will pursue the same course.

The Monroe doctrine finds its recognition in those principles of international law which are based upon the theory that every nation shall have its rights protected and its just claims enforced.

Of course this Government is entirely confident that under the sanction of this doctrine we have clear rights and undoubted claims. Nor is this ignored in the British reply. The prime minister, while not admitting that the Monroe doctrine is applicable to present conditions, states: "In declaring that the United States would resist any such enterprise if it was contemplated, President Monroe adopted a policy which received the entire sympathy of the English Government of that date." He further declares: "Though the language of President Monroe is directed to the attainment of objects which most Englishmen would agree to be salutary, it is impossible to admit that they have been inscribed by any adequate authority in the code of international law." Again he says: "They (Her Majesty's Government) fully concur with the view which President Monroe apparently entertained, that any disturbance of the existing territorial distribution in the hemisphere by any fresh acquisitions on the part of any European state, would be a highly inexpedient change."

In the belief that the doctrine for which we contend was clear and definite, that it was founded upon substantial considerations and involved our safety and welfare, that it was fully applicable to our present conditions and to the state of the world's progress and that it was directly related to the pending controversy and without any conviction as to the final merits of the dispute, but anxious to learn in a satisfactory and conclusive manner whether Great Britain sought, under a claim of boundary, to extend her possessions on this continent without right, or whether she merely sought possession of territory fairly included within her lines of ownership, this Government proposed to the Government of Great Britain a resort to arbitration as the proper means of settling the question to the end that a vexatious boundary dispute between the two contestants might be determined and our exact standing and relation in respect to the controversy might be made clear.

It will be seen from the correspondence herewith submitted that this proposition has been declined by the British Government, upon grounds which in the circumstances seem to me to be far from satisfactory. It is deeply disappointing that such an appeal actuated by the most friendly feelings towards both nations directly concerned, addressed to the sense of justice and to the magnanimity of one of the great powers of the world and touching its relations to one comparatively weak and small, should have produced no better results.

The course to be pursued by this Government in view of the present condition does not appear to admit of serious doubt. Having labored faithfully for many years to induce Great Britain to submit this dispute to impartial arbitration, and having been now finally apprized of her refusal to do so, nothing remains but to accept the situation, to recognize its plain requirements and deal with it accordingly. Great Britain's present proposition has never thus far been regarded as admissible by Venezuela, though any adjustment of the boundary which that country may deem for her advantage and may enter into of her own free will can not of course be objected to by the United States.

Assuming, however, that the attitude of Venezuela will remain unchanged, the dispute has reached such a stage as to make it now incumbent upon the United States to take measures to determine with sufficient certainty for its justification what is the true divisional line between the Republic of Venezuela and British Guiana. The inquiry to that end should of course be conducted carefully and judicially and due weight should be given to all available evidence records and facts in support of the claims of both parties.

In order that such an examination should be prosecuted in a thorough and satisfactory manner I suggest that the Congress make an adequate appropriation for the expenses of a commission, to be appointed by the Executive, who shall make the necessary investigation and report upon the matter with the least possible delay. When such report is made and accepted it will in my opinion be the duty of the United States to resist by every means in its power as a willful aggression upon its rights and interests the appropriation by Great Britain of any lands or the exercise of governmental jurisdiction over any territory which after investigation we have determined of right belongs to Venezuela.

In making these recommendations I am fully alive to the responsibility incurred, and keenly realize all the consequences that may I follow.

I am nevertheless firm in my conviction that while it is a grievous thing to contemplate the two great English-speaking peoples of the world as being otherwise than friendly competitors in the onward march of civilization, and strenuous and worthy rivals in all the arts of peace, there is no calamity which a great nation can invite which equals that which follows a supine submission to wrong and injustice and the consequent loss of national self-respect and honor beneath which are shielded and defended a people's safety and greatness.

PEACE, FRIENDSHIP, LIMITS, AND SETTLEMENT: TREATY OF GUADALUPE HIDALGO 1848

In the name of Almighty God:

The United States of America and the United Mexican States, animated by a sincere desire to put an end to the calamities of the war which unhappily exists between the two Republics, and to establish upon a solid basis relations of peace and friendship, which shall confer reciprocal benefits upon the citizens of both, and assure the concord, harmony and mutual confidence, wherein the two Peoples should live, as good Neighbors, have for that purpose appointed their respective Plenipotentiaries: that is to say, the President of the United States has appointed Nicholas P. Trist, a citizen of the United States, and the President of the Mexican Republic has appointed Don Luis Gonzaga Cuevas, Don Bernardo Couto, and Don Miguel Atristain, citizens of the said Republic; who, after a reciprocal communication of their respective full powers, have, under the protection of Almighty God, the author of Peace, arranged, agreed upon, and signed the following TREATY OF PEACE, FRIENDSHIP, LIMITS AND SETTLEMENT BETWEEN THE UNITED STATES OF AMERICA AND THE MEXICAN REPUBLIC

Article I

There shall be firm and universal peace between the United States of America and the Mexican Republic, and between their respective Countries, territories, cities, towns and people, without exception of places or persons.

Article II

Immediately upon the signature of this Treaty, a convention shall be entered into between a Commissioner or Commissioners appointed by the General in Chief of the forces of the United States, and such as may be appointed by the Mexican Government, to the end that a provisional suspension of hostilities shall take place, and that, in the places occupied by the said forces, constitutional order may be reestablished, as regards the political, administrative and judicial branches, so far as this shall be permitted by the circumstances of military occupation.

Article III

Immediately upon the ratification of the present treaty by the Government of the United States, orders shall be transmitted to the Commanders of their land and naval forces, requiring the latter, (provided this Treaty shall then have been ratified by the Government of the Mexican Republic and the ratifications exchanged) immediately to desist from blockading any Mexican ports; and requiring the former (under the same condition) to commence at the earliest moment practicable, withdrawing all troops of the United States then in the interior of the Mexican Republic, to points, that shall be selected by common agreement, at a distance from the sea-ports, not exceeding thirty leagues; and such evacuation of the interior of the Republic shall be completed with the least possible delay: the Mexican Government hereby binding itself to afford every facility in it's power for rendering the same convenient to the troops, on their march and in their new positions, and for promoting a good understanding between them and the inhabitants. In like manner, orders shall be despatched to the persons in charge of the custom houses at all ports occupied by the forces of the United States, requiring them (under the same condition) immediately to deliver possession of the same to the persons authorized by the Mexican Government to receive it, together with all bonds and evidences of debt for duties on importations and on exportations, not yet fallen due. Moreover, a faithful and exact account shall be made out, showing the entire amount of all duties on imports and on exports, collected at such Custom Houses, or elsewhere in Mexico, by authority of the United States, from and after the day of ratification of this Treaty by the Government of the Mexican Republic; and also an account of the cost of collection; and such entire amount, deducting only the cost of collection, shall be delivered to the Mexican Government, at the City of Mexico, within three months after the exchange of ratifications.

The evacuation of the Capital of the Mexican Republic by the Troops of the United States, in virtue of the above stipulation, shall be completed in one month after the orders there stipulated for shall have been received by the commander of said troops, or sooner if possible.

Article IV

Immediately after the exchange of ratifications of the present treaty, all castles, forts, territories, places and possessions, which have been taken or occupied by the forces of the United States during the present war, within the limits of the Mexican Republic, as about to he established by the following Article, shall be definitively restored to the said Republic, together with all the artillery, arms, apparatus of war, munitions, and other public property, which were in the said castles and forts when captured, and which shall remain there at the time when this treaty shall be duly ratified by the Government of the Mexican Republic. To this end, immediately upon the signature of this treaty, orders shall be despatched to the American officers commanding such castles and forts, securing against the removal or destruction of any such artillery, arms, apparatus of war, munitions, or other public property. The city of Mexico, within the inner line of entrenchments surrounding the said city, is comprehended in the above stipulations, as regards the restoration of artillery, apparatus of war, etc. The final evacuation of the territory of the

Mexican Republic, by the forces of the United States, shall he completed in three months from the said exchange of ratifications, or sooner, if possible: the Mexican Government hereby engaging, as in the foregoing Article, to use all means in it's power for facilitating such evacuation, and rendering it convenient to the troops, and for promoting a good understanding between them and the inhabitants.

If, however, the ratification of this treaty by both parties should not take place in time to allow the embarkation of the troops of the United States to be completed before the commencement of the sickly season, at the Mexican ports on the Gulf of Mexico; in such case a friendly arrangement shall be entered into between the General in Chief of the said troops and the Mexican Government, whereby healthy and otherwise suitable places at a distance from the ports not exceeding thirty leagues shall be designated for the residence of such troops as may not yet have embarked, until the return of the healthy season. And the space of time here referred to, as comprehending the sickly season, shall be understood to extend from the first day of May to the first day of November.

All prisoners of war taken on either side, on land or on sea, shall be restored as soon as practicable after the exchange of ratifications of this treaty. It is also agreed that if any Mexicans should now be held as captives by any savage tribe within the limits of the United States, as about to be established by the following Article, the Government of the said United States will exact the release of such captives, and cause them to be restored to their country.

Article V

The Boundary line between the two Republics shall commence in the Gulf of Mexico, three leagues from land, opposite the mouth of the Rio Grande, otherwise called Rio Bravo del Norte, or opposite the mouth of it's deepest branch, if it should have more than one branch emptying directly into the sea; from thence, up the middle of that river, following the deepest channel, where it has more than one to the point where it strikes the

Southern boundary of New Mexico; thence, westwardly along the whole Southern Boundary of New Mexico (which runs north of the town called Paso) to it's western termination; thence, northward, along the western line of New Mexico, until it intersects the first branch of the river Gila; (or if it should not intersect any branch of that river, then, to the point on the said line nearest to such branch, and thence in a direct line to the same;) thence down the middle of the said branch and of the said river, until it empties into the Rio Colorado; thence, across the Rio Colorado, following the division line between Upper and Lower California, to the Pacific Ocean.

The southern and western limits of New Mexico, mentioned in this Article, are those laid down in the Map, entitled "Map of the United Mexican States, as organized and defined by various acts of the Congress of said Republic, and constructed according to the best authorities. Revised edition. Published at New York in 1847 by J. Disturnell:" Of which Map a Copy is added to this Treaty, bearing the signatures and seals of the Undersigned Plenipotentiaries. And, in order to preclude all difficulty in tracing upon the ground the limit separating Upper from Lower California, it is agreed that the said limit shall consist of a straight line, drawn from the middle of the Rio Gila, where it unites with the Colorado, to a point on the Coast of the Pacific Ocean, distant one marine league due south of the southernmost point of the Port of San Diego, according to the plan of said port, made in the year 1782, by Don Juan Pantoja, second sailing-Master of the Spanish fleet, and published at Madrid in the year 1802, in the Atlas to the voyage of the schooners *Sutil* and *Mexicana:* of which plan a Copy is hereunto added, signed and sealed by the respective Plenipotentiaries.

In order to designate the Boundary line with due precision, upon authoritative maps, and to establish upon the ground landmarks which shall show the limits of both Republics, as described in the present Article, the two Governments shall each appoint a Commissioner and a Surveyor, who, before the expiration of one year from the date of the exchange of ratifications of this treaty, shall meet at the Port of San Diego, and proceed to run and mark the said Boundary in it's whole course to the mouth of the Rio Bravo del Norte. They shall keep journals and make out plans of their operations; and the result, agreed upon by them, shall be deemed a part of this treaty, and shall have the same force as if it were inserted therein. The two Governments will amicably agree regarding what may be necessary to these persons, and also as to their respective escorts, should such be necessary.

The Boundary line established by this Article shall be religiously respected by each of the two Republics, and no change shall ever be made therein, except by the express and free consent of both nations, lawfully given by the General Government of each, in conformity with it's own constitution.

Article VI

The vessels and citizens of the United States shall, in all time, have a free and uninterrupted passage by the Gulf of California, and by the river Colorado below it's confluence with the Gila, to and from their possessions situated north of the Boundary line defined in the preceding Article: it being understood that this passage is to be by navigating the Gulf of California and the river Colorado, and not by land, without the express consent of the Mexican Government.

If, by the examinations which may be made, it should be ascertained to be practicable and advantageous to construct a road, canal or railway, which should, in whole or in part, run upon the river Gila, or upon it's right or it's left bank, within the space of one marine league from either margin of the river, the Governments of both Republics will form an agreement regarding its construction, in order that it may serve equally for the use and advantage of both countries.

Article VII

The river Gila, and the part of the Rio Bravo del Norte lying below the southern boundary of New Mexico, being, agreeably to the fifth Article, divided in the middle between the two Republics the navigation of the Gila and of the Bravo below said boundary shall be free and common to the vessels and citizens of both countries; and neither shall, without the consent of the other, construct any work that may impede or interrupt, in whole or in part, the exercise of this right: not even for the purpose of favoring new methods of navigation. Nor shall any tax or contribution, under any denomination or title, be levied upon vessels or persons navigating the same, or upon merchandise or effects transported thereon, except in the case of landing upon one of their shores. If, for the purpose of making the said rivers navigable, or for maintaining them in such state, it should be necessary or advantageous to establish any tax or contribution, this shall not be done without the consent of both Governments.

The stipulations contained in the present Article shall not impair the territorial rights of either Republic, within its established limits.

Article VIII

Mexicans now established in territories previously belonging to Mexico, and which remain for the future within the limits of the United States, as defined by the present Treaty, shall be free to continue where they now reside or to remove at any time to the Mexican Republic, retaining the property which they possess in the said territories, or disposing thereof and removing the proceeds wherever they please; without their being subjected, on the account, to any contribution, tax or charge whatever. Those who shall prefer to remain in the said territories, may either retain the title and rights of Mexican citizens, or acquire those of citizens of the United States. But, they shall be under the obligation to make their election within one year from the date of the exchange of ratifications of this treaty: and those who shall remain in the said territories, after the expiration of that year, without having declared their intention to retain the character of Mexicans, shall be considered to have elected to become citizens of the United States.

In the said territories, property of every kind, now belonging to Mexicans not established there, shall be inviolably respected. The present owners, the heirs of these, and all Mexicans who may hereafter acquire said property by contract, shall enjoy with respect to it, guaranties equally ample as if the same belonged to citizens of the United States.

Article IX

The Mexicans who, in the territories aforesaid, shall not preserve the character of citizens of the Mexican Republic, conformably with what is stipulated in the preceding article, shall be incorporated into the Union of the United States and be admitted, at the proper time (to be judged of by the Congress of the United States) to the enjoyment of all the rights of citizens of the United States according to the principles of the Constitution; and in the mean time shall be maintained and protected in the free enjoyment of their liberty and property, and secured in the free exercise of their religion without restriction.

Article X

All grants of land made by the Mexican Government or by the competent authorities, in territories previously appertaining to Mexico, and remaining for the future within the limits of the United States, shall be respected as valid, to the same extent that the same grants would be valid, if the said territories had remained within the limits of Mexico. But the grantees of lands in Texas, put in possession thereof, who, by reason of the circumstances of the country since the beginning of the troubles between Texas and the Mexican Government, may have been prevented from fulfilling all the conditions of their grants, shall be under the obligation to fulfill the said conditions within the periods limited in the same respectively; such periods to be now counted from the date of the exchange of ratifications of this treaty: in default of which the said grants shall not be obligatory upon the State of Texas, in virtue of the stipulations contained in this Article.

The foregoing stipulation in regard to grantees of land in Texas, is extended to all grantees of land in the territories aforesaid, elsewhere than in Texas, put in possession under such grants; and, in default of the fulfillment of the conditions of any such grant, within the new period, which as is above stipulated, begins with the day of the exchange of ratifications of this treaty, the same shall be null and void.

The Mexican Government declares that no grant whatever of lands in Texas has been made since the second day of March one thousand eight hundred and thirty six; and that no grant whatever of lands in any of the territories aforesaid has been made since the thirteenth day may one thousand eight hundred and forty-six.

Article XI

Considering that a great part of the territories which by the present treaty are to be comprehended for the future within the limits of the United States, is now occupied by savage tribes, who will hereafter be under the exclusive control of the Government of the United States, and whose incursions within the territory of Mexico would be prejudicial in the extreme; it is solemnly agreed that all such incursions shall be forcibly restrained by the Government of the United States, whensoever this may be necessary; and that when they cannot be prevented, they shall be punished by the said Government, and satisfaction for the same shall be exacted: all in the same way, and with equal diligence and energy, as if the same incursions were meditated or committed within it's own territory against it's own citizens.

It shall not be lawful, under any pretext whatever, for any inhabitant of the United States, to purchase or acquire any Mexican or any foreigner residing in Mexico, who may have been captured by Indians inhabiting the territory of either of the two Republics; nor to purchase or acquire horses, mules, cattle or property of any kind, stolen within Mexican territory by such Indians;

And, in the event of any person or persons, captured within Mexican territory by Indians, being carried into the territory of the United States, the Government of the latter engages and binds itself, in the most solemn manner, so soon as it shall know of such captives being within it's territory, and shall be able so to do, through the faithful exercise of it's influence and power, to rescue them, and return them to their country, or deliver them to the agent or representative of the Mexican

Government. The Mexican Authorities will, as far as practicable, give to the Government of the United States notice of such captures; and it's agent shall pay the expenses incurred in the maintenance and transmission of the rescued captives; who, in the mean time, shall be treated with the utmost hospitality by the American Authorities at the place where they may be. But if the Government of the United States, before receiving such notice from Mexico, should obtain intelligence through any other channel, of the existence of Mexican captives within it's territory, it will proceed forthwith to effect their release and delivery to the Mexican agent, as above stipulated.

For the purpose of giving to these stipulations the fullest possible efficacy, thereby affording the security and redress demanded by their true spirit and intent, the Government of the United States will now and hereafter pass, without unnecessary delay, and always vigilantly enforce, such laws as the nature of the subject may require. And finally, the sacredness of this obligation shall never be lost sight of by the said Government, when providing for the removal of the Indians from any portion of the said territories, or for it's being settled by citizens of the United States; but on the contrary, special care shall then be taken not to place it's Indian occupants under the necessity of seeking new homes, by committing those invasions which the United States have solemnly obliged themselves to restrain.

Article XII

In consideration of the extension acquired by the boundaries of the United States, as defined in the fifth Article of the present treaty, the Government of the United States engages to pay to that of the Mexican Republic the sum of fifteen Millions of Dollars.

Immediately after this Treaty shall have been duly ratified by the Government of the Mexican Republic, the sum of three Millions of Dollars shall be paid to the said Government by that of the United States at the city of Mexico, in the gold or silver coin of Mexico. The remaining twelve Millions of Dollars shall be paid at the same place, and in the same coin, in annual installments of three Millions of Dollars each, together with interest on the same at the rate of six per centum per annum. This interest shall begin to run upon the whole sum of twelve millions, from the day of the ratification of the present treaty by the Mexican Government, and the first of the installments shall be paid at the expiration of one year from the same day. Together with each annual installment, as it falls due, the whole interest accruing on such installment from the beginning shall also be paid.

Article XIII

The United States engage moreover, to assume and pay to the claimants all the amounts now due them, and those hereafter to become due, by reason of the claims already liquidated and decided against the Mexican Republic, under the conventions between the two Republics, severally concluded on the eleventh day of April eighteen hundred and thirty-nine, and on the thirtieth day of January eighteen hundred and forty three: so that the Mexican Republic shall be absolutely exempt for the future, from all expense whatever old account of the said claims.

Article XIV

The United States do furthermore discharge the Mexican Republic from all claims of citizens of the United States, not heretofore decided against the Mexican Government, which may have arisen previously to the date of the signature of this treaty: which discharge shall be final and perpetual, whether the said claims be rejected or be allowed by the Board of Commissioners provided for in the following Article, and whatever shall be the total amount of those allowed.

Article XV

The United States, exonerating Mexico from all demands on account of the claims of their citizens mentioned in the preceding Article, and considering them entirely and forever cancelled, whatever their amount may be, undertake to make satisfaction for the same, to an amount not exceeding three and one quarter millions of dollars. To ascertain the validity and amount of those claims, a Board of Commissioners shall be established by the Government of the United States, whose awards shall be final and conclusive: provided that in deciding upon the validity of each claim, the board shall be guided and governed by the principles and rules of decision described by the first and fifth Articles of the unratified convention, concluded at the city of Mexico on the twentieth day of November one thousand eight hundred and forty-three; and in no case shall an award be made in favor of any claim not embraced by these principles and rules.

If, in the opinion of the said Board of Commissioners, or of the claimants, any books, records or documents in the possession or power of the Government of the Mexican Republic, shall be deemed necessary to the just decision of any claim, the Commissioners or the claimants, through them, shall, within such period as Congress may designate, make an application in writing for the same, addressed to the Mexican Minister for Foreign Affairs, to be transmitted by the Secretary of State of the United States; and the Mexican Government engages, at the earliest possible moment after the receipt of such demand, to cause any of the books, records or documents, so specified, which shall be in their possession or power, (or authenticated copies or extracts of the same) to be transmitted to the said Secretary of State, who shall immediately deliver them over to the said Board of Commissioners: *Provided* That no such application shall be made, by, or at the instance of, any claimant, until the facts which it is expected to prove by such books, records or documents, shall have been stated under oath or affirmation.

Article XVI

Each of the contracting parties reserves to itself the entire right to fortify whatever point within it's territory, it may judge proper so to fortify, for it's security.

Article XVII

The Treaty of Amity, Commerce and Navigation, concluded at the city of Mexico on the fifth day of April A.D. 1831, between the United States of America and the United Mexican States, except the additional Article, and except so far as the stipulations of the said treaty may be incompatible with any stipulation contained in the present treaty, is hereby revived for the period of eight years from the day of the exchange of ratifications of this treaty, with the same force and virtue as if incorporated therein; it being understood that each of the contracting parties reserves to itself the right, at any time after the said period of eight years shall have expired, to terminate the same by giving one year's notice of such intention to the other party.

Article XVIII

All supplies whatever for troops of the United States in Mexico, arriving at ports in the occupation of such troops, previous to the final evacuation thereof, although subsequently to the restoration of the Custom Houses at such ports, shall be entirely exempt from duties and charges of any kind: the Government of the United States hereby engaging and pledging it's faith to establish and vigilantly to enforce, all possible guards for securing the revenue of Mexico, by preventing the importation, under cover of this stipulation, of any articles, other than such, both in kind and in quantity, as shall really be wanted for the use and consumption of the forces of the United States during the time they may remain in Mexico. To this end, it shall be the duty of all officers and agents of the United States to denounce to the Mexican Authorities at the respective ports, any attempts at a fraudulent abuse of this stipulation, which they may know of or may have reason to suspect, and to give to such authorities all the aid in their power with regard thereto: and every such attempt, when duly proved and established by sentence of a competent tribunal, shall be punished by the confiscation of the property so attempted to be fraudulently introduced.

Article XIX

With respect to all merchandise, effects and property whatsoever, imported into ports of Mexico, whilst in the occupation of the forces of the United States, whether by citizens of either republic, or by citizens or subjects of any neutral nation, the following rules shall be observed:

I. All such merchandise, effects and property, if imported previously to the restoration of the Custom Houses to the Mexican Authorities, as stipulated for in the third Article of this treaty, shall be exempt from confiscation, although the importation of the same be prohibited by the Mexican tariff.

II. The same perfect exemption shall be enjoyed by all such merchandise, effects and property, imported subsequently to the restoration of the Custom Houses, and previously to the sixty days fixed in the following Article for the coming into force of the Mexican tariff at such ports respectively: the said merchandise, effects and property being, however, at the time of their importation, subject to the payment of duties as provided for in the said following Article.

III. All merchandise, effects and property, described in the two rules foregoing, shall, during their continuance at the place of importation, and upon their leaving such place for the interior, be exempt from all duty, tax or impost of every kind, under whatsoever title or denomination. Nor shall they be there subjected to any charge whatsoever upon the sale thereof.

IV. All merchandise, effects and property, described in the first and second rules, which shall have been removed to any place in the interior, whilst such place was in the occupation of the forces of the United States, shall, during their continuance therein, be exempt from all tax upon the sale or consumption thereof, and from every kind of impost or contribution, under whatsoever title or denomination.

V. But if any merchandise, effects or property, described in the first and second rules, shall be removed to any place not occupied at the time by the forces of the United States, they shall, upon their introduction into such place, or upon their sale or consumption there, be subject to the same duties which, under the Mexican laws, they would be required to pay in such cases, if they had been imported in time of peace through the Maritime

Custom Houses, and had there paid the duties, conformably with the Mexican tariff.

VI. The owners of all merchandise, effects or property, described in the first and second rules, and existing in any port of Mexico, shall have the right to reship the same, exempt from all tax, impost or contribution whatever.

With respect to the metals, or other property, exported from any Mexican port, whilst in the occupation of the forces of the United States, and previously to the restoration of the Custom House at such port, no person shall be required by the Mexican Authorities, whether General or State, to pay any tax, duty or contribution upon any such exportation, or in any manner to account for the same to the said Authorities.

Article XX

Through consideration for the interests of commerce generally, it is agreed, that if less than sixty days should elapse between the date of the signature of this treaty and the restoration of the Custom Houses, conformably with the stipulation in the third Article, in such case, all merchandise, effects and property whatsoever, arriving at the Mexican ports after the restoration of the said Custom Houses, and previously to the expiration of sixty days after the day of the signature of this treaty, shall be admitted to entry; and no other duties shall be levied thereon than the duties established by the tariff found in force at such Custom Houses at the time of the restoration of the same. And to all such merchandise, effects and property, the rules established by the preceding Article shall apply.

Article XXI

If unhappily any disagreement should hereafter arise between the Governments of the two Republics, whether with respect to the interpretation of any stipulation in this treaty, or with respect to any other particular concerning the political or commercial relations of the two Nations, the said Governments, in the name of those Nations, do promise to each other, that they will endeavour, in the most sincere and earnest manner, to settle the differences so arising, and to preserve the state of peace and friendship, in which the two countries are now placing themselves: using, for this end, mutual representations and pacific negotiations. And if, by these means, they should not be enabled to come to an agreement, a resort shall not, on this account, be had to reprisals, aggression or hostility of any kind, by the one Republic against the other, until the Government of that which deems itself aggrieved, shall have maturely considered, in the spirit of peace and good neighbourship, whether it would not be better that such difference should be settled by the arbitration of Commissioners appointed on each side, or by that of a friendly nation. And should such course be proposed by either party, it shall be acceded to by the other, unless deemed by it altogether incompatible with the nature of the difference, or the circumstances of the case.

Article XXII

If (which is not to be expected, and which God forbid!) war should unhappily break out between the two Republics, they do now, with a view to such calamity, solemnly pledge themselves to each other and to the world, to observe the following rules: absolutely, where the nature of the subject permits, and as closely as possible in all cases where such absolute observance shall be impossible.

I. The merchants of either Republic, then residing in the other, shall be allowed to remain twelve months (for those dwelling in the interior) and six months (for those dwelling at the sea-ports) to collect their debts and settle their affairs; during which periods they shall enjoy the same protection, and be on the same footing, in all respects, as the citizens or subjects of the most friendly nations; and, at the expiration thereof, or at any time before, they shall have full liberty to depart, carrying off all their effects, without molestation or hinderance: conforming therein to the same laws, which the citizens or subjects of the most friendly nations are required to conform to. Upon the entrance of the armies of either nation into the territories of the other, women and children, ecclesiastics, scholars of every faculty, cultivators of the earth, merchants, artisans, manufacturers, and fishermen, unarmed and inhabiting unfortified towns, villages or places, and in general all persons whose occupations are for the common subsistence and benefit of mankind, shall be allowed to continue their respective employments, unmolested in their persons. Nor shall their houses or goods be burnt, or otherwise destroyed; nor their cattle taken, nor their fields wasted, by the armed force, into whose power, by the events of war, they may happen to fall; but if the necessity arise to take anything from them for the use of such armed force, the same shall be paid for at an equitable price. All churches, hospitals, schools, colleges, libraries, and other establishments for charitable and beneficent purposes, shall be respected, and all persons connected with the same protected in the discharge of their duties and the pursuit of their vocations.

II. In order that the fate of prisoners of war may be alleviated, all such practices as those of sending them into distant, inclement or unwholesome districts, or crowding them into close and noxious places, shall be studiously avoided. They shall not be confined in dungeons, prison-ships, or prisons; nor be put in irons, or bound, or otherwise restrained in the use of their limbs. The officers shall enjoy liberty on their paroles, within convenient districts, and have comfortable quarters; and the common soldier shall be disposed in cantonments, open and extensive enough for air and exercise, and lodged in barracks as roomy and good as are provided by the party in whose power they are for it's own troops. But, if any officer shall break his parole by leaving the district so assigned him, or any other prisoner shall escape from the limits of his cantonment, after they shall have been designated to him, such individual, officer or other prisoner, shall forfeit so much of the benefit of this article as provides for his liberty on parole or in cantonment. And if any officer so breaking his parole, or any common soldier so escaping from the limits assigned him, shall afterwards be found in arms, previously to his being regularly exchanged, the person so offending shall be dealt with according to the established laws of war. The officers shall be daily furnished by the party in whose power they are, with as many rations, and of the same articles as are allowed either in kind or by commutation, to officers of equal rank in it's own army; and all others shall be daily furnished with such ration as is allowed to a common soldier in it's own service: the value of all which supplies shall, at the close of the war, or at periods to be agreed upon between the respective commanders, be paid by the other party on a mutual adjustment of accounts for the subsistence of prisoners; and such accounts shall not be mingled with or set off against any others, nor the balance due on them be withheld, as a compensation or reprisal for any cause whatever, real or pretended. Each party shall be allowed to keep a commissary of prisoners, appointed by itself, with every cantonment of prisoners, in possession of the other: which commissary shall see the prisoners as often as he pleases; shall be allowed to receive, exempt from all duties or taxes, and to distribute whatever comforts may be sent to them by their friends; and shall be free to transmit his reports in open letters to the party by whom he is employed.

And it is declared that neither the pretence that war dissolves all treaties, nor any other whatever shall be considered as annulling or suspending the solemn covenant contained in this article. On the contrary, the state of war is precisely that for which it is provided; and during which it's stipulations are to be as sacredly observed as the most acknowledged obligations under the law of nature or nations.

Article XXIII

This treaty shall be ratified by the President of the United States of America, by and with the advice and consent of the Senate thereof; and by the President of the Mexican Republic, with the previous approbation of its General Congress: and the ratifications shall be exchanged in the City of Washington, or at the seat of government of Mexico, in four months from the date of the signature hereof, or sooner if practicable.

In faith whereof, we, the respective Plenipotentiaries, have signed this Treaty of Peace, Friendship, Limits and Settlement, and have hereunto affixed our seals respectively. Done in Quintuplicate, at the City of Guadalupe Hidalgo, on the second day of February in the year of Our Lord one thousand eight hundred and forty eight.

N. P. TRIST

LUIS G. CUEVAS

BERNARDO COUTO

MIG ATRISTAIN

BOUNDARIES: GADSDEN TREATY 1853

In the Name of Almighty God

The Republic of Mexico and the United States of America desiring to remove every cause of disagreement, which might interfere in any manner with the friendship and intercourse between the two Countries; and especially, in respect to the true limits which should be established, when notwithstanding what was covenanted in the Treaty of Guadalupe Hidalgo in the Year 1848, opposite interpretations have been urged, which might give occasion to questions of serious moment: to avoid these, and to strengthen and more firmly maintain the peace, which happily prevails between the two Republics, the President of the United States has for this purpose, appointed James Gadsden Envoy Extraordinary and Minister Plenipotentiary of the same near the Mexican Government, and the President of Mexico has appointed as Plenipotentiary "ad hoc" His Excellency Don Manuel Diaz de Bonilla Cavalier Grand Cross of the National and Distinguished Order of Guadalupe, and Secretary of State and of the Office of Foreign Relations, and Don Jose Salazar Ylarregui and General Mariano Monterde as Scientific Commissioners invested with Full powers for this Negotiation who having communicated their respective Full Powers, and finding them in due and proper form, have agreed upon the Articles following:

Article 1

The Mexican Republic agrees to designate the following as her true limits with the United States for the future; Retaining the same dividing line between the two California's, as already defined and established according to the 5th Article of the Treaty of Guadalupe Hidalgo, the limits between

the Two Republics shall be as follows: Beginning in the Gulf of Mexico, three leagues from land, opposite the mouth of the Rio Grande as provided in the fifth article of the treaty of Guadalupe Hidalgo, thence as defined in the said article, up the middle of that river to the point where the parallel of 31°47′ north latitude crosses the same, thence due west one hundred miles, thence south to the parallel of 31°20′ north latitude, thence along the said parallel of 31°20′ to the 111th meridian of longitude west of Greenwich, thence in a straight line to a point on the Colorado river twenty english miles below the junction of the Gila and Colorado rivers, thence up the middle of the said river Colorado until it intersects the present line between the United States and Mexico.

For the performance of this portion of the Treaty each of the two Governments shall nominate one Commissioner to the end that, by common consent, the two thus nominated having met in the City of Paso del Norte, three months after the exchange of the ratifications of this Treaty may proceed to survey and mark out upon the land the dividing line stipulated by this article, where it shall not have already been surveyed and established by the Mixed Commission according to the Treaty of Guadalupe keeping a Journal and making proper plans of their operations. For this purpose if they should Judge it is necessary, the contracting Parties shall be at liberty each to unite to its respective Commissioner Scientific or other assistants, such as Astronomers and Surveyors whose concurrence shall not be considered necessary for the settlement and ratification of a true line of division between the two Republics; that line shall be alone established upon which the Commissioners may fix, their consent in this particular being considered decisive and an integral part of this Treaty, without necessity of ulterior ratification or approval, and without room for interpretation of any kind by either of the Parties contracting.

The dividing line thus established shall in all time be faithfully respected by the two Governments without any variation therein, unless of the express and free consent of the two, given in conformity to the principles of the Law of Nations, and in accordance with the Constitution of each country respectively.

In consequence, the stipulation in the 5th Article of the Treaty of Guadalupe upon the Boundary line therein described is no longer of any force, wherein it may conflict with that here established, the said line being considered annulled and abolished wherever it may not coincide with the present, and in the same manner remaining in full force where in accordance with the same.

Article 2

The government of Mexico hereby releases the United States from all liability on account of the obligations contained in the eleventh article of the treaty of Guadalupe Hidalgo, and the said article and the thirty-third article of the treaty of amity, commerce and navigation between the United States of America and the United Mexican States concluded at Mexico, on the fifth day of April, 1831, are hereby abrogated.

Article 3

In consideration of the foregoing stipulations, the government of the United States agrees to pay to the government of Mexico, in the city of New York, the sum of ten millions of dollars, of which seven millions shall be paid immediately upon the exchange of the ratifications of this treaty, and the remaining three millions as soon as the boundary line shall be surveyed, marked, and established.

Article 4

The Provisions of the 6th and 7th Articles of the Treaty of Guadalupe Hidalgo having been rendered nugatory for the most part by the Cession of Territory granted in the First Article of this Treaty, the said Articles are hereby abrogated and annulled and the provisions as herein expressed substituted therefore—The Vessels and Citizens of the United States shall in all Time have free and uninterrupted passage through the Gulf of California to and from their possessions situated North of the Boundary line of the Two Countries. It being understood that this passage is to be by navigating the Gulf of California and the river Colorado, and not by land, without the express

consent of the Mexican Government, and precisely the same provisions, stipulations and restrictions in all respects are hereby agreed upon and adopted and shall be scrupulously observed and enforced by the Two Contracting Governments in reference to the Rio Colorado, so far and for such distance as the middle of that River is made their common Boundary Line, by the First Article of this Treaty.

The several Provisions, Stipulations and restrictions contained in the 7th Article of the Treaty of Guadalupe Hidalgo, shall remain in force only so far as regards the Rio Bravo del Norte below the initial of the said Boundary provided in the First Article of this Treaty. That is to say below the intersection of the 31°47′30″ parallel of Latitude with the Boundary Line established by the late Treaty dividing said river from its mouth upwards according to the 5th Article of the Treaty of Guadalupe.

Article 5

All the provisions of the Eighth and Ninth, Sixteenth and Seventeenth Articles of the Treaty of Guadalupe Hidalgo shall apply to the Territory ceded by the Mexican Republic in the First Article of the present Treaty and to all the rights of persons and property both civil and ecclesiastical within the same, as fully and as effectually as if the said Articles were herein again recited and set forth.

Article 6

No Grants of Land within the Territory ceded by the First Article of This Treaty bearing date subsequent to the day Twenty fifth of September—when the Minister and Subscriber to this Treaty on the part of the United States proposed to the Government of Mexico to terminate the question of Boundary, will be considered valid or be recognized by the United States, or will any Grants made previously be respected or be considered as obligatory which have not been located and duly recorded in the Archives of Mexico.

Article 7

Should there at any future period (which God forbid) occur any disagreement between the two

Nations which might lead to a rupture of their relations and reciprocal peace, they bind themselves in like manner to procure by every possible method the adjustment of every difference, and should they still in this manner not succeed, never will they proceed to a declaration of War, without having previously paid attention to what has been set forth in Article 21 of the Treaty of Guadalupe for similar cases; which Article as well as the 22nd is here re-affirmed.

Article 8

The Mexican government having on the 5th of February 1853 authorized the early construction of a plank and railroad across the Isthmus of Tehuantepec, and to secure the stable benefits of said transit way to the persons and merchandise of the citizens of Mexico and the United States, it is stipulated that neither government will interpose any obstacle to the transit of persons and merchandise of both nations; and at no time shall higher charges be made on the transit of persons and property of citizens of the United States than may be made on the persons and property of other foreign nations, nor shall any interest in said transit way, nor in the proceeds thereof, be transferred to any foreign government.

The United States by its Agents shall have the right to transport across the Isthmus, in closed bags, the mails of the United States not intended for distribution along the line of communication; also the effects of the United States government and its citizens, which may be intended for transit, and not for distribution on the Isthmus, free of custom-house or other charges by the Mexican government. Neither passports nor letters of security will be required of persons crossing the Isthmus and not remaining in the country.

When the construction of the railroad shall be completed, the Mexican government agrees to open a port of entry in addition to the port of Veracruz, at or near the terminus of said road on the Gulf of Mexico. The two governments will enter into arrangements for the prompt transit of troops and munitions of the United States, which that government may have occasion to send from

one part of its territory to another, lying on opposite sides of the continent. The Mexican government having agreed to protect with its whole power the prosecution, preservation and security of the work, the United States may extend its protection as it shall judge wise to it when it may feel sanctioned and warranted by the public or international law.

Article 9

This Treaty shall be ratified, and the respective ratifications shall be exchanged at the City of Washington, within the exact period of six months from the date of its signature or sooner if possible.

In testimony whereof, We the Plenipotentiaries of the contracting parties have hereunto affixed our hands and seals at Mexico the—Thirtieth (30th)—day of December in the Year of Our Lord one thousand eight hundred and fifty-three, in the thirty third year of the Independence of the Mexican Republic, and the seventy-eighth of that of the United States

JAMES GADSDEN

MANUEL DIEZ DE BONILLA

JOSE SALAZAR YLARREGUI

J. MARIANO MONTERDE

TREATY OF PEACE (TREATY OF PARIS) 1898

The United States of America and Her Majesty the Queen Regent of Spain, in the name of her August Son Don Alfonso XIII, desiring to end the state of war now existing between the two countries, have for that purpose appointed as Plenipotentiaries: The President of the United States, William R. Day, Cushman K. Davis, William P. Frye, George Gray, and: Whitelaw Reid, citizens of the United States; and Her Majesty the Queen Regent of Spain,

Don Eugenio Montero Rios, President of the Senate,

Don Buenaventura de Abarzuza, Senator of the Kingdom and ex-Minister of the Crown,

Don Jose de Garnica, Deputy to the Cortes and Associate Justice of the Supreme Court,

Don Wenceslao Ramire de Villa-Urrutia, Envoy Extraordinary and Minister Plenipotentiary at Brussels, and

Don Rafael Cerero, General of Division;

Who, having assembled in Paris, and having exchanged their full powers, which were found to be in due and proper form, have, after discussion of the matters before them, agreed upon the following articles:

Article I

Spain relinquishes all claim of sovereignty over and title to Cuba.

And as the island is, upon its evacuation by Spain, to be occupied by the United States, the United States will, so long as such occupation shall last, assume and discharge the obligations that may under international law result from the fact of its occupation, for the protection of life and property.

Article II

Spain cedes to the United States the island of Porto Rico and other islands now under Spanish sovereignty in the West Indies, and the island of Guam in the Marianas or Ladrones.

Article III

Spain cedes to the United States the archipelago known as the Philippine Islands, and comprehending the islands lying within the following line:

A line running from west to east along or near the twentieth parallel of uncaptured war north latitude, and through the middle of the navigable channel of Bachi, from the one hundred and eighteenth (118th) to the one hundred and twenty seventh (127th) degree meridian of longitude east of Greenwich, thence along the one hundred and twenty seventh (127th) degree meridian of longitude east of Greenwich to the parallel of four degrees and forty five minutes (4° 45′) north latitude to its intersection with the meridian of longitude one hundred and nineteen degrees and thirty-five minutes (119° 35′) east of Greenwich to the parallel of latitude seven degrees and forty minutes (7° 40′) north, thence along the parallel

of latitude seven degrees and forty minutes (7° 40′) north to its intersection with the one hundred and sixteenth (116th) degree meridian of longitude east of Greenwich, thence by a direct line to the intersection of the tenth (10th) degree parallel of north latitude with the one hundred and eighteenth (118th) degree meridian of longitude east of Greenwich, and thence along the one hundred and eighteenth (118th) degree meridian of longitude east of Greenwich to the point of beginning.

The United States will pay to Spain the sum of twenty million dollars ($20,000,000) within three months after the exchange of the ratifications of the present treaty.

Article IV

The United States will, for the term of ten years from the date of the exchange of the ratifications of the present treaty, admit Spanish ships and merchandise to the ports of the Philippine Islands on the same terms as ships and merchandise of the United States.

Article V

The United States will, upon the signature of the present treaty, send back to Spain, at its own cost, the Spanish soldiers taken as prisoners of war on the capture of Manila by the American forces. The arms of the soldiers in question shall be restored to them.

Spain will, upon the exchange of the ratifications of the present treaty, proceed to evacuate the Philippines, as well as the island of Guam, on terms similar to those agreed upon by the Commissioners appointed to arrange for the evacuation of Porto Rico and other islands in the West Indies, under the Protocol of August 12, 1898, which is to continue in force until its provisions are completely executed.

The time within which the evacuation of the Philippine Islands and Guam shall be completed shall be fixed by the two Governments. Stands of colors, uncaptured war vessels, small arms, guns of an calibres, with their carriages and accessories, powder, ammunition, livestock, and materials and supplies of all kinds, belonging to the land and naval forces of Spain in the Philippines and Guam, remain the property of Spain. Pieces of heavy ordnance, exclusive of field artillery, in the fortifications and coast defences, shall remain in their emplacements for the term of six months, to be reckoned from the exchange of ratifications of the treaty; and the United States may, in the mean time, purchase such material from Spain, if a satisfactory agreement between the two Governments on the subject shall be reached.

Article VI

Spain will, upon the signature of the present treaty, release all prisoners of war, and all persons detained or imprisoned for political offences, in connection with the insurrections in Cuba and the Philippines and the war with the United States. Reciprocally, the United States will release all persons made prisoners of war by the American forces, and will undertake to obtain the release of all Spanish prisoners in the hands of the insurgents in Cuba and the Philippines.

The Government of the United States will at its own cost return to Spain and the Government of Spain will at its own cost return to the United States, Cuba, Porto Rico, and the Philippines, according to the situation of their respective homes, prisoners released or caused to be released by them, respectively, under this article.

Article VII

The United States and Spain mutually relinquish all claims for indemnity, national and individual of every kind, of either Government, or of its citizens or subjects, against the other Government, that may have arisen since the beginning of the late insurrection in Cuba and prior to the exchange of ratifications of the present treaty, including all claims for indemnity for the cost of the war.

The United States will adjudicate and settle the claims of its citizens against Spain relinquished in this article.

Article VIII

In conformity with the provisions of Articles I, II, and III of this treaty, Spain relinquishes in Cuba, and cedes in Porto Rico and other islands in the West Indies, in the island of Guam, and in the Philippine Archipelago, all the buildings, wharves, barracks, forts, structures, public highways and other immovable property which, in conformity with law, belong to the public domain, and as such belong to the Crown of Spain.

And it is hereby declared that the relinquishment or cession, as the case may be, to which the preceding paragraph refers, cannot in any respect impair the property or rights which by law belong to the peaceful possession of property of all kinds, of provinces, municipalities, public or private establishments, ecclesiastical or civic bodies, or any other associations having legal capacity to acquire and possess property in the aforesaid territories renounced or ceded, or of private individuals, of whatsoever nationality such individuals may be. The aforesaid relinquishment or cession, as the case may be, includes all documents exclusively referring to the sovereignty relinquished or ceded that may exist in the archives of the Peninsula. Where any document in such archives only in part relates to said sovereignty, a copy of such part will be furnished whenever it shall be requested. Like rules shall be reciprocally observed in favor of Spain in respect of documents in the archives of the islands above referred to.

In the aforesaid relinquishment or cession, as the case may be, are also included such rights as the Crown of Spain and its authorities possess in respect of the official archives and records, executive as well as judicial, in the islands above referred to, which relate to said islands or the rights and property of their inhabitants. Such archives and records shall be carefully preserved, and private persons shall without distinction have the right to require, in accordance with law, authenticated copies of the contracts, wills and other instruments forming part of notarial protocols or files or which may he contained in the executive or judicial archives, be the latter in Spain or in the islands aforesaid.

Article IX

Spanish subjects, natives of the Peninsula, residing in the territory over which Spain by the present treaty relinquishes or cedes her sovereignty, may remain in such territory or may remove therefrom, retaining in either event all their rights of property, including the right to sell or dispose of such property or of its proceeds; and they shall also have the right to carry on their industry, commerce and professions, being subject in respect thereof to such laws as are applicable to other foreigners. In case they remain in the territory they may preserve their allegiance to the Crown of Spain by making, before a court of record, within a year from the date of the exchange of ratifications of this treaty, a declaration of their decision to preserve such allegiance; in default of which declaration they shall be held to have renounced it and to have adopted the nationality of the territory in which they may reside.

The civil rights and political status of the native inhabitants of the territories hereby ceded to the United States shall be determined by the Congress.

Article X

The inhabitants of the territories over which Spain relinquishes or cedes her sovereignty shall be secured in the free exercise of their religion.

Article XI

The Spaniards residing in the territories over which Spain by this treaty cedes or relinquishes her sovereignty shall be subject in matters civil as well as criminal to the jurisdiction of the courts of the country wherein they reside, pursuant to the ordinary laws governing the same; and they shall have the right to appear before such courts, and to pursue the same course as citizens of the country to which the courts belong.

Article XII

Judicial proceedings pending at the time of the exchange of ratifications of this treaty in the territories over which Spain relinquishes or cedes her sovereignty shall be determined according to the following rules:

1. Judgments rendered either in civil suits between private individuals, or in criminal matters, before the date mentioned, and with respect to which there is no recourse or right of review under the Spanish law, shall be deemed to be final, and shall be executed in due form by competent authority in the territory within which such judgments should be carried out.

2. Civil suits between private individuals which may on the date mentioned be undetermined shall be prosecuted to judgment before the court in which they may then be pending or in the court that may be substituted therefor.

3. Criminal actions pending on the date mentioned before the Supreme Court of Spain against citizens of the territory which by this treaty ceases to be Spanish shall continue under its jurisdiction until final judgment; but, such judgment having been rendered, the execution shall be committed to the competent authority of the place in which the case arose.

Article XIII

The rights of property secured by copyrights and patents acquired by Spaniards in the Island of Cuba, and in Porto Rico, the Philippines and other ceded territories, at the time of the exchange of the ratifications of this treaty, shall continue to be respected. Spanish scientific, literary and artistic works, not subversive of public order in the territories in question, shall continue to be admitted free of duty into such territories, for the period of ten years, to be reckoned from the date of the exchange of the ratifications of this treaty.

Article XIV

Spain shall have the power to establish consular officers in the ports and places of the territories, the sovereignty over which has been either relinquished or ceded by the present treaty.

Article XV

The Government of each country will, for the term of ten years, accord to the merchant vessels of the other country the same treatment in respect of all port charges, including entrance and clearance dues, light dues, and tonnage duties, as it accords to its own merchant vessels, not engaged in the coastwise trade.

This article may at any time be terminated on six months' notice given by either Government to the other.

Article XVI

It is understood that any obligations assumed in this treaty by the United States with respect to Cuba are limited to the time of its occupancy thereof; but it will upon the termination of such occupancy, advise any Government established in the island to assume the same obligations.

Article XVII

The present treaty shall be ratified by the resident of the United States by and with the advice and consent of the Senate thereof, and by Her Majesty the Queen Regent of Spain; and the ratifications shall be exchanged at Washington within six months from the date hereof, or earlier if possible.

In faith whereof, we, the respective Plenipotentiaries, have signed this treaty and have hereunto affixed our seals.

Done in duplicate at Paris, the tenth day of December, in the year of Our Lord one thousand eight hundred and ninety eight.

WILLIAM R. DAY

CUSHMAN K. DAVIS

WM. P. FRYE

GEO. GRAY

WHITELAW REID

EUGENIO MONTERO RIOS

B. DE ABARZUZA

J. DE GARNICA

W. R. DE VILLA URRUTIA

RAFAEL CERERO

U.S. Relations with Cuba

Whereas the Congress of the United States of America, by an Act approved March 2, 1901, provided as follows:

Provided further, That in fulfillment of the declaration contained in the joint resolution approved April twentieth, eighteen hundred and ninety-eight, entitled, "For the recognition of the independence of the of people Cuba, demanding that the Government of Spain relinquish its authority and government in the island of Cuba, and to

withdraw its land and naval forces from Cuba and Cuban waters, and directing the President of the United States to use the land and naval forces of the United States to carry resolutions into effect," the President is hereby authorized to "leave the government and control of the island of Cuba to its people" so soon as a government shall have been established in said island under a constitution either as a part thereof or in an ordinance appended thereto, shall define future relations of the United States with Cuba, substantially as follow:

"I.—That the government of Cuba shall never enter into any treaty or other compact with any foreign power or powers which will impair or tend to impair the independence of Cuba, nor in any manner authorize or permit any foreign power or powers to obtain by colonization or for military or naval purposes or otherwise, lodgement in or control over any portion said island."

"II.—That said government shall not assume or contract any public debt, to pay the interest upon which, and to make reasonable sinking fund provision for the ultimate discharge of which, the ordinary revenues of the island, after defraying the current expenses of government shall be inadequate."

"III.—That the government of Cuba consents that the United States may exercise the right to intervene for the preservation of Cuban independence, the maintenance of a government adequate for the protection of life, property, and individual liberty, and for discharging the obligations with respect to Cuba imposed by the Treaty of Paris on the United States, now to be assumed and undertaken by the government of Cuba."

"IV.—That all Acts of the United States in Cuba during its military occupancy thereof are ratified and validated, and all lawful rights acquired thereunder shall be maintained and protected."

"V.—That the government of Cuba will execute, and as far as necessary extend, the plans already devised or other plans to be mutually agreed upon, for the sanitation of the cities of the island, to the end that a recurrence of epidemic and infectious diseases may be prevented thereby assuring protection to the people and commerce of Cuba, as well as to the commerce of the southern ports of the United States and the people residing therein."

"VI.—That the Isle of Pines shall be omitted from the proposed constitutional boundaries of Cuba, the title thereto being left to future adjustment by treaty."

"VII.—That to enable the United States to maintain the independence of Cuba, and to protect the people thereof, as well as for is own defense, the government of Cuba will sell or lease to the United States lands necessary for coaling or naval stations at certain specified points to be agreed upon with the President of the United States."

"VIII.—That by way of further assurance the Government of Cuba will embody the foregoing provisions in a permanent treaty with the United States."

Whereas the Constitutional Convention of Cuba, on June twelfth, 1901, adopted a Resolution adding to the Constitution of the Republic of Cuba which was adopted on the twenty-first of February 1901, an appendix in the words and letters of the eight enumerated articles of the above cited act of the Congress of the United States;

And whereas, by the establishment of the independent and sovereign government of the Republic of Cuba, under the constitution promulgated on the 20th of May, 1902, which embraced the foregoing conditions, and by the withdrawal of the Government of the United States as an intervening power, on the same date, it becomes necessary to embody the above cited provisions in a permanent treaty between the United States of America and the Republic of Cuba;

The United States of America and the Republic of Cuba, being desirous to carry out the foregoing conditions, have for that purpose appointed as their plenipotentiaries to conclude a treaty to that end,

The President of the United States of America, Herbert G. Squiers, Envoy Extraordinary and Minister Plenipotentiary at Havana,

And the President of the Republic of Cuba, Carlos de Zaldo y Beurmann, Secretary of State and

Justice—who after communicating to each other their full powers found in good and due form, have agreed upon the following articles:

Article I

The Government of Cuba shall never enter into any treaty or other compact with any foreign power or powers which will impair or tend to impair the independence of Cuba, nor in any manner authorize or permit any foreign power or powers to obtain by colonization or for military or naval purposes, or otherwise, lodgement in or control over any portion of said island.

Article II

The Government of Cuba shall not assume or contract any public debt to pay the interest upon which, and to make reasonable sinking-fund provision for the ultimate discharge of which, the ordinary revenues of the Island of Cuba, after defraying the current expenses of the Government, shall be inadequate.

Article III

The Government of Cuba consents that the United States may exercise the right to intervene for the preservation of Cuban independence, the maintenance of a government adequate for the protection of life, property, and individual liberty, and for discharging the obligations with respect to Cuba imposed by the Treaty of Paris on the United States, now to be assumed and undertaken by the Government of Cuba.

Article IV

All acts of the United States in Cuba during its military occupancy thereof are ratified and validated, and all lawful rights acquired thereunder shall be maintained and protected.

Article V

The Government of Cuba will execute, and, as far as necessary, extend the plans already devised, or other plans to be mutually agreed upon, for the sanitation of the cities of the island, to the end that a recurrence of epidemic and infectious diseases may be prevented, thereby assuring protection to the people and commerce of Cuba, as well as to the commerce of the Southern ports of the United States and the people residing therein.

Article VI

The Island of Pines shall be omitted form the boundaries of Cuba specified in the Constitution, the title thereof being left to future adjustment by treaty.

Article VII

To enable the United States to maintain the independence of Cuba, and to protect the people thereof, as well as for its own defense, the Government of Cuba will sell or lease to the United States lands necessary for coaling or naval stations, at certain specified points, to be agreed upon with the President of the United States.

Article VIII

The present Convention shall be ratified by each party in conformity with the respective Constitutions of the two countries, and the ratifications shall be exchanged in the City of Washington within eight months form this date.

In witness whereof, we the respective Plenipotentiaries, have signed the same in duplicate, in English and Spanish, and have affixed our respective seals at Havana, Cuba, this twenty-second day of May, in the year nineteen hundred and three.

H.G. SQUIERS

CARLOS DE ZALDO

THE "HAY–BUNAU–VARILLA CONVENTION"

Between the United States and Panama, signed at Washington, November 1, 1903

THE UNITED STATES of America and the Republic of Panama being desirous to insure the construction of a ship canal across the Isthmus of Panama to connect the Atlantic and Pacific oceans, and the Congress of the United States of America having passed an act approved June 28, 1902, in furtherance of that object, by which the President of the United States is authorized to acquire within a reasonable time the control of the necessary territory of the Republic of Colombia, and the

sovereignty of such territory being actually vested in the Republic of Panama, the high contracting parties have resolved for that purpose to conclude a convention and have accordingly appointed as their plenipotentiaries,

The President of the United States of America, JOHN HAY, Secretary of State, and

The Government of the Republic of Panama, PHILIPPE BUNAU–VARILLA, Envoy Extraordinary and Minister Plenipotentiary of the Republic of Panama, thereunto specially empowered by said government, who after communicating with each other their respective full powers, found to be in good and due form, have agreed upon and concluded the following articles:

Article 1

The United States guarantees and will maintain the independence of the Republic of Panama.

Article 2

The Republic of Panama grants to the United States in perpetuity the use, occupation and control of a zone of land and land under water for the construction, maintenance, operation, sanitation and protection of said Canal of the width of ten miles extending to the distance of five miles on each side of the center line of the route of the Canal to be constructed; the said zone beginning in the Caribbean Sea three marine miles from mean low water mark and extending to and across the Isthmus of Panama into the Pacific ocean to a distance of three marine miles from mean low water mark with the provision that the cities of Panama and Colon and the harbors adjacent to said cities, which are included within the boundaries of the zone above described, shall not be included within this grant. The Republic of Panama further grants to the United States in perpetuity the use, occupation and control of any other lands and waters outside of the zone above described which may be necessary and convenient for the construction, maintenance, operations, sanitation and protection of the said Canal or of any auxiliary canals or other works necessary and convenient for the construction, maintenance, operation, sanitation and protection of the said enterprise.

The Republic of Panama further grants in like manner to the United States in perpetuity all islands within the limits of the zone above described and in addition thereto the group of small islands in the Bay of Panama, named Perico, Naos, Culebra and Flamenco.

Article 3

The Republic of Panama grants to the United States all the rights, power and authority within the zone mentioned and described in Article 2 of this agreement and within the limits of all auxiliary lands and waters mentioned and described in said Article 2 which the United States would possess and exercise if it were the sovereign of the territory within which said lands and waters are located to the entire exclusion of the exercise by the Republic of Panama of any such sovereign rights, power or authority.

Article 4

As rights subsidiary to the above grants the Republic of Panama grants in perpetuity to the United States the right to use the rivers, streams, lakes and other bodies of water within its limits for navigation, the supply of water or water-power or other purposes, so far as the use of said rivers, streams, lakes and bodies of water and the waters thereof may be necessary and convenient for the construction, maintenance, operation, sanitation and protection of the said Canal.

Article 5

The Republic of Panama grants to the United States in perpetuity a monopoly for the construction, maintenance and operation of any system of communication by means of canal or railroad across its territory between the Caribbean Sea and the Pacific Ocean.

Article 6

The grants herein contained shall in no manner invalidate the titles or rights of private land holders or owners of private property in the said zone or in or to any of the lands or waters granted to the United States by the provisions of any Article of this treaty, nor shall they interfere with the rights of way over the public roads passing through the said zone or over any of the said lands or waters unless said rights of way or private rights shall conflict with rights herein granted to the United States in which case the rights of the United States shall be superior. All damages caused to the owners of private lands or private property of any kind by reason of the grants contained in this treaty or by reason of the operations of the United States, its agents or employees, or by reason of the construction, maintenance, operation, sanitation and protection of the said Canal or of the works of sanitation and protection herein provided for, shall be appraised and settled by a joint commission appointed by the Governments of the United States and the Republic of Panama, whose decisions as to such damages shall be paid solely by the United States. No part of the work on said Canal or the Panama railroad or on any auxiliary works relating thereto and authorized by the terms of this treaty shall be prevented, delayed or impeded by or pending such proceedings to ascertain such damages. The appraisal of said private lands and private property and the assessment of damages to them shall be based upon their value before the date of this convention.

Article 7

The Republic of Panama grants to the United States within the limits of the cities of Panama and Colon and their adjacent harbors and within the territory adjacent thereto the right to acquire by purchase or by the exercise of the right of eminent domain, any lands, buildings, water rights or other properties necessary and convenient for the construction, maintenance, operation and protection of the Canal and of any works of sanitation, such as the collection and disposition of sewage and the distribution of water in the said cities of Panama and Colon, which, in the discretion of the United States may be necessary and convenient for the construction, maintenance, operation, sanitation and protection of the said Canal and railroad. All such works of sanitation, collection and disposition of sewage and distribution of water in the cities of Panama and Colon shall be made at the expense of the United States, and the Government of the United States, its agents or nominees shall be authorized to impose and collect water rates and sewerage rates which shall be sufficient to provide for the payment of interest and the amortization of the principal of the cost of said works within a period of fifty years and upon the expiration of said term of fifty years the system of sewers and water works shall revert to and become the properties of the cities of Panama and Colon respectively, and the use of the water shall be free to the inhabitants of Panama and Colon, except to the extent that water rates may be necessary for the operation and maintenance of said system of sewers and water.

The Republic of Panama agrees that the cities of Panama and Colon shall comply in perpetuity with the sanitary ordinances whether of a preventive or curative character prescribed by the United States and in case the Government of Panama is unable or fails in its duty to enforce this compliance by the cities of Panama and Colon with the sanitary ordinances of the United States the Republic of Panama grants to the United States the right and authority to enforce the same.

The same right and authority are granted to the United States for the maintenance of public order in the cities of Panama and Colon and the territories and harbors adjacent thereto in case the Republic of Panama should not be, in the judgement of the United States, able to maintain such order.

Article 8

The Republic of Panama grants to the United States all rights which it now has or hereafter may acquire to the property of the New Panama Canal Company and the Panama Railroad Company as a result of the transfer of sovereignty from the Republic of Colombia to the Republic of Panama over the Isthmus of Panama and authorizes the New Panama Canal Company to sell and transfer to the United States its rights, privileges, properties and concessions as well as the Panama Railroad and all the shares or part of the shares of that company; but the public lands situated outside of the one described in Article 2 of this treaty now included in the concessions to both said enterprises and not required in the construction or operation of the Canal shall revert to the Republic of Panama except any property now owned by or in the possession of said companies within Panama or Colon or the ports or terminals thereof.

Article 9

The United States agrees that the ports at either entrance of the Canal and the waters thereof, and the Republic of Panama agrees that the towns of Panama and Colon shall be free for all time so that there shall not be imposed or collected custom house tolls, tonnage, anchorage, lighthouse, wharf, pilot, or quarantine dues or any other charges or taxes of any kind upon any vessel using or passing through the Canal or belonging to or employed by the United States, directly or indirectly, in connection with the construction, maintenance, operation, sanitation and protection of the main Canal, or auxiliary works, or upon the cargo, officers, crew, or passengers of any such vessels, except such tolls and charges as may be imposed by the United States for the use of the Canal and other works, and except tolls and charges imposed by the Republic of Panama upon merchandise destined to be introduced for the consumption of the rest of the Republic of Panama, and upon vessels touching at the ports of Colon and Panama and which do not cross the Canal.

The Government of the Republic of Panama shall have the right to establish in such ports and in the towns of Panama and Colon such houses and guards as it may deem necessary to collect duties on importations destined to other portions of Panama and to prevent contraband trade. The United States shall have the right to make use of the towns and harbors of Panama and Colon as places of anchorage, and for making repairs, for loading, unloading, depositing, or transhipping cargoes either in transit or destined for the service of the Canal and for other works pertaining to the Canal.

Article 10

The Republic of Panama agrees that there shall not be imposed any taxes, national, municipal, departmental, or of any other class, upon the Canal, the railways and auxiliary works, tugs and other vessels employed in the service of the Canal, store houses, work shops, offices, quarters for laborers, factories of all kinds, warehouses, wharves, machinery and other works, property, and effects appertaining to the Canal or railroad and auxiliary works, or their officers or employees, situated within the cities of Panama and Colon, and that there shall not be imposed contributions or charges of a personal character of any kind upon officers, employees, laborers, and other individuals in the service of the Canal and railroad and auxiliary work.

Article 11

The United States agrees that the official dispatches of the Government of the Republic of Panama shall be transmitted over any telegraph and telephone lines established for canal purposes and used for public and private business at rates not higher than those required from officials in the service of the United States.

Article 12

The Government of the Republic of Panama shall permit the immigration and free access to the lands and workshops of the Canal and its auxiliary works of all employees and workmen of whatever nationality under contract to work upon or seeking employment upon or in any wise connected with the said Canal and its auxiliary works, with their respective families, and all such persons shall be free and exempt from the military service of the Republic of Panama.

Article 13

The United States may import at any time into the said zone an auxiliary lands, free of custom duties, imposts, taxes, or other charges, and without any restrictions, any and all vessels, dredges, engines, cars, machinery, tools, explosives, materials, supplies, and other articles necessary and convenient in the construction, maintenance, operation, sanitation and protection of the Canal and auxiliary works, and all provisions, medicines, clothing, supplies and other things necessary and convenient for the officers, employees, workmen and laborers in the service and employ of the United States and for their families. If any such articles are

disposed of for use outside of the zone and auxiliary lands granted to the United States and within the territory of the Republic, they shall be subject to the same import or other duties as like articles imported under the laws of the Republic of Panama.

Article 14

As the price or compensation for the rights, powers and privileges granted in this convention by the Republic of Panama to the United States, the Government of the United States agrees to pay to the Republic of Panama the sum of ten million dollars ($10,000,000) in gold coin of the United States on the exchange of the ratification of this convention and also an annual payment during the life of this convention of two hundred and fifty thousand dollars ($250,000) in like gold coin, beginning nine years after the date aforesaid.

The provisions of this Article shall be in addition to all other benefits assured to the Republic of Panama under this convention.

But no delay or difference of opinion under this Article or any other provisions of this treaty shall affect or interrupt the full operation and effect of this convention in all other respects.

Article 15

The joint commission referred to in Article 6 shall be established as follows:

The President of the United States shall nominate two persons and the President of the Republic of Panama shall nominate two persons and they shall proceed to a decision; but in case of disagreement of the Commission (by reason of their being equally divided in conclusion) an umpire shall be appointed by the two Governments who shall render the decision. In the event of the death, absence, or incapacity of a Commissioner or umpire, or of his omitting, declining or ceasing to act, his place shall be filled by the appointment of another person in the manner above indicated. All decisions by a majority of the Commission or by the umpire shall be final.

Article 16

The two Governments shall make adequate provision by future agreement for the pursuit, capture, imprisonment, detention and delivery within said zone and auxiliary lands to the authorities of the Republic of Panama of persons charged with the commitment of crimes, felonies or misdemeanors without said zone and for the pursuit, capture, imprisonment, detention and delivery without said zone to the authorities of the United States of persons charged with the commitment of crimes, felonies and misdemeanors within said zone and auxiliary lands.

Article 17

The Republic of Panama grants to the United States the use of all the ports of the Republic open to commerce as places of refuge for any vessels employed in the Canal enterprise, and for all vessels passing or bound to pass through the Canal which may be in distress and be driven to seek refuge in said ports. Such vessels shall be exempt from anchorage and tonnage dues on the part of the Republic of Panama.

Article 18

The Canal, when constructed, and the entrances thereto shall be neutral in perpetuity, and shall be opened upon the terms provided for by Section I of Article 3 of, and in conformity with all the stipulations of, the treaty entered into by the Governments of the United States and Great Britain on November 18, 1901.

Article 19

The Government of the Republic of Panama shall have the right to transport over the Canal its vessels and its troops and munitions of war in such vessels at all times without paying charges of any kind. The exemption is to be extended to the auxiliary railway for the transportation of persons in the service of the Republic of Panama, or of the police force charged with the preservation of public order outside of said zone, as well as to their baggage, munitions of war and supplies.

Article 20

If by virtue of any existing treaty in relation to the territory of the Isthmus of Panama, whereof the obligations shall descend or be assumed by the Republic of Panama, there may be any privilege or concession in favor of the Government or the citizens and subjects of a third power relative to an interoceanic means of communication which in any of its terms may be incompatible with the terms of the present convention, the Republic of Panama agrees to cancel or modify such treaty in due form, for which purpose it shall give to the said third power the requisite notification within the term of four months from the date of the present convention, and in case the existing treaty contains no clause permitting its modifications or annulment, the Republic of Panama agrees to procure its modification or annulment in such form that there shall not exist any conflict with the stipulations of the present convention.

Article 21

The rights and privileges granted by the Republic of Panama to the United States in the preceding Articles are understood to be free of all anterior debts, liens, trusts, or liabilities, or concessions or privileges to other Governments, corporations, syndicates or individuals, and consequently, if there should arise any claims on account of the present concessions and privileges or otherwise, the claimants shall resort to the Government of the Republic of Panama and not to the United States for any indemnity or compromise which may be required.

Article 22

The Republic of Panama renounces and grants to the United States the participation to which it might be entitled in the future earnings of the Canal under Article 15 of the concessionary contract with Lucien N. B. Wyse now owned by the New Panama Canal Company and any and all other rights or claims of a pecuniary nature arising under or relating to said concession, or arising under or relating to the concessions to the Panama Railroad Company or any extension or modification thereof; and it likewise renounces, confirms and grants to the United States, now and hereafter, all the rights and property reserved in the said concessions which otherwise would belong to Panama at or before the expiration of the terms of ninety-nine years of the concessions granted to or held by the above mentioned party and companies, and all right, title and interest which it now has or may hereafter have, in and to the lands, canal, works, property and rights held by the said companies under said concessions or otherwise, and acquired or to be acquired by the United States from or through the New Panama Canal Company, including any property and rights which might or may in the future either by lapse of time, forfeiture or otherwise, revert to the Republic of Panama under any contracts or concessions, with said Wyse, the Universal Panama Canal Company, the Panama Railroad Company and the New Panama Canal Company.

The aforesaid rights and property shall be and are free and released from any present or reversionary interest in or claims of Panama and the title of the United States thereto upon consummation of the contemplated purchase by the United States from the New Panama Canal Company, shall be absolute, so far as concerns the Republic of Panama, excepting always the rights of the Republic specifically secured under this treaty.

Article 23

If it should become necessary at any time to employ armed forces for the safety or protection of the Canal, or of the ships that make use of the same, or the railways and auxiliary works, the United States shall have the right, at all times and in its discretion, to use its police and its land and naval forces or to establish fortifications for these purposes.

Article 24

No change either in the Government or in the laws and treaties of the Republic of Panama shall, without the consent of the United States, affect any right of the United States under the present convention, or under any treaty stipulation between the two countries that now exists or may hereafter exist touching the subject matter of this convention.

If the Republic of Panama shall hereafter enter as a constituent into any other Government or into any union or confederation of states, so as to merge her sovereignty or independence in such Government, union or confederation, the rights of the United States under this convention shall not be in any respect lessened or impaired.

Article 25

For the better performance of the engagements of this convention and to the end of the efficient protection of the Canal and the preservation of its neutrality, the Government of the Republic of Panama will sell or lease to the United States lands adequate and necessary for naval or coaling stations on the Pacific coast and on the western Caribbean coast of the Republic at certain points to be agreed upon with the President of the United States.

Article 26

This convention when signed by the Plenipotentiaries of the Contracting Parties shall be ratified by the respective Governments and the ratifications shall be exchanged at Washington at the earliest date possible. In faith whereof the respective Plenipotentiaries have signed the present convention in duplicate and have hereunto affixed their respective seals. Done at the City of Washington the 18th day of November in the year of our Lord nineteen hundred and three.

JON HAY

P. BUNAU–VARILLA

THE "HAY-HERRAN" TREATY

Between the United States and Colombia, Signed at Washington, January 22, 1903

THE UNITED STATES of America and the Republic of Colombia, being desirous to assure the construction of a ship canal to connect the Atlantic and Pacific oceans and the Congress of the United States of America having passed an Act approved June 28, 1902, in furtherance of that object, a copy of which is hereunto annexed, the high contracting parties have resolved, for that purpose, to conclude a Convention and have accordingly appointed as their plenipotentiaries,

The President of the United States of America, John Hay, Secretary of State, and

The President of the Republic of Colombia, Thomas Herran, Charge d'Affaires, thereunto specially empowered by said government, who, after communicating to each other their respective full powers, found in good and due form, have agreed upon and concluded the following Articles:

Article 1

The Government of Colombia authorizes the New Panama Canal Company to sell and transfer to the United States its rights, privileges, properties, and concessions, as well as the Panama Railroad and all the shares or part of the shares of that company; but the public lands situated outside of the zone hereinafter specified, now corresponding to the concessions of both said enterprises shall revert to the Republic of Colombia, except any property now owned by or in the possession of the said companies within Panama or Colon, or the ports and terminals thereof.

But it is understood that Colombia reserves all its rights to the special shares in the capital of the New Panama Canal Company to which reference is made in Article 4 of the contract of December 10, 1890, which shares shall be paid their full nominal value at least; but as such right of Colombia exists solely in its character of stockholder in said Company, no obligation under this provision is imposed upon or assumed by the United States.

The Railroad Company (and the United States as owner of the enterprise) shall be free from the obligations imposed by the railroad concession, excepting as to the payment at maturity by the Railroad Company of the outstanding bonds issued by said Railroad Company.

Article 2

The United States shall have the exclusive right for the term of one hundred years, renewable at the sole and absolute option of the United States, for periods of similar duration so long as the United States may desire, to excavate, construct, maintain, operate, control, and protect the Maritime Canal with or without locks from the Atlantic to the Pacific ocean, to and across the territory of Colombia, such canal to be of sufficient depth and capacity for vessels of the largest tonnage and greatest draft now engaged in commerce, and such as may be reasonably anticipated, and also the same rights for the construction, maintenance, operation, control, and protection of the Panama Railroad and of railway, telegraph and telephone lines, canals, dikes, dams and reservoirs, and such other auxiliary works as may be necessary and convenient for the construction, maintenance, protection and operation of the canal and railroads.

Article 3

To enable the United States to exercise the rights and privileges granted by this Treaty the Republic of Colombia grants to that Government the use and control for the term of one hundred years, renewable at the sole and absolute option of the United States, for periods of similar duration so long as the United States may desire, of a zone of territory along the route of the canal to be constructed five kilometers in width on either side thereof measured from its center line including therein the necessary auxiliary canals not exceeding in any case fifteen miles from the main canal and other works, together with ten fathoms of water in the Bay of Limon in extension of the canal, and at least three marine miles from mean low water mark from each terminus of the canal into the Caribbean Sea and the Pacific Ocean respectively. So far as necessary for the construction, maintenance and operation of the canal, the United States shall have the use and occupation of the group of small islands in the Bay of Panama named Perico, Naos, Culebra and Flamenco, but the same shall not be construed as being within the zone herein defined or governed by the special provisions applicable to the same.

This grant shall in no manner invalidate the titles or rights of private land holders in the said zone of territory, nor shall it interfere with the rights of way over the public roads of the Department; provided, however, that nothing herein contained shall operate to diminish, impair or restrict the rights elsewhere herein granted to the United States.

This grant shall not include the cities of Panama and Colon, except so far as lands and other property therein are now owned by or in possession of the said Canal Company or the said Railroad Company; but all the stipulations contained in Article 35 of the Treaty of 1846-48 between the contracting parties shall continue and apply in full force to the cities of Panama and Colon and to the accessory community lands and other property within the said zone, and the territory thereon shall be neutral territory, and the United States shall continue to guarantee the neutrality thereof and the sovereignty of Colombia thereover, in conformity with the above mentioned Article 35 of said Treaty.

In furtherance of this last provision there shall be created a Joint Commission by the Governments of Colombia and the United States that shall establish and enforce sanitary and police regulations.

Article 4

The rights and privileges granted to the United States by the terms of this convention shall not affect the sovereignty of the Republic of Colombia over the territory within whose boundaries such rights and privileges are to be exercised.

The United States freely acknowledges and recognizes this sovereignty and disavows any intention to impair it in any way whatever or to increase its territory at the expense of Colombia or of any of the sister republics in Central or South America, but on the contrary, it desires to strengthen the power of the republics on this continent, and to promote, develop and maintain their prosperity and independence.

Article 5

The Republic of Colombia authorizes the United States to construct and maintain at each entrance and terminus of the proposed canal a port for vessels using the same, with suitable light houses and other aids to navigation, and the United States is authorized to use and occupy within the limits of the zone fixed by this convention, such parts of the coast line and of the lands and islands adjacent thereto as are necessary for this purpose, including the construction and maintenance of breakwaters, dikes, jetties, embankments, coaling stations, docks and other appropriate works, and the United States

undertakes the construction and maintenance of such works and will bear all the expense thereof. The ports when established are declared free, and their demarcations shall be clearly and definitely defined.

To give effect to this Article, the United States will give special attention and care to the maintenance of works for drainage, sanitary and healthful purposes along the line of the canal, and its dependencies, in order to prevent the invasion of epidemics or of securing their prompt suppression should they appear. With this end in view the United States will organize hospitals along the line of the canal, and will suitably supply or cause to be supplied the towns of Panama and Colon with the necessary aqueducts and drainage works, in order to prevent their becoming centers of infection on account of their proximity to the canal.

The Government of Colombia will secure for the United States or its nominees the lands and rights that may be required in the towns of Panama and Colon to effect the improvements above referred to, and the Government of the United States or its nominees shall be authorized to impose and collect equitable water rates, during fifty years for the service rendered; but on the expiration of said term the use of the water shall be free for the inhabitants of Panama and Colon, except to the extent that may be necessary for the operation and maintenance of said water system, including reservoirs, aqueducts, hydrants, supply service, drainage and other works.

Article 6

The Republic of Colombia agrees that it will not cede or lease to any foreign Government any of its islands or harbors within or adjacent to the Bay of Panama, nor on the Atlantic Coast of Colombia, between the Atrato River and the western boundary of the Department of Panama, for the purpose of establishing fortifications, naval or coaling stations, military posts, docks or other works that might interfere with the construction, maintenance, operation, protection, safety, and free use of the canal and auxiliary works. In order to enable Colombia to comply with this stipulation, the

Government of the United States agrees to give Colombia the material support that may be required in order to prevent the occupation of said islands and ports, guaranteeing there the sovereignty, independence and integrity of Colombia.

Article 7

The Republic of Colombia includes in the foregoing grant the right without obstacle, cost, or impediment, to such control, consumption and general utilization in any manner found necessary by the United States to the exercise by it of the grants to, and rights conferred upon it by this Treaty, the waters of the Chagres River and other streams, lakes and lagoons, of all non-navigable waters, natural and artificial, and also to navigate all rivers, streams, lakes and other navigable water-ways, within the jurisdiction and under the domain of the Republic of Colombia, in the Department of Panama, within or without said zone, as may be necessary or desirable for the construction, maintenance and operation of the canal and its auxiliary canals and other works, and without tolls or charges of any kind; and to raise and lower the levels of the waters, and to deflect them, and to impound any such waters, and to overflow any lands necessary for the due exercise of such grants and rights to the United States; and to rectify, construct and improve the navigation of any such rivers, streams, lakes and lagoons at the sole cost of the United States; but any such water-ways so made by the United States may be used by citizens of Colombia free of tolls or other charges. And the United States shall have the right to use without cost, any water, stone, clay, earth or other minerals belonging to Colombia on the public domain that may be needed by it.

All damages caused to private land owners by inundation or by the deviation of water courses, or in other ways, arising out of the construction or operation of the canal, shall in each case be appraised and settled by a joint commission appointed by the Governments of the United States and Colombia, but the cost of the indemnities so agreed upon shall be borne solely by the United States.

Article 8

The Government of Colombia declares free for all time the ports at either entrance of the Canal, including Panama and Colon and the waters thereof in such manner that there shall not be collected by the Government of Colombia custom house tolls, tonnage, anchorage, light-house, wharf, pilot, or quarantine dues, nor any other charges or taxes of any kind shall be levied or imposed by the Government of Colombia upon any vessel using or passing through the Canal or belonging to or employed by the United States, directly or indirectly, in connection with the construction, maintenance and operation of the main work or its auxiliaries, or upon the cargo, officers, crew, or passengers of any such vessels; it being the intent of this convention that all vessels and their cargoes, crews, and passengers, shall be permitted to use and pass through the Canal and the ports leading thereto, subject to no other demands or impositions than such tolls and charges as may be imposed by the United States for the use of the Canal and other works. It being understood that such tolls and charges shall be governed by the provisions of Article 16.

The ports leading to the Canal, including Panama and Colon, also shall be free to the commerce of the world, and no duties or taxes shall be imposed, except upon merchandise destined to be introduced for the consumption of the rest of the Republic of Colombia, or the Department of Panama, and upon vessels touching at the ports of Colon and Panama and which do not cross the Canal.

Though the said ports shall be free and open to all, the Government of Colombia may establish in them such custom houses and guards as Colombia may deem necessary to collect duties on importations destined to other portions of Colombia and to prevent contraband trade. The United States shall have the right to make use of the ports at the two extremities of the Canal including Panama and Colon as places of anchorage, in order to make repairs for loading, unloading, depositing, or transshipping cargoes either in transit or destined for the service of the Canal and other works.

Any concessions or privileges granted by Colombia for the operation of light houses at Colon and Panama shall be subject to expropriation, indemnification and payment in the same manner as is provided by Article 14 in respect to the property therein mentioned; but Colombia shall make no additional grant of any such privilege nor change the status of any existing concession.

Article 9

There shall not be imposed any taxes, national, municipal, departmental, or of any other class, upon the canal, the vessels that may use it, tugs and other vessels employed in the service of the canal, the railways and auxiliary works, store houses, work shops, offices, quarters for laborers, factories of all kinds, warehouses, wharves, machinery and other works, property, and effects appertaining to the canal or railroad or that may be necessary for the service of the canal or railroad and their dependencies, whether situated within the cities of Panama and Colon, or any other place authorized by the provisions of this convention. Nor shall there be imposed contributions or charges of a personal character of whatever species upon officers, employees, laborers, and, other individuals in the service of the canal and its dependencies.

Article 10

It is agreed that telegraph and telephone lines, when established for canal purposes, may also, under suitable regulations, be used for public and private business in connection with the systems of Colombia and the other American Republics and with the lines of cable companies authorized to enter the ports and territories of these Republics; but the official dispatches of the Government of Colombia and the authorities of the Department of Panama shall not pay for, such service higher tolls than those required from the officials in the, service of the United States.

Article 11

The Government of Colombia shall permit the immigration and free access to the lands and workshops of the canal and its dependencies of all employees and workmen of whatever nationality under contract to work upon or seeking employment or in any wise connected with the said canal and its dependencies, with their respective families; and all such persons shall be free and exempt from the military service of the Republic of Colombia.

Article 12

The United States may import at any time into the said zone, free of customs duties, imposts, taxes, or other charges, and without any restriction, any and all vessels, dredges, engines, cars, machinery, tools, explosives, materials, supplies, and other articles necessary and convenient in the construction, maintenance and operation of the canal and auxiliary works, also all provisions, medicines, clothing, supplies and other things necessary and convenient for the officers, employees, workmen and laborers in the service and employ of the United States and for their families. If any such articles are disposed of for use without the zone excepting Panama and Colon and within the territory of the Republic, they shall be subject to the same import or other duties as like articles under the laws of Colombia or the ordinances of the Department of Panama.

Article 13

The United States shall have authority to protect and make secure the canal, as well as railways and other auxiliary works and dependencies, and to preserve order and discipline among the laborers and other persons who may congregate in that region, and to make and enforce such police and sanitary regulations as it may deem necessary to preserve order and public health thereon, and to protect navigation and commerce through and over said canal, railways and other works and dependencies from interruption or damage.

I. The Republic of Colombia may establish judicial tribunals within said zone, for the determination, according to its laws and judicial procedure, of certain controversies hereinafter mentioned. Such judicial tribunal or tribunals so established by the Republic of Colombia shall have exclusive jurisdiction in said zone of all controversies between citizens of the Republic of Colombia, or between citizens of the Republic of Colombia and citizens of any foreign nation other than the United States.

II. Subject to the general sovereignty of Colombia over said zone, the United States may establish judicial tribunals thereon, which shall have jurisdiction of certain controversies hereinafter mentioned to be determined according to the laws and judicial procedure of the United States.

Such judicial tribunal or tribunals so established by the United States shall have exclusive jurisdiction in said zone of all controversies between citizens of the United States, and between citizens of the United States and citizens of any foreign nation other than the Republic of Colombia; and of all controversies in any wise growing out of or relating to the construction, maintenance or operation of the canal, railway and other properties and works.

III. The United States and Colombia engage jointly to establish and maintain upon said zone, judicial tribunals having civil, criminal and admiralty jurisdiction, and to be composed of jurists appointed by the Governments of the United States and Colombia in a manner hereafter to be agreed upon between said Governments, and which tribunals shall have jurisdiction of certain controversies hereinafter mentioned, and of all crimes, felonies and misdemeanors committed within said zone, and of all cases arising in admiralty, according to such laws and procedure as shall be hereafter agreed upon and declared by the two Governments. Such joint judicial tribunal shall have exclusive jurisdiction in said zone of all controversies between citizens of the United States and citizens of Colombia, and between citizens of nations other than Colombia or the United States; and also of all crimes, felonies and misdemeanors committed within said zone, and of all questions of admiralty arising therein.

IV. The two Governments hereafter, and from time to time as occasion arises, shall agree upon and establish the laws and procedures which shall govern such joint judicial tribunal and which shall be applicable to the persons and cases over which such tribunal shall have jurisdiction, and also shall likewise create the requisite officers and employees of such court and establish their powers and duties; and further shall make adequate provision by like agreement for the pursuit, capture, imprisonment, detention and delivery within said zone of persons charged with the commitment of crimes, felonies or misdemeanors without said zone; and for the pursuit, capture, imprisonment, detention and delivery without said zone of persons charged with the commitment of crimes, felonies and misdemeanors within said zone.

Article 14

The works of the canal, the railways and their auxiliaries are declared of public utility, and in consequence all areas of land and water necessary for the construction, maintenance, and operation of the canal and other specified works may be expropriated in conformity with the laws of Colombia, except that the indemnity shall be conclusively determined without appeal, by a joint commission appointed by the Governments of Colombia and the United States. The indemnities awarded by the Commission for such expropriation shall be borne by the United States, but the appraisal of said lands and the assessment of damages shall be based upon their value before the commencement of the work upon the canal.

Article 15

The Republic of Colombia grants to the United States the use of all the ports of the Republic open to commerce as places of refuge any vessels employed in the canal enterprise, and for all vessels in distress having the right to pass through the canal and within to anchor in said ports. Such vessels shall be exempt from anchorage and tonnage dues on the part of Colombia.

Article 16

The canal, when constructed, and the entrance thereto shall be neutral in perpetuity, and shall be opened upon the terms provided for by Section I of Article three of, and in conformity with all the stipulations of, the treaty entered into by the Governments of the United States and Great Britain on November 18, 1901.

Article 17

The Government of Colombia shall have the right to transport over the canal its vessels, troops, and munitions of war at all times without paying charges of any kind. This exemption is to be extended to the auxiliary railway for the transportation of persons in the service of the Republic of Colombia or of the Department of Panama, or of the police force charged with the preservation of public order outside of said zone, as well as to their baggage, munitions of war and supplies.

Article 18

The United States shall have full power and authority to establish and enforce regulations for the use of the canal, railways, and the entering ports and auxiliary works, and to fix rates of tolls and charges thereof, subject to the limitations stated in Article 16.

Article 19

The rights and privileges granted to the United States by this convention shall not affect the sovereignty of the Republic of Colombia over the real estate that may be acquired by the United States by reason of the transfer of the rights of the New Panama Canal Company and the Panama Railroad Company lying outside of the said canal zone.

Article 20

If by virtue of any existing treaty between the Republic of Colombia and any third power, there may be any privilege or concession relative to an interoceanic means of communication which especially favors such third power, and which in any of its terms may be incompatible with the terms of the present convention, the Republic of Colombia agrees to cancel or modify such treaty in due form, for which purpose it shall give to the said third power the requisite notification within the term of four months from the date of the present convention, and in case the existing treaty contains no clause permitting its modification or annulment, the Republic of Columbia agrees to procure its modification and annulment in such form that there shall not exist any conflict with the stipulation of the present convention.

Article 21

The rights and privileges granted by the Republic of Colombia to the United States in the preceding Articles are understood to be free of all anterior concessions or privileges to other Governments, corporations, syndicates or individuals, and consequently, if there should arise any claims on account of the present concessions and privileges or otherwise, the claimants shall resort to the Government of Colombia and not to the United States for any indemnity or compromise which may be required.

Article 22

The Republic of Colombia renounces and grants to the United States the participation to which it might be entitled in the future earnings of the canal under Article 1 of the concessionary contract with Lucien N. B. Wyse now owned by the New Panama Canal Company and any and all other rights or claims of a pecuniary nature arising under or relating to said concession, or arising under or relating to the concessions to the Panama Railroad Company or any extension or modification thereof; and it likewise renounces, confirms and grants to the United States, now and hereafter, all the rights and property reserved in the said concessions which otherwise would belong to Colombia at or before the expiration of the terms of ninety-nine years of the concessions granted to or held by the above mentioned party and companies, and all right, title and interest which it now has or may hereafter have, in and to the lands, canal, works, property and rights held by the said companies under said concessions or otherwise, and acquired or to be acquired by the United States from or through the New Panama Canal Company, including any property and rights which might or may in the future either by lapse of time, forfeiture or otherwise, revert to the Republic of Colombia under any contracts of concessions, with said Wyse, the Universal Panama Canal Company, the Panama Railroad Company and the New Panama Canal Company.

The aforesaid rights and property shall be and are free and released from any present or reversionary interest in or claims of Colombia and the title of the United States thereto upon consummation of the contemplated purchase by the United States from the New Panama Canal Company, shall be absolute, so far as concerns the Republic of Colombia, excepting always the rights of Colombia specifically secured under this treaty.

Article 23

If it should become necessary at any time to employ armed forces for the safety or protection of the canal, or of the ships that make use of the same, or the railways and other works, the Republic of Colombia agrees to provide the forces necessary for such purpose, according to the circumstances of the case, but if the Government of Colombia cannot effectively comply with this obligation, then, with the consent of or at the request of Colombia, or of her Minister at Washington, or of the local authorities, civil or military, the United States shall employ such force as may be necessary for that sole purpose; and as soon as the necessity shall have ceased will withdraw the forces so employed. Under exceptional circumstances, however, on account of unforeseen or imminent danger to said canal, railways and other works, or to the lives and property of the persons employed upon the canal, railways, and other works, the Government of the United States is authorized to act in the interest of their protection, without the necessity of obtaining the consent beforehand of the Government of Colombia; and it shall give immediate advice of the measures adopted for the purpose stated; and as soon as sufficient Colombian forces shall arrive to attend to the indicated purpose, those of the United States shall retire.

Article 24

The Government of the United States agrees to complete the construction of the preliminary works necessary, together with all the auxiliary works, in the shortest time possible; and within two years from the date of the exchange of ratification of this convention the main works of the canal proper shall be commenced, and it shall be opened to the traffic between the two oceans within twelve years after such period of two years. In case, however, that any difficulties or obstacles should arise in the construction of the canal which are at present impossible to foresee, in consideration of the good faith with which the Government of the United States shall have proceeded, and the large amount of money expended so far on the works and the nature of the difficulties which may have arisen, the Government Colombia will prolong the terms stipulated in this Article up to twelve years more for the completion of the work of the canal.

But in case the United States should, at any time, determine to make such canal practically a sea level canal, then such period shall be extended for ten years further.

Article 25

As the price or compensation for the right to use the one granted in this convention by Colombia to the United States for the construction of a canal, together with the proprietary right over the Panama Railroad, and for the annuity of two hundred and fifty thousand dollars gold, which Colombia ceases to receive from the said railroad, as well as in compensation for other rights, privileges and exemptions granted to the United States, and in consideration of the increase in the administrative expenses of the Department of Panama consequent upon the construction of the said canal, the Government of the United States binds itself to pay Colombia the sum of ten million dollars in gold coin of the United States on the exchange of the ratification of this convention after its approval according to the laws of the respective countries, and also an annual payment during the life of this convention of two hundred and fifty thousand dollars in like gold coin, beginning nine years after the date aforesaid.

The provisions of this Article shall be in addition to all other benefits assured to Colombia under this convention. But no delay nor difference of opinion under this Article shall affect nor interrupt the full operation and effect of this convention in all other respects.

Article 26

No change either in the Government or in the laws and treaties of Columbia, shall, without the consent of the United States, affect any right of the

United States under the present convention, or under any treaty stipulation between the two countries (that now exist or may hereafter exist) touching the subject matter of this convention. If Colombia shall hereafter enter as a constituent into any other Government or into any union or confederation of States so as to merge her sovereignty or independence in such Government, union, or confederation, the rights of the United States under this convention shall not be in any respect lessened or impaired.

Article 27

The joint commission referred to in Articles 3, 7, and 14 shall be established as follows:

The President of the United States shall nominate two persons and the President of Colombia shall nominate two persons and they shall proceed to a decision; but in case of disagreement of the Commission (by reason of their being equally divided in conclusion) an umpire shall be appointed by the two Governments, who shall render the decision. In the event of death, absence or incapacity of any Commissioner or umpire, or of his omitting, declining or ceasing to act, his place shall be filled by the appointment of another person in the manner above indicated. All decisions by a majority of the Commission or by the umpire shall be final.

Article 28

This convention when signed by the contracting parties, shall be ratified according to the laws of the respective countries and shall be exchanged at Washington within a term of eight months from this date, or earlier if possible.

In faith whereof, the respective plenipotentiaries have signed the present convention in duplicate and have hereunto affixed their respective seals.

Done at the City of Washington, the 22d day of January in the year of our Lord nineteen hundred and three.

JOHN HAY

TOMAS HERRAN

TREATY OF RELATIONS BETWEEN THE UNITED STATES AND CUBA
Signed at Washington, May 29, 1934

THE UNITED STATES of America and the Republic of Cuba, being animated by the desire to fortify the relations of friendship between the two countries and to modify, with this purpose, the relations established between them by the Treaty of Relations signed at Habana, May 22, 1903, have appointed, with this intention, as their Plenipotentiaries:

[Names of Plenipotentiaries]

Who, after having communicated to each other their full powers which were found to be in good and due form, have agreed upon the following articles:

Article I

The Treaty of Relations which was concluded between the two contracting parties on May 22, 1903, shall cease to be in force, and is abrogated, from the date on which the present Treaty goes into effect.

Article II

All the acts effected in Cuba by the United States of America during its military occupation of the island, up to May 20, 1902, the date on which the Republic of Cuba was established, have been ratified and held as valid; and all the rights legally acquired by virtue of those acts shall be maintained and protected.

Article III

Until the two contracting parties agree to the modification or abrogation of the stipulations of the agreement in regard to the lease to the United States of America of lands in Cuba for coaling and naval stations signed by the President of the Republic of Cuba on February 6, 1903, and by the President of the United States of America on the 23rd day of the same month and year, the stipulations of that agreement with regard to the naval station of Guantanamo shall continue in effect. The supplementary agreement in regard to naval or coaling stations signed between the two Governments on July 2, 1903, also shall continue in effect in the same form and on the same conditions with respect to the naval station at Guantanamo. So long as the United States of America shall not abandon the said naval station of Guantanamo or the two Governments shall not agree to a modification of its present limits, the station shall continue to have the territorial area that it now has, with the limits that it has on the date of the signature of the present Treaty.

Article IV

If at any time in the future a situation should arise that appears to point to an outbreak of contagious disease in the territory of either, of the contracting parties, either of the two Governments shall, for its own protection, and without its act being considered unfriendly, exercise freely and at its discretion the right to suspend communications between those of its ports that it may designate and all or part of the territory of the other party, and for the period that it may consider to be advisable.

Article V

The present Treaty shall be ratified by the contracting parties in accordance with their respective constitutional methods; and shall go into effect on the date of the exchange of their ratifications, which shall take place in the city of Washington as soon as possible.

In faith whereof, the respective Plenipotentiaries have signed the present Treaty and have affixed their seals hereto.

Done in duplicate, in the English and Spanish languages, at Washington on the twenty-ninth day of May, one thousand nine hundred and thirty-four.

CORDELL HULL

SUMNER WELLES

M. MARQUEZ STERLING

ESTABLISHMENT OF THE BRACERO PROGRAM

Department of Foreign Relations

United Mexican States

Mexico City

Mexico City, *April 26, 1943.*

317

MR. AMBASSADOR:

With relation to the conversations held in this Department between representatives of the Embassy in Your excellency's charge and of the Farm Security Administration, on the one hand, and of the Departments of Gobernación, of Agricultura y Fomento, of Labor and Social Welfare and of this Department of Foreign Relations, on the other, with the object of examining the amendments which it would be proper to introduce in the arrangement of August 4, 1942, relative to agricultural workers who enter the United States to render their services, it is a pleasure for me to make the following statement to Your Excellency:

The Government of Mexico, which is pleased to render this collaboration to that of the United States of America, is grateful for the spirit of understanding evidenced by the representatives of the Embassy and of the Farm Security Administration and, in view thereof, takes the liberty of submitting to Your Excellency's approval the text which would amend the above-mentioned arrangement of August 4, 1942, in the understanding that these amendments will apply both to the workers who were engaged under the arrangement in question and to those who have been engaged and will continue to be engaged in accordance with the request of the United States Government. The amendments to the arrangement of August 4, 1942, are written in capitals:

[Here follows the text of the revised agreement, the English version of which appears in the next letter.]

In case Your Excellency, as I hope, considers the text of the arrangement acceptable as it is set forth in the foregoing sections, it will be sufficient for you to communicate it to me in writing for the same to come into force.

I renew to Your Excellency the assurance of my highest and most distinguished consideration.

E. PADILLA

His Excellency GEORGE S. MESSERSMITH,
Ambassador Extraordinary and Plenipotentiary
of the United States of America.
City.

Embassy of the
United States off America
México, D.F., April 26, 1943.
No. 1214
EXCELLENCY:

I have the honor to refer to the note No. 317 dated April 26, 1943 in which Your Excellency formulates certain proposals made by the Mexican Government for making the Agreement of August 4, 1942 between the Governments of the United States of America and Mexico a more workable instrument under which Mexican agricultural workers may be recruited in Mexico to work in the United States for a temporary period.

The United States representatives who have been discussing the proposed changes with the representatives designated by the Mexican Government for this purpose have been gratified by the generous spirit of cooperation which has animated these discussions and which has helped to bring them to a successful conclusion.

I am incorporating into this note the text of the Agreement of August 4, 1942 and indicating by underlining those additions or changes agreed upon by my Government:

"In order to effect a satisfactory arrangement whereby Mexican agricultural labor may be made available for use in the United States and at the same time provide means whereby this labor will be adequately protected while out of Mexico, the following general provisions are suggested:

"General Provisions

"1) It is understood that Mexicans contracting to work in the United States shall not be engaged in any military service.

"2) Mexicans entering the United States as a result of this understanding shall not suffer discriminatory acts of any kind in accordance with the executive Order No. 8802 issued at the White House June 25, 1941.

"3) Mexicans entering the United States under this understanding shall enjoy the guarantees of transportation, living expenses and repatriation established in Article 29 of the Mexican Federal Labor Law as follows:

'Article 29—All contracts entered into by Mexican workers for lending their services outside their country, shall be made in writing, legalized by the municipal authorities of the locality where entered into and visaed by the Consul of the country where their services are being used. Further more, such contract shall contain, as a requisite of validity of same, the following stipulations, without which the contract is invalid:

'I. Transportation and subsistence expenses for the worker, and his family, if such is the case, and all other expenses which originate from point of origin to border points and compliance of immigration requirements, or for any other similar concept, shall be paid exclusively by the employer or the contractual parties.

'II. The worker shall be paid in full the salary agreed upon, from which no deductions shall be made in any amount for any of the concepts mentioned in the above sub-paragraph.

'III. The employer or contractor shall issue a bond or constitute a deposit in cash in the Bank of Workers, or in the absence of same, in the bank of Mexico, to the entire satisfaction of the respective labor authorities, for a sum, equal to repatriation costs of the workers and his family, and those originated by transportation to point of origin.

'Once the employer established proof of having covered such expenses or the refusal of the worker to return to his country, and that he does not owe the worker any sum covering salary or indemnization to which he might have a right, the labor authorities shall authorize the return of the deposit or the cancellation of the bond issued.'

"It is specifically understood that the provisions of Section III of Article 29 above-mentioned shall not apply to the Government of the United States notwithstanding the inclusion of this section in the agreement, in view of the obligations assumed by the United States Government under Transportation (a) and (c) of this agreement.

"4) Mexicans entering the United States under this understanding shall not be employed to displace other workers, or for the purpose of reducing rates of pay previously established:

"(When the word 'employer' is used hereinafter it shall be understood to mean the Farm Security Administration of the Department of Agriculture of the United States of America; the word 'sub-employer' shall mean the owner or operator of the farm or farms in the United States on which the Mexican will be employed; the word 'worker' hereinafter used shall refer to the Mexican farm laborer entering the United States under this understanding.)

"*Contracts*

"a. Contracts will be made between the employer and the worker under the supervision of the Mexican Government. (Contracts must be written in Spanish.)

"b. The employer shall enter into a contract with the sub-employer, with a view of proper observance of the principles embodied in this understanding.

"*Admission*

"a. The Mexican health authorities will, at the place whence the worker comes, see that he meets the necessary physical conditions.

"*Transportation*

"a. All transportation and living expenses from the place of origin to destination, and return as well as expenses incurred in the fulfillment of any require-

ments of a migratory nature shall be met by the employer.

"b. Personal belongings of the workers up to a maximum so 35 kilos per person shall be transported at the expense of the employer.

"c. In accord with the intent of Article 29 of the Mexican Federal Labor Law, quoted under General Provisions (3) above, it is expected that the employer will collect all or part of the cost accruing under (a) and (b) of Transportation from the sub-employer.

"*Wages and Employment*

"a. (1) Wages to be paid the workers shall be the same as those paid for similar work to other agricultural laborers under the same conditions with the same area, in the respective regions of destination. Piece rates shall be so set as to enable the worker of average ability to earn the prevailing wage. In any case wages for piece work or hourly work will not be less that 30 cents per hour.

"a. (2.) On the basis of prior authorization from the Mexican Government salaries lower than those established in the previous clause may be paid those emigrants admitted into the United States as member of the family of the worker under contract and who, when they are in the field, are able also to become agricultural laborers but who, by their condition of age or sex, cannot carry out the average amount of ordinary work.

"b. The worker shall be exclusively employed as a agricultural laborer for which he has been engaged; any change from such type of employment or any change of locality shall be made with the express approval of the worker and with the authority of the Mexican Government.

"c. There shall be considered illegal any collection by reason of commission or for any other concept demanded of the worker.

"d. Work of minors under 14 years shall be strictly prohibited and they shall have the same schooling opportunities as those enjoyed by children of other agricultural laborers.

"e. Workers domiciled in the migratory labor camps or at any other place of employment under this understanding shall be free to obtain articles for their personal consumption, or that of their families, wherever it is most convenient for them.

"f. The Mexican workers will be furnished without cost to them with hygienic lodgings, adequate to the physical conditions of the region of a type used by a common laborer of the region and the medical and sanitary services enjoyed also without cost to them will be identical with those furnished to the other agricultural workers in the regions where they may lend their services.

"g. Workers admitted under this understanding shall enjoy as regards occupational diseases and accidents the same guarantees enjoyed by other agricultural workers under United States legislation.

"h. Groups of workers admitted under this understanding shall elect their own representatives to deal with the employer, but it is understood that all such representatives shall be working members of the group.

"The Mexican Consuls, assisted by the Mexican Labor Inspectors, recognized as such by the employer will take all possible measurers of protection in the interests of the Mexican workers in all questions affecting them, within their corresponding jurisdictions, and will have free access to the places of work of the Mexican workers. The employer will observe that the sub-employer grants all facilities to the Mexican Consuls and the Assistant Labor Inspectors of the Mexican Government for the compliance of all the clauses in this contract.

"i. For such time as they are unemployed under a period equal to 75% of the period (exclusive of Sundays) for which the workers have been contracted they shall receive a subsistence allowance at the rate of $3.00 per day.

"For the remaining 25% of the period for which the workers have been contracted during which the workers may be unemployed when such unemployment is not due to their unwillingness to work they shall receive lodging and subsistence without cost to them.

"Should the cost of living rise this will be a matter for reconsideration.

"The master contracts for workers submitted to the Mexican Government shall contain definite provisions for computation of subsistence and payments under this understanding.

"j. The term of the contract shall be made in accordance with the authorities of the respective countries.

"k. At the expiration of the contract under this understanding, and if the same is not renewed, the authorities of the United States shall consider illegal, from an immigration point of view, the continued stay of the worker in the territory of the United States, exception made of cases of physical impossibility.

"*Savings Fund*

"a. The respective agencies of the Government of the United States shall be responsible for the safekeeping of the sums contributed by the Mexican workers toward the formation of their Rural Savings Fund, until such sums are transferred to the Wells Fargo Bank and Union Trust Company of San Francisco for the account of the Bank of Mexico, S.A., which will transfer such amounts to the Mexican Agricultural Credit Bank. This last shall assume responsibility for the deposit, for the safekeeping and for the applications, or in the absence of these, for the return of such amounts.

"b. The Mexican Government through the Banco de Crédito Agrícola will take care of the security of the savings of the workers to be used for payment of the agricultural implements, which may be made available to the Banco de Crédito Agrícola in accordance with the exportation permits for shipment to Mexico with the understanding that the Farm Security Administration will recommend priority treatment for such implements.

"Numbers

"As it is impossible to determine at this time the number of workers who may be needed in the United States for agricultural labor employment, the employer shall advise the Mexican Government from time to time as to the number needed. The Government of Mexico shall determine in each case the number of workers who may leave the country without detriment to its national economy.

"General Considerations

"It is understood that, with reference to the departure from Mexico of Mexican workers, who are not farm laborers, there shall govern in understandings reached by agencies of the respective Governments the same fundamental principles which have been applied here to the departure of farm labor.

"It is understood that the employers will cooperate with such other agencies of the Government of the United States in carrying this understanding into effect whose authority under the laws of the United States are such as to contribute to the effectuation of the understanding.

"Either Government shall have the right to renounce this understanding, giving appropriate notification to the other Government 90 days in advance.

"This understanding may be formalized by an exchange of notes between the Ministry of Foreign Affairs of the Republic of Mexico and the Embassy of the United States of America in Mexico."

In Accepting the above text as the arrangement under which Mexican Agricultural workers shall be recruited and employed in agricultural work in the United States my Government agrees that all the conditions set forth in the revised agreement will apply equally to those agricultural workers already in the United States or on their way to the United States under individual work agreements

as well as those who may be recruited for such work in the future.

Accept, Excellency, the renewed assurance of my highest and most distinguished consideration.

G. S. MESSERSMITH

His Excellency

Señor Licenciado EZEQUIEL PADILLA,

Minister for Foreign Affairs,

México, D. F.

CONSTITUTIONAL CONVENTION OF PUERTO RICO

We, the people of Puerto Rico, in order to organize ourselves politically on a fully democratic basis, to promote the general welfare, and to secure for ourselves and our posterity the complete enjoyment of human rights, placing our trust in Almighty God, do ordain and establish this Constitution for the commonwealth which, in the exercise of our natural rights, we now create within our union with the United States of America.

In so doing, we declare:

The democratic system is fundamental to the life of the Puerto Rican community;

We understand that the democratic system of government is one in which the will of the people is the source of public power, the political order is subordinate to the rights of man, and the free participation of the citizen in collective decisions is assured;

We consider as determining factors in our life our citizenship of the United States of America and our aspiration continually to enrich our democratic heritage in the individual and collective enjoyment of its rights and privileges; our loyalty to the principles of the Federal Constitution; the coexistence in Puerto Rico of the two great cultures of the American Hemisphere; our fervor for education; our faith in justice; our devotion to the courageous, industrious, and peaceful way of life; our fidelity to individual human values above and beyond social position, racial differences, and economic interests; and our hope for a better world based on these principles.

Article I

The Commonwealth

Section 1.—The Commonwealth of Puerto Rico is hereby constituted. Its political power emanates from the people and shall be exercised in accordance with their will, within the terms of the compact agreed upon between the people of Puerto Rico and the United States of America.

Section 2.—The government of the Commonwealth of Puerto Rico shall be republican in form and its legislative, judicial and executive branches as established by this Constitution shall be equally subordinate to the sovereignty of the people of Puerto Rico.

Section 3.—The political authority of the Commonwealth of Puerto Rico shall extend to the Island of Puerto Rico and to the adjacent islands within its jurisdiction.

Section 4.—The seat of the government shall be the city of San Juan.

Article II

Bill of Rights

Section 1.—The dignity of the human being is inviolable. All men are equal before the law. No discrimination shall be made on account of race, color, sex, birth, social origin or condition, or political or religious ideas. Both the laws and the system of public education shall embody these principles of essential human equality.

Section 2.—The laws shall guarantee the expression of the will of the people by means of equal, direct and secret universal suffrage and shall protect the citizen against any coercion in the exercise of the electoral franchise.

Section 3.—No law shall be made respecting an establishment of religion or prohibiting the free exercise thereof. There shall be complete separation of church and state.

Section 4.—No law shall be made abridging the freedom of speech or of the press, or the right of the people peaceably to assemble and to petition the government for a redress of grievances.

Section 5.—Every person has the right to an education which shall be directed to the full development of the human personality and to the strengthening of respect for human rights and fundamental freedoms. There shall be a system of free and wholly non-sectarian public education. Instruction in the elementary and secondary schools shall be free and shall be compulsory in the elementary schools to the extent permitted by the facilities of the state. No public property or public funds shall be used for the support of schools or educational institutions other than those of the state. Nothing contained in this provision shall prevent the state from furnishing to any child non-educational services established by law for the protection or welfare of children.

Section 6.—Persons may join with each other and organize freely for any lawful purpose, except in military or quasi-military organizations.

Section 7.—The right to life, liberty and the enjoyment of property is recognized as a fundamental right of man. The death penalty shall not exist. No person shall be deprived of his liberty or property without due process of law. No person in Puerto Rico shall be denied the equal protection of the laws. No laws impairing the obligation of contracts shall be enacted. A minimum amount of property and possessions shall be exempt from attachment as provided by law.

Section 8.—Every person has the right to the protection of law against abusive attacks on his honor, reputation and private or family life.

Section 9.—Private property shall not be taken or damaged for public use except upon payment of just compensation and in the manner provided by law. No law shall be enacted authorizing condemnation of printing presses, machinery or material devoted to publications of any kind. The buildings in which these objects are located may be condemned only after a judicial finding of public convenience and necessity pursuant to procedure that shall be provided by law, and may be taken before such a judicial finding only when there is placed at the disposition of the publication an adequate site in which it can be installed and continue to operate for a reasonable time.

Section 10.—The right of the people to be secure in their persons, houses, papers and effects against unreasonable searches and seizures shall not be violated.

Wire-tapping is prohibited.

No warrant for arrest or search and seizure shall issue except by judicial authority and only upon probable cause supported by oath or affirmation, and particularly describing the place to be searched and the persons to be arrested or the things to be seized.

Evidence obtained in violation of this section shall be inadmissible in the courts.

Section 11.—In all criminal prosecutions, the accused shall enjoy the right to have a speedy and public trial, to be informed of the nature and cause of the accusation and to have a copy thereof, to be confronted with the witnesses against him, to have compulsory process for obtaining witnesses in his favor, to have assistance of counsel, and to be presumed innocent.

In all prosecutions for a felony the accused shall have the right of trial by an impartial jury composed of twelve residents of the district, who may render their verdict by a majority vote which in no case may be less than nine.

No person shall be compelled in any criminal case to be a witness against himself and the failure of the accused to testify may be neither taken into consideration nor commented upon against him.

No person shall be twice put in jeopardy of punishment for the same offense.

Before conviction every accused shall be entitled to be admitted to bail.

Incarceration prior to trial shall not exceed six months nor shall bail or fines be excessive. No person shall be imprisoned for debt.

Section 12.—Neither slavery nor involuntary servitude shall exist except in the latter case as a punishment for crime after the accused has been

duly convicted. Cruel and unusual punishments shall not be inflicted. Suspension of civil rights including the right to vote shall cease upon service of the term of imprisonment imposed.

No ex post facto law or bill of attainder shall be passed.

Section 13.—The writ of habeas corpus shall be granted without delay and free of costs. The privilege of the writ of habeas corpus shall not be suspended, unless the public safety requires it in case of rebellion, insurrection or invasion. Only the Legislative Assembly shall have the power to suspend the privilege of the writ of habeas corpus and the laws regulating its issuance.

The military authority shall always be subordinate to civil authority.

Section 14.—No titles of nobility or other hereditary honors shall be granted. No officer or employee of the Commonwealth shall accept gifts, donations, decorations or offices from any foreign country or officer without prior authorization by the Legislative Assembly.

Section 15.—The employment of children less than fourteen years of age in any occupation which is prejudicial to their health or morals or which places them in jeopardy of life or limb is prohibited.

No child less than sixteen years of age shall be kept in custody in a jail or penitentiary.

Section 16.—The right of every employee to choose his occupation freely and to resign therefrom is recognized, as is his right to equal pay for equal work, to a reasonable minimum salary, to protection against risks to his health or person in his work or employment, and to an ordinary workday which shall not exceed eight hours. An employee may work in excess of this daily limit only if he is paid extra compensation as provided by law, at a rate never less than one and one-half times the regular rate at which he is employed.

Section 17.—Persons employed by private businesses, enterprises and individual employers and by agencies or instrumentalities of the government operating as private businesses or enterprises, shall have the right to organize and to bargain collectively with their employers through representatives of their own free choosing in order to promote their welfare.

Section 18.—In order to assure their right to organize and to bargain collectively, persons employed by private businesses, enterprises and individual employers and by agencies or instrumentalities of the government operating as private businesses or enterprises, in their direct relations with their own employers shall have the right to strike, to picket and to engage in other legal concerted activities.

Nothing herein contained shall impair the authority of the Legislative Assembly to enact laws to deal with grave emergencies that clearly imperil the public health or safety or essential public services.

Section 19.—The foregoing enumeration of rights shall not be construed restrictively nor does it contemplate the exclusion of other rights not specifically mentioned which belong to the people in a democracy. The power of the Legislative Assembly to enact laws for the protection of the life, health and general welfare of the people shall likewise not be construed restrictively.

Section 20.—The Commonwealth also recognizes the existence of the following human rights:

The right of every person to receive free elementary and secondary education.

The right of every person to obtain work.

The right of every person to a standard of living adequate for the health and well-being of himself and of his family, and especially to food, clothing, housing and medical care and necessary social services.

The right of every person to social protection in the event of unemployment, sickness, old age or disability.

The right of motherhood and childhood to special care and assistance.

The rights set forth in this section are closely connected with the progressive development of the economy of the Commonwealth and require,

for their full effectiveness, sufficient resources and an agricultural and industrial development not yet attained by the Puerto Rican community.

In the light of their duty to achieve the full liberty of the citizen, the people and the government of Puerto Rico shall do everything in their power to promote the greatest possible expansion of the system of production, to assure the fairest distribution of economic output, and to obtain the maximum understanding between individual initiative and collective cooperation The executive and judicial branches shall bear in mind this duty and shall construe the laws that tend to fulfill it in the most favorable manner possible.

Article III

The Legislature

Section 1.—The legislative power shall be vested in a Legislative Assembly, which shall consist of two houses, the Senate and the House of Representatives whose members shall be elected by direct vote at each general election.

Section 2.—The Senate shall be composed of twenty-seven Senators and the House of Representatives of fifty-one Representatives, except as these numbers may be increased in accordance with the provisions of Section 7 of this Article.

Section 3.—For the purpose of election of members of the Legislative Assembly, Puerto Rico shall be divided into eight senatorial districts and forty representative districts. Each senatorial district shall elect two Senators and each representative district one Representative.

There shall also be eleven Senators and eleven Representatives elected at large. No elector may vote for more than one candidate for Senator at Large or for more than one candidate for Representative at Large.

Section 4.—In the first and subsequent elections under this Constitution the division of senatorial and representative districts as provided in Article VIII shall be in effect. After each decennial census beginning with the year 1960, said division shall be revised by a Board composed of the Chief Justice of the Supreme Court as Chairman and of two additional members appointed by the Governor with the advice and consent of the Senate. The two additional members shall not belong to the same political party. Any revision shall maintain the number of senatorial and representative districts here created, which shall be composed of contiguous and compact territory and shall be organized, insofar as practicable, upon the basis of population and means of communication. Each senatorial district shall always include five representative districts.

The decisions of the Board shall be made by majority vote and shall take effect in the general elections next following each revision. The Board shall cease to exist after the completion of each revision.

Section 5.—No person shall be a member of the Legislative Assembly unless he is able to read and write the Spanish or English language and unless he is a citizen of the United States and of Puerto Rico and has resided in Puerto Rico at least two years immediately prior to the date of his election or appointment. No person shall be a member of the Senate who is not over thirty years of age, and no person shall be a member of the House of Representatives who is not over twenty-five years of age.

Section 6.—No person shall be eligible to election or appointment as Senator or Representative for a district unless he has resided therein at least one year immediately prior to his election or appointment. When there is more than one representative district in a municipality, residence in the municipality shall satisfy this requirement.

Section 7.—If in a general election more than two-thirds of the members of either house are elected from one political party or from a single ticket, as both are defined by law, the number of members shall be increased in the following cases:

(a) If the party or ticket which elected more than two-thirds of the members of either or both houses shall have obtained less than two-thirds of the total number of votes cast for the office of Governor, the number of members of the Senate or of the House of Representatives or of both

bodies, whichever may be the case, shall be increased by declaring elected a sufficient number of candidates of the minority party or parties to bring the total number of members of the minority party or parties to nine in the Senate and to seventeen in the House of Representatives. When there is more than one minority party, said additional members shall be declared elected from among the candidates of each minority party in the proportion that the number of votes cast for the candidate of each of said parties for the office of Governor bears to the total number of votes cast for the candidates of all the minority parties for the office of Governor.

When one or more minority parties shall have obtained representation in a proportion equal to or greater than the proportion of votes received by their respective candidates for Governor, such party or parties shall not be entitled to additional members until the representation established for each of the other minority parties under these provisions shall have been completed.

(b) If the party or ticket which elected more than two-thirds of the members of either or both houses shall have obtained more than two-thirds of the total number of votes cast for the office of Governor, and one or more minority parties shall not have elected the number of members in the Senate or in the House of Representatives or in both houses, whichever may be the case, which corresponds to the proportion of votes cast by each of them for the office of Governor, such additional number of their candidates shall be declared elected as is necessary in order to complete said proportion as nearly as possible, but the number of Senators of all the minority parties shall never, under this provision, be more than nine or that of Representatives more than seventeen.

In order to select additional members of the Legislative Assembly from a minority party in accordance with these provisions, its candidates at large who have not been elected shall be the first to be declared elected in the order of the votes that they have obtained, and thereafter its district candidates who, not having been elected, have obtained in their respective districts the highest proportion of the total number of votes cast as compared to the proportion of votes cast in favor of other candidates of the same party not elected to an equal office in the other districts.

The additional Senators and Representatives whose election is declared under this section shall be considered for all purposes as Senators at Large or Representatives at Large.

The measures necessary to implement these guarantees, the method of adjudicating fractions that may result from the application of the rules contained in this section, and the minimum number of votes that a minority party must cast in favor of its candidate for Governor in order to have the right to the representation provided herein shall be determined by the Legislative Assembly.

Section 8.—The term of office of Senators and Representative shall begin on the second day of January immediately following the date of the general election in which they shall have been elected. If, prior to the fifteen months immediately preceding the date of the next general election, a vacancy occurs in the office of Senator or Representative for a district, the Governor shall call a special election in said district within thirty days following the date on which the vacancy occurs. This election shall be held not later than ninety days after the call, and the person elected shall hold office for the rest of the unexpired term of his predecessor. When said vacancy occurs during a legislative session, or when the Legislative Assembly or the Senate has been called for a date prior to the certification of the results of the special election, the presiding officer of the appropriate house shall fill said vacancy by appointing the person recommended by the central committee of the political party of which his predecessor in office was a member. Such person shall hold the office until certification of the election of the candidate who was elected. When the vacancy occurs within fifteen months prior to a general election, or when it occurs in the office of a Senator at Large or a Representative at Large, the presiding officer of the appropriate house shall fill it, upon the recommendation of the political party of which the previous holder of the office was a member, by appointing a person selected in the same manner

as that in which his predecessor was selected. A vacancy in the office of a Senator at Large or a Representative at Large elected as an independent candidate shall be filled by an election in all districts.

Section 9.—Each house shall be the sole judge of the election, returns and qualifications of its members; shall choose its own officers; shall adopt rules for its own proceedings appropriate to legislative bodies; and, with the concurrence of three-fourths of the total number of members of which it is composed, may expel any member for the causes established in Section 21 of this Article, authorizing impeachments. The Senate shall elect a President and the House of Representatives a Speaker from among their respective members.

Section 10.—The Legislative Assembly shall be deemed a continuous body during the term for which its members are elected and shall meet in regular session each year commencing on the second Monday in January. The duration of regular sessions and the periods of time for introduction and consideration of bills shall be prescribed by law. When the Governor calls the Legislative Assembly into special session it may consider only those matters specified in the call or in any special message sent to it by him during the session. No special session shall continue longer than twenty calendar days.

Section 11.—The sessions of each house shall be open.

Section 12.—A majority of the total number of members of which each house is composed shall constitute a quorum, but a smaller number may adjourn from day to day and shall have authority to compel the attendance of absent members.

Section 13.—The two houses shall meet in the Capitol of Puerto Rico and neither of them may adjourn for more than three consecutive days without the consent of the other.

Section 14.—No member of the Legislative Assembly shall be arrested while the house of which he is a member is in session, or during the fifteen days before or after such session, except for treason, felony or breach of the peace. The members of the Legislative Assembly shall not be questioned in any other place for any speech, debate or vote in either house or in any committee.

Section 15.—No Senator or Representative may, during the term for which he was elected or chosen, be appointed to any civil office in the Government of Puerto Rico, its municipalities or instrumentalities, which shall have been created or the salary of which shall have been increased during said term. No person may hold office in the Government of Puerto Rico, its municipalities or instrumentalities and be a Senator or Representative at the same time. These provisions shall not prevent a member of the Legislative Assembly from being designated to perform functions ad honorem.

Section 16.—The Legislative Assembly shall have the power to create, consolidate or reorganize executive departments and to define their functions.

Section 17.—No bill shall become a law unless it has been printed, read, referred to a committee and returned therefrom with a written report, but either house may discharge a committee from the study and report of any bill and proceed to the consideration thereof. Each house shall keep a journal of its proceedings and of the votes cast for and against bills. The legislative proceedings shall be published in a daily record in the form determined by law. Every bill, except general appropriation bills, shall be confined to one subject, which shall be clearly expressed in its title, and any part of an act whose subject has not been expressed in the title shall be void. The general appropriation act shall contain only appropriations and rules for their disbursement. No bill shall be amended in a manner that changes its original purpose or incorporates matters extraneous to it. In amending any article or section of a law, said article or section shall be promulgated in its entirety as amended. All bills for raising revenue shall originate in the House of Representatives, but the Senate may propose or concur with amendments as on other bills.

Section 18.—The subjects which may be dealt with by means of joint resolution shall be deter-

mined by law, but every joint resolution shall follow the same legislative process as that of a bill.

Section 19.—Every bill which is approved by a majority of the total number of members of which each house is composed shall be submitted to the Governor and shall become law if he signs it or if he does not return it, with his objections, to the house in which it originated within ten days (Sundays excepted) counting from the date on which he shall have received it.

When the Governor returns a bill, the house that receives it shall enter his objections on its journal and both houses may reconsider it. If approved by two-thirds of the total number of members of which each house is composed, said bill shall become law.

If the Legislative Assembly adjourns *sine die* before the Governor has acted on a bill that has been presented to him less than ten days before, he is relieved of the obligation of returning it with his objections and the bill shall become law only if the Governor signs it within thirty days after receiving it.

Every final passage or reconsideration of a bill shall be by a roll-call vote.

Section 20.—In approving any appropriation bill that contains more than one item, the Governor may eliminate one or more of such items or reduce their amounts, at the same time reducing the total amounts involved.

Section 21.—The House of Representatives shall have exclusive power to initiate impeachment proceedings and, with the concurrence of two-thirds of the total number of members of which it is composed, to bring an indictment. The Senate shall have exclusive power to try and to decide impeachment cases, and in meeting for such purposes the Senators shall act in the name of the people and under oath or affirmation. No judgment of conviction in an impeachment trial shall be pronounced without the concurrence of three-fourths of the total number of members of which the Senate is composed, and the judgment shall be limited to removal from office. The person impeached, however, may be liable and subject to indictment, trial, judgment and punishment according to law. The causes of impeachment shall be treason, bribery, other felonies, and misdemeanors involving moral turpitude. The Chief Justice of the Supreme Court shall preside at the impeachment trial of the Governor.

The two houses may conduct impeachment proceedings in their regular or special sessions. The presiding officers of the two houses, upon written request of two-thirds of the total number of members of which the House of Representatives is composed, must convene them to deal with such proceedings.

Section 22.—The Governor shall appoint a Controller with the advice and consent of a majority of the total number of members of which each house is composed. The Controller shall meet the requirements prescribed by law and shall hold office for a term of ten years and until his successor has been appointed and qualifies. The Controller shall audit all the revenues, accounts and expenditures of the Commonwealth, of its agencies and instrumentalities and of its municipalities, in order to determine whether they have been made in accordance with law. He shall render annual reports and any special reports that may be required of him by the Legislative Assembly or by the Governor.

In the performance of his duties the Controller shall be authorized to administer oaths, take evidence and compel, under pain of contempt, the attendance of witnesses and the production of books, letters, documents, papers, records and all other articles deemed essential to a full understanding of the matter under investigation.

The Controller may be removed for the causes and pursuant to the procedure established in the preceding section.

Article IV

The Executive

Section 1.—The executive power shall be vested in a Governor, who shall be elected by direct vote in each general election.

Section 2.—The Governor shall hold office for the term of four years from the second day of January of the year following his election and until his successor has been elected and qualifies. He shall reside in Puerto Rico and maintain his office in its capital city.

Section 3.—No person shall be Governor unless, on the date of the election, he is at least thirty-five years of age, and is and has been during the preceding five years a citizen of the United States and a citizen and *bona fide* resident of Puerto Rico.

Section 4.—The Governor shall execute the laws and cause them to be executed.

He shall call the Legislative Assembly or the Senate into special session when in his judgment the public interest so requires.

He shall appoint, in the manner prescribed by this Constitution or by law, all officers whose appointment he is authorized to make. He shall have the power to make appointments while the Legislative Assembly is not in session. Any such appointments that require the advice and consent of the Senate or of both houses shall expire at the end of the next regular session.

He shall be the commander-in-chief of the militia.

He shall have the power to call out the militia and summon the posse comitatus in order to prevent or suppress rebellion, invasion or any serious disturbance of the public peace.

He shall have the power to proclaim martial law when the public safety requires it in case of rebellion or invasion or imminent danger thereof. The Legislative Assembly shall meet forthwith on their own initiative to ratify or revoke the proclamation.

He shall have the power to suspend the execution of sentences in criminal cases and to grant pardons, commutations of punishment, and total or partial remissions of fines and forfeitures for crimes committed in violation of the laws of Puerto Rico. This power shall not extend to cases of impeachment. He shall approve or disapprove in accordance with this Constitution the joint resolutions and bills passed by the Legislative Assembly.

He shall present to the Legislative Assembly, at the beginning of each regular session, a message concerning the affairs of the Commonwealth and a report concerning the state of the Treasury of Puerto Rico and the proposed expenditures for the ensuing fiscal year. Said report shall contain the information necessary for the formulation of a program of legislation.

He shall exercise the other powers and functions and discharge the other duties assigned to him by this Constitution or by law.

Section 5.—For the purpose of exercising executive power, the Governor shall be assisted by Secretaries whom he shall appoint with the advice and consent of the Senate. The appointment of the Secretary of State shall in addition require the advice and consent of the House of Representatives, and the person appointed shall fulfill the requirements established in Section 3 of this Article. The Secretaries shall collectively constitute the Governor's advisory council, which shall be designated as the Council of Secretaries.

Section 6.—Without prejudice to the power of the Legislative Assembly to create, reorganize and consolidate executive departments and to define their functions, the following departments are hereby established: State, Justice, Education Health, Treasury, Labor, Agriculture and Commerce, and Public Works. Each of these executive departments shall be headed by a Secretary.

Section 7.—When a vacancy occurs in the office of Governor, caused by death, resignation, removal, total and permanent incapacity, or any other absolute disability, said office shall devolve upon the Secretary of State, who shall hold it for the rest of the term and until a new Governor has been elected and qualifies. In the event that vacancies exist at the same time in both the office of Governor and that of Secretary of State, the law shall provide which of the Secretaries shall serve as Governor.

Section 8.—When for any reason the Governor is temporarily unable to perform his functions, the Secretary of State shall substitute for him during the period he is unable to serve. If for any reason the Secretary of State is not available, the Secretary

determined by law shall temporarily hold the office of Governor.

Section 9.—If the Governor-elect shall not have qualified, or if he has qualified and a permanent vacancy occurs in the office of Governor before he shall have appointed a Secretary of State, or before said Secretary, having been appointed, shall have qualified, the Legislative Assembly just elected, upon convening for its first regular session, shall elect, by a majority of the total number of members of which each house is composed, a Governor who shall hold office until his successor is elected in the next general election and qualifies.

Section 10.—The Governor may be removed for the causes and pursuant to the procedure established in Section 21 of Article III of this Constitution.

Article V

The Judiciary

Section 1.—The judicial power of Puerto Rico shall be vested in a Supreme Court, and in such other courts as may be established by law.

Section 2.—The courts of Puerto Rico shall constitute a unified judicial system for purposes of jurisdiction, operation and administration. The Legislative Assembly may create and abolish courts, except for the Supreme Court, in a manner not inconsistent with this Constitution, and shall determine the venue and organization of the courts.

Section 3.—The Supreme Court shall be the court of last resort in Puerto Rico and shall be composed of a Chief Justice and four Associate Justices. The number of Justices may be changed only by law upon request of the Supreme Court.

Section 4.—The Supreme Court shall sit, in accordance with rules adopted by it, as a full court or in divisions. All the decisions of the Supreme Court shall be concurred in by a majority of its members. No law shall be held unconstitutional except by a majority of the total number of Justices of which the Court is composed in accordance with this Constitution or with law.

Section 5.—The Supreme Court, any of its divisions or any of its Justices may hear in the first instance petitions for habeas corpus and any other causes and proceedings as determined by law.

Section 6.—The Supreme Court shall adopt for the courts rules of evidence and of civil and criminal procedure which shall not abridge, enlarge or modify the substantive rights of the parties. The rules thus adopted shall be submitted to the Legislative Assembly at the beginning of its next regular session and shall not go into effect until sixty days after the close of said session, unless disapproved by the Legislative Assembly, which shall have the power both at said session and subsequently to amend, repeal or supplement any of said rules by a specific law to that effect.

Section 7.—The Supreme Court shall adopt rules for the administration of the courts. These rules shall be subject to the laws concerning procurement, personnel, audit and appropriation of funds, and other laws which apply generally to all branches of the government. The Chief Justice shall direct the administration of the courts and shall appoint an administrative director who shall hold office at the will of the Chief Justice.

Section 8.—Judges shall be appointed by the Governor with the advice and consent of the Senate. Justices of the Supreme Court shall not assume office until after confirmation by the Senate and shall hold their offices during good behavior. The terms of office of the other judges shall be fixed by law and shall not be less than that fixed for the term of office of a judge of same or equivalent category existing when this Constitution takes effect. The other officials and employees of the courts shall be appointed in the manner provided by law.

Section 9.—No person shall be appointed a Justice of the Supreme Court unless he is a citizen of the United States and of Puerto Rico, shall have been admitted to the practice of law in Puerto Rico at least ten years prior to his appointment, and shall have resided in Puerto Rico at least five years immediately prior thereto.

Section 10.—The Legislative Assembly shall establish a retirement system for judges. Retire-

ment shall be compulsory at the age of seventy years.

Section 11.—Justices of the Supreme Court may be removed for the causes and pursuant to the procedure established in Section 21 of Article III of this Constitution. Judges of the other courts may be removed by the Supreme Court for the causes and pursuant to the procedure provided by law.

Section 12.—No judge shall make a direct or indirect financial contribution to any political organization or party, or hold any executive office therein, or participate in a political campaign of any kind, or be a candidate for an elective public office unless he has resigned his judicial office at least six months prior to his nomination.

Section 13.—In the event that a court or any of its divisions or sections is changed or abolished by law, the person holding a post of judge therein shall continue to hold it during the rest of the term for which he was appointed and shall perform judicial functions assigned to him by the Chief Justice of the Supreme Court.

Article VI

General Provisions

Section 1.—The Legislative Assembly shall have the power to create, abolish, consolidate and reorganize municipalities; to change their territorial limits; to determine their organization and functions; and to authorize them to develop programs for the general welfare and to create any agencies necessary for that purpose.

No law abolishing or consolidating municipalities shall take effect until ratified in a referendum by a majority of the electors voting in said referendum in each of the municipalities to be abolished or consolidated. The referendum shall be in the manner determined by law, which shall include the applicable procedures of the election laws in effect when the referendum law is approved.

Section 2.—The power of the Commonwealth of Puerto Rico to impose and collect taxes and to authorize their imposition and collection by municipalities shall be exercised as determined by the

Legislative Assembly and shall never be surrendered or suspended. The power of the Commonwealth of Puerto Rico to contract and to authorize the contracting of debts shall be exercised as determined by the Legislative Assembly.

Section 3.—The rule of taxation in Puerto Rico shall be uniform.

Section 4.—General elections shall be held every four years on the day of November determined by the Legislative Assembly.

In said elections there shall be elected a Governor, the members of the Legislative Assembly, and the other officials whose election on that date is provided for by law.

Every person over twenty-one years of age shall be entitled to vote if he fulfills the other conditions determined by law. No person shall be deprived of the right to vote because he does not know how to read or write or does not own property.

All matters concerning the electoral process, registration of voters, political parties and candidates shall be determined by law.

Every popularly elected official shall be elected by direct vote and any candidate who receives more votes than any other candidate for the same office shall be declared elected.

Section 5.—The laws shall be promulgated in accordance with the procedure prescribed by law and shall specify the terms under which they shall take effect.

Section 6.—If at the end of any fiscal year the appropriations necessary for the ordinary operating expenses of the government and for the payment of interest on and amortization of the public debt for the ensuing fiscal year shall not have been made, the several sums appropriated in the last appropriation acts for the objects and purposes therein specified, so far as the same may be applicable, shall continue in effect item by item, and the Governor shall authorize the payments necessary for such purposes until corresponding appropriations are made.

Section 7.—The appropriations made for any fiscal year shall not exceed the total revenues, including available surplus, estimated for said fiscal year unless the imposition of taxes sufficient to cover said appropriations is provided by law.

Section 8.—In case the available revenues including surplus for any fiscal year are insufficient to meet the appropriations made for that year, interest on the public debt and amortization thereof shall first be paid, and other disbursements shall thereafter be made in accordance with the order of priorities established by law.

Section 9.—Public property and funds shall only be disposed of for public purposes, for the support and operation of state institutions, and pursuant to law.

Section 10.—No law shall give extra compensation to any public officer, employee, agent or contractor after services shall have been rendered or contract made. No law shall extend the term of any public officer or diminish his salary or emoluments after his election or appointment. No person shall draw a salary for more than one office or position in the government of Puerto Rico.

Section 11.—The salaries of the Governor, the Secretaries, the members of the Legislative Assembly, the Controller and Judges shall be fixed by a special law and, except for the salaries of the members of the Legislative Assembly, shall not be decreased during the terms for which they are elected or appointed. The salaries of the Governor and the Controller shall not be increased during said terms. No increase in the salaries of the members of the Legislative Assembly shall take effect until after the expiration of the term of the Legislative Assembly during which it is enacted. Any reduction of the salaries of the members of the Legislative Assembly shall be elective only during the term of the Legislative Assembly which approves it.

Section 12.—The Governor shall occupy and use, free of rent, the buildings and properties belonging to the Commonwealth which have been or shall hereafter be used and occupied by him as chief executive.

Section 13.—The procedure for granting franchises, rights, privileges and concessions of a public or quasi-public nature shall be determined by law, but every concession of this kind to a person or private entity must be approved by the Governor or by the executive official whom he designates. Every franchise, right, privilege or concession of a public or quasi-public nature shall be subject to amendment, alteration or repeal as determined by law.

Section 14.—No corporation shall be authorized to conduct the business of buying and selling real estate or be permitted to hold or own real estate except such as may be reasonably necessary to enable it to carry out the purposes for which it was created, and every corporation authorized to engage in agriculture shall by its charter be restricted to the ownership and control of not to exceed five hundred acres of land; and this provision shall be held to prevent any member of a corporation engaged in agriculture from being in any wise interested in any other corporation engaged in agriculture.

Corporations, however, may loan funds upon real estate security, and purchase real estate when necessary for the collection of loans, but they shall dispose of real estate so obtained within five years after receiving the title.

Corporations not organized in Puerto Rico, but doing business in Puerto Rico, shall be bound by the provisions of this section so far as they are applicable.

These provisions shall not prevent the ownership, possession or management of lands in excess of five hundred acres by the Commonwealth, its agencies or instrumentalities.

Section 15.—The Legislative Assembly shall determine all matters concerning the flag, the seal and the anthem of the Commonwealth. Once determined, no law changing them shall take effect until one year after the general election next following the date of enactment of said law.

Section 16.—All public officials and employees of the Commonwealth, its agencies, instrumentalities and political subdivisions, before entering upon their respective duties, shall take an oath to support the Constitution of the United States and the Constitution and laws of the Commonwealth of Puerto Rico.

Section 17.—In case of invasion, rebellion, epidemic or any other event giving rise to a state of emergency, the Governor may call the Legislative Assembly to meet in a place other than the Capitol of Puerto Rico, subject to the approval or disapproval of the Legislative Assembly. Under the same conditions, the Governor may, during the period of emergency, order the government, its agencies and instrumentalities to be moved temporarily to a place other than the seat of the government.

Section 18.—All criminal actions in the courts of the Commonwealth shall be conducted in the name and by the authority of "The People of Puerto Rico" until otherwise provided by law.

Section 19.—It shall be the public policy of the Commonwealth to conserve, develop and use its natural resources in the most effective manner possible for the general welfare of the community; to conserve and maintain buildings and places declared by the Legislative Assembly to be of historic or artistic value; to regulate its penal institutions in a manner that effectively achieves their purposes and to provide, within the limits of available resources, for adequate treatment of delinquents in order to make possible their moral and social rehabilitation.

Article VII

Amendments to the Constitution

Section 1.—The Legislative Assembly may propose amendments to this Constitution by a concurrent resolution approved by not less than two-thirds of the total number of members of which each house is composed. All proposed amendments shall be submitted to the qualified electors in a special referendum, but if the concurrent resolution is approved by not less than three-fourths of the total number of members of which each house is composed, the Legislative Assembly may provide that the referendum shall be held at the same time as the next general election. Each proposed amendment shall be voted on separately and not more than three proposed amendments may be submitted at the same referendum. Every proposed amendment shall specify the terms under which it shall take effect, and it shall become a part of this Constitution if it is ratified by a majority of the electors voting thereon. Once approved, a proposed amendment must be published at least three months prior to the date of the referendum.

Section 2.—The Legislative Assembly, by a concurrent resolution approved by two-thirds of the total number of members of which each house is composed, may submit to the qualified electors at a referendum, held at the same time as a general election, the question of whether a constitutional convention shall be called to revise this Constitution. If a majority of the electors voting on this question vote in favor of the revision, it shall be made by a Constitutional Convention elected in the manner provided by law. Every revision of this Constitution shall be submitted to the qualified electors at a special referendum for ratification or rejection by a majority of the votes cast at the referendum.

Section 3.—No amendment to this Constitution shall alter the republican form of government established by it or abolish its bill of rights.

Article VIII

Senatorial and Representative Districts

Section 1.—The senatorial and representative districts shall be the following:

I.—SENATORIAL DISTRICT OF SAN JUAN, which shall be composed of the following Representative Districts: The Capital of Puerto Rico, excluding the present electoral precincts of Santurce and Rio Piedras; 2.—Electoral zones numbers 1 and 2 of the present precinct of Santurce; 3.—Electoral zone number 3 of the present precinct of Santurce; 4.—Electoral zone number 4 of the present precinct of Santurce; and 6.—Wards Hato Rey, Puerto Nuevo and Caparra Heights of the Capital of Puerto Rico.

II.—SENATORIAL DISTRICT OF BAYAMON, which shall be composed of the following Representative Districts: 7.—The municipality of Bayamon; 8.—The municipalities of Carolina

and Trujillo Alto; 9.—The present electoral precinct of Rio Piedras, excluding wards Hato Rey, Puerto Nuevo and Caparra Heights of the Capital of Puerto Rico; 10.—The municipalities of Catano, Guaynabo and Toa Baja; and 11.—The municipalities of Toa Alta, Corozal and Naranjito.

III.—SENATORIAL DISTRICT OF ARECIBO, which shall be composed of the following Representative Districts: The municipalities of Vega Baja, Vega Alta and Dorado; 12.—The municipalities of Manati and Barceloneta; 13.—The municipalities of Ciales and Morovis; 14.—The municipality of Arecibo; and 15.—The municipality of Utuado.

IV.—SENATORIAL DISTRICT OF AGUADILLA, which shall be composed of the following Representative Districts: 16.—The municipalities of Camuy, Hatillo and Quebradillas; 17.—The municipalities of Aguadilla and Isabela; 18.—The municipalities of San Sebastian and Moca; 19.—The municipalities of Lares, Las Marias and Maricao; and 20.—The municipalities of Anasco, Aguada and Rincon.

V.—SENATORIAL DISTRICT OF MAYAGÜEZ, which shall be composed of the following Representative Districts: 21.—The municipality of Mayaguez; 22.—The municipalities of Cabo Rojo, Hor migueros and Lajas; 23.—The municipalities of San German and Sabana Grande; 24.—The municipalities of Yauco and Guanica; and 25.—The municipalities of Guayanilla and Penuelas.

VI.—SENATORIAL DISTRICT OF PONCE, which shall be composed of the following Representative Districts: 26.—The first, second, third, fourth, fifth and sixth wards and the City Beach of the municipality of Ponce; 27.—The municipality of Ponce, except for the first, second, third, fourth, fifth and sixth wards and the City Beach; 28.—The municipalities of Adjuntas and Jayuya; 29.—The municipalities of Juana Diaz, Santa Isabel and Villalba; and 30.—The municipalities of Coamo and Orocovis.

VII.—SENATORIAL DISTRICT OF GUAYAMA, which shall be composed of the following Representative Districts: 31.—The municipali-

ties of Aibonito, Barranquitas and Comerio; 32.—
The municipalities of Cayey and Cidra; 33.—The
municipalities of Caguas and Aguas Buenas; 34.—
The municipalities of Guayama and Salinas; and
35.—The municipalities of Patillas, Maunabo
and Arroyo.

VIII.—SENATORIAL DISTRICT OF HUMA-
CAO, which shall be composed of the following
Representative Districts: 36.—The municipali-
ties of Humacao and Yabucoa; 37.—The munici-
palities of Juncos, Gurabo and San Lorenzo; 38.—
The municipalities of Naguabo, Ceiba and Las
Piedras; 39.—The municipalities of Fajardo and
Vieques and the Island of Culebra; and 40.—The
municipalities of Rio Grande, Loiza and Luquillo.

Section 2.—Electoral zones numbers 1, 2, 3 and 4
included in three representative districts within
the senatorial district of San Juan are those presently existing for purposes of electoral organization in the second precinct of San Juan.

Article IX

Transitory Provisions

Section 1.—When this Constitution goes into
effect all laws not inconsistent therewith shall
continue in full force until amended or repealed, or
until they expire by their own terms. Unless otherwise provided by this Constitution, civil and criminal liabilities, rights, franchises, concessions, privileges, claims, actions, causes of action, contracts,
and civil, criminal and administrative proceedings
shall continue unaffected, notwithstanding the
taking effect of this Constitution.

Section 2.—All officers who are in office by
election or appointment on the date this Constitution takes effect shall continue to hold their offices
and to perform the functions thereof in a manner
not inconsistent with this Constitution, unless the
functions of their offices are abolished or until
their successors are selected and qualify in accordance with this Constitution and laws enacted
pursuant thereto.

Section 3.—Notwithstanding the age limit fixed
by this Constitution for compulsory retirement, all
the judges of the courts of Puerto Rico who are
holding office on the date this Constitution takes

effect shall continue to hold their judicial offices
until the expiration of the terms for which they
were appointed, and in the case of Justices of the
Supreme Court during good behavior.

Section 4.—The Commonwealth of Puerto Rico
shall be the successor of the People of Puerto Rico
for all purposes, including without limitation the
collection and payment of debts and liabilities in
accordance with their terms.

Section 5.—When this Constitution goes into
effect, the term "citizen of the Commonwealth of
Puerto Rico" shall replace the term "citizen of
Puerto Rico" as previously used.

Section 6.—Political parties shall continue to
enjoy all rights recognized by the election law,
provided that on the effective date of this Constitution they fulfill the minimum requirements for
the registration of new parties contained in said
law. Five years after this Constitution shall have
taken effect the Legislative Assembly may change
these requirements, but any law increasing them
shall not go into effect until after the general
election next following its enactment.

Section 7.—The Legislative Assembly may enact
the laws necessary to supplement and make effective these transitory provisions in order to assure
the functioning of the government until the officers provided for by this Constitution are elected
or appointed and qualify, and until this Constitution takes effect in all respects.

Section 8.—If the Legislative Assembly creates a
Department of Commerce, the Department of
Agriculture and Commerce shall hereafter be called
the Department of Agriculture.

Section 9.—The first election under the provisions of this Constitution shall be held on the date
provided by law, but not later than six months after
the effective date of this Constitution. The second
general election under this Constitution shall be
held in the month of November 1956 on a day
provided by law.

Section 10.—This Constitution shall take effect
when the Governor so proclaims, but not later
than sixty days after its ratification by the Congress of the United States.

Done in Convention, at San Juan, Puerto Rico, on the sixth day of February, in the year of Our Lord one thousand nine hundred and fifty-two.

RESOLUTIONS APPROVED BY THE CONSTITUTIONAL CONVENTION RELATING TO THE CONSTITUTION OF THE COMMONWEALTH OF PUERTO RICO

Resolution No. 22

Approved by the Constitutional Convention of Puerto Rico in the Plenary Session Held February 4, 1952

To determine in Spanish and in English the name of the body politic created by the Constitution of the people of Puerto Rico. WHEREAS, this Constitutional Convention, in accordance with the mandate of the people, is about to adopt the Constitution by virtue of which the Puerto Rican community will be politically organized;

WHEREAS, it is necessary to give an appropriate name in both English and Spanish to the body politic thus created;

WHEREAS, the word "commonwealth" in contemporary English usage means a politically organized community, that is to say, a state (using the word in the generic sense) in which political power resides ultimately in the people, hence a free state, but one which is at the same time linked to a broader political system in a federal or other type of association and therefore does not have an independent and separate existence;

WHEREAS, the single word "commonwealth," as currently used, clearly defines the status of the body politic created under the terms of the compact existing between the people of Puerto Rico and the United States, i.e., that of a state which is free of superior authority in the management of its own local affairs but which is linked to the United States of America and hence is a part of its political system in a manner compatible with its federal structure;

WHEREAS, there is no single word in the Spanish language exactly equivalent to the English word "commonwealth" and translation of "commonwealth" into Spanish requires a combination of words to express the concepts of state and liberty and association;

WHEREAS, in the case of Puerto Rico the most appropriate translation of "commonwealth" into Spanish is the expression "estado libre asociado," which however should not be rendered "associated free state" in English inasmuch as the word "state" in ordinary speech in the United States means one of the States of the Union;

THEREFORE, Be it resolved by the Constituent Assembly of Puerto Rico:

First: That in Spanish the name of the body politic created by the Constitution which this Convention is adopting for submission to the people of Puerto Rico shall be "Estado Libre Asociado," it being understood that in our case this term is equivalent to and an appropriate translation of the English word "commonwealth."

Second: That, as a consequence, the body politic created by our Constitution shall be designated "The Commonwealth of Puerto Rico" in English and "El Estado Libre Asociado de Puerto Rico" in Spanish.

Third: That the Committee on Style of this Convention is instructed to use these designations in the respective English and Spanish texts of the Constitution when submitting the documents for third reading.

Fourth: That this resolution shall be published in Spanish and in English as an explanatory and authoritative statement of the meaning of the terms "Commonwealth" and "Estado Libre Asociado" as used in the Constitution; and that it shall be widely distributed, together with the Constitution, for the information of the people of Puerto Rico and the Congress of the United States.

Resolution No. 23

Approved by the Constitutional Convention of Puerto Rico in the Plenary Session Held February 4, 1952

Final declarations of the Constitutional Convention of Puerto Rico.

WHEREAS, the Constitutional Convention of Puerto Rico, in fulfilling the important mission assigned it by the people, has approved a Constitution for the Commonwealth of Puerto Rico within the terms of the compact entered into with the United States of America;

WHEREAS, in accordance with the terms of the compact, said Constitution is to be submitted to the people of Puerto Rico for their approval;

THEREFORE, Be it resolved by this Constitutional Convention:

First: That, pursuant to the relevant regulations, a certified copy of the Constitution as approved be sent to the Governor of Puerto Rico so that he may submit it to the people of Puerto Rico in a referendum as provided by law.

Second: That copies of the Constitution be printed in Spanish and English, respectively, in numbers sufficient for general distribution to the end that it will become widely known. Third: That the following final declarations of this Convention be entered on its journal and also published:

(a) This Convention deems that the Constitution as approved fulfills the mission assigned it by the people of Puerto Rico.

(b) When this Constitution takes effect, the people of Puerto Rico shall thereupon be organized in a commonwealth established within the terms of the compact entered into by mutual consent, which is the basis of our union with the United States of America.

(c) The political authority of the Commonwealth of Puerto Rico shall be exercised in accordance with its Constitution and within the terms of said compact.

(d) Thus we attain the goal of complete self-government, the last vestiges of colonialism having disappeared in the principle of Compact, and we enter into an era of new developments in democratic civilization. Nothing can surpass in political dignity the principle of mutual consent and of compacts freely agreed upon. The spirit of the people of Puerto Rico is free for great undertakings now and in the future. Having full political

dignity the commonwealth of Puerto Rico may develop in other ways by modifications of the Compact through mutual consent.

(e) The people of Puerto Rico reserve the right to propose and to accept modifications in the terms of its relations with the United States of America, in order that these relations may at all times be the expression of an agreement freely entered into between the people of Puerto Rico and the United States of America.

Fourth: That a copy of this resolution be sent to the President of the United States and to the President of the Senate and the Speaker of the House of Representatives of the Congress of the United States.

KEY PROVISIONS OF THE CIVIL RIGHTS ACT OF 1964

Title I—Voting Rights

Barred unequal application of registration procedures, and rejections for minor errors; made a sixth-grade education a rebuttable presumption of literacy; required that literacy tests be administered in writing and that copies of the test and an individual's answers be furnished on request.

Title II—Public Accommodation

Barred discrimination in restaurants, hotels, motels, places of amusement, and gasoline stations if the discrimination were "supported by state laws or action," or involved interstate commerce. It specifically exempted owner-occupied lodging houses with five or fewer rooms for rent (the "Mrs. Murphy" clause) and private clubs.

Title III—Desegregation of Public Facilities

Permitted the Justice Department to initiate suits to secure desegregation of state or locally owned, operated, or managed public facilities—parks, playgrounds, swimming pools, libraries, etc.

Title IV—Desegregation of Public Education

Authorized the attorney general to file school desegregation suits on written complaint, but did not cover busing of pupils or other such steps to end "racial imbalance." Required the United States Office of Education to make a survey and report to Congress within two years on the progress of desegregation of public schools at all levels.

Title V—Civil Rights Commission

Extended life of the Civil Rights Commission through January 31, 1968, and broadened the Commission's duties by authorizing it to serve as a national clearinghouse on civil rights information.

Title VI—Federally Assisted Programs

Barred discrimination under any federally assisted activity against any person because of race, color, or national origin; ordered federal agencies extending aid to issue rules (to be approved by the President) to carry out the title's provisions.

Title VII—Equal Employment Opportunity

Barred discrimination by employers or unions with 100 or more employees or members, but the number would be reduced over four years to 25 employees/members or more.

Title VIII—Registration and Voting Statistics

Directed the Census Bureau to compile registration and voting statistics based on race, color, and national origin wherever recommended by the Civil Rights Commission.

Title IX—Intervention

Permitted the attorney general to intervene in private suits where person alleged denial of equal protection of the laws under the Fourteenth Amendment and where he found the case to be of "general public importance."

Title X—Community Relations Service

Provided for a Community Relations Service in the Commerce Department to help communities resolve discrimination disputes.

Title XI—Miscellaneous

Guaranteed jury trials for criminal contempt cases under any part of the act but Title I, with a limit on the sentences of six months in prison and a $1,000 fine. Title I or voting rights cases were covered by the 1957 jury-trial provision that a judge may try a case without a jury but that in such cases sentences

were limited to a $300 fine and forty-five days in prison; in voting rights cases tried by jury, sentences were limited to six months and a fine of $1,000.

Public Law 88-352.

THE NORTH AMERICAN FREE TRADE AGREEMENT (NAFTA)

On August 12, 1992, Canadian Minister of Industry, Science and Technology and Minister for International Trade Michael Wilson, Mexican Secretary of Trade and Industrial Development Jaime Serra, and United States Trade Representative Carla Hills completed negotiations on a proposed North American Free Trade Agreement (NAFTA). The text of the agreement was completed on September 13, 1993 and was presented to Congress in November 1993.

The Preamble and Part One (General Part) are presented here.

Preamble

The Government of Canada, the Government of the United Mexican States and the Government of the United States of America, resolved to:

STRENGTHEN the special bonds of friendship and cooperation among their nations;

CONTRIBUTE to the harmonious development and expansion of world trade and provide a catalyst to broader international cooperation;

CREATE an expanded and secure market for the goods and services produced in their territories;

REDUCE distortions to trade;

ESTABLISH clear and mutually advantageous rules governing their trade;

ENSURE a predictable commercial framework for business planning and investment;

BUILD on their respective rights and obligations under the General Agreement on Tariffs and Trade and other multilateral and bilateral instruments of cooperation;

ENHANCE the competitiveness of their firms in global markets;

FOSTER creativity and innovation, and promote trade in goods and services that are the subject of intellectual property rights;

CREATE new employment opportunities and improve working conditions and living standards in their respective territories;

UNDERTAKE each of the preceding in a manner consistent with environmental protection and conservation;

PRESERVE their flexibility to safeguard the public welfare;

PROMOTE sustainable development;

STRENGTHEN the development and enforcement of environmental laws and regulations; and

PROTECT, enhance and enforce basic workers' rights;

HAVE AGREED as follows:

PART ONE

GENERAL PART

Chapter One

Objectives

Article 101: Establishment of the Free Trade Area

The Parties to this Agreement, consistent with Article XXIV of the General Agreement on Tariffs and Trade, hereby establish a free trade area.

Article 102: Objectives

1. The objectives of this Agreement, as elaborated more specifically through its principles and rules, including national treatment, most-favored-nation treatment and transparency are to:

(a) eliminate barriers to trade in, and facilitate the cross border movement of, goods and services between the territories of the Parties;

(b) promote conditions of fair competition in the free trade area;

(c) increase substantially investment opportunities in their territories;

(d) provide adequate and effective protection and enforcement of intellectual property rights in each Party's territory;

(e) create effective procedures for the implementation and application of this Agreement, and for its joint administration and the resolution of disputes; and

(f) establish a framework for further trilateral, regional and multilateral cooperation to expand and enhance the benefits of this Agreement.

2. The Parties shall interpret and apply the provisions of this Agreement in the light of its objectives set out in paragraph 1 and in accordance with applicable rules of international law.

Article 103: Relation to Other Agreements

1. The Parties affirm their existing rights and obligations with respect to each other under the General Agreement on Tariffs and Trade and other agreements to which such Parties are party.

2. In the event of any inconsistency between the provisions of this Agreement and such other agreements, the provisions of this Agreement shall prevail to the extent of the inconsistency, except as otherwise provided in this Agreement.

Article 104: Relation to Environmental and Conservation Agreements

1. In the event of any inconsistency between this Agreement and the specific trade obligations set out in:

(a) Convention on the International Trade in Endangered Species of Wild Fauna and Flora, done at Washington, March 3, 1973;

(b) the Montreal Protocol on Substances that Deplete the Ozone Layer, done at Montreal, September 16, 1987, as amended June 29, 1990;

(c) Basel Convention on the Control of Transboundary Movements of Hazardous Wastes and Their Disposal, done at Basel, March 22, 1989, upon its entry into force for Canada, Mexico and the United States; or

(d) the agreements set out in Annex 104.1, such obligations shall prevail to the extent of the inconsistency, provided that where a Party has a choice among equally effective and reasonably available means of complying with such obligations, the Party chooses the alternative that is the least inconsistent with the other provisions of this Agreement.

2. The Parties may agree in writing to modify Annex 104.1 to include any amendment to the agreements listed in paragraph 1, and any other environmental or conservation agreement.

Article 105: Extent of Obligations

The Parties shall ensure that all necessary measures are taken in order to give effect to the provisions of this Agreement, including their observance, except as otherwise provided in this Agreement, by state and provincial governments.

Annex 104
Bilateral and Other Environmental and Conservation Agreements

1. The Agreement Between the Government of Canada and the Government of the United States of America Concerning the Transboundary Movement of Hazardous Waste, signed at Ottawa, October 28, 1986.

2. The Agreement between the United States of America and the United Mexican States on Cooperation for the Protection and Improvement of the Environment in the Border Area, signed at La Paz, Baja California Sur, August 14, 1983.

GLOSSARY

ACTO a one-act Chicano theater piece developed out of collective improvization.

ADELANTADO the commander of an expedition who would receive, in advance, title to any lands that he would discover.

AGRINGADO literally "Gringo-ized" or Americanized.

AUDIENCIA a tribunal that ruled over territories.

AZTLÁN originally the mythological land of origin of the Mechica nations, to which the Toltecs and the Aztecs belong; Chicanos identify this land of origin as the geographic region of the American Southwest, figuratively their homeland.

BABALAO a spiritual healer, witch, or advisor, especially in **SANTERÍA.**

BATOS LOCOS See *Pachucos.*

BODEGA a small general store.

BOHÍOS thatched-roofed huts used by the Caribbean Indians.

BOTÁNICA a shop that specializes in herbs, folk potions, and medicines.

BRACERO from *brazo,* literally someone who works with their arms or performs manual labor; originally applied to temporary Mexican agricultural and railroad workers, it is also occasionally used to refer to any unskilled Mexican workers.

BRAZO arm.

BULTO the wooden sculpture in the image of a Catholic saint.

CABILDO city council.

CACIQUE an Indian village chieftain.

CALAVERAS literally "skulls"; a type of folk poem.

CALÓ a Mexican–American dialect, often associated with **PACHUCOS.**

CAMPESINO peasant.

CANCIÓN song.

CAPILLA chapel.

CARPA from the Quechua word meaning an awning of branches, in Spanish it has come to mean a tent; circuses and tent theaters have come to be known as *carpas* by extension.

CARRETA cart.

CASTELLANOS pesos.

CAUDILLO chief or leader, originally of the rural poor, but today quite often said of any grassroots political leader.

CHARRERÍAS contests of the Mexican cowboys.

CHARRO a Mexican cowboy of the Jalisco region, maintaining the dress and customs often associated with mariachis.

CHICANO derivative of Mechicano, the same Nahuatl word that gave origin to the name of Mexico, the term originally meant Mexican immigrant worker in the early twentieth century, but became the name adopted by Mexican

Americans, especially during the days of the civil rights and student movements.

CHINAMPA   a man-made island or floating garden developed by Meso–American Indians as an agricultural technique.

CIMARRONES   runaway slaves.

COLONIA   literally a "colony" it refers to the enclave of Hispanic population within a city, much as the term barrio is used today (barrio means neighborhood in Spanish).

COMPADRAZGO   godparenthood; usually through the baptism of a child, **COMPADRAZGO** is the extension of kinship to non-relatives and the strengthening of responsibilities between kin.

CONFIANZA   trust, the basis of the relationships between individuals in many spheres of social activity, but especially among kin.

CONJUNTO   a Texas–northern Mexico musical style as well as the ensemble that plays it, made up usually of a guitar, a bass guitar, a drum, and a button accordion.

CORREGIDORES   regional government administrators.

CORRIDO   a Mexican ballad.

CORTES   Spanish legislative body.

CRIOLLISMO   Spanish American.

CRIOLLO   a creole, that is, someone of Spanish origin born in the New World.

CRÓNICA   a local color newspaper column often satirizing contemporary customs.

CRONISTA   the writer of *crónicas*.

CURANDERO   a folk healer that combines the practices of the Mexican Indians and Spanish folk healing.

DANZAS   Puerto Rican dance music.

EJIDOS   land parcels.

ENCOMENDERO   the owner of the *encomienda*.

ENCOMIENDA   developed during feudalism in Spain, the *encomienda* was booty given to a Spanish conqueror of a Moorish caliphate. The award was usually the land that had belonged to

the caliph. In the Americas, it was the land that had belonged to the conquered Indian nations.

EX-VOTO   a gift presented to a saint as a show of gratitude for a favor conceded.

FAMILIA, LA   the greater family, which includes the immediate nuclear household and relatives that are traced on both female and male sides.

FANEGA   a dry measure of about a hundred-weight, or 1.6 bushels.

FILIBUSTEROS   subversive agents.

FINCA   farm or ranch.

GALLEGO   the stock Galician Spaniard, known for his hard head and frugality in Cuban farce.

GRINGO   Anglo–American.

HACENDADOS   the owner of an *hacienda*.

HACIENDA   a large ranch derivative of the latifundia system.

HERMANDAD   brotherhood.

INDIGENISMO   an emphasis on American Indian and Pre-Columbian origins and identity.

INGENIOS   plantations, especially of sugar.

ISLEÑOS   descendants of the Canary Island settlers in southern Louisiana.

JÍBARO   originally an American Indian word for highlander, it is what Puerto Ricans call the rural mountain folk, but has also come to be symbolic of the national identity of Puerto Ricans.

KIVA   a secret underground ceremonial chamber, especially as used in Pueblo culture for ceremonies and meetings.

LATIFUNDIA   a large estate or ranch originating in ancient Roman civilization.

LECTORES   professional readers who would read books, magazines, and newspapers to cigar-rollers as they performed their laborious tasks.

LICEUM   secondary school.

MACANA   a wooden war club.

MANDA   a sacrificial offering to a saint in order to receive some favor.

MANIOC   source of commercial tapioca.

MAQUILADORA   a factory on the Mexican side of the border which performs part of the manual assembly of products at comparatively lower wages offered by the Mexican economy, said products are shipped back for finishing and marketing by the partner company in the United States.

MARAVEDÍ   a fictional unit and common denominator of all coins. The **CASTELLANO** contained 450 **MARAVEDÍS.**

MARIELITO   a Cuban refugee who arrived in the United States as a result of the Mariel boatlift.

MATADERO   slaughterhouse.

MERCEDES   land grants.

MESTIZO   an individual of mixed Spanish (or European) and American Indian heritage.

MILAGRO   a charm made out of tin, gold, or silver and shaped in the form of an arm, a leg, a baby, a house, representing the favor usually of healing desired from a saint.

MORADA   the meeting house of the Penitente lay brotherhood.

MULATA   the stock female Mulatto character in Cuban farce.

MÚSICA NORTEÑA   *conjunto* music from the northern region of Mexico (also includes Texas).

MUTUALISTA   mutual aid society, organizations that engaged in social activities and provided basic needs for immigrant workers and their families, including insurance and death benefits for members.

NACIMIENTO   a nativity.

NAÑIGUISMO   membership in the secret society of Abakúa, which combines elements of the Efik culture of the southern coast of Nigeria and Freemasonry.

NEGRITO   the stock character in black face of Cuban farce.

NITAINOS   principal advisors among the Arawak Indians, quite often in charge of the labor force.

NOPAL   the prickly pear cactus.

NORTEÑO   of northern Mexican origin.

NUYORICAN   literally New York-Rican, a term developed colloquially by Puerto Ricans born or raised in New York to distinguish themselves from those identifying with the island solely.

OBRAS BUFAS CUBANAS   Cuban farce.

ORISHAS   the African deities of *santería.*

ORQUESTA   a Mexican American musical ensemble that develops its style around the violin.

PACHUCO   the member of a Mexican American urban youth subculture, which characteristically developed its own style of dress (zoot suit), its own dialect *(caló)* and its own bilingual-bicultural ideology during the 1940s and 1950s.

PADRINOS   godparents.

PARENTESCO   kinship sentiment.

PARIENTES   blood relatives.

PASTORELA   the shepherds play, a folk drama reenacted during the Christmas season.

PATRIA   fatherland.

PATRIA CHICA   the home region within a country.

PELADITA   underdog Vaudevillian character.

PELADO   literally the "skinned one" or shirtless one, he was the stock underdog, sharp-witted picaresque character of Mexican vaudeville and tent shows.

PENITENTE   literally "penitent," it is the name of a religious brotherhood in New Mexico.

PIRAGUAS   a narrow, high-prowed canoe as used by the Caribbean Indians.

POSADA   a community Christmas pageant where carolers go door to door asking for shelter in reenactment of Joseph and Mary's search for lodging.

PRESIDIO   a fort, especially characteristic of frontier settlements.

PROMESA   literally a "promise," it is a sacrificial offering to a saint in order to receive some favor.

QUECHUA   language of the Mayans.

REAL   also known as a **TOMÍN**.

RENEGADO   a renegade, someone who denies his or her Mexican identity.

REPARTIMIENTO   a form of the *encomienda* which vested the rights over the Indians in the civil authorities.

REREDO   altar screen

RESIDENCIA   a device by the Crown implementing the policy of never entrusting the enforcement of decrees and laws to a single officer.

RETABLOS   paintings on panels behind the altar in a Catholic church.

REVISTA   a vaudeville musical revue.

SAINETE   short play.

SALSA   literally "sauce," it refers to Afro–Caribbean music.

SANTERÍA   a synchretic religious sect growing out of the original African religion and the Catholicism of slaves.

SANTERISMO   the same as *santería*.

SANTERO   in the Southwest, a sculptor of wooden saints; in the Caribbean, a devotee of an *orisha* in *santería*.

SANTOS   the sculpted figures representing saints of the Catholic church which are used in worship and prayer.

TAINO (ALSO NITAINO)   a group of sedentary tribes native to the Caribbean.

TOMÍN   in Spanish coinage, 1 peso was divided 8 **TOMINES**, each **TOMÍN** into 12 granos.

TRATADOS   treaties.

ULTRAISMO   avant-garde literary movement.

VAQUERO   cowboy.

VEGAS   plantations, especially of coffee.

YERBERÍAS   shops specializing in medicinal plants, herbs, and potions.

YERBEROS   folk healers and spiritualists who use herbs in their practices.

YUCA   manioc root.

ZARZUELA   a type of Spanish operetta.

ZEMÍES   gods of the Arawak Indians, also the small Taino religious figure made of clay that represented these gods.

GENERAL BIBLIOGRAPHY

A

Acosta-Belén, Edna, ed. *The Puerto Rican Woman.* New York: Praeger, 1986.

Aguilar Camín, Héctor, and Lorenzo Meyer. *In the Shadow of the Mexican Revolution. Contemporary Mexican History, 1910–1989.* Austin: University of Texas Press, 1993.

Alvarez, Robert R. *Familia: Migration and Adaptation in Alta and Baja California 1850–1975.* Berkeley: University of California Press, 1987.

Ameringer, Charles. *The Democratic Left in Exile: The Antidictatorial Struggle in the Caribbean, 1945–1959.* Coral Gables, FL: University of Miami Press, 1974.

B

Bannon, John Francis, ed. *The Spanish Borderlands Frontier 1513–1821.* Norman: University of Oklahoma Press, 1970.

Barrera, Mario. *Race and Class in the Southwest: A Theory of Racial Inequality.* Notre Dame, IN: University of Notre Dame Press, 1979.

Bean, Frank D., and Marta Tienda. *The Hispanic Population of the United States.* New York: Russell Sage Foundation, 1988.

Beardsley, John, and Jane Livingston. *Hispanic Art in the United States: Thirty Painters and Sculptors.* New York: Abbeville Press, 1987.

Bizzarro, Salvatorre. *Historical Dictionary of Chile.* Metuchen, NJ: Scarecrow Press, 1972.

Blasier, Cole. *The Hovering Giant: U.S. Responses to Revolutionary Change in Latin America.* Pittsburgh, PA: University of Pittsburgh Press, 1979.

Booth, John A., and Thomas Walker. *Understanding Central America.* Boulder, CO: Westview Press, 1989.

Boswel, T. D., and J. R. Curtis. *The Cuban American Experience.* Totowa, NJ: Rowan and Allenheld, 1984.

Bronx Museum of the Arts. *The Latin American Spirit: Art and Artists in the United States, 1920–1970.* New York: Harry N. Abrams, 1988.

Burns, E. Bradford. *Latin America: A Concise Interpretive History.* Englewood Cliffs, NJ: Prentice-Hall, 1986.

C

Camp, Roderick A. *Mexican Political Biographies, 1884–1935.* Austin: University of Texas Press, 1991.

Carter, Hodding. *Doomed Road of Em-* *pire: The Spanish Trail of Conquest.* New York: McGraw-Hill, 1963.

Castedo, Leopoldo. *A History of Latin American Art and Architecture from Pre-Columbian Times to the Present.* Translated by Phyllis Freeman. New York: Praeger, 1969.

Chase, Gilbert. *Contemporary Art in Latin America.* New York: The Free Press, 1970.

Chilcote, Ronald S. *Latin America: The Struggle with Dependency and Beyond.* New York: Schenkman, 1974.

Cockroft, James D., et al. *Dependence and Underdevelopment.* New York: Anchor Books, 1972.

Collier, Simon. *From Cortés to Castro: An Introduction to the History of Latin America.* New York: Macmillan, 1974.

Cope, R. Douglas. *The Limits of Racial Domination: Plebeian Society in Colonial Mexico City, 1660–1720.* Madison: The University of Wisconsin Press, 1994.

Cotera, Marta P. *Latina Sourcebook: Bibliography of Mexican American, Cuban, Puerto Rican and Other Hispanic Women Materials in the USA.* Austin, TX: Information Systems Development, 1982.

Crassweller, Robert D. *Peron and the*

Enigmas of Argentina. New York: Norton, 1989.

Crawley, Eduardo. *Nicaragua in Perspective.* New York: St. Martin's Press, 1979.

D

Damaz, Paul F. *Art in Latin American Architecture.* New York: Reinhold, 1963.

Diederich, Bernard. *Somoza and the Legacy of U.S. Involvement in Central America.* New York: E. P. Dutton, 1981.

Dixon, Marlene. *On Trial: Reagan's War Against Nicaragua.* San Francisco, CA: Synthesis Publications, 1985.

Dobyns, Henry F. *Peru: A Cultural History.* New York: Oxford University Press, 1978.

Dorner, Peter. *Latin American Land Reforms in Theory and Practice.* Madison: The University of Wisconsin Press, 1992.

Dunkerley, James. *Power in the Isthmus: A Political History of Central America.* London: Verso, 1988.

E

Enciclopedia de Cuba, La. 8 vols. Madrid: Playor, S.A., 1973.

F

Fagen, Richard R., Richard A. Brody, and Thomas J. O'Leary. *Cubans in Exile: Disaffection and the Revolution.* Stanford, CA: Stanford University Press, 1968.

Fitzpatrick, Joseph P. *Puerto Rican Americans. The Meaning of Migration to the Mainland.* Englewood Cliffs, NJ: Prentice Hall, 1987.

G

García, Mario. T. *Mexican Americans.* New Haven, CT: Yale University Press, 1989.

Gerhard, Peter. *The Northern Frontier of New Spain.* Princeton, NJ: Princeton University Press, 1982.

Gómez-Quiñones, Juan. *Roots of Chicano Politics, 1600–1940.* Albuquerque: University of New Mexico Press, 1994.

Gran enciclopedia Argentina. Buenos Aires: Ediar S.A., 1956.

H

Hall, Elvajean. *The Land and People of Argentina.* New York: Lippincott, 1972.

Harvey, H. R., ed. *Land and Politics in the Valley of Mexico.* Albuquerque: University of New Mexico Press, 1991.

Hendricks, G. L. *The Dominican Diaspora: From the Dominican Republic to New York City.* New York: Teacher's College Press of Columbia University, 1974.

Hernández, José M. *Cuba and the United States: Intervention and Militarism, 1868–1933.* Austin: University of Texas Press, 1993.

History Task Force of the Centro de Estudios Puertorriqueños. *Labor Migration Under Capitalism: The Puerto Rican Experience.* New York: Monthly Review Press, 1979.

Hostos, Adolfo de. *Diccionario histórico bibliográfico comentado de Puerto Rico.* San Juan: Instituto de Cultura Puertorriqueña, 1976.

J

Jonas, Susan. *The Battle for Guatemala: Rebels, Death Squads, and U.S. Power.* Boulder, CO: Westview Press, 1991.

K

Kanellos, Nicolás. *Biographical Dictionary of Hispanic Literature.* Westport, CT: Greenwood Press, 1985.

———. *Hispanic–American Almanac.* Detroit, MI: Gale Research Inc., 1993.

———. *A History of Hispanic Theater in the United States: Origins to 1940.* Austin: University of Texas Press, 1990.

Kanellos, Nicolás, and Claudia Esteva-Fabregat. *Handbook of Hispanic Cultures in the United States.* 4 vols. Houston: Arte Público Press, 1994.

Karnes, Thomas L. *The Failure of Union: Central America, 1824–1975.* Tempe: Arizona State University, 1976.

Kinsbruner, Jay. *Chile: A Historical Interpretation.* New York: Harper & Row, 1973.

Knight, Franklin W. *The Caribbean.* New York: Oxford University Press, 1990.

L

Llanes, J. *Cuban Americans, Masters of Survival.* Cambridge, MA: Harvard University Press, 1982.

Lomelí, Francisco, and Julio A. Martínez. *Chicano Literature. A Reference Guide.* Detroit, MI: Gale Research Inc., 1985.

López, Adalberto, ed. *The Puerto Ricans: Their History, Culture and Society.* Cambridge, MA: Schenkman, 1980.

Loveman, Brian. *Chile: The Legacy of Hispanic Capitalism.* New York: Oxford University Press, 1988.

M

MacLachlan, Colin M. *Spain's Empire in the New World. The Role of Ideas in Institutional and Social Change.* Berkeley: University of California Press, 1988.

Martz, John D. *Central America: The Crisis and the Challenge.* Chapel Hill: University of North Carolina Press, 1959.

————, ed. *U.S. Policy Toward Latin America: Quarter Century of Crisis and Challenge.* Lincoln: University of Nebraska Press, 1987.

Mecham, J. L. *Church and State in Latin America.* Chapel Hill: University of North Carolina Press, 1966.

Meier, Matt S. *Mexican American Biographies.* Westport, CT: Greenwood Press, 1988.

Meier, Matt S., and Feliciano Rivera. *Dictionary of Mexican American History.* Westport, CT: Greenwood Press, 1981.

Meléndez, Edwin, and Edgardo Meléndez, eds. *Colonial Dilemma. Critical Perspectives on Contemporary Puerto Rico.* Boston, MA: South End Press, 1993.

Moore, Joan, and Harry Pachón. *Hispanics in the United States.* Englewood Cliffs, NJ: Prentice Hall, 1985.

Morales, Julio. *Puerto Rican Poverty and Migration: We Just Had to Try Elsewhere.* New York: Praeger, 1986.

Morales Carrión, Arturo, ed. *Puerto Rico: A Political and Cultural History.* New York: W. W. Norton, 1983.

Munro, Dana G. *Intervention and Dollar Diplomacy in the Caribbean.* Princeton, NJ: Princeton University Press, 1964.

————. *The United States and the Caribbean Republics, 1921–1933.* Princeton, NJ: Princeton University Press, 1974.

N

Nisbet, Charles T. *Latin America: Prob-* *lems in Economic Development.* New York: The Free Press, 1969.

P

Parker, Franklin D. *The Central American Republics.* New York: Oxford University Press, 1971.

Parry, J. H., and P. M. Sherlock. *A Short History of the West Indies* London: Macmillan & Co., 1963.

Pastor, Robert A. *Condemned to Repetition: The United States and Nicaragua.* Princeton, NJ: Princeton University Press, 1987.

Paterson, Thomas G. *Contesting Castro. The United States and the Triumph of the Cuban Revolution.* New York: Oxford University Press, 1994.

Pedraza-Bailey, S. *Political and Economic Migrants in America.* Austin: University of Texas Press, 1985.

Perera, Victor. *Unfinished Conquest. The Guatemalan Tragedy.* Berkeley: University of California Press, 1993.

Pérez, Louis A. *Cuba: Between Reform and Revolution.* New York: Oxford University Press, 1988.

Portes, Alejandro, and Robert L. Bach. *Latin Journey: Cuban and Mexican Immigrants in the United States.* Berkeley: University of California Press, 1985.

R

Rausch, Jane M. *The Llanos Frontier in Colombian History, 1830–1930.* Albuquerque: University of New Mexico Press, 1993.

Ryan, Bryan, ed. *Hispanic Writers. A* *Selection of Sketches from Contemporary Authors.* Detroit, MI: Gale Research Inc., 1991.

S

Schoultz, Lars. *Human Rights and U.S. Policy Toward Latin America.* Princeton, NJ: Princeton University Press, 1981.

Smith, Hazel. *Nicaragua: Self-determination and Survival.* London: Pluto Press, 1993.

Smirnow, Gabriel. *The Revolution Disarmed, Chile 1970–1973.* New York: Monthly Review Press, 1979.

Solís, José. *Public School Reform in Puerto Rico: Sustaining Colonial Models of Development.* Westport, CT: Greenwood Press, 1994.

Suchlicki, Jaime. *Cuba: From Columbus to Castro.* Washington, DC: Pergamon Press, 1986.

W

Weber, David. *The Mexican Frontier, 1821–1846: The American Southwest Under Mexico.* Albuquerque: University of New Mexico Press, 1982.

————. *Myth and History of the Hispanic Southwest.* Albuquerque: University of New Mexico Press, 1988.

————. *The Spanish Frontier in North America.* New Haven, CT: Yale University Press, 1992.

Whitaker, Arthur Preston. *The United States and the Southern Cone: Argentina, Chile and Uruguay.* Cambridge, MA: Harvard University Press, 1976.

Who's Who Among Hispanic Americans, 1994–1995. Detroit, MI: Gale Research Inc., 1994.

Wolf, Eric. *Sons of the Shaking Earth:*

The People of Mexico and Guatemala—Their Land, History and Culture. Chicago, IL: University of Chicago Press, 1961.

Woodward, Ralph Lee, Jr. *Rafael Carrera and the Emergence of the Republic of Guatemala, 1821–1871.* Athens: University of Georgia Press, 1993.

Z

Zamora, Emilio. *The World of the Mexican Worker in Texas.* College Station: Texas A & M University Press, 1993.

ILLUSTRATIONS CREDITS

Illustrations appearing in the *Chronology of Hispanic-American History* were received from the following sources:

Archivo General de las Indias, Seville 25, 43; Arte Público Press Archives, University of Houston 10, 31 (left), 35 (left), 35 (right), 56, 57, 61 (left), 88, 91, 99, 107, 127, 129, 133, 134, 143, 150, 155, 160, 167, 174, 180, 181, 187, 188, 190, 194, 196, 198, 199, 206, 207, 214 (left), 214 (right), 219, 221, 228, 230, 234, 235, 236, 239, 245, 249, 265, 281; Biblioteca Nacional, Madrid xii, xvi, 13 (left), 27, 39; California Historical Society 67; Center for Puerto Rican Studies Library, Hunter College, CUNY 146, 177; CISPES 268; Columbus Memorial Library 68; Cuban Archives, Florida International University 108, 124 (left); Institute of Puerto Rican Culture, San Juan 84; Jesús Colón Papers, Center for Puerto Rican Studies Library, Hunter College, CUNY 237; The Library of Congress Historic American Buildings Survey, Prints & Photographs Division 80; The Library of Congress Prints & Photographs Division xxi, 4, 5, 11, 13 (right), 14, 15, 16, 23, 28, 31 (right), 32, 36, 37, 46, 54, 58, 59, 64, 66, 71, 73, 82, 100, 101, 122, 147 (left), 147 (right), 151, 168, 184, 197, 202, 203 (left), 203 (right), 211, 218, 271; The Library of Congress Rare Book and Special Collections Division xxxii, 7; Library of the Granger Collection 86; *Los Angeles Times* 164, 220; Ministry of Internal Relations, Caracas 61 (right); Museo Nacional de Artes Plásticas, Montevideo 85; National Archives 191 (left), 223, 224; National Institute for Fine Arts, Mexico City 117, 120, 141, 144, 159, 200; National Museum of History, Mexico City 50, 95, 96, 106, 116; National Palace, Madrid 8; Recovering the U.S. Hispanic Literary Heritage Project, University of Houston 140, 171; Secretariate of Culture, La Paz 41, 51; Smithsonian Institution 21; Special Collections, General Library, University of New Mexico 104, 162; *Texas Catholic Herald* 251, 253, 259, 267, 272, 273; U.S. Department of the Interior and National Park Service 29, 90.

CATEGORY INDEX

AGRICULTURE

1508   Sugar Comes to the Americas.

1509   Ponce de León Negotiates for Produce.

1689   First Land Grants.

1760   Texas Land Grant.

1800   Agricultural Products Cross Ocean.

1823–30   Anglos Flock to Texas.

June 25, 1856   Law Forces Redistribution of Church Lands.

1870   The Banana Trade.

1890   The United Fruit Company Is Created.

1899   The United Fruit Company's Influence.

January 6, 1915   Agrarian Reform in Mexico.

1918   The Rise and Fall of Sugar.

1930   The Hawley–Smoot Tariff Affects Sugar Industry.

1930   Southern Migrants Displace Mexicans.

October 1933   The San Joaquín Cotton Strike.

1934   Cárdenas Redistributes Land.

October 7, 1940   Agronomist Pedro Sánchez Is Born.

July 1942   The Bracero Program.

April 29, 1943   Congress Passes Act to Regulate Bracero Program.

1945   Revolution in Guatemala.

1952   Agrarian Reform in Bolivia.

1952   Agrarian Reform in Guatemala.

1953   Agrarian Reform in Bolivia.

1957   Land Redistribution Starts in Venezuela.

May 17, 1959   Cuba's Agrarian Reform Law.

1960   Employers Recruit Foreign Workers.

1961   Land Reform in Colombia.

1962   Chile Establishes Agencies for Land Reform.

1962   United Farm Workers Organizing Committee.

1963   Ecuador Passes Land Reform Act.

September 1963   López Tijerina Founds Alianza.

1965   El Teatro Campesino, Labor-Related Theatre Movement.

September 16, 1965   César Chávez and the Delano Grape Strike.

1967   Reform Leads to Assassination.

1969   Peru Begins Agrarian Reform.

1970   Ecuador Expropriates Land.

July 29, 1970   The Lettuce Boycott Leads to New Labor Law.

1972   Land Reform in the Dominican Republic.

May 1975   California Labor Relations Act.

1977   Ecuador Encourages Colonization of Amazon Region.

July 17–19, 1979   Sandinistas Come to Power.

1980   Land Reform in El Salvador.

February 24–25, 1994   Mexican Farmers Protest Agricultural Crisis, Blame NAFTA.

ANTHROPOLOGY

50,000–10,000 B.C. Asians Cross Bridge into West.

1500 B.C.–1000 A.D. Mayan Civilization Flourishes.

1150 B.C.–500 A.D. Olmecs Build Monuments.

1000 B.C.–1492 A.D. Civilizations Build on Iberian Culture.

200 B.C.–1200 A.D. Toltecs Known for Writing, Architecture.

1000 A.D. Incan Empire Flourishes.

1200 A.D. Aztec Expansion.

ART & ARCHITECTURE

1150 B.C.–500 A.D. Olmecs Build Monuments.

200 B.C.–1200 A.D. Toltecs Known for Writing, Architecture.

1503 Church Constructed in Santo Domingo.

1543 Painter Bernardo Bitti Is Born.

1563 Cathedral of Mexico Is Begun.

c. 1600 Painter and Poet Antonio Acero Is Born.

1611 Indian Folk Artist Tito Is Born.

1626 Quito School Leads Colonial Art.

1633 Antonio Acero Decorates Tomb.

1665 Bolivian Painter Pérez Is Born.

May 1, 1718 Expedition at San Antonio.

1722 Bolivian Painter Pérez Finishes Masterpiece.

December 23, 1751 Colonial Artist Campeche Is Born.

1756 Manuel Tolsá, Sculptor and Architect, Is Born.

1783 Fine Arts Schools Established.

1790 Colonial Artist Paints Royalty.

1796 Colombian Painter Espinosa Is Born.

June 10, 1822 Mexican Painter Juan Cordero Is Born.

1823 Argentine Painter Pueyrredón Is Born.

1830 Uruguayan Painter Juan Manuel Blanes Is Born.

July 17, 1833 Oller, Art Educator and Pioneer of Impressionism, Is Born.

1840 Landscape Artist Velasco Born in Mexico.

1851 Cordero's Painting on Exhibit.

February 2, 1851 José Guadalupe Posada, Mexican Illustrator, Is Born.

1854 Oller Receives Art Medal.

1860 Colombian Painter Andrés de Santa María Is Born.

November 10, 1869 Oller Knighted.

1874 Cordero's Last Mural.

July 28, 1874 Uruguayan Painter Torres-Garcia Is Born.

1882 Blanes Receives Art Medal.

November 23, 1883 Mexican Muralist Orozco Is Born.

December 8, 1886 Diego Rivera, Master Painter and Muralist, Is Born.

1888 Posada Starts Print Shop, Newspaper.

May 10, 1889 Venezuelan Painter Reverón Is Born.

December 2, 1891 Guatemalan Painter Mérida Is Born.

1893 Artist Wins First Prize.

1895 Posada Creates New Art Technique.

December 3, 1896 Muralist Xavier Guerrero Is Born in Mexico.

December 19, 1896 David Siqueiros, Modern Artist and Intellectual, Is Born.

1897 Cuban Painter Amelia Peláez Is Born.

1899 Ecuadorean Painter Egas Is Born.

August 26, 1899 Rufino Tamayo, Mexican Painter, Is Born.

1902 Alvarez Bravo, Mexican Photographer, Is Born.

1902 Argentine Painter Forner Is Born.

1902 Wilfredo Lam, Modern Artist, Born in Cuba.

1904 Painter Andrés de Santa María Becomes Director.

1905   Antonio Berni, Argentine Painter and Muralist, Is Born.

1905   O'Gorman, Mexican Muralist, Is Born.

July 6, 1907   Modern Artist Frida Kahlo Born in Mexico.

1911   Roberto Matta, Surrealist Painter, Born in Chile.

1912   René Portocarrero, Cuban Painter, Is Born.

1916   Debut Art Exhibition.

1919   Guayasamín, Prize-Winning Painter and Muralist, Is Born.

1922   Artists' Union Founded.

1923   Jesús Rafael Soto, Venezuelan Painter, Is Born.

1929   Artist Gironella Born in Mexico City.

1932   Painter Fernando Botero Born in Cuba.

1932   Painter Organizes Exhibition.

1934   Mexican Painter Cuevas Is Born.

1939   Painter Publishes Autobiography.

1947   Painter Jesús Rafael Soto Becomes Art Director.

1948   Oswaldo Guayasamín Completes Fresco, Wins Fellowship.

1950   Juan O'Gorman Has Exhibition, Designs Library.

1951   Painter Botero Has Exhibition.

1962   Painter Antonio Berni Wins Award.

1962   Painter Egas Accepts Merit Award.

1963   Painter René Portocarrero Wins Prize.

1964–65   Cuban Painter Wins Award.

1966   Siqueiros Receives Art Award.

1967   Siqueiros Awarded Soviet Prize.

1974   Museum Established for Mexican Painter.

1975   Alberto Gironella Illustrates Fuentes's Book.

1980   Nobel Peace Prize Awarded to Argentine.

1980   Photographer Bravo Establishes Museum.

BIOGRAPHY

c. 1451   Christopher Columbus Is Born.

c. 1460   Ponce de León Is Born.

1466   Aztec Emperor Moctezuma Is Born.

1470   Díaz de Solís Is Born.

1470   Spanish Missionary Bartolomé de las Casas Is Born.

1475   Núñez de Balboa Is Born.

1478   Francisco Pizarro Is Born.

1485   Hernán Cortés Is Born.

c. 1490   Explorer Cabeza de Vaca Is Born.

c. 1496   Prince Cuauhtémoc Is Born.

c. 1497   Pedro de Valdivia Is Born.

1498   Díaz del Castillo, Chronicler of the Conquest of Mexico, Is Born.

1499   Friar Bernardino de Sahagún Is Born.

1500   Conquistador de Soto Is Born.

c. 1500   Indian Chief Caupolicán Is Born.

1509   Conqueror of Colombia Is Born.

1510   Explorer Francisco Vásquez de Coronado Is Born.

1519   Naval Commander Menéndez Is Born.

August 7, 1533   Soldier and Poet Alonso de Ercilla Is Born.

1539   Spanish Chronicler Garcilaso de la Vega Is Born.

1543   Francis Drake Is Born.

1543   Painter Bernardo Bitti Is Born.

c. 1600   Painter and Poet Antonio Acero Is Born.

1611   Indian Folk Artist Tito Is Born.

1645   Sigüenza y Góngora Is Born.

November 12, 1651   Author, Poet Sor Juana Is Born.

1665   Bolivian Painter Pérez Is Born.

December 23, 1751   Colonial Artist Campeche Is Born.

May 8, 1753   Miguel Hidalgo y Costilla, Mexican Independence Leader, Is Born.

1756   Manuel Tolsá, Sculptor and Architect, Is Born.

June 9, 1756 Francisco de Miranda, Activist for Independence, Is Born.

November 15, 1776 "The Mexican Thinker" Is Born.

February 25, 1778 Liberator of Chile and Peru Is Born.

November 29, 1781 Andrés Bello Is Born.

July 24, 1783 Simón Bolívar, the Liberator, Is Born.

1793 Father Martínez Is Born.

November 3, 1793 Stephen Austin Is Born.

February 21, 1795 Santa Anna Is Born.

1796 Colombian Painter Espinosa Is Born.

1800 Leader of the Californios Is Born.

May 5, 1801 Governor Pico Is Born.

September 3, 1805 Poet Echeverría Is Born.

March 21, 1806 Liberal Leader Benito Juárez Is Born.

October 27, 1806 Texas Republic Founder Is Born.

July 7, 1808 Californio Politician Vallejo Is Born.

December 24, 1809 Kit Carson Is Born.

February 14, 1811 Domingo Faustino Sarmiento Is Born.

March 23, 1814 Writer Gómez de Avellaneda Is Born.

October 24, 1814 Rafael Carrera, Dictator of Guatemala, Is Born.

October 21, 1817 Antonio Coronel, California Politician, Is Born.

December 2, 1817 Argentine Writer José Mármol Is Born.

June 10, 1822 Mexican Painter Juan Cordero Is Born.

October 6, 1822 Manuel Alonso, Puerto Rican Poet and Physician, Is Born.

1823 Argentine Painter Pueyrredón Is Born.

February 28, 1823 Puerto Rican Nationalist Román Baldorioty de Castro Is Born.

May 16, 1824 Mexican Folk Hero Juan Nepomuceno Cortina Is Born.

April 8, 1827 Ramón Emeterio Betances, Puerto Rican Patriot, Is Born.

1830 Uruguayan Painter Juan Manuel Blanes Is Born.

September 15, 1830 Mexican Dictator Porfirio Díaz Is Born.

April 13, 1832 Writer Juan Montalvo Is Born.

February 7, 1833 Creator of Tradición Literary Genre Ricardo Palma Is Born.

July 17, 1833 Oller, Art Educator and Pioneer of Impressionism, Is Born.

November 10, 1834 José Hernández, Defender of Gauchos, Is Born.

April 1, 1837 Colombian Novelist Jorge Isaacs Is Born.

January 11, 1839 Eugenio María de Hostos Is Born.

1840 Landscape Artist Velasco Born in Mexico.

September 14, 1843 Puerto Rican Feminist Lola Rodríguez de Tió Is Born.

January 6, 1848 Peruvian Poet Manuel González Prada Is Born.

April 13, 1849 Cuban Philosopher Varona Is Born.

February 2, 1851 José Guadalupe Posada, Mexican Illustrator, Is Born.

January 28, 1853 National Hero Martí Is Born in Cuba.

May 6, 1857 Composer Juan Morel Campos Is Born.

July 26, 1857 Barbosa, Puerto Rican Doctor and Political Activist, Is Born.

October 17, 1859 New Mexico Governor Otero Is Born.

1860 Colombian Painter Andrés de Santa María Is Born.

1863 Patriot and Writer Marín Born in Puerto Rico.

January 18, 1867   Poet Rubén Darío, Promoter of Literary Modernism, Is Born.

February 22, 1870   Labor Organizer Pantín Is Born.

August 27, 1870   Amado Nervo, Mexican Modernist Poet, Is Born.

July 15, 1872   Writer and Humanist José Enrique Rodó Is Born.

January 1, 1873   Mexican Writer Azuela Is Born.

January 24, 1874   Historian Schomburg Is Born.

July 28, 1874   Uruguayan Painter Torres-Garcia Is Born.

May 14, 1876   Puerto Rican Poet Torres Is Born.

June 5, 1878   Bandit and Revolutionary General Villa Is Born.

December 31, 1878   Horacio Quiroga, Uruguayan Short-Story Writer, Is Born.

August 8, 1879   Revolutionary General Zapata Is Born in Mexico.

1880   Luisa Capetillo, Advocate for Women's Rights, Is Born.

February 28, 1882   Educator Vasconcelos Born in Mexico.

November 23, 1883   Mexican Muralist Orozco Is Born.

February 13, 1886   Argentine Novelist Güiraldes Is Born.

October 24, 1886   Delmira Agustini, Uruguayan Poet, Is Born.

December 8, 1886   Diego Rivera, Master Painter and Muralist, Is Born.

December 8, 1886   Mexican Composer Ponce Is Born.

September 26, 1887   Spanish Actor Moreno Is Born.

1888   Cuban Negro League Pitcher Is Born.

April 7, 1889   Nobel Winner Mistral Is Born.

May 10, 1889   Venezuelan Painter Reverón Is Born.

May 17, 1889   Mexican Poet and Educator Reyes Is Born.

September 12, 1891   Puerto Rican Activist Campos Is Born.

December 2, 1891   Guatemalan Painter Mérida Is Born.

March 16, 1892   César Vallejo, Poet and Political Activist, Is Born.

May 29, 1892   Poet and Feminist Storni Is Born.

October 24, 1892   Rafael Hernández, Composer of Popular Music, Is Born.

1895   Cuban Batter Oms Is Born.

March 8, 1895   Poet Juana de América Is Born.

June 14, 1895   José Carlos Mariátegui, Peruvian Activist, Is Born.

October 8, 1895   Juan Perón, Argentine General and Politician, Is Born.

August 7, 1896   Cuban Composer Lecuona Is Born.

November 11, 1896   Historian Carlos Castañeda Is Born.

December 3, 1896   Muralist Xavier Guerrero Is Born in Mexico.

December 19, 1896   David Siqueiros, Modern Artist and Intellectual, Is Born.

1897   Cuban Painter Amelia Peláez Is Born.

February 18, 1898   Luis Muñoz Marín, Puerto Rican Political Leader, Is Born.

March 20, 1898   Poet Luis Palés Matos Is Born.

1899   Cuban Actor O'Farrill Is Born.

1899   Ecuadorean Painter Egas Is Born.

February 6, 1899   Ramón Novarro, Silent Film Idol, Is Born.

June 13, 1899   Carlos Chávez y Ramírez, Composer of Classical Music, Is Born.

August 24, 1899   Writer and Poet Borges Born in Argentina.

August 26, 1899   Rufino Tamayo, Mexican Painter, Is Born.

October 19, 1899   Guatemalan Novelist Asturias Is Born.

December 31, 1899   Composer Silvestre Revueltas Is Born.

May 20, 1900 Writer Lydia Cabrera Born in Cuba.

1901 Puerto Rican Journalist and Activist Jesús Colón Is Born.

1902 Alvarez Bravo, Mexican Photographer, Is Born.

1902 Argentine Painter Forner Is Born.

1902 Wilfredo Lam, Modern Artist, Born in Cuba.

July 10, 1902 Cuban Poet Nicolás Guillén Is Born.

August 20, 1903 La Chata Noloesca, Stage Personality, Is Born.

March 26, 1904 Actor and Director "El Indio" Fernández Is Born.

July 12, 1904 Chilean Pablo Neruda, Poet and Nobel Laureate, Is Born.

December 26, 1904 Novelist Carpentier Born in Cuba.

1905 Antonio Berni, Argentine Painter and Muralist, Is Born.

1905 O'Gorman, Mexican Muralist, Is Born.

February 20, 1905 Folklorist and Scholar Campa Is Born.

August 3, 1905 Actress Dolores del Río Is Born.

November 17, 1905 Playwright and Diplomat Usigli Born in Mexico.

December 11, 1905 Gilbert Roland, the Cisco Kid, Is Born.

March 3, 1906 Enrique Laguerre, Puerto Rican Writer and Teacher, Is Born.

October 4, 1906 Educator and Civil Rights Advocate George Sánchez Is Born.

February 15, 1907 Movie Star César Romero Is Born.

April 24, 1907 Noted Cinema Photographer Figueroa Born in Mexico.

July 6, 1907 Modern Artist Frida Kahlo Born in Mexico.

July 18, 1907 Lupe Vélez, Screen Actress, Is Born.

September 17, 1907 Luis Leal, Scholar and Teacher, Is Born.

November 26, 1907 Lefty Gómez, Record-Holding Baseball Pitcher, Is Born.

March 3, 1908 Corretjer, Poet and Activist, Born in Puerto Rico.

November 4, 1909 Ciro Alegría, Peruvian Novelist, Is Born.

April 10, 1910 Franciscan Angélico Chávez, Religious Poet, Is Born.

June 8, 1910 Novelist María Bombal Is Born.

October 28, 1910 Cuban Boxer Eligio Sardiñas Is Born.

January 18, 1911 Peruvian Novelist Arguedas Is Born.

June 13, 1911 Physicist Alvarez, Nobel Prize Winner, Is Born.

June 24, 1911 Argentine Racing Driver Fangio Is Born.

1912 René Portocarrero, Cuban Painter, Is Born.

January 8, 1912 Actor, Director, and Producer José Ferrer Is Born.

May 9, 1912 Mexican Film Star Pedro Armendáriz, Sr., Is Born.

January 17, 1914 Héctor García Pérez, Civil Rights Leader and Government Official, Is Born.

August 26, 1914 Argentine Novelist Cortázar Is Born.

April 21, 1915 Anthony Quinn, Academy Award-Winning Actor, Is Born.

September 3, 1915 Américo Paredes, Folklorist and Teacher, Is Born.

November 15, 1915 Physicist and Teacher Alberto Baez Is Born.

February 10, 1916 Edward Roybal, U.S. Congressman, Is Born.

April 1, 1916 Composer Ginastera Born in Buenos Aires.

May 3, 1916 Mexican–American Politician González Is Born.

February 17, 1917 Julia de Burgos, Puerto Rican Poet, Is Born.

March 2, 1917 Desi Arnaz, Cuban Bandleader and Actor, Is Born.

August 15, 1917 Archbishop, Human Rights Advocate Romero is Born.

May 29, 1918 Bert Corona, Founder of Labor Groups, Is Born.

September 12, 1918 Writer Arreola Born in Mexico.

September 26, 1918 Fernando Alegría, Chilean Scholar and Novelist, Is Born.

October 17, 1918 Rita Hayworth, Dancer and Actress, Is Born.

1919 Guayasamín, Prize-Winning Painter and Muralist, Is Born.

October 4, 1919 René Marqués, Puerto Rican Playwright and Author, Is Born.

March 1, 1920 Julián Samora, Hispanic Sociologist, Is Born.

November 25, 1920 Actor Ricardo Montalbán Is Born in Mexico.

1923 Jesús Rafael Soto, Venezuelan Painter, Is Born.

January 20, 1925 Author and Priest Cardenal Born in Nicaragua.

May 25, 1925 Castellanos, Mexican Poet, Novelist, and Feminist, Is Born.

1926 Pentecostal Minister López Tijerina Is Born.

March 8, 1926 José González, Novelist and Short-Story Writer, Is Born.

May 3, 1927 César Chávez, Advocate for Farmworkers, Is Born.

June 19, 1927 Julián Nava, Educator and Ambassador, Is Born.

March 6, 1928 Novelist and Nobel Laureate Gabriel García Márquez Is Born.

May 9, 1928 Tennis Champion Pancho González Is Born.

June 14, 1928 Ernesto "Ché" Guevara, Castro Aide and Revolutionary, Is Born.

November 11, 1928 Carlos Fuentes, Novelist, Essayist, and Teacher, Is Born.

December 2, 1928 Mari Bras, Activist for Puerto Rican Independence, Is Born.

December 11, 1928 Director/Screenwriter Gutiérrez Alea Born in Cuba.

1929 Artist Gironella Born in Mexico City.

January 21, 1929 Rolando Hinojosa, Hispanic Writer, Is Born.

April 22, 1929 Cabrera Infante, Cuban Novelist and Critic, Is Born.

July 26, 1929 Flores, First Hispanic Bishop, Is Born.

1930 Spanish Cinematographer Almendros Is Born.

December 11, 1931 Actress Rita Moreno Is Born.

1932 Painter Fernando Botero Born in Cuba.

January 20, 1932 Poet Heberto Padilla Is Born.

1934 Mexican Painter Cuevas Is Born.

August 11, 1934 Educator and Author Carmelo Mesa-Lago Is Born.

August 18, 1934 Star Outfielder Roberto Clemente Born in Puerto Rico.

December 4, 1934 Guerrilla Guzmán Is Born.

August 20, 1935 Lionel García, Author and Veterinarian, Is Born.

October 23, 1935 Golfer Chi Chi Rodríguez Born in Puerto Rico.

November 1, 1935 Author Nicholasa Mohr Is Born.

December 22, 1935 Tomás Rivera, Leader in Chicano Literature, Is Born.

1937 Juan Marichal, Dominican Baseball Pitcher, Is Born.

March 21, 1937 Football Coach Thomas Flores Is Born.

October 30, 1937 Rudolfo Anaya, Novelist and Teacher, Is Born.

March 23, 1939 George Castro, Chemist and IBM Lab Leader, Is Born.

December 1, 1939 Lee Treviño, Champion Golfer, Is Born.

March 9, 1940   Raúl Julia, Puerto Rican Star of Stage and Screen, Is Born.

May 11, 1940   Novelist Victor Villaseñor Is Born.

June 26, 1940   Luis Valdez, the Father of Chicano Theatre, Is Born.

July 19, 1940   Singer Vikki Carr Is Born.

September 5, 1940   Raquel Welch, International Film Star, Is Born.

October 7, 1940   Agronomist Pedro Sánchez Is Born.

March 29, 1941   Ricardo Sánchez, Autobiographical Chicano Poet, Is Born.

August 2, 1942   Isabel Allende, Chilean Novelist, Is Born.

September 5, 1942   Symphony Conductor Eduardo Mata Born in Mexico City.

May 14, 1943   Cuban Singer Tania León Is Born.

July 4, 1943   Reporter, TV Personality Geraldo Rivera Is Born.

July 16, 1943   Reinaldo Arenas, Cuban Novelist, Is Born.

1945   Miriam Colón, Hispanic Theatre Leader, Is Born.

December 19, 1946   Miguel Piñero, Dramatist of Nuyorican School, Is Born.

February 24, 1947   Mexican–American Actor Olmos Is Born.

March 15, 1947   Federico Peña, Secretary of Transportation, Is Born.

June 11, 1947   Henry Cisneros, HUD Secretary, Is Born.

August 8, 1947   Alurista, Poet and Pioneer in Chicano Literature, Is Born.

January 29, 1948   TV and Radio Talk Show Host Cristina Saralegui Is Born.

February 6, 1949   Nuyorican Poet Victor Hernández Cruz Is Born.

September 5, 1950   Tato Laviera, Popular Hispanic Poet, Is Born.

August 24, 1951   Pulitzer Prize-Winning Writer Oscar Hijuelos Is Born.

September 24, 1951   Novelist Roberto Fernández Born in Cuba.

February 24, 1952   Judith Ortiz Cofer, Poet, Novelist, and Teacher, Is Born.

February 15, 1953   Biodiversity and Conservation Biologist Gómez-Dallmeier Is Born.

August 6, 1954   Poet and Teacher Lorna Dee Cervantes Is Born.

July 9, 1955   Jimmy Smits, Puerto Rican Actor, Is Born.

January 6, 1957   Nancy López, Golf Champion, Is Born.

August 27, 1961   Bowling Champion Monacelli Is Born.

CIVIL RIGHTS & DISCRIMINATION

1813   Children of Slaves Become Free.

1817   Cuban Slave Trade.

1820   Spain Bans Slave Trade.

1824   Constitution of the Central American Federation.

1829   Mexican Government Abolishes Slavery.

1835   Spain Bans Slave Trade.

September 17, 1868   Children of Slaves Freed.

1870   State-Owned Slaves Freed.

1872   Puerto Rican Civil Rights.

March 22, 1873   Puerto Rican Slavery Ends.

1886   Cuba Liberates Slaves.

1894   The Alianza Hispano Americano, Civil Rights Group, Is Founded.

June 14, 1895   José Carlos Mariátegui, Peruvian Activist, Is Born.

1901   Puerto Rican Journalist and Activist Jesús Colón Is Born.

October 4, 1906   Educator and Civil Rights Advocate George Sánchez Is Born.

1912   Ambassador Protests Mistreatment of Mexicans.

1926   Puerto Ricans Attacked in New York City.

1929   The League of United Latin American Citizens.

1930   Mexican–Americans Use Courts to Fight Segregation.

1938   Hispanic Civil Rights Congress Founded.

1941   Congress Outlaws Discrimination in Employment.

1941   George Sánchez Is President of LULAC.

June 3, 1943   The "Zoot Suit" Riots.

March 21, 1945   Parents Win Rights Case in California.

1950   Segregation Banned in Southwest.

1954   Supreme Court Rules on Hispanic Discrimination.

1954   U.S. Deports Mexicans.

1957   The Civil Rights Commission.

1965   Héctor García Pérez Awarded Panamanian Prize.

1965   The Voting Rights Act.

1966   Texas Tax on Voting.

1967   Héctor García Pérez Appointed by President Johnson.

1968   Civil Rights Act of 1968.

1968   Mexican American Legal Defense and Education Fund.

1970   Affirmative Action vs. Reverse Discrimination.

1970   Congress Amends Voting Rights Act.

1975   Ban on Literacy Tests for Voting Becomes Permanent.

1980   Reagan and Affirmative Action.

1984   Héctor García Pérez Recognized by U.S.

1991   New Civil Rights Action Sought.

March 1991   Minorities Riot.

ECONOMICS

February 14, 1503   Contract House Governs Commerce.

1508   Sugar Comes to the Americas.

1670   Spain and England Sign Treaty of Madrid.

1689   First Land Grants.

1701   House of Bourbon Takes Spanish Throne.

1760   Texas Land Grant.

1800   Agricultural Products Cross Ocean.

1838   Cuban Sugar Exports.

1840   Immigrants Aid Cuban Economy.

1860   The Cigar Industry.

1870   The Banana Trade.

1899   The United Fruit Company's Influence.

May 1902   Cuba Breaks with United States.

1914   Disputes Arise between U.S. and Panama.

1918   The Rise and Fall of Sugar.

1930   Coffee Crash Precipitates Revolution.

1930   The Hawley–Smoot Tariff Affects Sugar Industry.

1930   Trujillo, Dictator of Dominican Republic, Comes to Power.

1959   Countries Seek Free Trade Zone.

1960   The Rise of the Maquiladoras.

January 1960   Eisenhower Moves against Cuba.

May 8, 1960   Cuba Turns to Soviets for Help.

March 13, 1961   The Alliance for Progress.

1969   Border War Affects Common Market.

1969   Peru Begins Agrarian Reform.

May 1969   The Andean Group.

1970   Allende Elected to Govern Chile.

1976   Peso Devaluated.

1978   Hispanic Income Data.

1980   The Mexican Economy.

February 1982   Mexico Devalues Its Currency.

August 1982   Mexico Cannot Pay Foreign Debt on Time.

1989   Hispanic Family Income Data.

December 1990   Russia and Cuba Sign Treaty.

1991   NAFTA Proposal Expands Maquiladora Concept.

March 1991   Hispanic Unemployment High.

March 31, 1992 Russia Withdraws Economic Support for Cuba.

October 23, 1992 The Cuban Democracy Act.

January 1, 1994 NAFTA Takes Effect.

February 24–25, 1994 Mexican Farmers Protest Agricultural Crisis, Blame NAFTA.

March 23, 1994 Mexican Presidential Candidate Assassinated.

February 21, 1995 Mexico Receives International Loan Package.

EDUCATION

1505 School Established for Children.

1513 Bishop Establishes Secondary School.

1513 Indian Schools Teach Latin.

1523 Franciscans Establish Indian School.

1538 Dominican College Becomes University.

1551 King Charters Universities.

1600 Spanish Missions Run Schools.

1642 First Library Established in Puerto Rico.

1721 Cuban University Established.

1783 Fine Arts Schools Established.

1792 Mining Schools Established.

February 14, 1811 Domingo Faustino Sarmiento Is Born.

1825 Spain Forces Students Out of U.S.

January 11, 1839 Eugenio María de Hostos Is Born.

1843 University Founded.

September 5, 1848 Governor Rejects School for Puerto Rico.

1862 School Mandatory in Puerto Rico.

1865 Public Education in Puerto Rico.

February 28, 1882 Educator Vasconcelos Born in Mexico.

May 17, 1889 Mexican Poet and Educator Reyes Is Born.

November 11, 1896 Historian Carlos Castañeda Is Born.

March 12, 1903 University of Puerto Rico.

February 20, 1905 Folklorist and Scholar Campa Is Born.

March 3, 1906 Enrique Laguerre, Puerto Rican Writer and Teacher, Is Born.

October 4, 1906 Educator and Civil Rights Advocate George Sánchez Is Born.

September 17, 1907 Luis Leal, Scholar and Teacher, Is Born.

January 18, 1911 Peruvian Novelist Arguedas Is Born.

1912 Medical Institute Founded.

March 31, 1914 Octavio Paz, Nobel Laureate, Is Born.

August 26, 1914 Argentine Novelist Cortázar Is Born.

September 3, 1915 Américo Paredes, Folklorist and Teacher, Is Born.

November 15, 1915 Physicist and Teacher Alberto Baez Is Born.

February 17, 1917 Julia de Burgos, Puerto Rican Poet, Is Born.

September 26, 1918 Fernando Alegría, Chilean Scholar and Novelist, Is Born.

March 1, 1920 Julián Samora, Hispanic Sociologist, Is Born.

June 19, 1927 Julián Nava, Educator and Ambassador, Is Born.

November 11, 1928 Carlos Fuentes, Novelist, Essayist, and Teacher, Is Born.

1930 Mexican–Americans Use Courts to Fight Segregation.

August 11, 1934 Educator and Author Carmelo Mesa-Lago Is Born.

October 30, 1937 Rudolfo Anaya, Novelist and Teacher, Is Born.

March 21, 1945 Parents Win Rights Case in California.

February 24, 1952 Judith Ortiz Cofer, Poet, Novelist, and Teacher, Is Born.

August 6, 1954   Poet and Teacher Lorna Dee Cervantes Is Born.

1961   Aspira Promotes Education.

1967   School Programs Aid Bilingual Children.

August 1971   California Court Rules on School Financing.

1973   Court Decides Texas School Financing Issue.

1974–86   Carmelo Mesa-Lago Serves as Director.

1974   Congressional Act Supports Bilingual Education.

January 1974   Court Decision Backs Bilingual Programs.

1978   Writer Tomás Rivera Heads University.

1988   Cavazos Named Secretary of Education.

1991   Hispanic Sociologist Julián Samora Wins Award.

FILM & THEATER

1598   Soldiers Take Up Pens.

September 26, 1887   Spanish Actor Moreno Is Born.

1899   Cuban Actor O'Farrill Is Born.

February 6, 1899   Ramón Novarro, Silent Film Idol, Is Born.

August 20, 1903   La Chata Noloesca, Stage Personality, Is Born.

March 26, 1904   Actor and Director "El Indio" Fernández Is Born.

August 3, 1905   Actress Dolores del Río Is Born.

December 11, 1905   Gilbert Roland, the Cisco Kid, Is Born.

February 15, 1907   Movie Star César Romero Is Born.

April 24, 1907   Noted Cinema Photographer Figueroa Born in Mexico.

July 18, 1907   Lupe Vélez, Screen Actress, Is Born.

June 8, 1910   Novelist María Bombal Is Born.

1912   Film Career Begins for Spanish Actor.

January 8, 1912   Actor, Director, and Producer José Ferrer Is Born.

May 9, 1912   Mexican Film Star Pedro Armendáriz, Sr., Is Born.

April 21, 1915   Anthony Quinn, Academy Award-Winning Actor, Is Born.

March 2, 1917   Desi Arnaz, Cuban Bandleader and Actor, Is Born.

September 12, 1918   Writer Arreola Born in Mexico.

October 17, 1918   Rita Hayworth, Dancer and Actress, Is Born.

October 4, 1919   René Marqués, Puerto Rican Playwright and Author, Is Born.

November 25, 1920   Actor Ricardo Montalbán Is Born in Mexico.

1923   Mexican Film Idol Sees Success in Movie Role.

December 11, 1928   Director/Screenwriter Gutiérrez Alea Born in Cuba.

1930   Spanish Cinematographer Almendros Is Born.

December 11, 1931   Actress Rita Moreno Is Born.

1934   Movie Star César Romero Goes to Hollywood.

1936   La Chata Noloesca's Compañía Mexicana.

1940s   Actor Gilbert Roland Portrays the Cisco Kid.

March 9, 1940   Raúl Julia, Puerto Rican Star of Stage and Screen, Is Born.

May 11, 1940   Novelist Victor Villaseñor Is Born.

June 26, 1940   Luis Valdez, the Father of Chicano Theatre, Is Born.

September 5, 1940   Raquel Welch, International Film Star, Is Born.

1941   Compañía Mexicana Moves to New York.

1943   Film Star Dolores del Rio Returns to Mexico.

1945   Miriam Colón, Hispanic Theatre Leader, Is Born.

December 19, 1946   Miguel Piñero, Dramatist of Nuyorican School, Is Born.

1947   Actor Ricardo Montalbán Goes to Hollywood.

February 24, 1947   Mexican–American Actor Olmos Is Born.

1950   Puerto Rican Actor Ferrer Wins an Oscar.

1952   Anthony Quinn Wins the Oscar.

July 9, 1955   Jimmy Smits, Puerto Rican Actor, Is Born.

1956   Actor Anthony Quinn Takes Second Oscar.

1959   Director and Screenwriter Gutiérrez Alea Founds Institute.

1961   Puerto Rican Actress Moreno Wins Oscar.

1965   El Teatro Campesino, Labor-Related Theatre Movement.

1978   Cinematographer Wins Oscar.

1981   Ferrer Becomes Hall-of-Famer.

1987   Luis Valdez Writes Hollywood Screenplay.

1990   Hispanic Theatre Leader Wins Award.

February 14, 1995   Cuban Film Receives Oscar Nomination.

LABOR

1394   Portuguese Slave Trade.

September 3, 1501   African Slave Trade Authorized.

1510   First Slaves Sent to Gold Mines.

1512   Indians and the Laws of Burgos.

1517   Las Casas Asks for African Slaves.

1518   Crown Licenses Slave Traders.

1550   Indian Exploitation Continues.

1562   English Trader Imports Slaves.

1595   King Permits African Slave Trade.

1770   Slave Traffic Increases.

1792   Mining Schools Established.

1840   Immigrants Aid Cuban Economy.

1860   The Cigar Industry.

February 22, 1870   Labor Organizer Pantín Is Born.

1880   Luisa Capetillo, Advocate for Women's Rights, Is Born.

1900   Mexicans Hired by Railroads.

1901   Workers Group Joins AFL.

June 1903   Arizona Copper Miners Strike.

1907   Mexican Workers Repatriated.

1917   U.S. Restricts Immigration.

May 29, 1918   Bert Corona, Founder of Labor Groups, Is Born.

1921   Immigration Restrictions.

May 3, 1927   César Chávez, Advocate for Farmworkers, Is Born.

1930   Southern Migrants Displace Mexicans.

1931   Mexican–Americans Deported.

1933   Confederation Advocates for California Workers.

October 1933   The San Joaquín Cotton Strike.

January 1938   Pecan Shellers on Strike.

1940   Independent Labor Union Formed.

1941   Congress Outlaws Discrimination in Employment.

July 1942   The Bracero Program.

April 29, 1943   Congress Passes Act to Regulate Bracero Program.

1944   Operation Bootstrap in Puerto Rico.

1945   Revolution in Guatemala.

1950   Migrant Workers.

July 12, 1951   The Migratory Labor Agreement.

1960   Employers Recruit Foreign Workers.

1960   Labor Migration Patterns Change.

1960   The Rise of the Maquiladoras.

1965   El Teatro Campesino, Labor-Related Theatre Movement.

April 1965   The Maquiladora Program.

September 16, 1965   César Chávez and the Delano Grape Strike.

July 29, 1970   The Lettuce Boycott Leads to New Labor Law.

May 3, 1972   Farah Workers Strike in Texas.

1973   Hispanics Form Labor Group.

1973   Supreme Court Acts on Farah Case.

May 1975   California Labor Relations Act.

1977   INS Seizes Undocumented Workers.

1978   Hispanic Women in U.S. Work Force.

1980   Hispanics Are 40 Percent of Immigrants.

1991   NAFTA Proposal Expands Maquiladora Concept.

March 1991   Hispanic Unemployment High.

January 1, 1994   NAFTA Takes Effect.

LITERATURE

1498   Díaz del Castillo, Chronicler of the Conquest of Mexico, Is Born.

1519   Cortés Documents Conquests.

1533   Printers Operate in Mexico City.

August 7, 1533   Soldier and Poet Alonso de Ercilla Is Born.

1539   Spanish Chronicler Garcilaso de la Vega Is Born.

1543   Charles V Bans Books.

1555   Explorer's Document Is Published.

1568   Díaz del Castillo Writes Chronicle.

1569   Alonso de Ercilla Publishes Part I of Poem.

1598   Soldiers Take Up Pens.

1605   Spanish Chronicle Is Published.

1612   Franciscan Translates Spanish Books into Indian Language.

1645   Sigüenza y Góngora Is Born.

November 12, 1651   Author, Poet Sor Juana Is Born.

November 15, 1776   "The Mexican Thinker" Is Born.

November 29, 1781   Andrés Bello Is Born.

1792   Sigüenza y Góngora's Collection Burns.

September 3, 1805   Poet Echeverría Is Born.

February 14, 1811   Domingo Faustino Sarmiento Is Born.

March 23, 1814   Writer Gómez de Avellaneda Is Born.

1816   Lizardi's Masterpiece Published.

December 2, 1817   Argentine Writer José Mármol Is Born.

October 6, 1822   Manuel Alonso, Puerto Rican Poet and Physician, Is Born.

1829   Friar Bernardino de Sahagún's Work Published.

1832   Spanish Poem Published.

April 13, 1832   Writer Juan Montalvo Is Born.

February 7, 1833   Creator of Tradición Literary Genre Ricardo Palma Is Born.

November 10, 1834   José Hernández, Defender of Gauchos, Is Born.

April 1, 1837   Colombian Novelist Jorge Isaacs Is Born.

January 11, 1839   Eugenio María de Hostos Is Born.

September 14, 1843   Puerto Rican Feminist Lola Rodríguez de Tió Is Born.

January 6, 1848   Peruvian Poet Manuel González Prada Is Born.

1849   Alonso's Masterpiece Is Published.

April 13, 1849   Cuban Philosopher Varona Is Born.

January 28, 1853   National Hero Martí Is Born in Cuba.

1858   Mármol Named Library Director.

October 17, 1859   New Mexico Governor Otero Is Born.

1861   Avellaneda's First Novel.

1863   Patriot and Writer Marín Born in Puerto Rico.

1867   Isaacs Publishes Spanish American Classic.

January 18, 1867   Poet Rubén Darío, Promoter of Literary Modernism, Is Born.

August 27, 1870   Amado Nervo, Mexican Modernist Poet, Is Born.

1872   Martín Fierro, Part I, Is Published.

July 15, 1872 Writer and Humanist José Enrique Rodó Is Born.

January 1, 1873 Mexican Writer Azuela Is Born.

January 24, 1874 Historian Schomburg Is Born.

May 14, 1876 Puerto Rican Poet Torres Is Born.

December 31, 1878 Horacio Quiroga, Uruguayan Short-Story Writer, Is Born.

1879 Martín Fierro, Part II, Is Published.

1882 Montalvo Publishes Major Work.

1884 Francisco "Pachín" González Marín Is Published.

February 13, 1886 Argentine Novelist Güiraldes Is Born.

October 24, 1886 Delmira Agustini, Uruguayan Poet, Is Born.

April 7, 1889 Nobel Winner Mistral Is Born.

May 17, 1889 Mexican Poet and Educator Reyes Is Born.

March 16, 1892 César Vallejo, Poet and Political Activist, Is Born.

May 29, 1892 Poet and Feminist Storni Is Born.

March 8, 1895 Poet Juana de América Is Born.

June 14, 1895 José Carlos Mariátegui, Peruvian Activist, Is Born.

March 20, 1898 Poet Luis Palés Matos Is Born.

August 24, 1899 Writer and Poet Borges Born in Argentina.

October 19, 1899 Guatemalan Novelist Asturias Is Born.

1900 Writer José Enrique Rodó Publishes Masterpiece.

May 20, 1900 Writer Lydia Cabrera Born in Cuba.

July 10, 1902 Cuban Poet Nicolás Guillén Is Born.

July 12, 1904 Chilean Pablo Neruda, Poet and Nobel Laureate, Is Born.

December 26, 1904 Novelist Carpentier Born in Cuba.

November 17, 1905 Playwright and Diplomat Usigli Born in Mexico.

March 3, 1906 Enrique Laguerre, Puerto Rican Writer and Teacher, Is Born.

1907 Poet Agustini Is Published.

September 17, 1907 Luis Leal, Scholar and Teacher, Is Born.

March 3, 1908 Corretjer, Poet and Activist, Born in Puerto Rico.

November 4, 1909 Ciro Alegría, Peruvian Novelist, Is Born.

1910 Philosopher Varona Publishes Collected Works.

April 10, 1910 Franciscan Angélico Chávez, Religious Poet, Is Born.

June 8, 1910 Novelist María Bombal Is Born.

January 18, 1911 Peruvian Novelist Arguedas Is Born.

1913 Poet Establishes Magazine.

March 31, 1914 Octavio Paz, Nobel Laureate, Is Born.

August 26, 1914 Argentine Novelist Cortázar Is Born.

1915 Mariano Azuela Writes.

September 3, 1915 Américo Paredes, Folklorist and Teacher, Is Born.

1917 Horacio Quiroga Publishes Most Renowned Book.

February 17, 1917 Julia de Burgos, Puerto Rican Poet, Is Born.

1918 Vallejo Has First Book Published.

September 12, 1918 Writer Arreola Born in Mexico.

September 26, 1918 Fernando Alegría, Chilean Scholar and Novelist, Is Born.

October 4, 1919 René Marqués, Puerto Rican Playwright and Author, Is Born.

1920 Amado Nervo Publishes Poetry.

1925 Mexican Educator Vasconcelos Publishes Book.

January 20, 1925 Author and Priest Cardenal Born in Nicaragua.

May 25, 1925 Castellanos, Mexican Poet, Novelist, and Feminist, Is Born.

1926 Güiraldes' Prize-Winning Novel Published.

March 8, 1926 José González, Novelist and Short-Story Writer, Is Born.

March 6, 1928 Novelist and Nobel Laureate Gabriel García Márquez Is Born.

November 11, 1928 Carlos Fuentes, Novelist, Essayist, and Teacher, Is Born.

1929 Artist Gironella Born in Mexico City.

January 21, 1929 Rolando Hinojosa, Hispanic Writer, Is Born.

April 22, 1929 Cabrera Infante, Cuban Novelist and Critic, Is Born.

January 20, 1932 Poet Heberto Padilla Is Born.

August 11, 1934 Educator and Author Carmelo Mesa-Lago Is Born.

1935 Novelist Bombal Publishes First Novel.

August 20, 1935 Lionel García, Author and Veterinarian, Is Born.

November 1, 1935 Author Nicholasa Mohr Is Born.

December 22, 1935 Tomás Rivera, Leader in Chicano Literature, Is Born.

1937 Palés Matos Publishes Masterpiece.

October 30, 1937 Rudolfo Anaya, Novelist and Teacher, Is Born.

1939 Collected Works of Hostos Published.

1939 Painter Publishes Autobiography.

May 11, 1940 Novelist Victor Villaseñor Is Born.

1941 Ciro Alegría Publishes Famous Work.

March 29, 1941 Ricardo Sánchez, Autobiographical Chicano Poet, Is Born.

August 2, 1942 Isabel Allende, Chilean Novelist, Is Born.

July 16, 1943 Reinaldo Arenas, Cuban Novelist, Is Born.

1945 Mistral Awarded Nobel Prize.

December 19, 1946 Miguel Piñero, Dramatist of Nuyorican School, Is Born.

August 8, 1947 Alurista, Poet and Pioneer in Chicano Literature, Is Born.

1948 Oswaldo Guayasamín Completes Fresco, Wins Fellowship.

February 6, 1949 Nuyorican Poet Victor Hernández Cruz Is Born.

September 5, 1950 Tato Laviera, Popular Hispanic Poet, Is Born.

August 24, 1951 Pulitzer Prize-Winning Writer Oscar Hijuelos Is Born.

September 24, 1951 Novelist Roberto Fernández Born in Cuba.

1952 Writer Juan José Arreola Publishes Collection.

February 24, 1952 Judith Ortiz Cofer, Poet, Novelist, and Teacher, Is Born.

1953 Cuban Poet Wins Soviet Award.

1954 Juan José Arreola Wins Prize for Play.

August 6, 1954 Poet and Teacher Lorna Dee Cervantes Is Born.

1956 Mexican Poet Nominated.

1962 Enrique Laguerre Publishes Essay.

1962 United Farm Workers Organizing Committee.

1964 Cuban Poet Accorded Award.

1965 Novelist Fernando Alegría Publishes Book.

1967 Guatemalan Wins Nobel Prize.

1967 Guillermo Cabrera Infante Publishes Award-Winning Novel.

1967 Writer Alurista Founds Chicano Movement.

1970 Novelist Gabriel García Márquez Publishes Novel.

1971–72 Pablo Neruda Is Chilean Ambassador.

1971 Chilean Poet Awarded Nobel Prize.

1971 Cuban Poet Imprisoned.

1972 Mexican Rosario Castellanos Publishes Poems.

1972 Playwright Usigli Awarded National Prize.

1973   Author Mohr Publishes Award-Winning Book.

1973   Writer Hinojosa Publishes First Book.

1973   Writing Career Launched for Villaseñor.

1974–76   Cuban Novelist Imprisoned.

1974   Nuyorican Poet Has Award-Winning Year.

1978   Book on Luis Leal Published.

1978   José Luis González Wins Award.

1978   Writer Tomás Rivera Heads University.

1979   Poet Laviera Publishes Book.

1980   Hispanic Novelist Wins Award.

January 3, 1980   Poet Laviera at the White House.

1981   Nuyorican Poet Hernández Cruz in *Life*.

1982   García Márquez Wins Nobel Prize.

1982   Novelist Allende Publishes Poetic Work.

1983   Lionel García Wins Literary Award.

1988   Novelist Fernández Publishes Hit Book.

1989   Novelist Ortiz Cofer Wins Arts Fellowship.

1990   Nobel Prize Awarded to Octavio Paz.

1990   Writer Hijuelos Wins Pulitzer Prize.

1992   Poet Cervantes Wins Awards.

MEDIA (TELEVISION & JOURNALISM)

1722   Newspapers in Americas.

1806   Puerto Rican Press Expands.

February 2, 1851   José Guadalupe Posada, Mexican Illustrator, Is Born.

1855   Spanish Newspaper Founded in Los Angeles.

1866   El Cosmopolita Launched.

August 27, 1870   Amado Nervo, Mexican Modernist Poet, Is Born.

1888   Posada Starts Print Shop, Newspaper.

1901   Puerto Rican Journalist and Activist Jesús Colón Is Born.

July 10, 1902   Cuban Poet Nicolás Guillén Is Born.

1913   Poet Establishes Magazine.

March 2, 1917   Desi Arnaz, Cuban Bandleader and Actor, Is Born.

November 25, 1920   Actor Ricardo Montalbán Is Born in Mexico.

March 6, 1928   Novelist and Nobel Laureate Gabriel García Márquez Is Born.

April 22, 1929   Cabrera Infante, Cuban Novelist and Critic, Is Born.

January 20, 1932   Poet Heberto Padilla Is Born.

June 3, 1943   The "Zoot Suit" Riots.

July 4, 1943   Reporter, TV Personality Geraldo Rivera Is Born.

December 19, 1946   Miguel Piñero, Dramatist of Nuyorican School, Is Born.

January 29, 1948   TV and Radio Talk Show Host Cristina Saralegui Is Born.

1950   Arnaz Starts Production Company.

1955   Spanish-Language Television Begins.

July 9, 1955   Jimmy Smits, Puerto Rican Actor, Is Born.

1961   Colón's Essays Published.

1976   Octavio Paz Founds Magazine.

1979   Galavisión, Spanish-Language Television, Begins.

1987   Journalist Rivera Launches Talk Show.

January 1, 1987   Univisión Television Begins.

April 10, 1987   Telemundo Group Begins Broadcasting.

1989   Journalist Cristina Saralegui Launches Talk Show.

March 20–23, 1990   Cubans Respond to Newspaper Survey.

1993   Colón's Essays Published.

MUSIC

1700   Operas Continue to Cultivate.

1750   First Symphony Orchestra.

1824   First Conservatory Established.

May 6, 1857   Composer Juan Morel Campos Is Born.

1868   National Hymn Lyrics Written.

1877   Composer Juan Morel Campos Founds Society.

December 8, 1886   Mexican Composer Ponce Is Born.

October 24, 1892   Rafael Hernández, Composer of Popular Music, Is Born.

August 7, 1896   Cuban Composer Lecuona Is Born.

June 13, 1899   Carlos Chávez y Ramírez, Composer of Classical Music, Is Born.

December 31, 1899   Composer Silvestre Revueltas Is Born.

April 1, 1916   Composer Ginastera Born in Buenos Aires.

1921   Composer Chávez Wins Commission.

1928   Composer Becomes Musical Director.

1937   Composer Ginastera Debuts.

July 19, 1940   Singer Vikki Carr Is Born.

September 5, 1942   Symphony Conductor Eduardo Mata Born in Mexico City.

May 14, 1943   Cuban Singer Tania León Is Born.

1945   Ponce Becomes Musical Director.

1968   Cuban Singer Named Music Director.

1971   Argentine Composer Wins Pulitzer Prize.

1971   Singer Carr Founds Scholarship Foundation.

1985   Hispanic Singer Vikki Carr Wins Grammy.

1991   Conductor Mata Receives Award.

1994   Mata Named Conductor Emeritus.

POLITICS & LAW

1394   Portuguese Slave Trade.

c. 1451   Christopher Columbus Is Born.

c. 1460   Ponce de León Is Born.

1466   Aztec Emperor Moctezuma Is Born.

1470   Díaz de Solís Is Born.

1470   Spanish Missionary Bartolomé de las Casas Is Born.

1475   The Culture of Conquest.

1475   Núñez de Balboa Is Born.

1478   Francisco Pizarro Is Born.

1485   Hernán Cortés Is Born.

c. 1490   Explorer Cabeza de Vaca Is Born.

April 17, 1492   Monarchs Meet Columbus's Terms.

August 3, 1492   The Santa María, Niña, and Pinta.

October 12, 1492   Columbus Lands in Eastern Bahamas.

October 27, 1492   Columbus Expects Gold, Finds Poverty.

March 15, 1493   Voyagers Return to Spain.

May 1493   Pope Divides Lands, Seeks to Expand Church.

September 25, 1493   Columbus' Second Voyage.

November 1493   The Virgin Islands and Puerto Rico.

1494   Line of Demarcation Is Moved.

Summer 1494   Columbus Sails to Jamaica.

c. 1496   Prince Cuauhtémoc Is Born.

c. 1497   Pedro de Valdivia Is Born.

1498   Díaz del Castillo, Chronicler of the Conquest of Mexico, Is Born.

1499   Friar Bernardino de Sahagún Is Born.

1500   Conquistador de Soto Is Born.

c. 1500   Indian Chief Caupolicán Is Born.

September 3, 1501   African Slave Trade Authorized.

September 16, 1501   Queen Extends Encomienda to New World.

February 14, 1503   Contract House Governs Commerce.

1508   Cuba Circumnavigated.

1508   Ponce de León Governs Puerto Rico.

1508   Sugar Comes to the Americas.

1509   Conqueror of Colombia Is Born.

1509   First Outpost on Mainland.

1509   Ponce de León Negotiates for Produce.

1509   Spaniard Settles Jamaica.

1509   Spanish Kings to Administer Catholic Church in New World.

1510   Explorer Francisco Vásquez de Coronado Is Born.

1510   First Slaves Sent to Gold Mines.

1510   Velázquez Leaves to Conquer Cuba.

1511   Court System Is Established.

1511   Taínos Resist.

1512   Indians and the Laws of Burgos.

1512   Missions Expand.

1513   Indians Defeat Spanish Expeditions.

February 4, 1513   Discovery of Gulf Stream Promotes Commerce.

April 2, 1513   Ponce de León Lands in Florida.

September 25, 1513   Explorer Balboa Reaches Pacific Ocean.

September 27, 1514   Colonizing Patent Granted.

1515   Velázquez Establishes Cuban Cities.

February 1516   Rio de la Plata Discovered.

1517   Las Casas Asks for African Slaves.

1517   The Yucatan Peninsula.

1518   Cortés Leaves Cuba to Explore Mexico.

1518   Crown Licenses Slave Traders.

1519   Cortés Documents Conquests.

1519   Cortés Moves into Mexico.

1519   Naval Commander Menéndez Is Born.

1519   Texas Claimed for Spain.

November 8, 1519   Aztec Emperor Meets Spaniard.

1520   Florida Proved to be Part of Continent.

July 1, 1520   Aztecs Force Spaniards Out.

August 10, 1520   Magellan Sails from Spain.

1521   González de Avila Converts, Enslaves Indians.

1521   Ponce de León Dies.

August 13, 1521   Cortés Conquers Aztecs.

1522   Slaves Escape in Hispaniola.

1524   The Council of the Indies.

1524   Spanish Explore the North American Coast.

November 16, 1532   Spanish Horsemen Battle Incas.

1533   Caupolicán Becomes Chief.

1533   Colombia Produces Gold.

1535   Pizarro Founds City.

1535   Vice Royalties Are Founded.

1536   Cabeza de Vaca's Return Starts Rumors.

1536   Indians Destroy Buenos Aires Fort.

1537   Asunción Is First Permanent Settlement in La Plata.

August 6, 1538   Jiménez Explores Colombia.

May 18, 1539   De Soto Sails to Florida.

1540   Coronado Seeks Cities of Gold.

August 25, 1540   Coronado's Expedition Reaches Grand Canyon.

1541   Viceroy Orders Rebuilding of Buenos Aires.

February 12, 1541   City of Santiago Founded.

May 8, 1541   De Soto Crosses the Mississippi.

December 1541   Expedition Discovers the Amazon River.

1542   Coronado Returns.

1542   King Proclaims New Laws of Indies.

1542   Spanish Missionary Establishes New Laws.

September 28, 1542   Portuguese Sailor Enters California Port.

1543   Charles V Bans Books.

1543   Francis Drake Is Born.

1544   France and Spain Sign Peace Treaty.

1550   Indian Exploitation Continues.

1550   Slaves Rebel.

1551   King Charters Universities.

1553   Argentinean City Founded.

1555   Explorer's Document Is Published.

1560   Spanish Found Santa Elena.

1561   Naval Commander Menéndez to Lead Fleet.

1562   Bishop Orders Burning of Mayan Works.

1562   English Trader Imports Slaves.

August 28, 1565   Saint Augustine Is Founded.

1568   Díaz del Castillo Writes Chronicle.

1569   Inquisition Introduced to Americas.

1570   Courts Judge Threats to Religious Unity.

1573   Franciscans Establish Missions.

1577–89   Sir Francis Drake's Great Voyage.

1578   Second Part of Epic Poem Published.

1580   Puerto Rican Indians Fall to Disease.

1580   Spain Defeats Portugal.

1580   Spanish Conquest Is Completed.

1590   Juan de Fuca Sails North.

1595   King Permits African Slave Trade.

1596   Treaty of The Hague Is Signed.

1598   Soldiers Take Up Pens.

1605   Spanish Chronicle Is Published.

1610   New Mexican City Founded.

1639   Missions in Paraguay.

1670   Spain and England Sign Treaty of Madrid.

1678   British Assume Protectorate over Miskito Indians.

August 9, 1680   Santa Fe Falls.

1681   Spain Organizes Laws for Colonies.

1689   First Land Grants.

May 24, 1690   Spanish Settlement in Texas.

1691   Governor Named for Texas.

1691   Jesuit Establishes Missions in Arizona.

1693   Spanish Abandon Texas.

1701   House of Bourbon Takes Spanish Throne.

1716   Spaniards Reoccupy Texas.

1717   English Company Imports African Slaves in Americas.

March 9, 1731   Families Colonize San Antonio.

May 8, 1753   Miguel Hidalgo y Costilla, Mexican Independence Leader, Is Born.

June 9, 1756   Francisco de Miranda, Activist for Independence, Is Born.

1760   France Cedes Claims.

1760   Texas Land Grant.

1761   Alta California Is Founded.

1762   Cuba and the United States.

September 17, 1766   Presidio of San Francisco Founded.

1767   Jesuits Expelled.

1769   San Diego Mission Established.

July 3, 1769   Father Serra Founds Missions.

1770   Slave Traffic Increases.

1773   Alaskan Expeditions.

1774   Overland Route to California.

September 17, 1776   Moraga Founds San Francisco.

February 25, 1778   Liberator of Chile and Peru Is Born.

1779   Spain's Role in American Revolution.

1780   Incan Chief Battles Authorities.

1781   Forerunner of Los Angeles Is Founded.

1781   Spanish Strategy Aids Americans.

November 29, 1781   Andrés Bello Is Born.

1783   Spain Regains Florida.

July 24, 1783   Simón Bolívar, the Liberator, Is Born.

1790   Hispanic Settlements Increase.

1790   Northern Exploration.

1793   Father Martínez Is Born.

1793   Spain and France at War.

November 3, 1793   Stephen Austin Is Born.

February 21, 1795   Santa Anna Is Born.

October 1795   Pinckney's Treaty.

1796   Spain Allies with France.

1797   American Lodge Founded.

1798   The Alien Act.

1798   Naturalization Act.

1800   Leader of the Californios Is Born.

1800   Spain Cedes Louisiana.

March 21, 1801   Napoleon and the Treaty of Luneville.

May 5, 1801   Governor Pico Is Born.

March 27, 1802   The Treaty of Amiens.

1803   U.S. Buys Louisiana Territory.

1804   American Expansion Worries Spain.

October 21, 1804   The Battle of Trafalgar.

September 3, 1805   Poet Echeverría Is Born.

1806   Puerto Rican Press Expands.

March 21, 1806   Liberal Leader Benito Juárez Is Born.

October 27, 1806   Texas Republic Founder Is Born.

1807   Napoleon Invades; Wars of Independence Begin.

July 7, 1808   Californio Politician Vallejo Is Born.

December 24, 1809   Kit Carson Is Born.

April 19, 1810   French Rule Sparks Wars.

September 16, 1810   Hidalgo Leads Insurrection.

1811   Venezuela Declares Independence.

January 11, 1811   U.S. Seeks to Protect Floridas.

January 22, 1811   Mexican War Spreads to Texas.

February 14, 1811   Domingo Faustino Sarmiento Is Born.

May 14, 1811   Paraguay Leaves Spanish Control.

November 5, 1811   San Salvador Priest Calls for Independence.

1813   Children of Slaves Become Free.

1813   Paraguayan Independence.

November 1813   Morales Continues Hidalgo's Fight.

1814   Dictatorship Rules Paraguay.

October 24, 1814   Rafael Carrera, Dictator of Guatemala, Is Born.

1816   Provinces Proclaim Independence.

1817   Chile Liberated.

1817   Cuban Slave Trade.

October 21, 1817   Antonio Coronel, California Politician, Is Born.

1819   U.S. Buys Florida.

1819   U.S. Takes Over Spanish Sites.

June 23, 1819   Spain Seeks to Settle Texas.

1820   Spain Bans Slave Trade.

1821   Adams–Onís Treaty Approved.

1821   Santo Domingo Proclaims Independence.

June 1821   Bolívar Leads Gran Colombia.

July 28, 1821   Peruvian Independence.

September 16, 1821   Guatemalan Countries Proclaim Their Independence.

September 27, 1821   Iturbide Leads Mexico to Independence.

1822   Haiti Rules Dominicans.

1822   Iturbide Declares Himself Emperor.

March 8, 1822   U.S. Recognizes Independent Governments.

1823   California Missions.

1823   Guatemalan Territories Join Together.

1823   John Quincy Adams and Cuba.

1823–30   Anglos Flock to Texas.

February 28, 1823   Puerto Rican Nationalist Román Baldorioty de Castro Is Born.

March 19, 1823   Mexican Emperor Steps Down.

July 1, 1823   Central Americans Form Federation.

December 2, 1823   The Monroe Doctrine.

1824   Constitution of the Central American Federation.

1824   Seguín Becomes Mayor.

1824   Spanish Rule Comes to End.

May 16, 1824   Mexican Folk Hero Juan Nepomuceno Cortina Is Born.

July 19, 1824   Iturbide Killed by Firing Squad.

1825   Ferdinand VII Returns.

1825   Latin–American Congress Fails.

1825   Spain Forces Students Out of U.S.

August 6, 1825   Bolivia Becomes Independent.

1826   Congress of American Republics.

1826   Kit Carson Is Trapper, Guide.

1826   Spaniards Give Up Fortress.

April 8, 1827   Ramón Emeterio Betances, Puerto Rican Patriot, Is Born.

1828   Californio Political Leader Elected.

1828   Uruguay Gains Independence.

1829   Gran Colombia Splits.

1829   Mexican Government Abolishes Slavery.

September 1830   Venezuela, Ecuador Leave Gran Colombia.

September 15, 1830   Mexican Dictator Porfirio Díaz Is Born.

1832   Santa Anna Becomes President.

1834   Tacón Governs Cuba.

November 10, 1834   José Hernández, Defender of Gauchos, Is Born.

1835   Spain Bans Slave Trade.

1836   California Established.

April 21, 1836   Battles Between Texas and Mexico.

1837   First Spanish–American Railroad.

1838   Carrera Rules Guatemala.

May 30, 1838   Federation Authorizes Independence.

January 11, 1839   Eugenio María de Hostos Is Born.

1840   Carrera Overthrows Morazán.

1840   Immigrants Aid Cuban Economy.

1840   Puerto Rican Bans Enacted.

January 14, 1840   Northern Secessionist Movement Ends.

June 1841   The Santa Fe Expedition.

September 14, 1843   Puerto Rican Feminist Lola Rodríguez de Tió Is Born.

1844   Three Rule Dominican Republic.

March 1, 1845   Texas Annexed to U.S.

1846   U.S. Invades Mexico.

May 13, 1846   New Mexico Is Attacked.

June 10, 1846   The Bear Flag Revolt.

July 7, 1846   California Is Annexed.

1848   Anglos Follow Gold.

1848   Costa Rica Keeps the Peace.

1848   Invasions of Cuba.

1848   Mexico Offers Aid for Repatriation.

1848   Presidents Make Offers for Cuba.

February 2, 1848   Mexican–American War Ends.

September 5, 1848   Governor Rejects School for Puerto Rico.

April 13, 1849   Cuban Philosopher Varona Is Born.

1850   The Clayton–Bulwar Treaty.

1850   Compromise of 1850 Affects Slavery Issue.

May 20, 1850   The Foreign Miners Tax Law.

February 8, 1851   The California Land Act.

1852   England, France Propose Pact on Cuba.

1853   Juárez Jailed.

1853   Santa Anna Sells Land to U.S.

January 28, 1853   National Hero Martí Is Born in Cuba.

October 1854   The Ostend Manifesto and Cuba.

1855   California Anti-Vagrancy Act.

1855   Supreme Court Rules on Treaty.

1855   Tennessee Adventurer Heads Nicaragua.

June 25, 1856   Law Forces Redistribution of Church Lands.

1857   The Cart War.

1857   Mexico Adopts New Constitution.

July 26, 1857   Barbosa, Puerto Rican Doctor and Political Activist, Is Born.

1858   Mexican Civil War.

1858   Parties Unite to Make Nicaragua a Republic.

1859   Cortina Leads Rebellion in Texas.

July 12, 1859   Reform Laws Enacted in Mexico.

October 17, 1859   New Mexico Governor Otero Is Born.

1860   The Cigar Industry.

1861   The French Intervention.

1861   Spain Reoccupies Dominican Republic.

May 17, 1862   The Homestead Act.

1863   Patriot and Writer Marín Born in Puerto Rico.

1864   Juárez Opposes Maximilian.

1865   Public Education in Puerto Rico.

1865   The Triple Alliance War.

1867   Coronel Becomes Treasurer.

April 27, 1867   Troops Executed.

1868   Dominican Annexation Fails.

1868   National Hymn Lyrics Written.

1868   Sermiento Becomes President.

July 28, 1868   The Fourteenth Amendment.

September 17, 1868   Children of Slaves.

September 23, 1868   The Lares Revolt.

October 10, 1868   Struggle for Cuban Independence.

1869   Baldorioty Elected to Legislative Body.

1869   The Panama Canal.

November 10, 1869   Oller Knighted.

1870   Amnesty in Puerto Rico.

1870   The Banana Trade.

1870   Guatemala Dispossesses Mayas.

1870   State-Owned Slaves Freed.

February 22, 1870   Labor Organizer Pantín Is Born.

1871   Cuban Immigrants Found Institute.

1872   Puerto Rican Civil Rights.

July 15, 1872   Writer and Humanist José Enrique Rodó Is Born.

March 22, 1873   Puerto Rican Slavery Ends.

1875   Court Rules on Immigration.

1875   Pacheco Governs California.

November 1876   Díaz Takes Power in Mexico.

1877   The Salt War.

May 21, 1878   Cuba Returns to Colonial Rule.

June 5, 1878   Bandit and Revolutionary General Villa Is Born.

1879   The War of the Pacific.

August 8, 1879   Revolutionary General Zapata Is Born in Mexico.

August 29, 1879   The "Little War" in Cuba.

1880   Luisa Capetillo, Advocate for Women's Rights, Is Born.

1882   Dominican Republic Institutes Reign of Terror.

February 28, 1882   Educator Vasconcelos Born in Mexico.

1885   Central America Unity Attempt Fails.

1886   Cuba Liberates Slaves.

1887   Baldorioty Founds Autonomist Party.

1889   American Republics Form Union.

1889   Costa Rica Holds Free, Fair Elections.

1891   Party Organizes for Independence.

January 5, 1891   Separatist Clubs Approve Revolutionary Group.

September 12, 1891   Puerto Rican Activist Campos Is Born.

March 16, 1892   César Vallejo, Poet and Political Activist, Is Born.

May 29, 1893   Nicaragua Elects Zelaya.

1894   The Alianza Hispano Americano, Civil Rights Group, Is Founded.

January 12, 1895   War of Cuban Independence.

February 24, 1895   Martí and Weyler Battle.

June 14, 1895   José Carlos Mariátegui, Peruvian Activist, Is Born.

October 8, 1895   Juan Perón, Argentine General and Politician, Is Born.

1896   New York Puerto Ricans Form Junta.

1897   Otero Appointed Governor.

November 25, 1897   Spain Issues Letter of Autonomy.

1898   Cabrera Launches Guatemalan Dictatorship.

January 1, 1898   Cuban and Puerto Rican Independence Established.

February 15, 1898   U.S. Battleship Destroyed.

February 18, 1898   Luis Muñoz Marín, Puerto Rican Political Leader, Is Born.

April 11, 1898   U.S. Involvement in Cuban Revolution.

April 19, 1898   U.S. Declares War on Spain.

May 18, 1898 U.S. Army Moves into Puerto Rico.

August 12, 1898 Armistice Is Signed.

December 10, 1898 The Treaty of Paris.

1899 Pantín Founds Socialist Party.

1899 The United Fruit Company's Influence.

January 1, 1899 U.S. Institutes Military Rule.

1900 Civilians Govern Puerto Rico.

1901 Puerto Rican Journalist and Activist Jesús Colón Is Born.

1901 Treaty Permits U.S. to Build Canal.

March 1, 1901 Cuba and the Platt Amendment.

December 28, 1901 Cuba Elects Palma.

1902 Cuban Independence.

1902 The Reclamation Act.

May 1902 Cuba Breaks with United States.

November 1, 1903 The Hay–Bunau–Varilla Convention.

November 2, 1903 Panama, U.S. Negotiate on Canal.

1904 Roosevelt's Corollary to Monroe Doctrine.

1904 Union Party Takes Power in Puerto Rico.

July 12, 1904 Chilean Pablo Neruda, Poet and Nobel Laureate, Is Born.

1905 Palma Resigns.

1905 U.S. Moves in Dominican Republic.

November 17, 1905 Playwright and Diplomat Usigli Born in Mexico.

October 4, 1906 Educator and Civil Rights Advocate George Sánchez Is Born.

1907 Mexican Workers Repatriated.

1907 Nicaragua Invades Honduras.

November 14, 1907 United States, Mexico Hold Peace Conference.

March 3, 1908 Corretjer, Poet and Activist, Born in Puerto Rico.

December 16, 1909 United States Intervenes in Nicaragua.

1911 Roberto Matta, Surrealist Painter, Born in Chile.

May 21, 1911 Peace Treaty Signed in Mexico.

May 24, 1911 Díaz Is Ousted.

June 7, 1911 Madero, Supporters Enter Mexico City.

October 1, 1911 Mexico Elects Madero President in Landslide

November 6, 1911 Madero Takes Office.

1912 Ambassador Protests Mistreatment of Mexicans.

1912 Marines Are Sent to Cuba.

1912 New Party Established in Puerto Rico.

January 6, 1912 New Mexico Becomes a State.

June 1912 United States Takes Control in Nicaragua.

February 10, 1913 United States Backs Huerta.

February 19, 1913 General Forces Out Officials.

March 4, 1913 Wilson Backs New Policy toward Mexico.

1914 Countries Side with Allies in War.

1914 Disputes Arise between U.S. and Panama.

1914 President Wilson Sends Troops.

March 31, 1914 Octavio Paz, Nobel Laureate, Is Born.

April 21, 1914 Wilson Orders Marines to Veracruz.

August 14, 1914 Huerta's Army Surrenders.

August 14, 1914 Panama Canal Opens.

November 13, 1914 Constitutionalists Come to Power.

January 6, 1915 Agrarian Reform in Mexico.

February 20, 1915 The Plan de San Diego.

July 15, 1915 Dictator Huerta Steps Down.

September 3, 1915 Américo Paredes, Folklorist and Teacher, Is Born.

October 17, 1915 U.S. Recognizes Carranza Government.

1916 Mexican–American Governs New Mexico.

1916   U.S. Installs Military Government in Dominican Republic.

February 10, 1916   Edward Roybal, U.S. Congressman, Is Born.

March 9, 1916   Villa's Troops Attack.

May 3, 1916   Mexican–American Politician González Is Born.

September 16, 1916   Carranza Calls for Constitutional Congress.

1917   Acosta García Wins in Costa Rica.

1917   The Jones Act.

1917   The Mexican Constitution.

1917   Navy, Marines Go to Cuba.

1917   Otero Becomes U.S. Marshall.

1917   U.S. Restricts Immigration.

January 16, 1917   The Zimmerman Telegram.

February 1917   U.S. Immigration Act.

May 1917   The Selective Service Act.

May 1, 1917   Revolution Ends.

August 15, 1917   Archbishop, Human Rights Advocate Romero is Born.

May 29, 1918   Bert Corona, Founder of Labor Groups, Is Born.

May 21, 1920   Carranza Is Killed.

1921   Immigration Restrictions.

1922   Nationalist Party Founded in Puerto Rico.

December 1922   Central American Conference Adopts Accords.

1924   The Aprism Movement.

1924   Border Patrol Established.

1925   Activist Forms Political Group.

1925   Mexican Educator Vasconcelos Publishes Book.

1925   New Church Leader Disavows Rome.

May 25, 1925   Castellanos, Mexican Poet, Novelist, and Feminist, Is Born.

1926   Pentecostal Minister López Tijerina Is Born.

1926   Puerto Ricans Attacked in New York City.

July 31, 1926   Mexican Government Ends Catholic Practices.

May 3, 1927   César Chávez, Advocate for Farmworkers, Is Born.

June 19, 1927   Julián Nava, Educator and Ambassador, Is Born.

June 14, 1928   Ernesto "Ché" Guevara, Castro Aide and Revolutionary, Is Born.

July 17, 1928   Mexican President Assassinated.

November 11, 1928   Carlos Fuentes, Novelist, Essayist, and Teacher, Is Born.

December 2, 1928   Mari Bras, Activist for Puerto Rican Independence, Is Born.

1929   Depression Alters Migration.

1929   The League of United Latin American Citizens.

March 1929   Revolutionary Party Formed.

June 21, 1929   Government and Church Sign Peace Agreement.

1930   Coffee Crash Precipitates Revolution.

1930   The Hawley–Smoot Tariff Affects Sugar Industry.

1930   Juan Antonio Corretjer Heads Party.

1930   Mexican–Americans Use Courts to Fight Segregation.

1930   Puerto Ricans Go Back to Island.

1930   Southern Migrants Displace Mexicans.

1930   Trujillo, Dictator of Dominican Republic, Comes to Power.

1930   U.S. Controls Much of Puerto Rico.

1931   Mexican–Americans Deported.

January 20, 1932   Poet Heberto Padilla Is Born.

1933   Bolivia and Paraguay Fight Chaco War.

1933   Confederation Advocates for California Workers.

1933   Language Policy Changed.

1933   Somoza Wins Power in Nicaragua.

January 1933   The "Good Neighbor" Policy.

September 4, 1933   Batista Comes to Power in Cuba.

October 1933   The San Joaquín Cotton Strike.

1934   Cárdenas Redistributes Land.

1934   Communists Organize.

1934   Perón Starts Political Movement in Argentina.

May 29, 1934   Platt Amendment Annulled.

December 4, 1934   Guerrilla Guzmán Is Born.

September 4, 1935   Batista Tries to Overthrow Cuban President.

1936   Argentine Wins Peace Prize.

1936   Panama and U.S. Agree on Canal Zone Treaty.

1937   The Ponce Massacre.

1938   Hispanic Civil Rights Congress Founded.

January 1938   Pecan Shellers on Strike.

March 8, 1938   Mexican Oil Industry Nationalized.

1939   Spanish–American Nations Align with Allies.

March 23, 1939   George Castro, Chemist and IBM Lab Leader, Is Born.

1940   Bolivian Revolutionary Movement.

1940   Cubans Elect Batista.

1940   Independent Labor Union Formed.

1940   Industrialization and Urbanization in Mexico.

1940   Muñoz Marín Heads New Party in Puerto Rico.

1941   Congress Outlaws Discrimination in Employment.

1941   George Sánchez Is President of LULAC.

1941   Hispanics Support War Effort.

March 29, 1941   Ricardo Sánchez, Autobiographical Chicano Poet, Is Born.

July 30, 1941   The Office of Inter-American Affairs Is Established.

July 1942   The Bracero Program.

January 13, 1943   The "Sleepy Lagoon" Murder Case.

April 29, 1943   Congress Passes Act to Regulate Bracero Program.

June 3, 1943   The "Zoot Suit" Riots.

June 4, 1943   Perón Begins to Take Over.

July 16, 1943   Reinaldo Arenas, Cuban Novelist, Is Born.

1944   Batista Retires from Politics.

1944   Operation Bootstrap in Puerto Rico.

1945   Revolution in Guatemala.

1945   The United Nations.

March 21, 1945   Parents Win Rights Case in California.

1946   Mexican Political Party Takes New Name.

1946   Puerto Rican Independence Party Created.

1946   Truman Appoints Puerto Rican Governor.

February 24, 1946   Perón Elected President.

1947   The American G.I. Forum Movement.

1947   Puerto Ricans Fly Away.

March 15, 1947   Federico Peña, Secretary of Transportation, Is Born.

June 11, 1947   Henry Cisneros, HUD Secretary, Is Born.

July 4, 1948   Puerto Rican Politics.

1949–65   Muñoz Marín Is Governor.

1950s   Mexican Immigration Increases.

1950   Migrant Workers.

1950   Segregation Banned in Southwest.

July 3, 1950   Puerto Rico Becomes Commonwealth.

July 12, 1951   The Migratory Labor Agreement.

1952   Agrarian Reform in Bolivia.

1952   Agrarian Reform in Guatemala.

1952   McCarran–Walter Act Regulates Immigration.

1952   Revolutionary Movement Wins in Bolivia.

March 10, 1952   Batista Seizes Power Again; Castro Opposes.

July 25, 1952   Puerto Rican Commonwealth Takes Effect.

1953   Agrarian Reform in Bolivia.

July 26, 1953   Cuban Guerillas Take Up Arms.

1954   General Rules Paraguay.

1954   Supreme Court Rules on Hispanic Discrimination.

1954   U.S. Deports Mexicans.

March 1, 1954   Puerto Rican Nationalists Attack Congress.

December 2, 1956   Castro and His Men Land in Cuba.

1957   The Civil Rights Commission.

1957   Land Redistribution Starts in Venezuela.

1959   Activist Mari Bras Founds Movement.

1959   Countries Seek Face Trade Zone.

1959   Cuban Immigration.

1959   Union Organizer Corona Founds Political Association.

January 1, 1959   The Cuban Revolution.

May 17, 1959   Cuba's Agrarian Reform Law.

1960   The Chicano Movement.

1960   Employers Recruit Foreign Workers.

1960   Labor Migration Patterns Change.

1960   The Rise of the Maquiladoras.

January 1960   Eisenhower Moves against Cuba.

May 8, 1960   Cuba Turns to Soviets for Help.

July 6, 1960   Cuba Nationalizes U.S.-Owned Property.

1961   Aspira Promotes Education.

1961   Colón's Essays Published.

1961   Land Reform in Colombia.

1961   Trujillo Assassinated.

March 13, 1961   The Alliance for Progress.

April 1961   The Bay of Pigs Invasion.

1962   Chile Establishes Agencies for Land Reform.

1962   Dictator Heads El Salvador.

1962   Edward R. Roybal Becomes Congressman.

1962   Enrique Laguerre Publishes Essay.

1962   United Farm Workers Organizing Committee.

October 22, 1962   The Cuban Missile Crisis.

1963   Ecuador Passes Land Reform Act.

1963   La Raza Unida.

July 1963   OAS Votes to Sever Relations with Cuba.

September 1963   López Tijerina Founds Alianza.

1964   Congress Passes Historic Acts to Expand Opportunities.

1964   Revolutionary Movement Ousted in Bolivia.

1965   Cubans Transport Relatives to Miami.

1965   El Teatro Campesino, Labor-Related Theatre Movement.

1965   Héctor García Pérez Awarded Panamanian Prize.

1965   U.S. Military Intervenes in Dominican Republic.

1965   U.S. Revises Immigration Law.

1965   The Voting Rights Act.

April 1965   The Maquiladora Program.

September 16, 1965   César Chávez and the Delano Grape Strike.

1966   The Crusade for Justice and the Spiritual Plan of Aztlán.

1966   The Cuban Airlift.

1966   Ernesto "Ché" Guevara Is Commander in Chief.

1966   Puerto Rican Youths Riot in Chicago.

1966   Texas Tax on Voting.

October 1966   Reies López Tijerina Reclaims Forest.

1967   Colonel Sánchez Elected in El Salvador.

1967   Héctor García Pérez Appointed by President Johnson.

1967   New Dictator Heads Nicaragua.

1967   Reform Leads to Assassination.

1967   School Programs Aid Bilingual Children.

1967   Siqueiros Awarded Soviet Prize.

1968   Civil Rights Act of 1968.

1968   Mexican American Legal Defense and Education Fund.

1968   Torrijos Overthrows Civil Government in Panama.

1969 Border War Affects Common Market.

1969 El Salvador, Honduras Go to War.

1969 Peru Begins Agrarian Reform.

May 1969 The Andean Group.

October 2, 1969 Demonstrators Massacred in Mexico City.

1970 Affirmative Action vs. Reverse Discrimination.

1970 Allende Elected to Govern Chile.

1970 Authoritarian Regimes Rule Six Countries.

1970 Congress Amends Voting Rights Act.

1970 Ecuador Expropriates Land.

1970 Most Hispanics in U.S. Live in Nine States.

1970 Undocumented Immigration Rises.

July 29, 1970 The Lettuce Boycott Leads to New Labor Law.

August 20, 1970 Police Disrupt Chicanos' Vietnam War Protest.

1971–72 Pablo Neruda Is Chilean Ambassador.

1971 Cuban Poet Imprisoned.

August 1971 California Court Rules on School Financing.

1972 Dictator Molina Elected in El Salvador.

1972 Hispanic Woman Named U.S. Treasurer.

1972 Land Reform in the Dominican Republic.

1973 Court Decides Texas School Financing Issue.

1973 Supreme Court Acts on Farah Case.

1973 UN Action Supports Independence Movement.

September 11, 1973 Chile's Allende Killed in Military Coup.

1974–76 Cuban Novelist Imprisoned.

1974 Congressional Act Supports Bilingual Education.

January 1974 Court Decision Backs Bilingual Programs.

1975–77 Novelist Carlos Fuentes Is Ambassador.

1975 Abimael Guzmán Reynoso Heads Guerrilla Movement.

1975 Ban on Literacy Tests for Voting Becomes Permanent.

May 1975 California Labor Relations Act.

1976 Peso Devaluated.

1977 The Antonio Maceo Brigade.

1977 Canal Will Go to Panama in 2000.

1977 Ecuador Encourages Colonization of Amazon Region.

1977 Hispanics Form Congressional Caucus.

1977 INS Seizes Undocumented Workers.

1977 Romero Elected in El Salvador.

1978 Civil War Erupts in Nicaragua.

1978 Hispanic Income Data.

1978 Hispanic Women in U.S. Work Force.

1979 Nationalists Leave Prison.

July 17–19, 1979 Sandinistas Come to Power.

1980 Cubans in U.S. Elected to Office.

1980 Duarte Appointed President of El Salvador.

1980 El Salvador, Honduras End Dispute.

1980 Former Nicaraguan Dictator Assassinated.

1980 Hispanics Are 40 Percent of Immigrants.

1980 The Mexican Economy.

1980 Meza Takes Over Bolivia in Military Coup.

1980 Nava Named Ambassador to Mexico.

1980 Nobel Peace Prize Awarded to Argentine.

1980 Reagan and Affirmative Action.

1980 Reagan Supports Old Order, Except in Nicaragua.

1980 The Refugee Act of 1980.

April 1980 The Mariel Boatlift.

January 1981 U.S. Seeks Ouster of Sandinistas in Nicaragua.

November 17, 1981 Reagan Supports Contras.

1982 Hispanic Congressman Roybal Chairs Committee.

1982 Robles Co-Winner of Peace Prize.

February 1982 Mexico Devalues Its Currency.

April 14, 1982 Argentina Invades Malvinas.

August 1982 Mexico Cannot Pay Foreign Debt on Time.

1983 Contras Invade Northeastern Nicaragua.

January 8–9, 1983 Nations Pursue Peace in Central America.

1984 Duarte Elected in El Salvador.

1984 Héctor García Pérez Recognized by U.S.

1984 Ortega Heads Nicaragua.

May 10, 1984 World Court Tells U.S. to Stop Mining Ports.

October 1, 1984 The Iran–Contra Affair.

1985 Cuba Reacts to Radio Martí.

1986 Undocumented Hispanics Achieve Legal Status.

June 27, 1986 International Court Finds U.S. Breaches Law.

November 25, 1986 The Iran–Contra Affair.

1987 Costa Rica's President Awarded Peace Prize.

1988 Cavazos Named Secretary of Education.

1988 Ceasefire Negotiated in Nicaragua.

1989 Américo Paredes Wins Award.

1989 Christiani Leads El Salvador.

1989 First Cuban Member of Congress.

1989 Hispanic Family Income Data.

1989 Immigration Increases.

1989 Novello Named Surgeon General.

January 20, 1989 Puerto Rican Statehood.

December 1989 Noriega Captured as U.S. Invades Panama.

December 28, 1989 An Open Letter to Fidel Castro.

1990 Civilian Leads Chile.

February 1990 Chamorro Succeeds Ortega in Nicaragua.

March 20–23, 1990 Cubans Respond to Newspaper Survey.

December 1990 Russia and Cuba Sign Treaty.

1991 Américo Paredes Wins Mexican Award.

1991 NAFTA Proposal Expands Maquiladora Concept.

1991 New Civil Rights Action Sought.

1991 Puerto Ricans Favor Statehood.

March 1991 Hispanic Unemployment High.

March 1991 Minorities Riot.

July 17–22, 1991 Spain, Mexico Urge Castro to Democraticize Cuba.

September 11, 1991 Soviet Troops to Withdraw from Cuba.

1992 Guatemalan Woman Wins Peace Prize.

February 1992 FMNL, El Salvador Sign Peace Treaty.

March 31, 1992 Russia Withdraws Economic Support for Cuba.

September 12, 1992 Shining Path Leader Jailed.

October 23, 1992 The Cuban Democracy Act.

1993 Colombia Passes Anti-Discrimination Law.

1993 Colón's Essays Published.

1993 Federico Peña Named Secretary of Transportation.

1993 Henry Cisneros Named HUD Secretary.

1993 U.S. President Appoints Hispanics.

May 25, 1993 Carpio Governs Guatemala.

December 1993 Frei Wins Free Elections in Chile.

January 1, 1994 NAFTA Takes Effect.

February 24–25, 1994 Mexican Farmers Protest Agricultural Crisis, Blame

March 11, 1994 Frei Sworn In as Chilean President. NAFTA.

March 23, 1994 Mexican Presidential Candidate Assassinated.

April 24, 1994 El Salvador Holds Free Elections.

May 8, 1994 Balladares Elected President of Panama.

May 12, 1994 Mexico Holds First Presidential Debates.

May 16, 1994 Dominican Republic Holds Election.

August 8, 1994 César Chávez Wins Medal of Freedom.

August 14, 1994 Free Elections in Guatemala.

November 8, 1994 Save Our State Initiative Passes.

November 16, 1994 Courts Block Implementation of Proposition 187.

January 1995 Efforts to Curb Affirmative Action Laws Begin.

February 21, 1995 Mexico Receives International Loan Package.

RELIGION

1470 Spanish Missionary Bartolomé de las Casas Is Born.

1475 The Culture of Conquest.

May 1493 Pope Divides Lands, Seeks to Expand Church.

1499 Friar Bernardino de Sahagún Is Born.

1503 Church Constructed in Santo Domingo.

1505 School Established for Children.

1509 Spanish Kings to Administer Catholic Church in New World.

1511 First Bishop Named.

1512 First Cathedral Built.

1512 Indians and the Laws of Burgos.

1512 Missions Expand.

1513 Bishop Establishes Secondary School.

1521 González de Avila Converts, Enslaves Indians.

December 12, 1531 The Virgin of Guadalupe.

1542 Spanish Missionary Establishes New Laws.

1543 Charles V Bans Books.

1543 Painter Bernardo Bitti Is Born.

1569 Inquisition Introduced to Americas.

1570 Courts Judge Threats to Religious Unity.

1573 Franciscans Establish Missions.

1600 Spanish Missions Run Schools.

1639 Missions in Paraguay.

May 24, 1690 Spanish Settlement in Texas.

1691 Jesuit Establishes Missions in Arizona.

1716 Spaniards Reoccupy Texas.

May 1, 1718 Expedition at San Antonio.

1767 Jesuits Expelled.

1769 San Diego Mission Established.

July 3, 1769 Father Serra Founds Missions.

1793 Father Martínez Is Born.

November 1813 Morales Continues Hidalgo's Fight.

1823 California Missions.

1829 Friar Bernardino de Sahagún's Work Published.

June 25, 1856 Law Forces Redistribution of Church Lands.

1857 Father Martínez Is Excommunicated.

April 10, 1910 Franciscan Angélico Chávez, Religious Poet, Is Born.

1917 Brother Chávez Becomes Friar.

August 15, 1917 Archbishop, Human Rights Advocate Romero is Born.

1925 New Church Leader Disavows Rome.

January 20, 1925 Author and Priest Cardenal Born in Nicaragua.

1926 Pentecostal Minister López Tijerina Is Born.

July 31, 1926 Mexican Government Ends Catholic Practices.

June 21, 1929 Government and Church Sign Peace Agreement.

July 26, 1929 Flores, First Hispanic Bishop, Is Born.

May 5, 1970 First Mexican–American Bishop.

SCIENCE & MEDICINE

1645 Sigüenza y Góngora Is Born.

October 6, 1822 Manuel Alonso, Puerto Rican Poet and Physician, Is Born.

July 26, 1857 Barbosa, Puerto Rican Doctor and Political Activist, Is Born.

February 20, 1897 Telephone Service Begins in Puerto Rico.

June 13, 1911 Physicist Alvarez, Nobel Prize Winner, Is Born.

1912 Medical Institute Founded.

November 15, 1915 Physicist and Teacher Alberto Baez Is Born.

August 20, 1935 Lionel García, Author and Veterinarian, Is Born.

March 23, 1939 George Castro, Chemist and IBM Lab Leader, Is Born.

October 7, 1940 Agronomist Pedro Sánchez Is Born.

1947 Argentinean Wins Nobel Prize.

February 15, 1953 Biodiversity and Conservation Biologist Gómez-Dallmeier Is Born.

1970 Argentine Chemist Wins Nobel Prize.

1984 Argentinean Is Co-Winner of Nobel Prize.

1986 Physicist Alvarez Wins Nobel Prize.

1989 Biologist Gómez-Dallmeier Becomes Director at Smithsonian.

1989 Novello Named Surgeon General.

1990 IBM Chemist and Lab Leader Castro Named Fellow.

1991 Physicist Alberto Baez Is Co-Winner of Award.

SPORTS

1871 Hispanics in the Major Leagues.

1878 Cuban Starts Professional Baseball League.

1888 Cuban Negro League Pitcher Is Born.

1895 Cuban Batter Oms Is Born.

Summer 1900 Cuban Fencer Wins Medal.

Summer 1904 Olympic Gold Medalists.

November 26, 1907 Lefty Gómez, Record-Holding Baseball Pitcher, Is Born.

October 28, 1910 Cuban Boxer Eligio Sardiñas Is Born.

June 24, 1911 Argentine Racing Driver Fangio Is Born.

1919 Cuban Pitches in Two World Series.

Summer 1920 Olympic Medal Winners.

Fall 1923 Luque Wins Pitching Championship.

Summer 1924 Olympic Medal Winners.

1928 Oms Sets Baseball Record.

May 9, 1928 Tennis Champion Pancho González Is Born.

Summer 1928 Hispanics Win Olympic Medals.

1930 Uruguayan Soccer Champions.

July 15, 1931 Cuban Wins World Boxing Title.

Summer 1932 Olympic Medal Winners.

August 18, 1934 Star Outfielder Roberto Clemente Born in Puerto Rico.

October 23, 1935 Golfer Chi Chi Rodríguez Born in Puerto Rico.

1936 Olympians Win Medals.

August 31, 1936 Puerto Rican Boxer Is Champion.

1937 Juan Marichal, Dominican Baseball Pitcher, Is Born.

March 21, 1937 Football Coach Thomas Flores Is Born.

December 1, 1939 Lee Treviño, Champion Golfer, Is Born.

1948 Pancho González Is Tennis Champion.

Summer 1948 Hispanic Olympic Medalists.

1950 World Cup Winners.

1951 Cuban Player Has Most Stolen Bases.

July 10, 1951 Carrasquel Is First Hispanic in All-Star Game.

1954 Avila Wins Batting Championship.

1956 Luis Aparicio Is Baseball's Outstanding Rookie.

Fall 1956 Hispanics Take Medals in Summer Olympics.

January 6, 1957 Nancy López, Golf Champion, Is Born.

August 18, 1957 Fangio Wins World Race Car Championship.

1960   Miñoso Leads Leagues in Hits.

Summer 1960   Olympic Athletes Win Bronze Medals.

1961   Cepeda Hits Most Home Runs.

August 27, 1961   Bowling Champion Monacelli Is Born.

April 21, 1962   Carlos Ortiz Becomes Boxing Champion.

July 15, 1963   Marichal Throws No-Hitter.

1964   Tony Oliva Leads in Baseball Categories.

Summer 1964   Cuban, Argentine Win Silver Medals.

1966   Outfielder Clemente Named MVP.

1967   Rosemary Casals Becomes Tennis Champion.

1968   González Coaches, Becomes Hall-of-Famer.

Summer 1968   Olympic Medals Won by Hispanics.

February 18, 1969   Ramos Outboxes Cruz.

1971   Big Year for Mexican–American Golfer.

1972   Clemente Recognized by Hall of Fame.

February 19, 1972   Ramos Defeats Carrasco for Boxing Title.

Summer 1972   Athletes Win Olympic Medals.

1974   Jockey Runs for the Roses.

Summer 1976   Hispanics Are Olympic Medalists.

1978   Big Year for Mexican–American Golfer.

1978   Flores Coaches Oakland Raiders.

June 11, 1978   González Sets World Record in Walk.

Summer 1980   Cuban Athletes Win Medals.

1982   Cordero Named Top U.S. Jockey.

1983   Dominican Pitcher Is Hall-of-Famer.

1984   Baseball Hall of Fame Inducts Aparicio.

February 29, 1984   New World Walking Record.

Summer 1984   Cuba Boycotts Olympics.

1986   Argentina Repeats World Cup Win.

1990   Venezuelan Bowler Monacelli Is Bowler of the Year.

August 5, 1991   Cuba Wins Gold at Pan Am Games.

WOMEN'S ISSUES & FEMINISM

November 12, 1651   Author, Poet Sor Juana Is Born.

September 14, 1843   Puerto Rican Feminist Lola Rodríguez de Tió Is Born.

1880   Luisa Capetillo, Advocate for Women's Rights, Is Born.

May 29, 1892   Poet and Feminist Storni Is Born.

July 6, 1907   Modern Artist Frida Kahlo Born in Mexico.

June 8, 1910   Novelist María Bombal Is Born.

May 25, 1925   Castellanos, Mexican Poet, Novelist, and Feminist, Is Born.

November 1, 1935   Author Nicholasa Mohr Is Born.

August 2, 1942   Isabel Allende, Chilean Novelist, Is Born.

February 24, 1952   Judith Ortiz Cofer, Poet, Novelist, and Teacher, Is Born.

August 6, 1954   Poet and Teacher Lorna Dee Cervantes Is Born.

1972   Hispanic Woman Named U.S. Treasurer.

1978   Hispanic Women in U.S. Work Force.

1989   First Cuban Member of Congress.

1989   Novello Named Surgeon General.

SUBJECT INDEX

A

abolition of slavery, 80, 83, 84, 108, 109, 209
Academia Baixas, 112
Academia de San Alejandro, 132
Academia Nacional de Bellas Artes, 148
Academy Awards
  in 1950, 167, 229
  in 1952, 172, 233
  in 1956, 172, 238
  in 1961, 199, 244
  in 1978, 197, 262
  in 1992, 226
  in 1994, 193
  in 1995, 283
Academy of Fine Arts (Caracas), 122
Academy of San Alejandro, 148
Academy of San Fernando, 87, 104, 122
Academy-Institute Award, 221
The Account and Commentary (Cabeza de Vaca), 44
The Account of the Conquest (Jiménez de Quesada), 24
Accounting House of Seville, 10
Acero de la Cruz, Antonio, 48
Acosta, Julio, 176
activists, 145, 243
actors
  Chicano, 149, 214
  Cuban, 139, 157, 177, 204
  Mexican, 141, 152, 155, 156, 159, 172
  Puerto Rican, 167, 199, 213, 222, 224
  Spanish, 121, 166, 180

The Actors Studio, 222
actos, 248
Adams, John Quincy, 79
Adams-Onis Treaty, 71, 74, 77
adelantados, 34
Affirmative Action, 247, 255, 266, 283
AFL-CIO, 246
Afro-Caribbean culture, xxii
Afro-Caribbean literature, 230
Afro-Cuban culture, 153
Afro-Cuban folklore, 145
Afro-Cuban literature, 145, 153
Afro-Cuban music, 153
Afro-Cuban poetry, 149
Afro-Hispanic, 282
Agrarian Law of 1952, xxvi
agrarian reform
  in 1800s, 69, 101, 109
  in 1910s, 163, 172, 176
  in 1920s, 129, 184
  in 1930s, 204
  in 1940s, xxvi, xxxi, 223
  in 1950s, xxxii, 233, 235, 239, 241
  in 1960s, xxxv, 243–46, 252, 253
  in 1970s, 255–57, 259, 261, 263
  in 1980s, 264–65
  in 1990s, 280
Agrarian Reform Act of 1981, 263
Agrarian Reform Corporation, 245
agrarian revolt, 115
agribusiness, 231
agriculture, xix, xxxi
  in 1500s, 23, 24
  in 1700s, 53, 60
  in 1800s, 65, 109, 123, 140
  in 1920s, 184

  in 1930s, 196, 201, 203
  in 1940s, xxxiv, 212, 219, 222
  in 1950s, xxxii, 235, 239
  in 1960s, xxxv, 242, 248, 254
  in 1970s, xviii, 257, 261
  in 1990s, 279, 280
Agüeybana, 24
Aguila Azteca Medal, 173, 182, 277
Aguilar, Jose, 266
Agustini, Delmira, 119, 157
Ahrens, Marlene, 238
Ahuízotl, 9
Alaminos, Antonio de, 30
Alamo, 63, *90*
Alarcón, Alonso de, 53
Alarcón, Martín de, 54
Alaska, 58
Aldama, Andres, 266
Alegría, Ciro, 161, 216
Alegría, Fernando, 179, *180*, 249
Alessandri, Arturo, 245
Alexander von Humbolt Senior Research Award on Social Security, 205
Algarín, Miguel, 225
Alianza Federal de Mercedes, 186
Alianza Federal de Pueblos Libres, 186, 247
Alianza Hispano Americana, xix, 127, 229
Alianza Popular Revolucionaria Americana (APRA), xxxi, 129, 184
Alien Act of 1798, 64
Allende, Isabel, 163, 218, *219*, 268
Allende, Salvador, xxxv, 152, 218, 252, 255, 257, 259, 280
Allende, Tomás, 218

Alliance for Progress, xxxiv, 244
Almagro, Diego de, 12, *37*
Almeida, Rafael, 110
Almendros, Nestor, 196, *198, 262*
Alonso, Alicia, 231
Alonso, Manuel A., 78, 79, 96
Alta California, 57
Alurista, 227, 252
Alvarado, Juan Bautista, 65, 89
Alvarado, Pedro de, 20
Alvarez, Luis, 165, 272
Alvarez Bravo, Manuel, 147
Alvarez de Pineda, Alonso, 33
Alvarez de Sotomayor,
    Fernández, 148
Alverio, Roista Dolorea. *See*
    Moreno, Rita
Alvizu Campos, Pedro, 124, *124,*
    161, 183, 230
Amalgamated Clothing Workers of
    America, 258
Amalia (Mármol), 74
Amaru, Tupac, xxxi, 59
Amauta, 129, 184
Amazon River, 40
ambassadors, 189, 252, 257,
    260, 265
American Academy of Arts and
    Letters, 139
American Academy of Arts and
    Sciences Gold Medal, 167
American Book Award winners, 230
American common market, 279
American Council of Spanish-
    Speaking People, 157
American Federation of Labor, 109,
    146, 202
American Folklore Society, 173
American G.I. Forum, xix, 169, 225
American Legion posts, xix
American literature, 14
American Lodge, 56, 64
American Physical Society, 211
American Popular Revolutionary
    Alliance, 184
American Revolution, 59
Americanism, 60, 67, 87, 107,
    113, 115
Americanization, xix, xxiii
amnesty, 109
Anaya, Rudolfo A., 209, 264
Andean Group, 254
annexation of California, 94
annexation of Cuba, 100
annexation of Texas, 94

annexationism, xxii, 57, 71, 79, 94–
    96, 99, 107, 140, 144
anthropologists, 14, 21, 49
anticlericalism, 81, 162, 185,
    187, 195
anti-immigrant, 283
Antillean Federation, 83, 91
Antonio Maceo Brigade, 261
Apache Indians, 62
Aparicio, Luis, 238, 271
"Apeles of America." *See* Santiago,
    Miguel
APRA. *See* Alianza Popular
    Revolucionaria Americana
Aprism, xxxi, 184
Aprista party, 161
Aranda, Count of, 57
Arango, Doroteo. *See* Villa,
    Francisco "Pancho"
Araucan Indians, 20, 36
The Araucana (Ercilla y
    Zúñiga), 36, 46
Araucanians, 22, 35
Arawak Indians, xvi, xx, *xxi,*
    16, 26, 30
Arbenz, Jacobo, xxvi, 223, *223,* 233
Arce, José Manuel, 81
architects, 154, 229
architecture, xv, 3, 24, 45, 54, 56
ARENA party, xxx, 281
Arenas, Reinaldo, 221, 260
Areu, José, 149
Arévalo, Juan José, xxvi, 223
Arguedas, José María, 165
Arias Sánchez, Oscar, xxx, 270, 274
Ariel (Rodo), 111, 145
arielism, 111, 145
Armada de la Carrera de
    Indias, 32, 45
Armendáriz, Pedro, Jr., 167
Armendáriz, Pedro, Sr., 167
Armijo, Manuel, 93
armistice, 135
Army Appropriation Act, 147
Army of the Andes, xxxiii, 59
Arnaz, Desi, 177, 229, 232
Arreola, Juan José, 179, 233
art and artists, xv, xxii
    baroque, 48
    ceramist, 132
    colonial, 55, 62
    cubist, 119

etching, 128
fresco, 200
impressionist, 122
independence, 64
landscape, 84, 92, 98, 127
lithography, 98
muralist, 78, 112, 119, 131
surrealist, 193
ASCAP Composer's Award, 221
Aspira of America, 243
Assembly of Federated States, 83
Association of May, 67
astronomy, 3
Asturias, Miguel Angel, 143,
    143, 252
Asunción, 38
Atahualpa, xxxi, 6, 12, 35, *35*
Atalayismo, 161
Atchison, 144
Atelier de Gleyre, 88
Atheneum Society Experimental
    Theater, 181
Atracciones Noloesca, 149, 208
audiencia, 27
Austin, Moses, 63, 74
Austin, Stephen F., 63
Austrian kings, 53
Auténtico Party, 203
auto racing, 165, 240
automobile industry, xix
Autonomist Party of Puerto Rico,
    80, 121
Autonomous University of Santo
    Domingo, 38
autonomy, xxiii, 152, 212
autonomy movement, 80, 105
Avellaneda, Gertrudis Gómez
    de, 104
Avendaño, Angel, 190
Avila, Pedrarias de, 20
Avila, Roberto (Beto), 235–36
Avila Camacho, Manuel, 212
Axayácatl, 9
Axis powers, 217
Ayacucho, Battle of, 81
Aylwin, Patricio, xxxv, 276,
    279, 281
Aztec Confederation, 36
Aztec Eagle Medal, 277
Aztec Indians, xv, 4–6, 9, 13, 20,
    21, 32, 33, 44, 49, 141, 170,
    227, 250
Aztec smallpox epidemic, *21*
Aztlán, 227, 250
Azuela, Mariano, 111, 172

B

Baez, Alberto Vinicio, 173, *174*, 277
Báez, Buenaventura, xxii, 93, 107
Bahamas, 16
Balada de otro tiempo (González), 262
Balaguer, Joaquín, xxii, 244, 282
Balboa, Núñez de. *See* Núñez de Balboa, Vasco
Baldorioty de Castro, Román, 79, 105, 109, 120
Ball, Lucille, 177, 229
Ballad from Another Time (González), 262
"Banana Republics," xxvii, 109, 143
bananas, xxvi, xxvii, 109, 123
bandits, 81, 114, 156
The Banker Artist (Avellaneda), 104
Bañuelos, Ramona Acosta, 257
Barbie, Klaus, 265
Barbosa, José "Pepito" Celso, 102, 140
"Baroque of the Indies," 41
Barrientos, René, 248
Barrios, Justo Rufino, xxv, xxvi, xxviii, 109, 118
Barros, Francisca Llona, 218
Barth, John, 142
Barthelme, Donald, 142, 231
Barzón, El, 280
baseball
    Cuban, 114, 121, 128, 160, 180, 189, 231, 242, 248
    Dominican, 209, 247, 269
    Mexican, 235–36
    Puerto Rican, 205, 243
    Venezuelan, 238, 271
Baseball Hall of Fame, 160
basketball, 208, 228, 238, 243, 258
Bastidas, Rodrigo, 27
Batista, Fulgencio, 193, 200, *203*, 221
    and Castro, Fidel, xxiv, 235, 239
    comes to power, 202–3, 207, 212, 234
    and Guevara, Ché, 191
    loses power, 193, 240
Battle of Ayacucho, 81
Battle of Churubusco, *96*
Battle of Monterrey, *95*
Battle of San Jacinto, 63, 89
Battle of Trafalgar, 67
Battle of Yagueca, 27
Battle of Yauco, 27

Bautista, Daniel, 261
Bautista de Anza, Juan, 58
Bautista de Casas, Juan, 71
Bay of Pigs, xxiv, 243, 244, 246
Bean, Orso, 213
Bear Flag Republic, 94
Bear Flag Revolt, 70, 94
Before Columbus Foundation, 230
Bellán, Esteban, 110
Bellingradt, Helmut, 258
Bello, Andrés, 60, *61*, 71, 93, 123
Berni, Antonio, 154, 245
Bernstein, Leonard, 220
Best-Maugard, Adolfo, 119
Betances, Ramón Emeterio, xxiii, 83, *84*, 108
Betancourt, Rómulo, 239
Bicentennial Medallion, 205
Bignone, Reynaldo, 269
bilingual education, xx, 157, 174, 252, 260
bilingualism, 216, 227, 228, 230, 232, *259*, 260
Bill of Rights, Puerto Rico, 229
birth rates, xx
Bishop's Committee for the Spanish-Speaking, 195
bishops, 195, 256
Bitti, Bernardo, 41
Black Legend, 12
The Black Messengers (Vallejo), 179
Blades, Rubén, 282
Blair House, 125, 230
Blanes, Juan Manuel, 84, 117
Bleznick, Donald W., 160
bodegas, 92
bohíos, 16
Boland Amendment, xxx, 270, 273
Bolívar, Simón, 61, *61*, 64,
    and Gran Colombia, 77, 84
    and the Latin-American League, 82
    and Miranda, Francisco de, 56
    and San Martin, José de, xxxiii, 59
Bolivia, 82
Bombal, María Luisa, 163
Bonaparte, Joseph, xxxiii, 69
Bonaparte, Napoleon
    and Dominicans, 77
    and Louisiana, 45, 65
    and Mexico, xviii
    and Spain, xxxiii, 55, 63, 67, 69, 70
Bonnelly, Rafael, 244
books, 30, 36

books, banning of, 41
border, U.S.-Mexico, 94
Border Industrialization Program, 242
Border Patrol, 184, *184*
Borges, Jorge Luis, 142
"Borgesian," 142
Boria, Juan, 231
Bosch, Juan, 244, 249, 282
Bossi, Enrico, 120
Boston Braves, 180
Boswell, Herbert, Jr., 236
Botella, Juan, 243
Botero, Fernando, 200, 231
Bourbon monarchy, 53, 63
bowling, 244, 276
boxing, 163, 199, 209, 254, 258,
boxing, Olympic
    in 1928, 190
    in 1932, 201
    in 1936, 208
    in 1956, 231, 239
    in 1962, 244
    in 1964, 248
    in 1980, 266
    in 1984, 271
boycott, 256
Boyer, Jean Pierre, 77
Bracero Program, xx, *218*
    establishment of, 217
    and Gonzalez, Henry Barbosa, 175
    and "Public Law 45," 78, 219, 231
    and railroads, 144
    termination of, 242, 250
Bravo, Manuel Alvarez, 147, 266
Breton, André, 158
Breve historia de la literatura hispanoamericana (Leal), 160
Breve relación de la destrucción de las Indias (Las Casas), 28
Bridgman, George, 132
Brief History of Spanish American Literature (Leal), 160
Brief Relation of the Destruction of the Indies (Las Casas), 28
British colonies, 50
Broad and Alien Is the World (Alegría), 161
Brown, Jerry, Jr., 256, 261
Brown, Joe, 246
Browski, Félix, 144
Brunetto, Luis Angel, 184
Bryan-Chamorro Treaty, 171
Buenos Aires, 40

Buil, Brother, 8
Bunau-Varilla, Philippe, 326–31
Buñuel, Luis, 148, 158, 167
Burgos, Julia de, 177, *177*
Burgos, Laws of. *See* Laws of
    Burgos
Burnet, David G., 89
Bush, George, xxix, xxx, 270, 272,
    275, 277, 278
Bustamante, Anastasio, 63, 87
Bustamante, Jorge, 182
Byrne, William Matthew, Jr., 283

C

Caballero, Juan Pedro, 72
Cabeza de Vaca, Alvar Núñez, 13,
    26, 38, *38*, 44
Cabeza de Vaca, Ezequiel, 174
cabildo, 21, 70
Cabot, John, 34
Caboto, Sebastián, 38
Cabral, Donald Reid, 244
Cabrera, Delfo, 228
Cabrera, Lydia, 145
Cabrera Infante, Guillermo,
    195, 252
Cáceres, Ramón, 174
calaveras, 98
Calderón Sol, Armando, xxx,
    281, 282
California, 89, 94
California Agriculture Labor
    Relations Act, 256
California Anti-Vagrancy Act of
    1855, 100
California Labor Relations Act,
    189, 261
California Land Act, 98
Californios, 65, 69, 89
Calles, Plutarco Elías, xviii, 187,
    192, 195
Campa, Arthur León, 155, *155*
Campbell, Jeanette, 208
Campeche, José, 55, 62
Campos, Juan Morel, 114
Campos, Pedro Alvizu, xxiv
Canada, 360–62
Canal Zone, 169
Canal Zone treaty, 208
Canales, Antonio, 92
Canales, Nemesio R., 113
Canales Torresola, Blanca, 230
Cancel Miranda, Ramón, 237, 262

Cannery and Agricultural Workers
    Industrial Union, 203
Cansino, Eduardo, 180
Cansino, Margarita Carmen. *See*
    Hayworth, Rita
Capetillo, Luisa, 117
Capriles, Miguel de, 201
Caraballeda Declaration, xxix, 270
Cardenal, Ernesto, 185
Cárdenas, Cuauhtémoc, 281, 282
Cárdenas, Lázaro, 204
Cardona de Quiñones, Ursula, 93
Carewe, Edwin, 155
Carías, Tiburcio, xxviii, 202
Carib Indians, xx, 8, 26, 27
Caribbean Federation. *See* Antillean
    Federation
Caribbean Review, 113, 168
Carmelites, 49
Carpentier, Alejo, 153
Carr, Vikki, 215, 257, 272
Carranza, Venustiano, *171*
    and agrarian reform, 172
    assassinated, 182
    comes to power, 172, 173, 178
    and Constitutional Congress,
        175, 178
    and Huerta, Victoriano, 171, 173
    and Mexican Revolution,
        164, 178
    and Villa, Pancho, 114
    and Zapata, Emiliano, 115
    and "Zimmerman Telegram," 177
Carrasco, Pedro, 258
Carrasquel, Roberto (Chico), 231
Carrera, Rafael, xxv, 72, 73,
    73, 90, 92
Carson, Christopher (Kit), 70, 83
Cart War, 102
Cartas de relación (Cortés), 13, 32
Carter, Jimmy, xxviii, xxix, 230,
    261, 263, 266
Carthaginians, 4
cartographers, 9
Carvajal, Félix, 152
Carvajal, Gaspar de, 40
Carver, Raymond, 142
Casa de Contratación, 10, 22, 24
Casal, Julián del, 132
Casals, Rosemary, 252
Casals Festival, 219
Casanovas, Oscar, 208
Casillas Martínez Cardona,
    Florencia Bisenta de. *See*
    Carr, Vikki
Castañeda, Carlos Eduardo, 131

Castellanos, Rosario, 185, 258
Castillo, Ramón S., xxxiv, 129, 221
Castillo Armas, Carlos, xxvi, 223,
    224
Castro, Fidel, xxiv, xxv, 140, 201,
    222, *241*, 275, 277
    and Agrarian Reform Law, 241
    and Bay of Pigs, 244
    and Cuban Revolution, 203, 234,
        235, 239–40
    and Guevara, Ché, 191
    and "Law 851," 243
    and Soviet Union, 243
Castro, George, 211, 276
Cathedral of Mexico, xv, *46*
cathedrals, 27, 45
Catholic Church, xxv, 26, 69, 185,
    195, 257
Catholic Conference of
    Bishops, 250
Catholic monarchs, 4, 6, 8, 12, 14–
    15, 19, 22, 26, 78, 97
Catholicism
    and Cardenal, Ernesto, 185
    and Carrera, Rafael, 90
    and Chavez, Angélico, 163
    conversion of Indians to,
        xvi, 12, 53
    and encomienda, 23
    as religion of Central American
        Confederacy, xxv, 81
    suspended in Mexico, 187
    and Virgin of Guadalupe, 34
cattle, 26, 57, 58, 65
Cauce sin río: Diario de mi generación
    (Laguerre), 245
caudillos, xviii, xxiv, xxv, xxxi, xxxiii,
    192, 195
Caupolicán, 20, 22, 35, 36, 40
Cavazos, Lauro F., 274
Celts, 4
censorship, 68
census, 73
Centennial International Exposition
    in Philadelphia, 92
Center for Historical Studies
    (Madrid), 123
Central American Common
    Market, 253
Central American Conference, 183
Central American Court, 171, 183
Central American Court of
    Justice, 160
Central American Federation, xxv,
    77, 78, 81, 91, 118
Central American refugees, xx

Central Bank of Mexico, 281
Central Intelligence Agency (CIA), xxvi, xxxv, 223, 255, 259, 271
Cepeda, Orlando, 243
ceramists, 132
Cercle et Carré, 113
Cervantes, Lorna Dee, *236,* 237–38, 278
Céspedes, Carlos Manuel de, xxii, 108, *108*
Cession of Louisiana, 303–6
Cézanne, Paul, 88
Chaco War, xxxi, 201, 212
Chamorro, Violeta, xxx, 270, 276
Chapman, Leonard, xxviii, 256
Charles II, 49
Charles III, 53, 57
Charles IV, 55, 56, 63, 65
Charles V, 13, 20, 22, 34, 40
Charles Frankel Prize, 173, 274
Charrua Indians, 10
Charter of Punta del Este, xxxv, 244
Chata Noloesca, La. *See* Escalona, Beatriz
Chávez, Angélico, 162, *162,* 176
Chávez, Carlos, *141*
Chávez, César, 187, *188,* 214, 245, 250, 256
Chávez y Ramírez, Carlos, 141, 144, 183
Chi Chi Rodríguez Youth Foundation, 207
Chibcha Indians, 24
Chicago White Sox, 231, 242, 271
Chicano literature, 160, 194, 227, 252, 259
Chicano Moratorium to the Vietnam War, 256
Chicano movement, xx, 186, 216, 227, 242
Chicano protest, *253*
Chicano Student Movement of Aztlán, 227, 252
Chicano theater, 214, 274
Chicano Youth Liberation Conference, 250
Chichimeca Indians, xv, 49
children's literature, 162, 218
Chile, 73
Chilean Civil Code, 60
Chilean Communist Party, 152
Chilean National Prize, 153
Chinese exclusion laws, xix
Chivas, Silvia, 258
Christian Democratic Party, 259

Christianity, 22, 27, 28, 33
chroniclers, 45, 64, 111
Chronicles, 20, 38, 48
churches, 24, 45, 53, 78
Churubusco, Battle of, 96
Cíbola, 26
Cicuye Indians, 26
Cien años de soledad (García Márquez), 189, 218, 256
Cienfuegos, 160
Cigar industry, 104
cinema. *See* film
Cinematographic Art and Industry Institute, 193, 197, 240
Cinzano Prize, 175
Circle and Square, (Torres-Garcia), 113
Círculo de Trabajadores de la Habana, 109
Círculo y Cuadrado (Torres-Garcia), 113
circumnavigation, 33, 41, 46
The Cisco Kid, 156, 158, 212
Cisneros, Henry, 226, 279
citizenship, 108, 176, *273*
Ciudad Trujillo, 197
civil rights
   and Alianza Hispano Americano, 127
   and American G.I. Forum, 225
   Central American, xxviii
   Chicano, 186, 242, 257
   and Congreso de Pueblos de Haldas Hispana, 210
   and Crusade for Justice, 250
   and education, 223
   and Flores, Patrick F., 195
   and García Peréz, Héctor, 169
   and González, Henry Barbosa, 175
   and *Hernández v. Texas,* 236
   and Indians, xxxi, 233
   and League of United Latin American Citizens (LULAC), xx, 193, 216
   and López Tijerina, Reies, 186
   Mexican, xviii–xix, 94
   and Mexican American Legal Defense and Education Fund, 253
   movements, xix, xx, 169
   organizations, xix, 128, 196
   Puerto Rican, 111
   and Refugee Act of 1980, 266
   and Sanchez, George, 157, 216, 252

South American, xxxv, 255
   and strikes, 204
   and voting, 251, 260
Civil Rights Act of 1957, 239
Civil Rights Act of 1964, 247, 258, 359, 360
Civil Rights Act of 1968, 252
Civil Rights Act of 1991, 277
Civil Rights Commission, 239
Civil War, United States, 81
civil wars, xxix, 81, 103, 274
Claridad, 192
Classical period, xv
classicism, 60
Clayton-Bulwar Treaty, 97
Clemente, Roberto, 205, 251, 257
Cleveland Indians, 231
Clifton-Morenci strike, 149
Clinton, Bill, 175, 189, 226, 279, 282, 283
Cofer, John, 233
Cofer, Judith Ortiz, 233, *234,* 275
coffee, xxiii, xxvi, 65, 109, 157, 196
cold war, xxii, xxiv, xxviii, xxix, xxx, xxxiv, 266, 276, 278, 281
Colegio Antillano, 80
Colegio de México, 123
Coll y Cuchí, José, 183
Collazo, Oscar, 237, 262
College of William and Mary, 131
Collier Trophy, 165
Colombia, 326–31
Colón, Jesús, 145, *146,* 243, 279
Colón, María, 266
Colón, Miriam, 222, 276
Colona, Juan de, 14
colonialism, xxiii, xxiv, 91, 129, 198, 230
colonization, xvii, xx, xxiii, 7, 12, 24, 47, 52, 58, 79
colonizers, xvi, 24, 40
Colored Independents revolt, 166
Colosio, Luis Donaldo, 281, 282
Columbus, Christopher, xx, 6, 7, 8, 9, 15, *15,* 16, *16,* 19, 24, 30, 65, 78, 97
Comentarios reales (Garcilaso de la Vega), 39
common markets, 254
commonwealth, xxiv, 212, 229
Commonwealth of Puerto Rico, xxiii, 133, 212, 234
communications, xviii, xx
Communism
   Arenas, Reinaldo, and, 222

Central American, xxvii, 223, 255, 278
cold war and, xxvi, xxviii, xxiv
collapse of, xxx, 278
Cuban, 149, 221, 243, 244
and Nevuda, Pablo, 154
Puerto Rican, 204
Refugee Act of 1980, 266
and Rivera, Diego, 120
and Siqueiros, David Alfaro, 132
South American, xxxv, 255, 260
Communist Party, 145, 210
Communists, xxvi, 119, 152, 154, 158, 186, 223, 233
Community Action Program, 247
Community Service Organization, 188
Company of the Indies, 53
Compañía Mexicana, 150, 208, 216
Compilation of the Laws of the Indies, 52
composers
    Argentine, 175, 209, 257
    Cuban, 130, 221
    Mexican, 120, 141, 143, 183, 189, 223
    Puerto Rican, 102, 114, 126, 127
Compromise of 1850, 97
Concepción de Gracia, Gilberto, 224
Condorcanqui, José Gabriel. See Amaru, Túpac
conductors, 218, 220
Confabulario (Arreola), 179, 233
Confederación de Repúblicas Centroamericanas. See Central American Federation
Confederación de Trabajadores Generales, 212
Confederation of Mexican Farm Labor Unions, 201
Congreso de Pueblos de Habla Hispana, 210
Congress of American Republics, 83
Congress of Cúcuta, 77
Congressional Hispanic Caucus, 174, 261, 268
The Conquest of New Mexico (Pérez de Villagra), 47
conquistadors, xvi, xvii, 10, 13, 20, 22–24, 27, 31–33, 34, 38, 40, 47
conservatories of music, 81
Conservatorio Nacional de Cuba, 130

Conservatorio Nacional de Música, 120, 141
constitution
    Mexican, 102
    Puerto Rican, 229
Constitutional Convention of Puerto Rico, 344–58, 359
constitutionalists, 171, 172
Contadora Group, xxix, 269, 270
Contadora process, xxvi, xxix, xxx, 274
Contract House, 22, 24
Contras, xxvi, xxix, xxx, 266, 267, 269, 270, 272–74, 276
Contú, Norma, 279
Convent of San Francisco, 49
conventions
    Constitutional Convention of Puerto Rico, 344–58
    Constitutional Convention of Puerto Rico, resolutions, 358, 359
    Hay-Bunau-Varilla Convention, 326–31
Cooper, Gary, 159
copper, xx, xxxv, 255
Cordero, Angel, 260, 268
Cordero, Juan, 78, 97, 112
Corollaries to the Monroe Doctrine, 150, 154
Corona, Bert, 179, 210, 240
Coronel, Antonio, 73, 107
Corporación de Reforma Agraria, 245
corregidores, 60
Corretjer, Juan Antonio, 161, 196
corridos, 98, 214
Cortázar, Julio "Boom," 171
Cortes, 68, 80, 88, 111
Cortés, Hernán, xv, 7, 9, 13, 13, 14, 20, 31–33, 35
Cortijo, Rafael, 231
Cortina, Juan Nepomuceno, 81, 103
Cortina War, 103
The Cosmic Race (Valconceles), 118, 185
Costa, Afranio Da, 182
Costa Rica, 122
Costa Rican Constitution of 1848, 94
cotton, 65, 203
Council of Castile, 34
Council of the Indies, 8, 14, 34
Counter Reformation, 50
coup d'etat, 72
court system, 27

Courts of the faith, 46
Couture, Thomas, 88
Creoles, xxxi, 77
criollismo, 115
Cristero War, 187, 195
Cristiani, Alfredo, 275
The Cristina Show, 227
"The Crucifixion" (Pérez de Holguín), 50, 54
Crusade for Justice, 250
Cruz, Carlos "Teo," 246, 254
Cruz, Sor Juana Inés de la, 49, 50
Cruz, Victor Hernández, 228, 267
Crystal City, 246
Cuarteto Victoria, 127
Cuauhtémoc, 13, 20, 32, 33
Cuba
    circumnavigated, 24
    liberates slaves, 118
    and Platt Amendment, 146
    Treaty of Peace (Treaty of Paris), 321–24
    Treaty of Relations between the United States and Cuba, 339, 340
Cuba-Soviet Union relations, 191, 243, 276, 324–26
Cuba-United States relations, 243, 244, 246
Cuban Academy of Arts and Letters, 93
Cuban American culture, 232
Cuban Democracy Act, 278
Cuban embargo, xxiv, 247, 278
Cuban immigration, 240
Cuban Missile Crisis, xxiv, 246
Cuban National Union of Writers and Artists, 149
Cuban Revolution, xxiv, xxxi, 130, 134, 153, 191, 193, 200, 203, 232, 240
Cuban Revolutionary Party, 99
Cuentos de amor, de locura y de muerte (Quiroga), 115, 176
Cuevas, José Luis, 204, 260
Cuitlahuac, 33
cultural nationalism, xix, 142
culture conflict, 232
Cuza Malé, Belkis, 201
Cuzco School, 41

D

Daily Worker, 145

Dámaso de Alonso Luis. *See* Roland, Gilbert
Dance Theater of Harlem, 220, 252
dancers, 157, 180, 199
Daniels, Bebe, 121, 166
danzas, 102, 127
Darío, Rubén, 107, *107*
D'Aubuisson, Roberto, 281, 282
Davidovsky, Mario, 257
De Mille, Cecil B., 172
De Santa María, Andrés, 104, 176
Dean Dixon Achievement Award, 221
death squads, 282
debt-peonage, xxvi
Decreto Orgánico, 105
defense, 53
Delgado, José Matías, 72
Demiddi, Alberto, 253
democracy, xxvi, 163
Democratic Party, 103, 169, 174, 176, 245
Democratic Revolutionary Party, 281
Denís, Julio. *See* Cortázar, Julio
Dennis Gabor Award, 173, 277
deportation, xix, 199, 236
descamisados, 204
Desde mi belvedere (Varona), 162
desegregation, xx
Desilu Productions, 229
Desolación (Mistral), 122
Díaz, Adolfo, xxvii, 162, 168
Díaz, José, 219
Díaz, Manuel, 152
Díaz, Porfirio, xviii, 82, 86, *86*, 98, 113, 160, 162, 163, 164, 165
Díaz de Solís, Juan, 9, 31
Díaz del Castillo, Bernal, 20, 45
Díaz Saenz Valiente, Carlos Enrique, 228
dictators
   Argentina, xxxiv, 129, 269
   Bolivia, 248
   Chile, 252, 259
   Costa Rica, xxvi, 94, 122
   Cuba, xxiv, 212, 243, 276
   Dominican Republic, xxii, 93, 117, 197, 244
   Ecuador, 87
   El Salvador, 245, 257
   Guatemala, xxv–xxvi, 90, 132, 143
   Mexico, 86, 113
   Nicaragua, xxvii, 202, 252
   Panama, 253, 282

Paraguay, xxxiii, 72
Peru, 205
Diego, José de, 127, 134, 166
Diego, Juan, 34
Diepalismo, 134
Diocese of Juan Bautista, 27
diplomat, 155
directors, 152, 155, 167, 192, 214
discrimination, xviii, 229, 247, 278
   employment, 169, 216, 247, 258, 278
   of Hispanics, 213, 236
   housing, 252
   of Indians, 100, 280
   of Mexicans, xviii, xix, 74, 81, 100, 166, 213, 217, 221, 225, 246
   of Puerto Ricans, 124, 145, 186
   reverse, 255, 266
diving, 228, 238, 243, 253
Dr. Atl, 118, 119
doctors, 78, 83, 102, 111
Doesburg, Theo van, 113
Dollar imperialism, 168
Dominican Agrarian Institute, 257
Dominican Republic, 105, 117
Dominicans, 10, 27, 34, 38
Don Segundo Sombra, 119, 186
Draft Act on Peace and Cooperation, xxix, 270
Drake, Sir Francis, 41, 45, 46
Drama Desk Award, 260
Drug trade, xxx, 265, 275
Duarte, Eva "Evita," xxxiv, 130
Duarte, José Napoleón, 264, 271, *271*
Duchamp, Marcel, 158
Duvalier, Francois, xxviii, 202

E

Eastman Second Century Award, 226
Echeverría, Esteban, 67
economic integration, xxxi, 184, 253
Economic Opportunity Act, 247
economics, 53, 86, 140, 205, 261, 269, 278–80, 283
Ecuador, 84
Editorial Hispánica, 145
education, 247, 257, 258
   in Argentina, xxxiv, 130
   Aspira of America, 243
   bicultural, 157

bilingual, xx, 157, 174, 252, 260
   Crusade for Justice and, 250
   in Cuba, 88, 276
   desegregation in, xx, 196
   in Dominican Republic, xxii, 174
   in Guatemala, xxvi, 223
   Hispanics and, 216, 274, 275
   Indians and, 6, 9, 20
   Mexicans and, 117, 176, 213, 215, 223
   in Puerto Rico, xxxiii, 96, 103, 105–6, 133, 210
   religious, 30, 33, 204
   Vikki Carr Scholarship Foundation, 257
   for women, 91
educators, 73, 79, 156, 157, 160, 173, 185, 194, 204, 209, 216, 274
Egas, Camilo, 139, 245
Einstein Medal, 165
Eisenhower, Dwight D., 243, 246
ejidos, 204
El Ahorro Colective (Barbosa), 102
El artista banquero (Avellaneda), 104
El Cosmopolita, 106
El cuento hispanoamericano (Leal), 160
El gíbaro (Alonso), 79, 96
El Hijo Pródigo (Paz), 170
El incario y la Conquista (Guayasamín), 227
El libro blanco (Agustini), 119, 157
El Machete, 131
El Monte Berry strike, 201
El mundo es ancho y ajeno (Alegría), 161, 216
El Norte (Alegría), 161
"El Pensador Mexicano." *See* Fernández de Lizardi, José Joaquín
El Periquillo Sarniento, (Fernández de Lizardi), 59, 73
El Plan Espiritual de Aztlán, 250
El Postillón, 105
El Teatro Campesino, 248
Elías Sourasky Prize, 219
Elízara, José Mariano, 81
Ellis Island Medal of Honor, 196
Elvira o la novia del Plata (Echeverría), 67, 87
Elvira or The Bride of the River Plate (Echeverría), 67, 87
Emergency Tariff Bill, 179
Emmy Awards, 215, 226
employment, 262, 264, 277
encomendero, 23

encomienda, xvi, xx, 10, 11, 20, 22, 23, 26, 27, 31, 40, 42, 53
Endara, Guillermo, xxx
English as a Second Language, 252
English language, xxiii, 176, 202
epic poetry, 46, 47, 110
Equal Educational Opportunity Act, 260
equal employment, 258
Equal Employment Opportunity Commission, 247
equestrianship, 228, 248
Ercilla y Zúñiga, Alonso de, 36, *36,* 46
Erwin Piscator Dramatic Workshop, 222
Escalante, Jaime, 226
Escalona, Beatriz "La Chata Noloesca," 149, *150,* 208
Escobar, Sixto, 209
Escuela de Gramática, 30
Escuela Nacional de Pintura y Escultura, 204
Escuela Normal de Preceptores, 71
Escuela Normal Insular, 106
Escuela Oficial de Bellas Artes, 112
Escuela Superior de Guerra, 129
Espinosa, José María, 64
Esquivel, Juan de, 26
Estado Libre Asociado, 234
Estenssoro, Víctor Paz, xxxi, 212, 233, 235
Estrada, Juan, xxvii, 162
Estrada Cabrera, Manuel, xxvi, 132, 143
Estrada Palma, Tomás, 147, 148
ethnographers, 14
ethnography, 21, 84
ethnomusicologists, 153
evangelization, 4, 10, 19, 23, 26, 28, 52
excommunication, 102
exile, 221, 241
exile literature, 200, 221, 232, 257
exiles, xxxv, 57, 88, 227, 244, 261, 266
Espinoza v. Farah Manufacturing Company, 258
Estampas del Valle y otras obras (Hinojosa), 259
existentialism, 153
exploration, xvii
explorers
   in 1400s, xvi, xvii, 8, 9, 12, 13, 19, 20

in 1500s, 21, 24, 26, 30–35, 38– 40, 45, 47
in 1700s, 58, 62
in 1800s, 67, 70
expressionism, 104
expressionists, 164
expropriation, 89, 98, 103, 105, 148
expropriation of lands, xvii, xxvi, 109, 115, 243, 253, 257, 263
expulsion, religious, 57

F

Facundo o Civilización y barbarie 71 (Sarmiento), 71
The Fair (Arreola), 179
Fair Employment Practices Act, 216
Fair Labor Standards Act, 210
Fairbanks, Douglas, 159
Falkland Islands. *See* Malvina Islands
family, xix
Fangio, Juan Manuel, 165, 240
Farabundo Martí National Liberation Front (FMLN), xxix, xxx, 264, 266, 278, 281
Farah, William, 258
Farah Manufacturing Company, 258
Farah strike, 258
Farfán de los Godos, Marcos, 47
farm labor, 186
Farm Labor Supply Program. *See* Bracero Program
farm workers, 176, 188, 203, 214, 250, 256, 261
farmers, 280
farming, xx, 280
fascism, xxxiv, 129
Federación de Trabajadores, 140
Federación Libre de Trabajadores, 146
Federación Libre de Trabajadores de Puerto Rico, 109
Federación Panamericana de Trabajo, 109
Federal Alliance of Free Towns, 186, 247
Federal Alliance of Grants, 186
Federal Bureau of Investigation, 210
Federation of Agricultural Workers Union of America, 201
feminism, 49
feminists, 93, 117, 126, 163, 185, 234

fencing, 145, 152, 190, 201
Ferdinand of Aragon, 4, 6, 22
Ferdinand VII, xxxiii, 69, 70, 82, *83*
Fernández, Emilio "El Indio," 152, 158, 167
Fernández, Fernando, 158
Fernández, Roberto, 232, 274
Fernández de Cevallos, Diego, 282
Fernández de Lizardi, José Joaquín, 59, 73
Fernández Morales, Juanita. *See* Ibarbourou, Juana de
Ferrer, José, 167, *167,* 229, 266
feudalism, xvii, xx, xxvi, 205
Ficciones (Borges), 142
Fictions (Borges), 142
53rd Street Theater, 150, 216
Figueroa, Gabriel, 158
Figuerola, Enrique, 248
figure skating, 238–39
filibusteros,, 93
film
   Cuban, 157, 192–93, 283
   Mexican, 141, 147, 152, 155, 158, 159–60, 182
   Puerto Rican, 167
   Spanish, 121, 180, 196, 262
filmmakers, 214
filmwriters, 63
The Final Mist (Bombal), 163, 206
Fine arts academies, 60
First International Conference of American States, 121
Flores, Irving, 237, 262
Flores, Patrick F., 195, *196,* 256
Flores, Thomas, 209, 262
Flores Magón, Enrique, 163, *164*
Flores Magón, Ricardo, 163, *164*
Flores nacientes (González Marín), 118
Florida, 30, 33, 74
Florida territory, 74
folk heroes, 81
folk literature, 113
folklore, 114, 119, 149, 165
folklorists, 145, 155, 173, 274
Fonst, Ramón, 145, 152
Fontcubierta, Father, 52
football, 209, 262
Foraker Act, xxiii, 144
Forcella Pelliccioni, Enrique, 243
Ford, John, 155, 158, 167, 219
Ford Foundation, 253
foreign aid, xxxv
foreign debt, 191, 243, 265, 269, 283

Foreign Miners Tax, 97
Forner, Raquel, 148
Francis I, 41
Franciscans, 33, 46, 48, 50, 57, 58, 79, 162, 176
Free Associated State, 234
free trade, 240
freedom of press, xxvi
freedom of speech, xxvi
Frei, Eduardo, xxxv, 252, 259, 279, 280
Frémont, John C., 70, 94
French Illustration, 59
French Intervention, xviii, 69, 81, 86, 105, 113
French Revolution, 56
Frente Sandinista de Liberación Nacional, xxix
From My Belvedere (Varona), 162
From the Cables of Genocide (Cervantes), 238
FSNL. *See* Sandinistas
Fuca, Juan de, 47
Fuentes, Carlos, 192, 193, 260
Fujimoro, Alberto, 206

G

Gadsden Treaty, 98, 318–20
Galavisión, 262
Galtieri, Leopoldo, 269
Galve, Count of, 49
Gálvez, Bernardo de, 60
Gálvez, José de, 57, *57*
Gandia, Ovando, 248
Gante, Pedro de, 34
Garay, Juan de, 47
Garbo, Greta, 121, 166
Garcés, Pedro de, 58
García, Calixto, 108, 116
García, Félix Rubén. *See* Darío, Rubén
García, Lionel, 206, 269
García, Pablo Antonio, 64
García Lorca, Federico, 149
García Márquez, Gabriel, 163, 189, *190*, 218, 256, 268
García Meza, Luis, 265
García Moreno, Gabriel, 87
García Pérez, Héctor, 169, 248, 252, 271
García Robles, Alfonso, 268
Garcilaso de la Vega, Bernal, 38, 48
Gardner, John, 142
Garza Falcón, Blas María de la, 57

Gaspar y Francia, José, 72
gaucho literature, 119, 142
gauchos, 72, 89, 110, 119
Gaudí, Antonio, 112
Gautier Benítez, José, 161
Gaxiola, Alvaro, 253
General History of the Things of New Spain (Sahagún), 21, 84
General Treaty, 160
genocide, xx, 265
Georgetown University, 133
Geraldo, 221, 274
Gervex, Enrique, 104
Gil Samaniega, Ramón. *See* Novarro, Ramón
Ginastera, Alberto, 175, 209
Girl Scouts of America Award, 215
Gironella, Alberto, 193, 260
Godoy Alcayaga, Lucila. *See* Mistral, Gabriela
gold, xvi, xx, 26, 35
gold rush, 74, 94, 97
Golden Globe Award, 215, 226
Golden Glove, 205, 271
Golden Lyre Award, 219
golf, 207, 212, 239–40, 257
Gómez, Esteban, 34
Gómez, Jose, 266
Gómez, Máximo, 123, 166
Gómez, Miguel Mariano, 203
Gómez, Vernon Louis "Lefty," 160
Gómez-Dallmeier, Francisco, 235, *235*, 274
Gómez de Avellaneda, Gertrudis, 72
Gómez Farías, Valentín, 63
Gómez Reynel, Pedro, 47
Gonzáles, Pancho, 252
Gonzales, Paul, 271
Gonzales, Rodolfo "Corky," 250
González, Felipe, 277
González, Henry Barbosa, 175
González, José Luis, 186, *187*, 262
González, Raúl, 262, 271
González, Richard Alonso "Pancho," 190, *191*, 227
González de Avila, Gil, 33
González Marín, Francisco "Pachín," 105, 118
Gonzálcz Prada, Manucl, 95, 162
Good Government League, 226
Good Neighbor Policy, xxviii, xxxiv, 202, *203*, *206*
Gorbachev, Mikhail, 278
Gordon, William, 218
Goríbar, Nicolás Javier de, 48

Goths, 4
Gráfico, 139
Graham, Martha, 141
Grammy Award, 272
Gramsci, Antonio, 129
Gran Colombia, 77, 84
Grand Canyon, 26
Grant, Ulysses S., xxviii, 107, 109
grape boycott, 246
Grau San Martín, Ramón, 222
Greaser laws, 100
Great Depression, 196, *197*, 198, *202*
Great Society, 217, 247
Grenada War, xxix, 269
Griffith, D. W., 166
Grijalva, Juan de, 31
gringos, 114
Grito de Lares, 81, 83, 108, 109, 113, 161
Grito de Yara, 108
Group of 8, xxx, 270
Grupo de Oficiales Unidos, xxxiv, 129, 221
Guadalajara Summit, 277
Guadalajara Symphony Orchestra, 218
Guadalupe, Our Lady of. *See* Our Lady of Guadalupe
Guajardo, Jesús, 116
Guam, 321–23
Guantanamo Naval Base, 148
Guaraní Indians, 38, 48
Guardia, Tomás, xxvi, 94
guardianism, 161
Guatemala, 90
Guatier Benítez, José, 127
Guayama, 356, 357
Guayasamín, Oswaldo, 181, 227
Guerra Chiquita, 116
Guerrero, Vicente, 84
Guerrero, Xavier, 131
guerrilla movements, 205, 260, 278
guerrilla warfare, 192
Guerrillas of the Frente Farabundo Martí, 265
Guevara, Ernesto "Ché," 191, *191*, 251
Guggenheim International Award, 143, 148, 248
Guillén, Nicolás, 134, 148, 231, 235, 247
Güiraldes, Ricardo, 118
Gulf Stream, 30
Gunther, Yela, 125
Gutiérrez, José Angel, 246

Gutiérrez Alea, Tomás, 193, 196, 240, 283
Gutiérrez de Lara, José Bernardo, 71
Guzmán Reynoso, Abimael, 205, 260, 278

H

H-2 Program, 242
hacendados, xviii, xxv
haciendas, xvii, 34, 40, 42, 65, 86
Haitian Revolution, 153
Halasz, Laszlo, 220
Hall of Famers
  baseball, 205, 209, 257, 269, 271
  golf, 212, 240
  tennis, 190, 252
  theater, 167, 266–67
Harry Smith Point Leader Award, 244
Hatuey, 26
Havana, *44*
Havana Workers' Circle, 109
Hawkins, Jack, 41, 45
Hawley-Smoot Tariff, 196
Haworth, Volga, 180
Hay, John, 326–31, 331–39
Hay-Bunau-Varilla Convention, 326–31
Hay-Bunau-Varilla Treaty, xxviii, 147, 150
Hay-Herrán Treaty, 146, 150, 331–39
Hay-Paunceforte Treaty, 146
Haya de la Torre, Raúl, xxxi, 184
Hayes, Rutherford B., xxviii, 109
Haymes, Dick, 180
Hayworth, Rita, 180
Henderson v. Mayor of New York, 113
Henry, O., 156
Henry the Navigator, 6
Hepburn bill, 146
Heredia, Pedro de, 35
Hermanded General de Trabajadores, 179
Hermanos Areu, 149
Hernández, José, 89, 110, 115, 119, 142
Hernández, Juan, 266
Hernández, Pete, 235, 236
Hernández, Rafael, 126, *127*
Hernández Cruz, Victor. *See* Cruz, Victor Hernández

Hernández de Córdoba, Francisco, 31
Hernández Martínez, Maximiliano, xxviii, 196, 202
Hernández v. Texas, 235, 236
Herran, Thomas, 331–39
Herrera, Angel, 266
Heureaux, Ulises, xxii, 93, 117, 154
Hidalgo y Costilla, Miguel, 34, 55, 56, 63, 70, 72
Hijuelos, Oscar, 231, 276
Hills, Carla, 360
Hinojosa, Rolando, 193, 194, 259
Hispanic Civil Rights Congress, 210
Hispanic Institute, 122
Hispanic Media Image Task Force Imagen Award, 238
Hispanic Publishers, 145
Hispanic Woman of the Year, 215
Historia de la novela hispanoamericana (Alegría), 249
Historia de mi vida (Torres-García), 210
Historia general de las cosas de Nueva España (Sahagún), 21, 84
historians, 49, 131, 162
Historic or Orthodox Autonomist Party, 102
History of My Life (Torres-García), 211
History of the Spanish American Novel (Alegría), 249
Homage to Luis Leal (Bleznick and Valencia), 262
Homenaje a Luis Leal (Bleznick and Valencia), 262
Homestead Act, 105
homophobia, 222
Honduras, 157
Hoover Institution Prize, 205
Hope, Bob, 177
horse racing, 260, 268
Horta, Adolfo, 266
hospitals, 27
Hostos, Eugenio María de, 91, *91*, 92, 210
Hostos y Alvizu Campos (Corretjer), 161
The House of the Spirits (Allende), 268
Houssay, Bernardo A., 225
Houston, Sam, 63
Huácar, 12
Huayna Cápac, 6
Hudson, Henry, 34

Huerta, Victoriano, 114, 164, 168, 169, 171, 173
Huet, Gustavo, 201
Hughes, Langston, 149
Huitzilopchtli, xv
Huizar, Eleanor, 225
Humacao, 357
human rights, xxix, xxx, 265, 266, 278
human rights advocates, 178
human rights violations, 265
humanists, 49, 60, 122
Humberto, Fernando, 104
Humbolt, Alexander von, 62
Hurtado de Mendoza, García, 22

I

I Love Lucy, 178
Ibarbourou, Juana de, 128, *129*
Ide, William B., 94
identity crisis, xxv
Iglesias Pantín, Santiago, 109, 140
Iguala Plan, 77
illiteracy, xxxv
illustrators, 98
immigrants, 183, 195
immigration
  Anglo-American, 63
  Central American, xx, xxviii, xxix, 256
  census, 256
  Cuban, xxv, 57, 92, 104, 110, 240, 241, 248, 251, 266, 272
  deportation, 64
  European, xxiii
  labor and, 242, 264
  laws, 113, 176, 177, 183, 233, 249
  Mexican, xix, 97, 162, 164, 176–78, 183, 187, 193, 198, 199, 229, 240, 242, 275
  national quotas, xxiii
  novels and, 213, 232
  Salvadoran, 275
  undocumented, xviii, 256, 261, 266, 272, 283
Immigration Act, 177
Immigration and Nationality Act, 233, 242, 249
Immigration and Naturalization Service, xxviii, 256, 261, 266, 283
Immigration Reform and Control Act, 272

The Immobile Beloved One
  (Nervo), 182
imperialism, 107, 111
import duties, 279
impressionism, 87, 88, 99, 104, 150
impressionists, 88, 166
Inca Empire, 6, 36
Inca Indians, xxxi, 5, 12, 35, 38,
  60, 165
The Incan and the Conquest
  (Guayasamín), 227
The Incan's Florida (Garcilaso de la
  Vega), 38, 48
income data, 275
independence, 22, 82
  Californian, 94
  Chicano, 250
  El Salvador, xxv
  Mexican, 34, 55
  northern Mexico, 92
  Texan, 63, 69
independence movements, xxxiii, 58,
  60, 69, 70, 81, 128, 140, 183
  Argentina, 73
  Belize, 50
  Bolivia, 70, 82
  British Colonies, 56
  Central America, xxv, 50, 72, 77
  Chile, 59, 73
  Colombia, 64, 70
  Costa Rica, xxv
  Cuba, xxii, xxiii, 57, 73, 81, 82,
    88, 91, 93, 95, 97–99, 105, 108,
    110, 114, 123, 128, 132, 133,
    134, 141, 147, 148
  Dominican Republic, xxii, 78,
    105, 107
  Guatemala, xxv, 90
  Haiti, 65
  Mexico, xvii, 59, 63, 70–72,
    74, 77, 84
  Nicaragua, xxv
  Panama, xxviii, 150, 208
  Paraguay, 72
  Peru, 70, 77
  Puerto Rico, xxii, xxiii, xxiv, 80,
    81, 82, 83, 91, 92, 93, 105, 108,
    109, 111, 123, 124, 130, 132,
    133, 152, 161, 166, 186, 192,
    209, 212, 224, 228, 230, 236–
    37, 240, 259, 262
  Santo Domingo, 77, 105
  South America, xxxiii, 59, 62,
    78, 83, 88
  Texas, xvii, 63, 74, 89, 94
  United States, xvii

Uruguay, 73, 83
Venezuela, 56, 70, 71
*Independent School District (Texas) v.
  Salvatierra*, 196
Indians
  agrarian reform and, 101, 115,
    129, 184, 235, 263
  agriculture and, 65
  Araucan, xxi, 20, 36
  Arawak, *xxi*, 16, 26, 30
  assimilation and, 89
  Balboa and, 12
  Cabeza de Vaca and, 14
  Carib, 8, 26, 27
  civil rights and, 11, 28, 40, 205,
    233, 278, 280
  Colombia and, xxxi
  Columbus and, xx, *15*
  conquest of, xvii, 3–6, 9, 10, 13,
    20, 26, *28*, 32
  Cortés and, 9, 13, 33
  dictators and, xxvi, 132
  education and, 30, 34
  Guatemala and, 90, 143, 278
  land and, xx, *25*
  Laws of Burgos, 27, 285–96
  Mexico and, xx, 70, 282
  missionaries and, xxi, 10, 21–4,
    48, 50, 58
  Ponce de León and, 26, 30, 33
  population, xx, 279
  protection of 10–12, 28, 40, 50,
    95, 285–96
  rebellions, 14, 26, 27, 38, 40, 60,
    70, 93, 282, 283
  slavery and, xxii, 23, 31,
    33, 42, 55
  Spaniards and, xxv, 20, 26, *28*,
    38, 40, 45, 77
  Taíno, xx, 27
  Toltec, 3, 4, 5
  writers and, 143, 163, 185
indigenism, 86, 129, 248
indigenist literature, 161, 216
indigenist movements, 95
industrialization, xxiii, xxxiv, 212,
  222, 250, 254
Inquisition, Spanish, 12, 27, 46
Institute for Agricultural and
  Fishing Industry
  Development, 245
Institute for Tropical Medicine, 166
Institute of Tropical Zoology, 235
Institutional Revolutionary Party,
  195, 224, 254, 281, 282
Instituto Agrario Dominicano, 257

Instituto Colombiano de la Reforma
  Agraria, 243
Instituto de Desarrollo
  Agropecuario, 245
Instituto del Arte e Industria
  Cinematográfica, 193, 197, 240
Instituto Juárez, 143
Instituto Nacional de Bellas
  Artes, 141
Instituto San Carlos, 110
Inter-American Bank, xxxv, 255
Inter-American Conference,
  xxviii, 202
International Brotherhood of
  Teamsters, 256
International Centre for Research in
  Agroforestry, 216
International Court of Justice, xxx,
  270, 273
International Monetary Fund,
  265, 280
International Prize at the Sao Paulo
  Bienal, 166
International Union of American
  Republics, 121
interventionism, 78, 111, 150, 160,
  171, 172, 176, 183, 249
  French in Mexico, 104–5
  Guatemala in El Salvador, 90
  U.S. in Chile, xxxv
  U.S. in Cuba, xxiii, 128, 147,
    166, 203
  U.S. in Dominican Republic, xxii,
    154, 174, 244
  U.S. in Grenada, xxix, 269
  U.S. in Guatemala, xxv, xxvi, 223
  U.S. in Nicaragua, xxvii, 162,
    167, 270
  U.S. in Panama, 169, 208
  U.S. policy, xxviii, 151, 152, 202
Iran-Contra Affair, xxix, 270,
  272, 273–74
Isaacs, Jorge, 89, 107
Isabella of Castille, 4, 6, *8, 9,*
  22, 23, 24
Islam, 4, 38
Isthmian canal, 97
Iturbide, Agustín de, xvii, 55, 63,
  70, 77, 78, 81, 82, *82*

J

Jackson, Andrew, 74
Jamaica, 19, 26

Jane Addams Children's Book
    Award, 207, 258
jazz poetry, 228
Jefferson, Thomas, 64, 67
Jeronymites, 22, 30
Jesuits, 41, 42, 48, 49, 52, 53, 57
Jews, 22
jíbaro, 113
Jiménez, Juan Isidro, 155
Jiménez de Quesada, Gonzalo,
    xxxi, 24, 38
Job Corps, 247
John II, 19
John Paul II, 185
Johnson, Lyndon B., xxii, 170, 217,
    244, 247, 249, 252
Jones Act, xxiii, xxviii, 152,
    176, 202
journalism, 68, 87, 100, 145, 189,
    219, 243
journalists, 256, 275
    Cuban, 149, 153, 195, 200,
        227, 275
    Guatemalan, 143
    Peruvian, 129, 161
    Puerto Rican, 93, 105, 133, 161
    U.S., 221, 274
Juan Bobo, 113
"Juana de América." *See* Ibarbourou,
    Juana de
Juantorena, Alberto, 261
Juárez, Benito, xviii, 68, 81, 86,
    98, 103–5
Juárez García, Pablo. *See* Juárez,
    Benito
judo, 261
Judson, Edward, 180
Julia y Arcelay, Raúl Rafael
    Carlos, 213
Julián del Casal Prize, 200
July 26th Movement, 191
junta, 72
Junta Revolucionaria de Cuba y de
    Puerto Rico, 105
Junta Superior de Instrucción
    Pública, 106
Junta Suprema de Censura, 68
justice system, 27, 219
justicialismo, 204

K

Kahlo, Frida, 158, *159*
Kanellos, Nicolás, 279
kayac, 253

Kearny, Stephen, 94
Kennedy, Edward, 201
Kennedy, John F., xxiv, xxxiv, 170,
    244, 246
Kennedy, Robert F., 250
Khan, Aly, 180
Khrushchev, Nikita, 246
"Kid Chocolate." See Sardiñas,
    Eligio
Kieth, Minor Cooper, xxvii, 123
King, Billie Jean, 252
King, Rodney, 226, 277
King Ranch, 57
Kino, Eusebio, 52
Kirkpatrick, Paul, 277
Klee, Paul, 125
Knapp, Harry, 174
Knight, Ray, 240
Kohler, Georges J. F., 271
Korean War, 231
Krause, Martin, 120

L

La amada inmóvil (Nervo), 182
La araucana (Ercilla y
    Zúñiga), 36, 46
La Beach, Lloyd, 228
"La Borinqueña" (Puerto Rican
    national anthem), 107
La Carreta, 181, *181*
La Carreta Made a U-Turn
    (Laviera), 262
La casa de los espíritus (Allende), 268
La conquista de la Nueva Méjico
    (Pérez de Villagra), 47
La Democracia, 161
La feria (Arreola), 179
La Florida de Inca (Garcilaso de la
    Vega), 38, 48
La gaceta de Cuba, 149
La Noche Triste, 33
La Patria, 123
La Patria Ilustrada, 121
La Purísima Concepción, 79
La raza cósmica, 118, 170, 185
    (Vasconcelos)
La Raza Unida Party, 246
*La relación y comentarios (Cabeza de
    Vaca)*, *44*
*La Salle Museum of Natural
    History*, 235
La Torre del Viejo, 105
La última niebla (Bombal), 163, 206

labor
    Argentine, 204
    and Chavez, César, 250, 256
    Chicano, 242
    Chilean, 255
    Guatemalan, 223
    Mexican, 144, 176, 210, 219,
        229, 231, 242–43
    migration, 242
    migrant, 196, 229
    Puerto Rican, 109–10, 117, 125,
        212, 222
Labor Council of Latin American
    Advancement, 258
labor leaders, 91, 109, 117, 133,
    179, 187, 214
labor unions, 117, 119, 125, 131,
    146, 149, 179, 183, 201, 203,
    240, 280
Laguerre, Enrique, 156, 245
Laguna, Ismael, 246
Lam, Wilfredo, 132, 148, 165, 248
Lamar, Mirabeau Buonoparte, 93
Lamy, Jean Baptiste, 62, 102
land claims, 19, 105
land dispossession, xxvi
land expansion, 74
land exploration, *29*
land expropriation, xxvi, 233,
    235, 280
land grants, 52, 57, 63, 66, 186, 247
land parceling, *25*
land redistribution, 70, 239, 280
Landa, Diego de, 45
Landesio, Eugenio, 92
landholders, xxxi
Landini, Raul, 190
Laredo Brú, Federico, 203
las Casas, Bartolomé de, 8, 10, *11*,
    23, 27, 31, 40
Las Leyes de Indias, 11
Latifundios, 235
Latin America-United States
    relations, 217
Latin American Association for
    Free Commerce, 240
Latin American League, 82
Latin American Novel Contest of
    the Pan American Union, 216
Latin American Writers Institute
    Award (1992), 238, 278
"Latin lovers," 121, 158, 182,
    184, 225
Lau, Kinney, 260
Lau v. Nichols, 260
Lautaro, 20, 22, 36, 40

Laviera, Jesús Abraham "Tato," 230, *230*, 262, 266
law, 27, 52
Law 135 (Colombian), 243
Law 851 (Cuba), 243
Lawrence Berkeley Lab, 165
Laws of Burgos, 27, 285–97
    amendments to, 295
Laws of Reform, 69, 113
Laws of the Indies, 11
Le Clerc, François, 42
League of United Latin American
    Citizens, xx, 157, 193, 216, 229
Leal, Luis, 160, *160*, 262
Leaving Home (García), 269
Lebrón, Lolita, xxiv, 236–37, 262
Lecuona, Ernesto, 130
Lecuona's Cuban Boys, 130
Lehtinen, Ileana Ross, 264, 275
Leloir, Luis F., 255
Lenin Peace Prize, 247
    in 1953, 153
    in 1967, 132, 252
Lennon, John, 231
León, Tania, 219, *221*, 252
León Carpio, Ramiro de, 279
León Donoso, Pedro, 181
Lerdo de Tejada Law, 101
Letter of Autonomy, 132
Letters of Account (Cortés), 13, 32
lettuce boycott, 256
Lewis and Clark expedition, 67
Ley de Imprenta, 68
Liberal Club of Querétaro, 55
liberalism, 59
Liberating Revolution, 204
liberation theology, 185, 257
Liga de Béisbol Profesional
    Cubana, 114
Liga de Patriotas, 91
Lima, Peru, 36
Lima Group, xxix, xxx, 270
Linden Lane, 201
Line of Demarcation, 19
Lira Ponceña, 102, 114
literacy, 30, 260
literary critics, 179, 249
literature
    books banned, 40–41
    documents on exploration, 20, 32,
        38–39, 46
    gaucho, 71, 119, 142
    novels, 87, 89, 96–97, 156, 165,
        172, 186, 189, 206–8, 213, 216,
        222, 252, 256, 259, 268
    plays, 47, 258

poetry, 36, 49, 60, 67, 87, 122–
    23, 152–53, 170, 227, 238,
    257, 276
    and printing press, 68
    short stories, 118, 142, 145, 186
"Little War," 116
livestock industry, 53
Llorens Torres, Luis, 113, 166
Long, Stephen, 74
López, Nancy, 239–40, *239*, 261
López, Narciso, 95
López Tijerina, Reies, 186, 247
López v. Harlowe, 257
Los Angeles Drama Critics Circle
    Award (1978), 215, 225
Los Angeles Federation of Mexican
    Societies, 201
Los Angeles riots, 277
Los de abajo (Azuela), 111, 172
"los descamisados," 130
Los heraldos negros (Vallejo), 179
Los moros y los cristianos (Farfán de
    los Godos), 47
Louisiana, cession of, 303–6
Louisiana Purchase, xvii, 45,
    63, 65, 67
Louisiana Territory, 57, 65
Lovell, Santiago, 201
Lugones, Leopoldo, 142
Luque, Adolfo, 180, 184
Luque, Hernando de, 12, *37*
lyric poetry, 49

M

McCarran-Walter Act, 233
Maceo, Antonio, 123, *124*
Machado, Catherine, 238–39
Machado, Gerardo, 202, 207
Macho! (Vilaseñor), 259
McKinley, William, 103, 132, 134
McKinley Tariff, 104
McLeod, Hugh, 93
McWilliams, Carey, 217, 219
Madden, John, 209, 262
Madero, Francisco, xviii, 86, 114,
    115, 163, 165, 166, 168, 169
Madrazo y Kunts, Federico, 88
Madriz, José, 162
Magellan, Ferdinand, 33, 34
magic realism, 153, 163, 189, 193,
    218, 222, 256
maize, 3
Makeba, Miriam, 231
Malamud, Bernard, 201

Malintzin, 34
Malvina Islands, 269
mambo, 232
*The Mambo Kings Play Songs of
    Love* (Hijuelos), 276
Man and the Biosphere Biological
    Diversity Program, 235
Mango, 238
Manifest Destiny, xvii, 74, 94, 100
mannerism, 41, 50
Manso, Alonso, 27, 30
Mantilla, María, 157
Maoism, xxxii, 205, 260
mapuches, 40
maquilador, 250, *251*, 277, 279
maquiladoras, 242
Marcelilno, José, 272
Mari Bras, Juan, 192
María (Isaacs), 89, 107
Mariátegui, José Carlos, 95,
    128, 184
Marichal, Juan, 209, 247, 269
Mariel Boatlift, xxv, 222, 266, *267*
"Marielitos," 266
Mariles, Humberto, 228
Marino, Tony, 209
Mármol, José, 74, 103
Marqués, René, 181
Márquez, Gabriel. *See* García
    Márquez, Gabriel
Marsans, Armando, 110
Martí, José, xxiii, 98, *99*, 123,
    128, 157
Martín, Esteban, 35
Martín Fierro (Hernández), 89, 110,
    115, 119
Martinez, Armando, 266
Martínez, Estela, xxxiv, 130
Martínez, José Antonio, 62, 102
Martínez, Tomás, xxvii, 103
Martínez Asunsolo López Negrete,
    Lolita Dolores. *See* Río,
    Dolores del
Martínez de Irala, Domingo, 38
Marxism, xxix, xxxv, 129, 185, 191,
    205, 255, 266
Marxist-Leninist, 243
mason, 112
Massanet, Father, 52
the master teacher. See Alonso,
    Manuel A.
Mata, Eduardo, 218, 277, 279
Mata, Miguel, 78
mathematicians, 49
mathematics, Mayan, 3
Matta, Roberto, 164

Maximilian I, xviii, 69, 105, *106*
Mayan art, *4*
Mayan codices, 45
Mayan Indians, xxvi, 3, 5, 45, 109, 125, 185, 280, 283
Mayan palace, *5*
meat packing industry, xix
Mechicas. *See* Aztec indians
A Medal for Benny, 199
Medal of Freedom winners, 189, 196, 271, 282
medical profession, 78, 83
medicine, 271
Menchu, Rigoberta, 278
Mendes, Chico, 213
Méndez, José, 121
Méndez et al v. Westminster School District et al, 223
Mendieta, Carlos, 203
Mendoza, Antonio de, 26
Mendoza, Juan Fabila, 248
Mendoza, Pedro de, xxxi, 34, 38
Menéndez de Avilés, Pedro, 32, *32*, 41, 42, 45
Menéndez Pidal, Ramón, 123
Merced Theater, 74
mercedes, 52, 57, 63, 66 186, 247
Mérida, Carlos, 125
Merritt, Ezekiel, 94
Mesa-Lago, Carmelo, 204, 260
mestizaje, xvi
Mestizos, xvi, xviii, xxi, 23, 24, 30, 34, 39, 77, 86, 115, 118
Mexican Farm Labor Supply Program. *See* Bracero Program
Mexican Farm Labor Union, 201
Mexican Labor Agreement, 231
Mexican Revolution, xviii, xxxi
    art, 98, 131
    begins, 163
    chronicles of, 111
    and Díaz regime, 114
    and Huerta, Victoriano, 169
    and immigration, xix
    and independence, 70
    and Mexican Constitution, 176, 178
    and Plan de San Diego, 172
    and Villa, Pancho, 114
"Mexican Spitfires," 159
Mexican workers, 157
Mexican-American culture, xix
Mexican-American Legal Defense and Education Fund, 157, 253, 279

Mexican-American Political Association, 179, 240
Mexican-American War, 62, 69, 81, 94, 96, 97, 196
Mexican-American Youth Conference, 179
The Mexican Thinker (Fernández de Lizardi), 59
Mexico
    adopts constitution, 102
    establishes Bracero Program, 340–44
    explored by Hernán Cortés, 31, 32
    Gadsden Treaty (1853), 318–20
    invaded by U.S., 94
    North American Free Trade Agreement (NAFTA) and, 360–62
    Treaty of Guadalupe-Hidalgo and, 309–20
Mexico-United States relations, 160, 169, 217, 242
Michimalonco, 40
migrant labor, 229
migration, xxxiv, 242
    Puerto Rican, xxiii, 133, 183, 186, 222, 225, 240
    reverse, xxiii
Migratory Labor Agreement, 231
Miguel Luis Amunátegui Liceum, 91
militancy, Chicano, 247
Militaristic Period, xv
military control, xxxv
military service, 178
Milstein, César, 271
Minería Palace, 56
mines, 157
minimalism, 152
mining, xviii, xix, xxi, xxxi, 35, 42, 52, 62, 63, 65, 86, 97, 103, 115, 176, 184
Minnesota Twins, 248
minority class, 236
Miñoso, Orestes (Minnie), 231, 242
Miranda, Francisco de, 56, 64
Miró, Joan, 125
Miskito Indians, 50
Missile crisis, Cuban, 246
missionaries, xvi, 8, 10, 12, 21, 24, 30, 40, 46, 48, 52, 58, 79
missions, xvi, 24, 46, 48, 52–54, 57, 58, 66, 69, 79
Mississippi River, 22, 40
Mississippi Territory, 67

Mistral, Gabriela, 122, *122*, 152, 222
Mixtec Indians, 9
Mobile Act, 67
Moctezuma, 9, 13, 20, 32, 33
Moctezuma II, xv
modern art, 148
modernism, 95, 107, 113, 149, 152, 168
Mohr, Nicholasa, 207
Molina, Arturo Armando, xxix, 257
Monacelli, Amleto Andrés, 244, *245*, 276
Monastery of Santo Domingo, 30
Mondrian, Piet, 113, 119
Monet, Claude, 88
Monroe, James, 78, 81, 306–9
Monroe Doctrine, 81, 150, 154, 306–9
Montalbán, Ricardo, 182, 225
Montalvo, Juan, 87, 117
Montenegro, Roberto, 119, 131, 142
Monterrey, Battle of, *95*
Montesinos, Antonio de, 27
Montilla, Ricardo, 122
The Moors and the Christians (Farfán de la Godoza), 47
Moraga, José, 58
Moratorio, Carlos, 248
Morazán, Francisco, 73, 92
Morel Campos, Juan, 102
Morello de Auñón, Rubio, 50
Morelos y Pavón, José María, 55, 63, 72
Moreno, Antonio, 121, 166
Moreno, Luisa, 210
Moreno, Rita, 199, 244
moslems, 12, 22
Movimiento Estudiantil de Aztlán, 227, 252
Movimiento Nacionalista Revolucionario (MNR), xxxi, 233, 248
Movimiento Pro Independencia, 192, 240
Mozart Medal (1991), 219
Mulattoes, xxii, 30, 55, 124, 134, 149
Muñoz, Felipe, 253
Muñoz Marín, Luis, xxiii, 125, 133, *133*, 212, 228
Muñoz Rivera, Luis, 133, *134*, 152
muralists, 78, 117–19, 131, 139, 143, 147, 154, 181, 229
Murillo, Gerardo. *See* Dr. Atl

Museo de Arte
    Contemporáneo, 200
Museum of Mexican
    Photography, 266
Museum of Pre-Hispanic Art
    (Oaxaca), 143
music, xxii, 53, 55, 81, 102,
    114, 144
    classical, 102, 120, 126, 141, 219
    folkloric, 120
    popular, 126, 130, 215
    semi-classical, 130
Mussolini, Benito, xxxiv, 129
mutiny, 107
*My Penitent Land: Reflections on
    Spanish New Mexico*
    (Chávez), 163
Myrdal, Alva, 269

N

NAFTA. *See* North American Free
    Trade Agreement (NAFTA)
Napoleon. *See* Bonaparte, Napoleon
Napoleon III, 69, 105
Narváez, Pánfilo de, 14, 30
National Action Party, 282
National Archeological Museum
    (Mexico), 142
National Autonomous University of
    Mexico, 186
National Baseball Association, 110
National Baseball League, 114
National Border Program, 242
National College (Mexico), 120
National Congress of Spanish-
    Speaking People, 179
National Council of Women
    Achievement Award (1980), 221
National Farm Workers
    Association, 250
National Football League, 209
National Forest Project, 103
National Institute for Fine Arts
    Drama Festival (1954), 179
National Labor Relations Act, 261
National Liberation Army (Bolivia),
    191, 251
National Medal of Science
    (1964), 165
National Origins Quota Act, xix
National Preparatory School,
    119, 131
National Recovery
    Administration, 210

National Revolutionary Party,
    195, 224
National School of Fine Arts
    (Mexico), 142
National School of Painting and
    Sculpture (Mexico), 120
National Security Council, 270, 273
National University of
    Colombia, 189
nationalism
    Chicano, 248
    Mexican, 34, 114, 142, 163–64
    Peruvian, 129, 184
    Spanish, 12
    Texan, 69
Nationalist Party (Puerto Rico),
    124
nationalists, 79
nationalization of industries, xxxi,
    xxxiv, xxxv, 191
nationalizing, 204, 243, 259
naturalization, 264
Naturalization Act of 1798, 64
Nava, Julián, 189, 265
Naziism, xxxiv, 129, 265
Negri, Pola, 121, 166
negrito, 139
Negritude Law, 279
Negro Leagues, 121, 128, 231
Nelson, Lord, 67
Neruda, Pablo, 152, 257
Nervo, Amado, 110, 182
Neve, Felipe de, 58
New Laws of the Indies, 11, 40
New Mexico, 94
New Panama Canal Company, 146
New Realism, 154, 245
New Spain, 36
New York Drama Critics Circle
    Award (1974), 260
New York Yankees, 160
Newborn Flowers (González
    Marin), 118
newspapers, 49, 54, 68, 139
Nicaragua, 157
Nicaragua-United States relations,
    162, 167, 262
Nicaraguan Agrarian Reform
    Institute, 263
Nicaraguan protest march, *268, 272*
Nicaraguan Revolution, 185
Nicuesa, Diego de, 24
Nin, Joaquín, 130
Niña, 15
Nixon, Richard M., xxxv, 153, 255
No-transfer resolution, 71

Nobel Prize
    chemistry, 255
    literature, 122, 143, 152, 170,
        189, 222, 238, 252, 257,
        268, 276
    Peace, xxx, 208, 265, 269, 270,
        274, 278
    physics, 165, 272
    physiology and medicine,
        225, 271
Noloesca, La Chata. *See* Escalona,
    Beatriz
Noriega, Manuel, xxix, xxx, 253,
    275, 281
normal schools, 106, 149
The North (Alegría), 161
North, Oliver, 272, 273–74
North American Free Trade
    Agreement (NAFTA), xviii,
    277, 279–83, 360–62
Northwest Passage, 47
Novarro, Ramón, 141, 184
novelists
    Argentine, 118, 171, 186
    Chicano, 206
    Chilean, 163, 179, 206, 217,
        249, 268
    Colombian, 89, 107, 189,
        256, 268
    Cuban, 99, 153, 195, 221, 232,
        260, 274
    Guatemalan, 143, 252
    Hispanic, 193, 264
    Mexican, 111, 185, 192, 208,
        213, 260
    Peruvian, 161, 165, 216
    Puerto Rican, 156, 186, 233, 295
    Spanish, 59
Novello, Antonia, 275
novels of immigration, 232
nuclear arms, 269
"Nuestra America" (Martí), 99
Nuestra Señora de Guadalupe. *See*
    Our Lady of Guadalupe
Nuestra Señora de los Dolores, 52
Nuestra Señora de los Remedios, 52
Nuestro Tiempo, 193
Nueva Granada, 36
*Nueva Revista de Filología
    Española*, 123
Nuevas Leyes de las Indias (Las
    Casas), 11, 40
Núñez, Daniel, 266
Núñez de Balboa, Vasco, 10, 12, 30, *31*
Núñez de Vela, Blasco, 40
Nutka Convention, 58

Nuyorican literature, 145, 225, 228

O

O'Farrill, Alberto, 139, *140*
O'Gorman, Juan, 154, 229
O'Higgins, Bernardo, xxxiii, 59, 73
O'Higgins, Pablo, 147
Oakland Raiders, 209, 262
Obie Award
    in 1968, 215
    in 1974, 260
obras bufas cubanas, 139
Obregón, Alvaro, 192
Ocampo, Sebastián de, 24
Odria, Manuel, 205
Office of Economic
    Opportunity, 247
Office of Inter-American
    Affairs, 217
oil, xviii, xxxi, 184, 201, 210, 243,
    265, 269
Ojeda, Alonso de, 24
Oliva, Tony, 248
Oller y Cestero, Francisco Manuel,
    87, 88, 99, 109
Olmecs, 4
Olmos, Edward James, 225
Olmos, Pedro, 225
Olympic Games, 254
    in 1900, 145
    in 1904, 152
    in 1920, 182
    in 1924, 184
    in 1928, 190
    in 1932, 201
    in 1936, 208
    in 1948, 228
    in 1956, 238–39
    in 1960, 243
    in 1964, 248
    in 1968, 253
    in 1972, 258
    in 1976, 261
Oms, Alejandro, 128, 189
One Hundred Years of Solitude
    (García Márquez), 256
Oñate, Juan de, 47
Open Air Painting School, 131
operas, 53
Operation Bootstrap, xxiii, 133, 222
Operation Wetback, 236
Orden de Mérito Agrícola
    Medal, 216

Order of Vasco Núñez de Balboa,
    170, 248
Orellana, Francisco de, 40
Organization of American States,
    xxix, xxx, 121, 247, 270
Orozco, José Clemente, 118, 120,
    139, 153, 173, 181
Orquesta Filarmónica, 218
Orquesta Sinfónica de México, 141,
    144, 189
Ortega, Daniel, 271, 276
Ortiz, Carlos, 246
Ortiz Lugo, Jesús, 233
Ostend Manifesto, 100
Otero, Miguel A., Jr., 103, *104,*
    132, 176
Otero, Miguel A., Sr., 103, 132
Otero, Sellar & Co., 103
Otomís, 9, 44
Our America (Martí), 99
Our Lady of Guadalupe, 34
Our Time, 193
Outstanding Innovation Award
    (1978), 211
Ovando, Nicolás de, 22, 26
The Oxcart poster, *181*
Ozawa, Seiji, 220

P

Pachacuti, 6
Pacheco, Romualdo, 113
pachucos, 219
Pact of El Zajón, xxii, 108, 114
Padilla, Heberto, 200, 257
painters
    Argentine, 79, 148, 154, 245
    Bolivian, 49, 50, 54
    Chilean, 164
    Colombian, 48, 64, 104, 150
    Cuban, 132, 148, 166, 200, 231,
        246, 248
    Cuzco School, *42, 51*
    Ecuadorean, 139, 179–80, 245
    Guatemalan, 125
    Indian, 48
    Italian, 41
    Mexican, 78, 119, 131, 142, 158,
        193, 204, 260
    Puerto Rican, 55, 87
    Quito School, 48
    Uruguayan, 84, 112, 209–10
    Venezuelan, 122, 183, 225

Palace of Fine Arts (Mexico), 120,
    132, 141, 143
Palés, Vicente, 134
Palés Matos, Luis, 134, 209, 231
Palma, Ricardo, 87, *88*
Palma, Tomás Estrada, *147,* 154
Pan American Games, 278
Pan American Union, 121, 133,
    162, 216
Panama Canal, xxviii, 146, 150,
    157, 160, 169, 171, 176, 183,
    202, 261
Panama Canal Zone, 103, 176
Panama-United States
    relations, 169
Paraense, Guilherme, 182
*Paraguay: Image of Your Desolate
    Country,* 85
Paredes, Américo, 173, 274
Pareja, Father, 48
Paret y Alcázar, Luis, 55
Parra, Félix, 119
Partido Autonomista Histórico u
    Ortodoxo, 102
Partido de la Independencia, 166
Partido de la Revolución
    Mexicana, 224
Partido Independentista, 228
Partido Independentista
    Puertorriqueño, 224
Partido Nacional Revolucionario,
    xviii, 195, 224
Partido Nacionalista Puertorriqueño,
    161, 183, 196
Partido Obrero Social, 109
Partido Obrero Socialista, 140
Partido Popular Democrático, 212
Partido Puertorriqueño
    Republicano, 103
Partido Republicano, 140, 144, 212
Partido Revolucionario Cubano,
    123, 128
Partido Revolucionario Institucional,
    xviii, 195, 224, 254
Partido Socialista
    Puertorriqueño, 192
Partido Unión, 152
Party of the Democratic Revolution,
    281, 282
Party of the Mexican
    Revolution, 224
party politics, 246
Pastry War, 63
Paterson Poetry Prize (1992),
    238, 278
Paul VI, 195

Paz, Octavio, 170, 261, 276
Paz, Suni, 231
Paz Estenssoro, Víctor, xxxi
Peabody Award, 221
Peace Corps, 155
Peace, Friendship, Limits, and
    Settlement: Treaty of
    Guadalupe-Hidalgo, 309–20
pecan shellers, 210, *211*
Pedraza, José, 253
Pedrozo, Trinidad, 98
Peladita, 149
pelado, 214
Peláez del Casal, Amelia, 132
PEN Southwest Discovery Award
    (1983), 206, 269
Peña, Federico, 226, 279
Peña Gómez, José Francisco, 282
Peñalba, Rodrigo, 165
Peñarredonda, Magdalena, 132
Peralta, Victor, 190
Pérez, García, 252
Pérez, José Joaquín, 185
Pérez, Juan, 15
Pérez Balladares, Ernesto, xxx, 281
Pérez Capilla, Joaquín, 228, 238
Pérez de Holguín, Melchor, 49, 54
Pérez de Villagrá, Gaspar, 47
Pérez Esquivel, Adolfo, 265
Perla Theatre, 102
Perón, Juan, xxxiv, 129, 130,
    204, 224
Pershing, John J., 114, 164
petroleum, 86
Pezuela, Juan Manuel de la, 96
Philip II, 34
philosophers, 49, 92, 97, 162
photography, 147, 148, 158, 266
physicists, 165, 173, 272
Picasso, Pablo, 125, 139, 148
Pico, Pío de Jesús, 65, *67*, 83
Pico House, 66
Pierce, Franklin, 95, 98–100
Pinckney Treaty, 64, 297–303
Pinochet, Augusto, 259, 276, 281
Pinta, 15
Piñero, Jesús T., 224
Piñero, Miguel, 224, 260
Pinzón, Martín Alonso, 15
Pinzón, Vicente Yáñez, 15
piracy, 41
pirates, xxii, 32, 41, 42
Piscator Dramatic Workshop,
    181, 227
Pissarro, Camille, 88
Pittsburgh Pirates, 205, 251, 257

Pizarro, Francisco, xxxi, 6, 12, *13,*
    20, 21, 35, 36, *37*, 40
Pizarro, Sebastián Lorenzo, 55
Plan de Iguala, 77
Plan de San Diego, 172
Plan de San Luis, 163
Plan of Ayala, 115
Platt, Orville, 147, *147*
Platt Amendment, xxiii, xxviii, 146,
    147, 154, 166, 176, 202–4
playwrights, 47, 72, 99, 118, 139,
    155, 179, 181, 214, 224,
    248, 258
Plaza, Miguel I., 190
Plural, 170
*Poesía no eres tú: obra poética, 1948–
    1971* (Castellanos), 258
poetry, 36, 67, 87, 93, 110, 113,
    118, 119
poets
    Argentine, 67, 74, 126, 142
    Chilean, 122, 152, 222, 257
    Colombian, 48
    Cuban, 98, 108, 132, 148, 200,
        235, 247, 257
    Mexican, 49, 110, 115, 122, 170,
        182, 185, 216, 227, 237–38,
        238, 276, 278
    Nicaraguan, 107, 185
    Peruvian, 95, 126, 179
    Spanish, 36, 46, 49
    Uruguayan, 119, 128, 157
    Venezuelan, 60
Poindexter, John, 273
Police brutality, xix, 251, 256, 257
political activists, 161
Political Association of Spanish-
    Speaking Organizations, 246
politicians, 8, 69, 71, 73, 83, 113,
    129, 133, 174, 175, 226, 245,
    257, 264, 274
Polk, James K., xxiii, 95
poll taxes, 251
Ponce, Manuel M., 120, 141, 223
Ponce de León, Juan, xvii, 8, 24,
    30, *31*, 33
    discovers Florida, 30
    and treaty with Carib Indians, 26
Ponce Fire Brigade Band, 102, 114
Ponce Massacre, xxiv, 125, 183, 209
Pontifex Romana, 26
Popé, 50
Popi, 199
Popular Democratic Party, 133
population statistics, 256
Porterfield, L.B., 176

Portes Gil, Emilio, 187
Portocarrero, Pedro, 12
Portocarrero, René, 132, 166, 246
Pórtola, Gaspar de, 57
Posada, José Guadalupe, 98,
    118, 121
positivism, 123
positivist movement, 97
poverty, 163, 262, 275, 280
Prado Museum, 88, 148
pre-Colombian art, 125
pre-Colombian dance, 125
preachers, 186
prejudice, xix, xxiv, 177, 219
Premio Casa de las Américas, 194
Premio Quinto Sol, 194, 209, 259
President's National Salute to
    American Poets and Writers
    (1980), 209, 264
Presley, Elvis, 215
Press Prize (1958), 148
Prim, Juan, 87
printing, 35–36, 62
printing press, 30, 35–36, 62, 68
Prisoner of Zenda, 141
privateers, 41, 45
Pro Independence Movement, 240
Procedure for the Establishment of
    a Strong and Lasting Peace,
    xxx, 270
The Prodigal Child (Paz), 170
Professional School of Industrial
    and Fine Arts, 104, 150
professors, 179
Programa Nacional Fronterizo, 242
Proposition 187, 282
Public Law 45 (U.S.), 219
Public Law 78 (U.S.), 231
publishing, 30, 68, 208
Pueblo Nuestra Señora de los
    Angeles de la Portiúncula (Los
    Angeles), 60
Pueblos, 50
Pueblos Hispanos, 161
Puerto Rican Communist
    Party, 204
Puerto Rican independence, *237*
Puerto Rican Independence
    Party, 224
Puerto Rican national anthem, 107
Puerto Rican Nationalist Party, 183
The Puerto Rican Peasant
    (Alonso), 79
Puerto Rican Republican Party, 103
Puerto Rican Socialist Party,
    144, 192

Puerto Rican statehood, xxiv, 62, 103, 140, 144, 152, 228, 275, 277
Puerto Rican Traveling Theater, 222
Puerto Rico
  abolishes slavery, 112
  Constitutional Convention of Puerto Rico and, 344–58
  Constitutional Convention of Puerto Rico, resolutions and, 358, 359
  governed by Ponce de León, 24
  Treaty of Peace (Treaty of Paris) and, 321–23
Pueyrredón, Juan Martín de, 79
Pueyrredón, Prilidiano P., 79
Pulitzer Prize winners, 231, 257, 276
Purísima Concepción mission, 53

Q

Quechua Indians, 165
Quinn, Anthony, 172, 238
Quiroga, Horacio, 114, 176
Quito School, 48
Quivira, 26

R

racism, xvii, xviii, xix, xxiv, 110, 118, 145, 180, 282
Radio Martí, 272
railroads, xviii, xix, xxvii, xxxiv, 86, 89, 92, 97, 123, 144, 279
Raining Backwards (Fernández), 274
Ramírez, Alejandro, 68
Ramírez, Francisco P., 100
Ramírez, María Teresa, 253
Ramos, Armando, 254, 258
ranching, xviii, 103, 118
Rancho Real de Santa Petronila, 57
Raquel Welch Productions, 216
Reagan, Ronald, xxix, xxx, 263, 266, 267, 269, 270, 272, 274, 277
  cabinet, 274
  civil rights and, 266, 277
  Contras and, 270, 272
  Grenada and, 262
  Latin America and, 266, 270
  Sandinistas and, 263, 267
realist, 79

Rebuild LA Committee, 226
Rebull, Santiago, 119
Reclamation Act, 148
Recopilación de las leyes de las Indias, 52
redistribution of land, xxvi, xxxi, 101, 176, 223, 233
Reform and Control Act (1986), 174, 268
Reform Law of 1964 (Ecuador), 246
reform laws, 103, 246
Refugee Act, 266
refugees, xxix, 187, 266
  Cuban, 246
  economic, xix
  Mexican, 164
  political, xix, xxiv, xxv, xxviii
Reid Cabral, Donald, 249
Reinoso, Alonso de, 40
Relación de la conquista (Jiménez de Quesada), 24
religion, 30, 63, 94, 101, 103
Renoir, Pierre, 88
repartimientos, 23, 27, 42
repatriation, xix, 95, 157, 199
Republic of Jayuya, 230
Republic of Río Chama, 186, 251
Republic of Texas, 69, 89
Republic of the Río Grande, 92
Republican National Alliance (Arena), 281
Republican Party, 103, 212, 228
Reverón, Armando, 122, 238
reverse discrimination, 255, 266
Revista Chicano-Riqueña, 234
Revista de las Antillas, (Torres), 113, 168
Revolución Libertadora, 204
Revolutionary Junta for Cuba and Puerto Rico, 105
Revolutionary Movement Party, xxxi, 233
revolutionary movements, 239
  Cuba, 235, 241
  El Salvador, 281
  indigenous, 280
revolutions
  Bolivian, xxxi, 212, 233, 248
  Cuban, 212, 240
  French, 70
  Mexican, 70, 212
  Texas, 172
Revueltas, Silvestre, 143, 144, 189
Reyes, Alfonso, 122, 238

Reyes y Basoalto, Nefatlí Eliezer. See Neruda, Pablo
Ricardo, Ricky, 178
Richter, Hans, 196
Riffo, Eduardo, 228
The Ring, 199
Río, Dolores del, 155, 219
Río, Jaime del, 155
Rio de la Plata, 31
Rio Grande, 26
Río Piedras Massacre, 125
Ríos Montt, Efrain, 282
riots, 251
Rivera, Diego, 117, 119, 120, 125, 131, 147, 153, 154, 158, 183
  artist's union and, 183
  biography, 119
  Bravo and, 147
  Guerrero and, 131
  Kahlo and 158
  Mérida and, 125,
  O'Gorman and, 154
  Sigueros and, 131
  Vasconcelos and, 117
Rivera, Geraldo, 221, 274
Rivera, Julio Adalberto, 245
Rivera, Tomás, 208, 262
Riverbed without a River: A Diary of My Generation (Laguerre), 245
Roach, Hal, 159
Robinson, Jackie, 110
Robledo, Carmelo Ambrosio, 201
Rocambruna, José, 144
Rockefeller, Nelson, 181
Rodó, José Enrique, 111, 145
Rodríguez, Juan "Chi Chi," 207
Rodriguez, Washington, 248
Rodríguez de Cabrillo, Juan, 40
Rodríguez de Tío, Lola, 93, 107
Rodríguez Francia, José Gaspar, 72
Rohmer, Eric, 197
Roland, Gilbert, 156, 212
Rolf, James, 203
Roman Empire, 4
Romañach, Leopoldo, 132
romanticism, 68, 72, 87, 89, 107
Romero, Carlos Humberto, xxix, 261
Romero, César, 157
Romero, Roland Lee, 201
Romero y Galdamez, Oscar Arnulfo, xxix, 178, 213, 281, 281
Roosevelt, Franklin Delano, xxiii, xxviii, xxxiv, 202, 204, 217

Roosevelt, Theodore, 103, 146, 150,
    160, 174
"Roosevelt Corollary" to the
    Monroe Doctrine, 154
Rosas, Juan Manuel de, 67,
    68, 71, 74
Rosas, Manuelita, 79
Royal Decree of 1799, 82
Roybal, Edward R., 174, 245, 268
"Rúben's Wife" (Bolero), *200*
Rufino Tamayo Museum of
    Contemporary Art, 143, 260
Ruiz Belvis, Segundo, 108
Rullán Lequerica, José, 127
Rusiñol, Santiago, 104

S

Saavdera Lamas, Carlos de, 208
Sábato, Ernesto, 163
Sacasa, Juan B., xxvii, 202
Sahagún, Bernardino de, 21, 83
Saint Augustine, 45
St. Thomas Aquinas University, 38
Salazar, Rubén, 256
Salcedo, Manuel de, 71
Salinas de Gortari, Carlos,
    277, 280–83
Salinas Lettuce Strike, 256
Salt War, 114
Samora, Julián, 182, 277
San Alejandro Academy, 132
San Antonio de Béjar, 53
San Antonio de Padua, 79
San Antonio de Valero, 53
*San Antonio Independent School
    District v. Rodríguez*, 258
San Buenaventura, 79
San Carlos Academy, 78, 92, 118,
    119, 127, 131, 142, 147
San Carlos de Monterrey, 79
San Cayetano de Tumacácori, 52
San Diego de Alcalá, 79
San Diego mission, 58
San Fernando de Bexar, 55
San Fernando Rey, 79
San Francisco, 57, 58
San Francisco de Asís, 79
San Francisco de la Espada mission,
    53, *80*
San Francisco de los Tejas, 52
San Francisco Giants, 209, 243, 247
San Francisco Mime Troupe,
    214, 248

San Francisco Solano, 69, 79
San Gabriel Arcángel, 79
San Gabriel Mission, 65
San Jacinto, Battle of, 63, 89
San Joaquin Cotton Strike, 203
San José de Guadalupe, 79
San José de Imuris, 52
San Juan, 356
San Juan Bautista, 79
San Juan Capistrano, 79
San Juan Capistrano mission, 53
San Luis Obispo de Tolosa, 79
San Luis Rey, 66, 79
San Martín, José de, xxxiii, 59,
    59, 73, 77
San Miguel Arcangel, 79
San Nicolás de Bari, 24
San Rafael Arcángel, 79
San Xavier del Bac, 52
Sánchez, Fidel, 252
Sánchez, George I., 157
Sánchez, Pedro Antonio, 216
Sánchez, Ricardo, 216
Sandinista Front for National
    Liberation, 262
Sandinistas, xxvi, xxix, xxx,
    civil war and, 262, 276, 279
    Contras and, 269
    government, 263
    political party, 270
Sandino, César Augusto, 168, *168*
Santa Anna, Antonio López de,
    xvii, xxv, *64*, 65, 68, 69,
    86, 90, 98
    becomes president, 87
    birth of, 63–64
    portraits of, 78
    and Treaty of Velasco, 89
Santa Bárbara, 79
Santa Clara de Asís, 79
Santa Cruz, 79
Santa Elena, 45
Santa Fe de Bogotá, 38
Santa Fe Expedition, 69, 93
Santa Fe, New Mexico
    falls to the Indians, 50
    founded, 48
Santa Fe railroad, 144
Santa Gertrudis de Saric, 52
Santa Inés, 79
Santa María, 15
Santa María, Andrés de, 150
Santa María de Buenos Aires, 38
Santana, Pedro, xxii, 93, 105
Santiago, 40

Santiago, Isabel, 48
Santiago, Miguel de, 48
Santiago del Estero, 44
Santo Domingo, 24, 77
Santos Zelaya, José, xxvii, 127,
    157, 162
Sanz, Laureano, 68, 106
Sao Paolo Bienel, 183
Saralegui, Cristina, 227, *228*, 275
Saralegui, Francisco, 227
Sardiñas, Eligio "Kid Chocolate,"
    163, 199, *199*
Sarmiento, Domingo Faustino, 71,
    71, 72, 108
scholars, 21, 155, 160, 180
Schomburg, Arturo Alfonso, 112
school financing, 257, 258
School for Tropical Medicine, 166
School of Fine Arts, Bogotá,
    104, 150
schools, xxi, 24, 30, 34, 48, 62, 96
sciences, xv, 49, 225
scientific expeditions, 62
scientists, 49, 165, 173, 211, 216,
    235, 255
Scott, Winfield, 94
Scott Medal (1953), 165
screenwriters, 213
sculling, 228
sculptors, 148
sculpture, 3, 48, 56
Seattle Seahawks, 209
Sebastián de Elcano, Juan, 33
secessionist efforts, 93
segregation, xix, 196, 223, 229
Seguín, Erasmo, 79
Seguín, Juan N., 69, 81, 92
Selective Service Act, 178
Selvetti, Humberto, 238
Sendero Luminoso. *See*
    Shining Path
Separation of Church and
    State, 101–3
separatist clubs, 123
Sergeants' revolt, 202
Serra, Jaime, 360
Serra, Junípero, 57, 58, *58*, 79
Serrano, John, 257
Serrano, Jorge, 279
Serrano v. Priest, 257
service industries, xxiii
settlements, 19, 26, 34, 38, 41, 45,
    52, 55, 57, 62, 74, 103
    California, 57
    Caribbean, 41

exploration, 34
Florida, 45
Jamaica, 19, 26
La Plata, 38
Santiago, 26
United States, 26, 45, 74, 94
Texas 52, 55, 103
Seuphor, Michel, 113
Seven Cities of Cíbola (Gold),
    xvii, 38
Seven Treatises, 87, 117
Seven Years' War, 57, 65
Shakespeare, William, 111
Shining Path, xxxii, 205, 260, 278
shipping, 32, 41, 47
Short Eyes (Piñero), 260
short story writers
    Argentine, 114, 142
    Bolivian, 233
    Chilean, 218
    Colombian, 189
    Cuban, 222
    Mexican, 186
    Peruvian, 162
    Puerto Rican, 157, 186
    Uruaguayan, 110
Shout at Lares, xxiii
Shout at Yara, xxii
Shrine of the Virgin of
    Guadalupe, 34
Siete tratados (Montalvo), 87, 117
significant documents
    Bracero Program, 340–44
    Cession of Louisiana, 303–6
    Civil Rights Act of 1964,
        359, 360
    Constitutional Convention of
        Puerto Rico, 344–58
    Constitutional Convention of
        Puerto Rico, resolutions,
        358, 359
    Gadsden Treaty 1853, 318–20
    Hay-Bunau-Varilla
        Convention, 326–31
    Hay-Herran Treaty, 331–39
    Laws of Burgos, 285–95
    Laws of Burgos, amendments to,
        296, 297
    Monroe Doctrine, 306–9
    Peace, Friendship, Limits and
        Settlement: Treaty of
        Guadalupe-Hidalgo, 309–18
    Pinckney Treaty, 297–303
    Treaty of Friendship, Limits and
        Navigation (The Pinckney
        Treaty), 297–303

Treaty of Guadalupe, 309–18
Treaty of Guadalupe-Hidalgo,
    319, 320
Treaty of Peace (Treaty of
    Paris), 320–24
Treaty of Relations between the
    United States and Cuba,
    339, 340
Sigüenza y Góngora, Carlos de,
    44, 49, 62
silver, xvi, xx, 41
Simonetto de Portela, Noemí, 228
singers, 215, 219
Siqueiros, David Alfaro, 120, 131,
    153, 154, 251, 252
Siqueiros Cultural Polyforum, 132
Sisley, Alfred, 88
slavery
    abolition, xxii, xxv
    abolitionists, 80, 83, 109
    African, 22, *23*, 28, 31,
        47, 58, 79
    Argentina and 72
    Central American Federation
        and, 81
    Cuba and 73, 108, 109, 118
    England and, 45, 53, *54*
    Indians and, 10, 22, 23,
        23,26, 27, 42
    Mexico and, 55, 84
    Nicaragua and, 100
    Portugal and, 6
    Puerto Rico and, 108, 109,
        112, 209
    slave revolts, 33, 193
    Spain and, 26, 74, 89, 92
    United States and, 97, 100
Slavkin, Mark, 283
Sleepy Lagoon Defense
    Committee, 219
"Sleepy Lagoon" murder case, 219,
    220
Sloat, John, 94
Smits, Jimmy, 238
smuggling, 50
Snead, Sam, 212
soccer, 184, 190, 198, 229, 272
social castes, xvii
social classes, xix
social realist art, 154
socialism, xxiv, xxxv, 109, 117, 163,
    176, 191, 192, 205, 212, 224,
    255, 259
Socialist Party, 109, 140
Sociedad Anónima del
    Teléfono, 132

Sociedad José Guatier Benítez, 161
sociologists, 182, 277
Solano López, Francisco, 106
Somoza, Anastasio, xxvii, xxviii,
    185, 202, 262, 263
Somoza, Anastasio, Jr., xxvii, 202
Somoza, Luis, xxvii, 202
Somoza Debayle, Anastasio, xxviii,
    252, 262, 264
sonofilm, 163
Sores, Jacques, 42
Soto, Hernando de, xvii, 21,
    30, 39, 40
Soto, Jesús Rafael, 183, 225
South Sea Company, 53
Southern Pacific Railroad, 144
Southwest Booksellers Association
    Prize for Fiction, 206
Soviet Union, xxx
Soviet Union-Cuba relations, 191,
    243, 276
The Spanish American Short Story
    (Leal), 160
Spanish-American War, 133–
    35, 147
Spanish Civil War, 126, 132
Spanish empire, 47
Spanish Haiti, 77
Spanish International
    Communications Corporation,
    274
Spanish International Network, 274
Spanish language, xix, xx, xxii
Spanish-language television,
    238, 262
Spanish-Speaking Division, Office
    of Inter-American Affairs, 217
Spiritual Plan of Aztlán, 250
Spooner Amendment, 146
Stalin Peace Prize (1953), 153, 235
statehood
    California, 167
    New Mexico, 97, 167
    Puerto Rico, xxiv, 62, 103, 140,
        144, 152, 228, 275
    Texas, 94
steel industry, xix
Steinbeck, John, 162
Sterenson, Teafilo, 266
Stockton, Robert, 94
*Stories of love, of Madness and of
    Death* (Quiroga), 115, 176
Storni, Alfonsina, 126
Strait of Juan de Fuca, 47
strikes, 149, 203, 210, 250

Stroessner, Alfredo, 236
Suárez, Pino, 169
Sucre, Antonio José de, xxxiii, 62
sugar
    Americas and, 24
    Cuba and, 26, 91, 92, 148, 176,
        178, 191, 196, 243
    Guatemala and, 109
    Indians and, 22
    New World and, 65
    shipping and, 31
    slaves and, 58, 73
sugar beet growers, xix
Sugar Equalization Board, 178
Supreme Court, 100, 235, 260
Supreme Revolutionary Congress of
    San Diego, 172
surrealism, 126, 147, 148, 152,
    164, 193
Swanson, Gloria, 121, 166
swimming, 190, 208, 253
Symphony orchestras, 55
syncretic religions, xxii

T

Tacón, Miguel, 88
Taínos, xx, 27
Taller Torres-García, 113
Tamayo, Rufino, 142, 260
tariffs, 280
Tatham, Carlos, 152
Tavárez, Manuel G., 102
taxes, 53, 97, 104
Taylor, Zachary, 94
Teamsters Union, 101, 246
Teatro Campesino, El, 214
Teatro chicano, 248
Teatro de la Merced, 74
Teatro Experimental del Ateneo, 181
Teatro Hispano, 150, 216
Teatro Nacional, 149
Teatro Puerto Rico, 150, 216
Teatro Triboro, 150, 216
Tejada, Raquel. *See* Welch, Raquel
tejanos, 69
Telemundo Group, 274
Televisa, 262
television, xx, 221, 225, 227, 238,
    274, 275
Teller Amendment, 134
Tello, Rafael J., 144
Ten Years War, xxii, 108
Tenayuca, Emma, 210

tennis, 190, 227, 252
Tenochas. *See* Aztec Indians
Tenochtitlán, 10, 20
Tepeyac, 34
Terán de los Ríos, Domingo, 52
terrorism, xxiv
Texas
    annexed to U.S., 94
    claimed for Spain, 33
    independence of, 74
    rebellion of Cortina, 103
    reoccupied by Spaniards, 53
Texas Institute of Letters
    Award, 206
Texas Rangers, 81, 182
textiles, 65, 86, 279
theater
    agit-prop, 248
    Chicano, 214, 248
    hall of fame, 167, 267
    labor, 248
    Puerto Rican, 222, 181
    vaudeville, 150, 216
Theater World Award, 225
Three Trapped Tigers (Cabrera
    Infante), 195, 252
Three Years War, 103
Tierra Amarilla Courthouse
    Raid, 186
Tiguex Indians, 26
Tijerina, Reies López. *See* López
    Tijerina, Reies
Timicua Indians, 45
Tinoco, Federico, 122, 175
Tió, Bonocio, 93
Tito, Diego Quispe, 48
Tlaltelolco Massacre, 254
tobacco, 26, 65, 104
Tolsá, Manuel, 56
Toltecs, 4–6
Tony Award (1979), 225
Toor, Frances, 147
Topeka railroad, 144
Torchi, Luigi, 120
Torres, José, 239
Torres-García, Joaquín, 112,
    200, 210
Torricelli Bill, 278
Torrijos, Omar, xxviii, 253
track and field, 184, 228, 238, 248,
    253, 258, 261, 266
trade, 50, 53, 57, 121
Tradición, 87
Trafalgar, Battle of, 67
Transisthmian canal, xxviii, 109,
    146, 171

translation, 48
transportation, xviii, xxii
Treaty of Amiens, 67
Treaty of Amity, Commerce and
    Navigation, 314, 315
Treaty of Crespy, 41
Treaty of Friendship, Limits and
    Navigation (The Pinckney
    Treaty), 297–303
Treaty of Guadalupe-Hidalgo, xvii,
    94–96, 100, 101, 318
Treaty of London, 47
Treaty of Luneville, 65
Treaty of Madrid, 50
Treaty of Paris, 45, 134,
    135, 320–24
Treaty of Peace, 320–24
Treaty of Relations between the
    United States and Cuba,
    339, 340
Treaty of San Ildefonso, 65
Treaty of San Lorenzo. *See*
    Pinckney Treaty
Treaty of the Hague, 47
Treaty of Tlaltelolco, 269
Treaty of Tordesillas, 19
Treaty of Velasco, 89
Treaty of Versailles, 45, 60
Treaty of Vervins, 47
Treaty, Gadsden, 318–20
Treaty, Hay-Herran, 331–39
Treaty, Pinckney, 297–303
Tres tristes tigres (Cabrera Infante),
    195, 252
Treviño, Lee, 211, 257
Trío Borinquen, 127
Triple Alliance War, 106
"The Triumph of Science and
    Work over Ignorance and Sloth"
    (mural by Juan Cordero), 112
Trosky, Leon, 158
Truce of Antwerp, 47
*The True History of the Conquest
    of New Spain* (Díaz del
    Castillo), 20, 45
Truffaut, Francois, 197
Trujillo, Rafael, xxii, xxviii, 197,
    202, 244, 282
Truman, Harry S, 125, 183, 217,
    224, 230
Tun tun de pasa y griferia (Palés
    Matos), 134, 209
Tun Tun of Raisins and Negritude
    (Palés Matos), 134
Túpac Inca, 6

Tyler, John, 94

U

Ubico, Jorge, xxvi, xxviii, 109, 202
"Ultraísmo," 142
The Underdogs (Azuela), 111, 172
undocumented immigration, 256
undocumented workers, xxviii, 174,
    236, 242, 256, 261, 266, 268,
    272, 282
unemployment, 277
Unión de Puerto Rico, 124
Union of Technical Workers,
    Painters and Sculptors, 119,
    131, 183
unions, 176, 188, 203, 210, 212,
    214, 243, 246, 250, 258, 261
    agricultural, 188, 201, 203, 210
    farmworkers and, 188, 214,
        246, 250
    labor, 212, 243, 258, 261
    Mexico and, 176
    teamsters, 246
United Farm Workers, 188, 245–
    46, 248, 256
United Fruit Company, xxvi, xxvii,
    109, 123, 140, 176, 223, 233
United Nations, xxiv, xxix, xxx, 223,
    246, 270
United Officers Group (Argentina),
    129, 221
United Provinces of Central
    America, xxv, 77, 79, 91
United Provinces of the River
    Plate, 73
United States Border Patrol, 184
United States Civil War, 100
United States Commission on Civil
    Rights, 170, 252
United States-Cuba relations, 243,
    244, 246
United States Federal Reserve, 269
United States-Latin America
    relations, 217
United States Marines, xxvii, 166,
    167, 202
United States-Mexico relations,
    160, 169, 217, 242
United States National Security
    Council, xxix, 270, 273
United States-Nicaragua relations,
    162, 167, 262
United States of America Medal of
    Freedom (1984), 170, 271

United States of South America,
    xxxiii, 62
United States-Panama relations,
    169, 208
United States Senate Energy and
    Resources Committee, 275
United States Strategic Oil
    Reserve, 269
United States Synod of
    Bishops, 196
United States Treasury, 269
universalist, 113
Universidad Nacional Autónoma de
    México, 120, 223
universities, xxi, 38, 44, 54
University of Alcalá de Henares, 42
University of Chile, 60, 93
University of Mexico, 42
University of Puerto Rico, 88, 106,
    149, 156, 166, 192
University of Salamanca, 42
University of San Marcos, 42
University of Trujillo, 126
Univisión, 274
Urista, Alberto Baltasar. *See* Alurista
Uriza, Rubén, 228
Urquiza, Justo José de, 84
Uruguay, 83
Usigli, Rodolfo, 155, 258
USS Maine, 133, 134

V

Valdes Lacarra, Alberto, 228
Valdez, Luis, 214, *214*, 248, 274
Valdivia, Pedro de, xxxi, 20, 22, 40
Valencia, Juan O., 160
Valens, Ritchie, 215, 274
Valenti, Carlos, 125
Vallejo, César, 126, 179
Vallejo, Mariano G., 69, 94
The Valley (Hinojosa), 259
Van Gogh, Vincent, 104
Van Zo Post, Albertson, 152
vandals, 4
Vardon Trophy, 212
Vare Trophy, 240, 261
Varela, Antonio, 98
Varese, Edgard, 141
Vargas, Diego de, 50
Vargas Arroyo, Antonio, 98, 128
Varona, Enrique José, 97, 162
Vasconcelos, José, 117, 119, 125,
    170, 185

Vásquez, Horacio, 174
Vásquez Cam, Edwin, 228
Vásquez de Ayllón, Lucas, 30
Vásquez de Coronado, Francisco,
    xvii, 26, 40
vaudeville, 149, 150, 214, 216
Velasco, José María, 92, 119, 127
Velázquez de Cuéllar, Diego, 13,
    20, 26, *27*, 30, 193
Vélez, Lupe, 159
Venezuela, 84
Venezuelan Order of Andrés
    Bello, 200
Venice Biennale, 183
*Verdadera historia de la conquista
    de la Nueva España* (Díaz del
    Castillo), 20, 45
Verrazano, Giovanni, 34
Vespucci, Amerigo, 10, 24
veterinarians, 206
viceroyalties, 34, 36
Viceroyalty of Peru, 36
Viceroyalty of Río de la Plata, 36
Victoria, Guadalupe, 82
Vietnam War, 256
vigilantism, 172
Vikki Carr Scholarship Foundation,
    215, 257
Villa, Francisco "Pancho," 111, 114,
    116, 155, 164, 174
Villagrá, Francisco de, 22
Villalobos, María Guadalupe Vélez
    de. *See* Vélez, Lupe
Villaseñor, Victor, 213, *214*, 259
Villenueve, Marshall, 67
Virgin of Guadalupe, *35*, 70
Visigoths, 4
Viva Kennedy Clubs, 169
Volunteers in Service to
    America, 247
voting rights, 239, 251, 255
Voting Rights Act, 250, 260
Voting Rights Act Amendments of
    1975, 260
Voting Rights Act of 1970, 255
Vuelta (Paz), 170, 261

W

Walker, William, xxvii, 100, *100*,
    103, 185
Walker Commission, 146
War of Independence, 60, 69

War of Reform, 103
War of the Pacific, 95, 115
"War on Drugs," xxx
War on Poverty, 247
war veterans, 174
Washington, George, 60
The Way It Was and Other Sketches
   (Colón), 279
weightlifting, 238, 266
Weismuller, Johnny, 159
Welch, James, 215
Welch, Raquel, 215
welfare, 199
Welles, Orson, 180
West Side Story, 199, 244
Weyler, Valeriano, 128, 132
The White Book (Agustini), 119, 157
White House Hispanic Heritage
   Award, 182, 219
   in 1985, 182
   in 1990, 222, 276
   in 1991, 219, 277
Whitney, Gertrude Vanderbit, 112
Whitney, William Collins, 112
William E. Harmon Award
   (1927), 112
Wilson, Henry Lane, 168
Wilson, Michael, 360
Wilson, Pete, 283
Wilson, Woodrow, 103, 114, 164,
   169, 171, 174, 176
women's literature, 218
women's rights, 49, 91, 93, 117

Wood, Leonard, 148
wool, 65
Workers' Social Party, 109
World Bank, xxxv, 255
World Boxing Congress, 258
World Court, 271
World War I, 169
   Puerto Rican soldiers and, 169
   Puerto Ricans and, 176
World War II, 211, 216, 217,
   219, 222
writers
   Argentine, 74, 142
   Chilean 179
   Cuban, 72, 98, 197
   Ecuadoran, 87
   Guatemalan, 147
   Mexican, 110, 155, 179
   Mexican-American, 155, 173
   Peruvian, 128,
   Puerto Rican, 78, 91, 105, 112,
     156, 181, 207
   Uruguayan, 111

X

Xavier Villaurrutia Prize for Fiction
   (1978), 187, 262

Y

Yagueca, Battle of, 27

Yáñez Pinzón, Vicente, 9
Yauco, Battle of, 27
"yellow journalism," 219
Yo soy Joaquín/I Am Joaquín
   (Gonzales), 251
You Are Poetry: The Poetic Works,
   1948–1971 (Castellanos), 258
Young, Robert, 225
Yucatan Peninsula, 31

Z

Zabala, Juan, 201, 208
Zalamea, Jorge, 165
Zapata, Emiliano, 115, *116,*
   164, 280
Zapatista National Liberation
   Army, 280
Zapotecs, 68
Zárate, Ortiz de, 40
Zárraga, Angel, 119
zarzuelas, 102, 127
Zedillo, Ernesto, 282
Zeno Gandía, Manuel, 166
Zimmerman Telegram, 176
Zoot Suit Riots, 219, 221, *249*
Zorrilla, Alberto, 190
Zuloaga, Ignacio, 104
Zunis, 26
Zurbarán, Francisco de, 50